Mission and Memory

A History of the Catholic Church in Arkansas

Mission and Memory

A History of the Catholic Church in Arkansas

James M. Woods, Ph.D.

Prologue by Bishop Andrew J. McDonald

Diocese of Little Rock

1993

Published by August House, Inc.,
P.O. Box 3223, Little Rock, Arkansas, 72203.
501-372-5450

Printed in the United States of America

10 9 8 7 6 5 4 3 2 1

LIBRARY OF CONGRESS CATALOGING IN PUBLICATION DATA
Woods, James M., 1952-
Mission and Memory : a history of the Catholic church in
Arkansas / James M. Woods ; prologue by Andrew J. McDonald.
p. cm.
Includes bibliographical references and index.
ISBN 0-87483-264-0 : $24.95
1. Catholic Church–Arkansas–History. 2. Arkansas–Church history.
I. Title.
BX1415.A7W66 1993
282'.767–dc20 93-10687
CIP
Cover design: Harrill-Ross Studios
Typography: Heritage/North Little Rock

This book is printed on archival-quality paper which meets the
guidelines for performance and durability of the Committee on Production Guidelines
for Book Longevity of the Council on Library Resources.

AUGUST HOUSE, INC. PUBLISHERS LITTLE ROCK

This book is dedicated to my wife

Becky

who happily moved with me
for five summers to Little Rock
and lived with me during the composition
of this book. I could not have completed it
without her support, love, and prayers.

CONTENTS

ACKNOWLEDGEMENTS

A book of this size and scope could not have been completed without assistance from many people. I must first thank Bishop Andrew J. McDonald of Little Rock who commissioned the publication of this history of Arkansas Catholicism as part of the sesquicentennial celebration of the diocese, 1843-1993. Bishop McDonald read the entire manuscript and made some important contributions. Sr. Catherine Markey, O.S.B., Archivist for the Diocese of Little Rock, guided my research and made important comments and corrections to the entire manuscript. Portions of this manuscript were edited and commented on by William W. O'Donnell, K.S.G., Fr. George W. Tribou, and Msgr. J. Gaston Hebert.

Some people agreed to be interviewed on audio tape. These interviews were with: Bishop McDonald; Bishop Lawrence P. Graves, now retired, of Alexandria, Louisiana; Msgr. James E. O'Connell; Msgr. John F. O'Donnell; Msgr. John E. Murphy; Msgr. William E. Galvin; Fr. Lawrence Maus; Sr. Annella Willett, O.S.B.; William W. O'Donnell, K.S.G; Rose Capel; and Louis Belotti.

Many who work for the diocese at St. John's Catholic Center in Little Rock were helpful in many ways; these include Martha McNeil, Elizabeth Parker, James T. Davis, Deacon William M. Hartmann, Fr. Francis I. Malone, Fr. Scott Marczuk, John Sweeney, Ginny Cia, Antje Harris, Karen DiPippa, Carol Ann Blow, Sr. Henrietta Hockle, O.S.B., Sr. Maria Kleinschmidt, D.C., Anne Dierks, Gregory Wolfe, Dennis Lee, Fr. Stephen Binz, Deacon Lawrence Jegley, Rose Kennedy, Fr. Albert Schneider, Deborah Halter, Ed Sweeden, Deacon Johnson Mattingly, Betty Cox, and Loretta Maes. Fr. Thomas J. Sebaugh and Joey Halinski helped me a great deal with the computer as the work progressed.

While I mainly used his book, Fr. Hugh Assenmacher, O.S.B., provided me with some updated information on the Benedictine monks of Arkansas. For the material about the Carmelite monks at Marylake, I received help from Fr. Henry Bordeaux, O.C.D. Diocesan priests, Frs. James E. Mancini and L. Warren

Harvey, also provided some useful material.

I owe a great deal to my parents, Federal Judge Henry and Kathleen Woods, who loved and supported me during my five summers in Little Rock. My brother Thomas H. Woods and my sister Mary S. Woods did some necessary research for me. Ernest Dumas, now of the Journalism Department of the University of Central Arkansas, edited the entire manuscript and greatly improved its narrative flow. Jo Schneider of Catholic High School proofread the manuscript in its final form. I also received help from others including: Thomas Sexton, Diane Hanley, Stephen Hanley, Arthur Zorn, the late W.R. Stephens, and the late Jim Coleman. Russell Baker of the Arkansas History Commission and Joy Geisler, now retired, at the University of Arkansas at Little Rock Library, helped me with their wide knowledge of Arkansas sources.

I would also like to thank the staffs of different archives utilized outside of Arkansas; these include the Archives of the Archdiocese of Baltimore, the Archives of the Archdiocese of St. Louis, and the Archives of the University of Notre Dame. A special thanks to Dr. Charles E. Nolan, Archivist of the Archdiocese of New Orleans and Fr. John W. Bowen, S.S., Archivist for the Sulpician Archives in Baltimore. For material on the Diocese of Little Rock and the Indian Territory, later Oklahoma, this information was supplied by Fr. James D. White, historian for the Diocese of Tulsa. On the Society of St. Joseph, I was given material by Fr. Peter E. Hogan, S.S.J., Archivist for the Society of St. Joseph in Baltimore. Although I primarily used his book, Fr. Henry J. Koren, C.S.Sp., Archivist of the Congregation of the Holy Spirit, Pittsburgh, Pennsylvania, sent me some additional information on the Holy Ghost Fathers. Mr. Don Buske, archivist of the Glenmary Fathers in Cincinnati, also supplied me with information on their work in Arkansas.

For the various women religious orders, I relied on recent histories and these are mentioned in the notes. While I mainly used her history, Sr. Louise Sharum, O.S.B., sent me some updated information on her order, the Fort Smith Benedictines. I received information on these religious orders from these sisters living in Arkansas: Srs. Catherine Dominic Stack, O.P., and Mary Veronica Doolin, O.P., for the Dominican Sisters; Sr. Mary Magdalen Kelly, O.C.D., for the Discalced Carmelite Sisters; Sr. Theresa Maria Lalacette, O.L.C.R., for the Sisters of Our Lady of Charity; and Sr. Maria Liebeck, D.C., for the Daughters of Charity. Archivists outside of the diocese also supplied the author with material: Sr. Mary Collette Crone, S.C.N., Archivist, Motherhouse of the Sisters of Charity, Nazareth, Kentucky; Sr. Marie Richard Eckerle, S.S.N.D., Archivist of the Dallas Province of the School Sisters of Notre Dame; Sr. Mary Monica LeFleur, C.C.V.I., Sisters of Charity of the Incarnate Word, Congregational Archives, Houston, Texas.

The author also received assistance from Dr. John B. Boles of Rice University and Eric Wedig of the Tulane University Library. Also providing assistance was Thomas Stritch and Tim and Patty Brandyberry of South Bend,

Indiana. In Statesboro, Georgia, retired historian Msgr. Joseph N. Moody read the entire manuscript and added his expertise. Peggy Smith, secretary of the history department, typed the manuscript into the computer here at Georgia Southern University. My department head, Dr. Walter J. Fraser, made some scheduling adjustments to enable me to complete the book. My colleagues in the history department were all quite supportive. Thanks also to all my personal friends, especially Dr. Paul and Sue MacLeod, now of Grand Forks, North Dakota. I would also like to thank the Lord Jesus Christ who gave me the grace to complete the book.

Finally, I need to thank my wife Becky who traveled with me for five summers back and forth from Little Rock. This book would not have been written without her love, prayers, support, and encouragement.

Much, but not all of chapter two, was previously published under the same title as the chapter in the fall 1989 issue of the *Arkansas Historical Quarterly*.

PROLOGUE

THE MEMORY – THE MOMENT – THE MISSION ONE PLANTS, ANOTHER WATERS, GOD GIVES THE GROWTH

We can begin with Adam when God breathed life into him, so beautifully portrayed by the master painter Michelangelo on the ceiling of the Sistine Chapel. We can begin with Our Lord atop the mountain, "Go teach all nations." Although the Catholic Diocese of Little Rock was established 150 years ago, toward the middle of the nineteenth century, the Catholic presence in the state arrived within fifty years of Columbus. In June 1541, De Soto and his men, together with less than a dozen Catholic clergymen, arrived in what is now the state of Arkansas. Later, missionaries, pioneers, and immigrants endured the perilous journey from foreign lands to come to America and Arkansas. They came to the state not bearing gifts of gold, frankincense, and myrrh, but bearing the gifts of Faith, Hope, and Charity, virtues inspired by their Catholic Christianity.

This story is really a story representing these virtues. It took a great deal of faith to come to America and Arkansas. Even more faith was needed to preserve the faith of the forebears in their new environment. They labored with hope that their lives in this New World would provide themselves and their children more freedom and opportunities. They also practiced charity, as they shared their love and concern with their neighbors of different religious faiths.

Though Roman Catholics have never been numerous in Arkansas, their personal and institutional charity is well known. Catholics still staff Arkansas' oldest hospital and operate the oldest educational facility in the state.

As the pages of our history unfold, read them in the spirit in which they were lived and in which they were written. We have opened our hearts and our archives to Professor James M. Woods of Georgia Southern University. A native Arkansan, educated in the parochial schools in Little Rock, he is a man of integrity and honesty, and a professional historian. Read these pages with a generous heart and with the courageous spirit of the those who first came to Arkansas bringing their great gifts of FAITH, HOPE, and CHARITY.

INTRODUCTION

Mission and Memory: A History of the Catholic Church in Arkansas

This book is a traditional, narrative history of a unique and important topic. It chronicles the Catholic Diocese of Little Rock, which embraces the whole state of Arkansas, as seen through the ecclesiastical administrations of its five bishops from 1843 to 1993. The book's scope, however, is far beyond the contours of these diocesan episcopacies; it is the history of the Catholic presence in Arkansas. The first European explorers and settlers to the state were Roman Catholics, and members of this faith have been present in Arkansas for the past four and a half centuries. This Church history surveys the era from the earliest exploration of the region through the establishment of the diocese, a span of three centuries. The book examines the impact of immigrants and immigration upon Arkansas Catholicism, while also highlighting the Church's record on black evangelization and race relations. Catholic religious orders, both male and female, have contributed to the educational and charitable needs of the Arkansas citizenry; their accomplishments will also be presented.

This topic is unique and important for three reasons. While there have been several works on the history of the Baptist, Methodist, and Episcopal Churches in the state, there has never been a substantial treatment of Arkansas Catholicism. As Catholics have been such a minority for much of the state's history, it is easy to see why they have been previously ignored. Catholics are a minority with a long, and I believe, significant story that deserves to be told.

Another reason for the unique importance of this topic is that it is a contribution to the overall scholarship on Catholicism in the South, a historical field just beginning to flower. Aside from some detailed studies of the Church in Louisiana, Texas, and Florida, which contain sizable Catholic populations, little attention has been paid to areas where Catholics have not equaled more than 3 percent of the overall state population. The Mississippi Church during the antebellum era and through the Civil War has received some attention; and the Diocese of Nashville published a history of the Church in Tennessee up to 1970. Some nineteenth century southern Catholic prelates have attracted biographies; namely, Louis DuBourg of New Orleans, John England of Charleston, and Augustin Verot of Savannah, later of St. Augustine. There is no history of the Catholic Church in a southern state up to the present time in a single volume. Students of southern religion, immigration, and race relations will find this present book of real interest and value.

The topic is also salutary for a third reason; it serves to broaden the scope of American Catholic history. Numbers draw historical interest; large amounts of Catholics in the Northeast, Midwest, Southwest, and the Pacific Coast have long commanded the attention of American Catholic historians. While scholars like Randall M. Miller and Jon L. Wakelyn have produced some promising work on the Church in the Old South, there is no full substantive work on Catholics in the region, either before or after the Civil War. This book may be of real value for such a future synthesis. Beyond the region itself, mainline American Catholic history generally ignores the southern Catholic experience, because there has been so little written about it by professional historians. This work integrates the local Catholic Church with the universal Catholic Church, showing how events and movements outside of Arkansas have impacted the diocese. This contribution is not totally one-directional. Certain individuals and movements from Arkansas have also affected the larger Church.

This book is not an exhaustive survey of all things Catholic in Arkansas history. Given its length, this disclaimer might appear to be false modesty. To paraphrase a more famous historian, never has so much been written about so few. Yet, this book is not a history of the Catholic parishes or lay organizations. This survey is not a complete chronicle of the different orders who have served in the Arkansas Church; some published accounts of these religious societies already exist and they are quite useful for anyone interested in their activities. This history hopes not so much to be the last word, but merely the first—an extended invitation for future researchers to explore our intriguing past. Since this work is a commissioned study, an authorized account of Arkansas Catholicism by the Diocese of Little Rock, something needs to be said about the way the book was written and researched. While several archives were utilized (see the first page of the endnotes), the main material was taken from the Archives of the Diocese of Little Rock. Both Bishop Andrew J. McDonald and the archivist for the diocese, Sr. Catherine Markey, allowed this author absolute freedom to examine the historical documents necessary to complete the study. While Bishop McDonald and Sr. Markey read the material and made many useful comments and criticisms, the final content of this work was left to the discretion of the author. I am also in debt to the other archivists and many others in writing this book; they are named in the acknowledgements.

The irony of the Catholic Church in Arkansas is that while it has often been seen as a threatening religious minority, irreconcilable in belief with either sacred Scripture or the American republic, it remains the state's oldest Christian institution. Spanish explorers first brought Catholicism to the area, and the Church was present when the French founded the first permanent European settlement. Although the French-Spanish settlement of the Arkansas Post was only nominally Catholic during the eighteenth century, the Church was somewhat influential in areas of morality and law. The American acquisition in the early nineteenth century, and the accompanying influx of Anglo-American Protestants, altered forever the cultural and religious makeup of Arkansas. Nevertheless, the Church persisted, maintained by its courageous missionaries and bishops of the nineteenth century. These first two prelates in Arkansas were extremely important in attracting some Catholic immigration into the state. The twentieth century has no doubt brought new challenges and opportunities. Under this century's three bishops, Catholicism in Arkansas has enjoyed small, yet steady growth. Its impact historically has been far greater than its actual membership; the Church still operates and staffs the oldest continuous academy and hospital in the state.

The sesquicentennial year of 1993 marks an important date for the Diocese of Little Rock—150 years of substantial progress. By illuminating Arkansas' Catholic heritage, this book is a proud and integral part of this celebration.

BISHOP ANDREW J. McDONALD, D.D.
Fifth Bishop of Little Rock (1972-)

CATHEDRAL OF ST. ANDREW–LITTLE ROCK, ARKANSAS
DEDICATED 1880
Exterior View, May 1988

CINDY MOMCHILOV

CATHEDRAL OF ST. ANDREW–LITTLE ROCK, ARKANSAS
Interior View, May 1988

CINDY MOMCHILOV

Diocese of Little Rock Coat of Arms

The diocesan arms are composed of the Marian colors, silver (the same as white in heraldry) and blue. They honor Mary as the patroness of the United States under her title of the Immaculate Conception.

Since Peter is the "petra" (rock) upon which the church was founded by Jesus Christ, the diocese is appropriately represented by small reversed silver crosses in memory of his crucifixion with his head to the earth.

The cross in the form of the letter X is the Cross of Saint Andrew the Apostle, the patron of the diocesan cathedral and the baptismal patron of Bishop Andrew Byrne, its first Ordinary.

The star of six points is derived from the coat of arms of Pope Gregory XVI, who established the Diocese of Little Rock on November 28, 1843. The star also refers to the State of Arkansas which displays a circle of stars in its seal, though of five points.

CHAPTER I

Planting the Cross

The Catholic Church in Colonial Arkansas, 1541-1803

HAVING BEEN ROUTED by Indians along the gulf coast, Hernando De Soto, the Spanish conquistador and the new *adelantado* of Florida, pounded northward through the wilderness with five hundred desperate men and a herd of swine until the morning of May 21, 1541, when he stumbled upon the eastern bank of a river so wide and powerful that it took away the breath. The group peered across the muddy torrent at distant canebrakes and woods. De Soto and his bedraggled men were the first Europeans to gaze upon the land that would become Arkansas. While on a raft some ten years earlier, Spanish explorer Alvar Nunex Cabeza De Vaca had felt the power of the river even in its estuary. De Soto, a veteran of the Pizarro expedition, was sent to explore and colonize and to discover the mighty northern river, which might be a passageway to the Orient.[1]

With this goal in mind, De Soto set out in May 1539 from what is now Tampa, Florida, with six hundred Spaniards and a scattering of Portuguese, French, Italian, German, and English adventurers. In this company were also twelve Catholic clergy, eight secular or diocesan priests, and four regular or order priests (one Trinitarian, one Franciscan, and two Dominicans).[2]

To De Soto and other Spanish conquistadors, the extension of the reign of their earthly Spanish king included the extension of the heavenly kingdom of God, the most holy Catholic faith. Any pious, or even not so pious, Spaniard believed that the advancement of both Church and State was a single goal.

The two-year trek through the flat, wooded wilderness of Florida, Georgia, Alabama, and Mississippi extracted a heavy price from the would-be conquerors. An Indian attack, in October 1540 in Alabama, had killed twenty-two men and wounded 168.[3] It was a bedraggled group that camped on the eastern shore of the Mississippi. The once glistening silver armor was dulled by dirt and rust; the doublets of the soldiers and the cassocks of the priests were in shreds. A few wore only deer or bear skin or cloaks of moss and grass. Their numbers had been reduced to just over 500 by Indian attacks, hunger, and disease.[4] Despite the hardships, the members of the expedition were clearly impressed by the great river. Gentleman Fidalgo de Elvas wrote, "It was a dirty giant, sprawling out into the bayous and morass, revealing three little level islands of mud, choked elsewhere with canebrakes. The swiftness of its current was shown by the uprooted trees carried along like broken twigs."[5] This was the first European description of the Mississippi River and the first European view of Arkansas, a land that looked fair and pleasant. The adventurers immediately made plans to cross.[6]

In crude boats, De Soto and his men made their way across the mighty waterways and landed about forty miles south of the site of the present day city of Helena in southern Phillips County on June 18, 1541, almost 295 years to the day before Arkansas entered the Union.[7] It was sixty-six years before the first permanent English settlement in the New World.

After the crossing, they disassembled their boats and kept the materials. As they made their way west and southwest, they ran into a Quapaw Indian village, near present-day Helena, they called Casqui.[8] The Indians greeted the visitors as "children of the Sun," and begged them to call down rain upon their withering crops. Two blind men asked De Soto to restore their sight. De Soto took the opportunity to preach the Christian faith to these native Arkansans:

> that in the heavens above there was One who had the power, to make them whole and do whatever they could ask of Him, whose servant he was; that this great Lord made the heavens and the earth, and man after His image, that He had suffered on the cross to save the human race, and risen from the tomb on the third day in what of man there was of Him dying, what of divinity being immortal; and that, having ascended into heaven, He was there with open arms to receive all that would be converted to Him.[9]

Governor De Soto then commanded that a lofty cross be erected on one of the nearby Indian mounds. He told the Quapaws that Christians venerated the cross in memory of the true one on which Christ suffered for all people, including them. "From that time on," he declared, "they should thus worship the Lord, of whom he had spoken to them, that was in the Heavens, and should ask Him for whatsoever they stood in need of."[10] De Soto and his company then knelt before the cross, chanted in Latin *Te Deum Landamus,* a traditional Catholic hymn of thanksgiving and joy, and a request for continuance of God's grace and mercy. The Indians knelt, too. It was the first Christian religious ceremony ever held in Arkansas.[11] Though not a Mass (the materials necessary for one had been lost in the Indian attack in Alabama), the ceremony was obviously Catholic in tone and spirit. The date was June 25, 1541.[12]

De Soto then marched north to the eastern edge of Crowley's Ridge. Learning that mountains and possibly more food were towards the west, he turned southwestward until he crossed the Arkansas River south of present-day Little Rock in early September 1541. In the Ouachita Mountains, he came to a village that the Spanish narrator called Tonico, which was near "a lake of very hot water somewhat brackish."[13] Here they found streams of hot water and salt, and the priests blessed the water.[14] By November, the explorers had settled in for the winter east of Little Rock along the southern shore of the Arkansas River.[15]

When the journey continued down the Arkansas River the next spring, De Soto caught a fever and fell into a deep depression. After three years of wandering through a vast and dangerous wilderness, his expedition had yielded little but the discovery of De Vaca's great northern river. Unlike the Cortes expedition or that of Pizarro, of which he was a part, De Soto found no wealthy empires, the conquest of which might bring him and his company gold and glory. With death approaching, he summoned one of the nine surviving priests to hear his confession. The priest gave him the last sacramental rites of the Catholic Church. De Soto died on May 21, 1542, on the western side of the river he had discovered for Europeans. The river would be his final resting place. His men wanted to keep their commander's death hidden from the Indians.[16]

De Soto's hand-picked successor, Luis Moscoso de Alvarado, assumed command and set out to get his men back to Mexico. Moscoso led the expedition across southern Arkansas into northern Louisiana and traveled as far west as what is now Dallas before turning back and traveling back to the site of Helena. There the exhausted explorers built crude rafts to float down the Mississippi into the Gulf of Mexico. They arrived in Mexico City in September 1543. Of the original 600, only 311 men made it safely back to Spanish Mexico.[17]

Of the twelve priests who began the expedition in Florida, four survived to reach Mexico. They were the Franciscan, Juan de Torres; two Dominicans, Juan Gallegos and Luis de Soto; and one regular diocesan priest, Dionisio de Paris. Three priests died before De Soto did and five more perished en route to Mexico.[18] Since many of the sacred vessels and vestments necessary for Mass disappeared in the Indian attack in Alabama, there is no record of a Catholic Eucharistic service or Mass being conducted by De Soto's clergy in Arkansas.

The priests did hold public prayers, heard confessions, administered the sacraments to the ill and fatally wounded, and conducted burial services for the dead. They also preached to the Indians, and a few of the natives received baptism and accompanied the Spanish on their journey. Before they departed for Mexico, Moscoso decided to abandon these Christianized Indians to lighten the burden and reduce the number of mouths they had to feed.[19] While it might be easy to write off the De Soto expedition as a failure, both militarily and spiritually, De Soto did lift the cross of Christ in Arkansas and presented, however weak and shallow, a witness of Catholic Christianity.

With a vast empire stretching from Argentine to Florida, and greatly overburdened by these colonial possessions, Spain decided to abandon the river and the valley that it had uncovered for European eyes. Not for 130 years would another European visit the area that would become Arkansas, and this time the visitors would be fewer and from the north. They would be of a different language and nation, but they would share the religious faith of De Soto and his explorers.

France established a foothold in the New World in 1608 at Quebec along the St. Lawrence River. In the next half-century, the French pushed their settlements, political control, economic trade, and Catholic religion into what is now central Canada and the Great Lakes region. In 1673, French Colonial official Fontenac sent Jesuit Father Jacques Marquette and Louis Joliet to explore the Great River to the west and see if it flowed into the western sea, the Pacific.[20] If the French governor desired exploration, Fr. Marquette had the heart of the missionary. He wanted to spread the Catholic faith. He wrote in his journal:

> Above all I placed our voyage under the protection of the Blessed Virgin Immaculate, promising her that if she granted us the favor of discovering the Great River, I would give it the name of the Conception, and that I would also make the first Mission that I should establish among these new peoples, bear the same name.[21]

Whatever may have been Father Marquette's prayerful desire, the Great River he would encounter eventually received its name from the French spelling of the Illinois Indian name "Mitchi Sipi."[22]

Father Marquette was born in Laon, France, in 1637; he entered the Society of Jesus in 1654 and just after ordination, in 1666, he was sent to French Canada. Three years later, he was at the Indian mission Pionte du Sainte Espirit at the western end of Lake Superior.[23] Now in his mid-thirties, he was about to embark on his most famous voyage.

Marquette and Joliet set out in May 1673 and reached the Mississippi River via the Illinois River by June 17. After stopping at villages along the river, the two Frenchmen arrived in July at a Quapaw village that Marquette called

Mitchigamea.[24] This was probably the same Quapaw village, Casqui, that De Soto had visited more than a century earlier. Their reception was far from friendly:

> We had recourse to our Patroness and guide, the Blessed Virgin Immaculate; and we greatly needed her assistance, for we heard from afar the savages who were inciting one another to the fray by their continual yells. They were armed with bows, and arrows, hatchets, clubs and shields. They prepared to attack us, on both land and water; part of them embarked in great wooden canoes–some to ascend, others to descend the river, in order to intercept us and surround us on all sides . . . In fact, some young men threw themselves into the water, to come and seize my canoe; but the current compelled them to return to land. One of them hurled his club which passed over us without striking us. In vain I showed the calumet, and made them signs that we were not coming to war against them. The alarm continued, and they were already preparing to pierce us with arrows from all sides, when God suddenly touched the hearts of the old men, who were standing on the water's edge. This no doubt happened through their sight of our calumet, which they had not clearly distinguished from afar; but as I did not cease displaying it, they were influenced by it, and checked the ardor of their young men. Two of the elders even . . . entered the canoes and made us approach the shore, whereon we landed, nor without fear on our part. At first we had to speak by signs, because none of them understood the six languages which I spoke. At last we found an old man who could speak a little Illinois.[25]

Upon concluding a meal with them, Marquette informed his pacified hosts that he was on his way to the sea. He then spoke to them briefly about God and His plan of salvation through Jesus Christ, but he doubted whether the Indians fully understood what he was saying. Despite the language barrier, the Jesuit felt that his address "was seed cast onto the ground, which will bear fruit in due season."[26] He and Joliet spent the night at the Quapaw village, but he admitted in his account that both slept "with some anxiety."[27]

Francis Shaw Guy, an early historian of Arkansas Catholicism, maintains that Marquette celebrated Mass for his Indian host the following morning and that this was the first Catholic Mass on Arkansas soil. There is no evidence of it in Marquette's report to his superior.[28] Guy may have been engaged in wishful thinking; the first recorded Catholic Mass in Arkansas would not take place for more than a quarter-century.

The two explorers continued their journey downriver with ten Indians as guides. They arrived at the Quapaw village they called Arkansas, which was near the junction of the Arkansas and Mississippi Rivers. Presents were exchanged, and a meal was shared before Marquette made another attempt to preach to these Indians. He told them of:

> God, who had created them, had pity on them, inasmuch as, after they had so long been ignorant of Him, He wished to make Himself known to all; that he was sent by God for that purpose; and they should accept what he told them of God and acknowledge Him as their Supreme Lord.[29]

After speaking at length about God and the mysteries of the Christian faith, Marquette inquired about the people down the river. The Indians replied that they knew little of the people in that area, but that the sea could be reached in about ten days. Marquette and Joliet conferred and quickly agreed that the Great River did not flow into the Pacific but into the Gulf of Mexico, which was under Spanish dominion. Moving farther south might mean capture and imprisonment by the Spanish. Their mission had been to locate the Great River and determine where it emptied. There was no further reason to continue downriver. They began their trip back upriver on Monday, July 17, 1673.[30]

At the end of September, in the Lake Michigan area, they separated and Joliet went to report to colonial officials.[31] Marquette stayed in the Great Lakes region, and during the winter of 1673-1674, wrote an account of his odyssey for his superior, Fr. Claude Dablon, S.J. He continued his mission work in the area and died on March 29, 1675, a month short of his thirty-eighth birthday.[32] Marquette's stay in Arkansas was brief, even shorter than that of De Soto's, but it was more significant because it marked the beginning of a long history of French Catholic missionary work in the area. For the next 130 years of the Colonial era, French Catholic priests would be practically the only Christian clergymen to serve in Arkansas.

Within a decade after Marquette's exploratory trip down the Mississippi, Robert Cavalier, Sieur de La Salle, arrived at the Quapaw village of Kappa in eastern Arkansas to formally take possession of the land for France. In a ceremony on March 13, 1682, La Salle claimed Arkansas for King Louis XIV and successors.[33] As it was with Spain, once the land was under the French king, it was expected that the subjects would join the religion of that monarch, Catholicism. Father Zenobius Membre, O.F.M., a member of the Order of the Friars Minor or Franciscans, accompanied the expedition as chaplain and erected a cross. He spoke to the Indians "of the truth of God, and the mysteries of our redemption, . . . During this time they showed that they relished what I said by raising their eyes to the heaven and kneeling as if to adore . . . on our return from the sea, we found that they had surrounded the cross with a palisade."[34] In the Indian mind-set, however, the cross itself was to have a magical quality. Pere Membre observed that he saw them "rub their hands over their bodies after rubbing them over the cross."[35] La Salle then continued downriver and claimed all the Mississippi River Valley for his king in April 1682.

While in Arkansas, La Salle granted one of his lieutenants, Henri de Tonti (or Tonty), a seignorial grant over Arkansas, and it was on that basis that the first European settlement would be made in the lower Mississippi River Valley near the junction of the Arkansas and Mississippi Rivers. Tonti was born in Italy in either 1649 or 1650, but was reared in France where his parents were political refugees. He returned to Arkansas in the spring of 1686 while descending the Mississippi to link up with La Salle, who was to come up the river from its mouth. Both hoped to choose a suitable capital for the new French colony which they called Louisiana. La Salle never made the rendezvous because his ship was blown off course, and he landed on the coast of what would become Texas. After many mishaps and tragedies and a mutiny, La Salle eventually was assassinated by his own men on a prairie in east Texas. Meanwhile, at the mouth of the Mississippi, Tonti sent scouting parties along the Gulf coast in both directions in a vain attempt to locate La Salle. Despairing, Tonti reluctantly ascended the Mississippi to the mouth of the Arkansas in May 1686. Six of his men asked to stay and establish a post under his seignory grant from La Salle. The commander saw the importance of a post as an entrepot between the Illinois country and the proposed colony of Louisiana near the mouth of the Mississippi. Arkansas Post was created, some thirty-two years before the founding of New Orleans. Since the Spanish had been driven out of what is now New Mexico by the Indian pueblo revolt in 1680, this was also the only European settlement in the United States west of the Mississippi River.[36]

When he left the settlement in the late spring of 1686, Tonti apparently had major plans for his Post. He styled himself *seigneur de ville de Tonti* (lord of the town of Tonti). There never was really much of a town at the Post in the seventeenth century; a recent historian contends that between 1686 and 1699 "there is no evidence that the European population of the place ever exceeded six."[37] When two survivors of the ill-fated La Salle group straggled into the Post in July 1687, they found only two Frenchmen. One of the survivors was Pere Louis Cavalier, priest and brother of the deceased explorer.[38] Tonti, its absent lord, had great visions for the place because he had granted to the Jesuits in 1689 a large grant of land to establish "a chapel and a mission house," asking only that they "build two chapels, raise a cross fifteen feet high, and say a Mass for Tonti on his feast day, that of St. Henry."[39] Whatever his plans, the ensuing war with the Iroquois Indians cut French Canada off from the Mississippi River until 1693.[40] By 1696, Jean Couture, a lieutenant of Tonti and one of the original settlers, realized how vulnerable the Post was militarily so he deserted to the English during the first of these Anglo-French wars in North America.[41] (In Europe the war was called the War of the League of Augsburg; in North America, the English colonists called it King William's War because it broke out during the reign of King William and Queen Mary. It lasted from 1689 to 1697.

It would be the first of four English-French conflicts on the continent.) When Tonti returned in late 1698, he discovered that his town had been abandoned. He did not stay around to revive it, but relocated on the Gulf coast where he died from yellow fever in September 1704. It is believed that he was buried near what is now Biloxi, Mississippi, but his grave has never been located.[42]

Tonti did bring with him in late 1698 missionaries from the Quebec Seminary to work in the lower Mississippi valley. Three missionaries came to Arkansas on December 27, 1698, yet the Arkansas Indians appeared to be so sickly and few that the leader of the missionaries, Father Francois de Montigny, left Arkansas in search of a larger number of Indians.[43] In late January 1699, Fr. Antoine Davion settled east of the Mississippi River among the Tunica Indians. Parts of the tribe inhabited the southeastern corner of Arkansas, mainly what is now Chicot County. His companions, Fathers Jean Francois Buisson de St. Cosme and Francois de Montigny, worked among tribes up and down the river, outside the present boundaries of the state.[44]

Only an accident brought a priest to the Quapaw Indians of Arkansas. In early September 1700, a boat carrying Fr. Joseph de Limoges and two companions capsized in the Mississippi River. By clinging to a tree, they floated with the current for three hours before making shore. They built a raft that carried them down to the Quapaws. During his days on the raft, Fr. Limoges sought the intercession of St. Francis Xavier, who "had struggled for his life in the water for as many days on a piece of plank."[45] The Indians located his overturned canoe which had been stopped by driftwood. All that was saved was his chalice, the cup used for the altar wine. Father Limoges stayed only for a few days and continued his journey downriver.[46]

Another Jesuit, Father Jacques Gravier, stopped at the Quapaw Kappa village on October 31, 1700. He asked about any missionaries coming through, and a few older Indians remembered a "black robe chief" who had come about twenty-seven years earlier. This was an obvious reference to Fr. Marquette's visit in the summer of 1673. Gravier asked if there were any sick among the Indians and received no response. He ate with them and gave them instructions on Christianity. The next morning being the Feast of All Saints, he said Mass for the Indians. It was the first recorded Catholic Mass ever said within the present boundaries of Arkansas and the Catholic Diocese of Little Rock.[47] It was 159 years after De Soto's visit and 143 years before the Pope created a Catholic diocese for Arkansas.

The year 1700 also witnessed the arrival of the first Catholic priest assigned to the Arkansas Quapaw Indians. He also would be the first missionary in the lower Mississippi Valley to suffer a violent death for his work. Nicholas Foucault was born in Paris and traveled to the New World to be a missionary. Ordained in Quebec on December 3, 1689, he worked among the Catholic parishes about a decade before being sent by the bishop of Quebec to work in Arkansas. He arrived in late December 1700 and stayed until July 1702. There is a vague reference to Foucault's "mistreatment" by the Indians, and a letter from Governor d'Iberville asking that a priest be sent to Choctaw and Chickasaw. The French missionary left eastern Arkansas for the recently founded French settlement of Mobile with two French soldiers and a few Korea Indians who were related to the Quapaws.[48] South of the junction of the Arkansas and Mississippi Rivers, on the eastern shore of the Father of Waters, the Indians fell upon the priest and the French soldiers and killed them all.[49] Later, Father Antoine Davion "recognized the hats, plates, and the altar which was still set up, and a few papers written by M. Foucault."[50] Father Davion gave the remains a Christian burial, but it is impossible to find the final resting place of the man whom an early American Catholic historian called "the first martyr of the Seminary of Quebec in the Valley of the Mississippi."[51] Davion ended his report with a touch of bitterness: "Nothing is to be expected from the mission if this murder is left unpunished."[52]

Because the French held the Quapaw Indians responsible for the murder of Fr. Foucault and the documents themselves were not specific about the "mistreatment" he received while working among the Quapaw, the French wrote off Arkansas as a mission field for a quarter-century. Not until 1727, after a European settlement was revived in Arkansas, would there be an effort to send a Catholic priest to the region.

In the first years of the eighteenth century, France was preoccupied with the massive War of the Spanish Succession (1701-1713). Only after the Treaty of Utrecht in 1713 was France capable of developing and expanding its holdings in North America. In the lower Mississippi Valley there was the founding of Natchitoches on the Red River (1714) and New Orleans near the mouth of the Mississippi (1718).[53] Four years later, New Orleans was made the capital of the colony of Louisiana, which included the Mississippi River Valley from the Gulf to the Great Lakes. As part of this effort to develop the area, the recently crowned King Louis XV, in 1717, granted to a Scotsman named John Law a monopoly of trade for his Compagnie d'Occident, or Company of the West. Law recruited hundreds of Frenchmen and Germans to settle on the Arkansas, and false stories were circulated about silver mines in Arkansas.[54] The French also believed that gold mines were hidden up the Arkansas River in the northern tip of land claimed by Spain as part of Mexico. This was the rationale behind Bernard de La Harpe's exploratory trip up the Arkansas River in 1722.[55]

In August 1721, a group of Law's emigrants arrived at the place where Tonti's post had stood. La Harpe found forty-seven persons "of both sexes" at the post in March 1722. It had been a rough winter for these early European inhabitants of Arkansas because half of them had perished in just over six months.[56] In October, Jesuit Father Francois Xavier de Charlevoix visited the re-established French post on his way down the Mississippi on an inspection tour for the king. He recommended in his final report in 1723 that a priest be sent to Arkansas.[57] In the spring of the year that Charlevoix penned his report to

Louis XV, Jesuit Father Jean Le Boullenger baptized two French children and presided over two marriages when he stopped by Arkansas Post.[58]

Charlevoix's recommendation would be late in implementation because of the fighting between the religious orders over mission territory. In December 1723, it was decided that all the territory north, east, and west of Natchez to the Great Lakes would be for the Jesuits, and they would be directed by a superior based in New Orleans, who would oversee what became known as the Jesuit Louisiana mission. The southern area was given to the Capuchins, a branch of the Franciscan order. One Capuchin grumbled that "the Jesuits promise more than they can keep."[59] This made Arkansas Post part of this vast mission area, and for the next forty years, Arkansas would be served only by French members of the Society of Jesus. The first priest sent to Arkansas died en route from New Orleans. On May 25, 1727, three more Jesuits departed from New Orleans for mission work upriver. On July 7, 1727, two of them continued upriver after leaving Father Paul du Poisson at the Arkansas Post.[60] He was the first resident priest since Foucault's departure a quarter-century earlier.

Father du Poisson was born in Epinal, France, on January 27, 1692. In his mid-thirties when he came to Arkansas, du Poisson was described by a colleague as a person of "common sense, . . . a good, very zealous man."[61] He believed that he was to serve not only the French at the Post but the nearby Indians as well. When he visited the Indians, he told them that he had neither gifts nor presents and wanted only the chance to "talk to them about the Great Spirit whom they did not know and that I had brought only the things necessary for that purpose."[62] The Indians referred to the Frenchman as the "black chief" due to his long black cassock.[63] The Jesuit arrived in the middle of a heat wave in the summer of 1727 and found the settlement in great want and misery. He wrote his superior:

> The time I have had to give to the sick has not prevented me exhorting every Sunday and every feast day, an address during Mass and an address of instruction after Vespers. I have the consolation of seeing that the greater part of them have profited by it, and have come to the Sacraments, and that the rest are inclined to do so. It is indeed a reward for the greatest labor if they are followed by the conversion of even one sinner.[64]

The Jesuit's duties were not only religious. When Bertrand Dufresne du Demaine, acting judge at the Post since 1722, departed, du Poisson was called on to settle disputes. According to a recent historian of colonial law in Arkansas, "Father Paul du Poisson, the Jesuit missionary resident from 1727 to 1729, used his good offices to maintain order among the approximately thirty Frenchmen who had remained behind."[65]

Fortunately, Father du Poisson did have some clerical assistance during most of his tenure: 44 year old Jesuit Brother Philip Crucy who arrived at the Post in the latter part of 1727. Unhappily, neither stayed long. Crucy died in early November 1729 from what was described as heat stroke, perhaps exhaustion.[66] Soon after burying his assistant, du Poisson set out for New Orleans to confer with the authorities on Indian migration and other matters. He stopped in Natchez on November 26, 1729, and said Mass the next day, the first Sunday of Advent. The following Monday, having said Mass in the morning, he was on his way to give communion to the sick when a large Indian threw the priest to the ground and cut off his head with a big hatchet.[67] He was the first Jesuit to shed his blood for the gospel in the Mississippi River Valley and the second consecutive priest assigned to Arkansas to lose his life after a short stay at the Post. His death on November 28, 1729, was exactly 114 years to the day before Pope Gregory XVI set up the Catholic Diocese of Little Rock.[68]

Soon after du Poisson's death in 1731, the crown revoked the charter for the Compagnie d'Occident, and Louisiana again became a crown colony directly under the authority of the king.[69] The Jesuit reaction to du Poisson's death was different from that of The Quebec seminary to the earlier death. Instead of abandoning the region, the Jesuits sent Father de Guyenne in 1734. He did not stay long. By the end of the year, he was in the Illinois country.[70] Three years later, a Father Avond arrived at New Orleans from France and was sent upriver to Arkansas. This French Jesuit stayed for three years. His superior, Father Vitry, visited the thirty year old missionary in October 1738 and recorded the crudeness of life for a missionary in early Arkansas. He described Father Avond's dwelling:

> His lodging is a . . . hut, the walls of which are made of splinters of wood; the roof of cypress bark; the chimney of mud mixed with dry grass, which is the straw in this country. I had elsewhere lived in such dwellings, but nowhere did I get so much fresh air, the house is full of cracks from top to bottom. However I deem myself happy to find myself here in company with Fr. Avond, who is successfully procuring me for the recovery of my health all the help his charity can think of.[71]

Father Vitry stayed with his confrere only a month, and Father Avond probably left Arkansas sometime in 1740. He went to New Orleans, where he stayed until January 1745. Father Avond then returned to France where he died in 1761.[72] For a decade after Father Avond's departure, no Jesuit priest would be available for Arkansas. During the 1740s, only one Catholic priest stopped in Arkansas to perform the sacraments. Father M. Laurent, a Canadian missionary, had come to New Orleans in 1743. He arrived at Arkansas Post in July 1744 and baptized four children, one being Elizabeth, the daughter of Commandant Montcharvaux, and one being an Indian girl eight or nine years old.[73]

A census in 1746 revealed twelve habitant families, ten slaves, and twenty men at the garrison. Judge Morris Arnold estimates from that information that outside of the garrison, Arkansas Post had about forty-eight free inhabitants.[74] Including the slaves, the population was near sixty. That was some progress because Father du Poisson had found only thirty whites and blacks at the Post in 1727. On May 10, 1749, about 150 Indians made an all-out attack on the Arkansas Post which was thwarted with great difficulty. A census that year showed some of the damage to the white population. The whites were down from forty-eight to thirty-one, but the African population had increased from ten to sixteen.[75] For security reasons, the Post moved farther along the northern shore of the Arkansas River, where it would stay for seven years, when it would once again be moved closer to the Mississippi River along the southern shore of the Arkansas.[76] Moving the Post around did not end the problems. When the commander traveled to New Orleans in June 1751 to confer with the governor, all six soldiers in the garrison took the opportunity to desert.[77] Into that situation came the last resident Catholic priest of the French era. He was a Jesuit priest and would stay longer in Arkansas than any Catholic clergyman before the Pope set up the Diocese of Little Rock in 1843.

Father Louis Carette was born in France, July 17, 1712, and joined the Jesuit order on September 30, 1731. He came to New Orleans in 1750 and arrived in Arkansas later that year.[78] Father Carette did a splendid job at the Post. He worked hard at learning the Indians' language, served as notary, and settled legal disputes.[79] What most frustrated this hard-working Jesuit was the apathy and irreligious conduct of those who dwelled at the Post. Though he was there a long time, he could never get them interested in building a church or rectory. The only place available for Mass was the dining room of the garrison. It was not a good place as a Jesuit superior would report:

> This was not a suitable place, not only because it was a dining room, but on account of the bad conduct and freedom of language of those who frequented it; everything that was in the fort entered there, even to the fowls. A hen flying over the altar overthrew the chalice, which had been left there at the end of mass. The spectators were not affected by this, and of those who ought to have been most concerned about it, exclaimed: 'There! the good God's shop is upset.' To these sentiments, so little religious, corresponded a life as little Christian. Father Carette at last concluded that he must withdraw, at least until a chapel be built in the fort, and until they were disposed to respect religion, besides he was necessary for work from which better success was expected.[80]

Father Carette left Arkansas forever in August 1758 and took with him the church records of the Post. He would also leave Louisiana forever in 1763. A French Jesuit would write later that century that Carette "labored to correct the morals of the French, but reaped hardly any fruit from his toil."[81]

The year that Carette left Louisiana, 1763, was important because the Jesuit order was suppressed in the French colonies and expelled from North America. The reason is not the focus of this study, but apparently the sons of St. Ignatius Loyola ran afoul of both the king and the religious authorities.[82] France also lost her fourth and final war for North America with England, and according to the Treaty of Paris signed in 1763, all her North American holdings disappeared. Britain received all of French Canada and everything south of the Great Lakes and east of the Mississippi River, including what was once Spanish Florida. To compensate Spain for its loss of Florida, France gave all of Louisiana west of the Mississippi River, plus New Orleans, to them. This placed Arkansas under Spanish rule for the rest of the eighteenth century. However, before this transfer occurred, Arkansas would be visited by one last French Jesuit priest. Father Sebastien Meurin, traveling upriver from New Orleans, paused for a day at Arkansas Post on March 1, 1764, and baptized seven persons.[83] This would be the end of the French era of Arkansas history. Catholicism would have to depend upon the Spanish religious authorities.

New rulers usually mean change, but in Arkansas' case it meant neglect of ecclesiastical matters. The already hard-pressed mission field of the French Jesuits would be turned over to the Spanish Franciscan Capuchins. This alone reduced the number of missionaries in Spanish Louisiana from thirteen to nine.[84] The political transfer of Louisiana from France to Spain would not be easy. The French in New Orleans revolted and expelled the first Spanish governor in 1766-1767, and not until Lt. Gen. Alejandro O'Reilly arrived in 1769 was the revolt crushed. Spanish rule in French Louisiana would not be challenged after 1770.[85]

The Church followed the state in the Spanish colony, and not until 1770 was Arkansas' ecclesiastical status determined. When O'Reilly wrote a memorandum in February 1770 outlining where priests should be sent, he did not even include Arkansas, but later that year Arkansas Post became a mission of the parish of St. Genevieve, a town about one hundred miles south of St. Louis.[86] The priest there was supposed to go periodically to the Post. In the next twenty years, Arkansas saw only two priests on three occasions. Father P. Valentin, one of the few French Capuchin priests who stayed in the Spanish colony, visited the Post on April 19, 1772, to baptize three persons. The next month, this Franciscan Capuchin was in St. Louis to become the first resident priest for that small village. Only the Spanish Capuchin, Father Luis Guignes, O.F.M. Cap., pastor at St. Genevieve, even attempted to fulfill his duties at the Post. He presided at one marriage and baptized sixteen adults on July 19, 1786, and between January 12 and 26, 1789, he witnessed four marriages and baptized thirty-four persons.[87]

While Arkansas was part of St. Genevieve parish, 1770-1790, tremendous political changes occurred east of the Mississippi River. The thirteen British colonies from New England to Georgia revolted in 1775 and declared their independence in 1776. The eight-year conflict between England and her North American colonies drew France to the side of the Americans. France sought revenge on its longtime foe. On June 21, 1779, Spain declared war on England as an ally of France. In December 1780, Holland came into the war against Great Britain.[88] All the diplomatic activity meant that Spanish Louisiana, including Arkansas, could be open for an attack from the British-held territory east of the Mississippi River.

In the year that Spain declared war on England, Captain Balthazar de Villiers at Arkansas Post wrote Spanish Governor Bernardo de Galvez in New Orleans that he had moved the Post back from the Mississippi and farther along the north shore of the Arkansas River. This was its location between 1749 and 1756 and the location of Arkansas Post today. The move was not until May 1779, owing mainly to flood damage that spring, but it turned out to be a wise move militarily because war between Spain and England broke out a month later.[89] Though the move made the Post a little less vulnerable, the Post was still exposed because of its "isolation and the smallness of its garrison."[90] Not until 1781 did the Spanish raise the number of troops at the Post from eight to twenty.[91] They would need all the help they could get because British agent James Colbert, together with about seventy Chickasaw Indians, attacked the Post at 2:50 a.m. on April 17, 1783. By the middle of the morning, the forces at the Post repelled the attack and prevented a British capture.[92] The final peace treaty was signed in early September 1783. By the Treaty of Paris, the American republic received all the land east of the Mississippi River from Florida to the Great Lakes. For its part in the war, Spain won back both east and west Florida, which included the area from Baton Rouge to Mobile and the whole Florida peninsula. Spain would have control over all the coastline of the Gulf of Mexico.[93]

Owing to the weakness of the new American republic, Spain expanded its hold of territory to the eastern shore of the Mississippi. It controlled Natchez, and in 1795 built a fort at Chickasaw Bluffs, the present site of Memphis.[94] Arkansas Post's population expanded after the American Revolution. A 1777 census recorded only fifty whites and eleven slaves. Fifty years earlier, Father du Poisson had reported only thirty residents. By 1791, about 107 whites and 37 slaves lived there. In less than fifteen years, both the European and African populations had doubled. According to the same 1791 census, about eighty percent were of French descent, with Germans and Spanish making up the rest of the white population.[95] Seven years later, a new census revealed that the white population had more than tripled to 341 persons. There were fifty-six slaves and three free persons of color. The French accounted for about seventy percent of the whites. Along with the German and Spanish names, there was now an Anglo-American minority at the Post. They apparently crossed the Mississippi River into Spanish Arkansas.[96]

The last decade of the eighteenth century would also see a greater number of Catholic priests in Arkansas. In 1790, Arkansas Post was made part of a mission of New Madrid, a new town about two hundred miles south of St. Louis.[97] The Post was still a mission, for it had no resident priest, but the home parish was now closer and more accessible for visits by the parish priest.

The first priest in Arkansas from New Madrid was Father Pierre Gibault, who visited the Post in September 1792. A fifty-five year old native of Montreal, Gibault had been in the mission field since ordination in 1768. A decade later, he would be the only Catholic priest in the area north of the Ohio River, south of the Great Lakes, and east of the Mississippi River. In that capacity, he had encouraged the French settlers in Illinois to support the American cause during the Revolution.[98] The priest grew disillusioned with the new republic and its bishop in Baltimore, because in 1789 he crossed the Mississippi into Spanish territory where he was given the Post at New Madrid. He visited the Post six times between September 1792 and September 1793, presiding at twenty marriages and baptizing thirty persons. He never came back to Arkansas after 1793, although he continued to be the pastor at New Madrid until his death in 1802.[99]

A French Capuchin, Fr. Sebastien Flavien de Besancon, a fugitive from the French Revolution, came to assist at a marriage in April 1794 and stayed until July. He reported, even at that late date, Arkansas Post had no church, chapel, or confessional.[100] Since it was unclear how Fr. Flavien came to Arkansas or what diocese he was a part of, he had to go to New Orleans to receive full clerical faculties. He was later assigned to St. Charles along the German coast near New Orleans.[101]

The next Catholic priest to visit Arkansas, like Father Flavien, had fled the French Revolution, and like Father Gibault, had once served in the United States. Father Pierre Janin was a French diocesan priest who came to the United States in March 1792 with a group of priests from the Society of St. Sulpice. The Sulpicians were used by Bishop John Carroll of Baltimore to begin his seminary, St. Mary's. Father Janin and Sulpician Father Jean Francois Rivet were sent to the Indian missions of the far northwest. Father Janin came to his Post at Kaskaskia in October 1795.[102] Father Janin, in the words of his colleague Father Rivet, "had no aptitude for missionary work," especially when the Post was primarily for work among the Indians.[103] Within six months, he had abandoned his Post and crossed the Mississippi into Spanish Louisiana. He entered not only a new political domain but a new diocese.

In 1793, Pope Pius VI created the Diocese of Florida and Louisiana with New Orleans being the seat for the new diocese. This was to be the Catholic diocese for all the Spanish territory in North America. Luis Ignacio Penalver y Cardenas of Havana, Cuba, became the first bishop and arrived in New Orleans in July 1795.[104] In the spring of 1796, Father Janin was on his way to New Orleans when he received his assignment to Arkansas in Spanish-occupied Natchez. He agreed to it on May 17, 1796. The assignment meant that he had to go upriver to the Post, the first resident priest in Arkansas in almost forty years. The Spanish governor, Francisco Luis Hector de Carondelet, approved the appointment on May 31, and Bishop Penalver y Cardenas approved it the next day. Whether he was awaiting the final word on his appointment or he was merely slow, Father Janin did not arrive at the Arkansas Post until August 5, 1796.[105]

As the first resident priest since Carette left in 1758, Father Janin had to face a flock whose spiritual needs had been neglected for a generation. One of his first objectives was to build a church, but the French-born Spanish governor of Louisiana, Francois Louis Hector de Carondelet, felt that the Post would not be ready for one or two or three more years. The Arkansas Post pastor wrote to New Orleans complaining that his rectory was so rotten that he could not live in it. The government agreed in the summer of 1799 to rebuild the priest's house with a kitchen and an expanded room that would be used as a chapel. The most recent historian of this period contradicts earlier accounts and maintains that Janin failed to get a church built. This meant that throughout the whole Colonial period, the French, and then the Spanish, never built a Catholic church in Arkansas.[106] During his three and a half years, Janin presided over twenty-one marriages, baptized seventy-two infants and adults, and buried twenty-six persons.[107] Father Janin, who had ministered to Indians in his earlier post at Kaskaskia in Illinois, was happier serving the growing European-African settlement at Arkansas Post, and he all but ignored the surrounding tribes. Whatever future plans Father Janin might have had for building a church were over when the bishop of Spanish Louisiana and Florida transferred him to St. Louis in September 1799. He left on December 28, 1799.[108] There would be no resident Catholic priest in Arkansas for more than three decades.

Before the end of the Colonial era, another Catholic priest would visit Arkansas Post. Father Juan Brady, an Irishman working as a missionary in Spanish Louisiana and a member of the Order of Our Lady of Mt. Carmel, or Carmelites, came up the Mississippi River in 1802 from his parish, Our Lady of Mt. Carmel, in Avoyelles in what is now east central Louisiana. He ministered during the week of July 12-16 and for two days in August. He baptized forty-nine persons and witnessed three marriages.[109] Father Brady would be the last Catholic priest to serve in Arkansas before the United States acquired it.

For more than a century, France and Spain had sovereignty over the land that would become the state of Arkansas. Both of these Catholic countries, however, had sparingly sent missionaries. Consequently, Catholicism never became deeply rooted in the hearts and minds of the people. Throughout the eighteenth century, a Catholic priest served the area for twenty years. Religious activities were clearly the exception, not the rule. Not until the last decade of the century did Arkansas Post have more than a hundred European and African settlers, and no church was built. Lieutenant Governor Athanase de Mezieres at Natchitoches wrote in 1770 that the people who lived on the Arkansas River above the Post were mainly outlaws. "Most of those who lived there," he said, "have either deserted from the troops and ships of the most Christian King or have committed robberies, rape, and homicide, that River being the asylum of the most wicked persons, without doubt, in all the Indies."[110] Sixteen years later, Jean Filhiol, a Frenchman working for the Spanish and commandant of Ouachita Post or what is now Monroe, Louisiana, wrote that the people who lived up the Ouachita River in Arkansas "are the scum of all sorts of nations, several fugitives from their native countries, and who have become fixed here through their attachment to their idleness and independence, . . . As for their morals, hardly do they know whether they are Christian."[111] The lack of a priest meant that people were married before military officials, with the stipulation that they would be married by a priest if and when one arrived. The people grew accustomed to living together, and a few refused to get married even when a clergyman came.[112] As Judge Arnold has written, "Clearly, the inhabitants of Louisiana, and of Arkansas in particular, were not especially devout."[113] If the Church was not very effective, it was nonetheless important. According to French law, a priest could and did act as notary royal for all acts and contracts, and the Church did try to set a standard of morality.[114] The Church in both France and Spain demanded that the slaves be baptized and buried with the free persons in a Christian grave. The Church had a difficult time getting the slave owners to allow a priest to marry their slaves.[115] The Church did act as a beacon of morality and stability, albeit under difficult circumstances. As Judge Arnold has commented, "It is a tribute to the persuasiveness of the priests of Arkansas that they were able to impose as much order on the place as they were."[116] Yet it is true that the Church was weak, and except for some baptismal records from 1796-1802, there is "little left behind to indicate what influence it was in fact able to bear."[117]

On October 1, 1800, Spain secretly ceded to France all of Spanish Louisiana west of the Mississippi River. Spain already had pulled out of Natchez and Chickasaw Bluffs with the ratification of Pinckney's Treaty in 1796. Not until early 1803 did it become known that France controlled Louisiana. On April 30, 1803, France sold the area to the United States for $15,000,000. Not until November 30, 1803, did France take formal possession of Louisiana, and on December 20, 1803, an American governor assumed control over the area in a ceremony in New Orleans. On March 23, 1804, Lt. James B. Many of the American army, "bearing a commission from the French colonial prefect Pierre Laussat to act for the French Republic, received the dilapidated Fort San Estevan from Spanish Capt. Francisco Caso y Luengo who commanded there for Spain."[118] Quietly, an American military officer assumed control of Arkansas from a Spanish officer while carrying a French document. In this strange fashion, Arkansas formally came under the control of the United States.

French heritage in Arkansas mainly consists of the French spelling of the state's Indian name, and a few French place names like Lake Chicot and Chicot

County, Petit Jean, Cache River, Dardanelle, Des Arc, Maumelle, Mount Magazine, Fourche Bayou, Poteau Mountain and River, and Saline River and County.[119] At the time of the transfer, about 450 persons lived in the area, and of these about sixty were slaves.[120] Most of these persons called themselves Roman Catholics. They may have been Catholic in name but not in practice, but Catholicism was the first Christian church in what would become Arkansas. While Catholicism would later be characterized by some as something alien to the state, Roman Catholicism was present at the European discovery of Arkansas by De Soto and at Tonti's founding of Arkansas Post. Catholicism may not have not flowered in colonial Arkansas but it persisted and survived, even without much clerical presence. Even when it became a United States Territory, it was still the dominant religious faith of Arkansans of European descent. These early Arkansans had no idea how the change of ownership to the United States would profoundly alter their social, economic, and religious structures.

CHAPTER II

To the Suburb of Hell

Catholic Missionaries in Arkansas, 1803-1843

AN EARLIER HISTORIAN of Arkansas Catholicism has characterized the era from the Louisiana Purchase to the formation of the Little Rock Diocese as an "interim".[1] In this equivalent to a Biblical generation of forty years, Arkansas experienced tremendous political, social, economic, and religious changes. When this vast territory was purchased from Napoleon in 1803, Catholicism was the dominant religion of the non-Indian peoples of that portion which later became Arkansas. By the middle of the nineteenth century, less than one percent of the state population identified themselves as Roman Catholics–not a period of "interim" but one of profound transformation. There was metamorphosis from a remote European colony inhabited by a handful of French and Spanish settlers to a booming American frontier state, flooded by an Anglo-American migration from east of the Mississippi River. Two institutions of differing fortunes, African slavery and the Catholic Church, persisted into the American period. While slavery in Arkansas waxed, Catholicism waned. This Church went from a state-supported, nominally-dominant spiritual institution to a beleaguered denomination. That status had not substantially changed a century and a half after creation of the Arkansas diocese in 1843.

Fifteen years after an American officer appeared at the Arkansas Post to assume control of the area, President James Monroe signed the act creating the Arkansas Territory. On June 15, 1836, President Andrew Jackson approved the act making Arkansas the twenty-fifth state in the Federal Union.[2] It was the sesquicentennial of the founding of the first European outpost in Arkansas in 1686 by Henri de Tonti. As Judge Morris Arnold has observed, the Anglo-American legal system had now completely supplanted the older Franco-Spanish legal tradition.[3] These legal-political changes merely reflected the immense demographic-social upheaval occurring in Arkansas. Since the 1790s, Arkansas experienced incredible growth in its white and black populations. In 1791, a Spanish census had found only 170 whites and thirty-seven slaves; eleven years later, Frenchman Francois Marie Perrin du Lac estimated that the Arkansas Post had a population of about 450.[4] The first United States census in Arkansas in 1810 found a population of 1,062: 924 whites, 136 African slaves, and two free persons of color. Ten years later, just a year after the creation of the Arkansas Territory, the white population jumped to 12,579; the slave to 1,617; and fifty-nine free blacks. By 1830, the white population rose to 25,671; 4,579 slaves; and 141 free persons of color. During the 1830s, the population grew so rapidly that by 1840 the white population tripled to 77,174; the slave population quadrupled to 19,935; and free blacks more than tripled to 465.[5] In less than a half-century, Arkansas' non-Indian population grew from 144 to almost 100,000, practically all occurring after the cession of Louisiana, and consisting of Anglo-American settlers from the older southern states.[6]

These new settlers brought not only their hopes, dreams, families, property, and slaves, but also their culture and Protestant faith. The 1850 census was the first to note religious breakdown; there were 1,600 Catholics, or one percent out of a total white population of 162,189. At mid-century, there were only seven Catholic churches, in contrast to 168 Methodist churches, 114 Baptist churches, and 52 Presbyterian churches.[7] Catholics were a dwindling religious denomination in an increasingly large pool of Protestants.

While the decline in Arkansas Catholicism is principally attributable to the influx of Anglo-American Protestants, there was also a substantial amount of ecclesiastical confusion, neglect, and bickering, beginning at the time of the cession of Louisiana. With the departure of Bishop Penalver y Cardenas from New Orleans in 1801, the young diocese soon became embroiled in a factional dispute over control of St. Louis Cathedral, the main church of the New Orleans See. By the spring of 1805, there was an open schism which was not healed for almost forty years.[8] During that time, Pope Pius VII placed the whole Louisiana Purchase under the temporary supervision of the Bishop of Baltimore.[9] It would be another decade before the Vatican named forty-nine year old Haitian-born Louis William Dubourg as Bishop of New Orleans. Dubourg was no stranger to the diocese for he had been serving as Apostolic Administrator since 1812.[10] Dubourg's diocese covered the Louisiana Purchase and what would be much of Alabama and Mississippi. In the seven years that Dubourg served as bishop, only one priest came into Arkansas, Father L.A. Chaudorat. He was a French priest who stayed only a year, but was the first priest at the Post since Father Juan Brady in 1802. Father Chaudorat had come to the United States in 1817 as a seminarian, and had been ordained for the Kentucky Catholic Diocese of Bardstown. Unhappy with his duties there, he migrated across the Mississippi River into the New Orleans diocese to take up self-appointed pastoral duties at the Arkansas Post, arriving there in April 1820 and staying until the following spring.[11] A later Arkansas missionary claimed that Chaudorat was "extremely avaricious;" charging "enormous sums" for baptizing, stealing the public mail, and leaving laden with money.[12] Twelve years after he left, Father Chaudorat was still remembered for his greed by French settlers at the Post.[13] These complaints, however, must be considered in light of the character of the settlers at the Post. Englishman Thomas Nuttall visited the Post in 1819 and caustically commented, "The love of amusements, here, as in most French colonies, is carried to extravagance, particularly gambling and dancing parties or balls."[14] Chaudorat may have fit well into this environment, and when he departed in 1821, the Arkansas Post would not see a resident Catholic priest for a decade.

On July 14, 1823, Father Joseph Rosati was named coadjutor to the Bishop of New Orleans with residence in St. Louis and ecclesiastical jurisdiction north of the state of Louisiana.[15] Rosati's jurisdiction also covered the western half of what is now the states of Wisconsin and Illinois. Three years later, this area was formally constituted the Diocese of St. Louis, and Rosati would be consecrated as its first bishop in May 1826.[16]

Joseph Marie Rosati was born in Naples, Italy, in 1789 and became a Catholic priest in the Congregation of the Missions in 1811. (This Congregation was also known as the Lazarists or Vincentians.) He arrived in the United States in 1817 with Bishop Dubourg to serve this mission territory. A year later, he was named as one of the first faculty members of the new Congregation of the Missions' seminary at St. Mary of the Barrens in Perry County, Missouri. In 1821, he became seminary rector, then coadjutor, and finally bishop of the new diocese at the age of thirty-seven.[17] Until the establishment of an Arkansas See, Bishop Rosati maintained a twenty-year interest in placing missions in the southern part of his ecclesiastical domain. (A mission is a small parish which the priest visits regularly on Sunday or only on an occasional basis.)

An 1819 travel guide mentions Arkansas Territory's "principal villages are the Post of Arkansas, situated about sixty miles above the mouth of the river, Davidsonville, on the Big Black river, and small village at the commencement of the high lands of the Arkansa (sic), at a place called the Little Rock."[18] This would be the travel itinerary for Rosati's first sanctioned missionary tour of Arkansas. In early September 1824, he dispatched two young Vincentians; one priest and one sub-deacon. Father Jean Marie Odin, a twenty-four year old Frenchman ordained for only fifteen months, would lead the expedition, and his companion would be the twenty-seven year old sub-deacon from Pennsylvania, John Timon.[19]

Commissioned formally by Rosati on August 24, 1824, the two Lazarist clerics began their journey southward from St. Mary of the Barrens on September 8, 1824.[20] Entering Arkansas from its northeastern corner, they found five French families eighteen miles from Davidsonville, just inside the Territory. Odin later reported that "after spending a few days with them, we started toward Bate [Batesville], a town situated on the White River, and toward Little Rock, a small town built on the banks of the Arkansas River, and seat of the government."[21] Father Odin would be the first Catholic priest to visit Little Rock.[22] Odin and Timon then traveled down the Arkansas River to the Arkansas Post and across land to a Quapaw Indian village near Helena. Here they met a Quapaw Indian chief named Sarasin,[23] who greeted them with great love and affection. Odin celebrated Mass for the tribe on a rustic altar in a wigwam. They planned to visit the Ouachita River region, but the miserable condition of their horses, the lack of money, and a terrible fever which beset Odin convinced them to return. They were back at St. Mary's by the first part of November 1824.[24]

Bishop Rosati felt heartened by the reception the clerics Odin and Timon received in Arkansas, but discouraged about sending any more missionaries to the area. Before they arrived back at St. Mary's, he wrote Mother Philippine Duchesne of Sacred Heart sisters in St. Louis:

> Messrs. Odin and Timon in their trip to the Arkansas found the most beautiful dispositions above all in the Americans who until now profess no sect; . . . Our men were received with the greatest respect by the Savages who showed an extraordinary penchant for civilization and the Catholic religion. But no workers, no means. Let us pray for the Master of the Harvest to send us some. [25]

A year later, the Italian-born bishop wrote to Father Peter Caprano, the Secretary of the Office of Propaganda in Rome, that one priest for Arkansas "would not be sufficient in this vast territory which increases so rapidly in population . . . Till now I have not been in a position to do anything, having neither the priests nor the means."[26] In the same letter, he noted that Odin and Timon had baptized about two hundred people while in Arkansas, and that the Quapaw Indians desired to have a priest live among them.[27]

After their tour of frontier Arkansas, Odin and Timon would enjoy distinguished careers in the young American Catholic Church. Odin became a missionary in Texas and was named the Vicar Apostolic in 1842. In 1848, he was consecrated as the first Bishop of Galveston, the diocese for all of Texas. Thirteen years later, Pope Pius IX named him the second Archbishop of New Orleans, the position he held until his death in 1870.[28] Ordained as a Vincentian priest in 1826, Timon became the first Superior for the American province of the Congregation of the Missions in 1835. He, too, served as a missionary to Texas from 1838 to 1841, but returned as superior for the Lazarists until 1847 when he was named the first Bishop of the Diocese of Buffalo, New York, serving until his death twenty years later.[29]

Soon after assuming office, Bishop Rosati wrote the Society of the Precious Blood in Europe two appeals for priests to be sent explicitly to Arkansas, but no priest ever came. On June 13, 1829, the bishop directed Father Jean Martin of Avoyelles, Louisiana, to make a missionary tour of Arkansas. Father Martin did travel to the Arkansas Post, Pine Bluff, and even to Little Rock, yet returned to Louisiana in late January 1830. Msgr. Holweck, an early historian of the Archdiocese of St. Louis, described Fr. Martin as a "poor man" of "stubborn and scrupulous disposition," who "did not know how to treat the long neglected and careless Catholics of Arkansas."[32]

After Father Martin abandoned Arkansas, Bishop Rosati turned once again to Europe for help. He wrote the Leopoldine Society in Vienna, Austria, on March 10, 1830, appealing for financial assistance:

> In the territory of Arkansas and especially at the Post, there are many Catholics of French extraction. These Catholics have no priest with them, and are visited once a year by a priest of the Seminary . . . The small number of priests in my diocese, and the lack of means to support them in a land of great poverty, have so far prevented me from sending these Catholics to a resident priest. If Providence should bless with means, I would gladly place two priests in those regions, where religion could make wonderful progress, and to erect there a convent-school for girls.[33]

Eighteen months later, the Leopoldine Society sent a generous gift amounting to $2,500.00 quite a large sum of money at that time.[34] Rosati now had the means, but needed the men.

To lead this new mission, Rosati chose the rector of the cathedral in St. Louis, Father Edmund Saulnier. A native of Gascony province in France, Saulnier had taught languages at St. Louis College from 1819 to 1825 when he was named rector of the cathedral. He had asked to be sent out of St. Louis, yet desired some post in Missouri or Illinois. To his chagrin, he was sent to the wilds of Arkansas. Rothensteiner, the historian of the Archdiocese of St. Louis, described him as a "loquacious Gascon" who "never could get along with any assistant. He often quarrelled with his bishop . . . he consistently complained of his 'beggarly income'."[35] These personal failings of Saulnier would hamper the mission in Arkansas for, true to the comment of Rothensteiner, he would not be able to get along with his assistant in Arkansas, Father Pierre F. Beauprez. Beauprez hailed from Flanders and spoke Flemish, French, and German fluently, but English quite poorly. Beauprez had just been ordained on November 20, 1831, and eight days later, Rosati sent him as a companion with Saulnier to Arkansas. The two men met each other for the first time at St.

Genevieve and began their journey south.[36]

The missionaries arrived at the Post on December 14, 1831, and their reception was as cold as the weather. There was no chapel or rectory, and they had to rent a hut for the Sunday Mass scheduled for December 18. No one came because the ground was covered with sleet.[37] Besides the apathy of the people and the wintry conditions, another problem was the unhappy relationship of Saulnier and Beauprez. It was as frigid as the outside temperature. Saulnier wrote the bishop on Christmas Eve:

> My companion, Mr. Beauprez, seems to be a good man who follows the rules of his profession, but appears to be much attached to his own opinions and hates to give them up. Besides, he is not very active; if the house would fall on his back, he would hardly move. Although he is only a novice, he wants to be my equal.[38]

Upon hearing that many French were living near Pine Bluff, Saulnier informed the bishop in this same letter that he would minister there, leaving Beauprez at the Arkansas Post. Saulnier also hoped to establish a mission from Pine Bluff to Little Rock since "there are many ignorant Protestants there, and very few Catholics; but the priest would have to know English well and be a good controversialist."[39] In leaving the Post for Pine Bluff, Saulnier believed he was getting the easier assignment for "the inhabitants of the Post are very indifferent and ignorant; they have forgotten nearly everything."[40] Saulnier failed to realize how abandoned they had been.

In a postscript to his Christmas Eve letter, Saulnier happily noted more than fifty people were at Christmas Mass. Saulnier later told the parishioners that a church and house were necessary if a permanent priest was to be acquired. The people responded well and began to gather $167.00 for a church building and $47.00 to support the priest. The people wanted both priests to stay, but Saulnier responded that there were too few Catholics and the other priest was needed in other areas.[41] The two priests were still not getting along as a Saulnier letter revealed. "For nearly six days there has been an altercation between us and on New Year's day, we were both in ill humor; I even feared at one time he was going to leave me, as he threatened to do about the 2nd and 3rd of January."[42] Six days after writing that letter, on January 13, 1832, Saulnier wrote Rosati that since the people of the Post preferred a Frenchman over a Flemish prist, he changed his mind and decided to send Beauprez up the river to Pine Bluff.[43]

Believing that the Post would not even support one priest, Saulnier left for New Orleans to solicit more funds. He wrote to Rosati in late February that he had raised $400.00.[44] Beauprez traveled to Pine Bluff in February, baptizing children and adults; he stayed at Pine Bluff until the following summer.[45] From Pine Bluff in mid March, Beauprez complained to Rosati about Saulnier. "Mr.

Saulnier is a good man, but singular in his actions. If I crack a joke, he does not understand it; if I say something serious, it is a phantom to him. If I try to engage him in conversation on the duties of our ministry, I can hardly get a word out of him . . . he treats his dog better than me."[46]

In March, Saulnier was back at the Post with his additional collections from New Orleans, plus money he gathered at the Post. He proudly reported to Rosati that he now had over $800.00.[47] In a letter dated April 9, 1832, Saulnier revealed that he had found a census which Fr. Martin had conducted in January 1830. Although rather rudimentary, the first census of Arkansas Catholics conducted after the Louisiana Purchase reports as follows:

	Whites	**Blacks**
Arkansas Post	247	108
Jefferson County	204	60
Little Rock	38	3
Fort Smith	33	3

Saulnier commented, "this census does not to seem to be exact; there may be one thousand and more."[48]

Saulnier had plans to build a church and a rectory for $1,200.00; he also wrote the Sisters of Charity about a school.[49] About a month later, he revealed to Rosati that about $1,300.00 was spent for a two-story house, stable, kitchen, and smokehouse.[50] Instead of using the money for a church, the reason given for its collection, he spent the entire sum for a rather regal rectory.

Soon after moving into these comparatively sumptuous quarters, Saulnier decided to abandon Arkansas after a tragic-comedic episode with a married couple he was trying to reconcile. The husband pulled a loaded pistol and threatened to kill the priest for giving the wife some bad advice. The young man eventually calmed down, and no one was physically harmed, but the incident so unnerved Saulnier he wanted to leave.[51] Beauprez hurried downriver to the Post to dissuade him from departing, but Saulnier remained firm in his decision. This greatly disturbed Beauprez, and he pleaded to Rosati that summer:

> The departure of my confrere, Mr. Saulnier, afflicts and discourages me much . . . Here I am in this wretched country, abandoned, alone. With tears in my eyes I have wished a hundred times that I never heard mention of America, never had seen it . . . Father, for the love of my salvation, have pity on me. Take me from this suburb of hell![52]

Beauprez and Saulnier might have had their differences, but to be completely abandoned in this huge country genuinely frightened the young Flemish priest.

Despite Beauprez's pleadings, Saulnier left Arkansas for good on July 14,

1832, and arrived in St. Louis by August 3rd.[53] On August 17, Rosati reassigned him to Vide Poche, or Carondolet, Missouri, a town just south of St. Louis.[54] Beauprez remained at the Arkansas Post for a few more months. The situation appeared hopeless, and he wrote Rosati October 1st, "I go to the Post every Sunday to say Mass, but I have to say it to the bare walls, a sad spectacle!"[55] Rosati removed him within days with the short note: "You may go down to Donaldsonville and then come up to the Seminary. I appoint you to Apple Creek,"[56] a German parish in Perry County, Missouri, where the Flemish priest could use his fluent German.[57] Beauprez left the Arkansas Post on October 25[58] and headed south by boat to Donaldsonville, Louisiana. He never returned to the St. Louis diocese and on February 2, 1833, Bishop Rosati reluctantly transferred him to the New Orleans diocese.[59] Rosati must have been discouraged by these turn of events. Despite his best efforts, he could not keep a priest in Arkansas for more than a year. After almost three decades of American occupation, there was still no resident priest for the ever dwindling Catholic population. One collected a great deal of money to build a church and instead purchased a very elaborate rectory for himself; both Father Chaudorat and Father Saulnier were perceived as very greedy clerics.

A lesser man might have written off the Territory of Arkansas, but Rosati determinedly sent another Catholic priest to serve his flock in the southern part of his diocese. Father Ennemond Dupuy was a native of Lyon, France, and had been ordained at the same time as Beauprez on November 20, 1831, but had stayed at the seminary to work on his English. On October 4, 1832, Bishop Rosati commissioned him to go to Arkansas and presented him with $450.00 to sustain his mission.[60] After collecting his belongings at the seminary, Dupuy boarded a ship travelling south on the Mississippi River to its junction with the Arkansas. Dupuy outlined his difficult journey in a long letter to his bishop written at the Arkansas Post October 29, 1832:

> On the 27th of this month the steamboat cast me and my belongings on the shore of the Mississippi and my horse into the water; the stupid boat hands tried to make it walk over a board which was so narrow that even a bird could hardly walk over it without slipping. Besides, it was 12:50 A.M. The next morning I started, but my horse so stiff in consequence of the boat ride and the fall into water, and the road was so bad, that I could make only eighteen miles. The road is so dreadful that, without exaggeration, you have to make twelve miles in the mud up to your knees . . . I had to pay half a dollar to cross the White River and several lakes or creeks, in water up to the girth. At last I found a miserable hut in which a Creole lives, who made me pay only a dollar and a quarter to keep me and my horse overnight. Next morning, (it was Sunday), I left and arrived at the Post about noon. Of the inhabitants some were out hunting, others were busy at the gin mill,

> others trying and selling their horses, others playing billiards . . . At the first report that a new priest had come to take the place of those who had left, a crowd gathered around me, asking me a thousand questions: who I was, what had become of Mr. Saulnier, etc.; then they turned around and laughing and saying: 'This one won't stay long.'[61]

Dupuy left the next day for Pine Bluff, and there his reception was quite warm. He found the people "much more simple, more religious, and less arrogant."[62] Chaudorat and Saulnier did damage at the Arkansas Post for Dupuy observed that "at the Post, with few exceptions, everybody looks at me with evil eye on account of those who were here before me."[63] Dupuy discovered that Beauprez had promised the people at Pine Bluff that he would return, yet he left with all the sacred vessels and vestments.[64] The years without priest or clergy had greatly weakened the Catholic faith. In a letter to the bishop dated January 7, 1833, Dupuy stated, "It will take ten years of work, of patience, of bodily sufferings, and heartache, before we may look for any spiritual improvement amongst these people . . . It is useless to speak to them of abstinence, fasting, or confession, or of the duty to marry before a priest . . ."[65] He wrote the bishop in April that he was of good heart, but saddened that nearly half the population of Arkansas Post died during the winter without asking for the last sacramental rites. He also reported that his income amounted to only $3.00, and his expenses were over $300.00. He asked Rosati for an assistant who must "be a man, stouthearted, disinterested, and gentle."[66] He hoped his friend, Father Jean Bouillier, CM of Old Mines, Missouri, would stop and see him in May, but he never came.[67]

In the latter part of August, Dupuy was back in St. Louis to receive from Rosati a land deed to build a church in Little Rock. He traveled down the Mississippi River to New Orleans to stay two and a half months with a priest friend at a parish along the German coast. He did not return to Pine Bluff, Arkansas, until December 16, 1833.[68] By the following April, he had built a small church house which was well attended even by a few Protestants. This small building constructed in 1834 was the first Catholic church ever built in Arkansas, just three miles south of Pine Bluff on the Arkansas River. Father Dupuy was pleased with the progress at Pine Bluff, but disappointed with the Arkansas Post, where the people were not interested in going to confession, or hearing Mass, even during Lent. Thus, he did not celebrate Mass there.[69] In a letter to the bishop dated July 9, 1834, Dupuy hoped to build a newer, bigger church at Pine Bluff; unfortunately, he discovered that his deed for a church in Little Rock was actually for an area thirty-six miles northeast of Little Rock on the road to Batesville. "I doubt," he wrote, "there will be enough people there to build a chapel."[70] In the same letter he wrote, "Yesterday, I had a wedding, the first since I have been in this mission. When I came here, the people believed that marriages contracted before a priest were no good."[71]

In the summer of 1834, the French priest made his first visit to Little Rock, five years after Father Martin's short sojourn. Father Dupuy was visibly impressed with the beauty and location of "Petit Rocher"[sic]. He described the people as gentle, but found that "prejudice against the true religion is deeply rooted. Numbers of these circuit riding preachers pass here; all they do is spread calumnies against the Church."[72] In his view, most of the Protestants were Deists, and the Catholics were not much different. "Amongst those whom I visited, and who have not seen a priest since the coming of Father Martin, I baptized only one infant."[73] There is no indication in Father Dupuy's correspondence that he said Mass while in Little Rock.

After recovering from a serious illness, Father Dupuy journeyed from Pine Bluff to St. Louis in September, where he extracted a promise of an assistant from Bishop Rosati. He was back in Pine Bluff by November 1834,[74] and Rosati commissioned an assistant for him on April 13, 1835. Father Charles Rolle, a native of Lorraine, France, and newly ordained, arrived in Pine Bluff in late May.[75] The two French priests made splendid confreres, and Dupuy wrote in Latin to his bishop on July 2nd that "Illum amo, vivere cum co mihi est dulce." ("I love him, it is sweet to me to live with him.")[76] This happy situation lasted all too briefly, for while on call to a sick person, Father Rolle suffered a heatstroke and died on July 22, 1835.[77] Soon after this tragedy, Dupuy became quite ill and wrote the bishop in late August that he was near death.[78] Before he became ill, some prominent men, Chester Ashley in Little Rock and Samuel Roane in Jefferson County, promised him twelve lots of land in Little Rock worth $2,000.00 to establish a boarding school for boys and girls in the Arkansas capital.[79]

An excited Dupuy hurried to St. Louis after his recovery to inform Rosati of this proposition, but the bishop was skeptical. He felt that "to establish a school in a town so remote and at such an expense when the religious orders at St. Louis were short of teachers, was too perilous a venture."[80] A disappointed Dupuy returned to Arkansas to continue his lonely mission.[81] He noted the completion of the new church at Pine Bluff, and the next day wrote that even the people at the Post were interested in building a church.[82] In January 1836, he informed the bishop that he had twenty Christmas communicants and had visited a group of Catholic settlers in late December along the Ouachita River to refute ministers who had been "tormenting" the Catholics.[83]

In January 1836, a constitutional convention met in Little Rock to write a state constitution to be presented to Congress with its appeal for statehood. Dupuy was alone and brooding over the bishop's rejection of the offer of Ashley and others for a boarding school in Little Rock. He wrote Rosati on January 19, 1836, "Since you refused the offers which they made to me, they [will] now, at Little Rock, build a college which will be governed 'dogmatized' and 'moralized' by Protestants alone."[84] (Actually, there would not be a college in Little Rock until September 1859, when the Masonic Order opened St. John's Military Academy.)[85]

In May, Dupuy wrote his bishop about a visit to Fort Smith where he had witnessed a wedding. He reported that Catholics there did not want to raise money for a church unless there were plans for a school. He also accurately complained that little could be done for the Catholic cause in Arkansas by one priest.[86] A few weeks after these melancholy expressions, Arkansas became the twenty-fifth state on June 15, 1836. Even after this important political development, Dupuy labored throughout the summer and fall without any clerical assistance. After four long and lonely years in Arkansas, Dupuy was at the end of his rope. On November 5, 1836, he appeared before Rosati begging for an assistant. To placate the desperate missionary, the St. Louis prelate ordained one of his deacons, Peter Donnelly, on November 20, and four days later assigned him to serve in Arkansas.[87] Instead of being Dupuy's salvation, it would be the beginning of the end of his missionary tour.

The new partnership looked quite promising at first. Dupuy wrote Rosati from Pine Bluff in early January 1837, "everything is growing better and better. Mr. Donnelly looks to be satisfied with the place, and the people like him well enough, too. I hope firmly that our hardships will be in the advancing of the knowledge of Christ and his glory in these remote countries."[88] On March 6, Dupuy left for New Orleans to raise money. In his absence, Donnelly, who wrote phonetically in an Irish brogue, expressed his disappointment that in the last four months they had not ventured from Jefferson County.[89]

Dupuy wrote Rosati in early April of his return and also provided a census of the Catholic population. He believed that the population was about six hundred, mostly in Jefferson County. Others were at the Post in Arkansas County, in Little Rock in Pulaski County, and about ten families along the Ouachita River. There were some others scattered throughout the state, and he recommended the location of missions to serve them. Dupuy thought a church could be built in the French settlement of New Gascony about fifteen miles downriver from Pine Bluff. He felt that the Post, sixty miles downriver, could have a church but the people there "never pull together; I tried it more than ten times, but I did not succeed."[90] He also stated that "Little Rock would be a good place, but a chapel needs to be built first. Money for a school could not be raised in either St. Louis or New Orleans" and he added, "Mr. Donnelly is not capable to teach what is required because he cannot write his own language correctly; besides his health is poor."[91]

A few days after Dupuy's long and informative letter, Antoine Barraque of New Gascony sent a petition signed by sixteen families there asking that Rosati place Donnelly in their community.[92] Donnelly may well have been behind such a petition, for later that year he left for St. Louis to talk to the bishop. The result was that on September 2, 1837, a decree was issued which made Donnelly head of the mission in Arkansas and transferred Dupuy to the Diocese of New Orleans.[93] Before leaving, Dupuy poured out his heart to Rosati over the shameful way he had been so quickly pushed aside after laboring heroically in Arkansas for almost five years.[94] Donnelly's coup may have succeeded in removing Dupuy, yet it also created division among the Catholics in Jefferson County. Factions arose favoring either Dupuy or Donnelly, and Donnelly was mean-spirited enough to write the bishop that people were trying to get up a petition for Dupuy, yet no one would sign it.[95] This was untrue, for there are petitioners for Dupuy in the archives of the St. Louis archdiocese. Throughout the months of August to November 1837, Rosati continued to receive petitions from the competing groups.[96] Father Dupuy eventually became pastor at St. Gabriel's in Iberville, Louisiana, a post he was still holding as late as 1859.[97] For better or worse, Father Peter Donnelly was now the only Catholic pastor in Arkansas.

Donnelly undoubtedly exhibited a great deal more energy and industry than Dupuy. By late October, he had raised $900.00 for a church in New Gascony and was holding regular church services at a home there after November 26, 1837.[98] In early January, he traveled to the ill-omened Arkansas Post and collected $630.00 there in just a week, although visiting only half the people.[99] In February, carpenters were beginning the school building at the mission three miles south of Pine Bluff, and the building was ready by the following fall.[100] Later, Father Donnelly journeyed to Little Rock to raise money for a church there. He arrived on Friday, March 23, 1838, and the next day persuaded some prominent Protestants and Catholics to pledge $650.00 for the construction of a church. On Sunday, the Feast of the Annunciation, Fr. Donnelly said the first recorded Catholic Mass in the city of Little Rock on the second floor of Mr. A. G. Dugan's house and store near Main and Second Streets. March 25 was exactly the same day that Father Andrew White, S.J., celebrated a Catholic Mass in Maryland in English Colonial America two hundred years previously.[101] (The Feast of the Annunciation is a celebration of the event in Scripture of the Angel announcing to Mary that she is to be the Mother of the Redeemer.)

Later that year, a new school building was completed at New Gascony, and Mother Agnes Hart and four other nuns of the Sisters of Loretto arrived in Arkansas on October 11, 1838, to open the first Catholic school in Arkansas on November 19.[102] In late November 1838, Donnelly wrote Rosati that the money pledged for the church in Little Rock was in the hands of Mr. Dugan, but Donnelly's failing health would prevent him from doing more. He wanted to turn over the mission in Pine Bluff to the Congregation of the Mission.[103] Two weeks later, Donnelly happily reported that the school was doing well; in fact, the Methodist school had closed since the Catholic school had started. He also bought a lot for a chapel at Napoleon, a town on the Mississippi below the mouth of the Arkansas River. However, he complained that if his health did not improve by the spring, he would have to return to St. Louis.[104]

On January 2, 1839, Donnelly asked to return to his native Ireland. Bishop Rosati granted the request on May 21, 1839, and informed him that he would be replaced by two French priests.[105] On May 26, 1839, Donnelly penned his last letter from Arkansas expressing the hope that the new missionaries will complete the work of building a church in Little Rock to be named, St. Peter's on the Rock, for his own patron saint.[106]

Rosati's last two missionaries to Arkansas, before the creation of the Diocese of Little Rock in 1843, were originally diocesan priests from Besancon, France. Father Joseph Richard-Bole and Father August Simon Paris arrived in St. Louis on November 16, 1838. Six months later, they were given their assignment to Arkansas. They said the first Mass at Napoleon in May, and by early June 1839, they were in Pine Bluff.[107] Donnelly and the two French priests were not compatible. Richard-Bole wrote Rosati that Donnelly had placed $500.00 down for a $1,000.00 lot in Little Rock and now expected the Diocese of St. Louis to pay the other half.[108] Richard-Bole reports that Donnelly was "at first glad to see us, but when we spoke to him of his promises, impossible to realize with empty wishes, where there are no means to accomplish them, he changed his behavior."[109] For whatever reason, Donnelly did not leave until November 1839, and during that time, relations with the two French priests continued to worsen. Donnelly did not return to Ireland but to Missouri, where he was assigned the parish at Gravois, now Kirkwood, Missouri. He took up his duties there by late January 1840.[110]

Richard-Bole and Paris soon split their assignments in Arkansas using the Jefferson County churches as their hub. Richard-Bole was pastor at Arkansas' original Catholic church near Pine Bluff, now called St. Mary's. From there, he also conducted a mission to Little Rock. Father Paris was stationed at New Gascony with his mission at the Arkansas Post.[111] In late January 1840, Richard-Bole informed his St. Louis superior that he intended to sell the land Donnelly purchased and buy some land elsewhere in the city. He did not expect much could be done for Little Rock until there was a resident priest assigned there, along with one at St. Mary's near Pine Bluff, and one at the Post.[112] Three months later, he wrote again from St. Mary's that he would be going again to Little Rock to labor there. "The people have been very negligent, and we need the assistance of your prayers. I shall now start to build the church of which I wrote to you in my preceding letter."[113] Apparently, the prayer worked, for Father Simon Paris wrote to Bishop Antoine Blanc of New Orleans that the church in Little Rock would be completed by early the next year, and the Post would have a church finished by March 1841. In the same letter, he revealed that certain Protestant groups were quite agitated in Little Rock because a Catholic school would open there in January 1841. What worried Father Paris was that sickness and a "lack of trade" had taken many Catholics from this state, and the French priest further commented that he has had "five diseases in the previous four months."[114] Paris seemed rather discouraged for he wrote the New Orleans prelate, "If my superior would replace me, I would leave this mission."[115]

Despite this Frenchman's discouragement, some real progress was being made in the area of Catholic education. The Sisters of Loretto, an order out of Kentucky, sent Mother Agnes Hart, together with Sisters Eulalia Kelly, Louisa Phillips, Teresa Mattingly, and Alodia Vessels to St. Mary's to found a Catholic school along the banks of the Arkansas just south of Pine Bluff. An advertisement in the *Arkansas Gazette* declared that the school for young ladies would open on November 19, 1838. To allay some fears of Protestant parents it stated, "No undue influence will be used over them to embrace Catholicity, nor will they be permitted to embrace it except by the expressed permission of their parents."[116] They began with just thirty students.[117] On August 20, 1839, Mother Hart died and her position as Mother Superior was taken by Sr. Eulalia Kelly.[118] More sisters came and from this group, Sr. Alodia Vessels was authorized to be the Superior of a group of three sisters to found St. Joseph's Catholic School in Little Rock in 1841. In 1842, Father Paris moved from New Gascony to the Arkansas Post where he had a house built for him. That same year, the Sisters of Loretto abandoned their St. Mary's Academy near Pine Bluff to move to the Post to open St. Ambrose Female Academy under the direction of Mother Superior Teresa Mattingly.[119] Both of these schools, in Little Rock and at the Arkansas Post, operated for three years until lack of funds forced the Sisters of Loretto to abandon Arkansas in 1845.[120] Father Joseph Richard-Bole did build a church in Little Rock, not in the year Father Paris claimed, for he did not buy the property until 1842. It was known as St. Joseph's, and the church, school grounds, and convent were all sold to a New Orleans priest, Father Constantine Maenhaut, in 1845. The church stood at the northwest corner of Louisiana and Seventh Streets, across the street from where the present cathedral now stands.[121]

At the fifth Provincial Council of Baltimore on May 16, 1843, the Holy See in Rome was asked to establish four new dioceses for the United States: Chicago, Pittsburgh, Milwaukee, and Little Rock. On September 30, 1843, word came from Cardinal Giacomo Fransoni, Prefect of the Sacred Congregation of the Propaganda Fide, that Father Andrew Byrne, pastor of St. Andrew's Church in New York City, would be named to the new Arkansas See.[122] On November 28, 1843, Pope Gregory XVI formally approved the creation of the diocese. The decree stated:

> Therefore, after mature deliberation, . . . and on the advice of our venerable brethren, we deem it useful to erect the episcopal See of Little Rock. Therefore, on our own initiative, and from certain knowledge and from the plentitude of Apostolic power, we determine and erect in virtue of these present letters the new Episcopal See of Little Rock whose diocese embraces the State of Arkansas and whose

title is derived from the so-named city of Little Rock.[123]

Once these developments became known, Father Richard-Bole was extremely disappointed, for he fully expected to become the first bishop. Both he and Father Paris left the diocese in 1844.[124] As Monsignor Holweck points out, with Bishop Byrne's appointment, "the old French and Creole regime is buried forever."[125] The future of Arkansas Catholicism would be in the hands of the new Bishop Byrne. The establishment of the Arkansas diocese would not fundamentally alter the religious impact of the American acquisition. More than a century and a half later, Catholics would remain a small religious body within a society formed and shaped by an overwhelmingly Protestant faith and culture.

C H A P T E R I I I

A Bishop in the Wilderness

Bishop Byrne and the New Diocese, 1844-1862

ON A CERTIFICATE dated March 11, 1844, Bishop John Hughes of New York wrote, "The Right Reverend Andrew Byrne, first pastor of the Church of the Nativity in this City, was on Yesterday, the Tenth, consecrated by me, in our Cathedral, first Bishop of the new See at Little Rock, State of Arkansas."[1] Andrew Byrne was one of three priests elevated to the American hierarchy in Old St. Patrick's Cathedral that day. One other person, John McCloskey, would later become the second Archbishop of New York and the first American to become a cardinal.[2]

There is no certainty as to the exact date of the birth of Arkansas' first bishop. The official baptismal records give the date as December 3, 1802, two days earlier than the usual date given.[3] Given the fact that his baptismal name was Andrew and that it was customary in Ireland to name children after the feast day on which they were born, and November 30 being the feast day of St. Andrew the Apostle, it is plausible to assume that Andrew Byrne was born on November 30, 1802, just four days before his baptism. On the baptismal records, his parents are listed as Robert Byrne and Margery Moore Byrne, and he was born in the town of Navan in the County of Meath. Navan is located just about forty miles northwest of Dublin. Little is known of Byrne's early life or his education. As a young seminarian in the Diocesan Seminary in Navan, he heard newly named Bishop John England of Charleston speak of the need of priests for his diocese. Byrne responded to his call, arriving in Charleston in the early 1820s.[4] Bishop England ordained him a deacon in April 1827, and on November

11, 1827, Byrne was elevated to the priesthood in the Diocese of Charleston.[5]

The Diocese of Charleston covered not only South Carolina as it does today, but also North Carolina and Georgia. Father Byrne served as a missionary in both of the latter states and in 1829 almost perished from exhaustion in North Carolina.[6] In 1830, Byrne became pastor of the Irish church of St. Mary's in Charleston and was later named Vicar General. Three years later, he traveled with Bishop England to the Second Provincial Council of Baltimore as the personal theologian to the bishop.[7] Subsequently, Byrne fell into some type of dispute with Bishop England, which may have involved a personal rivalry with a Father Richard Baker, who replaced Byrne as vicar general. England, therefore, gave Byrne permission to leave the Diocese of Charleston on April 13, 1836.[8]

Father Byrne moved to the Diocese of New York and made a name for himself as an organizer and preacher. In metropolitan New York, he served at the Church of St. James, then began the parish of the Nativity, and later served as founding pastor of St. Andrew's Church.[9] Bishop Hughes sent Byrne to recruit priests for the New York diocese in Ireland. In his letter of introduction, he described Byrne as "a good and zealous priest."[10] On May 1, 1842, Byrne delivered a memorable and moving eulogy upon the death of Bishop John England. His letter to Bishop Francis Patrick Kenrick of Philadelphia played an important role in deciding the succession to the See at Charleston.[11] His connections with Bishop Hughes, his proven abilities as a preacher and pastor, and his past association with the South, may have made Byrne a natural choice to head the new diocese on the southern frontier.

Byrne departed for Arkansas in the spring of 1844, along with two priests from the Diocese of New York, Fathers Francis Donohoe and John Corry. They arrived in Little Rock on June 4, 1844. Father Joseph Richard-Bole had departed Little Rock, but was still in Arkansas. He appeared at the Sisters of Loretto convent in Arkansas Post on July 20, 1844. Byrne, as with Dupuy more than a decade earlier, had to deal with irate Catholics in Little Rock who were angry that Father Richard-Bole had left with the money and the deed for the church of St. Joseph in Little Rock.[12] Byrne visited the Sisters of Loretto at the Arkansas Post later that summer, and he "found them in great want".[13] Sr. Teresa Mattingly wrote that fall that Father Richard-Bole had grossly overcharged them on many items, and Mother Superior Eulalia Kelly wrote Bishop Antoine Blanc of New Orleans the following March from the Arkansas Post that they were robbed and plundered by that intriguing man who owed them over $1,000.00.[14] This was the last straw. The order abandoned its schools and convents in Little Rock and the Arkansas Post by the end of spring 1845.[15]

There were other deprivations facing the new bishop. Father John Corry had traveled with the bishop to Fort Smith, where the priest began, but did not finish construction of a church at Third and Hickory Streets. Father Corry also purchased one hundred acres of land near Fayetteville. However, he remained only nine months in the state, then returned to New York to take up his priestly duties in Albany by mid-1845.[16]

Bishop Byrne almost perished during his first few months in Arkansas. In July 1844, he had written Bishop Blanc of New Orleans about visiting Arkansas Post and New Gascony and about spending the late summer and early fall in the northwestern counties. While on a trip to Fort Smith, Van Buren, and Fayetteville, the new bishop became ill in Fayetteville and later in Van Buren. He could not return to Little Rock until September 28.[18]

Father Peter M. Walsh of Albany, New York, arrived that fall to assist Bishop Byrne with his first ordination. Although some of the secondary literature states that the first ordination in Arkansas was on All Saints Day, November 1, 1844, Bishop Byrne's own journal is in contradiction. Under the date October 23, Byrne wrote, "I arrived this day at the Post of Arkansas in company with the Rev. Mr. Walsh, and on the 28th gave tonsure to Mr. John Whalen, and tonsure, minor orders, deaconship to Mr. Thomas McKeone on the first of November, and on Sunday, the 3rd, priesthood."[19] Under the same entry Byrne noted that he left Father Walsh at the Arkansas Post and brought the newly ordained Fr. McKeone and seminarian Whalen back with him to Little Rock.[20] As there were few Catholic seminaries at that time, after study under the bishop, a priest candidate would often be elevated from minor orders, to diaconate, then to priesthood, whenever the bishop felt he was ready.

In late 1844, Byrne purchased the lot where he planned to build his own church, since Richard-Bole had sold the property of St. Joseph's Church at Seventh and Louisiana to Father Constantine Maenhaut of New Orleans. Bishop Byrne purchased a lot at the southeast corner of Second and Center streets, one block south of the newly erected state capitol.[21] Before the church and rectory were completed, he stayed for a time at the Anthony Boarding House, then with Catholic lawyer David W. Carroll, and finally at a small house on east Markham Street.[22]

During the first few months of 1845, Bishop Byrne attempted to visit his diocesan domain, the entire state of Arkansas. Since Arkansas was a frontier state with a virtually nonexistent transportation system, this was no easy task.[23] During the summer and early fall of 1845, Byrne journeyed to New York to raise money and purchase books and sacred items necessary for the liturgy. Prior to his departure, the Sisters of Loretto were permitted to leave his diocese.[24] Byrne returned with a young seminarian, John Monaghan, who became a deacon on December 19, 1845, and a priest the next day.[25] Byrne was overwhelmed by the needs and wants of this diocese, as indicated in a December 1845 letter to Archbishop Samuel Eccleston of Baltimore, "I can assure you that within the whole diocese of Little Rock, there exists no means to erect a single altar. The Catholic population does not exceed seven hundred souls, and they are scattered in every County in the State."[26]

So disconsolate had the new bishop become that during the Sixth

Provincial Council in Baltimore in early 1846, Byrne attempted to have the diocese dissolved and placed once again under St. Louis. He hoped to be transferred to the newly created Diocese of Buffalo. This plan was presented to Monsignor Choiselat Gallien of the Society of the Propagation of the Faith in Paris. He had given his brother bishops "a faithful statement of my situation . . . the number of Catholics scattered over the state would not form, if all were together, one large congregation in another diocese. The bishops petitioned the Holy See for my transfer to Buffalo and to place Arkansas again under the jurisdiction of the Bishop of St. Louis."[27]

Byrne would wait almost a year and a half to hear from the Holy Father. Meanwhile, he believed that he would be leaving for Buffalo and so did some of his fellow bishops. Bishop John Joseph Chanche of Natchez, Mississippi, wrote Bishop Blanc of New Orleans, "The news of Bishop Byrne's departure has gotten out, betrayed by some priest in his diocese."[28] While Byrne awaited word, he continued to struggle with pastoral problems. Thomas McKeone, the first priest ordained in Arkansas, fled to New Orleans against Byrne's "positive prohibition." Byrne wrote Blanc, "Father McKeone has influenced others to leave this poor diocese."[29] Actually, Byrne too hoped to flee Arkansas, for he wrote to a priest friend in New Orleans, "While I do not need to go to New York, I do not want to stay in my diocese."[30] He wrote those words, interestingly enough, just seven days after he had formally consecrated the first Cathedral of St. Andrew the Apostle on November 1, 1846.

In the spring of 1846, Byrne had given another one of his seminarians, John Whalen, minor orders and on October 19 promoted Patrick Canavan to the diaconate. On the day he consecrated his own cathedral, Byrne used the occasion to ordain Canavan to the priesthood. That day, the Feast of All Saints, was exactly 146 years after the first recorded Catholic Mass in Arkansas, performed by Father Jacques Gravier, S.J., on November 1, 1700.[31] The ordination ceremony was described in detail by the *State Democrat* in Little Rock:

> The New Roman Catholic Church of this City was dedicated on Sunday, the 1st, to the Service of the Most High, under the patronage of St. Andrew the Apostle. The ceremony was witnessed by a very large congregation, composed of all denominations, who seemed highly pleased with the proceedings. At the close of the consecration of the Church the Right Reverend Bishop Byrne ascended the platform of the altar and gave a very satisfactory explanation of the nature of ceremony, and the advantages springing from the use of one common language in the Church. He was followed on the same subject by Mr. Shafer, in the German language. At the gospels, an able discourse was delivered on the nature of the sacrifice, and the dignity of the Christian priesthood, to which state the Bishop, on this occasion, promoted a

deacon. It was the first ordination in the Catholic Church witnessed by many of our citizens. The Rev. Mr. Walsh preached at vespers, which were sung with much effect . . . The Church is well-situated, and when the interior is finished, will add much to the beauty of that part of our City in the vicinity of the Capitol.[32]

Soon after this ceremony, Byrne departed for southeastern Arkansas where he visited Catholic congregations in Pine Bluff, New Gascony, Arkansas Post, Helena, Napoleon, and a small Catholic community known as St. Rose in Arkansas County.[33]

As Byrne waited for news of his transfer, he still attended his duties, starting a Classical and Philosophical Institute for young men on east Markham in January 1847, under the direction of the newly ordained Father John Monaghan. The school advertised that it could accommodate sixty students, and the education would be "all that is required of young men for commercial business and learned professions."[34] This institute apparently floundered and collapsed for there is no mention of it in a Catholic Almanac of 1850.[35] Although a group of leading citizens in Benton and Washington Counties pleaded with the bishop to start a Catholic college in Fayetteville,[36] no such institution was established. Using money from a wealthy relative and French missionary aid from the Society for the Propagation of the Faith, Bishop Byrne purchased from the federal government on November 28, 1847, a huge plot of land near Fort Smith on which to build a college and seminary.[37] As with other U.S. dioceses, money was granted from France through the French-based Society for the Propagation of the Faith and from the Leopoldine Society in Vienna, Austria.[38] Byrne wrote Archbishop Eccleston of Baltimore in late 1845 that the money he receives from Europe is used to purchase land for churches and schools. "I have used only twenty dollars for my own support."[39]

Throughout the year 1847, Byrne continued to wait for news of his transfer as he labored in the Arkansas vineyard, visiting many areas of his diocese.[40] Father McKeone, the first priest ordained in Arkansas (1844), returned from New Orleans in early 1847, but died in the spring while serving the immigrant Irish settlement at Rocky Comfort in present day Sevier County. Informing Bishop Blanc of this news in May 1847, Byrne noted that Father McKeone had traveled as much as five hundred miles visiting groups of scattered Catholics across the southern counties of the state.[41] In the same letter, Byrne was perturbed greatly by Rome's silence on his transfer, since it had been over a year since the last Provincial Council had recommended the action.[42] Rumors floated about concerning his move. Bishop-designate Jean Marie Odin of Galveston wrote Bishop Blanc in September 1847 stating he believed, "They should leave Byrne in Arkansas, for it is a shame to abandon that country."[43] Rome agreed with this former missionary priest to Arkansas. On September 5, 1847, John Timon, Odin's seminarian companion on that 1824 missionary tour in Arkansas, was named as the first Bishop of Buffalo, New York.[44] It is not clear when Byrne received this news, but he wrote in late December, "It pleases God that I should stay in Little Rock. May His Holy Will be done."[45]

With the transfer question solved, Byrne resolutely concerned himself with care for the struggling diocese. In early 1848, he acquired Father Patrick McGowan from the Diocese of Charleston.[46] Byrne now had four other priests to work with him. Francis Donohoe and Peter Walsh came in 1844; John Monaghan was ordained in 1845; and Patrick Canavan in 1846. Within the next two years, he would lose two of these priests. Bishop Byrne expelled Father Canavan in 1849 for various infractions–marrying Catholics and non-Catholics without dispensation, not visiting his missions in New Gascony, and fraternizing with a woman named Mary Lawless, who claimed to be a Sister of Mercy, but could provide no proof. She likewise was asked to leave the diocese.[47]

The other priest, Father Francis Donohoe, one of the two original clergy Byrne brought with him to Arkansas, died during the summer of 1850. A humble and learned man, Bishop Hughes reluctantly allowed Byrne to take Donohoe to the wilds of Arkansas. Since 1845, Donohoe had served periodically as a missionary to Rocky Comfort, previously served by the now deceased Father McKeone. Father Donohoe had worked out of the cathedral in Little Rock while conducting a horseback mission to Rocky Comfort, a distance of almost two hundred miles. Monsignor John Michael Lucey, writing almost forty-two years later, maintained that Donohoe died while journeying to Rocky Comfort on a warm summer's day. Attempting to cool his thirst, the priest drank some buttermilk which had spoiled in the hot sun, and somewhere in Clark County, Donohoe "rode to a beautiful spot, which he had often remarked as a fine location for a church, stopped beneath a magnificent oak, cut a cross in its bark, and placing the saddle under his head, laid himself down and died."[48]

Both of these losses came as Byrne was pushing to have a college located on the land near Fort Smith. The legislature did grant his request for a charter, but only after more lay people were added to its Board of Trustees. A state Senate report expressed concern lest the trustees be controlled "by a foreign potentate, the Pope of Rome." A select committee of both houses added some lay and non-Catholic trustees and the charter passed easily.[49] Another project failed in the 1848-1849 legislature. Byrne attempted to incorporate the diocese, giving him and his successors sole ownership of its property. The House of Representatives turned it down by a vote of 57 to 10.[50] Although Byrne was merely trying to maintain clerical control over church lands and property, to non-Catholics, this proposal gave too much power to a man bound in obedience to a foreign leader. In spite of this setback, Byrne proudly announced, in the spring of 1849, that the College of St. Andrew would open near Fort Smith in the fall.[51]

The Church had been making some growth in Fort Smith. Father Peter Walsh was sent there in 1847 to oversee the completion of St. Patrick's church, dedicated by the bishop on March 5, 1848.[52] At the eastern end of the state, Father Patrick McGowan was stationed first at Helena, then in 1850 at New Gascony, where he served almost all of east central Arkansas, including Helena, Pine Bluff, New Gascony, and Napoleon. Father Monaghan was sent to Fort Smith to run the College of St. Andrew leaving only Byrne and Donohoe at the cathedral in 1849.[53]

The bishop would use his journey to the Seventh Provincial Council of Baltimore in May 1849 to find financial support and more seminarians. He arrived at the council one day late,[54] to pour out his troubles to his fellow bishops from whom he undoubtedly received a sympathetic hearing. After the council, Byrne went to Philadelphia where his fellow bishop, Jean Odin of Galveston, noted that he had raised a good deal of money for Arkansas.[55] Money was not Byrne's only object; he managed to recruit three seminarians and one priest. The seminarians were Edward Corcoran, Richard Nagle, and John Craigle, who were added to two seminarians at St. Andrew's, John Whalen and John O'Reilly. There is no record that Craigle was ordained for the Diocese of Little Rock. Byrne also brought with him Father Theopholus Marivault to work in the Indian Territory from Fort Gibson. Marivault did not stay long, for Byrne wrote later that he had deserted the mission after only a few months.[56]

Bishop Byrne, during the first six months of 1850, ordained three men to the priesthood: John Whalen in March, and John O'Reilly and Edward Corcoran in June.[57] During the summer, the Arkansas prelate entered the political contests by denying he was behind the candidacy of attorney David W. Carroll for the state House of Representatives. Carroll was a migrant from Maryland and a distant relative of America's first Catholic Bishop and Archbishop John Carroll. Byrne's letter, dated July 1, 1850, appeared the next day in the official newspaper of the state Democratic party, the Little Rock *Arkansas Banner*. In this small note, Byrne wrote, "I do not interfere in politics. Six years of residence in Little Rock ought to satisfy the smallest spirit of my conduct in regard to politics."[58]

Instead of quieting the controversy, Bishop Byrne's note only served to draw more political fire. A few days later, a letter appeared in the Little Rock *Arkansas Gazette* attacking both Carroll and Byrne for being more loyal to an "anti-Republican Foreign Prince than American democracy . . . Besides who could trust a man who signs his name with a dagger!"[59] Another letter writer responded a week later in the *Gazette* declaring that Catholics still possess legal rights to public office and anyone "with a moderate amount of intelligence" can see that Byrne did not sign his letter with a dagger but a cross.[60] A few weeks later, a writer identifying himself only as "Fellow Citizen" wrote a long piece in the *Gazette* attacking Byrne for trying to slip through the legislature a papal-controlled college, thwarted only by a legislature which made him add more laymen to the Board of Trustees. This writer also attacked Byrne for trying to have all property placed in his hands in order to gather more land for the Pope. No true Protestant minister would seek such power for himself. This same writer castigated Byrne for using money from Leopoldine Society in Austria to buy this land. The purpose of this Society was "to reduce America to papal bondage."[61]

The stir about Byrne and Catholics quieted for a time, but this type of invective would be heard again in Arkansas and throughout much of the nation, especially during the "Know-Nothing" crusade later in the decade. Since few Catholic immigrants came to Arkansas, this state remained a staunchly Protestant culture which continued to view Roman Catholics and Catholicism with great fear and alarm.[62]

Mid-century brought some changes to the American Catholic Church which affected the Diocese of Little Rock. Until 1847, there was only one archdiocese in the United States, Baltimore, and all the bishops of the United States had to relate to the Metropolitan See in Maryland. In 1847, the second archdiocese was created in St. Louis with jurisdiction over much of the upper Mississippi River Valley. Peter Richard Kenrick, the successor of Bishop Rosati, would now be the Archbishop of St. Louis. The other bishops still had to relate to the Baltimore See, but at the Seventh Provincial Council in 1849, that council asked the Holy See to create archdioceses at New York, Cincinnati, and New Orleans. On July 19 Pope Pius IX approved this request, and now the Diocese of Little Rock was placed in a new southern province under the Archbishop of New Orleans. The other Sees in this new southern province were Galveston (state of Texas), Natchez (state of Mississippi), and Mobile (state of Alabama). The Archdiocese of New Orleans would continue to include all the state of Louisiana. However, after July 29, 1853, all the state of Louisiana above the thirty-first parallel would now be part of the Diocese of Natchitoches, which would also be part of this new southern province.[63] Little Rock would remain as part of this province for the next 122 years.

Byrne knew he needed an order of sisters to conduct academies for young ladies if he wanted to bring Catholic education to Arkansas. It had been over five years since the Sisters of Loretto had left in 1845. Byrne turned to a recently created dynamic order out of Dublin, Ireland, the Sisters of Mercy, founded by Mother Catherine McAuley in 1831.[64] In late 1850, he journeyed to Ireland and approached the Mother Superior of the Sisters of Mercy convent on Baggott Street, Dublin, who sent him to another Mercy convent in Naas, County Kildare. Mother Mary Vincent Whitty of Naas allowed the Arkansas bishop to address the sisters.[65] According to one writer Byrne "spoke forcibly and well of the good to be accomplished in the wild region committed to his spiritual care, the great necessity for educated teachers for children and thoroughly instructed religion to enlighten adults ignorant of everything concerning their salvation."[66] While many wanted to respond, the Mother

Superior allowed only four sisters and five postulants to accompany Bishop Byrne back to Arkansas. The local bishop in Ireland had wanted to send some Mercy sisters to New Zealand. With regard to Arkansas, "he had some scruples and misgivings. The wild, terrible, and often romantic stories that had reached him . . . (made) him doubt whether he ought to allow the Sisters to risk themselves in such lawless regions."[67] The Irish bishop finally relented, saying that he would have never allowed the sisters to leave except that "I shall stand responsible to God for the good which I know they will accomplish."[68]

Bishop Byrne excitedly wrote Archbishop Blanc in New Orleans in late November, congratulating him on his ecclesiastical promotion and reporting that he now has a "colony of the Sisters of Mercy for my diocese."[69] This group of sisters, under the direction of Mother Superior Teresa Farrell, R.S.M., left Ireland for Arkansas on November 30, 1850, the feast day of St. Andrew the Apostle and quite possibly the forty-eighth birthday of Bishop Byrne.[70]

The Arkansas bishop and his Irish Mercy nuns arrived in New Orleans on January 23, 1851. They soon departed by riverboat for Little Rock, setting foot in the Arkansas capital on February 5, 1851.[71] The Little Rock *Arkansas Banner* effusively welcomed Byrne and the sisters saying, "Let it not be said that the children of Arkansas must be sent out of State to receive a finished education."[72] Not all were glad to see the Mercy sisters in Arkansas. "Fellow Citizen" penned a letter printed in the Little Rock *Arkansas Gazette* which asked rhetorically whether there were not enough paupers in Ireland for the Sisters of Mercy to handle rather than having them come so far to Arkansas.[73]

To house the sisters, Byrne had been working to purchase back the old St. Joseph's church and Loretto convent located at the northwest corner of Louisiana and Elizabeth Streets, now Seventh and Louisiana. Since Father Richard-Bole had sold it to Father Constantine Maenhaut of New Orleans, Byrne made contact with Maenhaut's agent in Little Rock, attorney Lemuel R. Lincoln. Lincoln acted not only as agent for Maenhaut, but also as custodian and renter of the property.[74] Byrne had asked Lincoln for a price, and Maenhaut informed Byrne through Lincoln that he wanted $4,000.00. Byrne gave a counter-offer of $2,000.00, and eventually the property sold for that amount plus a stipulation that three thousand Masses be said for Maenhaut. The transfer of the property to the diocese was not finalized until August 13, 1851.[75] The new school, Academy of St. Mary, opened on the site September 1, 1851.[76] As the convent had to undergo some repairs before the sisters could move in, they lived in a house behind the cathedral while the bishop resided with David W. Carroll. On November 1, 1851, the Mercy sisters moved into the old convent once occupied by the Sisters of Loretto.[77]

Before the school year began at the new St. Mary's Academy, an impressive event was held on June 22, 1851, at the old Cathedral of St. Andrew at Second and Center. Five postulants of the Sisters of Mercy received their habits at a ceremony which was a first for Arkansas and the diocese. Bishop

Martin J. Spalding, the Bishop of Louisville and the future Archbishop of Baltimore, became the first American bishop to visit the state and assist a Little Rock prelate in performing this Catholic ritual. Bishop Spalding's address, as reported by a local newspaper, expounded on the scriptural basis for celibacy and the nobility of the vocation chosen by the sisters.[78] At the ceremony were the three priests who had come from Ireland with Byrne and the sisters, each of which had the first name of Patrick: Father Martin, Father Reilly, and Father Behan.[79] A female academy in Little Rock was soon followed by a school for males. St. Andrew's Boarding and Day School opened in January 1852, headed by Fathers John O'Reilly and Edward Corcoran. The school soon changed its name to St. John's Male Academy and then to St. Patrick's Male Academy by the middle of the 1850s.[80]

Priests and nuns were not the only people Byrne inspired to leave their homeland. Since Ireland was at that time suffering a terrible famine due to the potato blight, Byrne was able to persuade many of his countrymen to come to the Arkansas frontier and settle on his land near Fort Smith. Father Thomas Hore (spelled Hoar in some accounts) led some three hundred souls from Ireland to Arkansas in the summer of 1850. About twenty colonists had perished by the time their ship landed in New Orleans on September 4.[81] By December, about one hundred had made it to the Arkansas capital. The *Arkansas Gazette* welcomed them, but warned they were coming "at a season when the inclemency of the weather forbids operations being commenced . . . we hope that the doors of hospitality will at once be thrown open wide, and the hand of friendship promptly offer every aid and assistance."[82]

The months of travel had greatly weakened them physically, and soon a cholera epidemic broke out among their number, which contributed to the subsequent tension between the new arrivals and the residents. The old church and convent on Seventh and Louisiana was transformed into a hospital for the sick. In February 1851, a contemporary described these poor Irish as having only "withered leaves for their bed, ragged garments their covering, and the winter sunlight as it streamed through the shattered windows, the only fire to warm them, and death itself entering almost every pew."[83] By the time Father Hore and an advance party left in mid-February, some seventeen or eighteen had already died.[84] The attitude toward these immigrants had changed by that point as indicated by a letter signed by "Justice" in the *Arkansas Gazette:*

> Out of the number of Irish emigrants who remain after Mr. Hore and his crowd fled in dismay, and almost despair, . . . a number are now groaning under the tortures of disease in various hovels about this City; some convalescents are walking shadows; and a few, very few, are able to do a day's labor.[85]

About eight families stayed in Little Rock; some decided that Arkansas itself was too unhealthy and migrated to St. Louis and Iowa, yet most did go on to the Fort Smith area. The 1860 census found 158 Irish families living near Fort Smith in Sebastian County.[86]

The appearance of the new Catholic institutions and new Irish Catholic immigrants did not go unnoticed in the community. They were probably welcomed by most Arkansans to such an undeveloped part of the country; others were not as pleased. Reverend Joshua F. Green, of the Presbyterian Church in Little Rock, made a strong attack upon Bishop Spalding, his sermon, and Roman Catholicism in general.[87] Reverend Green went on to write a twenty-three page pamphlet attacking Catholicism, which he wanted the *Gazette* to publish serially. In refusing, William Woodruff, the founder of the *Gazette*, editorialized, "These columns are not designed, and we trust never will be perverted, to the persecution of any class of our countrymen, who hold different tenets of religious faith."[88] Green then challenged Fr. Patrick Behan to a public debate. Bishop Byrne apparently advised Behan to refrain from this contest, perhaps fearing it would heighten sectarian tensions.[89]

Another controversy arose in the fall of 1851 when Lemuel R. Lincoln, once publicly attacked as an "aristocratic Protestant," converted to Catholicism near the time of his death in October 1851. Byrne refused to allow the Odd Fellows, Lincoln's fraternal organization, to perform the funeral rites and instead gave him a Catholic burial. Byrne was criticized in the local press for "interference."[90] Though the Reverend Green still continued his attacks on the Church, his unexpected death in Memphis on August 1, 1854, during the cholera epidemic, temporarily ended attacks on Catholicism in Arkansas.[91]

Bishop Byrne had more personal difficulties than anti-Catholicism; he was seriously injured in the spring of 1853 after being thrown from his horse. He wrote the Propaganda Fide Office in Rome about this accident in late May, promising to abide by whatever decision seemed best. Whether the Arkansas bishop was using this accident to ask for relief from his duties is not clear, yet the office in Rome apparently believed that Byrne, once again, was attempting a transfer and it so informed Archbishop Blanc by an August 1853 letter. On January 9, 1854, the Propaganda Fide Office asked Byrne to secure another priest for his mission chores.[92]

Despite his injury, Byrne continued to perform his duties faithfully. He proudly informed Archbishop Blanc in May 1853 that there were thirty-six students at St. Anne's Mercy Academy in Fort Smith.[93] Byrne ordained Father Richard Nagle on July 31, 1853, a gain offset by the loss of Father John Whalen who spent many months away from Arkansas in New York claiming to be ill. An exasperated and skeptical Byrne wrote Blanc in March 1854, that in Whalen's case, there was "no sickness till I insisted he return."[94] The Arkansas bishop misjudged the situation as Whalen was truly ill and died in New York City on July 18, 1854.[95] Vicar General John J. O'Reilly became involved in a bitter altercation with the bishop and left in the spring of 1854. Byrne bitterly wrote his Provincial Metropolitan, "I shall find no hesitation with parting with him, and religion will not suffer by his absence."[96] Father Patrick Behan, the new Vicar General, in 1854 sadly reported that Fr. Edward Corcoran had died suddenly, yet he gave no further details. These losses were replaced when Byrne returned from Ireland that fall with two more priests, Fathers Philip Shanahan and Lawrence Smyth. There were now eight diocesan clergy, including Byrne, and one Jesuit missionary priest stationed in Fort Smith but working outside the diocese in the Indian Territory.[97]

Although the Little Rock Catholic diocese remained a small struggling Catholic community, beginning in 1840, Catholicism nationally rode a huge wave of immigration. More immigrants came during the years 1845-1854 in proportion to the resident population than at any time in our history. Total yearly immigration first reached 100,000 in 1842, and by 1847 it had doubled to 200,000. Immigration exceeded 400,000 annually during the period 1851-1854.[98] These newcomers talked and acted strangely, took jobs away from native-born Americans, caused wages to decrease, and corrupted the Republican political institutions with their lock-step voting for urban machines. Most of these immigrants came from the Catholic southern counties of Ireland, bringing with them a religious faith long-held suspect by Anglo-Saxon Protestant America. Anti-foreign and anti-Catholic sentiment sometimes erupted into violence as mobs rampaged through immigrant neighborhoods attacking, and in some cases, torching Catholic churches and convents. In the early 1850s, this bigotry found its political expression in the American party, usually called the "Know Nothings." The members were sworn to secrecy and turned away all inquires about their activities with the statement, "I know nothing."[99]

Based largely in the northeast where most immigrants settled, the American party established some pockets of strength in the slaveholding South. There were more foreign-born in New Orleans than Boston in 1850.[100] In the South, the foreign-born population was at five percent, while the national average was eleven percent. In Arkansas the foreign population in 1850 was just over one percent (1.2%), and the Catholic population was also negligible (.98%).[101] This was, in fact, the fewest number of foreign-born in the slaveholding South.[102]

Although Arkansas was far from being inundated by Catholic immigrants, the Know-Nothing American party operated as a new political opposition to the state's dominant Democratic party. Since the national Whig party had collapsed in the early 1850s, the Republican and American parties had sprung up to take its place. Since most southerners believed that the Republicans were closet abolitionists, the only acceptable political organization to which a southern Whig could belong was the American party.[103] This was the reason that long-time Whig activist, editor, attorney, and Masonic leader, Albert Pike helped initiate the American party movement in Arkansas. A huge rally in Little Rock in August 1855 launched the new state party. By the fall of 1855, the *Arkansas*

Gazette in Little Rock had become its main party organ. The position of the *Gazette* is surprising in view of Woodruff's editorial just four years earlier. In addition, the new editor, Christopher Columbus Danley, had denounced the political movement in 1854 as one full of political and religious bigotry.[104]

The Know Nothing movement in Arkansas stayed quite active for about a year after its initial rally. Most of the Whig papers became Know Nothing organs with the *Arkansas Gazette* as the bellwether. Editor Danley was soon joined by Solon Borland, a former United States Senator from Arkansas, who had just returned a year earlier from a disastrous stint as foreign minister to Central America.[105] Catholics and Roman Catholicism would receive steady and quite vitriolic attacks from the Whig press.

The charges were varied and wide ranging: the Pope was the enemy of all democratic republics, Catholics are taught to hate Protestants, Catholics cheat at poker, Catholics were disloyal during the recent war with Mexico, Catholics don't support slavery, Catholics were against Bible reading in the schools, the Pope is the anti-Christ subverting political and religious liberty, and Catholics are his pliant tools in this plot.[106] Protestants were also cautioned against sending their children to Catholic schools.[107] One writer in the *Gazette* suggests that Catholics be allowed to practice their religion but not to hold political power. A passage of this letter contains some of the common theses usually mentioned in the attacks:

> The Holy Scriptures abundantly show that the Man of Sin, the Anti-Christ, is the Roman Catholic Church, with the Pope at its head . . . enjoying their religious privileges . . . Let them pray to the virgin as much as they please, repeat their Pater Nosters and Ave Marias, make confessions to their priests, count their beads, bow to the host, pray souls out of purgatory, put girls away in nunneries, and Priests abstain from marriage, and claim apostolic succession, and keys of St. Peter . . . I say let them do these and few hundred more mummaries, and do it in quietness, grasping at no political power, and no one will molest or disturb them.[108]

Reverend J.D. Moore of Little Rock and Reverend D.L. Saunders of Huntsville, both ran a series of articles attacking Catholics. Moore's pamphlet, "Is the Catholic Church the True Church?" was serialized in the *Gazette* from November 1855 to March 1856. Reverend Saunders' work, "Roman Catholicism: Repugnant to and Subversive to American Liberty and American Republicanism" ran in the above named newspaper during the spring and early summer of 1856.[109]

These religious attacks should not obscure the fact that a political campaign was in progress rather than merely a religious crusade. Democratic Governor Conway received his fair share of abuse for quitting Methodist services to attend Catholic Masses. Editor Borland pointed out that since Conway was not married and was seen talking with Bishop Byrne, perhaps the Catholic cleric had persuaded the Governor to follow his own brand of "connubial felicity."[110] The state Democratic paper, the Little Rock *True Democrat,* replied in kind saying that the *Gazette* editor had no right to criticize the governor's attendance at Catholic Masses since Borland was an "expelled, fallen-from-grace, backslidden Baptist," who was now living with "an indecent and lewd woman."[111] Later in the campaign, the *Gazette* charged that the Democrats and Catholics fear neither the penitentiary or hell, for "they believe the Governor can pardon them out of the penitentiary and they believe their priests can pray them out of hell."[112]

Democrats defended Catholics and their civil liberties, claiming that the American party was a northern-based movement which sought political power by playing upon Protestant prejudice. The real enemy was the "abolitionist" Republican party. The rancor over the Irish and the Catholics was only a tactic to keep the South divided in the face of its real political enemies.[113] The *True Democrat* quoted a statement by the bishops in the New Orleans province denying that the Pope had any claim to temporal authority beyond the Papal states.[114] These attacks caused Catholics in the nation and in the state to identify themselves with the Democratic party. Catholic David W. Carroll was a prominent state Democrat; Creed Taylor, a Catholic convert and Jefferson County planter, served as the chairman of the state Democratic convention in 1856.[115] The defeat of the Know Nothings in the August state election and in the presidential contest in November, spelled the doom of the party as a major opposition force to the Democrats.[116] Prejudice against Catholics did not cease in Arkansas, but it was never again the official agenda of a major political party.

Throughout the Know Nothing movement, Byrne kept a low profile. In June 1857, an American party politician described Byrne to Editor Danley as a "kind and generous man, of excellent sense, and agreeable manners, he believed him to be a sincere Christian." In the same article, Danley apologized for some things said in the last political contest, and he ended by saying, "I have seen nothing in the character of Bishop Byrne to disturb the opinion expressed of him by our friend."[117] Things had simmered down enough for Father Behan to deliver a lecture in December 1858 at St. Andrew's Cathedral on "Sources of Protestant Prejudices Against the Catholic Church."[118] Religious and sectarian fires had cooled by the end of the decade.

In the midst of the Know Nothing furor, Byrne left Arkansas to attend the first meeting of the Southern provincial council in New Orleans. The Bishops' First Plenary Council was held in Baltimore in May 1852. This council of all the American Catholic prelates had recommended, among other things, that bishops in the various provinces meet at least once every three years.[119] There had been some scheduling problems in 1855, and Archbishop Blanc wrote Byrne in April of that year to assure him that there would be no meeting of the council without him.[120] The official call went out in October 1855, and the bishops of the southern province met for the first time in New Orleans on January 20, 1856. Presided over by Archbishop Blanc, this first meeting included Bishops Andrew Byrne of Little Rock, Jean Odin of Galveston, Michael Portier of Mobile, and Auguste Martin of Natchitoches. The Natchez Diocese of Mississippi was not represented because its second bishop, James O. Van de Velde, had died the previous November. The meeting also had representatives from the various religious congregations working in the province. At its close, January 27, the bishops expressed support for the Holy Father with regard to the recent (1854) promulgation of the Doctrine of the Immaculate Conception; talked of better ways of choosing future bishops; recommended that a seminary for the province be established; urged that sacraments of baptism and matrimony be held only in a church; and attacked all secret societies. The council also declared that the Holy Father did not desire any temporal sovereignty outside of the Papal states.[121]

Once back in Arkansas, Bishop Byrne soon faced internal ecclesiastical problems. In August 1856, Fr. Richard Nagle left his mission at Napoleon and the Arkansas Post, telling Byrne that he would leave the diocese, with or without the bishop's permission. Byrne angrily wrote Blanc that this "disobedient and refractory priest" will not cooperate with the bishop "who educated and ordained him."[122] Nagle claimed his health required him to move north where he later joined the Diocese of Dubuque. The dispute between Byrne and Nagle persisted for years and both sent letters to Rome. The issue was not resolved till 1860, when Byrne gave his formal permission and Nagle refunded some of the money spent in educating him.[123] Considering the financial plight of the diocese and its lack of priests, Byrne's attitude is understandable. During the summer of 1856, a Fr. McIntyre from Nova Scotia asked to be admitted into the diocese.[124] Unfortunately, this Canadian priest did not work well in the missionary diocese and was dismissed a few months later.[125]

Byrne became seriously ill in the fall of 1856 and spent many months in Fort Smith. The priest caring for him reported to Blanc in November that Byrne "is so reduced, you would not recognize him. He is unable to hold a pen, . . . he is stricken with a severe fever."[126] Byrne was not able to return to Little Rock until January. He then wrote the New Orleans archbishop that progress was being made at St. Mary's in Little Rock with the remodeling and expansion. His letter ended, "I care not what trials and privations I have to meet, . . . provided I can establish and uphold these institutions that are destined to instruct and win souls to our Blessed Redeemer."[127] Bishop Byrne travelled once again to Ireland that year and returned with an unnamed seminarian. Desirous of solid tangible progress in Helena, an important Mississippi River town in eastern Arkansas, the Arkansas bishop purchased land from two wealthy and prominent men in Phillips County.[128] In January 1858, four Sisters of Mercy moved into their new Helena quarters and that fall opened an Academy of St. Catherine.[129]

Father Patrick Behan, sent there as chaplain, became the first priest in more than eight years to remain longer than a few months.[130]

Byrne's additional school in Helena was offset by the failure of the second male academy in Little Rock, which is no longer mentioned after 1859. However, the College of St. Andrew's in Fort Smith had a boys' boarding school with a seminary attached.[131] In the fall of 1858, Byrne toured the northwestern counties as he waited for the second provincial council scheduled for February 1859, but postponed until January 1860.[132]

Byrne journeyed to Ireland for the last time in 1859 and returned with three postulants for the Mercy sisters. Father Behan, who died in September 1859,[134] was replaced with Father Peter Clarke, another Irish priest who had come to the United States through Canada.[135] Father Clarke had been stationed in Pine Bluff and New Gascony. Father Behan, working close by in Helena, had written Byrne to watch Clarke, "for him to lie is the rule, the truth is the exception."[136] Father Clarke soon proved the truth of Behan's assessment. By the spring of 1860, Byrne was asking Clarke to send him the collection money due the diocese. The bishop estimated the amount owed the diocese to be $600.00. After Clarke sent what Byrne considered an "insulting and wicked note," the Arkansas prelate suspended him in late June, informing another priest that "there is no truth in him, he is drinking too much, and putting the entire collection in his pocket, . . . and, by accident caused the death of a negro."[137] Clarke apparently borrowed a slave and failed to return him. As a result of Clarke's negligence, the poor bondsman perished. The records are not exactly clear with regard to the details.[138] The errant priest was brought back to the cathedral and replaced by Father Lawrence Smyth.[139]

Byrne attended his last provincial council in New Orleans on January 22-29, 1860. This was presided over by Archbishop Blanc and attended by Bishop Odin of Galveston, Bishop Martin of Natchitoches, and two new bishops, William Henry Elder of Natchez and John Quinlan of Mobile. The council announced guidelines for Catholic burials, decreed that religious writings must be approved by the local ordinary of the diocese, and adopted some regulations applicable to diocesan priests.[140]

Byrne had now been in the diocese for about sixteen years. He had established three female academies run by the Sisters of Mercy in Little Rock, Fort Smith, and Helena. Although he had failed twice to establish a male academy in Little Rock, near Fort Smith he had founded Arkansas' first Catholic college with a small seminary and boys' boarding school.[141] The Catholic population basically had not grown since 1850, constituting only about one percent of the population in 1860.[142] There were now eight priests working in the diocese and one priest who worked out of Fort Smith in the Indian Territory west of Arkansas.[143] The legislature approved the incorporation of the Sisters of Mercy and the Governor signed the act on January 2, 1861. Four months later, on the eve of the Civil War, Bishop Byrne signed over to the

Sisters of Mercy the property of the school and convent on Louisiana and Elizabeth Streets.[144] In late June 1860, Archbishop Blanc died in New Orleans. His replacement was Jean M. Odin, formerly Bishop of Galveston and the first Catholic priest to visit the town of Little Rock. Byrne wrote a congratulatory letter on the occasion of his consecration on May 19, 1861.[145]

The American Civil War began on April 12, 1861, with the assault on Ft. Sumter. The country was about to enter upon its greatest ordeal; not only was the nation torn asunder, so also were most religious bodies with the exception of the Catholic Church. The Civil War would also have profound consequences for Arkansas and its minute Catholic minority. One of the first casualties of the war was the College of St. Andrew, which did not reopen after the academic year of 1860-1861 because so many young men went off to war.[146] Bishop Byrne's health had deteriorated from long years of travel and exposure in frontier Arkansas. He wrote Archbishop Odin his last letter in early December 1861 and lamented that illness had sapped him of his strength. He wrote at the bottom of the page, "Blessed be God forever for his felicity!"[147] This was the last documented letter written by this zealous man of God.

In March 1862, Byrne received a letter from R.A. Bakewell, a Catholic lawyer and former Missouri newspaper editor, pleading for a priest in Jacksonport, a river town in northeastern Arkansas. Bakewell wanted a priest to come at least four times a year, since there were ten adult Catholics and two Catholic families in Jacksonport. "They are poor, but they will support a priest."[148] Apparently Byrne had no priest available to meet this modest request.

Sensing perhaps that the end was near, Byrne, in June 1859, had his Will prepared. All the lands of the Church were deeded to his successor, and until that person was named, to the Archbishop of New Orleans and his successors. While he was visiting the Mercy sisters at St. Catherine's in Helena in May 1862, Bishop Byrne became seriously ill. The sisters must have sensed that their bishop did not have long to live, for they summoned Helena's resident priest, Father Philip Shanahan, to give the bishop the sacrament of Anointing, then called Extreme Unction. He died on June 10, 1862, and was buried in the garden of St. Catherine's convent. Nineteen years later, his remains were removed by his successor, Bishop Edward Fitzgerald, and placed in a crypt below the new cathedral. The reinterment on the feast day of St. Andrew, November 30, 1881, was some seventy-nine years after his birth in Ireland.

An earlier historian of Arkansas Catholicism described Byrne as a man with a "magnetic personality which drew men irresistibly to him–his sociable disposition, gentlemanly bearing and well-known ability won for him the affection of people of every creed. Physically, he was a giant; but this only made more difficult the duty of traversing his vast diocese on horseback." The *Arkansas Gazette,* once the state's leading "Know Nothing" mouthpiece, eulogized him, "The deceased was emphatically a good man, pure in heart, gentle and lovely in all his actions; no one knew him but to like him; naught could be said but in his praise."

Privately, Byrne suffered a great deal in this frontier diocese during the last eighteen years of his life. He sought to leave the diocese on at least one occasion. However, his discontent should never overshadow what Byrne accomplished as Arkansas' first Catholic bishop. Three female academies were begun and one continues to this day, 130 years after his death. He founded Arkansas' first Catholic college and seminary at Fort Smith and managed to keep a Catholic boys' school in Little Rock during most of his tenure as bishop. These objectives were achieved when there were never more than ten Catholic priests in Arkansas at one time; most of the time, there were probably about half that number. He did not spare himself in working diligently for his flock. He traveled many times back to the northeast and even across the Atlantic to Ireland to recruit priests and nuns for his poor diocese on the southern frontier. The outbreak of the Civil War must have added to his woes, even though the war had barely touched the state at the time of Byrne's death. The Federal troops had conquered the northern third of the state and would be in Helena a little over a month after Byrne's death.[153] Arkansas' first Catholic prelate never lived to see the real suffering and destruction the war would bring to his adopted state.

Bishop Byrne knew full well the burden of being Catholic in a strongly Protestant culture. He never involved himself in political disputes and always tried to avoid situations which might lead to increased sectarian tensions. He endured the Know Nothing episode with a dignity that earned the respect of sworn enemies of the Church. Byrne left posterity with no public or private record of his views on slavery. He never owned slaves, and the only time the institution was mentioned involved the incident with Father Clarke of Helena, discussed previously. Byrne, like many of fellow Catholic bishops, looked on slavery as a political and economic issue, not a religious and moral concern. He understood how Catholics were suspiciously viewed by many Americans of Protestant persuasion. Bishop Byrne persevered against great odds and won for himself his crown of glory, laying foundations so secure that even years of civil war and the five years absence of a bishop would not totally uproot the Little Rock diocese. To his successor fell the task of building the Arkansas Catholic Church from the ashes of war and neglect.

Bishop Andrew Byrne, D.D.
First Bishop of Little Rock
(1844-1862)

Bishop Edward M. Fitzgerald, D.D.
Second Bishop of Little Rock
(1867-1907)

Rev. Patrick Reilly
Administrator of the Diocese
of Little Rock
(1862-1867)

Bishop John Baptist Morris, D.D.
Coadjutor Bishop
(June, 1906-February 21, 1907)
Third Bishop of Little Rock
(1907-1946)

Bishop Albert Lewis Fletcher, D.D.
Auxiliary Bishop
(1940-1946)
Fourth Bishop of Little Rock
(1946-1972)

Bishop Lawrence Preston Graves, D.D., J.C.L.
Auxiliary Bishop of Little Rock
(1969-1973)
Bishop Emeritus of Diocese of Alexandria, Louisiana

St. Mary's, Plum Bayou

The oldest existing church structure in Arkansas. The church was moved from St. Mary's Landing as the river encroached on the land. Now on the list of Historic Buildings in Arkansas, it had a varied history as its congregation moved and the building was vacant at times as testified by Bishop Fletcher's notes with his 1920 snapshots.

Interior taken Fall of 1920
by Bishop Fletcher

Exterior taken Fall of 1920
by Bishop Fletcher

Little Rock: The first Cathedral of St. Andrew (?)
Located at the northeast corner of Second and Center Street

"This cut shows the two-story wing addition built by
Bishop Fitzgerald for the accommodation of the clergy."

Source for quote: HISTORY OF CATHOLICITY IN ARKANSAS,
The Guardian, Little Rock 1925

Little Rock: "Old St. Mary's"

This was the home of the Mercy Sisters and Mount St. Mary's prior to its moving to its present site in Pulaski Heights in 1907. The sisters arrived in Little Rock in 1951 and started the school as soon as they came.

Little Rock: St. Vincent Infirmary

The first home of the hospital staffed by the Sisters of Charity of Nazareth. The Sisters started the hospital in 1888 which was funded by Alexander Hagar in gratitude for Little Rock's escaping the Yellow Fever Epidemic.

Rev. Matthew Saettle, OSB
Missionary in Arkansas
especially 1887-1917

Rev. John Eugene Weibel
Missionary of northeast Arkansas
especially 1879-1908

Rev. Lawrence Smythe
Diocesan priest
Fort Smith, Immaculate Conception
(1864-1900)

Rev. Msgr. John Lucey
Diocesan priest
Pine Bluff, St. Joseph
(1872-1914)

Dedication of Kerens' Memorial Chapel
Eureka Springs, 1909
Later became St. Elizabeth's Church

CHAPTER IV

Abandoned At Home, A Presence in Rome

The Arkansas Church Through the Civil War and the First Vatican Council, 1862-1870

A CENTURY AGO, John Gilmary Shea, the dean of American Catholic historians, wrote, "The troubled condition of the country and the difficult communication delayed the appointment of a successor to Right Reverend Andrew Byrne."[1] No one really expected that it would be almost five years before the Diocese of Little Rock would see another prelate. Proper authorities had to be notified, however, of the passing of Bishop Byrne, and Father Lawrence Smyth, writing from Little Rock, duly informed the metropolitan of the southern province in New Orleans, Archbishop Jean M. Odin, on July 7, 1862, that "our venerable Bishop died on the tenth of June at Helena."[2]

While it would take more than four years for the Holy Father to name a successor to Byrne, it would take four months to name even an apostolic administrator for the Arkansas diocese. That choice normally would fall to the metropolitan of the province, Archbishop Odin, who was in Europe and not due to return to New Orleans until early 1863. Under those circumstances, the person who would name the administrator would be the senior bishop in the province, Bishop Auguste Martin of Natchitoches, Louisiana. Bishop Martin thus appointed Patrick Reilly, who had been the vicar general of the diocese since the mid-1850s, as apostolic administrator on October 12, 1862.[3]

Father Reilly hailed from the small village of Kilmessan in County Meath, about thirty miles west of Dublin. It was probably no more than fifteen miles from Navan, also in County Meath, which was the birthplace of Bishop Byrne. He was born on March 10, 1817, and while attending Maynooth Seminary College in 1850, he heard the appeal from Bishop Byrne to come to the New World and serve as a missionary priest on the Arkansas frontier. He came with two other seminarians and a whole group of Sisters of Mercy in 1851.[4] Reilly was ordained by Byrne on his feast day, March 17. Reilly's first assignment was principal of a boys' school and chaplain for the Sisters of Mercy in Little Rock.[5] By 1856, he would become vice president and then president of the College of St. Andrew in Fort Smith. Vicar general of the diocese within four years of ordination, Reilly served as rector at the cathedral from 1858 until the death of Byrne in 1862.[6] As a person already of some authority in the diocese, it was little wonder that this Irish priest became apostolic administrator.

Though Father Reilly had enjoyed some authority under Bishop Byrne, he was still somewhat unsure of the exact nature of his administrative powers. Apparently responding to Reilly's written inquiry, Bishop Martin wrote the Arkansas cleric from Natchitoches in early December 1862, "All priests hold from you alone their jurisdiction, and you can suspend priests for a time or altogether from the ministry."[7] The Louisiana bishop reminded Reilly that this "authority is not yours, it is Christ's and is in your keeping."[8] His final advice was for Reilly to reside in the "episcopal town."[9] Seven months later, Martin was still advising Reilly on baptisms and marriage dispensations and assuring him that "the names of three candidates for the See at Little Rock will be shortly sent to Rome and I hope that the appointment is not delayed too long."[10]

Reilly assumed ecclesiastical power at a difficult time. The country was in the midst of a civil war, and Arkansas was a battleground between invading Federal troops and Confederate defenders. U.S. General Samuel R. Curtis had taken Fayetteville in March, after the Union victory at Pea Ridge, and his forces had moved freely across the northern third of Arkansas toward the Mississippi River. On July 12, 1862, just a little over a month after Byrne died, Federal troops occupied Helena without firing a shot, and they would successfully fend off a Confederate attempt to retake the town on July 4, 1863. In December 1862, Confederate General Thomas C. Hindman failed to drive the Federal troops out of northwest Arkansas at Prairie Grove, and so Arkansas would remain throughout the war partly occupied by Federal soldiers and partly held by the Confederate government. After the Union victory at Vicksburg on July 4, 1863, the Union forces under Brig. General Frederick Steele were free to move to eastern Arkansas to take Little Rock, which they accomplished by September 10, 1863. This would relegate what was left of Confederate Arkansas to the southern and southwestern sections of the state, a situation that remained unchanged until the war's end in 1865.[11]

Just before the war ended, David W. Carroll became the first Catholic to win a major political office in Arkansas. At a special election in November 1864, Carroll, who was living in Pine Bluff, was chosen to represent southeast Arkansas in the third Confederate Congressional District. He served during the last session of the Confederate Congress from January 11 to March 18, 1865. He would be the first Arkansas Catholic to win election to an out-of-state legislative body.[12]

The Civil War closed the College of St. Andrew after the spring term in 1861 (see the previous chapter), yet the Sisters of Mercy managed to keep all three of their convent schools in operation throughout the war. From the galleries of the Academy of St. Catherine in Helena, the sisters observed the Confederate army's unsuccessful attempt to retake this strategic town on the Mississippi River. One Federal official saw their white veils in the breeze and mistakenly believed that the sisters were giving signals to the Confederates. The officer later complained to the nuns that because they had been so well treated by the United States army, it was ungrateful for them to communicate in that fashion with the "enemy."[13] Just weeks before the capture of Little Rock by the Federals, Mount Saint Mary's was still advertising its opening for the fall term in September 1863.[14] In the Arkansas capital, the Sisters of Mercy used their convent at Seventh and Louisiana as a hospital for Confederate soldiers. One early historian of the Mercy sisters reported that right across the street from the hospital, where the cathedral now stands, was a conveniently located coffin factory to provide for the proper burial of the deceased.[15] Father Pierre F. Dicharry of the Natchitoches diocese served as the chaplain for a Louisiana regiment during the war and filled in as chaplain at the Mercy hospital during the battle for Little Rock.[16]

When Federal troops finally entered the Arkansas capital after September 10, 1863, an early historian for the Mercy nuns contended that Union troops "bivouacked" on the convent grounds and "helped themselves to whatever was movable." Some sisters later remembered the Federal troops peering through the windows of the convent at daybreak and asking, "What place is this?"[17] The Federal authorities, however, treated the Sisters of Mercy with great respect, and so did the Catholic Irish soldiers, who were always in awe of the religious habit.[18]

Father Reilly, meanwhile, was consumed with the trying financial and clerical needs of the diocese. He communicated regularly with Father John Dunne, rector of Carlow Seminary College in Ireland, about future priests for Arkansas. In April 1863, Dunne wrote Reilly that D.J. Cogan would be ordained that summer and sent to Arkansas by August.[19] Two months later, Dunne happily informed Reilly that Cogan had been ordained and would be leaving soon. He also said that Francis Laughran would be ready the next year and Mr. Phelan and Mr. Kavanaugh within two years, although Mr. Kavanaugh's health was poor.[20] The following spring, Dunne reported to Reilly that Laughran was almost ordained, but that he had not received the money he needed to travel to

Arkansas. Then he reported that for reasons he did not understand, the Bishop of Ireland would not ordain Laughran to the priesthood nor promote Kavanaugh and Phelan to the diaconate. He said that he would write to Rome to receive special permission to ordain them himself if it was necessary.[21]

But the next month, Dunne could happily report that he had received the money for Laughran's expenses and, "Laughran will be ordained, please God next Sunday. Mr. Phelan will be released from his mission when he returns to the Diocese the money advanced to him." Dunne was still concerned about Kavanaugh's health and did not think that he would be able to serve in Arkansas.[22]

Money was always a problem for this missionary diocese on the frontier, and the Civil War and its disruptions did nothing to improve its impoverishment. As one early chronicler of the Mercy sisters put it, "Little assistance was then to be had from the people of Arkansas; the Catholics are few and poor."[23] Through a Mr. Kavanaugh, who was working for the F.L. Brauns Company in Baltimore, hundreds of dollars came into the diocese from the Vienna-based Leopoldine Society.[24] From Paris, France, the Society for the Propagation of the Faith sent more than 48,000 francs between January 1864 and May 1866.[25] By the end of 1866, it would send another 10,000 francs.[26] All of this money, of course, had to be changed to American dollars on the international monetary exchange.

As the Civil War wound down in 1864, the Catholic Almanac reappeared after missing publication for two years. The editions of 1865 and 1866 reveal almost nothing about the Arkansas Catholic Church, and the 1865 edition reported that the editors could obtain no information about the diocese.[27] Yet the 1864 edition did contain the only real information about Arkansas Catholicism during the Civil War. Father Reilly was listed as administrator of the diocese, and he served at the cathedral with two assistants, Fr. Peter Clarke and Fr. D.J. Cogan, the young priest who had come from Ireland. Father Lawrence Smyth was at St. Patrick's Church in Fort Smith and Father Patrick McGowan at New Gascony, below Pine Bluff along the Arkansas River. Father Phillip Shanahan was still stationed at Helena, and there were three convent schools: Helena (St. Catherine's), Little Rock (St. Mary's), and Fort Smith (St. Anne's).[28] Only two priests came into the diocese during Reilly's tenure as administrator; Cogan in 1863 and Laughran, who arrived either in late 1865 or early 1866. As late as April 23, 1865, Reilly complained "of the three priests we expected from Carlow only one came, and I may have to let him go."[29] Laughran must have come after that date, for he appears in the 1867 edition of the Almanac.[30] It was clear that the man "I may have to let go" was Cogan; Dunne had warned Father Reilly that while he believed Laughran was "sensible, intelligent, and pious," Cogan's "zeal may overstep his discretion."[31]

That assessment seemed to be prophetic. As soon as Reilly had assigned Cogan to Helena in 1864, the two men would become involved in a dispute.

From Helena, in the fall of 1864, Cogan wrote to Archbishop Odin attacking Reilly's style of administration. Cogan maintained that Reilly was frustrating his work at Helena and not doing enough to build churches and promote Catholicism in the state. Cogan complained, "We have only four missions to which priests are assigned."[32] Archbishop Odin apparently brought up these concerns to Reilly, as the diocesan administrator defended his efforts the following spring and said that he would like to get rid of Cogan, but that it would leave only four other priests for all of Arkansas. Reilly maintained that what the diocese really needed was not complaining priests, but an early appointment of a bishop.[33] This did not end the dispute. The Helena-based priest fired off four letters to Archbishop Odin attacking Father Reilly in June and July 1865. He considered Reilly an autocrat who interfered with his ministry to the people of Helena. How the diocesan administrator interfered with Cogan's pastoral duties is never completely spelled out in his letters to the Archbishop of New Orleans. Father Reilly again defended himself in letters to Odin in October 1865, and in March 1866, and opined that Cogan merely had a rebellious attitude.[34]

By the summer of 1866, Reilly had enough of Cogan and attempted to remove him from his post at Helena. Cogan's parishioners wrote a long petition to Reilly on July 14, 1866, contending that Father Cogan:

> has done more in the interests of Religion and the church, and for education than any of his predecessors. He has established a fine boys school, St. Paul's Academy, and has assisted much in improving the condition of the Convent and its school. Under his visitation, the Church has nearly doubled in numbers; he has the confidence and respect of not only his congregation, but that of the Protestant Community as well.[35]

The petition had its desired effect. Cogan remained in Helena another two years.[36]

On the day of the petition from Fr. Cogan's angry parishioners, the Little Rock *Arkansas Gazette* revealed that, according to the Cincinnati *Catholic Telegraph*, the Rev. Edward Fitzgerald, pastor of St. Patrick's Church in Columbus, Ohio, had been appointed Bishop of Little Rock by the Holy Father. "We trust that he may be a worthy successor of the late Bishop Byrne," the *Telegraph* said.[37]

Edward M. Fitzgerald was born in the city of Limerick on the Shannon River near the west coast of Ireland. All the sources agree on the birthplace of Arkansas' second bishop and the month and the year of his birth, October 1833. They could not agree on the date. They gave his birth date variously as October 13, 16, 26, and 28. A baptismal certificate from Ireland in the Diocese of Little Rock archives has Edward Mary Fitzgerald, the son of James Fitzgerald and Joanna Pratt, being baptized on October 26, 1833, by Father Robert Cussen at St. Michael's Church in Limerick. Although the document listed his godparents as Thomas O'Mealy and Fanny Walsh, an exact date of birth was not given. Fitzgerald may have been born on October 13, the feast day of St. Edward on the old Catholic calendar, yet there is evidence that he believed that his birth date fell on October 28. As with Arkansas' first bishop, Andrew Byrne, we are aware only when young Edward Fitzgerald was baptized, not when he was born.[38]

Little is known of Fitzgerald's early life except that his father was Irish and his mother, though living in Ireland, was of German descent. He migrated to the United States as a teenager with his parents in 1849 and entered St. Mary of the Barrens Seminary in Perryville, Missouri, the following year. At this illustrious Lazarist seminary, the only active seminary west of the Mississippi River at that time, young Fitzgerald had as his teacher, Professor John J. Lynch, the future first Archbishop of Toronto. In 1852, he transferred to Mount St. Mary's Seminary in Cincinnati, where he studied under Father Sylvester Rosecrans, the future first Bishop of Columbus, Ohio, and brother of the future Union General, William Rosecrans. After 1855, he completed his theological studies at Mount St. Mary's College and Seminary in Emmitsburg, Maryland. Archbishop John B. Purcell ordained the twenty-three year old Irishman on August 22, 1857, as a priest of the Archdiocese of Cincinnati.[39]

His first and only assignment as a priest was to St. Patrick's Church in Columbus, Ohio. That congregation was so deeply divided that it had been placed under an interdict by Archbishop Purcell. The archbishop had removed a popular pastor, Father James Meagher, and a portion of the congregation had refused to accept this situation or the archbishop's replacement. Fitzgerald was sent to heal the division and bring the parish back under the rightful authority of the ordinary of Cincinnati. Although he was just a young priest, Father Fitzgerald had within two months, "conciliated the two factions in the congregation, induced the ringleaders to make confessions, and settled the parish finances."[40] He proved so popular and able that Archbishop Purcell left him at that church for more than nine years. It was during that time, on October 11, 1859, that Fitzgerald became a naturalized American citizen.[41]

With a note on June 22, 1866, the Holy Father informed Father Fitzgerald of his appointment to the See at Little Rock, but the actual date of the papal bull appointing him was April 24. After some thought, the young priest responded by September 1 to Cardinal Alessandro Barnabo of the Propaganda Fide Office in Rome rejecting the appointment. The news that Fitzgerald had refused the diocese depressed and angered the clergy in Arkansas. A forlorn and frustrated Reilly wrote Odin on September 6, 1866, that all:

> our hopes were blasted, for a time at least, on hearing that Father

Fitzgerald has refused to take us under his pastoral care. What is sad for me is that I see religion suffering and can do nothing to remedy the defects. Convents in need of support, in fact, everything going back.[44]

From Fort Smith, on the day that Fitzgerald had rejected the appointment, Father Lawrence Smyth had pleaded with Archbishop Odin to push Fr. Reilly for the position of bishop. "He has not the gift of eloquence," Smyth noted, "but he has ruled this Diocese as Vicar General for many years in the past, and he has the full confidence of the people of this Diocese, Protestant and Catholic, clergy and laity. He knows the resources and wants of the Diocese."[45] In the same letter, Smyth said that almost all of the Catholic congregations in Arkansas were Irish or of Irish descent, with only a few Americans and about a dozen French families around the old Arkansas Post.[46] Six days later, Smyth angrily called on Odin to put Reilly's name before the Holy See because "I fear a strange man who knows nothing of the workings of this Diocese."[47] Smyth mentioned that he had been in the Arkansas diocese for nine years and feared that Fitzgerald might face political opposition because he was coming from a northern diocese to a southern see. "In God's name," Smyth begged the archbishop to forward the name of the administrator.[48] The Fort Smith priest ended his letter bitterly, "If we had been a rich diocese, we wouldn't be left four years without a Bishop."[49]

Whether Archbishop Odin complied with Fr. Smyth's urgent pleading is not clear, but that option apparently closed when Father Fitzgerald attended the Second Plenary Council in Baltimore and decided to accept the Arkansas appointment.[50] In addition to having Fitzgerald accept the bishopric at Little Rock, the Second Plenary Council formally accepted the profession of the Doctrine of the Immaculate Conception, issued by Pope Pius IX in 1854; condemned secret societies, indifference and secularization, spiritism and the occult; and called for more missions to blacks and Indians.[51] While the latter call was not fully heeded by much of the American Catholic Church, Bishop Fitzgerald, as we shall see in a later chapter, did take these concerns to heart. Even though Fitzgerald wrote in his register that he had informed Rome of his change of mind on the position at Little Rock, he was still expressing doubts about his abilities. He also said that he had not heard from the Holy See by that date, December 7, 1866.[52]

Shortly afterward, he received a *mandamus* (literally meaning "we command"), a direct order to accept the Arkansas diocese under holy obedience. Fitzgerald did not mention the *mandamus* in his register, but from a letter sent to him by Archbishop Odin in mid-December, it was clear that the order had reached the New Orleans prelate, who had relayed it to Archbishop Purcell, who then presented this extraordinary command to his priest in a letter on December 10, 1866.[53]

Once his acceptance became known, Fitzgerald's friends in the priesthood and hierarchy sent letters of congratulations and encouragement. On Christmas Eve, Bishop John Lynch, later Archbishop of Toronto, expressed these sentiments in a letter:

> When I heard of your nomination some months ago to the See of Little Rock, I felt very pleased and would have written to congratulate you, but I restrained myself, afraid to influence you in any way, knowing by experience the burden and responsibility of a Bishop, and the difficulties of your future diocese. However, you have done well to yield to the advice of the Bishops and thus have a guarantee of doing the will of God.[54]

Another friend, a monk in a Cistercian Abbey in England, wrote Fitzgerald on New Year's Day 1867, "You having first declined the dignity, and the second time received the Apostolic Letters accompanied by a command to accept immediate consecration, gives you the assurance that your election is of God."[55] Considering the difficulties that Fitzgerald would have to face in his new diocese, he would need to lean on these encouraging words once he became bishop.

On February 3, 1867, at St. Patrick's Church in Columbus, Edward M. Fitzgerald was consecrated as the second Bishop of Little Rock by Archbishop John B. Purcell of Cincinnati, who was assisted by Bishop John Lynch of Toronto and Auxiliary Bishop of Cincinnati Sylvester Rosecrans, himself to be appointed the first Bishop of Columbus a year later. Patrick John Ryan delivered the sermon. He later became coadjutor Bishop of St. Louis and the second Archbishop of Philadelphia in 1884. Fitzgerald would be the first student of Bishop Lynch and Bishop Rosecrans to be made a bishop.[56] A now-exuberant Fitzgerald wrote his metropolitan in New Orleans two days later of his consecration and reported that he would be in his diocese by the first of March. He concluded by mentioning that he would be "the Benjamin of the American hierarchy, and perhaps the youngest Bishop in the Catholic world."[57]

According to Fitzgerald's own register, he left Columbus on February 27, 1867, and arrived at Cincinnati by March 3 to preach at the cathedral where he asked for money for his new mission diocese. He traveled by boat to Louisville, where he boarded a train that took him through Nashville and eventually to Memphis. There he took a steamer to Helena, where he entered his diocese for the first time on March 12. He remarked that much of the city was under water from spring floods, but that the Mercy convent and St. Catherine's Academy were above water. At the convent, he spoke to Mother Superior Teresa M. Farrell and her five sisters, two novices, and two postulants who also lived there. He met Father Cogan, saw his boys' school, and found the Academy of St. Catherine not doing well financially. Before leaving on March 13, Bishop Fitzgerald said a Mass for the repose of the soul of his predecessor, Andrew

Byrne. He left Helena with Father Cogan the next day en route to the diocesan See.[58] Fittingly, Fitzgerald entered his new diocese in the town where Byrne had died. He took up the burden at the very spot where Byrne had laid it down almost five years earlier.

The Ides of March found Fitzgerald and Cogan in Napoleon, Arkansas, which also was experiencing heavy flooding. Fitzgerald met the pastor, Father Laughran, at Napoleon. On March 16, the new bishop sailed past the remains of the Arkansas Post, which was deserted after Union troops burned and destroyed it in January 1863. Fitzgerald's register recorded his sorrow at seeing the ruins of the earliest European settlement in the state. The Post had been the center of Catholicism in colonial Arkansas.[59]

Continuing up the Arkansas River, Fitzgerald arrived in Pine Bluff to find that the pastor, Father Peter Clarke, had left to meet him at the Arkansas capital. He finally arrived at his ecclesiastical See of Little Rock at 2 p.m., March 17, 1867, the feast day of St. Patrick, the patron saint of his homeland. A committee of lay Catholics headed by Mr. Patrick May met him. That evening, Father Reilly conducted a joyous Mass of celebration at the Cathedral of St. Andrew with Father Cogan delivering the homily.[60] Fathers Reilly and Cogan evidently had managed to put at least some of their differences behind them.

Fitzgerald would soon discover what five years with no bishop and a Civil War could do to a diocese. Only six priests ministered to the scattered flock: Fathers Reilly in Little Rock, Smyth in Fort Smith, McGowan in New Gascony, Clarke in Pine Bluff, Laughran in Napoleon, and Cogan at Helena.[61] The census of 1860 had estimated the number of Catholics to be just under three thousand, yet Fitzgerald claimed only fifteen hundred in a letter to Archbishop Purcell in late March 1868.[62] Unfortunately, Fitzgerald would soon see his small number of priests decrease once again. Laughran, the young priest from Carlow, asked for and received his *exeat* from Fitzgerald on March 18, 1867, only a day after Fitzgerald's arrival in Little Rock. At the end of the month, Fitzgerald reported to a French missionary society that he believed he had the smallest diocese in America with only five priests.[63] He reassigned Father Clarke from Pine Bluff to Helena to serve with Father Cogan, yet neither would stay in the diocese over the next year and a half. Father Cogan left in March 1868, in an exchange with the Diocese of Dubuque for Father Philip Shanahan, who had left the diocese in 1866. The official Catholic directories would record this clerical swap.[64] Father Cogan soon developed his own difficulties with Bishop Fitzgerald. The Helena priest felt that the bishop was wrong to close St. Catherine's Academy and his boys' school in Helena in 1868 simply because they were not making money. Bishop Fitzgerald thought that the financially strapped diocese could no longer afford the luxury of institutions that could not pay their way.[65] Father Clarke, who had a difficult time as a priest under Bishop Byrne seems to have left the diocese forever, for his name will never again appear under Little Rock in the *Official Catholic Directory* after 1869.

On January 4, 1868, Fitzgerald also dismissed Fr. H. Lipowsky, whom he had assigned the post at Napoleon the previous April.[66]

Fitzgerald's first duty, however, was to get out and see his diocese and meet his Catholic flock. He journeyed to Fort Smith where he found the antebellum church in ruins. He immediately began a collection among the Catholics, bought new property, blessed the grounds, and mentioned that the future dimensions would be 80 x 35 x 22.[67] He returned in August 1867 to dedicate the church, although the building was not completed until October.[68]

After his initial trip to Fort Smith, Fitzgerald returned that year, 1867, to perform the Easter Triduum at St. Andrew's Cathedral. From there, he toured southwestern and southern Arkansas, where on May 18 he said Mass at the Cumberland Presbyterian Church in Washington, Arkansas, a rare ecumenical event for that period.[69] The Washington (AR) *Telegraph* reported this religious event and remarked, "Our citizens rarely have the opportunity, thus afforded, in participating in a solemn service of a Church most misunderstood, but which has numbered among its members many of the eminent and pious benefactors of the human race."[70] Still, Fitzgerald recorded in his register that he had found only five Catholics in Washington, outside the Federal troops stationed at a nearby military post. In Camden, however, Fitzgerald found thirty resident Catholics together with fifty Union soldiers who were of his same faith. He also wrote that he was allowed to preach to the people in front of the Ouachita County Courthouse.[71] By June 9, 1867, Pentecost Sunday, Fitzgerald was back in Little Rock; but by the end of the month, he was in Pine bluff speaking at the Church of St. Joseph. From there, he went to Helena and to De Valls Bluff in early July, recording his opinion that De Valls Bluff could support a priest if he could obtain one.[72] Later, he raised a seminarian, James Quinn, from minor orders to deaconship in only three days, July 29-31, 1867.[73]

By January 1868, the bishop was already busy trying to recruit clergy for his ecclesiastical domain. He was in touch with Michael Smyth from Ireland and John B. Duggan, who was studying at Spring Hill Seminary in Mobile, Alabama. By March, he had admitted Father Thomas McGovern into the diocese, and in April, he ordained Quinn.[74] By July, Fitzgerald had ordained Duggan to the priesthood, and the new addition to St. Andrew's Cathedral had been completed. In an account of this ceremony, a newspaper mentioned the participants as Fathers Patrick Reilly, Philip Shanahan, Lawrence Smyth, Patrick McGowan, Thomas McGovern, and a new priest, James S. O'Kean. This latter priest had come into the diocese after serving in Memphis, Tennessee, and one source claims that he was a distant relative to Bishop Fitzgerald's successor, John B. Morris.[75] That fall, Fitzgerald and O'Kean traveled to northeast Arkansas, where they chose Pocahontas as the site for the first church in that area. The local paper, the *Black River Standard* proudly reported, "The establishment of a Catholic Church in our town is a fixed fact . . . Fr. James Kean (sic) will be entrusted with the pastoral charge of the Church."[76]

The article also observed that they were impressed with both Bishop Fitzgerald and Father O'Kean, describing them as "very circumspect and very respectful, courteous gentlemen."[77]

Indeed, Fitzgerald was very circumspect and courteous in a state where Catholics were such a decided minority. In a time when great value was placed on oratorical ability, Fitzgerald proved to be a superb preaching prelate. The *Arkansas Gazette*, in January 1869, mentioned that the Catholics at St. Andrew's had filled up their new addition, and the paper attributed the congregation's growth in large part to Bishop Fitzgerald, "who is a fine reasoner, and it is always pleasant to hear his fine discourse."[78]

The bishop also continued the splendid Catholic tradition of trying to provide good schools. Fitzgerald did have one early casualty. The Civil War had wrecked the plantation economy of the Mississippi Delta, forcing the closure of St. Catherine's in Helena and leaving only the convent schools in Little Rock and Fort Smith.[79] At Little Rock were St. Andrew's Day School for boys and two schools run by the Sisters of Mercy, St. Joseph's for girls and St. Mary's for older girls. At Fort Smith, there was Immaculate Conception School for boys to complement the girls' academy of St. Anne's, conducted by the Mercy sisters.[80]

Bishop Fitzgerald continued to gather priests and build churches. In August 1869, he dedicated the first Catholic church in Hot Springs, which would have as its resident pastor, Father Patrick Geraghty.[81] With Father Geraghty and another new priest, William O'Higgins, who was stationed in Little Rock, the diocese would have nine priests by the end of the 1860s. For a year following October 1869, Fitzgerald was out of the diocese, leaving his vicar general, now the Very Rev. Reilly, in charge.[82] Fitzgerald would be in Rome attending the first General Ecumenical Council of the Catholic Church in three centuries and the first council in the modern era. At this assembly of Catholic prelates from around the world, Fitzgerald would earn a place in American and Catholic history by demonstrating immense courage as a man and loyalty as a bishop.

On December 8, 1866, Pope Pius IX invited all bishops to Rome to celebrate what was believed to be the eighteenth centenary of the martyrdom of St. Peter and St. Paul on June 29, 1867. While the Arkansas bishop could not attend, five American archbishops and eighteen bishops did.[83] The Holy Father at that time announced his intention to call a General Council of the Church to begin on the Feast of the Immaculate Conception in 1869. An American theologian, Father James Corcoran of the Diocese of Charleston, was one of the experts preparing a *"schema"*, or agenda, for the Council, beginning on December 30, 1868.[84] On December 8, 1869, the First Council of the Vatican opened. There were 689 prelates present, among them six archbishops, forty bishops, and one mitered abbot from the United States.[85]

By January, however, it was clear that the main document from the council would be on the theology of the Church, specifically the question of papal infallibility. Many bishops, especially those from Italy, France, Spain, Ireland, and Latin America, favored a formal declaration of the doctrine. Those who opposed the declaration generally were bishops from countries where most of the population was non-Catholic: Germany, England, and the United States. There were some exceptions. For example, a strong minority of French episcopates was in opposition, while Archbishop Henry E. Manning of Westminster, England, who would become a cardinal in 1875, was one of the strongest proponents of the declaration on papal infallibility.[86]

American bishops were divided. Archbishops Francis Blanchet of Portland and Jean M. Odin of New Orleans, and Bishops Michael Heiss of La Crosse; William H. Elder of Natchez; Louis de Goesbriand of Burlington, Vermont; Auguste Martin of Natchitoches; Claude Dubuis of Galveston; and Eugene O'Connell of Grass Valley (later Sacramento), California, strongly supported the declaration on infallibility.[87] A petition signed by three American archbishops and seventeen bishops on January 12, 1870, did not necessarily doubt the doctrine of infallibility, but questioned its practical wisdom because they worried that it would hurt evangelization efforts in the United States. The archbishops who signed the document were Peter R. Kenrick of St. Louis, John B. Purcell of Cincinnati, and John McCloskey of New York. Among the seventeen bishops, Edward Fitzgerald of Little Rock was the only bishop in the New Orleans province to sign this document.[88] Fitzgerald was also the youngest bishop from the United States at the council, having turned thirty-six in the fall of 1869. James Gibbons, later cardinal from Baltimore, was a titular bishop and the vicar apostolic for North Carolina. At only thirty-five, Gibbons had the rank of a bishop and ruled the area of North Carolina, but it had not been erected as a diocese.[89]

Bishop Fitzgerald was not an outspoken leader of the opposition. That role fell to Archbishop Peter R. Kenrick of St. Louis and Bishop Augustin Verot of Savannah, Georgia.[90] On March 10, 1870, a group supporting papal infallibility asked the council to suspend its agenda and bring up the question as soon as possible. Five days later, another petition signed by American Archbishops Kenrick and Purcell and Bishop Fitzgerald suggested that the agenda be maintained. The former position passed, but the question would not be openly discussed before the council until May 14, nearly two months later.[91]

The opinions of the opposing American bishops ran the gamut: from men like Bishop Thaddeus Amat of Monterrey, California, who maintained that the decree was inopportune; to men like Verot of Savannah, Kenrick, Michael Domenec of Pittsburg, and Bernard McQuaid of Rochester, New York, who believed that the doctrine could not be supported in Scripture or tradition. Others, like Archbishop Purcell and Bishop Richard Whelan of Wheeling, West Virginia, felt that the Pope should get universal consent from the bishops before declaring a doctrine as part of the dogma of the Church.[92] By early July, the debate had ended. When Archbishop Kenrick learned that he would not again be allowed to speak in opposition, he took the extraordinary step of publishing a tract against the declaration in Naples on July 8. Kenrick heatedly argued that infallibility had to be tied to the consent of all the other bishops in the world.[93]

Two letters from Bishop Fitzgerald at the First Vatican Council survive. In late April, he wrote his friend, Mother Mary Alphonsus Carton at the Sisters of Mercy convent in Little Rock, that he had wanted to apply for a leave of absence, but had decided against it after hearing that Archbishop Purcell's application had been turned down (although the Cincinnati prelate had health reasons). It was not that the Arkansas bishop did not enjoy Rome; he wrote, "I am so charmed with Rome, I would wish to stay, were that possible."[94] He also enjoyed the pageantry of the liturgies, "The ceremonies of Holy Week were gorgeous and sublime. The music–beyond my expectations of what music was."[95] With some humor, he added, "Every one nearly, when I meet him, has heard of Arkansas and by then I faced sympathy." In this long and informative letter, Fitzgerald jokingly commented about not being in the good graces of the Pope (quite possibly, he was referring to his position on infallibility):

> There is no danger that the Holy Father will take me from Arkansas, except to put me in the prisons of the Inquisition, perhaps. I have not been in his good book since coming to Rome. There are others here who would wish to put an end to my banishment, but I will not leave Arkansas, except I am allowed to lay down my crozier altogether.[97]

The statement about his willingness to stay in Arkansas was remarkable, given the fact that the Holy See had given him a *mandamus* to go there only three and a half years before. Almost two months later, on June 17, 1870, Fitzgerald again wrote Mother Mary Alphonsus Carton, "We shall adjourn, most probably, after June 29th. If not, I intend asking to go home after that date."[98] That may have been wishful thinking because the council would last until July, and he would be there until the end.

A more personal account of Bishop Fitzgerald at the Vatican Council comes from Hubert Larkin, a Catholic reporter, who wrote his reminiscences soon after the prelate's death in 1907. Larkin met the Arkansas bishop in an obscure church in Rome in December 1869. Fitzgerald was praying with "three or four rough looking fellows."[99] Larkin was immediately impressed with Fitzgerald, whom he pictured as a "stalwart, manly man, a typical missionary bishop who had served his apprenticeship in rough and lonely country missions."[100] Larkin later learned that Fitzgerald represented a rather poor diocese, and thus had to be frugal to live in an expensive city like Rome. Larkin even suspected that Fitzgerald had been helped financially by the Pope to enable him to attend the council.[101] Larkin visited the residence where Fitzgerald lived alone and described the "solitary apartment" as "bare of all but absolutely necessary furniture, a rather large sized crucifix and a few books."[102] His assessment of the bishop was complimentary, "Bishop Fitzgerald had all the marks, the sincerity, the humility, and the strong faith and unobtrusive piety of the apostolic age."[103] In the private and public spheres of life, Fitzgerald exhibited himself to be a man of courage, conviction, humility, and faith.

While the dissenter's position would not be accepted by the council, the assembly did modify the declaration in many ways. The Pope could only make pronouncements on faith and morals; he must state that he was speaking *ex cathedra,* literally meaning "from the throne," as chief shepherd of the Church; he must speak to the universal Church, not just a particular region; and he must clearly state that he binds all the faithful to accept what he is proclaiming. But the Holy Father's position was not made in any way dependent upon, or conditional upon, the consent of the bishops. He might consult his fellow shepherds, yet he was not required to do so.[104] The doctrine, as it was voted on, reads as follows:

> That is why, by attaching ourselves, faithfully to the tradition which comes down to us from the origins of the Christian faith, for the glory of God our savior, the exaltation of the Catholic religion, and the salvation of the peoples, with the approval of the sacred council, we teach and define that it is a divinely revealed dogma that the Roman Pontiff, when he speaks *ex Cathedra* that is, when exercising his office as Shepherd and Teacher of all Christians, by virtue of his supreme apostolic authority, he defines a doctrine concerning faith and morals which is held to be true by the universal Church–thanks to the divine assistance promised to blessed Peter, he enjoys that infallibility which the Divine Redeemer wished to confer on his Church for the definition of doctrines of faith and morals; and therefore the definitions of the same Roman Pontiff are, by themselves and not be virtue of the consent of the Church, irreformable.[105]

On July 13, the first vote was taken. 451 voted *placet,* or "it pleases," and eighty-eight voted *non placet,* or "it does not please." Sixty-two prelates expressed *placet juxta modum,* or "it would please with modification," and seventy bishops absented themselves from the assembly. Of the twenty-eight American prelates, eighteen voted *placet,* three voted *placet juxta modum,* and seven voted *non placet.* Two opponents, Archbishop Purcell of Cincinnati and Bishop Whelan had either left Rome by this time or absented themselves from the voting.[106] Pope Pius IX ordered another vote, and the prelates must take a *placet* or *non placet* position. Fifty-five prelates, including three American prelates, Archbishop Kenrick and Bishops Verot and Domenec, sent a letter to the Holy Father on July 17 saying that they would not attend because they could not vote for it; Fitzgerald also sent a separate note asking that his name not be called on July 18 because he could not vote for it.[107] Arkansas' bishop must have changed his mind, because the next day he appeared and asked the usher to call his name for the vote.[108]

All of the original eighteen who voted *placet* on July 13 were there to repeat their vote five days later. Of the American prelates who had voted *placet juxta modum* five days earlier, all three voted for the declaration. Some bishops who had been absent came and voted *placet,* and these included the young James Gibbons. Eventually twenty-five American bishops voted *placet* in the final count. Of the seven members of the American hierarchy who voted *non placet* earlier, one, Bishop William McCloskey of Louisville, changed his vote. Five of the other seven refused to appear, and these included Archbishop Kenrick and Bishops Verot, Domenec, McQuaid, and Ignatius Mrak of Marquette, Michigan.[109] Only one attended that day and repeated his vote against the doctrine–Bishop Edward M. Fitzgerald of Little Rock.

Reporter Larkin recalled the scene almost fifty years later:

> Four hundred and ninety-one Bishops recorded their votes consecutively in favor of the definition when the name Eduardus Fitzgerald was called out by the secretary of the Council. The Bishop of Little Rock rose to his feet, and said "non placet," breaking the solidarity of the vote, inviting the curiosity of all, and the indignation of a few.[110]

From the back of the hall, in his big booming Irish brogue, Fitzgerald became a footnote in the history of the universal Catholic Church. The final vote was 533 voting *placet* and two voting *non placet.* Joining Fitzgerald in his vote was Bishop Luigi Aloisio Riccio of Cajazzo in Sicily, Italy. Fitzgerald was the only English-speaking bishop in the world to vote against the promulgation of the doctrine on papal infallibility.[111]

Immediately after casting his vote, the large-framed Irishman walked up to the front of the assembly, knelt before the papal throne and submitted, "Holy Father, now I believe."[112] As remarkable as his vote was, it is also noteworthy to observe that Fitzgerald humbled himself enough to submit to the desires and wishes of the Pope and accepted the view of an overwhelming majority of his fellow members of the Catholic hierarchy from all over the world. Fitzgerald showed himself to be a man of strong conviction, yet not so obstinate as to demand that the Church do everything his way. He also demonstrated his loyalty to the Church and the Holy Father by immediately submitting so that there would be no scandal or division within the body of Roman Catholicism. No doubt his final *non placet* did require singular courage, because as one Arkansas non-Catholic writer observed, "in an age of spineless yes-men, time-serving sycophants, and vacillating crowd-pleasers," Arkansas can proudly claim a man like Bishop Fitzgerald.[113]

Bishop Fitzgerald arrived at De Valls Bluff in eastern Arkansas early on October 27, 1870, a year to the day since leaving the diocese.[114] He went to Little Rock that afternoon. That night, well-wishers, Catholic and non-Catholic alike, crammed into the old St. Andrew's Cathedral to welcome home this Christian leader. Father W. O'Higgins made the formal welcoming address.[115] Bishop Fitzgerald made a short reply. "One year's absence today separated us; but never during the year have you at Little Rock, or the Diocese of Little Rock, been absent from my mind," he said.[116] While mentioning that he had the opportunity to see such famous places as Rome, Naples, Milan, Venice, Assisi, Loretto, Paris, London, and his beloved homeland of Ireland, he said, "All these delightful and pleasant stopping places have but served to remind me of the end of my journey–home."[117] Fitzgerald then performed a Eucharistic adoration service known as Benediction and went to a large private reception in his home.[118]

A few American archbishops and bishops made many speeches concerning the First Vatican Council, all submitting to the formal declaration of the doctrine of papal infallibility. These included Bishop Verot and Archbishops Kenrick and Purcell.[119] Fitzgerald made no such speeches initially because he did not need to formally submit, having done so in person before the Holy Father. On May 18, 1871, he did give a speech at the cathedral about his trip to Rome and the Vatican Council. The *Arkansas Gazette* reported, "the speaker handled his subject in a masterly manner . . . To attempt to give a synopsis of his remarks would not do justice to the speaker, his subject, or ourselves. To appreciate it properly, it had to be heard."[120] In the papers of Bishop Fitzgerald, however, is a handwritten address entitled, "The Vatican Council: Ten Years After." It obviously was not the speech that Fitzgerald gave in 1871, and no record of that speech has been found. But the lengthy address ten years later provides some reflections on the First Vatican Council, papal infallibility, and the reasons for his vote on July 18, 1870.

He spoke in awe of the pageantry and spectacle of the first council in three centuries, "The Ecclesiastical chiefs of 200,000,000 people representing every variety of language and of race; representatives too of the oldest form of Christianity."[121] Papal infallibility was not an invention of the council, he observed, but an elaboration of divinely revealed doctrine in both sacred Scripture and tradition, since the Divine Redeemer had promised the Holy Spirit to the Church to be with it and guide it. He said, "It is implicit that the same Spirit protect his flock from any serious danger to their faith and morals." Fitzgerald maintained that while the Church must ever deal with errors and heresies, the Holy Spirit would ever keep it "the pillar and the ground of truth."[122] Despite what some might say, the council did not make the Pope into a god and say that he was without sin or that he could not make "errors and blunders in ecclesiastical legislation or Ecclesiastical-political matters."[123] Fitzgerald himself was at first concerned about some of the earlier proposals of infallibility, which tended to make it seem that the Pope was infallible in his person or in all his decisions. Once some restrictions and conditions were inserted, he no longer had reservations about the doctrine itself.[124]

Yet the next question to Fitzgerald was whether it was right and prudent to make the declaration at that point in the history of the Church. As he put it:

> it is one thing to hold a given doctrine as the most probable . . .; quite a different thing to aid by my vote, (sic) to impose a new obligation on Catholics, and as it appeared to me then, to place a new obstacle in the path of others seeking a union with the Catholic Church. It was this latter consideration, chiefly, which put me, with a minority of the Bishops in what was called the opposition.[125]

Fitzgerald was well aware that he was living in a country, and especially a state, with an overwhelming Protestant majority and culture. To declare the doctrine of papal infallibility at that time could, in his view, do nothing but hamper efforts to bring more non-Catholics into the fold. This led him to cast his vote against the declaration on both July 13 and July 18, 1870.[126] Bishop Fitzgerald's concern about evangelization was real, and it determined almost all his actions at the First Vatican Council. For example, an American historian of the council recorded that in April 1870, Fitzgerald had decried the use of excessive "anathemas" in council documents; he felt that they were an embarrassment and would "only drive away those whom the Church was trying to win to itself."[127]

A few years after the council, Father Peter Benoit, a British priest of the newly founded Order of St. Joseph, visited the Arkansas bishop to talk about evangelization among black Catholics. Father Benoit's diary recorded a conversation with Bishop Fitzgerald on April 18, 1875. The bishop talked about his vote at the First Vatican Council and recalled a writer who had said that of the two who had voted *non placet*, "one had been in a lunatic asylum and the other was fit for it."[128] Benoit wrote later that the bishop added, "more seriously that he did not go a distance of 6,000 miles to vote at the will of anyone but to give his own conscientious vote."[129] Fitzgerald impressed Benoit as a man "in every way a most worthy Bishop, zealous, pious, and talented."[130] His vote at the First Vatican Council would not be the last time Fitzgerald demonstrated independence of mind and will.

It is arguable on hindsight that the ordinary of Little Rock was correct in believing that the declaration of infallibility would hurt evangelization in his strongly Protestant country and state. Nevertheless, Fitzgerald would go along with the rest of the Church and courageously face the challenge of preaching every aspect of the Catholic faith in a culture and society that could be either hostile or indifferent. Of his remaining thirty-seven years as Bishop of Little Rock, he would strive earnestly to enlarge his flock in a strongly non-Catholic enclave known as Arkansas.

C H A P T E R V

"Bishop Fitzgerald is Worthy of the Highest"

An Administrative Survey of the Diocese, 1870-1900

UPON HIS RETURN from Rome, Bishop Fitzgerald must have been mildly surprised, but delighted, that in his absence he had not lost any of his nine priests.[1] Writing some twenty years later, Father John M. Lucey cited the 1870 census to show that while Arkansas had a population of 484,981, only 2,000 were Catholics.[2] Bishop Fitzgerald would not admit such numbers until late 1874.[3] With heartfelt gratitude, Fitzgerald wrote the French missionary society on August 21, 1871, "We, in the United States, are deeply indebted to the Association, and the Diocese in Little Rock in particular, owes almost everything."[4] Fitzgerald attended his first provincial council in New Orleans in January 1873, the first such meeting since 1860, no doubt enjoying this opportunity to meet fellow bishops of the New Orleans Province.[5]

Progress continued, but difficulties persisted. By 1873, Fitzgerald had lost Fathers William O'Higgins from Little Rock and John B. Duggan from Pine Bluff. These losses were offset in 1872 by the addition of Fr. Michael Smyth, who joined his brother Lawrence (sometimes spelled Laurence) Smyth in ministering in Fort Smith and into the Indian Territory. In November of that year, Fitzgerald ordained John Michael Lucey at Fort Smith. Lucey was assigned to St. Joseph's Church at Pine Bluff, a post he would hold for more than forty years. The year 1873 found Bishop Fitzgerald and Vicar General Reilly in Little Rock, Father Patrick McGowan serving New Gascony and all of Jefferson

County, Father Philip Shanahan at Helena, Father James Quinn in southeastern Arkansas and Napoleon, Father James O'Kean at Pocahontas and northeastern Arkansas, and Fr. Patrick Geraghty at Hot Springs and Camden in southern and southwestern Arkansas.[6] Fitzgerald dedicated a church in Camden in May 1873, and the local paper reported that he "spoke in a happy style before a large and appreciative audience."[7] With some pride, Fitzgerald reported to the French missionary society in November 1874 that, counting himself, he had nine priests, thirty-one sisters, and twenty churches–fifteen completed and five still under construction. There were three hundred pupils in the four Catholic schools of St. Mary's and St. Joseph's in Little Rock, and Immaculate Conception and St. Anne's in Fort Smith.[8]

One responsibility that Fitzgerald definitely wanted to be rid of was the Indian Territory. In an 1872 letter, he blamed Reilly for taking on this responsibility, but it is not clear when the area was actually placed under the authority of the Diocese of Little Rock. Bishop Byrne brought Father Theophilus Marivault, S.J., to work there, but Marivault left after a few months. From 1852 through 1857 the *Metropolitan Catholic Almanac* listed Fr. Jean Baptiste Miege, S.J., as living in Fort Smith and visiting the Indian Territory. Even after 1857, some of the Indian area was being visited from St. Andrew's College in Fort Smith.[9] In September 1860, Father Miege wrote Bishop Byrne thanking him for being "so kind to take care of those Indians who live on the borders of Arkansas."[10]

At the Conference of Bishops in New Orleans in January 1873, Fitzgerald asked the Archbishop of New Orleans to petition Rome to remove the area from his jurisdiction. Fitzgerald revealed this in a letter to the French missionary society, and in the same letter, he estimated the number of Catholics there to be five hundred soldiers and one thousand Indians.[11] By the time that Father Isidore Robot, a French Benedictine priest, arrived in the Indian Territory in the fall of 1875, Fitzgerald was writing the society that "the Holy See is contemplating putting the Indian Territory, now under my jurisdiction, under the charge of a community of French Benedictines, Reverend Isidore Robot as provincial."[12] Fitzgerald wrote Father Charles Ewing of the Bureau of Catholic Indian Affairs in February 1875 that he had sent Fr. Michael Smyth from Fort Smith to minister to the Osage Indians. Bishop Fitzgerald wrote the Bureau of Catholic Indians Missions in 1879 that since Father Robot appeared in 1875, Father Smyth "has not set his foot across the line."[13] In 1876, the Holy See finally made the Indian Territory a separate ecclesiastical area, a Prefect Apostolic under Father Robot, but still connected with the New Orleans Metropolitan See.[14]

Yet the young bishop, now only turning forty, went through a profound spiritual crisis about his faith, ministry, and service in the Arkansas wilderness. He poured out his soul to his former pastor and friend, Archbishop John Purcell of Cincinnati, on December 8, 1873:

> I am most thoroughly unhappy, and there is nothing for me to do, no prospect for the future. I have tried writing and travel as a means of directing my mind, to no purpose. Not a single moment in my working life is free from fretting, and I often feel my mind will give way. I am useless to others, useless to myself, and, from not having anything to do, I find in me a growing dislike in making exertions of any kind, a bad sign in me, no longer a young man. I have hither been able to handle petty annoyances, which we meet with in the course of our lives, but for the nearly past, I am overwhelmed with despondency and gloom.[15]

Fitzgerald was depressed, too, by the slow recovery of Arkansas from the Civil War; the state was embroiled in the political and economic turmoil of Reconstruction. Also, the nation was in a deep economic depression known as the Panic of 1873. It was reflected in Fitzgerald's lengthy letter to his former archbishop. "Our state is not improving," Fitzgerald complained, "It is feared that the people of this state have actual want of the necessities of life . . . For our farmers do not raise their bread stuff, they buy from the proceeds of cotton. The cotton so low, the negroes refuse to pick it. The farmer, . . . has no money."[16] He confessed to Purcell that of the fourteen chapels he had built since coming to Arkansas, only ten remained in operation. In Little Rock, his largest congregation in the state, there were fewer than three hundred adult members.[17] This echoed complaints that Bishop Byrne had made to the Vatican about the small number of Catholics in Arkansas, which made it difficult to justify a separate diocese. Still he felt, "We have cause to be thankful, when we think of cities, places, like poor plagued Memphis, for instance, has gone through."[18] Fitzgerald referred to the yellow fever epidemic that had attacked Memphis the previous summer and autumn, the first of three such ravages in the 1870s. Despite such gratitude, Fitzgerald found it "impossible to throw off this all-pervading depression under which I labor."[19] He ended this long, revealing correspondence on a note of humility asking, "If you know of anything reprehensible in me, I beg of you, not to spare the rod!"[20]

Fitzgerald was in the midst of a profound mid-life or mid-ministry crisis. The letter showed him to be a man willing to take correction. Apparently, he was not sharing a momentary depression. Months before, Bishop Joseph Durenger of Fort Wayne, Indiana, had written Purcell, "I don't wonder Bishop Fitzgerald feels discouraged in his small diocese, but then Arkansas has all the requirements for future prosperity."[21]

Fitzgerald's own superior, the metropolitan of his province, the Archbishop of New Orleans, Napoleon Joseph Perche, wrote him a long letter, apparently in response to a letter similar to the one that Fitzgerald had written to Purcell. Perche told the Arkansas bishop that he "underestimated himself . . . "What you feel is a spirit of despondency and we can always banish it as with any other temptations."[22] He urged the young bishop to get out and visit his flock around the state, in which he saw many advantages. "The presence of a Catholic Bishop always produces great impressions, even among Protestants. In some places you could give talks, . . . for Americans are fond of lecturers. You have all that is required of an orator. Besides your visits could give energy and courage to your priests and Catholics."[23] He ended his note by reminding Fitzgerald not to get too involved with activities at the expense of prayer and theological study.[24]

Given the circumstances of his diocese, there seems to have been every reason for Bishop Fitzgerald to feel discouraged. In January 1873, he maintained that there were only 2,500 Catholics in the state, and they were "mostly immigrants and strangers to the land."[25] That October, he wrote the French missionary society that in Arkansas "the Catholics are very few and scattered,"[26] a comment that still seems current even after more than a century has passed. A year later, he wrote to France claiming that the situation had deteriorated further, because he believed that five hundred Catholics had fled the state for better economic opportunities, leaving the Catholic population at two thousand.[27] Despite these grim conditions, Fitzgerald would not only persevere, but forge ahead over the next quarter-century to make real improvements in the conditions of the Church in his adopted state.

How hard it was for him and many of his fellow Catholic priests in Arkansas in the 1870s is revealed in the memoirs of an Irish-born priest who had worked in Memphis during the yellow fever epidemics. He had served also as an itinerate missionary in several counties in eastern Arkansas. Father Denis A. Quinn is listed in the 1875 *Official Catholic Directory* as serving missions at "Madison, Taylor Creek, and several stations on the Mississippi and St. Francis Rivers, and along the Memphis and Little Rock Rail Road."[28] Writing in 1887 from Providence, Rhode Island, Father Quinn provided a rare glimpse into the experience of a missionary priest in a state still rural and quite primitive, and strongly Protestant in its religious orientation.

Father Quinn served at St. Brigid's Parish in Memphis as a priest for the Diocese of Nashville. He survived the calamitous yellow fever plagues of 1873, 1878, and 1879. Between ravages, he served for four years, 1874-1878, as a traveling Catholic missionary for eastern Arkansas. From his reminiscences, it is difficult to distinguish which assignment was more dangerous, the plagues of Memphis or the wilderness of Arkansas. His book, *Heroes and Heroines of Memphis,* is still a classic eyewitness account of the yellow fever tragedy. An addendum to the work, "A Graphic Description of Missionary Life in Eastern Arkansas," contains the material concerning his sojourn in the state.[29] According to Father Quinn, he served in the counties of Crittenden, Cross, St. Francis, Mississippi, Craighead, Poinsett, Prairie, and Woodruff.[30]

Quinn describes in detail what a missionary priest needed in his journey through eastern Arkansas. His small hand luggage or "valise" was one of a "bivalve formation" for "secular appurtenances."[31] The "ecclesiastical" part of his luggage included:

> An altar stone, chalice, paten, crucifix, missal, and stand, (vestments one color for all occasions), chasuble, maniple, stole, cincture, alb, amice, cassock, burse, . . . chalice covering, three altar-linens, finger-towel, three altar cards, one papal prayer, altar wine, altar breads (large and small), a pair of army candlesticks, with two candles, ritual, purple stole, breviary, book of epistles and gospels, a little bell, three sermons, (lectures if possible) . . . With the above, should also be carefully packed a number of rosary-beads, scapulars, agnus (sic) Deis, lace pictures; near which should be orderly shelved, a baptismal registry, a number of catechisms, polemic tracts, and a sufficient number of controversial works, such as *The Faith of Our Fathers, Catholic Belief, Why I am a Catholic,* etc., etc. The Missionary should never forget to bring about his person, a pix (sic) and replenished oil stokes, and a small vial of baptismal water.[32]

For his secular wants, Quinn included "three or four days' supply of Graham crackers, a patent alcohol stove, with supply, small tea or coffee pot, a can of beef, a fan to ward off mosquitoes."[33] After all this equipment has been "systemically adjusted," according to Quinn, there will be plenty of room for a moderate variety of under-clothing, hose, handkerchiefs, towels, gents' toilet and dressing case."[34] Quinn felt a "revolver or shot gun" might be needed to ward off "wild animals or robbers," yet he felt that it would not be fitting for a priest to be so armed. He did think that an umbrella would come in handy, and he admitted, "some of the above mentioned articles might be left out."[35]

Father Quinn's journal was filled with humorous anecdotes and observations about his time in the state. Quinn stressed the importance of removing your hat upon entering a country boarding house. "This simple act of politeness affords a pleasing surprise to the unbelieving country 'folk' who heretofore imagined every Priest had two horns on his forehead. Indeed, a tumor on the temple of a certain Bishop has excited a good deal of suspicion in this regard."[36] Little wonder that the Irish-born missionary believed that "the many unfounded prejudices that the people have been taught to believe regarding the Pope and the Priests, the Confessional, and other doctrines of the church, seriously mar the progress of Catholicity in these regions."[37]

Father Quinn had to endure cold, hunger, and heat, but he considered the weather more reliable than the schedule along the Little Rock-Memphis Railroad.[38] He maintained that while St. Paul had given a "sad recital" of his "persecutions, shipwrecks, and wonderful escapes, . . . except for flagellations alone, I would venture to undergo all the others rather than remain one night a helpless victim to a swarm of Arkansas mosquitoes."[39] Somewhat bitterly, Quinn contrasted the lot of the country missionary priest with that of the more sedentary urban pastor. "The city Priest seldom or never meets any one that will dispute his doctrine, calling, or revenue. His person and his words are considered sacred. The country missionary has everywhere to defend his church, and doctrine."[40] Quinn was impressed with the faith of the handful of Irish Catholic immigrants had who bravely settled in "that dreary wilderness."[41]

While he found traveling in rural Arkansas rough going, he described Little Rock as "a beautiful city" of sixteen thousand inhabitants, and he also marveled at the scenery around Fort Smith and Hot Springs.[42] Quinn preached and said Mass in log cabins, little wooden churches, Baptist churches, and even Masonic halls.[43] He found it both "strange and ludicrous" to hear himself "addressed in all manners of titles, ecclesiastical, professional, military and civic . . . Judge, professor, squire, . . . colonial or captain; while parson, brother, or priest Quinn"[44] by those who were members of other Christian churches. He also found it interesting that many people would attend both the Methodist and Baptist revival meetings, and that a few would be baptized twice in revivals only weeks apart.[45] As a priest trained in a sacramental theology, he found this odd, but for rural Arkansans, the immersions were a faith response to the preaching of the gospel. Denominational lines between Protestant churches also were blurred in the minds of many of these country folk.

The Irish-born missionary was also pessimistic about the growth of Catholicism in Arkansas. He thought that even after six years of the administration of Bishop Fitzgerald, only 1,400 Catholics were in the whole state. When he wrote his book in 1887, he maintained that the directory reported 8,200 Arkansas Catholics, an increase that he attributed mostly to the influx of German immigrants.[46] By the time his book was written, Bishop Fitzgerald had been bishop for twenty years, and the body of priests of the diocese were "a zealous and enlightened body of men." Quinn wondered, given these conditions, whether Catholicism "would have made greater progress in any other State or Territory, yea, even in the wilds of Africa or Cochin-China."[47] On average, there had been only twenty priests a year in Arkansas, and these men had to struggle "against the prejudices ingrafted by no less than twenty thousand Preachers."[48] He firmly believed that "had not God favored the Bishop of this diocese with a robust frame and unflinching perseverance, beyond a doubt, the paucity of the Catholic population at present would be very discouraging."[49] Further, he wrote, "I make no hesitation in reasserting that the Diocese of Little Rock is of all the Missions of the States and Territories, the most arduous and unhealthy. If it were not for the annual income of 'Propaganda' funds, the Priest of this diocese could not subsist."[50] Father Quinn ended his account by praising the abilities of Bishop Fitzgerald as person, priest, and preacher. "Besides being, like his diocese, a solid 'little rock' of authority for all knotty questions in theology, philology, and christian classics, Bishop Fitzgerald ranks amongst the best conversationalists, and is, perhaps, one of the first English scholars in the land."[51]

In the last half of the 1870s, the Catholic Church in Arkansas made some real gains amid troubling setbacks. Fr. Philip Shanahan, the longtime pastor at Helena and the priest who gave Bishop Byrne his last sacraments, had to leave the state in September 1875 owing to ill health. He died in Celedonia, Minnesota, in 1889, and his place at Helena was taken by Father J.M. Boetzkes.[52] The Sisters of Mercy convent in Fort Smith burned on December 8, 1875.[53] On St. Patrick's Day, 1876, Bishop Fitzgerald ordained to the priesthood Thomas Reilly. This gain was offset by the death of Fr. James O'Kean, the first Catholic pastor of northeastern Arkansas, who died in the summer of 1874 while stationed in Little Rock. He was so loved in the Pocahontas area that the railroad depot across the Black River is a little town known as O'Kean, named for this early Catholic missionary priest.[54] Bishop Fitzgerald wrote the French missionary society in the fall of 1876 that, in his opinion, his diocese was the smallest and poorest in the United States.[55] In January 1877, the Mercy sisters in Little Rock opened Arkansas' first orphanage, so the *Arkansas Gazette* asked its readers "to be liberal in assisting this noble charity."[56] By 1878, ten orphans were under the care of the Sisters of Mercy, yet it does not seem to have survived beyond that date.[57] Late in 1877, the *Gazette* also reported that the Benedictines, a Catholic monastic order, had purchased 15,000 acres in Logan County from the Little Rock and Fort Smith Railroad for a large colony of German Catholics.[58] This would cause the number of Catholics to increase, according to Bishop Fitzgerald's reports to France, from only 2,500 in December 1877 to over 6,200 by November 1881.[59]

In the late 1870s, the Arkansas prelate launched a building project to reflect the new growth and maturation of the Church. The Catholic population in the capital city had long outgrown the small wooden structure built by Bishop Byrne some thirty years earlier, though Fitzgerald had added a new north wing and a second story for the priests in the late 1860s.[60] The bishop announced at Hopefield (a town just across the Mississippi River from Memphis) in April 1878, in the presence of Father Denis A. Quinn, that he would build a permanent structure in Little Rock to serve as the cathedral for the diocese.[61] At 5:00 p.m. on July 7, 1878, on the Feast of the Most Precious Blood on the old Catholic calendar, a parade proceeded from the old church down Second Street to Louisiana, turned right and marched to the northeast corner of Seventh and Louisiana, just across the street from what was then St. Mary's Academy and the Sisters of Mercy convent. The cornerstone was laid and with it a tin box containing copies of Little Rock's newspapers, coins, and a scroll giving the date of the dedication, and the fact that it occurred under the administrations of President Rutherford B. Hayes, Governor William R. Miller, and Mayor John R. Fletcher. Thomas Harding, a parishioner of St. Andrew's and an architect with the firm Thompson and Harding, designed the English gothic structure. Father James Callaghan, then editor of the Cincinnati *Catholic*

Telegraph, gave the main address, which was followed by a reception at the Mercy convent.[62]

As Fitzgerald was beginning work on the new cathedral, a report appeared in the *Arkansas Gazette* in August 1879 asserting that "all manner of effort" had been used to bring Bishop Fitzgerald to Cincinnati to succeed his aging, ill friend and former prelate, Archbishop John Purcell, who would die within a year. The *Gazette* was proud that Fitzgerald had turned down this offer even though it meant that "he would be raised to the dignity of an Archbishop." "Few decline such honors," the *Gazette* said. "Bishop Fitzgerald is worthy of the highest."[63] Was the archbishopric offered to him, and did he decline to stay at a more humble position in a poorer diocese? Cincinnati's archdiocese was being rocked by a scandal involving Archbishop Purcell and the failure of his brother's bank.[64] While that situation might have made the offer less inviting, it nevertheless would have been a significant promotion for a man known mostly as the *non placet* bishop at the First Vatican Council. Bishop William McCloskey of Louisville, Kentucky, did mention to Fitzgerald that fall that he was on the list for the Cincinnati archbishopric:

> Should you be appointed to Cincinnati, you ought not, I think, to refuse. One reason for selecting you was the fact that apart from your knowing the Diocese and being known in it, you have probably at least twenty-one years of life; your youth and strength would be the next best thing to putting a saint in.[65]

Fitzgerald was the choice of the bishops of the Cincinnati Province, and his name was one of three sent to Rome for consideration, although he had his name removed from consideration.[66] For a man who had to be given a *mandamus* to go to Arkansas, Rome apparently must give him another one to force him to leave.

Fitzgerald had some projects to complete in Arkansas, and one of them was the new cathedral at Little Rock. The building that arose on the corner of Seventh and Louisiana was made of granite quarried from the Fourche Mountains, three miles southeast of downtown Little Rock.[67] As with most church structures, the floor plan was that of a cross; it was 140 feet in length and 86 feet across the transept and was made of wood from around the state. The huge altar was donated by a local couple, Alexander and Catherine Hager.[68] According to one source, it was the first building constructed of Arkansas granite.[69]

On November 27, 1881, almost thirty-eight years after Pope Gregory XVI established the Arkansas See, Bishop Fitzgerald presided over the formal dedication of the Cathedral of St. Andrew the Apostle, the patron saint of the diocese. The day was also the First Sunday of Advent, the beginning of the Catholic liturgical year. Joining in the celebration were his fellow prelates,

William McCloskey of Louisville, John Neraz of San Antonio, and John Watterson of Columbus, Ohio. The sermon for the Mass was given by coadjutor Bishop Patrick John Ryan of St. Louis, who in three years would become the second Archbishop of Philadelphia.[70] Fitzgerald had the remains of Arkansas' first bishop removed from Helena to the new cathedral on November 30, the Feast of St. Andrew the Apostle. Much of the interior was designed later by Father James F. Callaghan, who would leave the Archdiocese of Cincinnati to become vicar general of Little Rock from 1890 to 1899.[71]

Just as the cathedral construction got under way, Father Patrick Reilly, who had run the Diocese of Little Rock between 1862 and 1867 and who had since served as vicar general, was forced by bad health to leave Arkansas. He returned to his native Ireland where he died on April 29, 1882.[72] His place as vicar general was taken in 1881 by Father Aegidius Hennemann, O.S.B., who served until 1883, when he was succeeded by Rev. Dr. Michael M. Halliman, formerly a diocesan priest from St. Louis. Dr. Halliman served until Father Callaghan assumed the post at the beginning of the 1890s.[73] Fitzgerald himself passed one milestone as he celebrated his twenty-fifth anniversary as a priest in November 1882.[74] In December 1882, Archbishop William Elder of Cincinnati, who had taken the archbishopric in 1880, wrote Fitzgerald this congratulatory note, "I learn from various quarters how your diocese is growing; your institutions, and other works are multiplying; how your foresight and your patience have prepared considerable means to accomplish what is beginning to be needed."[75]

The decade of the 1880s would be one of real growth as Catholic immigrants continued to arrive and Catholic institutions continued to expand. In November 1880, Fitzgerald wrote the French missionary society that he had twenty-one priests and two seminarians, plus two new religious orders, the Order of St. Benedict (O.S.B.) and the Congregation of Holy Ghost (C.S.Sp.). He also reported that his income from the Catholic diocese of Arkansas for that year was $17,500.00, but that his expenses were $26,870.00.[76] A year later, he wrote the society that he estimated the Catholic population in the state to be 6,200 out of a total population of 808,197; even after thirty years, the Catholic population had not changed significantly. It was still below one percent of the total population; out of a white population of 591,531, Catholics were 1.04 percent, up a small bit from .98 percent of the white/free population in 1850.[77] In January 1882, he wrote the French society, "The growth is nearly altogether due to new colonists from Canada, Switzerland, Germany, and Holland, with a few French, Italian, and Poles. The people here, . . . are very poor, and for years to come, they will not be able to help maintain religion or its ministers."[78] By November 1882, Bishop Fitzgerald was revising his estimate of Catholics up to 6,500, with thirty-three churches, twenty-four priests, sixteen schools, six convents, and four religious orders. He also proudly reported that the exterior of his new cathedral was completed, and that work was progressing on the interior.[79] By the middle of the decade, the *Official Catholic Directory* reported 8,285 Catholics with twenty-three priests and convents in Little Rock, Fort Smith, Hot Springs, Helena, Pine Bluff, Morrilton, and Conway.[80]

As the Church developed during the 1880s, so too did Bishop Fitzgerald's prestige among his fellow bishops. Since the illness of Archbishop Napoleon J. Perche of New Orleans prevented him from going to Rome with his fellow archbishops to meet with Pope Leo XIII, Bishop Fitzgerald represented the province at the Vatican, the first time that he had been to Rome since his *non placet* vote thirteen years earlier. That meeting, in October 1883, came as Fitzgerald turned fifty years old. He left his new vicar general, Rev. Dr. Halliman, in charge of the diocese.[81] For the Third Plenary Council in November 1884, Fitzgerald was chosen to give the opening sermon on the "Holy Sacrifice of the Mass."[82] The sermon was published the next year in a memorial volume of the Third Plenary Council.[83]

Fitzgerald again played the role of dissenter from a position taken by a majority of the prelates. The American bishops called for a Catholic school in every parish and for committing much of the resources of the American church for the next eighty years to parochial schools. Backed strongly by men like Bishop Bernard McQuaid of Rochester, New York, and by most other bishops, the position passed overwhelmingly. Bishop Fitzgerald, however, opposed the measure declaring, "We were ordained to teach catechism not to teach school. If we know that children are learning the catechism it is enough."[84] His fellow bishops, nonetheless, voted for the program requiring almost all parents to send their children to Catholic schools.[85] Though he did not agree with the policy, Fitzgerald did his best to implement it in his scattered, poor, and rural diocese.

His minority opinions did not necessarily damage his prestige among his fellow bishops. In early 1887, Fitzgerald heard that his name had been forwarded to Rome for the position of coadjutor Bishop of New Orleans, a position as assistant to the ill Archbishop Francis Xavier Leray, with immediate right of succession to the archbishopric upon Leray's death. On February 14, 1887, he penned a strong letter of protest to Cardinal James Gibbons of Baltimore, who had just been raised from archbishop to cardinal the previous June. Fitzgerald stated:

> I will do whatever the Holy See commands, but I should much prefer remaining where I am . . . I am not fit to be an Archbishop, being but a plain man, good enough, perhaps for Arkansas . . . I am now twenty years in Arkansas, . . . I can now be a Bishop instead of a money maker . . . The Diocese is just 'out of the woods'.[86]

Fitzgerald observed that he was not French, a detriment in New Orleans, and that he could only speak French in a halting manner. That would be a problem in an archdiocese where the Arkansas bishop believed only thirteen priests of the 106 were English speaking.[87] "I should wish to be allowed to remain here, . . . after twenty years struggle, and after desperate efforts, the finances are in good shape, but this is owing not so much to our advancement, but to the advance of the value of real estate property."[88] He ended by begging Gibbons to block his appointment, for he was not ready to start a new career at a large archdiocese where, owing to his demeanor, ethnic background and language difficulty, he would not really fit in. Besides, he believed that New Orleans needed a younger man with more energy to get it out of some financial difficulty. Fitzgerald recommended instead Dutch-born Bishop Francis Janssens of Natchez, a man ten years younger.[89] No coadjutor bishop was named for Archbishop Leray, and he died in September 1887 while on a visit to his native city in France. Rome would take almost a year before assigning Janssens, the man Fitzgerald had proposed a year and a half earlier.[90]

This was the second time that Fitzgerald had rejected an archbishopric outside Arkansas, yet each was not as inviting as it seemed. After spending so many years getting Arkansas on its feet, Fitzgerald was unwilling to adjust to, and possibly even rescue, larger archdioceses. It says something, however, about Fitzgerald's favorable financial reputation that he was considered for both posts. Also important was the fact that his dissent at Vatican I had not ruined his prospects for advancement.

In his response to the Fitzgerald letter, dated March 1, 1887, Cardinal Gibbons reported that he had done as the Arkansas bishop requested and had recommended Janssen. In the same letter, Gibbons reported that he had come from Rome, where he had prevented the Holy Office from condemning the Knights of Labor, other labor organizations, and the doctrines of reformer Henry George, which he said would have been "unjust, unwise, dangerous to religion, and unnecessary."[91] He promised to send Fitzgerald a copy of his letter to Pope Leo XIII, and he believed that he had laid the condemnation of labor unions to rest.[92]

On March 19, the Feast of St. Joseph, Fitzgerald wrote to Gibbons thanking him for defending Henry George, and especially the Knights of Labor, because "you defended the cause of the poor and laborers." He worried that "there is a great danger in the United States, and in some other Catholic countries, that the poor will persuade themselves that the Church is in league with the rich to oppress them."[93] These comments indicated that Fitzgerald's horizons stretched beyond his diocese and that he embraced the cause of the poor and laboring classes in America. In his path breaking 1891 encyclical *Rerum novarum*, Pope Leo XIII would express some of the same concerns.

In a letter the day after his note on the Knights of Labor, Fitzgerald begged Gibbons to do all in his power to block any move by the Holy See to place him in another diocese.[94] Despite these protestations, Archbishop Patrick John Ryan of Philadelphia wrote Fitzgerald in late July 1887 that he would like to see him as coadjutor bishop at New Orleans or as Bishop of Harrisburg,

Pennsylvania. Ryan concluded by saying, "I think if you would consent, there would be little difficulty in obtaining a transition to Harrisburg . . . I believe you would be happier there than at Little Rock."[95] To all these pleadings, Fitzgerald turned a deaf ear, for he was still working on such projects as founding what would become Arkansas' oldest hospital.

In March 1886, Bishop Fitzgerald made public the Will of a Alexander Hager, dated April 23, 1882. The Will stipulated that it was not to be made public until the death of his wife, Catherine. Hager bequeathed $75,000.00, quite a bit of money in those days, to found a hospital in Little Rock under the direction of any religious order that Bishop Fitzgerald chose. Hager had made a secret vow to God that if he spared the Arkansas capital from the ravages of yellow fever, which was afflicting the city of Memphis, he would use his money to establish a hospital for Little Rock. Since providence had protected Little Rock, Hager wished to fulfill the vow in his Will.[96] In May 1888, the Sisters of Charity of Nazareth, Kentucky, arrived to assume their ministry at the hospital which opened on July 14, 1888.[97] First called Charity Hospital, it was known by 1889 as Little Rock Infirmary. By 1890, it had become St. Vincent's Infirmary. That year, it would be joined by St. Joseph's Hospital in Hot Springs under the direction of the Sisters of Mercy.[98]

As the decade of the 1880s came to a close, the diocese marked the closing of an era with the death of Fr. Patrick McGowan, an Arkansas priest for forty years, and the last one to have served under Bishop Byrne. He died in Hot Springs in November 1889, only days shy of his eighty-second birthday. He had come to Arkansas in 1847 and had served at New Gascony in Jefferson County on the Arkansas River from 1849 until early 1889. Known as one of the patriarchs of Catholicism in Arkansas, McGowan had served at a church built before there was a Little Rock diocese.[99]

At the start of the 1890s, the *Official Catholic Directory* reported that Arkansas had twenty-nine priests, forty-six churches, and twenty-five academies and schools. Based upon Fitzgerald's estimates, he reported that nine thousand Catholics lived in Arkansas.[100] In his annual report to the French missionary society in November 1890, Bishop Fitzgerald put the number of Catholics in Arkansas at ten thousand, with fifty-two churches, thirty priests, two hospitals, twenty-nine white schools, and six colored schools. Catholics still numbered about one out of every 125 persons, and they were mostly poor. Other religious denominations, he thought, had more wealth, prestige, refinement, and education. While admitting that arrayed against Arkansas' Catholics were many Protestant churches, he nevertheless believed, "The chief danger to the Faith is widespread indifferentism, and the infidelity of the day. I cannot claim to see we are making much headway at all."[101]

Are Fitzgerald's numbers correct? If his claim of ten thousand Catholics was correct, they would have been 0.98 percent of the white population in 1850 and 1.2 percent in 1890. The census did not substantiate Fitzgerald's estimates.

It asked how many were communicants or members, and only 3,835 claimed to be Catholic. The church-going Catholics in the census amounted to only 0.34 percent and 0.47 percent of the white population.[102] Fitzgerald's judgment that Catholics in Arkansas were not making much headway was quite an understatement.

Why the large discrepancy between Fitzgerald's estimates and the census records? The census may have listed those who considered themselves regular members or who had received communion the previous Sunday. That might be what people thought census workers were asking. Fitzgerald probably based his figures on parish estimates from local priests. These numbers might have been on the rolls of the parish, but people were not attending Mass regularly. If that is the case, only about 38 percent of Arkansas' Catholics considered themselves to be actual members or regular communicants of the Catholic religion, hardly an impressive number. The state's rural nature, its poor roads, and the scattered and isolated condition of so many Catholics, may explain why so few considered themselves real church members.

The census data also reinforces, somewhat, Fitzgerald's contention that infidelity and indifference to religion were widespread. To a modern mind, this might seem to be merely the assertions of a pious and zealous Church bishop. Neither the United States, nor the South, nor even Arkansas, could have been considered a real center of Christian apostasy in 1890. In the nation as a whole, only 32.85 percent of the people claimed to be members or communicants of churches. In the South (looking only at the eleven states of the old Confederacy), the average was a bit higher, 35.26 percent. Yet Arkansas' average was the least in the whole South, 26.26 percent. Only two southern states had a percentage lower than the national average, Tennessee (31.21 percent) and Texas (30.29 percent), but both were much higher than Arkansas. Of the people who considered themselves to be church members, 43.5 percent were Baptists, 41.6 percent were Methodists, and 6.1 percent were Presbyterians. While Catholics were only 1.3 percent of the church-going population, they were larger than the Episcopalians, who were only 0.80 percent of the church members.[103] What the numbers mean is that while only 38 percent of Catholics identified themselves that way, the percentage for Protestant churches was lower. Despite their small numbers, Catholics in Arkansas appeared comparatively to be quite committed.

One indication of the growth and prestige of Catholics in Arkansas was the election of William Leake Terry of Little Rock to the United States House of Representatives in 1890. Terry would be the first, and so far, the only Catholic ever elected to the United States Congress from Arkansas. A convert to Catholicism, Terry was a member of a distinguished family in Little Rock. Born in North Carolina in 1850, he moved with his family to Tippah County, Mississippi, in 1857 and from there to Little Rock in 1861. He was a forty year old practicing attorney at the time of his election. Terry's district was Little

Rock and the west central counties along the Arkansas River to the Oklahoma line.[104] This particular district, as the subsequent chapter will demonstrate, contained a significant amount of newly arrived German-speaking Catholic immigrants. Terry represented the fourth district in Congress as a conservative Democrat until his defeat in the Democratic primary in 1900.[105]

Arkansas had another and much more famous convert to Catholicism in Federal Judge Isaac Parker, the legendary "hanging judge." Judge Parker died on November 17, 1896, but two days before his death, he converted to Catholicism and was baptized by Father Lawrence Smyth of Immaculate Conception Church in Fort Smith, the man who conducted Parker's funeral one day after the famous jurist's death. Parker's decision to convert may have been largely influenced by the faith of his Catholic wife, Mary O'Toole Parker.[106]

Father Smyth may have also been a factor in Parker's conversion, as he was a popular priest and a powerful pulpit orator. The Irish-born priest also had a reputation for long-winded sermons, and on hot summer days this could be a real source of irritation to his parishioners. His brother, Father Michael Smyth, lived with him in the rectory and had a weakness for the bottle. Father Lawrence often had to fetch him from the local jail. The story is told that during Sunday Mass on a hot summer morning, when Fr. Lawrence was giving one of his elaborate sermons, an inebriated Fr. Michael Smyth crawled unseen up to the choir loft to listen. While many of the Immaculate Conception congregation were fervently praying that the priest would finally conclude his sermon, a voice in Irish brogue came forth from above, "O.K. Larry, you have done spoke long enough, now just get on with the rest of the Mass." To the parishioners, it must have seemed like an answered prayer, God speaking in an audible voice to finally quiet Father Lawrence's lengthy oration. Moreover, God had revealed himself to be Irish after all! Alas, it quickly became apparent that the origin of this utterance was not divine.[107]

Long-winded or not, Fr. Lawrence Smyth was selected as a spokesperson for the clergy and people of the diocese in congratulating Bishop Fitzgerald on his twenty-fifth anniversary as the Catholic ordinary of Arkansas. Not yet sixty years old, Fitzgerald held a huge celebration in Little Rock on February 3, 1892. The main celebration was a Pontifical High Mass at 10:30 a.m. that morning at St. Andrew's Cathedral. In attendance were bishops from the dioceses of Mobile, Natchez, Nashville, Columbus, Indianapolis, Wichita, and the Indian Territory, reconstituted since 1889 as the Oklahoma Territory. Archbishop Janssens of New Orleans delivered the homily, and Father Lawrence Smyth presented the address on behalf of the clergy and people of Arkansas.[108] At 3:00 p.m. the day before, Fitzgerald received a cablegram from Rome, from His Holiness Pope Leo XIII, congratulating him on his twenty-five year reign.[109] Bishop Fitzgerald's address gave a brief history of the diocese, which was not yet fifty years old. When he came, there had been only five priests, and now there were thirty-two; once there were only three schools, and now there were thirty-one. Fifty-eight Catholic churches or chapels were scattered throughout the state.[110] A large banquet at Mount St. Mary's hall and a musical concert at the cathedral followed the ceremony.[111]

In a long article about the affair, Father John M. Lucey described Bishop Fitzgerald as a "learned, logical, and convincing pulpit orator," but he noted that during his long years at the rectory on Second Street, there had been "many opportunities to practice the virtue of self-denial." Whenever a priest of the diocese happened to stay there, the bishop would invariably offer his bed to the visitor. "But the honoree never accepted a second time. No combination of bedstead and mattress was ever known to afford as little solid comfort to a tired sleeper; yet the Bishop's most refreshing slumbers were evidently enjoyed in this lowly and primitive condition."[112]

During his address at the Mass, Bishop Fitzgerald observed that the next year, 1893, would be the fiftieth anniversary of the Little Rock diocese. He said that he would like to have another celebration in November 1893 marking that event.[113] He would not have that opportunity. In December 1892, the Vatican, through Archbishop Janssens of New Orleans, ordered Fitzgerald to proceed to Dallas to become temporary administrator for the newly created Diocese of Dallas. Bishop Fitzgerald arrived there on New Year's Day, 1893, and stayed there for almost the entire year. Thomas Brennan had been consecrated as the first Bishop of Dallas on April 5, 1891, and he had been present at Fitzgerald's silver jubilee celebration in February 1892. On November 17, 1892, Brennan was forced to resign due to a number of factors. Although energetic and linguistically talented, Bishop Brennan had incurred a large debt and had alienated a significant portion of his laity and clergy during his short tenure.[114]

Bishop Fitzgerald was greeted by a generally hostile and divided Catholic citizenry. Matters were complicated by the former bishop's refusal to relinquish full property rights of the diocese until December 5, 1893. The Arkansas prelate spent almost the whole year there dealing with the problem. Finally, Father Edward Dunne, from the Archdiocese of Chicago, was chosen as the new bishop, arriving in December 1893. A petition from twenty-five Catholics of Dallas to the Vatican in February 1893 described Fitzgerald as having "a careful and considerate, but just judgment." They also wrote, "He guided us safely in our financial affairs."[115] But not everybody in Dallas was pleased with Fitzgerald. A letter to Rome signed by John Moore in April stated, "I would not like to see the Diocese to which I belong, to be, for any considerable length of time, under the administration of a *non-placet* Bishop!"[116] Fitzgerald wrote Rome in September that he hoped they would come up with a bishop for Dallas soon, because he did not like being a bishop of one diocese and an administrator of another, especially at his advanced age. His task, he said, was not made easier by the "contrariety" shown him by "former Bishop Brennan and his followers."[117]

From Dallas, Bishop Fitzgerald learned that the French missionary society would no longer support the Diocese of Little Rock financially. In a letter of November 1893, Fitzgerald accepted the decision with some chagrin, but he said that he hoped that the society would at least support the new Diocese of Dallas, which was just getting started.[118] Back in Little Rock, a year later, he wrote in a more bitter tone to the society that he wished it had not cut off the Arkansas Church at a time of great need. "Have you not heard that the United States is suffering a financial and business depression in all portions of the country, the like of which we have not seen since 1873?"[119] He referred to the Panic of 1893, the worst depression in America up to that time. The plea seemed to fall on deaf ears, for this would be the last letter in the French missionary file from Arkansas. For better or worse, after its first half-century, the Diocese of Little Rock would no longer receive missionary funds from France.

All during the 1890s, Fitzgerald attended conferences and performed duties beyond the boundaries of his diocese. He met with fellow bishops of the New Orleans Province in October 1890, and they issued decrees forbidding Catholics from joining Masonic orders, but not other social or labor organizations.[120] He traveled the state visiting his people and presiding over the sacrament of confirmation. The Pine Bluff *Press Eagle* described a confirmation class at St. Joseph's Church in May 1892 and quoted from Fitzgerald's sermon. While there are numerous records of his sermons in manuscript, this is a rare published account of his homilies. The Catholic prelate used the example of the Memphis railroad bridge as:

> indisputable evidence of the existence of an architect or designer-much more then, should be accepted the complicated universe as an evidence of the existence of a God. If there is a God, his plan of creation must be known and obeyed or ruin awaits. He has made known his plan and our respective duties, by means of his church, which he established by his own hands.[121]

Two years later, he represented Archbishop Janssens and the New Orleans Province at the Conference of Archbishops in Philadelphia.[122] In the summer of 1897, Fitzgerald communicated with Cardinal Gibbons and his fellow bishops in the New Orleans Province on a replacement for Archbishop Janssens.[123]

By the turn of the century, Bishop Fitzgerald had seen much material progress in Arkansas Catholicism. The number of Catholics went from 1,500 to 10,000 members. When Bishop Fitzgerald first came in 1867, he found only a half-dozen priests for the whole state; now there were twenty-one diocesan priests and twenty-two priests belonging to either the Order of St. Benedict (Benedictines) or the Congregation of the Holy Ghost (Holy Ghost Fathers). In 1867, he had only two seminarians, but now five were studying for the diocesan priesthood, and twenty seminarians were at the Subiaco Benedictine Abbey.

Only nine church buildings existed when he arrived, but now there were fifty-one edifices with more than forty chapels and missionary stations attached to standing parishes.[124] By 1900, 150 sisters were working in the diocese, and five academies were in operation. The Sisters of Mercy operated St. Mary's Academies in Little Rock and Hot Springs, St. Anne's Academy in Fort Smith, plus St. Joseph Infirmary in Hot Springs. The Sisters of Charity of Nazareth ministered not only at St. Vincent's Infirmary, but conducted an industrial school for blacks in Pine Bluff. They also conducted Annunciation Academy in Pine Bluff and Sacred Heart Academy in Helena. Altogether, these academies had about 250 students. Although Fitzgerald had not favored parish schools at the Third Provincial Council in 1884, by century's close, there were thirty-two parish schools with 1,837 pupils.[125] Despite this growth, Fitzgerald's own estimate of ten thousand Catholics in the 1900 *Official Catholic Directory* still put the Catholic percentage at less than one percent of the total population of 1,318,000.[126]

On January 17, 1900, Fitzgerald's very active thirty-three years as bishop came to an abrupt end. According to Father Eugene J. Weibel while visiting the Swiss-German Benedictine missionary priest in northeastern Arkansas, in Jonesboro, between noon and 1:00 p.m. Fitzgerald exclaimed, "I feel ill," and collapsed to the floor of the rectory. Weibel managed to get the now rather hefty prelate to a sofa. Fitzgerald could not speak and pointed to his right arm. Father Weibel grasped the arm and found it limp. With Fitzgerald's permission, Weibel administered the sacrament of extreme unction, or the anointing of the sick as it is now called, to his bishop.[127] Fitzgerald recovered enough to be moved first to Little Rock and then to Hot Springs, where he would stay under the care of the Sisters of Mercy at St. Joseph's Infirmary. He was in Hot Springs by February 3, 1900.[128] So ill was the bishop, that for months he seemed on the verge of death. Confusion would reign for the next several months over who had real power in the diocese.

Father James Callaghan had served as vicar general from 1890 until December 1899, but he died prior to Fitzgerald's sudden illness. According to one source, Father Fintan Kraemer, O.S.B., a thirty-two year old German Benedictine and pastor of St. Edward's German Catholic parish in Little Rock, had been offered the position of vicar general upon the death of Father Callahan.[129] A prominent Little Rock newspaper in February reported that Father Patrick Enright, pastor of St. Andrew's Cathedral, would be the vicar general and that Father Eugene J. Weibel had received a telegram on April 24, 1900, purportedly from the ill bishop, confirming the Enright appointment.[130] One Arkansas priest was so upset about this that he wrote the Vatican in late February that Father Enright is "by disposition, by training, and especially by habits, absolutely unfit, totally incompetent, and altogether unreliable."[131] A week later, on May 1, Bishop Fitzgerald released a document to the press saying that Fr. Fintan Kraemer would act as vicar general with a board of consultors, which included Kraemer, Fathers John Lucey of Pine Bluff, Lawrence Smyth of Fort Smith, and James Brady of North Little Rock, or Argenta as it was then known.[132] Later that month, the priests in northeastern Arkansas claimed that newspapers were quoting Father Lawrence Smyth, one of the consultors, as saying that the bishop's letter was in error, that Father Enright was the vicar general and "no power but the Pope of Rome can change it."[133] The priests wrote to the other bishops of the New Orleans Province asking that they intervene. They felt they had to take this step because they did not know "whether our Bishop really receives our letters, we think we are justified to write to you, Rt. Rev. Provincial Bishops."[134]

Bishop Fitzgerald recovered enough in early May to travel outside Hot Springs and dedicate a church in Engelburg, a German community in north Randolph County. He also visited a convent a few miles south in Pocahontas and presided over confirmation ceremonies in Pocahontas and Jonesboro.[135] He soon suffered a relapse that would confine him to Hot Springs until his death in 1907. In a petition on May 22, the priests in northeastern Arkansas begged the bishops of the New Orleans Province to have Rome appoint a coadjutor bishop for the diocese. They would accept him, "be he Irish, German, or Dutch, but we fear any stranger!" A coadjutor was needed immediately to end "the chaos."[136]

The "chaos" continued into the summer. By that time, the diocese appeared to be divided between priests of different ethnic backgrounds and positions. One group of predominantly diocesan priests from Ireland or of Irish descent were set against German or Swiss-German priests who were primarily in the Benedictine Order and Holy Ghost Congregation. The Irish apparently recognized the diocesan priest Enright as vicar, while the others saw Benedictine Kraemer as the true leader. In June 1900, Father Enright moved Father Brady from North Little Rock to Fort Smith to serve with Father Lawrence Smyth after the death of Father Michael Smyth, his brother. The Smyth brothers had served as priests at Immaculate Conception Church in Fort Smith for over three decades. Smyth and Brady worked there now, and according to local papers, recognized Enright as vicar, while Fr. Pius Zyssig, O.S.B., at St. Boniface German Catholic Church, told the papers that he acknowledged Kraemer, his fellow Benedictine, as the vicar.[137]

Father Kraemer apparently was recognized officially by Bishop Fitzgerald because from 1901 to 1906, the time when a coadjutor bishop was finally named, the Benedictine priest was listed in the *Official Catholic Directory* as the vicar.[138] The letters in the Fitzgerald papers in the diocesan archives demonstrate that Kraemer acted as vicar and wrote many letters to Fitzgerald telling him of his activities and appointments. The Benedictine priest often signed his correspondence as vicar general.[139] This could not have been possible unless Fitzgerald officially permitted him to exercise this role.

Father Kraemer's promotion by the summer of 1900 really signaled the end of Bishop Fitzgerald's active ministry as bishop, even though the prelate would not die until February 1907. That Fitzgerald chose a young, German Benedictine priest as his vicar, is indicative of the growth of the German and Swiss-German contingent in the ranks of Arkansas' Catholics. Before one can completely close Bishop Fitzgerald's career, there must be narrative of his role in bringing in non-Irish Catholic immigration into the state and his efforts to evangelize blacks. Both of these efforts will be treated in subsequent and different chapters.

No doubt, Edward M. Fitzgerald was a unique Catholic bishop for his time and the most significant prelate in the history of the Arkansas Church. Only thirty-three years old at the time of his appointment, he was sent to Arkansas under holy obedience to become the youngest Catholic bishop in the United States, if not the world. He distinguished himself by being only one of two bishops in the world, and the only English-speaking bishop to cast his *non placet* on the issue of infallibility. This action, together with his unusual position on Catholic education at the Third Plenary Council and his sympathy for the early labor movement, clearly mark him as one of the most liberal American Catholic bishops of the nineteenth century. One person in Dallas, more than twenty years after the First Vatican Council, referred to him as the *non placet* bishop, but he showed his total loyalty to the Church by implementing and defending doctrines and decrees from which he publicly dissented.

Bishop Fitzgerald also showed extreme loyalty to his diocese and his adopted state as he repeatedly turned down promotions and passed over opportunities to leave Arkansas. He asked that his name be removed for consideration to two archdioceses, Cincinnati and New Orleans. Fr. Eugene Weibel, the longtime Swiss-German missionary in Arkansas, wrote in his 1927 memoirs that Archbishop Patrick Ryan of Philadelphia had told him that Fitzgerald had turned down three or four appointments to other dioceses and that Archbishop Ryan had personally asked him, on behalf of the Holy See, to assume the position of bishop for the newly created Diocese of Kansas City in 1880.[140] As the *Arkansas Gazette* said in 1879, "Few men decline such honors." Yet he was not an icon. He had real difficulties and personal disappointments that he shared openly with his fellow prelates. Father John M. Lucey wrote with great truth at Fitzgerald's silver jubilee as bishop in 1892, "His progressive American ideas give him an independence of character and broad liberality which are recognized by non-Catholics, while those of his own flock have willingly paid him the tribute of their regard and affection."[141]

Arkansas' second Catholic prelate was more than a unique man of broad mind and great character; he exerted tremendous effort in the material growth of Arkansas Catholicism. Numerous churches and schools, two hospitals, and an industrial school for blacks were all opened during his tenure. He did all this even though Catholics were less than one percent of the state's population.

That is a remarkable achievement. Bishop Byrne had laid the foundation for the Arkansas Catholic Church, but it was during the long reign of Bishop Fitzgerald that the structure took form. Much of that form would also be influenced by the Catholic immigrants who came to the state between 1860 and 1920.

CHAPTER VI

"Strangers to the Land"

Immigrants and Their Impact on Arkansas Catholicism, 1860-1920

BISHOP EDWARD FITZGERALD wrote the Propagation of the Faith Missionary Society in France, in January 1873, that his diocese still needed its financial assistance, as Catholics in Arkansas "were mostly immigrants and strangers to the land."[1] While the good bishop was trying undoubtedly to elicit sympathy for his strapped Church in Arkansas, he was also expressing a profound truth about the nature of Catholicism in both America and Arkansas. European Catholics brought their faith to these shores, and Arkansas shared in that experience. This chapter will focus on foreign immigration and its impact on the Catholic Church in Arkansas. While Arkansas and the whole South did not attract as many immigrants as other areas of the United States, Arkansas had more foreign-born between 1860 and 1920 than at any time in its history. While not large, this migration had a great bearing upon the development of Arkansas Catholicism.

In 1850, Arkansas had the fewest foreign-born residents of the thirty-one states in the federal union, fewer than three of the four organized territories; only 1,628 out of a total white population of 162,189, or about one percent. Only the Oregon Territory had fewer. That statistic alone does not tell the whole story, because North Carolina had more foreign-born in its white population in the Union, less than half of one percent. (Throughout the chapter, the author will compare the foreign-born to the total white population of a particular community. Since these immigrants from Europe are overwhelmingly white, their percentages will be compared to the total white population because the immigrants themselves, the native-born whites and the blacks, would identify them as whites. These immigrants primarily mixed with the native white population and categorized themselves later as white. For this reason, a good perspective of the impact of immigration would be to compare its numbers with that of the existing white population.) Nationally, the foreign-born to white population that year equalled about 11.3 percent, while in the fifteen slave states, it amounted to only five percent. Excluding the border slave states of Delaware, Maryland, Kentucky, and Missouri, and considering the eleven states of the future Confederacy, the number of foreign-born to whites was only 3.4 percent, and over three-fifths of that group was in two states, Louisiana and Texas. In Arkansas, over three-fifths of the foreign-born came either from Germany or Ireland, and their numbers were roughly equal.[2]

Hoping to expand the number of Catholics in the state, Bishop Andrew Byrne, using money from a wealthy relative and from foreign missionary societies, purchased a huge section of land south of Fort Smith in 1847. In early 1851, groups of Irish colonists moved from Rocky Comfort in southwestern Arkansas to the land of Bishop Byrne. Here, Byrne built his St. Andrew's College and St. Anne's Academy. A few of the Catholic families who came from Rocky Comfort to Fort Smith included the Luceys, Breens, Scullys, Donohoes, Lynches, plus Michael Manning, who died in 1891. Mr. Manning claimed to be the first Catholic in the town of Fort Smith. [3]

Not all were pleased with this Irish colony, and a few citizens brought a lawsuit challenging the legality of the transfer of land. Byrne hired Samuel Hempstead, a prominent Little Rock attorney, to argue the case in state court in the early 1850s. Both the state district court and the Arkansas Supreme Court upheld the Catholic diocese's claim to the land.[4] To secure funds for the financially strapped diocese, newly arrived Bishop Fitzgerald gave power of attorney to John Dodson to sell off portions of the land on July 15, 1867. The city of Fort Smith purchased a square mile of this property, and for decades, this part of the city was known as the "Catholic mile" or the "Fitzgerald addition."[5]

Byrne's attempts at bringing his former countrymen and women to Arkansas did have a small impact on the population, according to the 1860 census. The number of foreign-born in the state rose to 3,740, or 1.1 percent of a white population of 324,143. Arkansas now had more foreign-born than North Carolina and Florida, but its percentage of foreign-born only outmatched that of North Carolina, 0.5 percent. Florida's foreign-born were 4.2 percent of the white population. Arkansas now had more foreign-born than four of the eight organized territories–Colorado, Dakota, Nevada, and Washington–but all the territories had a greater percentage of foreign-born than did Arkansas. Nationally, the foreign-born were 15 percent of the white population, but in the fifteen slave states they were 6.7 percent. Considering the eleven soon-to-be Confederate states alone, foreigners were 4.2 percent with Louisiana and Texas having most of the total foreign-born.[6] One result of Byrne's efforts was the Irish were now the largest group of immigrants, comprising 35 percent of the foreign-born; the German-born now 30.5 percent.[7]

This Irish lead would not be sustained through the next decade. In the years immediately after the Civil War, many Germans arrived. Religiously, they were either Lutheran Christians or Reformed Jews. Many were artisans and merchants, and they swelled the ranks of the German communities in Little Rock and Fort Smith. The counties containing these cities, Pulaski and Sebastian, had the highest percentages of Germans in the state.[8] In 1866, a German-language newspaper, the *Staates-Zeitung*, made an appearance in Little Rock and published a few issues. It surfaced again in November 1869 and lasted about eighteen months. Frederick Allsopp, the historian of the Arkansas press, wrote in 1922 that no issues had survived.[9] By 1870, a flourishing German Lutheran church and a Reformed Jewish synagogue were conducting services in German in the capital. Local newspapers often used such adjectives as reliable, thrifty, and hard-working to describe these immigrants. No doubt a few were put off by the rollicking, beer-swilling, *Gemuetlichkeit* (a congenial atmosphere or conviviality) that Germans displayed on Sunday afternoons and on holidays, yet most people in Little Rock and Fort Smith respected these newcomers.[10]

For their part, the Germans not only sought to preserve their culture in their own language newspapers, religious denominations, and festivals, but they also participated actively in holiday celebrations and communal picnics. No parade was considered complete without a German brass band and "occasionally a German grand marshall."[11] They also kept abreast of events in the fatherland. A huge torchlight parade with brass bands greeted the news in the Arkansas capital of the Prussian victory over France in early 1871. The celebrants heard speeches celebrating the event in German and English, and after these talks, Roman candles and a fireworks display ended the festivity.[12] Germans also were noted not only for love of their homeland, but for their adopted country. Germans wanted their neighbors to understand that they greatly appreciated the political, religious, and economic liberty granted to them by citizenship in the United States.[13]

Despite the greater presence of Germans in the state, the number of foreign-born in Arkansas jumped to 5,026 or up to 1.3 percent of a total white population of 362,115. This marked a growth of two-tenths of one percent from 1860. The Germans took the lead, now making up 31 percent of the foreign-born and the Irish 28.4 percent. This was at a time when the foreign-born nationally made up 16.5 percent of the white population. Within the now-defeated eleven Confederate states, the foreign-born amounted to 3.8 percent, Arkansas still had more foreign-born than North Carolina and Florida, but as with the decade earlier, its percentage of foreign-born was only larger than that of North Carolina, 0.4 percent. The immigrants in Arkansas numbered more than those in three territories: Dakota, Washington, and Wyoming, yet these places each had a greater percentage of foreign-born.[14] Only Florida had fewer people than Arkansas in the South. It seemed that the only way for the state to grow economically was to attract more immigrants.[15]

While the immigrants provided cheap labor to fuel the industrial engine of the North, the South was stripped of its slave labor force and was totally lacking in capital. The South now hoped to lure immigrants to develop its own still untapped natural resources. White southerners, however, were not looking for just any immigrants. The Germans had won great respect from native-born Americans for their hard work and frugality. These were the kind of people a poor state like Arkansas both desired and needed. To attract the foreigners, the legislature passed and Governor Elisha Baxter signed on April 28, 1873, a law promising to reimburse James P. Henry $15,000.00 to produce twenty thousand English pamphlets and five thousand German pamphlets extolling the beauty and climate of Arkansas to prospective immigrants born in other parts of America and Europe.[16] Despite the effort, the Arkansas government never attracted many people from Germany, because in the words of Jonathan J. Wolfe, the historian of German migration into Arkansas, "The state legislature never was able to part with a sufficient amount of cash to advertise effectively in Europe."[17] By the time the campaign got under way in the fall of 1873, both the United States and Germany had entered a depression known as the Panic of 1873. Moreover, the South as a whole, and Arkansas in particular, was at a disadvantage in attracting immigrants, because they could not afford to give away land. The whole region was saddled with huge debts from the Civil War and Reconstruction. In spite of these difficulties, between 1875 and 1890, Arkansas attracted more German immigrants than any former Confederate state except Texas.[18] Many of these Germans were Catholics, pulled to the state by the railroads and pushed out of their homeland by religious persecution.

Railroad construction came late to Arkansas. By the Civil War, only thirty-eight miles of track were operating in the state, from Hopefield across the Mississippi River at Memphis, to Madison on the St. Francis River. A track had been graded between Little Rock to De Valls Bluff on the west bank of the White River, about forty-five miles, but work on that line had been halted in July 1861 due to the war.[19] After the Civil War, both Congress and the Arkansas legislature granted the railroad sufficient land grants and capital to allow more rail lines to be completed. On April 11, 1871, the last spike was driven, completing the Little Rock-to-Memphis railroad.[20] On February 10, 1873, the St. Louis, Iron Mountain, and Southern Railway connected Little Rock to St. Louis, crossing the northeastern quadrant of the state.[21] This left much of the western part of the state isolated. Through the efforts of Jesse Turner, a Van Buren lawyer and merchant, and Asa Robinson, a Northern entrepreneur, a Little Rock-to-Fort Smith railroad was completed by June 10, 1876.[22] The line started just across the Arkansas River from Little Rock at Hunkersville (later Argenta and then North Little Rock), and followed westward along the northern bank of the Arkansas River, roughly corresponding to the route of the present Interstate 40 from Little Rock to Fort Smith.

In the fall of 1875, the Little Rock and Fort Smith Railroad Company brought editors from northern and northwestern states to see firsthand the land along the railroad. The group traveled along the route from what is now North Little Rock to Altus, then the west end of the line, from September 25-30, 1875. This excursion by the railroad helped spread publicity about the Arkansas River Valley throughout the country and into the German-language press.[23] A real estate dealer, Colonel T.P. Mills, collected many of these reports and editorials and published them the following year.[24] The route between St. Louis to Texarkana across the southwestern section of the state had been completed by March 20, 1874.[25] As the United States celebrated its centennial in 1876, Arkansas had two main rail lines, east and west from Memphis to Fort Smith-Van Buren and diagonally from the northeast to the southwest.

Land in Arkansas in the mid-1870s sold for as little as fifty cents to $2.00 an acre. Some good lands sold for $1.25 an acre and could be had for a 20 percent down payment with the rest to be paid off in five years at 6 percent interest. Underdeveloped federal land could be had for free if one agreed to live on the land for five years and pay his taxes. To claim this land one did not have to be a citizen, but only declare the intention to become one eventually.[26]

As generous as these conditions seem, they alone did not bring immigrants to Arkansas. Both the state and federal governments played a passive role, preferring to let the liberal land ownership laws lure the prospective settler. Railroads had a strong economic interest in seeing that people settled along their lines, and they were willing to pay to see that it happened. The railroads often provided the transportation necessary to sell its immense land grants to settlers in the state, often between $2.00 and $6.00 an acre with payment schedules as generous as the state and federal governments. The Little Rock and Fort Smith Railroad would go out of its way to lure immigrants, foreign and domestic; it was to these lands that the main German migration would flow.[27] That these German migrants between 1875-1890 were Catholics rather than Lutherans and Jews, owed much to the encouragement of two very different men working on opposite sides of the Atlantic, Bishop Edward M. Fitzgerald of Little Rock and Chancellor Otto von Bismarck of Germany.

Like his predecessor, Fitzgerald wanted to broaden the base of Catholicism in Arkansas. As Msgr. John M. Lucey wrote in 1911 in one of the earliest treatments of immigration into Arkansas, "The cooperation of Bishop Fitzgerald with the immigration societies, railroad land agents, and the general movement of the times, made this and subsequent colonization of Germans, Poles, and other nationalities successful ventures."[28] The Arkansas prelate only cooperated with the railroad companies, land agents, and others to attract people to Arkansas; he was in no way responsible for the wave of German Catholics who were fleeing their homeland for America. That responsibility lay at the doorstep of the man who ruled a now united Germany.

The establishment of a Prussian-dominated Germany in 1871 brought political, economic, and religious unrest to the Second Reich. Not every German was pleased to be dominated by an autocratic Prussian bureaucracy run by the authoritarian Chancellor Bismarck. As already mentioned, Germany suffered from the international economic depression of 1873, and the economic unrest and restlessness caused some to migrate from Germany in hopes of finding better opportunities. The German government's own plans for rapid industrialization also caused many artisans and small farmers to lose their positions and land. Population growth and the German tradition of giving each son an equal portion of land meant that sons were given so little land that they could not really sustain themselves and their families. More generous landholding grants had real appeal to these Germans. Many also were willing to emigrate from Germany to avoid the universal draft into the harsh Prussian-dominated German army.[29] Fr. Lawrence Maus, whose parents had migrated as children from Germany, recalled a story about a family in Cologne that disguised their son as a girl to keep him out of the draft. When the boy reached puberty, they sent him to America with his uncle and aunt. Not until the vessel cleared Europe, did the relatives allow the boy to shed his feminine clothes and dress as a young man.[30]

Another reason to leave Germany in the 1870s and early 1880s was the religious persecution of the Catholic Church through Bismarck's policy of *Kulturkampf*, or culture struggle. The declaration of the doctrine of papal infallibility in 1870, plus the feeling that Catholics in Germany could never be totally loyal to the State while they preserved their allegiance to a foreign prince, the Pope of Rome, provided Bismarck the rationale for his assault upon the Church. Bismarck also knew that the Pope was allied diplomatically with France, his main enemy in Europe. For these and other reasons not so obvious, Bismarck launched his assault first in 1872 by expelling the Society of Jesus (Jesuits) from Germany. The next year, he removed Catholic dioceses from the control of the bishops and the Pope. By 1875, all religious orders were dissolved except those working directly in hospitals. All marriages were made civil, not religious events, and Catholic schools were abolished. Bishops, priests, nuns, and laypersons by the hundreds were jailed for their faith while others fled the country. Not until the death of Pope Pius IX in 1878 did the situation improve. By 1881, Bismarck had signed a new agreement with Pope Leo XIII restoring to Catholics most of their religious freedom and to the Church some of its property. By the early 1880s, most of the jailed Catholics had been released, and by 1887, most of the anti-Catholic laws had been repealed.[31]

From this exodus of Germans, two main groups of Catholic colonies came to Arkansas, one associated with the Order of St. Benedict and the founding of

New Subiaco Abbey in Logan County, and the other with the Congregation of the Holy Spirit and the St. Joseph Colony in Conway and Morrilton. Both groups received land grants from the Little Rock and Fort Smith Railroad during the late 1870s. In the early 1880s, a predominantly Swiss-German colony formed in northeastern Arkansas along the St. Louis, Iron Mountain, and Southern Railway and also around Pocahontas, Engelberg, and Imboden in Randolph County; Jonesboro in Craighead County; Paragould in Greene County; and Weiner in Poinsett County. A German Lutheran colony formed in the same period around what is now Stuttgart in Arkansas County and Ulm in Prairie County and eventually would pioneer a successful rice-production industry. A small German Lutheran colony would be established in the town of Dresden in Pope County in 1882.[32] Since this work is about the history of Arkansas Catholicism and not German migration *per se*, this author will concentrate on the German Catholic immigrant communities. As the Benedictine colony came first, it seems fitting to begin with its story.

The Benedictine mission in Arkansas originated with the Abbey of Maria Einsiedeln or Hermitage of Mary near Lake Zurich in Switzerland. Founded as a Benedictine abbey in 934 A.D., the monastery had in turn founded St. Meinrad's Abbey in southern Indiana in 1854.[33] Abbot Martin Marty of St. Meinrad's Abbey had dreams that the Lord would use the Order of St. Benedict to convert the pioneer western United States to Christianity just as it had converted the barbarians after the collapse of the western Roman Empire. Abbot Marty visited the Dakota Territory in July 1877, when he stopped by the editorial office of a German newspaper known as *Amerika* published in St. Louis. Although he was having doubts about starting a mission in the northern plains, he wanted a place for the Abbey to expand its mission to the west. Editor Anton Hellmich mentioned that, on the previous day, Col. William Slack of the Little Rock and Fort Smith Railroad and Bishop Edward M. Fitzgerald of Little Rock had stopped by proposing a German Catholic colony for Arkansas. After getting the parties together, they agreed to meet and discuss the proposal at another time.[34]

On November 5, 1877, four months after the chance meeting in St. Louis, the railroad and the Benedictine order reached an agreement on a future colony for the state. The railroad allowed the Benedictines to select the site, and all migrants to the colony would have to be approved by both the Benedictines and the railroad. The land would be sold to settlers at $2.00 an acre, with a one-quarter down payment and the rest of the money due in six years at 6 percent interest. The railroad donated 2,500 acres for the building of a church, school, and rectory, and another seventeen thousand acres was set aside for the immigrants. The Benedictines also would receive 640 acres for their monastery and the Benedictine sisters another one hundred acres for a convent. The monastic lands were not to be sold, but used to financially support the monastery.[35] Editor Hellmich announced the colony in the November 28 issue of *Amerika*. What he probably did not know was that the date of the issue of that paper, the real beginning of the Benedictine colony in Arkansas, was the 34th anniversary of the creation of the diocese. Hellmich resigned as editor of *Amerika* to help foster this settlement. He arrived in Little Rock in January 1878 to take up his duties at the railroad office.[36]

To choose a site for the monks, Abbot Marty selected Father Isidor Hobi, described by one Benedictine historian as a "congenial and devoted monk."[37] The very day that *Amerika* carried the advertisement for the new colony, November 28, 1877, Fr. Hobi left St. Meinrad's en route to Arkansas. The railroad had 150,000 acres along the line to show him, and Father Hobi started down the Arkansas River Valley from Little Rock on December 1. After considering the area between what is now Clarksville and Ozark, Hobi felt that the mountains were too close and that it might not sustain the colonists. The tract that the railroad had given was so extensive that it even contained land south of the Arkansas River. On December 5, 1877, just four miles east of Paris in Logan County, Hobi decided to locate the monastery. Three days later, he was back in Little Rock concluding the arrangement. While in St. Louis on December 20, he wrote the abbot declaring that the area he chose was a "paradise fallen from heaven."[38]

Father Hobi may have selected the field, but someone else would have to till it. Abbot Marty chose thirty-seven year old Father Wolfgang Schlumpf, O.S.B., to lead the first group of Benedictines to Arkansas. Fr. Wolfgang would surely be the Father of Arkansas Benedictine monasticism. Born Jakob Schlumpf in 1831 in the village of Steinhausen in the Province of Canton Zug in Switzerland, he was admitted as a novice to the Abbey of Maria Einsiedeln in 1852. There he was given his monastic name of Wolfgang. Ordained a priest in 1857, he was sent to St. Meinrad's five years later. Fifteen years after arriving at the Indiana Abbey, he had become the business manager of the monastery and held the position of subprior, or second assistant to the abbot. Described by one contemporary Benedictine official as a "rigorous gentleman," it was he whom Abbot Marty chose to lead the first group of monks to the rugged Southwest. Fittingly, on Ash Wednesday, March 6, 1878, Fr. Schlumpf departed with two other monks for their Lenten journey to the Arkansas wilderness.[39]

Nine days after they left St. Meinrad's, the three monks arrived at the site described by Fr. Hobi as "paradise fallen from heaven." After looking about the landscape at dusk on the evening of March 15, they wondered if they had arrived at the same location. Often ribbed good-naturedly about his claim of a "paradise," Fr. Hobi always maintained that it was indeed there, "but the sinfulness of the monks and settlers hid the reality from their eyes and caused him to doubt his word."[40] On March 19, the Feast of St. Joseph, Father Schlumpf said the first recorded Mass in Logan County. Bishop Fitzgerald arrived on May 26 to dedicate the site to the Lord, and on August 15, the small wooden church of St. Benedict witnessed its first Catholic Mass. Later that fall,

Abbot Marty designated the small community, St. Benedict's Priory, with Father Schlumpf given the title of prior, a position he held until 1881.[41]

By the end of 1878, fewer than half of the three hundred families who had made down payments had arrived. The Arkansas legislature appropriated more money to advertise in Europe, and Hellmich went there during the summer of 1879 to inspire more migration. A few more did come in the early 1880s, yet unfortunately, letters from recently arrived migrants tended to counter all the good reports about the colony. The colony soon became known as "stupid immigrant's folly" and "that rocky desert," a reputation reinforced by the dishonesty of some land and railroad agents.[42] Bismarck also had begun to ease his persecution of the Catholic Church by 1881, abandoning it completely by the middle of the decade. This policy change, plus returning prosperity in Germany, provided prospective immigrants less reason to leave. St. Benedict's colony also tended to attract artisans, not farmers, and thus, too many had little knowledge about cultivating crops. Even those who were farmers back in Germany were unfamiliar with the land and climate of their new home. They eventually learned to grow cotton and grains and then diversified their crops into fruits and vegetables. The settlers were poor, but not destitute; a drought in 1881, however, brought real suffering. These Germans worked diligently six days a week, and then on Sundays, they both prayed and played. After attending Sunday morning Mass, they often had picnics, music and dancing, and they drank beer and played cards. One hot summer afternoon in Logan County, the sheriff and a posse arrested the Catholic pastor and many of the men for drinking beer and playing cards under the trees. They had broken two state laws: consuming alcohol and playing cards on the Sabbath. The men and their monk-pastor were taken to nearby Paris before the local magistrate, but there seems to be no record of further legal proceedings.[43]

This incident says a great deal about the cultural differences between the German and Swiss-German Catholics in largely Anglo-Saxon Protestant Arkansas. By 1890, Logan County's foreign-born amounted to 3.2 percent of the white population, at the time when the state percentage was 1.7 percent. Pulaski County had the highest percentage of foreign-born, 11 percent, but German and Swiss-Germans made up 52.1 percent of this group. In Logan County, almost 90 percent of the foreign-born were from Germany or Swiss-Germans, making them stand out even more in this rural county.[44] (The number of foreign-born in the different counties and their percentages, and the German-speaking group–Germans, Swiss-Germans, and Austrians–are laid out in Table 6A.)

These two groups, German immigrants and Anglo-American natives, were segregated by nationality, religion, education, and most of all, language. Both sides were guilty of maintaining such separation for about forty years, at least until World War I. Germans tended to view their less-educated and less-cultured American neighbors with a disdain that bordered on outright contempt. To the

Germans, *die Amerikaner* were crude, vulgar, *ungebildet* (uneducated), from an inferior culture and society. They saw little reason to fraternize. Fr. Hugh Assenmacher, O.S.B., the historian of Arkansas Benedictines, maintains that this separation was kept in the face of the recommendations by the monks. "The settlers fought English in their schools and in their sermons in church. They condemned monk-pastors who urged their people to learn English in order to participate in local affairs. These pastors were regarded almost as traitors."[45] Reinforcing this separation was religion; not only were the Germans aliens, they belonged to a Church that many of these Protestants believed was alien.[46]

For their part, the less educated and refined Protestant Arkansans often looked with bemused curiosity at these people whom they falsely called "the Dutchmen."[47] What people do not understand they often hold in contempt, and these Anglo-Saxon neighbors had neither the time nor the opportunity to learn German to communicate with these immigrants. To many of them, the practices and customs of the Germans were outlandish and humorous. Rude comments, jokes, long stares, and insulting imitations only aggravated the Germans and caused them to despise the Americans. Among many Protestants, there was also a long-standing religious suspicion about the Pope of Rome and his "monastic minions," and the Germans tended to associate becoming an American with becoming a Protestant, which they were not willing to do.[48] The historian of German migration into Arkansas claims that the German Lutherans also suffered much cultural isolation, and they did not leave their religious congregations for light reasons. Both German Catholics and Lutherans made few converts to their faiths owing to the huge cultural and language gaps, yet toleration between the groups came with time.[49]

Still, the gap was large enough to produce some amusing episodes. At a sewing bee between Anglo-American and German ladies, one native-born American woman asked a German lady what she was making. The German replied in her broken English that she was making clothing for her son for the Holy Sacrifice of the Mass on Easter. This comment soon became twisted to mean that the Germans were practicing child sacrifice as part of the Catholic ritual for Easter. That morning, a huge crowd gathered around the church, and it included the sheriff and deputies to stop this event should it occur. They must have stood by in bemused wonder as the Mass continued in Latin and the sermon was presented in German. When the service appeared to be over, the observers sheepishly left.[50] Not all was misunderstanding and conflict. At Charleston, in the neighboring county of Franklin, Protestants put up over $170.00, a lot of money at that time, to help build Sacred Heart Catholic Church.[51] A monk-priest serving at St. Benedict's Priory in 1885 wrote friends back in Switzerland that the Protestants whom he met in Charleston and in other places were "good natured, polite, sober, hospitable, intelligent, even nice people. I seldom have services without having some Protestants attending, . . .

Catholics are respected in this country."[52]

The last two decades of the nineteenth century would see much growth around the Benedictine monastery and settlement. The founder, Father Schlumpf, returned in January 1885 to serve as prior again. Under his guidance, the Priory of St. Benedict experienced real growth and development. In May 1886, it became totally independent of St. Meinrad's with the power to have its own novitiate to train future monks and priests. Brother Benedict Bulle, one of the settlers from Europe, became the first professed monk at the Priory of St. Benedict and stayed there until his death in 1931. Two young novices entered in March 1887. One was the future Father Fintan Kraemer, who would administer the Diocese of Little Rock for six years during the illness of Bishop Fitzgerald. In October 1887, a St. Benedict's College, the forerunner of what would be known as New Subiaco Academy, opened with five students. In October 1890, the first priest was ordained at St. Benedict's, Father Gregory Luthiger. Unfortunately, within two years he was dead.[53] In 1892, Bishop Fitzgerald began to send his seminarians for the Diocese of Little Rock to St. Benedict's Priory to receive priestly training. For the next eighteen years, until Bishop Morris established St. John's Seminary in Little Rock, the priests for the Diocese of Little Rock actually were trained within the boundaries of the state.[54]

The year that Bishop Fitzgerald began to send his seminarians to the monastery was also the year that Pope Leo XIII raised its status to a full Benedictine abbey. The change came not only in its ecclesiastical rank, but in its name as well. Abbot Fintan Mundwiler, who had succeeded Abbot Marty at St. Meinrad's in 1880, chose a new title for the monastery, New Subiaco Abbey. Abbot Mundwiler had written the Vatican recommending that the priory be raised to a full Benedictine abbey, yet he did not want them to keep the name St. Benedict, because there already was a St. Benedict's Abbey near Atchinson, Kansas. Mundwiler, however, wanted the name to somehow be associated with St. Benedict, so he asked that it be designated New Subiaco Abbey, after St. Benedict's first abbey of Subiaco in Italy. Pope Leo XIII accepted Mundwiler's recommendation regarding both the status and the name change.[55]

On March 24, 1892, the monks elected Father Ignatius Conrad, O.S.B., as Arkansas' first Benedictine abbot, a position that he would hold for the next thirty-three years. Only forty-six years old at the time of his election, he was a Swiss-German who came from a family of eight children. He and three of his other brothers all became Benedictines. An older brother, Father Frowin Conrad, founded and became the first Abbot of Conception Abbey in Missouri. His baptismal name was Nicholas, yet his monastic name became Ignatius when he entered Maria Einsiedeln. Father Ignatius was sent across the Atlantic in 1875 to New Engelberg Abbey in Nodaway County, Missouri, where he mastered the English language, taught Latin, and became a skilled carpenter and builder. All of these skills, plus his ability to delegate authority and get along with people helped him win the love and affection of many. Before his election as abbot in Arkansas, he served for fourteen years as the rector of St. Joseph's Cathedral in the Diocese of St. Joseph, Missouri, where he earned a reputation as a popular pastor-preacher. Before his election as abbot in March 1892, he had visited the Arkansas Benedictine monastery only once, two months earlier when he was visiting his friend, Father Gall D'Aujourd'hui. While he had not come to the state frequently, to be elected as their first abbot, he must have been known and respected by the Arkansas monks.[56]

Abbot Conrad's relations with Bishop Fitzgerald were quite cordial. When much of the monastery was destroyed by a great fire in December 1901, the bishop sent $10,000.00 to allow them to build a permanent monastery, which was completed by 1904.[57] This four-story Romanesque edifice is still a landmark in Logan County. Father Schlumpf stayed on at Subiaco, as the prior or the chief assistant to Abbot Conrad, for two more years. In 1894, he returned to St. Meinrad's Abbey in Indiana, and a year later, he journeyed back to his native land to serve the rest of his monastic life in the same place where he began it, in Maria Einsiedeln. There he died in 1904, the same year that Subiaco completed its beautiful permanent structure.[58]

Growth in education and missionary work became the main concerns of the new abbot. The school became a scholastic academy for boys between the ages of eight and twelve, and four years later, the legislature allowed it to confer degrees as a collegiate institution. The monastery could never completely sustain a college, and the great fire in December 1901 suspended the school for the rest of the academic year. It reopened in the fall of 1902, and the following year it published its first catalog. For decades it would remain a boys' academy with some commercial classes offered beyond the high school diploma, but all college classes were offered only to those who were entering the monastery to become priests.[59]

The Benedictines did not confine their activities to the monastery and serving the settlers in Logan County. In 1885, Bishop Fitzgerald asked for a German priest to serve a new German Catholic parish that was to be set up in Little Rock. Aware of the growth of a German contingent in St. Andrew's Parish in Little Rock, Bishop Fitzgerald had prevailed upon Father Aegidius Hennemann, O.S.B., to serve with him at the cathedral in 1878. A year later, Fr. Hennemann transferred his monastic base from St. Benedict's Abbey in Munich, Germany, to St. Meinrad's in Indiana. In 1880, Father Hennemann was appointed vicar general by Bishop Fitzgerald after Father Reilly had to retire. Father Hennemann also founded St. Boniface Church in Dixie and St. Elizabeth Church in Oppelo, small rural communities south of the Arkansas River some fifty miles west of Little Rock. Fr. Hennemann contracted tuberculosis and had to resign as vicar general in early 1883 to go to a sanatorium in New Orleans. There he died on Christmas day 1883.[60]

Father Felix Rumpf, O.S.B., then became the assistant pastor at St.

Andrew's for the German Catholics; yet a distinct German parish was still needed in Little Rock. In 1884, Bishop Fitzgerald donated three city lots, valued then at $400.00 each, across from the U.S. arsenal, now MacArthur Park and the Arkansas Arts Center. Father Rumpf served as the first pastor of the newly created St. Edward's parish, named in honor of the bishop's patron saint. In 1886, St. Boniface Catholic Church was founded in Fort Smith, and there, too, Bishop Fitzgerald donated a whole city block for the parish church and school. By 1890, the Benedictines were serving in Morrison Bluff, Altus, Hartman, Clarksville, Paris, and Charleston, and missions that Fr. Hennemann founded around Dixie.[61]

Still, Paris and all of Logan County remained isolated until the end of the nineteenth century. The first telephone hook-up to the monastery in May 1898 brought news of the outbreak of the Spanish-American War. The next year, a railroad line came into Paris, linking Little Rock and Fort Smith by rail along the south side of the Arkansas River. No longer would supplies and heavy equipment be dropped off at Spadra, ferried to the south side of the river to Morrison Bluff, and then brought fifteen miles over land to the monastery.[62] By the turn of the century, except for their mission in Altus and a few other places, the Benedictines served all the German Catholic communities along the south side of the Arkansas River from Little Rock to Fort Smith.[63]

North of the river, the Germans would be served by another religious order, the Congregation of the Holy Spirit, which also established a predominantly German Catholic colony only months after the Benedictines arrived. The man most responsible for founding the Holy Ghost Colony in Arkansas was the German-born Father Joseph Strub, C.S.Sp., a member of the Congregation of the Holy Spirit. This religious society originated in France in 1703, yet it had almost died out by the middle of the nineteenth century until revived by a Jewish convert to Catholicism, Francois Libermann. Father Libermann became Superior of the congregation in 1848, and through his efforts, the Holy Ghost Fathers (as they were frequently called) expanded from France into Germany, the Pacific Islands, and Africa. Joseph Strub was born in the French province of Alsace in 1833, yet he entered the Spiritan seminary in Germany in 1854. He finished his theological studies in Africa, being ordained in Dakar, Senegal, on Holy Saturday (Easter eve) 1858. After ministering in Africa for five years, Father Strub was sent back to Germany due to his poor health. In 1871, he became the provincial general for the German province of the Holy Ghost Fathers. By November 1873, Bismarck had expelled the group from Germany. Early the next year, Father Strub, the head of the German province, arrived in the United States to assume the leadership of a new American province, a position he held until his death in 1890. The Holy Ghost Fathers eventually set up their American headquarters in Pittsburgh, Pennsylvania, where they founded the Catholic College of the Holy Ghost, later Duquesne University, in 1878. That same year, their new American provincial founded the Catholic colony of St. Joseph in Arkansas.[64]

How Fr. Strub came to know about lands in Arkansas is not completely known, yet it is likely that he read the advertisement in the November 28, 1877, issue of *Amerika,* a national German weekly. Father Strub arrived in Little Rock on February 2, 1878, to confer with Hellmich and Bishop Fitzgerald. Fr. Strub liked what he heard from both men and returned to Pittsburgh to gain the approval for the colony from his local congregation and his superiors in Paris. After receiving affirmative answers from both quarters, he returned to Little Rock in late May to choose a location and close the deal with the railroad. Like the Benedictine priest before him, he rode the rails to Fort Smith and back for two weeks before deciding to locate the colony at the newly developed town of Conway.[65] Conway had been founded in 1872 and its county, Faulkner, had been established in 1873. What attracted the German priest to the area was the fact that the area was underdeveloped, yet located in the central part of the state, only thirty miles from the state capital.[66]

As with the Benedictine colony, Strub obtained generous amounts of land from the Little Rock and Fort Smith Railroad in June 1878. His grant was to follow the railroad for sixty-eight miles, from ten miles west of what is now North Little Rock to Galla Creek, a few miles east of present-day Russellville in Pope County. The grant was fifteen miles wide, and Strub was given six hundred acres near Conway to build a church, school, convent, rectory, and "monastery." Strub was given the right to sell the lands to anyone he chose, and he and his order would receive a twenty cents an-acre commission on all the land they sold.[67] Father Strub estimated that the land would be over 200,000 acres, but Father Henry Koren, C.S.Sp., the historian of the Holy Ghost Fathers in the United States, asserts that the total was nearer 720,000 acres. The provincial may have been excluding "lands already sold, lakes, rivers, bottom lands, . . . and other areas not suitable for cultivation."[68] Since this land grant would comprise a good duchy back in Germany, Father Strub earned the title within the Holy Ghost Fathers as "The Duke of Arkansas."[69] Jonathan Wolfe maintains that the Holy Ghost Fathers did not get as much land as the Benedictines because they could not promise that they could send nuns to the settlement.[70]

Unlike the Benedictine colony, the St. Joseph colony attracted a fair number of non-Germans. The Poles, headed by a Polish nobleman and his wife, Count Timothy and Maria Choinski, arrived just as the colony started. A political refugee from his homeland, Count Choinski had been in America with his wife since 1869. Appalled at the working and living conditions of his fellow Polish immigrants, he wanted to find a place where they could have their own land and live in a healthier environment. While living in Milwaukee, Choinski read in a Chicago-based Polish newspaper about inexpensive railroad lands for sale in Arkansas. Choinski wrote the editor of the *Arkansas Gazette* making inquiries, and the editor referred his letter to William D. Slack, land agent for the Little Rock and Fort Smith Railroad. In March 1878, Choinski reached Little Rock, where he purchased 11,000 acres of land. Choinski's land grant went along the railroad from about ten miles northwest of Little Rock westward to where it crossed for a few miles the Pulaski-Faulkner County line. A town called Warren was in the area and here Choinski picked the base for a settlement in May 1878. That fall, 169 Polish families, or about 330 settlers, arrived. Many had expected, or may have been led to believe, that farms and other things would be ready for them to receive. Instead, they discovered that the land was uncleared, and they had to spend weeks in a railroad depot and a rundown pavilion in Warren.

When Choinski arrived later in the year with more colonists, only eighty-five families remained. The railroad did send some lumber, which allowed them to begin building homes, and most of the settlers received farms averaging eighty acres per family. Fifty-one when he began this venture, Choinski stayed at the settlement until his death in 1890. The Poles changed the name of the town to Marche, and it received its first post office by that name in 1896; the town, however, never became large enough to win legal incorporation. In the fall of 1878, Father Strub brought Father Anthony Jaworski, who was the first in a series of Holy Ghost Polish priests, to serve the settlers. During World War I, many settlers lost their land to the government when it built Camp Pike, but the small settlement of Marche persists to this day.[71]

Since the Poles occupied some of the land that Strub had been granted, it was widely believed that they came because of his recruitment. Actually, they only came about the same time as Strub. Strub tried to bring in French-speaking settlers around the town of Louisburg (now spelled Lewisburg) just west of Morrilton, but only thirty-five families actually came.[72]

Still, most of the people who came to what would be called the St. Joseph Colony were Germans, and they would settle around the towns of Conway, Atkins, Morrilton, and Russellville. Despite the numerous land sales, the Congregation of the Holy Ghost found itself strapped for funds by the spring of 1879. The previous year had brought a poor harvest, and fifteen brothers and priests in the area now needed support. Since neither the settlers nor the diocese could adequately support them, they depended totally on the funds from the congregation. To meet this financial crisis, Father Strub responded in a typical Catholic fashion; he organized a national lottery. The first and second prizes were farms to be given away at eighty and forty acres each. A poor German woman from St. Louis won the first prize, and a black man from Little Rock took the second prize. Father Strub netted $4,000.00 from the lottery, and he used the money to support the priests and build churches and schools in the area.[73]

The influx of settlers had a profound impact on a few of the communities in the Arkansas River Valley. Conway's population went from 1,200 to 2,000 in one year, between 1878 and 1879. In Morrilton, the German immigrants were practically the first citizens. When they arrived in late 1878, they found only a railroad station and three or four log cabins. In January 1879, Father Strub decided to switch the base of the colony from Conway to Morrilton, which was a more central location in his land grant. He exchanged his 600 acres in Conway for an 880-acre tract near Morrilton. There, Strub set up a novitiate and a seminary at a place he called Marienstatt, or Mary's Place. This would be the first Catholic seminary in the Diocese of Little Rock. In March 1879, the novitiate opened with three novices and one postulant. A year later, there were eight Holy Ghost priests and brothers and seven novices and postulants.[75]

This whole Holy Ghost colony of German settlers soon acquired the title of the St. Joseph Colony. There are probably many reasons for such a title. In Germany, a national Catholic organization was known as St. Joseph's Union.[76] An American counterpart to this organization in the northeastern states held lectures and socials and sponsored insurance and other benefits for its members in case of sickness and death. Within German Catholic communities throughout the United States, "membership in the St. Joseph's Society was almost universal."[77] Local Arkansas chapters were formed starting in 1882, and by 1890, they were in every part of the state. That year, the *Deutsche Roemisch-Katholische Staatsverband von Arkansas* was organized at St. Benedict's Priory in Logan County.[78] As the colony's title, St. Joseph's would have a definite appeal to many German Catholics throughout Europe and America. Another reason might have been simply that Father Strub's own patron saint was Joseph. The only real remembrance from the whole colony is the St. Joseph Catholic Church and School which still exists in Conway. The original St. Joseph's Church in that city, which was completed in 1879, was considered at the time to be one of the most beautiful in the state. Built in a Gothic style at 40 by 62 feet with an 80-foot bell tower, the church originally cost $2,000.00. Bishop Fitzgerald arrived on February 23, 1879, to dedicate it and brought with him the choir from the cathedral.

Bishop Fitzgerald also dedicated the first church at Marche, the Church of the Immaculate Heart of Mary. In May 1880, when he arrived at Marche, the Polish were so eager to show their devotion that they unharnessed the horses and drew the episcopal carriage themselves to the church for high Mass.[79]

The dedication of the Morrilton church was just as dramatic. There in 1881, the Governor, secretary of state, and other high dignitaries came to see the Arkansas Catholic bishop bless the church, school, and convent. In the two-mile procession from the railroad station to the church, Fitzgerald was proceeded by twenty "Catholic Knights" on horseback and six hundred Catholics followed his carriage to the church. During the ceremony, a German boy of twelve spoke for all when he told the Catholic prelate, "Most Reverend Bishop, we thank you for coming today. We revere and love you as much as we did the persecuted bishops in our former Fatherland. You are our shepherd now, we will be yours in life and death."[80] Bishop Fitzgerald was so overcome that he had Father Strub reply for him.[81] Because Fitzgerald was part German through his mother's side of the family and had come from a land where his fellow religionists had suffered persecution for centuries, it is understandable that Arkansas' second Catholic bishop found it so emotionally difficult to respond.

Father Strub's colony achieved so much fame back in Germany that Bismarck's government officially warned citizens against going there. This provoked a response from the Catholic Center Party in the German Reichstag, or National Assembly, "It is not the Holy Ghost Fathers, but the Prussian policy and its wretched *Kulturkampf* that are depopulating the country and causing our best people to migrate to the U.S.A., where those religious men offer them the comforts of religion which they cannot have in the homeland."[82] While this exchange may have provided more advertising for the Arkansas colony, it would backfire on the congregation later. Fr. Koren, historian of the Holy Ghost congregation in the United States, cites the German historian, Josef Rath, who maintains that when the Holy Ghost Fathers requested permission in 1885 to serve in one of the German colonies in Africa as missionaries, Bismarck refused. Rath believed that the Iron Chancellor resented the congregation for its success in drawing many Germans to a Catholic colony in Arkansas.[83]

Not all was sweetness and light for those who had migrated to St. Joseph's Colony. The drought of 1881 and a tornado in 1883 destroyed the original St. Joseph's Church in Conway. Father Charles Steurer, C.S.Sp., wrote the Leopoldine Society in Vienna, Austria, in late August 1883 asking for help to rebuild it.[84] Fr. Frederick Bosch, C.S.Sp., at Marienstatt near Morrilton, wrote the same society the next spring thanking them for helping maintain churches and schools in Conway, Morrilton, and St. Vincent's, a small German community north of Morrilton. Father Bosch thought the colony was flourishing, even among "the Protestants and heathens."[85] Fr. Steurer in Conway was not as optimistic. He wrote in July 1884 to thank the Vienna-based society for help, but he was surprised to discover that he "conducts more funerals than baptisms here; not since my missionary work in Africa have I seen anything like this place."[86] Steurer believed that the Germans would make it, because they possessed "good virtues and keep good moral conduct."[87] As for himself, he must listen to confessions in three languages, German, English, and because a few lived near Conway, Polish. As for the Americans and their religious beliefs, Father Steurer wrote the Leopoldine Society, "they are either Methodists, Baptists, or nothing."[88]

By the middle of the 1880s, the flow of immigrants from Germany had virtually ceased, and an epidemic in 1884 and another drought in 1887 reduced the colony's numbers. By 1889, only ninety-five Catholic families were in the Morrilton area, ninety were in the St. Vincent's and Atkins area, and about one hundred families lived around Conway. The new pastor at Conway, Fr. Eugene Schmidt, C.S.Sp., maintained in September 1889 that only eighty Catholic families were in St. Joseph's Catholic parish.[89] The Marienstatt novitiate closed in 1884 and moved back to Pittsburgh, but the church and school continued. Unfortunately, a tornado took down both the school and church in early May 1892. The pastor, Father Matthew Heizmann, C.S.Sp., was ordered by his superiors not to rebuild, but join his parishioners with those of Sacred Heart Church in Morrilton. He was also to move into the rectory there with the other priest. Only the landmark, Monastery Ridge, north of Morrilton, remains as a relic of Marienstatt and the Holy Ghost novitiate that once stood there.[90]

By 1890, the Arkansas River Valley from Fort Smith-Van Buren to Little Rock had the heaviest population of foreign-born and the largest concentration of German-speaking people in Arkansas. While the percentage of foreign-born in the white population was 1.7 percent, those born in Germany, the Swiss-Germans, and a few Austrians made up 49.2 percent of the foreign-born. In 1860 or 1870, they had made up about one-third of the total foreign-born; by 1890, they were almost half of the total. As shown in Table 6A, the foreign population was greatest in Pulaski (Little Rock) and Sebastian (Fort Smith) Counties, and Germans were nearly half of it. Yet, the more rural Arkansas River counties of Conway, Faulkner, Logan, Pope, Johnson, Perry, and Franklin not only had higher percentages of foreign-born than the state average, but a high percentage of German or Swiss-German-Austrian-born. In Conway and Logan Counties, they made up over 80 percent of the foreign-born, while in Faulkner, Pope, and Perry Counties, they made up more than two-thirds. The census of 1890 showed another area of German and Swiss-German foreign-born in the northeastern corner of Arkansas. In Randolph County, 2.3 percent of the residents were foreign-born and over 83 percent of this number were Germans and Swiss-Germans. The German population spilled over into the neighboring counties of Greene, Craighead, and Poinsett.

Unlike the other German settlements, this area of German immigration was not associated with a Catholic religious order or congregation. Like the Little Rock and Fort Smith Railroad, the St. Louis, Iron Mountain, and Southern Railway had received generous land grants and had sent an agent to Europe to enlist immigration. The agent could enlist only ten families in Germany. Jonathan Wolfe, the historian of German migration, points out how inefficient this recruitment was compared with the success of the Benedictine and Holy Ghost colonies. The Catholic Church was more effective in attracting immigrants, according to Wolfe, owing to its "great resources and organization that reached down to the local level both in this country and in Europe."[91] Most of these German immigrants came, not so much from Europe, but from St. Louis and other areas of German concentration in Illinois, Indiana, and Pennsylvania. They came to northeastern Arkansas in the early 1880s to obtain inexpensive land or as workers on the railroad.[92] They became prominent minorities in towns such as Pocahontas and founded communities such as Engelberg, eight miles north of Pocahontas. Small German settlements appeared at Imboden in Lawrence County and Weiner in Poinsett County. A sizable minority of Germans lived in Paragould in Greene County and Jonesboro in Craighead County. (This is presented in Table 6A.)

Not only did German-Swiss and German-Austrian immigrants make up almost half the foreign-born in Arkansas in 1890, Arkansas had a higher percentage of these German-speaking foreigners than any state in the South. As revealed in Table 6B, while states like Texas and Louisiana had far greater numbers of German-speaking foreign-born population, only South Carolina, which also had a small foreign-born population, came close to having such a large percentage of German-speaking foreigners.[93]

In addition to the German and Swiss-Germans who swelled the ranks of Arkansas Catholics, two Swiss-Germans and one German played prominent and important roles in the Diocese of Little Rock during the years 1880-1920. The first was Fr. Eugene John Weibel, who was born in 1853 and entered the Abbey of Maria Stein (Our Lady of the Rock) in 1871. Though the local anti-Catholic government suppressed the monastery in 1875, he was ordained on August 15, 1876. Weibel soon was sent to St. Meinrad's Abbey where he arrived in December 1878. Two months later, he was en route to Logan County to serve among the early Benedictine missionaries. While going through Little Rock, Weibel was accosted by a city policeman and taken to Bishop Fitzgerald. The officer believed that Weibel had been the man who had recently posed falsely as a priest begging for money. Weibel was disoriented when he arrived at 2:00 a.m. at the train station. Weibel did not know enough English to clear up the matter. He would later be teased for having been introduced to Bishop Fitzgerald by a policeman. Fitzgerald quickly cleared up the matter and sent him to St. Benedict's Priory, where he arrived on February 10, 1879. Bishop Fitzgerald visited the priory two months later, and in a private moment, asked him to serve as a missionary either in Pocahontas or Hope. Father Weibel told the prelate he would think about it. It took him months to make up his mind, but on December 1, 1879, Weibel stepped off the train in Pocahontas to begin nearly thirty years of ministry in the area; when he did this, he became a diocesan priest, having left the Benedictine order.[94]

Father Weibel can rightly be called the Catholic apostle for northeastern Arkansas. He built churches, convents, schools, and St. Bernard's Hospital in Jonesboro. Churches in Paragould, Hoxie, Jonesboro, Engelberg, Walnut Ridge, and Corning were all founded by this industrious missionary. He brought an order of sisters to Pocahontas in 1887, and they eventually became part of the Benedictine Sisters of Mount Olive (Olivetans), an order of nuns founded in the 1300s. He constructed a convent for these nuns, first in Pocahontas and then in Jonesboro. Writing the Leopoldine Society in Vienna on November 30, 1898, he wrote that when he arrived in Pocahontas in 1879, only eighteen Catholics lived in the area, and there was no priest for 150 miles. Afterward, he would build fifteen churches and chapels, seven schools, and five convents. Seven priests would be ministering the territory that he once covered alone, and sixty sisters would be serving in the region.[95] Although Weibel maintained in his autobiography, *Forty Years Missionary in Arkansas,* that he always hated to beg, on the same page he recalled a story told to him about someone in Paragould who had swallowed a coin. A child nearby spontaneously exclaimed, "Call Father Weibel. He can get money out of anyone."[96]

Transferred to Hot Springs by Bishop Morris in 1908, Fr. Weibel had as one of his early assistants Father Walter Tynin, the first native-born Arkansan ordained for the Diocese of Little Rock. Tynin's parents were Swiss-German immigrants and Weibel had baptized their infant son Walter in Jonesboro in 1889. Twenty-two years later, the same son was a newly ordained priest and serving under the man who brought him into the Church.[97] At Hot Springs, Father Weibel continued his building programs with a new church, school, and parish center at the new St. John the Baptist Catholic parish. He retired from active ministry in 1918, but continued to serve as chaplain at the Good Shepherd convent and St. Joseph's Hospital in Hot Springs for another three years.[98] He retired completely to his native Switzerland, reentering the Benedictine order at Maria Einsiedeln in the early 1920s. Yet, he returned to Arkansas to celebrate his fifty years as a priest on August 31, 1926, at a gala festival at Pocahontas, which was attended by Bishop Morris and many people in the area. He left Arkansas forever the next year to write his memoirs, *Forty Years Missionary in Arkansas,* in the Abbey of Maria Einsiedeln, where he died on March 3, 1934.[99]

Another notable Swiss-German missionary priest was Father Matthew Saettele, O.S.B., who is sometimes known as "Arkansas' Greatest Catholic Missionary."[100] Born in 1857, he was ordained a priest at Maria Einseideln in Switzerland in 1883. In 1885, he journeyed to Arkansas to serve under Father Schlumpf's chief assistant at St. Benedict's Priory. Assigned as assistant pastor at St. Edward's parish in Little Rock in 1887, Father Saettele found city living distasteful and returned to Logan County the next year. In 1889 he went to Altus, where he began a career that lasted from 1889 to 1917 as a missionary in the rural areas of Arkansas.[101]

For the next nine years he ministered at Altus, where he built St. Matthew's Church in 1891, a mission to serve the newly arriving Austrian miners at Coal Hill five miles east of Altus in Johnson County. He also cared for the Church of Holy Redeemer in Clarksville in Johnson County and St. Wenceslaus in Dardanelle in Yell County. In the same county, he founded St. Patrick's Church for a small group of Irish settlers at Centerville. He built a convent and school at St. Boniface Church in Dixie and a new rectory in Oppelo at St. Elizabeth's Church.[102]

In 1898, he became pastor of St. Paul's Catholic Church in Pocahontas, where he built one of the most beautiful churches in the state. The church is made of granite and is outwardly in the Gothic style; its interior, however, is one of the finest examples of Swiss-German design. (St. Edward's in Little Rock, completed a few years later, also follows this style.) During his decade as pastor at Pocahontas, Father Weibel reported in one of his letters to the Leopoldine Society in Vienna in November 1900, that Saettele was offered the position as coadjutor bishop, but turned it down because he did not desire high positions. Father Weibel quoted Saettele as saying that he would have returned to Switzerland if he had not felt so needed in the Arkansas diocese.[103]

From Pocahontas, Bishop Morris sent him to Lake Village, in the southeast corner of the state. There he repaired the church and built a school, convent, and rectory. He went on to build other mission churches at Arkansas City, Stamps, Warren (in Bradley County, not the old Warren renamed Marche in Pulaski County), Grady, and Dermott. At one time, he was handling fifty-five churches and missions across southern Arkansas from the Mississippi River to the Oklahoma line, virtually one-third of the land area of the state.[104] By the middle of 1913, Saettele was reporting to the Leopoldine Society that he had moved from Lake Village to McGehee because that seemed to be a more central location for his missions.[105] In 1917, at the age of sixty, his health finally broke and he was ordered to live in more healthful and less humid environs. From 1917 to 1927, he worked in the Texas Panhandle as a missionary before resuming work in Arkansas at Searcy at the age of seventy. Bishop Morris made him chaplain of the Franciscan Boys' School there, a position of supposed semi-retirement. Father Saettele could not be still; he erected St. James' Church at Searcy in 1928, the forty-second church he had built in his lifetime. He died there two years later at the age of seventy-three.[106]

Another Benedictine would play a powerful role in the diocese once Bishop Fitzgerald became ill in 1900. Father Fintan Kraemer was born April 18, 1868, in Leistadt, Germany. He migrated to St. Benedict's colony in 1883 and settled on a farm with his family near Paris. He entered St. Benedict's in 1887 as one of the first candidates for the monastery. On March 21, 1888, he made his final vows as a Benedictine and was ordained for the priesthood on May 24, 1892. Sent to serve at St. Edward's Church in Little Rock a year later, Father Kraemer would stay there for the next fifteen years. He eventually became pastor and then vicar general in January 1900, one month after the death of Vicar General Father James Callaghan. After a few months of controversy, Father Kraemer, by the summer of 1900, had his role confirmed as the administrator until Fitzgerald recovered or a new bishop was named.[107]

Kraemer's term as administrator would be similar to that of Father Patrick Reilly's five-year reign between the death of Bishop Byrne and the coming of Bishop Fitzgerald. There is, of course, one large difference. Bishop Fitzgerald was still alive, and Father Kraemer did not enjoy full power, as he had to confirm his actions with a very ill and greatly incapacitated bishop who lived not in Little Rock, but in Hot Springs. Father Kraemer still held the position of pastor of St. Edward's and lived in the rectory. Kraemer did manage to get an assistant in 1902, Father Aloysius Baumgaertner, O.S.B., to serve with him, and his new assistant probably handled the day-to-day operations of the parish. A year later, Father Baumgaertner was replaced by Father Maurus Rohner, O.S.B., who helped oversee the final construction of the present St. Edward's Catholic Church by 1908.[108]

Kraemer's tenure as administrator would not be easy. The diocese was still somewhat ethnically divided, and his main rival during the 1900 controversy, Fr. Patrick Enright, was stationed just blocks away at St. Andrew's Cathedral.[109] Father Kraemer was quite young, not yet even thirty-one when he became vicar, and only thirty-two when he had the whole diocese put into his hands. That was, of course, a year younger than Edward Fitzgerald when he was handed the long-neglected Diocese of Little Rock. Father Kraemer, however, was not Bishop Fitzgerald. Some people may have felt that someone older and wiser should have been given the reins of the Church. Still, Fr. Kraemer carried on as best he could. He continued to send letters to the Leopoldine Society in Vienna soliciting funds for both St. Edward's and the whole diocese.[110] He also sent frequent correspondence to Bishop Fitzgerald about the affairs of the diocese; he seemed to be careful not to make a major move without his bishop's knowledge.[111] Father Kraemer's name was not sent to Rome for the position of coadjutor bishop, and there is some evidence that he was not liked by a few priests, whether owing to his age or manner of administration, it is not clear.[112]

Once Bishop Morris arrived, Father Kraemer continued working at St. Edward's and saw the new church completed by 1908. In February 1907, Morris asked him to begin ministering specifically to the small number of black Catholics in Little Rock and in 1908, named him the first pastor of St. Bartholomew's, a black Catholic parish in Little Rock. Father Kraemer built the first chapel for that congregation on Gaines Street and said the first Mass there on January 10, 1909. By this time, he was no longer vicar general, having been replaced by Msgr. John M. Lucey in June 1907. By the fall of 1909, Father Kraemer was in Armstrong Springs near Searcy trying, unsuccessfully as it turns out, to start a religious order known as the Brothers of St. Paul. After this project failed, Kraemer was sent by Abbot Conrad of Subiaco to St. Mary's Church in Nevada, Missouri, in 1912, and he would not work in Arkansas again for the next twenty-two years. After assignments in Ohio and Texas, he returned to Subiaco on Thanksgiving 1934, and died on his sixty-seventh birthday, April 18, 1935.[113]

In addition to being "apostles, missionaries, and administrators," the German Catholics also produced the first Catholic oriented weekly in Arkansas history. A Lutheran paper, the *Staates-Zeitung,* reappeared in 1877. It lasted until the United States entered World War I in 1917.[114] Apparently to provide a paper for the German Catholic immigrants, the *Arkansas Echo* appeared in 1891. Published like its competitor at Little Rock, this paper lasted until 1932. While not associated with the Diocese of Little Rock, it was clearly directed toward a Catholic audience. In 1922, newspaper historian Frederick Allsopp termed the still existing *Arkansas Echo* "the representative paper of the German people."[115] While the German and Swiss-German immigrants did have an important impact on Arkansas Catholicism, their large migration to the state had ended by 1890.

Historians of American immigration patterns traditionally see the 1880s as a decade of transition from Old to New Immigration. Most of the immigrants in the previous half-decade came from Ireland, Germany, Great Britain, or Scandinavia. After that date, more immigrants would come from southern and eastern Europe: Italians, Poles, Czechs, Slovaks, Greeks, and Russians. Also German-speaking Austrians would migrate to the U.S.[116] Since the Austrian migration to Arkansas was meager,[117] this shift in immigration patterns greatly affected the German communities in Arkansas, whether Catholic, Lutheran, or Jewish. As the historian of this German migration into Arkansas put it:

> Cut off from a course of people fresh from the homeland and full of enthusiasm for keeping up old customs, the distinctive life of the immigrant community would weaken. Eventually the language and the old customs would be lost . . . By 1890 the enclaves had become well-developed. After 1890 they were to die.[118]

Arkansas did experience some of this immigration shift during the 1890s. Some Austrians came to work as miners at Coal Hill in Johnson County in the early 1890s. Father Saettele had founded the church of St. Wenceslaus in Dardanelle, located in Yell County, for some "thirty families of Bohemians" who moved there in 1895 from the Austro-Hungarian Empire.[119] In December 1898, Father Placidus Oechsle, O.S.B., at Altus, wrote the Leopoldine Society that most of the parishioners at his mission church of St. Matthew's at Coal Hill were poor Austrians who could not afford to support a church, school, or convent. Moreover, he wrote, "The Company is not Christian and is paying them the poorest of wages, and is exploiting them."[120] A bitter strike erupted the following year, and it did not end until 1901 "with no real agreement, and conditions have not improved," according to Father Oechsle.[121] By October 1908, this Benedictine priest reported that the company had closed the mines.[122]

In the fall of 1894, the Slovac Colonization Company from Pittsburgh planted about twenty-five families in the southern part of Prairie County about twelve miles above Stuttgart. Father J. Simonik wrote the Leopoldine Society on June 27, 1895, asking for money, and he listed his location as Slovactown, Arkansas. The following April, John Adelsponger wrote Bishop Fitzgerald from Stuttgart asking for a priest for Slovactown, explaining that two priests had been there but "one left some time ago and the other has been living on a farm until recently, but is now gone, nobody knows where."[123] They would wait twenty-one years for a resident pastor, while priests from Stuttgart, like Father Joseph A. McQuaid, who built the first church there in 1900, ministered to them. Father Saettele mentioned Slovactown as one of his mission stations in 1911, but not until 1917 would Father Louis Glinski become the first resident pastor at SS. Cyril and Methodius Church in what would become known as the town of Slovac.[124] Bishop Fitzgerald blessed the second church at the growing Polish community at Marche on May 25, 1896; Father Hippolytus Orlowski happily recorded this event in his November 26 letter to the Leopoldine Society. The present Church of the Immaculate Heart of Mary in Marche was finished and dedicated in 1933.[125]

By far, the largest group to come during this wave of new immigrants were Italians, and Arkansas was no exception to this national pattern. The largest Catholic immigrant colony to be founded between 1890 and 1915 was at Sunny Side Plantation near Lake Village, which resulted in the founding of two Italian communities at completely opposite ends of the state by 1900. Compared with the rest of the country, including many of the south central states, few Italians migrated to Arkansas.[126] Most of these Italians, by 1910, lived in three areas of the state. About one hundred Italians lived in Little Rock engaged in small businesses, fruit vending, and barbering. Another large group lived in Tontitown, a few miles northwest of Springdale in Washington County. A third group continued to reside in the Lake Village area in Chicot County.[127] Five years later, a small colony of about twenty Italian families set up the Little Italy settlement, twenty-five miles west of Little Rock in Perry County. Most of the story of the Italian Catholic immigrants to Arkansas is linked to the Sunny Side Plantation colony at Lake Village and the career of Fr. Peter Bandini, who founded Tontitown as a spinoff from this colony.

After the Civil War, John C. Calhoun, grandson of the famous South Carolina statesman, bought the old Florence Plantation on the southern end of Lake Chicot near Lake Village. Calhoun also bought most of the other plantations in the area with the help of Austin Corbin, a wealthy banker and railroad owner from New York. By 1887, Calhoun had bought more than 10,000 acres around Lake Chicot and renamed the place Sunny Side Plantation. Calhoun needed more laborers to work on this large estate, and Corbin saw the influx of immigrants into the Northeast as a way to provide a labor force for his Arkansas plantation.[128] Although Chicot County had a large black population, making up 87.8 percent of the total county population, blacks were reluctant to work on a major plantation partially owned and run by a northern man they did not know and would have little contact with.[129]

Determined to solve his manpower shortage, Corbin turned to the Italian Bureau of Labor, which was established in New York City in 1894. The Italian officials were willing to help relocate Italian immigrants from urban to rural America. They would rather see their countrymen have their own land and laboring in the fresh air than working in grimy sweatshops and living in teeming tenement houses in northeastern cities. Whether these officials were ignorant or blind to the truth is not clear. Instead of helping these immigrants to become self-sufficient farmers, they were placing their fellow countrymen in a position to become peon labor on a large plantation in the Mississippi Delta.[130]

The agreement, drawn up in January 1895, called upon the Italian government to send about one hundred families a year for the next five years. The laborers were to rent the acres at $5.00 to $7.00 an acre with an option to buy land at $160.00 an acre in twenty-two years at 5 percent annual interest. "Although still exorbitant, rent was more acceptable to the immigrants because they could better control their expenses and take advantage of every lump of soil."[131] The company promised to supply mules, heating for the church, a water filter, and salaries for a priest, teacher, and gardener. What they did not know was that the company would tell them what to grow and how much, and the company operated the only gin, packing house, and railroad in the region. The company also owned and operated the only store.[132]

The massive Italian immigration to America had less to do with religious persecution than the economic dislocation caused by the Italian government's rush to industrialize its economy and consolidate its agriculture. This policy drove millions of Italians off their lands to look for work in the bustling cities. Not all could find work in the new factories, and with their land sold or confiscated and having no chance of employment in the area, many immigrants were lured across the Atlantic to North and South America. Once in their new lands, they were often the victims of squalor, destitution, disease, and crime. To help these immigrants in both Italy and in their places of destination, Bishop John Baptist Scalabrini of Piacenzia, a diocese in northern Italy, founded the St. Raphael Society. The society gave food, shelter, and help with employment for immigrants and their families. To help staff this society, Bishop Scalabrini also founded an order of priests called the Missionaries of St. Charles to follow the immigrants to their new lands and serve as their chaplains. The order was founded in the late 1870s, and in 1887 Pope Leo XIII formally approved the group, which came to be known as the Scalabrini Fathers.

One of the earliest members of the Scalabrini Fathers was Father Peter Bandini. Born of noble parents in Forli, Italy, in 1853, he was ordained September 30, 1878, and joined the newly formed Scalabrini Fathers in 1880. After laboring at the Italian ports for years, Father Bandini came to New York in early 1891 to found a St. Raphael Society there to help Italian immigrants when they arrived. In one year, his office helped more than 20,000 Italian immigrants find aid and employment. He did this while he was pastor of an Italian Catholic parish, Our Lady of Pompeii, in Manhattan.[133]

Father Bandini came to believe that this work alone was not adequate. Like the Italian officials at the Bureau of Labor, he hoped to place his fellow countrymen in a more healthful environment where they could be farmers. Bishop Fitzgerald happened to be writing Archbishop Corrigan of New York requesting an Italian priest to work at this colony, as he did not have an Italian priest in Arkansas. In early 1896, Archbishop Corrigan brought the matter up with Father Bandini who readily agreed to go to Arkansas.[134] At the time Bandini agreed to go, the first group of settlers from Italy, seventy-three families or about four hundred people, had arrived in Chicot County on December 4, 1895. Little preparation was made for these people, and the first year was miserable. They were not given their promised twenty acres a family, but only twelve, which made it harder to sustain their families. Almost all had no knowledge of growing cotton, which is what the company wanted them to produce. Many died from disease that year because of poor sanitation. By the time Bandini arrived on January 2, 1897, with a second group of about 376 settlers, the whole colony was in chaos, and order had broken down because the settlers were refusing to work.[135]

Although Bandini did get the settlers back to work and restored clean and adequate water, the experiment was already in trouble. Corbin had died in a carriage accident in June 1896, and his heirs took little interest in the plantation project. A major flood on the Mississippi River destroyed the drainage system and the cotton crop. With so much standing water and no way to remove it, more immigrants died from disease. The immigrant priest was so upset in late 1897, that he strongly criticized the Italian embassy for not ordering an on-site inspection of Sunny Side. Father Bandini, himself, had to flee in late August 1897 to regain his health. He journeyed to the Ozarks, where he came to believe that this is where the colony needed to locate; a place where they could live in a healthier environment and experiment with crops with which they were more familiar, such as grapes and fruits. Bandini had returned to Sunny Side to encourage the settlers to follow him to the Ozarks when news came that the whole plantation had been sold to O.B. Crittenden & Company of Greenville, Mississippi, as of February 1, 1898. The new company promptly changed the terms of the previous contract, saying that their mules, the filter for the water, and the salaries for the priest, teacher, and gardener would not be paid by the company, but had to come from the colonists' income. With this news, Bandini had little difficulty persuading about half the colony to follow him, like Moses, to the promised land of the Ozarks. While most of those who left followed Bandini, a few moved farther north and founded the settlement of Rosati near Knobview, Missouri.[136]

On February 28, 1898, Bandini's band of Italians began their 350-mile trek from the southeastern corner to the northwestern corner of Arkansas. The colonists stopped east of Little Rock, because the men found temporary work in the factories and railroads, and Fr. Bandini spoke at every Catholic church along the route soliciting funds for the move. By April 6, 1898, they were in Springdale, in Washington County, where Bandini purchased about eight hundred acres of state government land with the money he had collected. This tract had been set up by the state for Confederate veterans, but few had come forward to claim or develop it.

Like the early settlers all across the frontier, the Italians had to clear the land to build rudimentary structures for their families. Within a few years, a church, school, and convent were set up. Fr. Bandini used his rectory as an orphanage, at one time taking care of ten children whose parents had perished at Sunny Side. The first church was burned by those who did not like to see the Italians in the area. Everything in the church except the statue of St. Joseph was destroyed, so he became the patron saint of the new church. Bandini used the occasion to warn those who were hostile that the settlers would be armed in the future and would protect their families and property. No major trouble occurred after this incident. Bandini had the colonists growing apples in 1899, but a disease so hurt the crop in 1904, that they switched to growing grapes for juice and wine production. In 1921, Welch Grape Juice Company located a plant in Springdale, which gave the colony a secure economic future even though prohibition cut into the production of wine.[137]

Meanwhile, back at Sunny Side Plantation, no more settlers came between January 1897 and June 1900. Thirty-one two-parent families, and four single-parent families, were still working on the plantation.[138] Sunny Side imported a few Italian settlers every year from 1900 until 1914. The attraction of the colony was no doubt diminished by a United States government investigation of Crittenden & Company for inducing immigrants into debt peonage, a violation of federal law. The government filed charges against the company in 1907, and Crittenden was found not guilty. Two years later, the government investigated again, but filed no formal charges. In 1910, the Crittenden company announced that it would charge no rent, but would require tenants to share the profits from a quarter of their crop, causing them to become in fact sharecroppers. The resentful Italians began drifting away from the plantation. By the late 1930s, only two Italian families were still working at Sunny Side, while other Italian families stayed in the Lake Village area and bought other lands or acquired new jobs. By the end of World War II, the Kansas City Life Insurance Company, the last owner of Sunny Side, had sold off the acres of this once large plantation, breaking it up into smaller farms. Today, a few Italian families in Chicot County can trace their heritage to the Sunny Side Plantation experiment.[139]

Father Bandini continued to oversee the growth and development of Tontitown. In 1903, he opened a school with Bernadette Brady, a woman of Irish-American and Indian descent, as the first mistress. The Sisters of Mercy arrived in 1906 and stayed for six years. They opened an academy for girls from ages six through high school and a school for boys up to the age of twelve. Until the Sisters of Mercy came, Father Bandini also taught in the local school. For a time, from 1912 to 1914, the academy at Tontitown had a few of the Sisters of the Incarnate Word who had fled the revolution in Mexico. Ursuline sisters came in 1914 and stayed for ten years. Father Bandini served as both the religious and political leader. He gave the town its name and served as its major for more than a decade. In 1911, he organized the Tontitown Grape Growers Association to protect and market their major cash crop.[140]

Father Bandini achieved some national and international fame for his work at Tontitown. In May 1905, Baron Edmundo Mayor des Planches, the Italian ambassador to the United States, went to the remote area to pay tribute to the immigrants at Tontitown and their remarkable priest. He was greeted by a cheering crowd of Italians waving American and Italian flags.[141] Father Daniel E. Hudson, C.S.C., editor of the Notre Dame-based *Ave Maria* magazine, visited the colony in late 1908 and wrote a favorable piece about his visit when he returned to South Bend, Indiana. In the issue of January 9, 1909, he counted the colonists "among the most happy, law-abiding, thrifty, and pious citizens of this country."[142] Father Bandini thanked Hudson for his article, and a Catholic from Little Rock, John Mathews, wrote to the *Ava Maria* editor, "Fr. Bandini deserves the best you can say about him."[143] Other honors would come to Fr. Bandini from both his Church and his native land. Pope Pius X sent him a pontifical award for service to the Church in 1911, and Queen Margherita of Italy presented him "a beautiful set of vestments and robes with the Italian royal arms embroidered on them . . . the Italian government presented him with a gold medal in recognition of his work at Tontitown, accompanied with some financial aid for bringing more colonists from Italy."[144]

In early December 1916, Father Bandini suffered a stroke and was sent to St. Vincent's Infirmary in Little Rock, where he died after a second stroke on January 2, 1917.[145] Bishop Morris, who had a few personality disputes with Father Bandini, nevertheless praised him at his funeral as a man who "loved his people, and his love for them was so great that he lived with them, sharing their trials and tribulations and rejoicing with them in their moments of happiness and cheer." He continued, "He was a good and faithful soul, and the best known Italian priest in the United States."[146] The distinct Italian settlement that Fr. Bandini began in 1898 still exists in the Ozarks of northwestern Arkansas. It is also the only place in the state named after the Sicilian-born Italian soldier who, in 1686, founded the first European settlement in what would become Arkansas.

The last Catholic immigrant colony in Arkansas was the Little Italy colony in eastern Perry County near Little Rock. On December 23, 1915, five Italian Catholic families, Busato, Perrini, Belotti, Granato, and Segalla, all from Chicago or northern Michigan, came to live in Perry County. The land they bought had originally been part of the initial land grant of the Little Rock and Fort Smith Railroad. The land's ownership went to the Fourche River Lumber Company and eventually to the Arkansas Farms Company. The latter company advertised in Chicago newspapers that farms of forty would be sold for $10.00 an acre. Louis Belotti, the only original survivor of this first group, came to Arkansas from Chicago in 1914 when he was four years old. His oldest brother and sister were born in Italy, and his family came to Chicago from northern

Italy around 1904. After a decade in Chicago, his father feared that continued living in that city would mean his children would wind up in jail. He and the five other families decided to get out of the urban squalor and embark on a journey to Arkansas.

They arrived at their destination just two days before Christmas with almost nothing except the land they had purchased in inaccessible rural Arkansas. No roads went into this mountainous area, and like other rural immigrants who were allowed to buy cast-off land, they had to clear it themselves. More Italians, the Cia, Chairo, and Ghidotti families, came from Chicago, and one family, Zulpo, migrated to Little Italy from Lake Village. Like their countrymen at Tontitown, they turned to grape growing as a real money crop, and by 1920, they had four wineries in operation. The immigrants called it *Alta Villa* meaning high place or high village, but the name that has become its designation is Little Italy. Prohibition cut into its wine production, but Belotti still remembers that they produced and sold wine illegally during those years. Although the wineries resumed operation in the 1930s, none were surviving by 1942.

To serve the religious desires of the people, a priest from Little Rock, then the newly ordained Father Albert L. Fletcher, visited the new colony in the early 1920s. The community had never had a resident priest, but its first church was a Catholic church that it bought in Ola and moved fifty miles to Little Italy in 1922. This wooden church of St. Francis of Assisi served as their place of worship until a modern brick structure replaced it in 1969. Like Tontitown, Little Italy still exists as a distinct ethnic community on top of a mountain in Perry County.[147]

When you look at the actual number and percentages of foreign-born in Arkansas, immigrants did not make a major impact upon the population growth. In 1880, the number of foreign-born to the white population was just 1.7 percent, a small but substantial increase over the 1.3 percent the previous decade.[148] Ten years later, the number of foreign-born still made up 1.7 percent of the state white population. Still that is not the total story, for by 1890, the census returns show that Arkansas had more foreign-born than four other former Confederate states and that its percentage of foreign-born was higher than five of them. The number of foreign-born in the whole Confederacy was 3.3 percent of the white population.[149] (The numbers and the percentage of foreign-born in the Confederate states are in Table 6C.)

By 1900, the percentage of foreign-born in Arkansas fell to 1.5 percent and stayed at that figure ten years later.[150] This is another indicator that the second wave of immigration did not equal the impact on Arkansas of the earlier immigration, especially during the 1870s and 1880s.

The 1920 census is important in U.S. history for two major reasons. For the first time, more people lived in the cities than the rural areas, and the census came at the end of the great wave of European immigration. In 1890, the number of foreign-born in the U.S. was 16.8 percent of the overall white population; by 1920 it had dropped to 14.6 percent.[151] When one considers the percentages of foreign-born in the former Confederate states, the foreign-born amounted to 3.4 percent of the total white population in 1920, up one-tenth of one percent from 1890. Texas accounted for the increase, as it was the only southern state to gain in percentage of foreign-born between 1890 and 1920. (The numbers of foreign-born in these states and their percentages to the white population are in Table 6D.)[152] By 1920, the foreign-born in Arkansas was 1.1 percent of the total white population. Despite this drop of four-tenths of one percent from 1910, its share was still higher than in five other Southern states. The South, and Arkansas in particular, failed to participate much in the great European immigration that washed ashore in America between 1840 and 1920.

This would have important ramifications for the Catholic Church in Arkansas. Statistically, the state had the same percentage of foreign-born to white population in 1920 that it did in 1860, despite the efforts of the railroads, state government, colonization societies, and Bishop Fitzgerald. Though the foreign-born were far from being religiously homogeneous, nevertheless, had Arkansas been able to attract numerous immigrants, many of whom were Catholics, the base of the Church would have expanded. This should not obscure, however, the real contributions that the Irish, Germans, Swiss-Germans, Poles, Slovacs, Italians, and other foreign-born Catholics made to the Diocese of Little Rock. They built churches, opened schools, supported the Church's various charitable institutions, and shared their customs, cultures, and religious faith with their new neighbors. As the Catholic Church in Arkansas began to move into the twentieth century, its policy decisions and growth would be affected by a Tennessee-born bishop of Irish descent.

Table 6A

WHITE GERMAN-SPEAKING & FOREIGN-BORN POPULATION IN SELECTED ARKANSAS COUNTIES 1890 LITTLE ROCK TO FORT SMITH

COUNTY	WHITES	FOREIGN-BORN	% FB TO WHITES	GERMAN	% GER. FB TO WHITES	% GER TO FB
CONWAY	11,788	578	4.7	467	3.9	80.7
CRAWFORD	19,410	187	.9	71	.3	37.9
FAULKNER	14,994	298	1.9	223	1.4	74.8
FRANKLIN	19,256	317	1.6	202	1.0	63.7
JOHNSON	16,125	435	2.6	251	1.5	57.0
LOGAN	19,646	637	3.2	572	2.9	89.7
PERRY	4,597	87	1.8	59	1.2	67.8
POPE	17,837	340	1.9	234	1.3	68.8
PULASKI	25,329	2,807	11.0	1,465	5.6	52.1
SEBASTIAN	29,398	1,379	4.6	658	2.2	47.7
YELL	15,652	135	.8	16	.09	11.0
NORTHEAST ARKANSAS GERMANS						
CRAIGHEAD	11,506	171	1.4	63	.5	36.8
GREENE	12,747	166	1.3	80	.6	48.1
POINSETT	3,726	95	2.5	51	1.3	53.0
RANDOLPH	13,890	325	2.3	270	1.9	83.0
EAST CENTRAL ARKANSAS (LUTHERAN)						
ARKANSAS	7,899	315	3.9	215	2.7	68.0
PRAIRIE	7,011	180	2.5	81	1.1	45.0
JEFFERSON	10,951	614	5.6	222	2.0	36.1
STATE TOTAL	818,752	14,264	1.7	7,018	.8	49.2

U.S. Department of the Interior, *The Eleventh Census of the United States 1890* 10 volumes (Washington, D.C.: Government Printing Office, 1892-1894) 1:476-477, 2:613-614.

Table 6B

PER CENT OF GERMAN-AUSTRIAN-SWISS GERMAN TO THE FOREIGN POPULATION IN THE SOUTH

1890

	NB OF G-A-SG*	% FB TO WHITE	% G-A-SG TO WHITES	% OF G-A-SG TO FB
ALABAMA	4,316	1.7	.51	29.2
ARKANSAS	7,018	1.7	.85	49.2
FLORIDA	2,066	10.1	.84	9.0
GEORGIA	3,955	1.2	.40	32.5
LOUISIANA	15,717	8.9	2.81	31.5
MISSISSIPPI	2,539	1.4	.46	31.9
N. CAROLINA	1,174	.3	.11	31.7
S. CAROLINA	2,624	1.3	.56	41.8
TENNESSEE	6,571	1.4	.49	32.8
TEXAS	5,9,312	8.7	3.30	38.7
VIRGINIA	4,670	1.8	.45	25.4

* This number computed, not given in the Census. I added the number of those claiming to be born in Germany, Austria, or Swiss Germany.

U.S. Department of the Interior, *The Eleventh Census of the United States, 1890* 10 volumes (Washington, D.C.: Government Printing Office, 1892-1894) 2:600-601.

Table 6C

PERCENTAGE OF FOREIGN-BORN TO WHITE POPULATION IN THE SOUTH

1890

STATE	WHITE POPULATION	FOREIGN-BORN	% OF FB
ALABAMA	833,718	14,777	1.7
ARKANSAS	818,752	14,264	1.7
FLORIDA	224,949	22,932	10.1
GEORGIA	978,357	12,137	1.2
LOUISIANA	558,395	49,747	8.9
MISSISSIPPI	544,851	7,952	1.4
N. CAROLINA	1,055,382	3,702	.3
S. CAROLINA	462,008	6,270	1.3
TENNESSEE	1,336,637	20,092	1.4
TEXAS	1,745,935	152,956	8.7
VIRGINIA	1,020,122	18,374	1.8

U.S. Department of Interior, *The Eleventh Census of the United States, 1890* 10 volumes (Washington, D.C.: Government Printing Office, 1892-1894) 1:469.

Table 6D

PERCENTAGE OF FOREIGN-BORN TO WHITE POPULATION IN THE SOUTH

1920

STATE	WHITE POPULATION	FOREIGN-BORN	% OF FB
ALABAMA	1,429,370	17,662	1.2
ARKANSAS	1,265,782	13,975	1.1
FLORIDA	595,145	43,008	7.2
GEORGIA	1,672,928	16,186	0.9
LOUISIANA	1,051,740	44,871	4.2
MISSISSIPPI	845,943	8,019	0.9
N. CAROLINA	1,776,680	7,099	0.3
S. CAROLINA	812,137	6,401	0.7
TENNESSEE	1,870,515	15,478	0.8
TEXAS	3,557,646	360,519	10.1
VIRGINIA	1,587,124	30,785	1.9

pp. 1328, 1329, 1332, 1333, 1342, 1347, 1353, 1360, 1361, 1363, 1367.

Churches . . . in Wood

Ratcliff, Logan County, St. Anthony; second church

New Dixie, Perry County, St. Boniface; first church

Pine Bluff, Jefferson County, St. Peter; first church

Pine Bluff, Jefferson County, St. Joseph; first church

Brinkley, Monroe County, St. John the Baptist

Churches . . . in Stone and Brick

Hot Springs, Garland County, St. John the Baptist

Altus, Franklin County, Our Lady of Perpetual Help

Fort Smith, Sebastian County, Christ the King; first church

Fort Smith, Sebastian County, Immaculate Conception

Helena, Phillips County, St. Mary's

Little Rock, St. John's Seminary, Downtown Campus

Became the site of Catholic High in 1930

Theology Hall

Gymnasium

Lecture Hall

Little Rock, St. John's Seminary, Pulaski Heights
relocated in 1917

Fitzgerald Hall

Byrne Hall

Morris Hall

Aerial view of campus, 1950's

Little Rock, St. John's Seminary, Pulaski Heights

on the grounds of the former seminary which closed in 1969
(views taken 1993)

West side of the campus

East side of the campus

CINDY MOMCHILOV

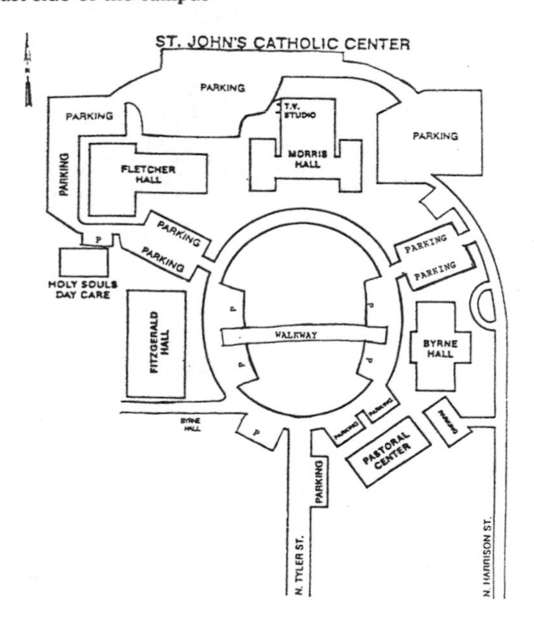

Schematic drawing showing
position of all buildings
on the grounds

Little Rock College

O'Hern Debating Team, 1913

Paragould, An early First Communion Class

C H A P T E R   V I I

Buildings and Bigotry

The Early Episcopacy of Bishop Morris, 1905-1929

AS BISHOP FITZGERALD lay stricken in St. Joseph's Infirmary at Hot Springs on Wednesday, September 20, 1905, three bishops of the New Orleans Province, Nicholas Gallagher of Galveston, Edward Allen of Mobile, and Edward Dunne of Dallas, arrived to discuss the perilous condition of the province. The metropolitan of the province, Placide Louis Chapelle, was dead and the senior bishop, Edward Fitzgerald, was permanently enfeebled. Chapelle had been Archbishop of New Orleans for eight years, and most of that time he was out of his See serving as apostolic delegate extraordinary for Cuba, Puerto Rico, and the Philippines. Affairs both within the province and archdiocese had been neglected. This particularly affected Arkansas because Bishop Fitzgerald had lain ill for more than five years and no coadjutor had been named. By the time that Chappelle had returned to New Orleans in early 1905, he felt compelled to make a pastoral tour. While he was on that journey, a yellow fever epidemic erupted in New Orleans. Disregarding all warnings, the archbishop arrived in the stricken city in late July and succumbed to the dreaded disease on August 9, 1905. Gustave Rouxel, Auxiliary Bishop and administrator of the New Orleans Archdiocese, informed Fitzgerald of this news in a letter on August 18.[1] Now, the province had no metropolitan and its senior bishop, was, in the words of a paper in San Antonio, "an invalid."[2]

Things did not get better after the meeting of the three bishops. Bishops Allen, Gallagher, and Dunne, together with the very infirmed Fitzgerald, did not make up a quorum, because three other bishops were still in Europe and two others could not make the meeting.[3] Another meeting was scheduled for late November in Hot Springs. Eventually, Gallagher, the senior bishop in the province after Fitzgerald, changed the meeting date to December 13 and moved the location to New Orleans. The Galveston bishop notified Fitzgerald of this decision on November 20.[4]

Seven of the nine bishops of the province appeared in New Orleans on December 13, and they worked through Christmas until December 28. In addition to Gallagher, Dunne, and Allen, Bishops Cornelius Van de Ven of Natchitoches, Theophile Meerschaert of Oklahoma City, John Forest of San Antonio, and Thomas Heslin of Natchez attended. Bishop Fitzgerald and Peter Verdaguer, vicar apostolic of South Texas, which became the Diocese of Corpus Christi in 1912, could not attend due to illness. Following a custom sanctioned by the Third Plenary Council and approved by Rome, the priests who served as consultors of the diocese and the bishops of the province would send a list of episcopal candidates to the Pope.[5] For New Orleans, the bishops' list included Bishop Meerschaert, the first choice, with the second and third positions falling to Heslin and Dunne, respectively. The priests' list included Bishop James Blenk of Puerto Rico, a member of the Society of Mary religious order who had worked in New Orleans, Bishop Meerschaert, and a Father Lavall from New Orleans. For the Diocese of Little Rock, the bishops' list put Fr. Patrick Horan of Our Lady of Good Counsel parish in Little Rock at the top, with Monsignor John Baptist Morris, vicar general of the Diocese of Nashville second, and Father James Brady of Immaculate Conception parish and pastor at St. Edward's Infirmary in Fort Smith third. The priests' list to Rome for Arkansas included Fr. Fintan Kraemer, O.S.B., then administrator of the diocese; Eugene Weibel, O.S.B.; and Father Horan. The fact that Horan was first on the bishops' list, and the only candidate to show up on both lists, meant that he was indeed a strong candidate. Only thirty-nine years old, he held a doctorate in Theology from the College for the Propagation of the Faith, the seminary in Rome for training missionary priests.[6]

Bishop Dunne of Dallas wrote Fitzgerald on December 30 informing him of the names sent to Rome to be his coadjutor. Dunne mentioned that the most heated debate at the meeting was not over the successors for the Archdiocese of New Orleans and the Diocese of Little Rock, but whether to recommend to the Holy See the creation of an archbishopric at Galveston for the dioceses that were multiplying in Texas. "I held the making of an Archiepiscopal See in Texas as premature," Dunne wrote, and his position was the one adopted by the council.[7] While Dunne mentioned in his letter that he hoped that Dallas, not Galveston, would be the place for the archdiocesan See, it would be neither city. San Antonio was made into an archdiocese in 1926, separating the dioceses in Texas and Oklahoma from the New Orleans Province.[8] Rome responded quickly on the See at New Orleans; Bishop James Blenk of Puerto Rico was elevated to archbishop on April 20, 1906.[9]

An *Arkansas Gazette* article from Rome on March 26, 1906, reported that the Congregation for the Propagation of the Faith would recommend to Pope Pius X that Msgr. John B. Morris, vicar general of the Diocese of Nashville, be the new coadjutor bishop with right of succession to the Diocese of Little Rock. Prematurely, Fitzgerald wired a note of congratulations that day to Morris, although the appointment was not yet certain. Five weeks later, on May 3, Morris wrote Fitzgerald telling him that he had not received official news of his appointment from Rome; that would not come for another eleven days.[10]

It is difficult to ascertain why Rome chose Morris over Horan. Both men had studied in Rome, but Horan was familiar with Arkansas, having been ordained and worked there since 1893. One explanation might be that Morris, unlike Horan, was born in the United States and in the South and was an outsider to the diocese.[11]

On the feast day of St. Peter and St. Paul, June 29, 1866, Anne Morris gave birth to her first son on the family farm near Hendersonville, Tennessee. The previous day's feast was that of the martyrdom of John the Baptist. The child's father, John Morris, was born on a farm in northwestern Ireland near Athenry in Galway County. Migrating to America as a young man, he had settled in northwestern Virginia in what is now West Virginia. He joined the Union Army in 1861 and fought in campaigns in Kentucky and Tennessee. While he was in Kentucky, he met and married his wife, Anne Morrissey. Her background is less clear. Thomas Stritch, her grandson, believed that she was born in Ireland and had migrated with her family to Canada and then Kentucky, where she met her future husband. John Morris saved his income, and when he left the army in the fall of 1863, he used his muster pay to purchase a farm near Hendersonville. He brought both his wife and her mother to live with him on the farm. There, Ann Morrissey Morris gave birth to the first of their nine children, the eldest being the future Bishop of Little Rock.[12]

The future bishop was baptized by an Italian-born Dominican priest named James A. Orengo, who was legendary for his mission work in Tennessee from 1848 to 1873. Young John Morris served as an altar boy under Father Joseph Jarboe, a Dominican priest who accompanied fellow Dominican Bishop Richard P. Miles to the newly erected Diocese of Nashville in 1838. Tutored at home, Morris received his first holy communion in 1879 at the age of thirteen and did not receive any formal education until he was sent to St. Mary's College in Lebanon, Kentucky, in 1882. Five years later, the year of the death of his mother, he received his degree. After her passing, his father moved the family to Nashville to a house on Summer Street a block from the cathedral. There, the younger Morris made his decision to enter the priesthood. Bishop Joseph Rademacher not only accepted the young man as a candidate for the Diocese of Nashville, but sent him to Rome to study at the College for the Propagation of the Faith. There, he was fortunate to have as one his teachers of dogma, Cardinal Francesco Satolli, the first and future papal apostolic delegate to the

United States, from 1893 to 1896. Ordained a priest in Rome on June 11, 1892, he said his first Mass at the Blessed Sacrament Chapel in St. Peter's. He was first appointed assistant pastor at St. Mary's Cathedral, and Bishop Thomas S. Byrne of Nashville made him his personal secretary two years later. In 1895, the twenty-nine year old priest became rector of the cathedral. On June 11, 1900, eight years to the day after Morris' ordination, Bishop Byrne made him vicar general of the Diocese of Nashville. On December 3, Morris gained the title of monsignor from Pope Leo XIII upon the request of Bishop Byrne.[13]

It was while Morris was performing his duties for the Tennessee diocese that he was called by Rome to be the coadjutor Bishop of Little Rock with right of succession. The date of his appointment from Rome was April 20, 1906, although Morris was not notified until May 14. He immediately left for Hot Springs, where he conferred briefly with Bishop Fitzgerald, and then he returned to Nashville to begin plans for his consecration.[14] On June 11, 1906, fourteen years to the day after his ordination, six years to the day after he became vicar general at Nashville, and just seventeen days short of his fortieth birthday, John Baptist Morris was consecrated as Bishop of Little Rock at St. Joseph's church in Nashville. Presiding were Bishops Thomas Byrne of Nashville, Edward Allen of Mobile, and Nicholas Gallagher of Galveston, with Archbishop Henry Moeller of Cincinnati delivering the homily. (Given Bishop Fitzgerald's Cincinnati roots, this must have pleased the elderly prelate.) Others in attendance included Bishops Edward Dunne and Thomas Heslin, and Abbots Ignatius Conrad of New Subiaco Abbey and Bernard Menges of the St. Bernard's Abbey in Alabama.[15]

Bishop Morris celebrated his first pontifical high Mass at St. Andrew's Cathedral on June 24, 1906, with an impressive ceremony that began about 10:00 a.m. Both Little Rock dailies gave the ceremony extensive coverage, with the *Arkansas Gazette* printing a picture of the new prelate on the morning of the ceremony. Morris was quoted as saying, "From today on my chief hope and desire shall be to labor earnestly for the welfare of this diocese. The advancement of the church in Little Rock is henceforth the chief ambition of my life and toward the fulfillment of this end I shall bend all my energies."[16]

The new bishop did not stay long in Arkansas. He visited the monastery and seminary in Logan County and wrote to the ill Bishop Fitzgerald in Hot Springs, "I found everything in Logan County quite splendid."[17] On September 3, 1906, he left Little Rock for Rome, sent by Bishop Fitzgerald. He reported later that month to Fitzgerald, that he was in Baltimore visiting some friends before going on to New York and from there to Europe. Morris' next letter was from Rome, where he told Fitzgerald that he had seen the Holy Father and obtained for him an apostolic blessing. In early December, Morris wrote from New York that he would be back in Little Rock by December 19.[18] He left affairs in the diocese in the hands of the vicar general, Fintan Kraemer, O.S.B., who continued to run the day-to-day operations of the diocese.[19]

Morris' last letter to Fitzgerald is dated January 18, 1907, and he wrote that Father James Brady, one of the candidates the bishops had recommended to Rome, had asked for a leave of absence. Morris refused until he had received from the priest a full financial account of his ministry at Fort Smith.[20] While Morris was in Europe in October 1906, it was Father Horan, at Our Lady of Good Counsel in Little Rock, who would replace Brady at Immaculate Conception, yet Horan did not actually leave for his new assignment at Fort Smith until December.[21]

Father Brady was born in 1867 in Ireland and attended All Hallows College in Dublin before his ordination in 1891. He came to serve in the Diocese of Little Rock where he was first assigned to the cathedral, and then to St. Patrick's Church in North Little Rock. During the short-lived division between Kraemer and Enright in 1900, he had supported the Irish faction. The leader of that faction, Father Enright, sent Father Brady to Immaculate Conception parish in Fort Smith to work with Father Lawrence Smyth and to serve also as a chaplain at the new hospital there, St. Edward's. Brady became pastor at Immaculate Conception after the death of Lawrence Smyth in November 1900, just five months after the death of his brother, Father Michael Smyth. Apparently an able and attractive priest, Father Brady must have had a good reputation, for he appeared on the bishops' list as a possible successor to Fitzgerald. On March 6, 1906, Father Brady claimed to have an early tip that he was to succeed Fitzgerald as the new coadjutor bishop, but an article the next day quoted "prominent clergymen of the Diocese who do not believe it."[22]

Bishop Morris wrote Father Brady in late July 1906 that business affairs in Fort Smith "are in bad shape, I fear, and you must help me clear up the tangle."[23] By his return in December, he still had not received any financial records from the Fort Smith priest. By late January 1907, an exasperated Morris wrote Brady that since August, he had refused to send the financial records requested and if he had failed to do so, "you will be *ipso facto* suspended."[24] Morris gave him more time, warning him of suspension again in a letter dated February 8. On February 15, he formally suspended Brady from the diocese and ordered him to give all his records, financial and otherwise, to the new pastor, Father Patrick Horan. Actually, Father Brady had left Immaculate Conception in October 1906 and moved to Tontitown near Fayetteville. He was married in June 1907 before a justice of the peace in Missouri and left the priesthood. He eventually became reconciled to the Church just prior to his death in 1937, in Bellevue, Illinois.[25]

Brady's initial suspension came around the time of the fortieth anniversary of Bishop Fitzgerald's consecration, which fell on Sunday, February 3, 1907. The event was marked by a special Mass said by Father Kraemer at St. Joseph's Infirmary in Hot Springs. Now seventy-three, Fitzgerald was paralyzed and near death. Clergymen from around the state were in Hot Springs that day to give homage to the bishop who had worked so hard to advance Catholicism in Arkansas. Telegrams came from around the country, and as a token of esteem, the newspapers reported the elderly prelate was given "an elegant carriage and a beautiful pair of horses purchased with a purse of $1,500.00 raised at the suggestion of Father Michael McGill of Hot Springs."[26]

Roughly two and a half weeks after this celebration, Fitzgerald died around 9:30 a.m. on Thursday, February 21, 1907. Bishop Morris and Father Kraemer had been summoned from Little Rock to Hot Springs as death approached. Fitzgerald was given last sacraments by Morris, who was assisted by Fathers Horan, Kraemer and McGill. On Sunday, February 24, 1907, his remains were brought by a special train from Hot Springs to Little Rock, where a newspaper reported that more than five thousand people came to the Rock Island Station to receive the beloved bishop. From Sunday afternoon through Wednesday morning, the body lay in state at the cathedral that he had built a quarter-century earlier. At 9 a.m. on Wednesday, a pontifical high Mass was said in his honor. Bishop Heslin of Natchez was the principal celebrant, assisted by Fathers Horan, McGill, and Winand Aretz. Father Kraemer served as master of ceremonies, and the funeral sermon was preached by Bishop Gallagher of Galveston, then the senior bishop of the New Orleans Metropolitan Province. Other bishops in attendance included Morris, Meerscheart, Janssen, and Cornelius Van de Ven of Natchitoches; Abbot Ignatius Conrad, O.S.B., of New Subiaco Abbey was also there. Some forty priests from Arkansas, Texas, and Tennessee were in the congregation. The cathedral was thronged with Catholics and non-Catholics. After the Mass, Fitzgerald was laid to rest beside Arkansas' first Catholic prelate, Andrew Byrne, beneath the cathedral, the future resting place of all of Arkansas' deceased bishops.[27]

Bishop Fitzgerald was not soon forgotten. At a memorial Mass a year later, Father Kraemer delivered a long eulogy that was published in the local paper. The German Benedictine related an account of Fitzgerald's personal bravery. In 1878, when Memphis was suffering under the terrible yellow fever epidemic, word came to the rectory at St. Andrew's that a person was dying of the dreaded disease in Little Rock. As a Catholic, this man called for the last sacraments. With Fitzgerald was the elderly vicar general, Patrick Reilly, and a newly ordained priest. Fitzgerald told Father Reilly that he was too old to attend the man, and the young priest was too needed in Arkansas for him to go. Fitzgerald said that he would go, and no amount of complaints or objections would stop him. Fitzgerald attended to the dying man's spiritual needs, and God spared the bishop from the yellow fever.[28] While this might seem to be only a pious story, when one considers the number of brave and resourceful actions that Fitzgerald took as bishop, his conduct at the Vatican Council and his unique views on various questions, such courage would be totally in character. As Father Kraemer put it, "After forty years of hard and apostolic labor, Bishop Fitzgerald accomplished a great work, and if any Bishop ever deserves the title of having been a successful Bishop, it is Bishop Fitzgerald."[29]

With Fitzgerald's passing, the Catholic Church in Arkansas fell completely into the hands of John Baptist Morris. The year Morris had become coadjutor bishop, 1906, was also the year the Census Bureau conducted a special report on the religious bodies in the United States. The report provides an numerical assessment of Catholicism in Arkansas during the transition from the era of Fitzgerald to the era of Morris. According to this special report of the census, Catholics had 31,434 members attending seventy-two churches and halls for Sunday Mass. Yet, these numbers need to be kept in perspective. The overwhelming religious faith in the state was either found among the Baptists, who numbered 187,134 and worshipped in 2,655 churches, or the Methodists, who amounted to 134,096 and had 2,153 churches.[30] These census numbers do not correspond with diocesan estimates. The 1907 *Official Catholic Directory,* put the number of Catholics in Arkansas at around 20,000.[31] These latter numbers are probably more accurate. Still, the Catholic Church in Arkansas appeared to be a growing Church, far behind the dominant Baptists and Methodists, but now roughly equal to that of the Presbyterians. This was a major change for the Presbyterian Church in Arkansas, as they had once been one of the three major Protestant denominations in the state in the mid-nineteenth century.[32]

Baptists, white and black, made up almost half the church-going population in Arkansas, 46.3 percent, with the Methodists falling into second place with about a third of the church members. All the other denominations were distant. Those calling themselves Catholic made up 7.7 percent of those who claimed a particular church membership, yet this percentage was still higher than some other Protestant churches.[33] Arkansas ranked thirty-ninth among the then forty-five states in the proportion of Catholics to the general population. Those with a smaller Catholic population included by rank: Alabama, Mississippi, Virginia, Tennessee, Georgia, and South Carolina.[34] That Arkansas ranked as high as it did is likely due to the efforts of Bishop Fitzgerald and the railroads in bringing Catholic immigrants to Arkansas.

The number of church-goers in Arkansas was still far below the national average and the lowest in the South. The number of church-goers rose from 26.3 percent in 1890 to 30.0 percent by 1906. The national average was 39.1 percent, and the average for the eleven southern states was close at 39.0 percent. Only Louisiana had a church-going population over 50 percent. Of the remaining ten southern states, five were above and five were below the national average.[35] Too much could be read into this statistic; Arkansas, after all, was a rural state with poor roads. Moreover, the state's predominate Protestant faiths did not stress church attendance as much as other religious denominations. Yet, it is still striking that the state had the poorest church attendance in the whole South in 1906.

Whatever its size or growth, the Catholic Church found itself in much better financial shape after the forty years of Bishop Fitzgerald. The large-framed, Irish-American cleric had found a diocese destitute and left it in with financial reserves. Indicative of this situation is the fact that the bishop's brother, Joseph Fitzgerald, operating through his New York attorney, D.O. Loughlin, contested the last will of Bishop Fitzgerald. Fitzgerald gave $5.00 to his brother and left the rest to Right Rev. John B. Morris, the Catholic Bishop of Little Rock. Witnesses at the ceremony included Father Michael McGill, then pastor at St. Mary's Catholic Church in Hot Springs, and an attorney, George G. Latta. Both McGill and Latta testified in legal documents accompanying the Will that Bishop Fitzgerald was of sound mind even though he was so paralyzed that he requested assistance, and Father McGill helped him sign it with an "x" mark. The Will was presented before the Pulaski County probate court on March 20, 1907.[36]

Soon after the Will appeared, Joseph Fitzgerald's attorney wrote Bishop Morris, "I did not suppose that any one conversant at all with church history in this country did not know that your predecessor was considered the wealthiest Bishop in the country."[37] The lawyer also quoted an unnamed Catholic editor who said, "At the time of his death Bishop Fitzgerald was a man of great wealth."[38] Mr. Loughlin went on to tell the Arkansas bishop, "His brother (Bishop Fitzgerald's) holds to that opinion, and that the property was in his name (Bishop Fitzgerald's), and that, therefore, as his brother and nearest relative, he is entitled to a share of that property."[39] For the next three months, strongly worded and lengthy letters passed between Morris and Loughlin with the bishop reminding the lawyer that the bishop owned the property for the Church and that it went always to his successor and could not be divided among the bishop's relatives and friends.[40] The matter apparently was settled out of court, for that was the recommendation of the bishop's lawyer, William E. Hemingway of Little Rock. Hemingway assured Morris on September 17 that he could prove that the late bishop's Last Will and Testament was valid and that the property was deeded to him as the Catholic Bishop of Arkansas, nonetheless:

> In view of the magnitude of the estate, of the certain expense to which you would be put by litigation, of the possible losses that you might sustain by reason of having your title somewhat clouded, and of the scandal that would result from the contest, we are of the opinion that a settlement of the terms offered would be wise . . . While we think you would win your suit, it would cost you as much money to win it as to settle.[41]

Bishop Morris was quite willing to use the money saved by Fitzgerald to expand Catholic institutions and services. One of his priorities was to establish a Catholic orphanage. Morris had reserves, but he was determined not to do it alone. He began his campaign for the orphanage with a letter to the Catholic clergy and people of Arkansas on June 4, 1908. By May 1909, he reported that most of the building was complete, and the profits from the Catholic Fourth of July picnic that year would be dedicated entirely to the new St. Joseph's Orphanage.[42] While the bishop had hoped that the building would open by August, it would be late October before he saw its doors open.[43] He personally selected the site on 720 acres, five miles northwest of Little Rock, much of what is now Camp Pike, west of the city of North Little Rock. This four-story edifice of eighty-two rooms could accommodate 250 persons. The Benedictine sisters of Fort Smith took charge of the facility with only three sisters, who were joined by another sister in January 1910, when the facility housed twenty-five orphans. First known as St. Joseph's Orphan Asylum, it became known as St. Joseph's Orphanage.[44] The Orphanage was supported not only by Arkansas' Catholics, but by many non-Catholics as well. One strong supporter was the Little Rock Board of Trade, the forerunner of the Little Rock Chamber of Commerce. The Board of Trade, on June 20, 1912, set up a committee to raise funds to help the orphanage.[45] Although the German Catholic population had a newspaper, the *Arkansas Echo,* since 1891, Morris was determined to have a Catholic paper published by the diocese and appealing to a much wider English-reading audience. For this reason, one of his earliest projects was the establishment of a newspaper called *The Southern Guardian* on March 25, 1911. More than four years later, it became known as merely *The Guardian,* with Msgr. John M. Lucey, the vicar general since 1907, as the first editor (for five months). In the opening editorial, Lucey outlined the purpose: "The *Southern Guardian* will be Catholic, by Catholic it is meant Roman Catholic, loyal to the Roman Pontiff, the supreme head of the church, to the Bishop and clergy of the Diocese, and to the Catholic laity in their varied interests."[46]

The first five years of Bishop Morris' reign saw the creation of Arkansas' second Catholic college and the creation of a seminary, both in Little Rock. Little Rock College was located on a block bordered by Twenty-fifth, Twenty-sixth, Gaines, and State Streets. Father D.W. O'Hern served as first president, and Father Winand Aretz was vice president. These clerics, together with five lay professors, made up the faculty for the first academic year of 1908-1909. Only twelve students enrolled when the doors opened on September 14, 1908, with the catalog describing courses in mechanics, chemistry, electricity, mineralogy, geology, and astronomy, as well as a classical humanities curriculum. The college was open to only males and was a day school for its first year. There was also a college preparatory program or a high school for boys.[47] The next academic year, 1909-1910, eight boarding students at the school were housed at the old Mount St. Mary's Academy at Seventh and Louisiana Streets, across from the cathedral, about two miles from campus. St. Mary's had moved out to its present location in Pulaski Heights, which was on the northwestern edge of Little Rock. By the end of the first year, the bulletin of Little Rock College listed forty-seven students. After two years as president, Father D.W. O'Hern was replaced by a young, energetic priest from New York, Fr. Herbert A. Heagney, who served as president of the school from 1910 to 1923.[48]

As the college opened for its fourth year in 1911-1912, it was joined by another institution, the Seminary of St. John the Baptist. In the first half-century of the diocese's existence, the diocese either had to have the bishop train the priests, as Bishop Byrne did sometimes, or send seminarians to other seminaries. They could also try and attract some priests from Irish missionary colleges and perhaps import some priests from other dioceses. After 1892, seminarians for the diocese had been sent to the Subiaco monastery in Logan County. Morris, apparently following the belief that the priests should know his people and the bishop his priests, decided to found a seminary in Little Rock. The first classes were held on September 19, 1911, at the location of Little Rock College. Father Winand Aretz was named Rector, with Msgr. Patrick Enright and Rev. Paul Krueger serving as the total faculty for ten seminarians.[49] By 1916, the increase of students at both Little Rock College and St. John the Baptist Seminary caused both institutions to move to new facilities in Pulaski Heights. St. Joseph's Orphanage moved to the old college and seminary building.[50] In 1920, change came again, as St. Joseph's Orphanage moved back into North Little Rock, and the seminary went back to old facilities at State and Gaines. Little Rock College stayed at its location in Pulaski Heights, an isolated spot seven and a half miles from downtown Little Rock.[51]

After World War I, Bishop Morris searched for financial support for the seminary and a way to increase the number of seminarians and the scope of its ministry. In 1919, the bishop began accepting seminarians from other dioceses. Morris wanted the Catholic Church Extension Society to designate St. John's Seminary as a place where the Society would send seminarians to prepare to serve in mission fields in the United States. Since the Diocese of Little Rock was still considered a mission field with so few Catholics in the general population, it appeared to be an ideal spot to send young men for American missions. In November 1922, the Catholic Church Extension Society granted this request. The seminary became St. John's Home Mission Seminary, training priests from all over the United States to serve in mission dioceses. In 1922-1923, the seminary had sixty-two students, with Monsignor Aretz still serving as rector and having a priest faculty of seven. In its first twelve years, it had trained forty-five priests, thirty-eight for the Diocese of Little Rock and seven for other dioceses.[52]

Little Rock College went through many changes in its first years of operation. At its new facilities in northwestern Pulaski Heights, only two buildings were ready for occupancy by the fall of 1916. Fitzgerald Hall, the first building completed, contained twenty-five classrooms, laboratories on the first floor, classrooms on the second floor, a bookstore and drawing rooms, and a fourth floor reserved for dormitory rooms and a chapel. Fitzgerald Hall was trimmed with granite taken from a quarry in the Fourche Mountains. Byrne

Hall, directly across a grassy oval, was the dining hall and housed more boarding students. Morris Hall, the central administration building, was completed and occupied by the fall of 1917. That year, the United States entered World War I, a war in which 132 students and alumni would serve.[53] A student army corps was set up at the Pulaski Heights campus in 1918, and the next year, it became a Reserve Officer's Training Corps, which continued for another eleven years. When the college moved to the forty acre plot in Pulaski Heights, it also added a pre-engineering program. In 1919, it started a pre-medical program and five years later, a pharmacy program which lasted three years. By 1924, with a young priest named Albert L. Fletcher serving as president and chemistry professor, this Catholic institution of higher education was granting Bachelor of Arts and Bachelor of Science degrees. A history of the diocese published in 1925 maintained that about half of the students were of other faiths, an important witness in a state with such a small Catholic population.[54]

This witness was important, because Arkansas experienced a strong revival of militant anti-Catholicism which had remained dormant since the 1850s. Although the small Catholic minority had remained a suspicious group to the largely evangelical Protestant population, the state did not experience the anti-Catholic vituperation of the American Protective Association, an organization that flourished in the Midwest in the late 1880s and early 1890s. In certain areas of the upper Midwest, anti-Catholic groups circulated a document in 1892 which claimed to have exposed a papal plot to instigate a Catholic rebellion in the United States to bring about the extermination of Protestants. The forgery received so much currency in the anti-Catholic press that it caused panic. It was said that farmers in Illinois avoided leaving their homes because the Romanists planned to put them to the torch. A rural schoolteacher in Minnesota armed herself for a week in anticipation of the expected Catholic attack. The A.P.A., however, made very little headway below Kentucky. Historian John Higham points out, "Southerners were generally very apathetic toward anti-Catholicism and viewed the A.P.A. as a Republican tool."[55] While Higham's comment was written in the mid-1950s, recent historic scholarship on American political history has confirmed his observation. Republicans in the latter part of the nineteenth century tended to represent middle-class, nativistic, northern Protestants who believed that the growing influx of immigrants threatened their job status and the country's republican institutions. Those on the margin of society and the political system, southern whites and Catholic and Jewish immigrants, identified with the Democratic Party. This kind of "cultural-political division" was prevalent until the end of the nineteenth century.[56] As Arkansas was strongly Democratic, anti-Catholicism did not seem to be a useful issue to use to gain political power in the state.

One important cause of the new anti-Catholicism may have been the work of the frustrated radical agrarian politician from Georgia, Tom Watson.

Through *Watson's Jeffersonian Magazine*, a journal that sold well throughout the South, he launched his anti-Catholic campaign in August 1910, with a series of articles entitled, "The Roman Catholic Hierarchy: The Deadliest Menace to Our Liberties and Civilization." This was only the beginning of a crusade that reached fever pitch over the next few years, with articles about baby murders in convents, priests raping women in confessionals, and priests being described as "chemise-wearing bachelors," "bull-necked convent-keepers," "shad-bellies," and "foot-kissers." He even brought out a pamphlet of "nasty-questions" priests ask women in the confessional; this could be obtained from Watson for the modest price of twenty-five cents. In 1911, Watson organized "Guardians of Liberty," an organization dedicated to exposing the Catholic conspiracy in America. This organization, according to Watson's biographer, C. Vann Woodward, flourished until the United States entered World War I. By 1915, Watson had added Jews to his list of enemies.[57]

Watson's description of Catholics as a "menace" to American liberty would soon find an echo in a magazine published in the Missouri Ozarks called *The Menace*. In November 1911, Wilbur Franklin Phelps, a country newspaper editor in Aurora, Missouri, founded a national "patriotic" weekly to expose the threat posed by the Roman Catholic Church and its political machine. Clearly, this Missouri paper drew its inspiration from Watson, because on its masthead were the words, "Roman Catholic Political Machine: The Deadliest Menace to American Liberties and Civilization." This weekly magazine would soon enjoy phenomenal growth; by 1914, it had more than a million subscribers.[58] As with Watson's magazine, *The Menace* carried the usual lurid stories of convents and rectories, and bitterly attacked Catholics as hapless dupes of a greedy and lecherous clerical clique ruled by the immoral Whore of Babylon, the Pope of Rome. Higham reported that *The Menace* sometimes dressed its anti-Catholicism in a progressive cloak: the Catholic Church was combining with big business to break the power of labor unions; Catholic bishops were behind assaults on progressive legislation; no real democracy was possible unless Catholic power was held in check. The Johns Hopkins University historian also reported that *The Menace* soon had imitators published in other small towns in Minnesota, Indiana, North Carolina, and Magnolia, Arkansas.[59]

The newspaper in Magnolia, called *The Liberator*, was published and edited by Reverend Joseph Addison Scarboro (1857-1932), a minister of the Landmark Baptist faith, a splinter group from the Southern Baptists. In the two copies in the state archives, *The Liberator* was, by October 1913, a four-page paper that drew heavily from Watson's magazine and *The Menace*. Scarboro's paper had much the same tone as these other papers. It called for a meeting November 1-3, 1913, at the state Capitol to form a statewide chapter of an organization called the American Liberty League. There seems to be no news report that the meeting ever took place, although an announcement of the meeting is also found in the papers of Bishop Morris. Rev. Scarboro wrote

Major Charles B. Taylor in Little Rock calling for a meeting on October 30-31 at the Capitol, now the Old State House, of "patriotic Americans for the purpose of organizing the state to meet the aggression of Roman Catholicism against American liberties and institutions."[60] While it is unclear whether the meetings took place, anti-Catholicism would be manifested in the Arkansas Convent Inspection Act of 1915, otherwise known as the Posey Act.

Robert Randolph Posey was from Sheridan in Grant County, about thirty-five miles due south of Little Rock. A public school teacher who had learned enough law to be certified as an attorney, Posey won election to the state House of Representatives in 1912. In his first session, Posey introduced a bill to grant power to the local sheriff or constable to inspect convents, hospitals, asylums, seminaries, and rectories. The purpose, as stated in one section, was "to afford every person within the confines of said institutions, the fullest opportunity to divulge the truth to their detention therein." Whatever its stated intentions, its real target was, in the words of a commentator in the *Arkansas Gazette,* "the Roman Catholic institutions of the state."[61] The bill called for an inspection by a sheriff, police, or constable at any time, day or night, if twelve citizens petitioned such authorities for one. The bill sparked a large debate in the House and passed there, but it apparently was not acted on in the state Senate.[62]

Two years later, however, Posey reintroduced the bill and got it through both houses of the General Assembly. It was signed by Governor George Washington Hays in early March 1915.[63] The diocesan Catholic weekly, *The Southern Guardian,* had vigorously attacked the bill in January and February and called on the Governor to veto it. When the bill passed, the paper gave a roll count of the vote in both houses, and this revealed the strong urban vs. rural split over the vote. Country legislators generally voted for the measure.[64] Mrs. Olivia B. Clarendon, a Catholic laywoman from Hot Springs, wrote a long, biting letter to the Governor attacking him for signing a bill that he knew was illegal and a violation of religious freedom. If Catholic institutions were under such suspicion, she asked, why did Protestants go to Catholic hospitals and schools? "The new law," she wrote, "is anti-Catholic, concocted by anti-Catholics, sent to Arkansas by anti-Catholics, passed by many anti-Catholics in the legislature, backed by many anti-Catholics, especially anti-Catholic preachers."[65] She asserted that Arkansas had the dubious distinction of beginning "an official persecution of the Catholic Church in the so-called land of the free."[66]

The Governor, a strong and dedicated Missionary Baptist, had also signed Arkansas' statewide prohibition law, which made it illegal to buy or manufacture liquor in the state after January 1, 1916; he also vetoed a bill allowing pari-mutuel horse racing in Hot Springs. In the religious context of his time and within the Governor's own sincere religious faith as a Missionary Baptist, he performed a good service for the state, establishing prohibition, blocking horse-race gambling in Hot Springs, and allowing the inspection of Catholic convents, monasteries, and rectories. His only biographer, however, sees Governor George W. Hays as a man who "found it almost impossible to stand firm when powerful pressure groups sought to exert influence."[67] Abbot Ignatius Conrad of Subiaco wrote J.B. Cook, the sheriff of Logan County, inviting him to come and fulfill his duties under the new law. In a tongue-in-cheek manner, the Benedictine abbot cautioned him to be sure and come only in the daylight "so that you may see everything desirable without trouble."[68]

There was some heated opposition to the Posey Act in non-Catholic circles. State Senator George Jones of Pulaski County called it a violation of the federal and state constitutions and state Senator Lewis Josephs of Miller County, the only Jewish member of the Arkansas General Assembly, called it a clear violation of religious freedom.[69] That fall, Bishop Morris responded to a friendly note given to him by the president of the Hot Springs branch of the Arkansas National Bank. Morris wrote the banker in November 1915, "I am sure I share your views, and those of all fair minded men, when I insist that religious liberty is not for ourselves alone, but for everybody else who has a conscience and is sincere in his beliefs."[70] While the state law was not widely enforced, it remained a statute until repealed, quietly it seems, in 1937.[71] Arkansas was not the only state to pass convent inspection bills; laws were passed in Alabama and Georgia in the same time period, no doubt owing to the powerful influence of Tom Watson and his assaults on Catholicism.[72]

The Posey Bill was not the only example of strong anti-Catholicism in the state just prior to World War I. In Pulaski County, just before local elections in January 1916, a pamphlet appeared denouncing Catholics and their growing influence in the Arkansas Democratic Party. The four-page pamphlet pointed out that James S. Mahoney was secretary of the state Democratic Party and that Harmon Dearst held a county Democratic post, both "Romanists" and not loyal Americans. This pamphlet, authored by "Patriots of Pulaski County," called for the voters in the January 16, 1916, county election to support only "Protestants and Prohibitionists."[73] A bizarre and somewhat comical incident happened that fall at a football game in Russellville. Little Rock College was playing the Russellville Aggies (later Arkansas Tech), and the Catholic school was winning in the third quarter. They had just scored another touchdown when irate fans came out of the stadium and started jeering at them from the sidelines. The victorious Little Rock College squad was eventually followed to the railroad station by a large number of fans hurling remarks like "mackerel snatcher" and other "gibes and missiles."[74]

Amid this mounting anti-Catholicism, a well-publicized religious debate occurred between Subiaco Benedictine monk, Father Boniface Spanke and Otis L. Spurgeon, a professional anti-Catholic speaker from Des Moines, Iowa. Spurgeon was associated with a group called the Knights of Luther and served also as a writer for *The Menace*. A Morrilton minister had invited him to address his congregation, and his talks created quite a sensation in a town that already had a sizable German Catholic minority.[75] To respond to Spurgeon, a young Swiss-German monk from Hartmann, Arkansas, decided to rebut. Born Anthony Spanke, he was the first student at the Subiaco school to join the monastery (1892), and he was given the monastic name of Boniface. Like his patron saint, Spanke was a missionary-evangelist and a fighter, combating not only anti-Catholicism, but his monastic superiors as well. Using funds from the Catholic Church Extension Society, Father Spanke constructed a "Gospel Wagon," a portable church pulled by horses on a wagon complete with a collapsible altar on which to say Mass, a small kitchen, and living quarters. Covered by a tin roof, it could protect a small crowd from rain or shield them from the sun. Dedicated to Jesus Christ and blessed by the abbot on August 1913, Spanke enthusiastically rode off from Subiaco to evangelize rural Arkansas towing a 4,500-pound church/rectory on wheels.[76] Spanke's mission throughout Arkansas was cut short when the Benedictine was at Conway in November and heard that Spurgeon had followed his successful speaking mission in Morrilton with a series of vicious attacks on the Catholic priesthood, the Pope, and the Knights of Columbus. Deciding not to let this challenge go unheeded, Spanke drove the "Gospel Wagon" back to Morrilton. Spanke and Spurgeon met in December 1913, but decided to put off their debate until after Christmas. The debate began on January 13, 1914, and lasted nine days. On the tenth day, the jury deliberated over who had won. This religious boxing match resulted in a hung jury, although nine thought Spurgeon had won the debate and three gave it to the young Benedictine monk. Great publicity surrounded the debate with reporters from around the state and nation reporting the blow-by-blow doctrinal argument. It certainly attracted interest. A huge tent had to be rented from Kansas City to take care of the crowd of more than two thousand. Both Spurgeon and Spanke engaged in rough verbal tactics, and a few newspapers refused to print some of Spurgeon's charges.[77]

Bishop Morris, however, was none too pleased with Spanke's performance, and in early March, asked Abbot Ignatius to recall the young monk to the abbey and sell the horses and wagon. Father Boniface was recalled, the horses were sold, and for a time, the "Gospel Wagon" was parked at the abbey. Eventually, it was given to St. Joseph's Orphanage in North Little Rock as playground equipment.[78] At the end of March, Bishop Morris wrote a friend in Canada, "Yes, a debate took place, a hung jury. The general impression here is that the debate was a mistake."[79]

Sensational debates were not a way Bishop Morris hoped to mitigate anti-Catholicism; he was sure that such things only fueled animosities. He put his trust in building an educated clergy and laity with the seminary and Little Rock College.[80] Father Aretz, a close friend and secretary to Bishop Morris, wrote a man in Rogers in January 1914 declining an offer for another religious debate in that northwest Arkansas town. Aretz wrote, "It is my opinion that no good comes from religious discussions, and that it only results in misunderstandings and bitterness, which is foreign to the Christian spirit."[81] The Tennessee-born prelate also kept up contacts with prominent non-Catholics, men such as Little Rock attorney George Rose, Governor Charles Brough (1917-1921), Senator William Kirby, William Kavanaugh, and Senator Joseph Taylor Robinson.[82]

Another way to mitigate anti-Catholicism was for the bishop to participate in certain civic affairs. For example, on September 13, 1909, he made a major address before the Little Rock Board of Trade where he called upon the state government to recruit more people from other parts of the United States and Europe and to improve its roads.[83] This strong position for good roads meant he was asked years later to give the invocation at the Arkansas Good Roads and Driving Convention in Little Rock, April 12-13, 1914.[84] Despite the work of this lobbying group, Arkansas' highways remained dismal during Morris' years as bishop, up to and including World War II. His nephew remembers one of the things that infuriated his uncle was the total lack of adequate road transportation.[85]

Morris also stayed scrupulously out of partisan politics, unless the government intruded into the affairs of the Church as it did with the Posey Bill in 1915. Charles Brough solicited his help in his bid for the governorship, and William Kirby tried to enlist his help in his bid for the United States Senate in the special election of 1913. As he would with other politicians, Morris wrote Kirby that while he wished him well, "the only position I can prudently assume is one of neutrality."[86]

Regarding neutrality, the bishop was a citizen from a neutral country in Rome just at the outbreak of World War I in August 1914. The bishop was actually in Rome as part of his second *ad limina* visit to the Holy Father. In 1904, Pope Pius X had ordered new rules requiring archbishops and bishops in non-mission countries to report personally to the Pope on the conditions in their dioceses. In 1908, the Vatican removed the United States from the status of being a mission country, requiring American bishops to journey to the Holy See. Morris had come in 1909, and then five years later, just in time for the war.[87] Some twenty-five years later, Bishop Morris recalled that he and Fr. Winand Aretz traveled to Naples where they had an uncomfortable trip aboard a slow and very crowded Italian ship.[88]

When the United States entered this conflict in April 1917, Bishop Morris hoped to undermine any lingering suspicions about Catholics by showing that both he and his fellow religionist were good patriots in time of war. The Arkansas bishop, like all the other Catholic bishops, supported the war and the creation of the National Catholic War Council in 1917. To help the war effort, the diocese sold the government land around St. Joseph's Orphanage to establish Camp Pike to train troops.[89] In the fall of 1917, Morris was invited to speak at a Liberty Fund rally in St. Louis; he turned down the invitation saying,

"I can be of more service by encouraging from the pulpit, . . . You can be sure I will do what I can to encourage the sale of bonds."[90] The Arkansas bishop was so supportive of the war that he allowed his priests, in the summer of 1918, to serve in the role of Four Minute Men, government-sponsored programs to rally people to the war cause, buy Liberty bonds, and give to the Red Cross.[91]

While Morris sought to assure his fellow Arkansans that Catholics could be counted on in wartime, his fellow Catholics who were Swiss-German or of German ancestry had a more difficult time proving their loyalty. The German-speaking monks and their German-speaking parishioners in western Arkansas came under increased scrutiny. On April 13, 1917, just seven days after President Wilson signed the declaration of war, local government officials entered the Subiaco Abbey to destroy its wireless set because it supposedly was receiving orders from the German Imperial Government. The sheriff had no knowledge of how to dismantle the machine and asked the monks standing nearby, "If I were to chop it up with my axe, would that be dismantling it?"[92] Rumors then surfaced that the large supplies being delivered to the monastery were really ammunition from Germany for an uprising. To spike such rumors, Prior Augustine Stocker wrote an editorial in *The Guardian* in 1918, strongly denying any support for Germany and mentioned that government officials had inspected Subiaco Abbey the previous week. He ended the editorial with this plea:

> Why should we be suspected of disloyalty? We are all American citizens, and most of us were never Germans in the political sense. It was from Switzerland that the abbey got most of its members until the monastery could produce American-born recruits. We appeal then, to our fair minded fellow-citizens to discontinue the unjust whisperings that would make us traitors.[93]

The monks did what they could to assure their fellow Americans of their loyalty. Monks addressed patriotic rallies. A few people were surprised that they could even speak English. A cadet corps was organized at the academy, and it marched in local parades and rallies. Once when the corps was marching down the road in their khaki uniforms, they stopped at a farmer's house to ask for water. The farmer and his family were soon running out the back door screaming that the "Germans" had finally "invaded" Arkansas! By 1921, wartime suspicion of Germans had subsided and life returned to normal for the abbey.[94]

If wartime hostility to Germans in Arkansas and the nation subsided after the war, nativism and political anti-Catholicism persisted in the nation. In 1921, Congress, for the first time in U.S. history, limited annual immigration to 350,000; three years later, it slashed that number to 165,000 and put the country's immigration policy on a quota system. Immigrants from Britain and northern Europe had higher quotas for immigration than those of southern and eastern Europe. The Johnson-Reed Act, passed in 1924, banned immigration from Africa and Asia.[95]

These immigration restrictions were vigorously supported by a new hate organization, the Ku Klux Klan. The modern Klan originated in Georgia in 1915, and the organization grew quickly in its first decade. By the middle of the 1920s, it had two to five million members and was quite powerful in states like Texas, Oklahoma, Oregon, and Indiana. In 1922, the Oregon Klan elected a Democratic governor named Walter Pierce, who pushed through the state legislature the next year a law requiring all students to attend public schools, which the U.S. Supreme Court declared unconstitutional in 1925.[96]

Though quite strong in other areas of the country, the Klan was never dominant in Arkansas, though it could be influential locally. Thomas J. Terral of Little Rock defeated the Klan-endorsed candidate, William L. Cozort of Johnson County, in the 1924 Democratic primary. Terral was hardly anti-Klan, he had become an honorary member of the secret organization in Louisiana; yet, the Arkansas Klan had rejected his membership application in 1923. Nevertheless, Terral was not the official "Klan" candidate, and no Klan-supported candidate won the state's highest elected office.[97] Nevertheless, the Klan could be strong in many locales and even in Little Rock. Catholic layman, John Healey of Griffin, Leggett, Healey, and Roth Funeral Homes, remembers his father being told by the local Klan that they would see him put out of business.[98]

A real test of anti-Catholicism and the power of the Klan came in 1928 when Alfred E. Smith, a Catholic and a proponent of the repeal of prohibition, won the Democratic presidential nomination. Identified as the candidate of "Rum and Romanism," Smith faced rough sledding in the Protestant-Prohibition South. Even before Smith's nomination, ex-Governor George W. Hays, who had signed the Posey Bill and statewide prohibition, called upon his fellow Arkansans to support Smith if he won the Democratic nomination.[99]

A major reason that Smith won such support from the state's Democratic Party was that he chose an Arkansan, Senator Joseph Taylor Robinson, as his vice presidential candidate. Robinson was then the leader of the Senate Democrats, and the Arkansas Protestant and prohibition supporter won Smith's notice and approval when he confronted Democratic Senator Thomas Heflin of Alabama over the issue of Catholicism. Heflin had a long career of Catholic bashing, and the Senate had long endured his tirades against Catholics, the Pope, and the Knights of Columbus, a Catholic laymen's organization. In early 1928, Robinson publicly rebuked his fellow Southern Democrat and won backing from the rest of his party. Smith rewarded the Arkansas senator with a place on the national ticket, the first Southerner to be so honored in sixty-four years.[100] Bishop Morris congratulated Senator Robinson for standing up to Heflin writing, "We are proud of you and proud too that this splendid thing was done by a Senator from Arkansas."[101] Governor Harvey Parnell and other state

Democratic political leaders quickly fell into line behind the Smith-Robinson ticket.[102]

Anti-Smith action in Arkansas was more religiously than politically based. Anti-Smith Democrats had been organized in Asheville, North Carolina, in July 1928, by Methodist Bishop James Cannon Jr. of Richmond and Baptist minister A.J. Barton of Atlanta. The group refused to support Smith due to his Catholicism and his call for prohibition repeal. They pledged to work for the Republican presidential candidate, Herbert Hoover, and those southern Democrats still committed to prohibition. The group in Arkansas was headed by Joe T. Robinson's own minister, the Rev. Hubert D. Knickenbocker of the First Methodist Church in Little Rock, the largest Methodist congregation in the state.[103] The Catholic paper, *The Guardian,* was surprisingly quiet during the campaign, although they did speak favorably on the career of Smith, the first Catholic ever nominated to the country's highest office.[104]

Hoover captured the election in a landslide, taking 58 percent of the popular vote and sweeping the electoral college, 444 to 87. Smith won only two states outside the South. Five of the former Confederate states voted for the Republican: Texas, Tennessee, Florida, North Carolina, and Virginia. Arkansas was one of the six states to remain loyal to the national ticket, and the Democratic vote that year was about the same as those of 1920 and 1924.[105] Arkansas clearly was not a center of this type of political anti-Catholicism, although any such feelings in that direction were no doubt blunted by the natural desire to see an Arkansas senator win the vice-presidency.

World War I and its aftermath brought major changes in the way the American Catholic Church acted and spoke. To coordinate activities better during the war, the Catholic bishops set up the National Catholic War Council in 1917. After the war, in September 1919, the bishops decided to make this wartime umbrella organization permanent and rename it the National Catholic Welfare Council. Three years later, it became the National Catholic Welfare Conference. As one writer has put it, the organization was to be the Catholic Voice of America, a way to offset the power of the Protestant Federal Council of Churches founded in 1908. It had a paid administrative secretary with oversight and administrative power over five major departments: education, lay activities, legislation, press, and social action.[106]

At the outset, a few bishops felt a bit threatened by the actions of this new Church organization. Bishop Morris was one of them. He had no problems with setting up the organization *per se,* but he did not want to see it become too powerful. Morris expressed his reservations about the N.C.W.C. to Archbishop Henry Moeller of Cincinnati in September 1922. He feared that in the future, it might "restrict the activity of a Bishop in his Diocese."[108] Morris' letter came only months after Cardinal William O'Connell of Boston and Cardinal Dennis Dougherty of Philadelphia had tried to have the Pope suppress the N.C.W.C.; Archbishop Henry Moeller had been one of the ones who rushed to Rome to defend the N.C.W.C. to the Holy Father and Vatican officials. Moeller had taken with him a petition signed by 90 percent of the American bishops asking that the Pope not suppress the N.C.W.C.[108] Morris' name was not on that petition. He turned down a request to sign and wrote Bishop James Hartley of Columbus, Ohio, in May 1922 that he did not want to sign anything that could be interpreted as hostile to the Vatican and the Pope's governance of the Church in America. Without being specific, Morris ended his letter to the Ohio bishop saying that while he did not join in the effort to suppress the N.C.W.C., "You are aware that I am not in total harmony with the operations of the Welfare Council."[109] In one area, Morris was in harmony with it; both would lobby Congress and the State Department concerning the Church-State conflict in Mexico.[110] As early as 1917, Morris had become concerned about religious freedom below the Rio Grande and had written Secretary of State Robert Lansing about the imprisonments of the Archbishop of Guadalajara and the Bishop of Zacatecas.[111]

The decade after World War I saw not only changes in the American Catholic Church on the national level, but changes within the Metropolitan Province of New Orleans. In January 1918, the Holy Father created the Diocese of Lafayette, removing the territory west of the Atchafalaya River from the New Orleans archdiocese. Eight years later on August 3, 1926, the Holy See established the Metropolitan Province of San Antonio, which included all the Catholic dioceses in Texas and Oklahoma. This left within the New Orleans Metropolitan Province the dioceses of Alexandria (formerly Natchitoches, covering northern Louisiana), Lafayette, Natchez, Mobile, and Little Rock.[112]

The postwar decade also witnessed another transition; many immigrant priests, such as Matthew Saettele and Eugene J. Weibel, died or were in the twilight of their years.[113] The death in 1926 of Abbot Ignatius Conrad of New Subiaco Abbey also heralded the passing of the immigration era of the Arkansas Church. Abbot Conrad left Arkansas in May 1925 to attend a Congress of abbots to elect a new abbot primate for the worldwide Benedictine order. While visiting Einsiedeln Abbey in Switzerland, the founding abbey for the Arkansas Benedictines, he became ill in October and died the following March 13. On December 1, 1925, at a new election sanctioned by Pope Pius XI, Edward Burgert, prior at the abbey since 1923, was elected Subiaco's second abbot, a position he would hold until February 1939.[114]

Another indication of this transition from an immigrant to native church in the 1920s, was the death of Vicar General Winand Aretz in late 1929. Little is known of his early life except that he was born in 1882 in Holland, came to the United States, but arrived at Subiaco Abbey from St. Meinrad's Abbey in Indiana. After completing his training at Subiaco, Aretz was the first priest whom Bishop Morris ordained for the Diocese of Little Rock, which he did on his fortieth birthday, June 29, 1906. Aretz soon became a close adviser and confidante of the bishop. He became chancellor of the diocese in 1910 and served as the first rector of St. John's Seminary, a position he held until his death. He was with Bishop Morris in Rome in 1914 at the outbreak of World War I. In 1923, he became a monsignor and in 1926, the vicar general of the diocese. While Morris was away in Rome in the fall of 1929, Monsignor Aretz had a heart attack and died on October 1. Clearly, the diocesan paper was correct when it said in his obituary that he was second only to the bishop in the diocese.[115]

Nonetheless, the Catholic Church in Arkansas did grow between 1919 and 1929, at least according to the numbers in the *Official Catholic Directory*. In 1909, the number of diocesan and religious order priests had been equal, thirty-six, bringing the number of priests in the diocese to seventy-two. They served eighty-five churches with a Catholic population estimated at 21,000. By 1919, those numbers had not changed greatly, with thirty-six religious-order priests and forty-two diocesan priests ministering in 102 churches, to an estimated 23,000 Catholics. By 1929, the *Official Catholic Directory* was reporting that the Arkansas diocese had ninety-one priests; sixty diocesan and thirty-one in religious orders, serving 110 churches and a Catholic population estimated at 26,591. One remarkable change was that in 1907, the year Bishop Morris took over completely as bishop, the religious-order priests had outnumbered those of the diocese, thirty-four to twenty-six. By 1929, diocesan priests outnumbered those in the religious orders almost two to one.[116] No doubt, the establishment of the local seminary aided this growth in diocesan clergy.

Also in the postwar decade, a new school for boys opened near Searcy at a place known earlier as Armstrong Springs. Opened and operated by the Franciscan Brothers of the Poor from Mount Alverno in Cincinnati, it was christened the Morris School for Boys in November 1922.[117] In August 1928, it was announced that Little Rock College would begin to admit women. In early 1929, Bishop Morris had the cathedral renovated, its first renovation since it was built in 1881. The work included installing a new pipe organ.[118]

By the summer of 1929, Morris was sixty-three years old, fully bishop of the diocese for more than twenty-two years. He could point to some real accomplishments. Despite a resurgent anti-Catholicism, he had established Little Rock College in Pulaski Heights, St. John the Baptist Seminary, and the Morris School for Boys near Searcy. He started a regular diocesan Catholic newspaper, *The Guardian*, and had seen the number of priests in the diocese grow by more than 50 percent, from sixty priests in 1907 to ninety-one in 1929.[119] If he thought the worst of his years were past him, he would be wrong. In the fall of 1929, the United States experienced a great economic catastrophe, the Great Depression, and on the heels of that would come another war, much larger than the earlier conflict. He would live to see that war brought to a successful end by the United States and its allies, yet not much beyond that point. Before this era can be covered, however, another important segment of the story must be told: the efforts of Bishops Fitzgerald and Morris to evangelize blacks into the Catholic Church during an era of Southern segregation. While Fitzgerald would make some bold beginnings, it would be under Morris that the ministry to blacks would really take shape.

CHAPTER VIII

Converting the "Colored"

Catholic Efforts To Evangelize Black Arkansans, 1866-1929

IN A LETTER dated February 15, 1929, Bishop James A. Griffin, of Springfield, Illinois, commended Bishop Morris of Little Rock for his work in rural Arkansas. "I especially admire your great interest in our colored brethren."[1] In recognition of his work for evangelization of blacks, Katharine Drexel, who founded the Sisters of the Blessed Sacrament for the Indian and Colored People in 1891, asked that Bishop Morris speak at the dedication of three new English Gothic buildings at Carrollton and Washington Avenues in New Orleans on the new campus of Xavier University of Louisiana. Xavier, founded in 1915 by Mother Drexel's order, continues to be the only predominately black Catholic college in the United States. It was then being moved from its older facilities on Magazine Street to this new location. Since Mother Mary Katharine was from Philadelphia, she invited her metropolitan Cardinal Dennis Dougherty to dedicate the new facility. After the dedication, Bishop Morris gave the main address on October 12, 1932.[2]

In his remarks, he praised the spirit of Catholic education inspired by the two great commands of the Savior, love of God, and love of neighbor. Morris compared the plight of black Catholics in the South to that of many white Catholics, who had drifted away from the Church because "of the impossibility of bringing church and school to them."[3] That a major church campus for black Catholics would be dedicated in the fall of 1932, during the very depths of the depression, is quite remarkable. Almost as remarkable is the choice of the main speaker, a Catholic bishop from Arkansas, not one of the most significant sees in American or Southern Catholicism. That Morris spoke at the invitation of one of the more significant missionaries to black Catholics is a notable event in his career and an acknowledgement of his and his predecessor's efforts to evangelize blacks.

From the founding at Jamestown in the early seventeenth century through the Civil War, the Catholic religion, in what would become the United States, only affected a significant amount of blacks in the states of Louisiana and Maryland. The American Catholic Church, with the exception of a few pious clergy and some slaveholding Catholics, made no organized effort to evangelize blacks. The priority of the northern Church was to care for the overwhelming wave of Catholic immigrants between 1815-1865, most of whom did not come to the South. The Catholic Church in the slaveholding South had other problems. Historian Stephen Ochs aptly explained, "The weak condition of the Catholic Church in the antebellum South prevented it from adequately meeting the needs of either blacks or whites."[4]

Organized efforts to evangelize blacks into the Catholic Church date from the Second Plenary Council in Baltimore, in October 1866. Archbishop Martin J. Spalding, a slaveholder's son who had served at the Baltimore See since 1864, placed the topic of black evangelization on the Council agenda. The Council responded by calling for measures to bring blacks, most of whom had just been released from slavery, into the Catholic fold. With the exception of Bishops Augustin Verot of Savannah and Patrick Lynch of Charleston, both of whom had vigorously championed the Confederacy, most prelates paid little heed to the Council's call to shepherd the long-suffering African-American into the Catholic fold.[5] Some fifty years ago, historian E. Merton Coulter had opined that the hierarchy "had little success because in fact they made little effort."[6] While this judgment is both accurate and harsh, some explanation should be made.

The Catholic Church outside of the South continued to receive immigrants for a half-century after the Civil War, and committed itself to a costly alternative school system at the Third Plenary Council in 1884 to preserve Catholicism in a Protestant land. The Catholic bishops of the late nineteenth and early twentieth centuries were more concerned with keeping the baptized Catholic immigrants within the faith of their ancestors than evangelizing blacks into Catholicism. Ochs, in his mammoth study of the struggle for acceptance of a black priesthood, pointed out that most of the Catholic bishops came from immigrant stock in economic competition with blacks; many were imbued with the cultural racism of the late nineteenth century and found it difficult to accept blacks as being equal to whites.[7] The Third Plenary Council did provide for an annual collection for blacks and Indians on the first Sunday of Lent. A Commission for such missions was established and was originally headed by Cardinal James Gibbons.[8]

The Commission dispensed funds and collected money for the missions, and asked for information from the bishops as to the status of black missions. Nine years before the Third Plenary Council, Bishop Edward M. Fitzgerald had expressed strong interest in missionary work among blacks in Arkansas. Peter Benoit, a British priest of Angle-Belgian heritage, visited with the Arkansas bishop. He represented the newly founded St. Joseph's Society of the Sacred Heart for Foreign Missions, founded in England in 1866, in the London suburb of Mill Hill. For this reason, they are often called Mill Hill Fathers or English Josephites. Their founder, Father Herbert Vaughan, had come to America in 1871 with four missionary priests. He sent Father Benoit on a tour of the South in the first three months of 1875 to sound out various bishops about receiving Josephites in their dioceses. Although Vaughan had conceived of the Society for African Missions, he was willing to minister to blacks in the United States. Father Benoit was trying to identify bishops who would welcome members of the missionary society. About half of the southern prelates were interested in having Mill Hill Fathers work in their dioceses. Bishop Fitzgerald was most supportive, offering the English Josephites a whole stretch of Arkansas for mission work among blacks. No other southern bishop made such a generous offer. Because the society was new and had so many other pressing needs and concerns worldwide, the Josephites would not answer this invitation until May 1, 1898.[9]

It would not be the Josephites who established the first Catholic mission and schools for blacks in the Diocese of Little Rock. That honor belongs to the Congregation of the Holy Spirit and their imaginative leader, German-born Father Joseph Strub, C.S.Sp. As mentioned in an earlier chapter, Father Strub had been instrumental in attracting many German Catholic immigrants to settle along his land grant from the Little Rock and Fort Smith Railroad. His Holy Ghost Congregation staffed parishes from Marche to Morrilton. Together with Father Benoit and the Josephites, Bishop Fitzgerald had been eager for missionary work among blacks, going so far in 1878 as to offer the Holy Ghost Fathers all missions to blacks in the diocese, plus a grant of one thousand acres of delta land in southeast Arkansas.[10] Father Strub also approached Bishop Fitzgerald in 1878 with the idea of opening a German church and a mission to blacks in Little Rock. However, Fitzgerald was engaged in building the cathedral which was completed in 1881. He did not want to split the Little Rock church while raising funds for this project.[11] A German parish would be established in 1884 after the cathedral was constructed, but a black Catholic mission in Little Rock would have to wait thirty years from the time Strub first presented the project to Fitzgerald.

Father Strub did establish a black Catholic colony of about twenty families from Memphis to Plumerville, just east of Morrilton. None were Catholics, but all were interested in learning about Catholicism if a school and a church could be provided. Strub reported in March 1879 that he had baptized two black girls in Morrilton and that his seminary, Marienstatt, near Morrilton, would be opened that month. He wrote in September that two black men, ages twenty-four and twenty-seven, had been accepted to become either brothers or priests in the Holy Ghost Congregation. This is the first entry of black Catholics into a Catholic seminary to operate within the boundaries of the Diocese of Little Rock.[12]

Other firsts would follow at the Holy Spirit colony. The first Catholic school for blacks opened in the early 1880s at Conway, Arkansas, and was conducted by the Sisters of St. Joseph from Cluny, France. This first Catholic school for blacks in Arkansas had to close in the spring of 1883, but Fr. Strub managed to get funds from the newly created commission for black Catholic missions to reopen the school by the fall of 1884. By the spring of 1883, the colony around Marienstatt was operating the first Catholic school where white and black children attended school together. The white children were the children of the German immigrants, and the black children were mostly Protestants. To keep black children in the school, Father Strub provided free tuition from Holy Spirit funds and from the newly created Commission for Catholic Missions to the Colored People and Indians.[13]

These early schools in Conway and Morrilton would not endure; the droughts in 1881 and 1887 hurt the colony, and the Marienstatt seminary and monastery closed in 1884. Few conversions came from the schools, and black Protestant ministers preached against the Catholic schools and religion. By 1898, both the Morrilton and Conway schools for blacks had disappeared. The Holy Ghost Fathers would not work again among blacks in Arkansas until 1917, when they established a black Catholic parish in Fort Smith.[14] By 1898, Bishop Fitzgerald was centering his attention more to black evangelization efforts in Pine Bluff, not Conway and Morrilton.

Since the diocese was engaged in black education and greatly desired to convert the blacks to Catholicism, Bishop Fitzgerald decided to solicit help from the newly created Commission for the Catholic Missions to the Colored People and Indians. The earliest records of the commission, in the Sulpician archives in Baltimore, contain a letter from Bishop Fitzgerald, dated May 7, 1887, asking for funds for black missions. Four months later, he wrote that he had started one school already "for colored children;" yet, he ended with a comment which echoes the words of Ochs writing a century later, "Diocese is so numerically small . . ., that we are not able to meet the needs of the white Catholic population."[15]

The following spring, Bishop Fitzgerald wrote that he had Catholic schools for black children at Morrilton with fifty-two children, at Conway with thirty-six pupils, and at Hot Springs with fifty-five children. He also reported that the school in Pocahontas had closed because of "opposition made, I am sorry to say, by Catholics, who were not called on to contribute one single cent to its support."[16] In one of the first evaluations of black Catholic schools in Arkansas, Bishop Fitzgerald touched one major problem in establishing schools, the opposition of many white Catholics who did not want to have a black Catholic school. The bishop inferred that the whites were mistakenly fearful that the black schools would drag down their own white schools. There may also have been racism involved. Many white Catholics, influenced by the prevailing white culture of the South, held the view that education was not a real priority for blacks. Throughout the 1890s, Bishop Fitzgerald continued to seek money to keep struggling black Catholic schools alive, but there was little money sent from the Commission for Catholic Missions. By the 1890s, foreign missionary sources had either ended or were targeted to the German or Swiss-German missions.

Catholic schools for blacks were organized within the state in the last decade of the nineteenth century. In a long report dated April 16, 1891, Bishop Fitzgerald related that schools were flourishing in Pine Bluff, Morrilton, Conway, and Hot Springs. Fitzgerald also maintained prejudice was so strong against blacks that forty black families left from Morrilton and seventy others were leaving Conway for the African nation of Liberia. Whether this was true or just a rumor has been difficult for this author to ascertain. Fitzgerald claimed that many of these families had been the mainstay of the Catholic schools in the area. A Catholic school for blacks started in Pocahontas with thirty-two students; yet, another school he opened in Little Rock, in October 1890, had to shut down after three months due to lack of patronage from blacks.[17] A second Catholic parochial school for blacks would not be established in Little Rock until the episcopate of Bishop Morris. Fitzgerald informed the commission in 1896, that there were six Catholic schools for blacks, at Pine Bluff, Morrilton, Hot Springs, Pocahontas, Jonesboro, and Wynne. Except for Hot Springs and Morrilton, all were in eastern or southeastern Arkansas. Two years later, the number of black Catholic schools was reduced to three: Pine Bluff, Morrilton, and Pocahontas. By the turn of the century, the year Bishop Fitzgerald suffered his stroke, that number was down to just two, Pine Bluff and Pocahontas. In 1906, the year Morris came to Arkansas, Father Finton Kraemer wrote the last report of Fitzgerald's episcopate to the commission and stated that two Catholic schools from 1900 still were in operation. In the reports the diocese filed between 1889-1906, the number of black Catholics ranged between fifty to 250. The 1906 estimate was three hundred out of a black state population of 375,000.[18]

Pine Bluff soon emerged as the primary focus of work among black Catholics in the diocese; Bishop Fitzgerald's report of 1897 had referred to Pine Bluff as "the *colored* center of the State, and we feel that our influence over them should radiate from there."[19] Bishop Fitzgerald founded a black Catholic parish, St. Peter's, in 1895. A small frame church was replaced nine years later by a brick frame church with "pews, main altar, a set of stations of the cross costing $350.00, more or less."[20] Monsignor John Michael Lucey, longtime pastor at St. Joseph's Catholic Church in Pine Bluff, took a great interest in the missions to the blacks. Between 1890 and his death in 1914, he would be at the center of the diocesan concerns about black Catholic missions.

Born of Irish immigrants at Troy, New York, on September 29, 1843, John Michael Lucey had a colorful life before and after his ordination. His family left central New York for southwestern Arkansas to join the Irish colony at Rocky Comfort in what is now Sevier County. Three years later, his family moved to Fort Smith, where young John Michael entered the Catholic primary school associated with St. Andrew's Catholic College. His boyhood memories centered on growing up in Fort Smith and his early days at St. Andrew's. When the Civil War closed that institution in May 1861, the seventeen year old Lucey enlisted in the Fort Smith guards and saw action at Wilson's Creek and Prairie Grove. Dismissed from active service in 1863 due to injuries, he returned to now federally occupied Fort Smith, and two years later, enrolled in Fordham University from which he received a B.A. degree in 1868.

After graduation, he spent another two years training for the Catholic priesthood at Mount St. Mary's Seminary near Cincinnati, but was dismissed due to ill health and partial deafness. Back in Fort Smith, Lucey recovered his health, but not his total hearing. Still desirous of becoming a priest, he concluded his theological training directly under Bishop Fitzgerald in Little Rock. Though Lucey never totally recovered his hearing, Fitzgerald desperately needed priests and ordained him on November 10, 1872, at Immaculate Conception Catholic Church in Fort Smith. One month later, Lucey was assigned to St. Joseph's Church in Pine Bluff, a post he would hold for over forty years. Lucey was active in many areas of diocesan history; the preservation of this history was one of his major contributions. He sketched the first history of the diocese in 1892 and wrote the first history of Arkansas Catholicism (1908) and of European immigration (1911) in the *Publications of the Arkansas Historical Association*. He was quite active in Confederate veterans' affairs, serving many times as chaplain-general of the Arkansas Division of the United Confederate Veterans. He served in 1911 as the first editor of the Diocesan Catholic newspaper, *Southern Guardian*. In November 1903, Pope Pius X raised him to the rank of Monsignor, and on June 18, 1907, Bishop John B. Morris made him vicar general for the diocese, a position he held until his death in 1914.[21] In contrast to many of his white contemporaries, Lucey was an outspoken opponent of racial segregation and disenfranchisement. He severely condemned lynching in 1901 as no less than murder. This courageous stand attracted an editorial rebuke from the Little Rock *Arkansas Gazette* the very next day.[22]

Father Lucey served as the initial pastor for St. Peter's Catholic Church in Pine Bluff. Fitzgerald's report, in 1895 to the Catholic Commission to Blacks and Indians, listed him as the pastor of this church as well as St. Joseph's

Church. Lucey had become associated with the Pine Bluff Colored Industrial Institute established in 1889. It was located on the east side of Main Street across from Wiley Jones Park. Lucey had been instrumental in opening this institute with four Sisters of Charity of Nazareth. Originally secretary to the Board of Trustees, by 1898 he was a member of the Board of Trustees and overseer of the day-to-day operations of the institute, together with six Sisters of Charity of Nazareth. The institute was the principal ministry to blacks by the Diocese of Little Rock. Catholics and non-Catholics were served according to reports presented by Bishop Fitzgerald and Father Kraemer in 1899 and 1900.[23]

The Pine Bluff Colored Institute had a chapel and an Irish-born Josephite priest, Father Thomas J. Plunkett, as chaplain. Father Plunkett, S.S.J. (Society of St. Joseph), arrived in Pine Bluff in May 1898 after his ordination and built the first chapel there by 1900. Both his salary and the construction costs for the chapel came from the Commission for Catholic Missions to the Colored People and Indians. Father Plunkett left Pine Bluff in October 1900 for Nashville, Tennessee, where he stayed for twenty years and is known as the Father of the Colored Missions in Tennessee.[24]

A joint committee from the Arkansas General Assembly visited the Colored Institute in February 1899 according to an article in a Pine Bluff paper. They came away quite pleased with what they witnessed; in particular, they praised the zeal of the Sisters of Charity. This same article ended with a brief description of the curriculum, "The youth of both sexes are taught how to meet the demands of life and take care of themselves, self-respecting and self-supporting citizens. To this end, girls are taught the different branches of domestic science, cooking, dressmaking, etc., the boys are taught various trades."[25] In the racist culture of the post-Reconstruction South, these were the acceptable trades for black citizens.

More changes came to the institute in 1901, when the white Sisters of Charity were replaced by the black Sisters of the Holy Family, the second oldest black women's Catholic religious community in the United States, founded in New Orleans in 1842. Two other Josephite priests came to St. Peter's after Thomas Plunkett; Fathers James Nally, S.S.J., and John J. Ferdinand, S.S.J., by October 1902. It was Father Ferdinand who, in 1903, built a permanent brick church at St. Peter's.[26] Within two years, he would have an assistant, John Henry Dorsey, the second black priest in the American Province of the Society of St. Joseph and the third full-blooded African American priest in the United States. On June 22, 1902, John Henry Dorsey, S.S.J., was the first African American to be ordained in the twentieth century.[27] Within two and a half years, he became the first African American priest to be a pastor of a Catholic parish with a school staffed by black sisters attached to it, tending a congregation composed mostly of black Catholics.

Father John Henry Dorsey was one of the twin sons born in Baltimore, Maryland, on January 28, 1874, to Daniel and Emmaline Dorsey, a Catholic couple who raised their four children in their faith. At St. Francis Xavier parish in Baltimore, he received the sacrament of confirmation at the hand of Cardinal James Gibbons. He attended the minor seminary for the Josephites, Epiphany Apostolic College, and completed his theological training at St. Joseph's Seminary, the major training seminary of the Josephite order. Dorsey's ordination came at a time of real turmoil within the newly created society. Father John Slattery, S.S.J., the first American Provincial of the Society of St. Joseph, 1893-1904, was about to leave the order, and his place would be taken by Father Thomas Donovan, S.S.J. Turmoil in the leadership of the order did not matter to this young Catholic priest, described in contemporary accounts as having a "sonorous voice" with "elegant and flowing diction." Though only five feet, eight inches tall, Dorsey had "arching heavy eyebrows, intense eyes, a strong chin, and with a missionary cross hung around his neck and stuck into the sash of his cassock, he projected an air of authority."[28]

Soon after his ordination, Dorsey made a whirlwind speaking tour in Louisiana, Texas, Alabama, and Georgia, attracting hordes of blacks. Booker T. Washington was so impressed with Dorsey, that he invited him to give the 1903 commencement address at Tuskegee Institute. Pierre Le Beau, a Louisiana-born Josephite priest, was working in black churches in Louisiana, and remarked after hearing Dorsey speak, "If we had colored priests, we could convert the South."[29] Dorsey spent seventeen months in Mobile, Alabama, at the St. Joseph's College, a school run by the Society of St. Joseph's for black Catholics. By September 1904, Dorsey was reassigned to Pine Bluff by the new Superior of the American Josephites, Thomas Donovan. This would be Dorsey's first parish assignment, and the first time a black Catholic priest was sent to work in the South.[30]

Although welcomed initially by the white mayor of Pine Bluff, Dorsey would soon find himself in a very troubling situation. His fellow black ministers viewed Dorsey's arrival as a potential threat to their churches, and he became their implacable enemy. One of their most effective arguments was that the Catholic Church had only white clergymen, while in black Protestantism, they had ministers of their own race. Dorsey's very presence contradicted this position. This was not a time of ecumenical dialogue between Catholics and Protestants. Dorsey's other problem was Monsignor John M. Lucey. Monsignor Lucey was more than thirty years older than Dorsey and was one of the consultors in the diocese, a position especially powerful since 1900 because of Bishop Fitzgerald's illness. Monsignor Lucey had been the most prominent Catholic in Pine Bluff over the previous three decades, and it may have been difficult to accept any other priest except as a possible rival. As Ochs has pointed out, Lucey had not gotten along with any of Josephite priests who came to Pine Bluff in 1898, complaining of their lack of conversions, parish finances, and their close association with the sisters. Lucey confided to a friend that, by late 1901, he had regretted inviting the Society of St. Joseph to Pine Bluff.[31]

Things certainly did not get better when Father Dorsey arrived. Fathers Ferdinand and Dorsey did not get along from the outset. Ferdinand wrote Father Donovan that Dorsey spent all his time "from early morning till late at night with the Sisters." The black priest then inexplicably left for a mission to Fort Smith without telling anyone. On February 10, 1905, Provincial Superior Father Donovan assigned Father Ferdinand to Dallas making Father Dorsey, by default, the first black Catholic pastor of a parish in American Catholic history.[32]

Donovan had asked Lucey about appointing the young black priest to this position, and Lucey had warmly endorsed the proposal. By the end of the year, Lucey began to complain about Dorsey. The next year, 1906, was a transitional one; John B. Morris was made coadjutor in June and became bishop with the death of Fitzgerald in February 1907. Morris formed a close relationship with Lucey and appointed him vicar general in June 1907. Thus, in any dispute between Lucey and Dorsey, Morris would probably back his own, newly-appointed vicar general. That dispute was not long in coming. In his 1907 report to Bishop Morris, Vicar General Lucey complained that during Dorsey's first year as pastor, attendance was declining, and there were frequent unexplained and unsanctioned pastoral absences.[33]

One of the main problems between Dorsey and Lucey arose from the former's relationship with the Sisters of the Holy Family. Lucey maintained in his 1907 report that Mother Mary Austin, the Superior of the Holy Family sisters, wrote him fearing "criminal intimacy" between Dorsey and one of her sisters. For that reason, she replaced all of the nuns at Pine Bluff. Father Lucey received permission from Bishop Morris in the fall of 1906 to have his white assistant or himself hear the confession of the sisters. Over the course of the school year, 1906-1907, relations between Dorsey and the sisters did not go well. The local superior, Sister Regina, and Sister Columbe soon were at odds with Dorsey, while the other four sisters supported him. Historian Stephen Ochs interviewed one surviving parishioner who maintained that the two sisters who disliked Dorsey were "creole ladies from head to toe, who disliked real colored people," and wanted a white priest.[34] According to Ochs, they had the backing of Bishop Morris, who revealed his dissatisfaction with Dorsey in particular, and the Josephites in general, in a letter in May 1907 to Father John Murphy, American Superior of the French-based Congregation of the Holy Spirit. Morris felt that the South was not ready for black priests, and that segregation must continue until southern attitudes change. Bishop Morris asked Father Donovan to remove Dorsey in July 1907, "alleging concern for Dorsey's happiness in view of southern racial norms, which isolated him from the white clergy."[35]

Dorsey responded by professing enjoyment in his position and a desire to stay, a request Donovan granted. This angered Morris who felt that by failing to grant his request, Father Donovan was interfering with a bishop's control over a priest of his diocese. An ultimatum was issued–if Donovan did not remove Dorsey, the Holy Family sisters must leave. The divisions within the parish were affecting parish life. St. Peter's recorded no baptism nor first holy communion during the year 1907, a strong indicator of real division and lack of growth in this particular mission. As Stephen Ochs points out, "Morris viewed Dorsey as the culprit in the conflict."[36]

Two events in the summer of 1907 precipitated Dorsey's removal. One was Dorsey's illness; he had suffered for years with appendicitis, but distrusted southern doctors and hospitals. He wrote Donovan on July 18, 1907, "They wanted to butcher me in Pine Bluff, but I politely refused;" he had surgery at Mercy Hospital in Chicago.[37] Monsignor Lucey was upset that Dorsey had left without telling him or Morris; Dorsey claimed that he did tell Lucey and asked him to look after his parish. While recovering from his surgery, Dorsey exchanged views with Donovan concerning Pine Bluff. Donovan placed Dorsey in this old station at St. Peter's.[38]

New allegations made to Morris and Donovan by Lucey ended Dorsey's Arkansas career. The vicar general brought a serious charge against Dorsey, contained in a letter to Donovan dated September 6, 1907, and in Monsignor Lucey's report to Bishop Morris dated November 18, 1907. Lucey accused Dorsey of illicit sexual relations with an Adeline Robinson, a black Catholic convert, a teacher in the black public schools, and a morphine addict. Lucey maintained that he had witnesses to this affair: Mrs. Perry, Miss Robinson's sister, and a Dr. G.W. Bell. Mrs. Perry claimed that she turned the woman out of her house because Miss Robinson would not break off her affair with Father Dorsey. Lucey claimed that it was this well known affair which had scandalized the parish and caused a number of people to stay away from the church.[39]

Father Dorsey denied these charges. Faced with deciding between his new vicar general and a parish priest, the bishop informed Dorsey that he would not allow him to stay at Pine Bluff. Dorsey wrote a defense against these charges in a letter to Donovan dated September 16, 1907, denying a sexual affair with Miss Robinson. He claimed that Mr. Perry, brother-in-law of Miss Robinson, was a "bigoted Baptist" who did not want to see his sister-in-law join the Catholic Church, and that he had exposed Dr. Bell for overcharging on drugs. Dorsey believed that Bell was now a part of the conspiracy to get him removed. Dorsey also quoted Bishop Morris as saying that the time was not ripe for black priests and would not be for another fifty years. Dorsey ended his letter, "Once again, I am the victim of southern prejudice."[40]

This did not end the affair. Although his faculties in the diocese would not extend past October 16, 1907, Dorsey wanted to stay in Pine Bluff past Christmas. The ailing superior who died in January 1908 had no choice but to transfer the priest, even though a number of prominent black citizens petitioned Donovan to keep Dorsey at St. Peter's. It contained the names of every black physician except Dr. Bell, two directors of the Colored Institute, and the former and current principal of the state black normal college, forty-six citizens in all. Father William A. Murphy, S.S.J., Dorsey's successor at St. Peter's, claimed later on that Dorsey's real crime "was his black skin," and Lucey's "evil, suspicious mind." Father Murphy even advocated abandoning Arkansas altogether, but the Josephites would stay for another twenty-one years at St. Peter's.[41]

The whole Dorsey-Lucey affair did the Pine Bluff Catholic mission little good. By 1910, the numbers in Lucey's Colored Institute had dwindled to under fifty. In 1904, then Vicar General Father Fintan Kraemer had reported that the Colored Institute had 250 students enrolled. Undeniably, the Lucey-Dorsey fight alienated many black citizens. With so few students, the Holy Family sisters could no longer feasibly stay in Pine Bluff. Lay teachers had to be hired; therefore, few black students could afford the school. Not until 1913 would Lucey persuade the Sisters of the Holy Ghost and Mary Immaculate from San Antonio to teach at the school. Lucey himself did not live long after the Texas nuns arrived. He died in Santa Rosa Hospital in San Antonio on June 20, 1914. The *Official Catholic Directory,* after 1916, no longer referred to a Colored Industrial Institute but to St. Peter's Catholic School.[42]

Father Dorsey would make one more visit to the diocese for a preaching mission at St. Peter's on a rainy night in January 1915. Between 1913 and 1917, Dorsey had conducted a series of successful preaching tours on "Why I am a Catholic," "Bible Readings," and "Heaven, Hell, and Purgatory," throughout the South, particularly along the Gulf Coast areas of Louisiana, Alabama, and Mississippi. Father John J. Albert, S.S.J., a native of Brooklyn, was a year younger than Dorsey and had been a classmate in the seminary. He invited Dorsey, in 1913 and 1915, to speak at St. Peter's, describing himself to the bishop as a good friend of Father Dorsey. The bishop was not pleased, since the invitation was not cleared with him. He feared Dorsey's appearance would reopen old wounds. Besides, he had explicitly denied an earlier request from Father Albert in November 1913 to bring Dorsey in for a week's preaching mission. Dorsey's career had a tragic ending. The new Josephite Superior Louis Pastorelli relieved Dorsey of mission work and assigned him on August 29, 1918, to work in a black parish in Baltimore called St. Monica's. There, in September 1924, in a dispute over a disciplinary action at the parish school, a child's father, an ex-convict, grabbed a large piece of wood and struck the priest over the head; the partially paralyzed priest died two years later on June 30, 1926, in a sanitarium.[43] There would be no other black priest assigned to an Arkansas parish for over forty years.

Bishop Morris was still interested in founding missions for blacks in Arkansas. In his Commission report of 1907, a black parish in Little Rock was given as his main priority. St. Bartholomew's parish was established in January 1908, with former Father Fintan Kraemer serving as the first pastor. Father Kraemer's place was soon taken by newly ordained German-born priest, Father

Paul B. Krueger in the summer of 1910. Father Krueger's stint in the diocese was all too short and somewhat tragic. Born in Germany in 1884, he transferred to Mount St. Mary's Seminary near Cincinnati, Ohio, from an Austrian seminary. Looking for a missionary diocese which needed German-speaking priests, he asked to enter the Diocese of Little Rock in the spring of 1910. Morris gladly ordained him in June and assigned him to St. Bartholomew's and to the Little Rock College faculty. Two years later, the bishop sent him to Rome, where he obtained a doctorate in Moral Theology from the North American College. Shortly after graduation in late June 1914, he went to visit his parents in Germany. World War I broke out, and he was drafted into the German army. He had not been in the United States long enough to obtain citizenship. After he wrote Bishop Morris for proof that he was an ordained priest, he was released from actual fighting, but was forced to stay in the army as a chaplain. After the war, he could not return, since the Senate rejected the Treaty of Versailles, and the United States remained technically at war with Germany. By the time war between the United States and Germany was officially over in 1921, the young priest had died in his native country on the Feast of Our Lady of Sorrows, September 15, 1920.[44]

At the suggestion of Father Krueger, Bishop Morris had asked the predominately Dutch-Germanic Society of the Divine Word to take over the parish. The society accepted this responsibility on October 10, 1910. The first member of that congregation was Father Joseph Hoeflinger, S.V.D. (Society of the Divine Word). Servants of the Holy Ghost missionary sisters from Illinois came in September 1910 to take charge of the school from the Benedictine sisters of Shoal Creek, Arkansas, who conducted St. Bartholomew's first school year of 1909-1910.[45]

St. Bartholomew's was one of the first black missions of the Society of the Divine Word, founded in 1875, which had come to the United States by 1897. In 1905, they opened their first mission to black Catholics in Mississippi; five years later, St. Bartholomew's would be their first parish in Arkansas. The Society of Divine Word earned the reputation for having "German tenacity." Father Matthew Christman, S.V.D. (1887-1929), founded Sacred Heart College, a Divine Word Seminary in Greenville, Mississippi, in 1920. Three years later, it had to move to Bay St. Louis, Mississippi, because of Ku Klux Klan agitation. Now located on the Mississippi Gulf coast, it was renamed St. Augustine's Seminary, a place which opened its doors to black candidates at a time when the Josephites did not.[46]

The German people and nation, since the rise and fall of Hitler's Nazi regime, have been too often branded as racist. The irony is that this German-American religious order, the Society of the Divine Word, led the way in training blacks to the Catholic priesthood in southern Mississippi in the 1920s. German and Swiss-German missionary priests wrote appeals for money to the Austrian Leopoldine Society. They often commented upon the plight of southern blacks vis-a-vis southern prejudice. Father Eugene Weibel reported in a letter dated 30 November 1898 that whenever he opened his "Negro schools", he received "threatening letters from a great many whites, . . . this makes the work all the more gratifying and the schools thus deserve assistance."[47] Father Matthew Saettele, O.S.B., the great Benedictine missionary, was pastor at St. Paul the Apostle Church in Pocahontas when he wrote in 1901 that state law required that they have separate schools for blacks, which made it even more expensive for the Church. Five years earlier, writing from St. Boniface Church in Dixie, in Perry County, Arkansas, he warned "to have Negro children integrated with the white children is forbidden by state law."[48] Father Saettele often mentioned the plight of the blacks in his letters to Austria. He wrote from Pocahontas in 1905, "The Negro school has about thirty-five children and is dependent on aid from the outside. Without the school, they would grow up without anything, they would be destitute . . . Slavery is still much to be thought of here, and therefore, the pitiful, dark children are abused by the whites."[49] In 1910, while at Lake Village in Chicot County, the Benedictine observed that in his massive district, "there are a large number of Negroes, and no one cares about their spiritual well-being." In the same letter, he mentioned that he would like to start a Catholic school for blacks in Chicot County. He had the endorsement of Bishop Morris if the Leopoldine Society could help out.[50] In the same year, the black school at Pocahontas disappeared from the *Official Catholic Directory*.[51]

The two decades between 1910 and 1930 would not be happy ones for blacks in the South or Arkansas. Lynching continued to be used all too frequently against blacks. Around Elaine, Arkansas, in southern Phillips County, over two hundred blacks were killed in a series of racial disturbances in 1919.[52] At its national convention in Cleveland, Ohio, in June 1919, the National Association for the Advancement of Colored People focused a great deal of its attention on the atrocities happening to blacks in the South, with particular attention to lynching. Daniel Rudd, a prominent black Catholic layman, was sent to that convention by Bishop Morris. Rudd was born a slave on August 7, 1854, near Bardstown, Kentucky. His parents, Robert and Elizabeth Rudd, were slaves who were baptized Catholics and were united in holy matrimony. From their union came twelve children. Upon emancipation, young Daniel moved to Springfield, Ohio, where he completed his education while living with an older brother, Robert Rudd. In 1886, he founded a newspaper in Springfield, Ohio, called the *Ohio State Tribune*, a paper directed primarily at black citizens in his adopted state. Later that year, he changed the title and direction of his paper, calling it the *American Catholic Tribune*. He called on blacks to join the Catholic faith. As the paper stated proudly on its editorial page, "The only Catholic Journal owned and operated by Colored Men."[53] The paper moved to Cincinnati in 1887, where it enjoyed the support of Archbishop William Elder, once the Catholic Bishop of Mississippi. Rudd declared in an editorial in 1891,

"The Catholic Church alone can break the color line. Our people should help her to do it."[54]

Rudd organized and led the first black Catholic laymen's congress held in Washington, D.C., between January 1-4, 1889. This meeting was unique. It was not only the first congress of black Catholics, but also was the first national congress of Catholic laymen. In yet another first, the first African-American priest, Father Augustin Tolten, said the opening Mass, and Cardinal Gibbons of Baltimore welcomed the eighty black Catholics to this event. The group received a special message of support and an apostolic blessing from Pope Leo XIII. Their successful conference was culminated by a visit of Rudd and other leaders with out-going Democratic President, Grover Cleveland, at the White House.[55] That Cleveland, who had hired a substitute in the Civil War and was elected with a great deal of southern white support, would entertain a delegation from the first ever black Catholic congress was truly a remarkable event. For Daniel Rudd, born a slave in Kentucky, it was quite probably the high point of his life, saving perhaps his emancipation. One of the other leaders in the congress was Dr. William S. Lofton, a dentist in Washington, D.C. Born a slave in Arkansas in 1862, he migrated to Washington as a teenager, where he converted to Catholicism. Dr. Lofton was one of the first graduates of Howard University's School of Dentistry. He gave a major address at the second black Catholic laymen's congress held in Cincinnati, July 8-10, 1890.

Rudd's *American Catholic Tribune* left Cincinnati in 1894 for Detroit, where the paper was published for another five years. After it suspended operation in 1899, Rudd moved to the South. The 1910 census had him operating a lumber mill in Bolivar County, Mississippi. By 1919, Rudd had moved to Madison, Arkansas, in St. Francis County. There he served as an accountant for a well-to-do black farmer and merchant, Scott Bond, and his son, Theo Bond.[57] In May 1919, Rudd asked Bishop Morris for $60.00 to attend the N.A.A.C.P. National Convention, June 21-24, 1919, as a representative of the diocese. Morris denied his request to be an official representative of the diocese, but gave him a check for $60.00 to cover his expenses as "I have great personal confidence in you." Rudd went to the convention and sent a great deal of printed material to Bishop Morris.[58] The following year, while working as an accountant for John Gannon, a prominent black farmer-merchant in Marion, Arkansas, in Crittenden County, Rudd asked for financial assistance to attend a black Catholic laymen's convention in September 1920 at Washington, D.C. Morris wrote back, "Our colored population is not more than five hundred souls. So far as I know, I am not sure, this would not entitle us to a delegate."[59] Six years later, Bishop Morris appointed Rudd as a delegate to represent the black Catholics of Arkansas at the Eucharistic Congress in Chicago; Rudd wrote back in July that the appointment came too late for him to attend.[60] Rudd continued to live in eastern Arkansas until 1932, when he suffered a stroke and went to live with relatives in Bardstown, Kentucky. There, this father of the first laymen's congress of black Catholics and the first black editor of a national Catholic newspaper, died on December 3, 1911, at the age of seventy-nine. [61]

Bishop Morris was not content with supporting certain black laymen. He founded three black Catholic parishes between 1917-1929; two of these parishes were staffed by members of the Congregation of the Holy Ghost, a religious society which had founded many churches for German immigrants in the 1870s and 1880s, along the Little Rock and Fort Smith Railroad. During the Dorsey-Lucey affair, Morris had conferred with the provincial of this society, Father John Murphy, about the Holy Spirit Fathers working in Pine Bluff. However, Morris decided to keep the Josephites at St. Peter's.

In 1910, the Spiritans, as the Congregation of the Holy Spirit is sometimes called, elevated a new provincial in Father Eugene Phelan, C.S.Sp. During his twenty-three year tenure, he began to have the Spiritans staff black Catholic parishes in the South.[62] In 1910, Bishop Morris asked the Holy Spirit Fathers to operate a black Catholic parish in Fort Smith. Although this offer was accepted, no priest was sent to the area until 1917. Father Henry Koren, C.S.Sp., the official historian of the Spiritans in America, knows no reason as to the delay.[63] Father John M. Lundergan, C.S.Sp., who called his parish St. John the Baptist after the bishop's patron saint, started in 1917 with only thirty-five Catholics out of a city population of about five thousand blacks. Bishop Morris and Mother Katharine Drexel contributed money for the purchase of the land for a church and school, dedicated in 1920. By 1927, the school had sixty-six students, of which fifty-five were non-Catholics. The parish itself consisted of only seventy Catholics, but its Catholic population had doubled in the ten year period.[64]

Ten years after founding St. John the Baptist parish, the Holy Spirit Fathers founded their second black Catholic parish in the Diocese of Little Rock, in Helena, at the opposite end of the state. Helena was a town along the Mississippi River, existing on an agricultural economy, with a large black population. Provincial Father Phelan sent Father Henry Thessing, C.S.Sp., a native Arkansan, to Helena in the fall of 1927. He could only find five blacks who called themselves Catholic in all of Helena. Undaunted, Father Thessing built a small frame church in the black area of Helena with funds the bishop received from the Commission for Catholic Missions to the Colored People and Indians and the American Board for Catholic Missions. In order to complete this structure in a year, Father Thessing lived in great poverty which injured his health.

Father Thessing was replaced a year later by Father Timothy A. Murphy, who celebrated the first Mass in the church on October 8, 1928. The first week, seven people attended and the next week, only five. Soon, no one came at all; he had to borrow the altar boys from St. Mary's, the Catholic church attended by whites. Murphy queried blacks as to their reasons for not attending his church, for even blacks baptized as Catholics were not coming. He found that rumors were circulated by black ministers that Catholics were not Christians, that one had to pay to become a Catholic, and pay even more money to get themselves or relatives from purgatory to heaven. Other stories making the rounds were that Catholics wanted to place blacks back in slavery and that joining them would be a sure way to go to hell. Father Murphy fought these allegations with pamphlets explaining the Catholic Church; he went from house to house handing this literature to black citizens. On Christmas Day, 1928, he had his first convert; by August 1, 1929, ten people had converted to Catholicism, and together with the original five Catholics in Helena, Father Murphy now had a thriving parish of fifteen! Father Murphy's hard work and persistence had literally started the parish from nothing. When he left in 1933, there were fifty members of the parish, enough for the church to survive. It was a tenfold increase from the time Fr. Thessing had found only five black Catholics in 1927. Helena's black Catholic church was called St. Cyprian's, after the bishop, saint, and martyr from the North African city of Carthage, who lived and died during the first half of the third century A.D. Two teaching sisters arrived in 1937 and that fall, St. Cyprian's black Catholic school opened its doors, giving new life and educational benefits to the black citizens of Helena.[65]

In 1929, Bishop Morris opened a black Catholic parish in North Little Rock. The first Catholic parish established in the city was St. Patrick's in 1880, and the second was St. Mary's founded in 1901.[66] The Society of the Divine Word agreed to staff the black parish, as the priests from St. Bartholomew's had been visiting black Catholics on the north side of the river for years. Father Joseph Haarmann, S.V.D., wrote Morris from Cleveland, Ohio, in May 1929, that he would be ready to assume his duties. Bishop Morris had big plans for this parish christened St. Augustine's. Father Haarmann said the first Mass on September 9, 1929, and the school opened the very next day.[67] Morris and the new Divine Word pastor had differences. Morris complained to Haarmann's Provincial, Father Bruno Hagspiel, S.V.D., that the North Little Rock pastor had expensive tastes for a black Catholic parish in a poor diocese at the time when the nation was in the grips of a severe depression. Morris wrote in January 1931 that Haarmann "ran up bills for others to pay . . . a good priest, a zealous priest, but no administrator."[68] The provincial soon replaced Haarmann with Father A. G. Steig, S.V.D., who served as pastor at St. Augustine's for the next fifteen years, and who continued to keep the school operating for the rest of Morris' episcopate.[69]

What is striking about these new Catholic parishes in Helena and North Little Rock, is that they were named for early Catholic saints and bishops of North Africa. As Father Cyprian Davis, O.S.B., the historian of American black Catholics points out, other Catholic ethnic groups named churches for their European patrons: the Irish for St. Patrick's, the Germans for St. Boniface, or the Italians for St. Joseph. Black Catholics consciously reached back to an earlier age, when the Christian Church had strong areas of strength in what is now North Africa. This African connection was made by the naming of various black Catholic parishes after Sts. Augustine, Monica, Cyprian, Cyril of Alexandria (an Egyptian), Perpetua and Felicity (early Catholic Christian martyrs in the ancient city of Carthage in North Africa, c. 202 A.D.), and St. Benedict the Moor, a descendant of black slaves from North Africa. Prominent black Catholic parishes in America are named for these saints. One Catholic Church in Harlem is called St. Benedict the Moor. Father Dorsey, S.S.J., served at St. Monica's Catholic Church in Baltimore. The Seminary for the Divine Word Society at Bay St. Louis is called St. Augustine's.[70] A Father Davis writes, "Black Catholics had fashioned for themselves a rootedness in Christian antiquity that neither the Irish nor the Germans possessed; they had made a link with Africa that no black Baptist or AME church member could ever forge. They had a ready-made history that the average American Catholic lacked."[71]

The Society of the Divine Word not only started a parish at North Little Rock in the late 1920s, but also took over the church at Pine Bluff in 1928. Father John F. Thompson, S.S.J., arrived at St. Peter's in September 1926, the last Josephite to serve the parish. He was only thirty-three years old and had been a priest for a little more than two years. Within a year and a half of his arrival, there was a major division within the church. In April 1928, one faction wrote Monsignor Winand Aretz, vicar general at the time, requesting that Father Thompson be removed since the parish was in total confusion. Thompson had insulted members of the parish and was prejudiced against blacks.[72] Father Thompson denied all these charges in a four-page response. He had his own list of supporters and ended his letter by saying that he disliked his assignment, having been falsely told that he would be there for only three months. If the bishop wanted him to leave "my feelings will not be hurt, and I could leave on very short notice."[73]

Eventually, the affair escalated to the point that Father Thompson had the police arrest a parishioner, a Mr. Seymour Jones, for sending him a threatening letter. A delegation came to Little Rock in August to meet with the bishop about the affair and to call upon him to remove Fr. Thompson.[74] The bishop settled the dispute by having the charges dropped against Jones and removing Father Thompson as pastor. The dispute between Mr. Jones and Father Thompson was the final straw for the Josephite order in Arkansas. Divine Word Father Bruno Drescher now took up his duties October 12, 1928.[75] Three decades of an all-too-stormy relationship between the Society of St. Joseph and the Diocese of Little Rock now ended, but not without some results. The Archives of the Josephites reveal that in the thirty years at St. Peter's, there were 347 baptisms and of these, 204 were converts.[76]

In January 1927, Morris delineated his view of what he called "Negro Mission Work" in a long address to the Commission for Catholic Missions to the Colored People and Indians, outlining problems with promoting efforts at black Catholic evangelization. Morris accurately pointed out that blacks in Arkansas were primarily farmers, sharecroppers, who worked at the lowest end of the economic scale. In the cities they were relegated, due to prejudice, to mechanical trades, railroad work, and postal services. The little education for blacks in Arkansas in the late 1920s was provided by the state government, although the black Baptists and Methodists did operate colleges for blacks in Little Rock. Morris was incorrect on this point. There was a state college for blacks in Pine Bluff, and the African Methodist Episcopal Church was operating Shorter College in North Little Rock.[77]

Morris pointed out that the first thing one must consider in evangelization efforts is that "the negro is not a pagan, but rather as intensely Protestant as his white neighbors."[78] He observed what historians and sociologists have long known, "In both the city and country, the foundation of the colored man's social life is built around the church. And the Negro Protestant is, so far as I can see, untouched by the indifferentism so prevalent among the whites."[79] Morris also points out that another significant institution within the black community is the fraternal societies and/or lodges. For a black to become a Catholic, means a virtual separation from much of his own community. Segregation laws in Arkansas and the South made it more expensive to maintain separate churches and schools for blacks. Morris echoed Stephen Och's comment about the antebellum Catholicism in the South and Bishop Fitzgerald's comment to the same commission forty years earlier. Arkansas and other southern dioceses "are all poor missionary districts with a tremendous burden of trying to supply the needs of the scattered white Catholics and helping them to provide for themselves the very necessities of religion. To this burden is added the necessity of maintaining separate schools and churches for the colored people."[80] Morris concluded with an optimistic hope that the Catholic Church "has a great future among the colored people. For the negro . . . must first be won over through sympathetic interest in him and made to feel that the Church will not play him false, . . . the negro has a pride of race and quickly senses lack of sympathetic interest."[81]

By the year 1929, Morris could see some real progress in his efforts to minister to the few black Catholics in Arkansas. When he came in 1906, there had been only two black Catholic churches and schools in the state; the one in Pocahontas closed within a few years. He had established four more black Catholic churches and schools, three operated by the Society of the Divine Word: St. Bartholomew's in Little Rock, St. Augustine's in North Little Rock, and after 1928, St. Peter's in Pine Bluff. The Holy Spirit Congregation, still important in maintaining many Catholic churches along the Little Rock and Fort Smith Railroad, had two black Catholic churches at opposite ends of the state; one with a church and school, St. John the Baptist in Fort Smith, and one black Catholic congregation in Helena at St. Cyprian's. The amazing thing is that not only would these churches survive the Great Depression, but they continued after the bishop's death in 1946.

CHAPTER IX

Talks, Trials, and Transition

The Latter Years of Bishop Morris, 1929-1947

THE YEAR 1929 was of great significance to the episcopate of Bishop Morris. He set up his fifth black Catholic parish, renovated the cathedral, and journeyed to Rome for his fifth *ad limina* visit to the Holy Father. Having attended seminary in Rome and having made *ad limina* visits in 1909, 1914, 1919, and 1924, Morris was no stranger to the eternal city. As he was in Rome at the outbreak of World War I in 1914, he would be there, on his last visit, just in time to see the outbreak of World War II in 1939. In 1929, he was meeting Pope Pius XI for the second time.[1] Although he had been the Catholic bishop of Arkansas for only twenty-three years, Morris had met three Popes: Pius X (1903-1914), Benedict XVI (1914-1922), and Pius XI (1922-1939). Morris would live long enough to serve under yet another Pope, Pius XII (1939-1958), although the outbreak of World War II precluded his personally meeting this last pontiff during the 1939 *ad limina* visit. Nevertheless, the Tennessee native served under four pontiffs, more than any other Arkansas bishop in the 150 year history of the diocese.

In another way, 1929 marked a turning point in Bishop Morris' episcopate. When he returned to Little Rock from Rome, Morris felt the loss of his dear friend and chief subordinate, Vicar General Winand Aretz, upon whom he had depended to help him run the diocese. After Aretz's death, Morris would look for, and soon find, another trusted aid, Albert L. Fletcher. So much faith would Morris invest in this man, that he would recommend to Rome that Monsignor Fletcher be named his auxiliary bishop, a position he acquired in

1940. Trying to avoid the problems that had followed Fitzgerald's stroke forty years earlier, Morris knew that his age and growing infirmity might create real problems. Now that he was in the twilight of his life and service to the Catholic Church, Bishop Morris wanted it to be quite clear that one person was in charge. Indeed, there would be no doubt about this because the man would bear the title of auxiliary bishop.

In the year 1929, the country entered its greatest economic upheaval, the Great Depression, which would last until the United States entered World War II twelve years later. The war energized our country's manpower, economy, and society. For sixteen of the seventeen remaining years of Morris' career as bishop, these concerns would consume the attention of citizens of state and nation. The national depression, threatening world events, and finally, America's plunge into war, would alarm Arkansas' aging Catholic shepherd.

While he was between sixty-three and eighty, years when most people enjoy retirement, Morris was called on to deal with these crises. A nation during a depression and war needs reserves of inspiration, and Morris' reputation for wit and after-dinner oratory fetched him many invitations to speak at Catholic events around the country. Priests who still recall Bishop Morris during these years are more apt to remember his quick and ill temper, which flared more and more as he experienced the pain of infirmity and old age. Others would remember a manner more crotchety and a style more autocratic as he struggled with advancing medical problems, but the flow of his pen remained steady. He kept up an undiminished tide of pastoral letters, musings to a wide circle of friends in the American Catholic hierarchy, and correspondence with his family, in which he poured our his deepest feelings and opinions.

One must remember also that no one served longer, actively in the diocese than did John Baptist Morris. Technically, Bishop Fitzgerald lived longer as reigning Catholic bishop, but in the last seven years of his life, he was incapacitated and did not run the diocese in any meaningful way. Not so with Morris. While he delegated power to his auxiliary bishop during the last six years of his reign, he kept a loose, yet steady hand on the overall affairs of the diocese. Almost until the day he died, October 22, 1946, he wrote letters and directed major decisions in the Church. To be sure, it must have been difficult to yield power due to his advancing age.

Yet, the last seventeen years for Bishop Morris were not all sorrow and suffering. He celebrated his twenty-fifth year as bishop in 1931, and in 1942, he had a grand celebration of the fiftieth anniversary of his ordination to the priesthood. He also presided at the centennial celebration of the creation of the Diocese of Little Rock in 1943. This era of turmoil and trouble brought some institutional losses, yet mainly the diocese witnessed continued growth.

Morris returned from Rome to learn not only of the death of his beloved vicar general, but of a staggering blow to the nation's economic structure, the stock market crashes of October 1929. The stock market plummet did not cause the economic crisis that came to be known as the Great Depression, but it indicated that the economy was in grave trouble. It got worse. By the end of the year, unemployment stood at 8 percent; by the spring of 1933, it would be at 33 percent, the highest in American history. In Arkansas, more than a third of the state's work force lost their jobs between 1929 and 1932, and income was lower in Arkansas than in any state except Mississippi. Cotton prices fell from twenty cents a pound in 1927, to five cents by 1932, which alone was a tremendous loss of income because 80 percent of Arkansans were farmers in 1930. Nearly half the state's businesses had closed by the end of 1931.[2] Catholics were about 1 percent of the population in 1930, and they were not the wealthiest people. Aside from a few individuals, Catholic citizens were either first or second generation immigrants.

The diocese itself was far from financial collapse, yet it was hardly brimming with monetary funds. Morris had spent a great deal of money, which was left to him by Bishop Fitzgerald, on diocesan projects such as Little Rock College (Arkansas' second Catholic institution of higher education), the diocesan newspaper, *The Guardian*, and a residential seminary. The first to take a direct hit from the Depression was Little Rock College. In a front-page article in *The Guardian* on July 12, 1930, Bishop Morris announced the closing of the college. Its Pulaski Heights campus would be turned over to the seminary, and the old seminary building at Twenty-fifth and Gaines Streets would become Catholic High School for Boys at Little Rock.[3] A prefigurement of this closing came when Little Rock College School of Pharmacy closed in the spring of 1927 after three years of operation, leaving Arkansas without a school of pharmacy until 1946.[4] As the Civil War had closed the first Catholic college, St. Andrew's in Fort Smith, so the Great Depression would end the Diocese of Little Rock's second, and apparently last, attempt to found a Catholic institution of higher learning in Arkansas.

As the Depression worsened in January 1931, Bishop Morris sent a circular to his priests asking if there were people in the churches who needed financial assistance, how many heads of families had lost their jobs, and if there were church members who were destitute. Priests replied, and Morris often responded with the amounts they requested. There was no public campaign, and the private way that it was done preserved the pride and dignity of those receiving the aid. This was before the creation of broad public assistance programs (the seriousness of the Depression created the welfare system); and in 1931, many Americans thought the acceptance of any aid was demeaning. While this appears to have been a one-time effort to deal with the problems of unemployed Catholics, it indicates that Morris cared for his people's welfare and sought to help them in ways that did not embarrass or offend them.[5] It should also be remembered that the funds of the Diocese of Little Rock were not limitless.

Depression or not, Morris intended to celebrate his twenty-fifth jubilee as bishop at ceremonies on May 6-7, 1931. On Wednesday evening, May 6, the public celebration began with many dignitaries on hand at the old Little Rock High School on Park Street between Fourteenth and Sixteenth Streets. This show of public support included the mayor of Little Rock and Governor Harvey Parnell.[6] At a major ceremony the next morning at the seminary campus in Pulaski Heights (now St. John's Catholic Center), Archbishop Samuel Stritch of Milwaukee helped celebrate the pontifical high Mass. Like Bishop Morris, he was a native of Tennessee. He was also related to the Arkansas bishop by marriage. (One of Morris' younger sisters, Ellen, married Thomas Stritch, older brother of Archbishop Stritch.)[7] Together with Morris' metropolitan archbishop, John Shaw of New Orleans, Archbishop Stitch celebrated the pontifical high Mass on the morning of May 7, not at the cathedral as Bishop Fitzgerald had done some forty years earlier, but outside, on a special pavilion with a temporary altar constructed on the oval of St. John's Seminary. Twenty-seven bishops and seven archbishops, including Cardinal Dennis Dougherty of Philadelphia, attended the ceremony. That night, six hundred guests attended a banquet at the Arlington Hotel in Hot Springs.[8] Having the concluding dinner at Hot Springs was appropriate because Morris was returning to the city where he began in Arkansas, where Fitzgerald had died, and which he had visited when he knew he was the bishop-elect. Four years later, on May 21, 1935, Morris would give the main address in Milwaukee, on the twenty-fifth anniversary of the priestly ordination of Archbishop Stritch.[9]

Archbishop Stritch was not Morris' only close and powerful friend in the Catholic Church. Although Morris kept a high level of correspondence with other prelates, so large that the correspondence fills a complete box in the Diocese of Little Rock archives, one of the strongest friends in the American hierarchy was Cardinal Dennis Dougherty of Philadelphia.

As mentioned at the beginning of the last chapter, Morris spoke at a building dedication at Xavier University in New Orleans in the presence of Archbishop Shaw of New Orleans and Cardinal Dougherty, a year and a half after his own twenty-fifth anniversary as a bishop. Dougherty was only one year senior to Morris and shared with him an Irish background and modest beginnings. The men had studied together in Rome, and both felt strongly called to be missionaries, although in completely different areas. Cardinal Dougherty had been bishop in the Philippines between 1903-1916 before returning to the United States to become the Bishop of Buffalo, New York. Morris served as a priest and bishop in two missionary dioceses, Tennessee and Arkansas. Morris' correspondence with Dougherty lasted from 1918 until the Arkansas bishop died in 1946. With no other prelate did he correspond as frequently. Dougherty invited him to his installation as Archbishop of Philadelphia in 1918, and the two remained friends throughout their careers.[10]

Since Morris needed both financial and clerical assistance to run the diocese, it was in his interest to foster closer relations with dioceses that had money and men to spare for priestly work. On occasion, he went to St. Charles Borremeo Seminary, near Philadelphia, to ask the seminarians to think about becoming priests for his diocese. Morris wrote Dougherty in 1936, "I am indeed gratified for your kindness in permitting me to go to Philadelphia in search of candidates for our Seminary."[11] Dozens came from the Philadelphia area, but only about two dozen actually remained to serve in Arkansas.[12]

During the 1930s, Morris was invited to speak at functions around the United States and beyond. While Morris was in Rome at his *ad limina* visit in August 1934, Cardinal George W. Mundelein was celebrating his episcopal silver jubilee and had rented out the *Colegio Santa Maria del Lagoa* house for graduate students in Rome. Bishop Morris gave the principal speech and paid tribute to his friend as the "Cardinal of the Home Missions." (Chicago was the home of the Catholic Extension Society, headed by Auxiliary Bishop William O'Brien.)[13] When German-born Joseph F. Rummel was installed as the ninth Archbishop of New Orleans on May 15, 1935, Bishop Morris delivered the sermon. In his homily, the Arkansas prelate pointed out that when he first went to a meeting of the Province of New Orleans in 1906, almost all the other bishops were twenty years older than he; now, twenty-nine years later, he was the senior bishop of the provinces of both New Orleans and San Antonio.[14]

The following year, Bishop Morris was called on to give other lectures and homilies around the country. On May 6, 1936, at the installation of William Adrian as Bishop of Nashville, Bishop Morris delivered the homily. At the centennial celebration of the Diocese of Nashville on October 3, 1937, the Arkansas prelate delivered the main speech, as he was the first native Tennessean to be named to the Catholic hierarchy.[15] On October 17-20, 1938, at a National Eucharistic Congress in New Orleans, he gave the main bishop's discourse honoring the Holy Father, Pope Pius XI. He also gave oral presentations on the golden anniversary of the founding of St. Vincent's in Little Rock and of the Olivetan Sisters of St. Benedict at Holy Angels convent in Jonesboro, Arkansas.[16] From 1939, until his death seven years later, Morris would cut back his traveling and speaking engagements due to his declining health, especially an ailing knee that really began to hamper his movement by the late 1930s.[17]

One of Bishop Morris' last public addresses was an attack on Nazi Germany and its war upon its Jewish population. After the famous attack on the Jews, *Kristallnacht*, the Night of the Broken Glass, November 9-10, 1938, the state commander of the American Legion, B.A. Brooks of Fayetteville, asked Morris by telegram to address a rally called an "Arkansas Christian Protest of Treatment of Jews in Germany and Prayers for Their Deliverance." Brooks wrote that while many public officials, Christians and Jews alike, would be on hand, the major speeches would be given by Governor Carl Bailey, Reverend J.K. Cooper of Pulaski Heights Methodist Church, and Bishop John B.

Morris.[18] The presentation, held at the Little Rock High School auditorium, was presented on the evening of November 23, 1938. Bishop Morris eloquently and vigorously denounced the Nazi persecution of "a defenseless and innocent race" and actions contrary "to the principles of the country and the Church to which I belong."[19] Morris said that all humans shared certain God-given, inalienable rights that could not be taken from them. "We, the people of this nation, can, by rising up as one man, in union with the free peoples of other nations, give expressions of our detestation of such injustice," he declared.[20] Morris said that Americans should protest the persecution of the Jews "lest by our silence we appear to give assent to the perpetration of a grave injustice to a free people." Free people, he asserted, must be "tolerant of others' rights, but not their injustices."[21] He recalled that the Holy Father, Pope Pius XI, a year earlier had condemned Nazism as being rooted in paganism and contrary to Christian faith and charity.[22]

This would be his last major address. It was rare then to hear from American Catholic bishops such a strong condemnation of the anti-semitism of Nazi Germany. Cardinal George Mundelein of Chicago had raised a diplomatic storm by referring to Hitler as an "inept paper hanger." Germany protested and withdrew its ambassador to the Holy See.[23] While Morris' remarks did not receive distant attention or reaction, a survey of American Catholic bishops of that time produced no address matching his powerful attack on Nazi anti-semitism.[24]

Bold action accompanied the bold voice. In the depths of the Depression, Morris opened a black Catholic orphanage on land he had bought southeast of Pine Bluff. Fr. Bruno Drescher, S.V.D., a priest for almost thirty-five years and the pastor of St. Peter's Black Catholic Mission since 1928, had broached the idea to Morris. On St. Patrick's Day, 1931, Morris committed diocesan funds and obtained money from the Catholic Extension Society and the Commission for Catholic Missions to the Colored People and Indians. He bought a 582-acre farm and built an orphanage and work building. The Arkansas bishop hoped that the farm could help sustain three hundred people.[25] Bishop Morris wrote E.A Burrow, editor of the *Ozark* (AR) *Spectator* in 1934, that as a Southerner and a native of middle Tennessee:

> I have always been anxious to do something for the colored people, and while I have built several churches and schools in various places, I feel that the door to heaven is open also by giving these poor people food and clothes, and hence the inspiration for the orphanage. It is the first of its kind in this part of the country . . . I hope, through its large farm, it may succeed and become the home of many homeless and destitute children.

St. Raphael's Catholic Colored Orphanage opened on October 23, 1932, with about eight children. Father Drescher served as both pastor and director, and the orphanage was soon staffed by three nuns from the Benedictine convent in Fort Smith. Although the experiment started out with great excitement–one report in 1933 claimed that it was revitalizing St. Peter's Catholic parish and the black Catholic community in Pine Bluff[27]–a few problems at the outset hurt this noble cause. Father Drescher's superiors in the Society of the Divine Word informed Bishop Morris on June 10, 1933, that they were pulling him out of his work at St. Raphael's, but keeping him as pastor at St. Peter's. Curious about this move, Bishop Morris sent Father Gregory H. Keller and consultors with the Southeastern Deanery to investigate. On June 22, 1933, Father Keller, who headed the investigation, wrote the bishop, "Personally, I think that the orphanage is the greatest work that has been attempted for the colored people of Arkansas in its history."[28]

Bishop Morris wrote the Provincial of the Divine Word asking that Father Drescher be retained at St. Raphael's and sent them a copy of Fr. Keller's report and letter. This was all for naught, as Father Drescher wrote Morris on September 14 that he would like some rest from his duties and that he would abide by the decision of his superiors.[29] Father Drescher stayed in Pine Bluff as pastor of St. Peter's, but Edward Rinck, a major financial supporter of the project and of Father Drescher, was angry and wrote letters to Bishop Morris and the Divine Word Fathers asking that either Morris make Drescher a diocesan priest or the Society reinstate him at St. Raphael. Mr. Rinck wrote Monsignor Albert L. Fletcher, Chancellor of the Diocese, that he did not blame Morris, but the Society. Still, he wanted Morris to make Drescher a diocesan priest. Monsignor Fletcher informed Mr. Rinck a few days later, that in view of the fact that Father Drescher had been in the Society for almost thirty-five years and did not really want to leave it, he would not try to change the man's mind and interfere in what he believed to be a matter between Drescher and his provincial.[30]

While it was not apparent at the beginning, Drescher's departure as director and pastor at St. Raphael's was probably a mortal blow. He had built up the trust of the black community in the previous five years at St. Peter's. Drescher was a hard-working German who ran the place well and got along with the Benedictine sisters; he would not be replaced easily. His immediate replacement, a diocesan priest, Father John J. Hesselbrock from Cincinnati, stayed only four months. Two other priests, both diocesan, came later. Fr. Henry W. Nix stayed from February 1934 until he was replaced in June 1935 by Fr. Thomas Reynolds, who did a reasonably good job of running the orphanage. The problem was finding someone who could direct the overall facility. Eventually, a Mr. Anthony J. Tucchi directed the farm, and the priest the orphanage, but the farm's income proved not to be as dependable as Morris had hoped.[31]

What killed St. Raphael's in the end was that blacks, unlike whites, were unwilling to place their children in an institution run by whites whom they did not know or trust and operated by a Church they did not belong to. The orphanage had started with eight children in the fall of 1932; by the spring of 1937, only twenty-two children were in a facility that could accommodate 150 orphans.[32] At the end of 1937, Morris decided to change the nature of the facility, and the chancellor, Monsignor Fletcher, informed Reynolds of the decision on December 18. Fletcher wrote that "the unexpected difficulty in obtaining orphans and the uncertainty of support from the farm, has prompted him to make the arrangements for changing the character of the institution."[33]

Bishop Morris poured out his disappointment in April 1938 to Auxiliary Bishop William O'Brien of Chicago, head of the Catholic Extension Society. He said that he had founded a black Catholic orphanage, "but I did not find this work promising because the Colored People of this section have peculiar ideas about orphans. They don't like to send them to institutions but take them into their own homes and, I believe, look after them very well."[34] In the same letter, he said that he was turning the institution into a vocational school for boys that would be run by the Franciscan Brothers from Ohio, the same community that directed Morris School in Searcy. By 1940, the letterhead of the institution called it St. Raphael's Community Center for Colored Education, and it was still operating on the land on which the orphanage had been founded.[35] It had been an expensive experiment. Morris himself admitted in his 1938 report to the American Board for Catholic Missions that he had "discovered that I did not know as much about colored people as I thought."[36]

The Arkansas bishop, however, did not give up trying to establish schools and churches for blacks in Arkansas. In early 1940, Morris persuaded the Holy Ghost Fathers, real pioneers of black Catholic evangelization in Arkansas and an order already operating black Catholic parishes in Fort Smith and Helena, to open a new church in Hot Springs. Father John M. Haines, C.S.Cp., became the first pastor of St. Gabriel's Church. Haines arrived in the resort city on March 25, 1940, the Feast of the Annunciation, and within eight months, he had erected a small wooden church in the black section of town. Father Haines said his first Mass in that building on December 1, 1940. He was surprised to learn that the Sisters of the Good Shepherd had started a small black Catholic school called St. Augustine's in 1938, and that the school had been open until 1943, when the Sisters of the Good Shepherd turned the facility over to the Sister Servants of the Holy Heart of Mary. Then, the school became a formal part of St. Gabriel's parish, and the school changed its name to that of the parish. Father Haines served as pastor at St. Gabriel's until his death on June 27, 1947, after serving all thirty years as a priest working in black Catholic parishes across the South.[37]

In 1941, Bishop Morris established a black Catholic mission church in El Dorado called Holy Martyrs of Uganda Church, named for the black African Saint, Charles Lwanga, and twenty-one companions who were martyred for their Catholic faith in 1886.[38] This parish was organized on May 1, 1941, and on Pentecost Sunday, June 1, 1941, Father Raymond M. Marmon, a diocesan priest, took over the church. He pastored it for the next eleven years. On January 24, 1952, the Franciscan Fathers took over the parish from the diocese.[39]

America's entrance into World War II, and the financial and other demands that it placed on the diocese, affected Morris' ability to found many more black churches. Bishop Morris sold most of the farm in 1944 and moved much of the project into Pine Bluff, where it continued as a trade school for blacks into the postwar era, with the title St. Raphael's Colored Trade School, still operated by the Franciscans. The building and land still contained a church mission building also called St. Raphael's.[40] This ended the orphanage experiment called St. Raphael's.

In 1945, Morris founded his eighth and last black Catholic mission in the Diocese of Little Rock, St. John the Baptist Church in Lake Village, in the southeastern corner of the state. The pastor was the Franciscan Father Angelus Schaefer, O.F.M.[41] In his last written report to the American Board for Catholic Missions on September 25, 1945, Morris said that he would like to have black Catholic churches in Jonesboro and Forrest City, but, as usual, he did not have either the "men or money" for these projects.[42]

Bishop Morris had come to the diocese with only two fledgling black parishes; at his death forty years later, he had nine black churches in Little Rock, North Little Rock, Fort Smith, Helena, Hot Springs, El Dorado, and Lake Village. At Pine Bluff, St. Peter's still included St. Raphael's black mission church, south of the city. Catholic schools were in all but the two newest parishes, El Dorado and Lake Village, and St. Raphael's Mission. Bishop Morris was interested in setting up black Catholic parishes which would stand for some time; in this sense, he had some real success, in that most of these parishes lasted at least two decades after his death, and some are still operating to this day. (Their stories will be continued in subsequent chapters.)

Institutionally, the Church grew during the Morris years, but the number of Catholics at the end still stood at between one and two percent of the population. In 1920, the Catholic population was 23,192, or 1.3 percent of the state population of 1,752,204. Of the white population alone–Catholics were overwhelmingly white–the Catholic percentage rose to 1.8 percent. Just after World War I, the Arkansas diocese had 104 churches, forty-five with resident priests. Within the diocese were eighty priests, forty-four diocesan or secular priests, and thirty-six in religious orders. Religious sisters, including novices and postulants, numbered 448.[43]

The *Official Catholic Directory* for 1930, ten years later, put the number of Catholics in Arkansas at 26,610, or 1.4 percent of a general population of 1,854,482. When only whites are included, the numbers rise to about 1.9 percent. There were 111 churches in the state, fifty with resident priests. There were ninety-one Catholic priests, fifty-eight diocesan or secular priests, and thirty-three members of religious orders. Over six hundred religious nuns, postulants, and novices served in the diocese, and fifty-two parishes had schools.[44]

Little growth occurred during the next ten years. Catholics numbered 33,374 in 1940; 1.7 percent of the state population of 1,949,511, a gain of three-tenths of one percent. Of the white population, Catholics made up 2.2 percent of the state. There were now 125 churches, fifty-nine with resident priests. The number of priests working in the diocese stood at 141. There were eighty-four diocesan or secular priests, fifty-seven members of religious orders, and 664 religious women, nuns, postulants, and novices.[45] A couple of trends are noteworthy. The number of clergymen almost doubled between the wars, and the number of nuns grew by a third.

The priest numbers grew as Bishop Morris put money and effort into the seminary. Located in the attractive Pulaski Heights area of Little Rock, the seminary continued to grow throughout the 1930s, helped no doubt by an article in 1935 about the institution in *Extension Magazine*, the monthly national journal of the U.S. Catholic Extension Society. A film about St. John's Home Missions Seminary, in the fall of 1938, reported that ninety-seven seminarians from dioceses around the United States were at the institution, and that in less than thirty years, it had trained 196 men for the priesthood.[46] It was Bishop Morris' proudest accomplishment. The diocesan newspaper referred to the seminary and its grounds in 1942 as "the Heart of the Diocese."[47]

One matter in which the bishop could not take pride was the affair between him and Monsignor Patrick F. Horan, which concluded in 1936, the thirtieth year of Bishop Morris' reign. Horan was born in Ireland, December 2, 1866. His name appeared on both the bishop's and priests' lists for the Diocese of Little Rock in December 1905. He had been transferred from Our Lady of Good Counsel Parish in Little Rock, where he was the founding pastor in 1894, to Immaculate Conception Church in Fort Smith by late 1906. Known by his parishioners and many other people around the diocese as "Doctor Horan," he proved to be both an able preacher and a popular pastor. Rumors had floated about the diocese that Horan would become the new bishop. Whatever jealousies existed between Bishop Morris and Father Horan, they had been kept under wraps for twenty years. By the mid-1920s, the bishop had made him head of the western deanery and petitioned the Holy See to grant him the title monsignor, which was done in 1928. Horan had become a consulter of the diocese and member of the Diocesan Financial Board, and he was the permanent pastor of the largest and wealthiest church in Fort Smith.[48] Horan was still acting in that capacity when the diocese published a history of Catholicism in Arkansas in 1925. That book described Horan as a talented preacher and speaker and a man with a remarkable memory. He was fluent in Latin, German, and Italian, and he had a huge personal library. Both an eccentric and eclectic person, Horan was one of the outstanding personalities in the history of Arkansas' Catholic clergy.[49] A parishioner recalled that the pastor had been given a Kaiser automobile by a local car dealer. A few days later, the dealer was shocked to see Fr. Horan driving the automobile without doors. When he asked why the doors were missing, Horan replied that he found them too confining. If he were involved in an accident, he could get out of the car faster. Older Catholics in Fort Smith who remember "Doc" Horan fondly remember his talent and charm.[50]

What triggered the conflict was Morris' decision in 1927 to split Immaculate Conception parish and create Christ the King parish. Fort Smith had a traditionally German Catholic parish since the late 1880s and a black parish since 1917. Horan saw no reason for another parish and felt his position being undermined. Morris thought that Fort Smith was growing so much that it was worthy of another Catholic church.[51] This dispute would lock these powerful and proud Irishmen in a struggle lasting more than eight years. Differences had been simmering for decades and with Morris' move, the pot boiled over.

Horan was bold. He wrote the bishop in November 1927 that he would like to request of the apostolic delegate that the diocese be divided and that Fort Smith be made the seat of a new diocese of western Arkansas. Horan even said that he would ask the apostolic delegate to name Father Thomas S. Griffins, another diocesan priest, as the first bishop of Fort Smith. Horan considered the division necessary for two reasons. The Church in western and northwestern Arkansas was declining because the bishop was concentrating his projects and money in Little Rock. For another thing, Horan asserted about his ordinary, "You dislike the people of the Northwest and are cordially hated in return."[52] Apparently, the Fort Smith pastor felt that if the bishop could split and divide his parish, he was requesting that Morris' diocese also be divided.

By the early 1930s, Morris and Horan were quarrelling over Horan's desire to borrow $125,000.00 from a local bank, based on the credit of the diocese to build a new church and school. With the country in a depression and the diocese in need of funds, Morris was appalled at the idea. Other complaints concerned Horan's attack on the diocesan tax to support the Little Rock Seminary and the poor quality of priests sent to work as his assistants. One young assistant priest, Father Thomas Keaney, contended in a letter to the bishop in December 1932 that the Fort Smith pastor was constantly attacking Morris and had turned the whole parish against the prelate. He said Horan consistently refused to follow diocesan policies. Father Keaney wondered if the Fort Smith pastor was "demented." All of this was not Keaney's imagination. A parishioner from that era confirmed that many in the parish affected indifference or hostility to the bishop owing to the influence of Monsignor Horan.[53] On the same day of Keaney's letter, Morris wrote to the apostolic delegate alleging that since coming to the diocese, Horan had given him nothing but "passive opposition" despite their having been classmates in Rome and giving Horan many honors and positions in the diocese. In February 1933, Morris asked for, and received from Horan, his resignation as head of the western deanery and consulter for the diocese, though he remained pastor at Immaculate Conception.[54]

Relations worsened over the next two and a half years. Horan sent a long letter to his prelate in June 1935, complaining about his administration and the assistants the bishop had sent to him. The tenor of this correspondence suggests that Morris considered this and other actions of Horan to be a direct challenge to his authority. Bishop Morris called for a meeting of the consulters of the diocese in Little Rock for October 27; and on October 31, Morris removed Horan from the pastorate at Fort Smith. Horan did not go easily. He had a petition signed by hundreds of people in Fort Smith, Catholics and non-Catholics alike, requesting his reinstatement. Monsignor Horan went to Washington, D.C., to meet with the apostolic delegate, Cardinal Ameto Giovanni Cicognani, on Thanksgiving Day. Cardinal Cicognani wrote Morris on December 10 that since he had received so many letters and complaints from the people of Fort Smith concerning Monsignor Horan, "I trust that the removal of Msgr. will not prove detrimental to the spiritual interests of the parish and its people."[55]

Soon after meeting with the apostolic delegate, Horan was hospitalized in the nation's capital with what doctors called acute diabetes. While Horan was in the hospital, Morris sent the apostolic delegate an eight-page, single-spaced letter outlining his problems with Horan since 1927.[56] The apostolic delegate then responded to Horan's petition by asserting that he had no grounds to counteract the bishop's authority. Horan received the letter back in Fort Smith, and in early January, he wrote the Italian Cardinal declaring his submission to his decision. On February 25, Horan formally asked for a three-month leave of absence to return to Ireland, because he was ill and wanted to see his native land again. Chancellor Albert L. Fletcher, acting in the name of the bishop, readily agreed two days later. Unfortunately, the longtime pastor of Immaculate Conception never made it back to the land of his birth. He died in a Catholic hospital in New Orleans on March 19, 1936, the feast day of St. Joseph.[57]

This whole affair does not reveal either man in his best light; personality conflicts seldom do. As with Morris' dispute with Father Dorsey, Morris saw it as a challenge to his authority, which it was in large degree. The removal and death of Monsignor Horan nevertheless had a cost. Replacing this popular pastor no doubt strained the relationship between the Fort Smith Catholic community and the rest of the diocese for years to come.

Just as this painful affair ended, two new Catholic women's organizations appeared in the diocese in the middle of the 1930s. The Catholic Business Women's Club of Greater Little Rock was formed at the cathedral school on Friday, June 3, 1936. This organization was open to all Catholic business and professional women in the greater Little Rock area. It remains an active organization after more than fifty years.[58] In the fall of 1937, Bishop Morris endorsed the creation of a Diocesan Council of Catholic Women, directing all Catholic women's organization's in the state to be merged into this new organization which would be affiliated with the National Council of Catholic Women. The first state board meeting for Diocesan Council of Catholic Women was held at the Marion Hotel in Little Rock on January 31, 1938.[59] Earlier in his administration, the Bishop had not been enthusiastic about a national Catholic bishops' organization; however, by the late 1930s, he was encouraging the women of the diocese to organize across the state and be affiliated with an organization which was part of the National Catholic Welfare Conference.[60]

Bishop Morris himself was under great personal strain during his last decade as bishop, because his knee was so painful that he had to walk with a cane. "Old Wounded Knee" he comically called himself in letters to his relative, Archbishop Stritch.[61] Morris always had a bad temper, but the pain and the problems that came with aging made him more crotchety. At times, he could strike out violently at his priests. Clergymen who knew Morris during this period usually recall his dressing someone down in public or even striking them with his hands or cane. Monsignor John Murphy remembered that at an ordination-day dinner with the bishop in 1938, Morris hit Father Joseph F. Murphy with his cane because the priest had not visited the bishop when he was last in town.[62] Msgr. William Galvin of Fort Smith recalled that Morris verbally assailed his vicar general, Monsignor Albert Fletcher. Ever the cool gentleman, Fletcher merely got up, put on his hat and coat, and left. Morris later apologized to Fletcher for the outburst.[63] Morris was especially hard on his personal secretary, Father Francis A. Allen. Allen was so disturbed that he went to his physician for stress. The doctor ordered two weeks of vacation for the shaken priest. When Allen returned to the bishop's residence by St. Andrew's Cathedral, the bishop met him at the door and asked what the doctor had told him. When Allen replied, "two weeks vacation," Morris responded, "Good, where can we go?" Msgr. James O'Connell said he would never forget the look on Allen's face.[64] Morris' reputation for striking out at his priests spread. Auxiliary Bishop William O'Brien of Chicago, head of the Catholic Extension Society and a close friend of Morris, wrote him in 1941 that he was most impressed with Morris' new auxiliary bishop, but found him a little bashful, "not like his Ordinary, who is ready to beat one with a stick every now and then."[65]

To Morris' family, however, he showed a different face. A box in the archives is filled with correspondence with his family. His nephew, Thomas Stritch, remembers his uncle John's bad temper, but he also recalls riding with the bishop in his automobile; Morris frequently stopped and gave money from his own pocket to beggars and other needy people.[66] His generous side is revealed in a letter to a cousin, Patrick Morrissey, in Galloway, Ireland. Morris wrote that while a bishop may appear to have a lot, "personally, I can say that I have nothing on my own . . . I have had a multitude of calls from within and without the Diocese. This makes things difficult for me to help others, as much as I should wish to give to all who ask."[67] Bishop Morris really poured out his heart to his sister, Sister Madeleine Morris, a member of the Daughters of Charity, who lived in a convent near Paris, France. In August 1936, he wrote to her about his fear of communism and his sadness about the violence in Spain. Later that year, he wrote that the situation in Spain, Germany, and Russia was getting worse and that "there is growing tendency to evil in the world."[68] Morris would only wait less than three years after writing those words to witness the outbreak of another great evil, World War II.

It was while he was in France visiting his sister, that World War II broke out on September 3, 1939. Morris had traveled to Europe with his secretary, Father Allen, and Monsignor John J. Healy to make what would be his last *ad liminia* visit to the Holy Father. Pope Pius XII had been elected in March, and the aging bishop wanted to meet his fourth pontiff, but that did not occur. Morris had left New York on July 25, 1939, and after a long stay in England, he journeyed to Paris, where he arrived on August 21. The American government warned citizens that a general European war might break out and recommended that they return home. Morris had planned to leave for Rome on the morning of September 1, but that day Germany invaded Poland, beginning the European stage of the war. (The Asian-Pacific stage began in 1937 when Japan invaded China.) Morris altered his plans for Rome and attempted to leave from France that day. The French passenger ship would not really leave until September 3, when France and Britain declared war on Germany. That whole week, from Sunday, September 3, through Saturday, September 9, the boat on which the three Arkansas Catholic clerics traveled moved warily across the Atlantic looking for German submarines, but the ship never came under fire. Bishop Morris was met at the dock in New York on September 9 by Monsignor Fletcher, whom Morris had ordered by cable to meet Fletcher and drive him back to Arkansas. They reached Little Rock on Tuesday afternoon, September 12.[69]

Upon his return, Morris waited for an answer from Rome on the appointment of an auxiliary bishop for the diocese. Morris' knee was not getting better, and he was seventy-three. In case he became incapacitated, he would need to have someone help him manage the diocese, someone with the rank of bishop so no one could question his authority. Morris was sure whom he wanted; namely, his vicar general, Albert Lewis Fletcher. Morris had long admired this priest, telling his friend, Auxiliary Bishop William O'Brien of Chicago, after his return from Europe in 1939, "My vicar general carried on famously while I was away. I sometimes think if I had a dozen men like him, I should not need anyone else."[70] On Monday afternoon, December 11, 1939, Fletcher was notified from Rome that he was to be Arkansas' fourth Catholic bishop, its first auxiliary bishop.[71] He was also to be the first native Arkansan ever raised to bishop.

Fletcher was born in Little Rock on October 28, 1896, into one of Arkansas' prominent families. The family had come to Lawrence County in 1820. A cousin was John Gould Fletcher (1886-1950), a poet and writer, who had won the Pulitzer Prize for poetry in 1939 and was Arkansas' most distinguished man of letters.[72] Albert L. Fletcher's father was Thomas Fletcher, a physician who married Helen Wehr. Both were converts to Catholicism, the only members of this distinguished family who were. Thomas and Helen Fletcher had four children, Albert being the oldest. Just four months after his birth in Little Rock, he moved with his family to Paris, Arkansas, where Father Thomas Kellar, O.S.B., baptized him on March 12, 1897. Albert spent his boyhood in Paris, Logan County, and Tontitown, Washington County. (After he entered Little Rock College in 1912, his parents moved to Mena.) At college, Fletcher played for the baseball and football teams. He graduated in 1917 with a major in Chemistry and entered St. John's Seminary, where he completed his theological studies and was ordained by Bishop Morris on the feast day of the Sacred Heart of Jesus, June 4, 1920. Fletcher said his first Mass two days later at St. Agnes Church in Mena. For four summers, 1919-1922, he studied at the University of Chicago and earned a Master of Science degree in 1922.

Albert would be the only male in his family to survive after 1922. Philip died at the age of fifteen, drowning while trying to rescue an altar boy at a parish picnic, in Mena, in 1918. In 1922, George died in Rome while studying for the priesthood. Fletcher's only sister, Marie Fletcher Frame, was married and living in North Little Rock when he was made bishop.[73]

Fr. Fletcher taught chemistry and biology at Little Rock College from 1920-1923, while serving at times as substitute pastor for the Little Italy congregation in Perry County, about forty miles west of the Capital, and in Carlisle, a town about forty miles east of Little Rock. In 1923, he became president of Little Rock College, a position he held for two years, until he became vice chancellor for the diocese. A year later, in 1926, he became chancellor, and seven years later in 1933, Morris made him vicar general, a position that had been vacant since the death of Monsignor Winand Aretz in 1929. At the request of Bishop Morris, the Pope bestowed the title Monsignor in 1934. That same year, Fletcher traveled with the bishop to Rome as his secretary on *ad limina* visit.[74] After six years as vicar general, on the tenth anniversary of the death of his father, Fletcher was notified of his appointment as auxiliary bishop.[75] All of his education, except for four summers in Chicago, was in Arkansas, and all his clerical assignments, except for substitute ones, were in and around Little Rock. If, as bishop, Fletcher would be charged in some quarters with provincialism, there would be a basis for it. From his ordination, until his appointment as auxiliary bishop, Fletcher had traveled very little in the United States or within the Diocese of Little Rock.

It was an important day in Arkansas Catholic history, April 25, 1940.

Some four centuries after De Soto first came to the area, and almost ninety-seven years after the creation of the diocese, a native Arkansan was raised to the hierarchy of the Catholic Church. Witnessing this event were seven archbishops, thirty-one bishops, fifty monsignors, three abbots, seventy-eight priests, and more than two hundred religious sisters. The most significant visitor was Cardinal Ameto Giocanni Cicognani, the apostolic delegate to the United States. It was the first time that the Holy Father's representative in the United States had ever come to Arkansas. Archbishop Joseph Rummel of New Orleans gave the main address at the consecration Mass, which was attended by Governor Carl Bailey and Mayor Robert Satterfield of Little Rock. Fletcher thanked God, the Holy Father, and all the well-wishers and supporters who had loved him. A large luncheon followed at Robinson Auditorium, and that night, the new auxiliary bishop attended a banquet at Mount St. Mary's with over two hundred sisters who had attended the consecration.[76]

With Fletcher now holding the auxiliary position, Morris could feel good about turning over to him the day-to-day operations of the diocese. Fletcher continued as vicar general as well as auxiliary bishop, and depending upon Morris' health, would essentially run the diocese. Morris would live another six years, and at times, worked and made important decisions, but most affairs of the diocese were now handled by the auxiliary bishop.

The diocese was not the only institution where the leadership was in transition. Abbot Edward Burgert, O.S.B., had succeeded the founding abbot of Subiaco Abbey, Abbot Ignatius Conrad, in 1925. Born in nearby Paris in 1887, Burgert was not even forty when he became Subiaco's second abbot. In his fourteen years as abbot, the Benedictine monastery went through some hard times; a devastating fire in December 1927 and the Great Depression damaged the financial resources of the abbey. Recovering from the fire and dealing with the Depression and its impact on abbey finances, caused Abbot Edward Burgert much pain. When Abbot Columbian Thius, president of the Swiss-American Benedictine Congregation, visited Subiaco in late 1935 and 1938, Abbot Edward mentioned his desire to resign. By the end of 1938, he wrote to the Holy See, and the Vatican notified him in February 1939 that it accepted his resignation. On February 22, 1939, he resigned as abbot, but continued as a Benedictine monk and pastor in Arkansas and Texas for nearly thirty more years. He died in Refugio, Texas, on January 23, 1968.[77] At the election on March 23, 1939, his position was taken by Father Paul Nahlen, O.S.B.

Father Nahlen's parents had come from the German Rhineland and had settled in the Holy Ghost colony in Faulkner County. Young Martin Nahlen was born there in November 1882. At the age of fourteen, his parents, poor, hard-working farmers, sent the boy to Subiaco Academy, where he graduated in 1900. He entered the monastery, taking the name Paul, and was ordained to the priesthood in 1908. After serving as a teacher and disciplinarian at the academy, Father Paul Nahlen went to Corpus Christi, Texas, in 1927 to serve as pastor. He had returned to Subiaco for the important election in 1939 and became its third abbot.[78]

Elected as abbot at the age of fifty-six, Nahlen was a tough taskmaster who was legendary in his devotion to duties and community prayer. It was said that no one could beat him to chapel for morning community prayer, no matter how late he had arrived the previous evening from some outside engagement. In a car, he would say the rosary before anything else, including conversation. The historian of Subiaco also reported that traveling with the abbot could be a real test of faith for any monk, "not because the monks disliked prayers while traveling, but because the abbot was more insistent of getting to his destination than on safe driving and drove with childlike abandon."[79] Considering the abbot's driving habits, the praying apparently continued long after the formal prayers ended.

This hard-driving abbot was determined to get Subiaco out of its financial difficulty. Fund-raising operations were held on the Fourth of July, Labor Day, and Thanksgiving. He was famous for getting local businessmen to donate prizes, and it was said that they grew to fear the appearance of Abbot Paul, because they knew how persuasive he could be in getting donations. At the first Fourth of July picnic in 1939, despite still unsettled economic conditions, the abbot raffled off a new car donated by a local car dealer.[80] Through fund-raising, cost cutting, and some good investments, Abbot Paul not only paid the debt incurred during his predecessor's reign (the debt had risen to $220,000.00 by 1937), but by 1946, he retired the debt to the Massachusetts Mutual Company which had hung over the community for twenty years. By February 1946, Abbot Paul sent to Abbot Ignatius Staub, O.S.B, of Einsiedeln, all the money the Arkansas monastery had owed the Swiss abbey since the 1920s, a total of $9,932.29.[81]

But Subiaco's salvation was not due only to the work of Abbot Paul Nahlen. The abbot received great financial assistance from an important and wealthy Catholic layman from Fort Smith, Mr. Charles Jewitt, who was a Knight of St. Gregory and of the Holy Sepulcher. Mr. Jewitt served as chair of the Board of Trustees of St. John's Home Missions Seminary and contributed money for a new school for Immaculate Conception in Fort Smith and for a church for West Memphis.[82] It was Mr. Jewitt who helped rebuild the eastern wing of the abbey after the damaging fire of 1927. That project was completed by 1940. Mr. Jewitt also provided scholarships for many boys to attend Subiaco and provided the financial help necessary to construct an abbey press building in 1946. In 1940, the first *Abbey Message* appeared as a small pamphlet, and it became a newspaper by the fall. So it would remain until 1958, when it became a monthly magazine.[83] A new water supply system was also installed in the grounds between 1946-1948, and since the abbey would be more financially solvent, it would be ready for the building expansion in the post-war era.[84]

War would be upon America after the Japanese attack on Pearl Harbor on

December 7, 1941; the United States now entered a massive two-front war in Europe and the Pacific. The American Catholics, who had been as divided as the country over President Roosevelt's foreign policies, joined their fellow citizens to fight in the largest war of the century. George Q. Flynn described this era in the Church as a time for a "Theology of War." Catholics were most anxious again to prove that they were loyal in times of national conflict.[85]

Soon after the war began, Major Thomas Lewis of the Selective Service complimented Catholics for their loyalty during the two world wars, asking if any Catholics would be able to claim to be conscientious objectors. Fletcher denied that "Catholics can be classified as Conscientious Objectors for they certainly have nothing in the doctrines of the church to warrant such an attitude."[86] Fletcher shared that attitude with much of the American Catholic leadership. Fletcher wrote Father Edward McCormack, a military chaplain from Arkansas stationed in North Carolina, who was about to head to Europe in 1944, that "I do hope and pray that the Lord will help us end this war victoriously sooner than we might expect. If any one starts talking disarmament and junking our navy after this war is over, I think he should be shot for treason."[87]

One part of the war effort many Arkansans were not happy about was having the camps for Japanese internees from the west coast within the state. The Japanese-Americans were held in camps at Rohwer, in Desha County, and Jerome, in Chicot County, both in southeastern Arkansas. Methodists were the only religious group willing to publicly give these Japanese-Americans any religious ministry, and even the Methodists backed off a bit in their work owing to public opinion. The Japanese-Americans stayed in these camps from the summer of 1942 to the summer of 1944.[88]

Behind the scenes, the Catholic diocese was trying to meet the spiritual needs for these persecuted fellow citizens, some of whom were Catholic. Fletcher wrote the Maryknoll Fathers on the west coast in November 1942 asking them to send a priest who knew Japanese to the camps. Eventually, Father Hugh Lavery, M.M. (Maryknoll Missionaries), sent a Father Leo J. Steinbeck, M.M.[89] Fletcher reported to the Maryknoll Fathers in February 1943 that only fifty Catholics were at both camps. Fletcher reported that Father Steinbeck would live in the rectory with Father Charles Stanowski in McGehee. The diocese, he said, was ready to contribute financially to provide a Catholic chaplain for the relocated Japanese-Americans. Father Steinbeck was not the first or last Maryknoll priest assigned to the Japanese-Americans. The 1944 and 1945 editions of the *Official Catholic Directory* listed Father John F. Swift, M.M., and Father Edmund L. Ryan, M.M., respectively, as working in the Japanese relocation camps.[90] When these "refugees" were allowed to return to their homes, the camps were taken over by German and Italian prisoners. Father Steinbeck left for California, and Father (now Monsignor) John Murphy served as their chaplain for the war's duration.[91]

If the Japanese-Americans were persecuted and interned, there was no real animosity shown to Americans of German ancestry, not anything like the previous World War. The isolation and segregation had been removed over the previous quarter-century. No one questioned whether the "monks" at Subiaco were loyal. At the abbey, a para-military unit was formed called the Victory Corps and it stressed physical and moral fitness.[92] It was during World War II that the abbey had its most famous novice. Fred Demara, alias Robert L. French, was made famous by the 1959 book, The *Great Imposter*, by Robert Crichton. This best selling book was made into a movie of the same title in 1960, with Tony Curtis playing Demara. During the fall and winter of 1943-1944, Demara entered Subiaco Monastery before it was discovered that he was both a forger and a liar.[93]

As the rest of the country's eyes were turned to the war, the Diocese of Little Rock conducted two major celebrations. The first was the fiftieth anniversary of the ordination of Bishop Morris to the priesthood on June 11, 1942. A dinner the previous evening at the Lafayette Hotel in Little Rock featured remarks from Morris' relative, Archbishop Stritch, who now presided over the Catholic Church in Chicago. The next day, a major ceremonial Mass was held with Stritch and three of his fellow archbishops, Joseph Rummel of New Orleans, Edward Mooney of Detroit, and John Floresch of Louisville. Ten other prelates attended this celebration Mass at the cathedral. A banquet followed in Byrne Hall at St. John's Seminary. As Morris spoke that warm summer afternoon, the newspapers were filled with news about the American naval victory at Midway. Bishop Morris thanked everyone and praised the loyalty of Catholics, both to their country and to the Holy Father.[94]

Less than a year and a half later, the Diocese of Little Rock celebrated its centennial. Morris, who had been ill for months before this happy occasion, reported a few days later in a letter, "Well, I made it." The actual date of the centennial, November 28, 1943, was on a Sunday, but Bishop Morris actually celebrated a centennial Mass at St. Andrew's Cathedral on November 30, the feast day of St. Andrew the Apostle. While Morris was at the ceremony, he did not preach the sermon, Fletcher did. The diocese had a list of things planned to mark its one hundred year history over the next year, but the aging and often infirm prelate no doubt was just glad that he had lived to be the bishop to celebrate the centennial. Morris confided to Bishop O'Brien of Chicago that while the Mass for the centennial went well, "I felt pretty fatigued when it was over; I made out wonderfully well, better than I even expected."[95]

Morris was still the bishop and he exerted his authority whenever his health permitted. When his rector of the seminary, Monsignor James Gaffney, had to resign due to illness in September 1944, he called up Father (now Monsignor) James E. O'Connell, then principal of Catholic High School, to come down to the bishop's house. A native of Boston, and ordained for the Diocese of Little Rock in 1934, O'Connell was only in his thirties. The priest reported to the bishop in his upstairs bedroom. Bishop Morris informed him that he was to be the new rector for St. John's Seminary. When the young priest demurred, saying that he was not the right man for the position, the bishop gruffly barked, "I will do the thinking here, I make the decisions! You will report to Seminary immediately!"[96]

Despite such occasional assertions of power, Auxiliary Bishop Fletcher reported to Auxiliary Bishop O'Brien of Chicago in the spring of 1945 that Bishop Morris was "getting more helpless all the time. It's becoming more difficult to care for him."[97] Morris' last major public event was the Mass to celebrate the twenty-fifth anniversary of the auxiliary bishop's priestly ordination, June 4, 1945. Morris acknowledged in his sermon that when one is an auxiliary bishop, it can be difficult to carve out an exact role. He praised Fletcher for having played that role "carefully and properly."[98] Later that summer, Japan surrendered, ending World War II, but within two months came tragic personal news for Bishop Morris. His beloved sister, Madeleine Morris, had died in her convent in Paris on July 23.[99] This telegram reached Little Rock in October, adding a deep personal wound to a bishop already quite ill. Another indication of Morris' growing health problems was that Fletcher, not he, represented the diocese at the November meeting of the American bishops.[100] This would be Fletcher's first meeting as a bishop with the American Catholic hierarchy.

As 1946 dawned, Morris received the good news that Pope Pius XII had named Archbishop Samuel Stritch of Chicago a cardinal of the Roman Curia. Bishop O'Brien wrote the aging and infirm Arkansas bishop:

> Aren't you the one more than anyone else who helped him become a priest? Aren't you the one they say that got him to go to Rome for his studies? Why, man alive, outside of the Holy Father, Pius XII, you, the Bishop of Little Rock, are more responsible for the naming of Samuel Cardinal Stritch than anyone else.[101]

While Morris shared in the joy of his prominent in-law, he could not go to Chicago to witness his installation as a cardinal on February 18, 1946. Morris wrote two months later that he was in such poor health that he could hardly get around.[102] Later that year, Morris again was invited to a Stritch celebration, his twenty-fifth anniversary as a member of the Catholic hierarchy, on November 19.[103] Chicago Auxiliary Bishop O'Brien must have known that his invitation was a formality, but Morris responded on September 17 with a note that he would not be able to make the trip, much to his regret.[104] This would be his last letter. On Tuesday afternoon, October 22, at around 4:30 p.m., John Baptist Morris died at the age of eighty.[105] After a little more than a century, Arkansas now lost its third bishop.

Fitzgerald and Morris each served as bishop for about forty years. In

1906, when Morris came to the diocese as coadjutor bishop (bishop with right to succession), there were only sixty priests; thirty-four of them in religious orders and twenty-six with the diocese, and two hundred religious sisters.[106] At the end of Morris' reign forty years later, the *Official Catholic Directory* for 1946 reported 154 priests working in Arkansas: eighty-four as Diocesan priests and forty-nine in religious orders. About ten were working outside the diocese (usually priest-monks from Subiaco Abbey who worked at parishes out of state or diocesan priests serving in the military) and eleven were retired, sick, or absent. In that year, 1946, at St. John's Home Missions Seminary, thirty-eight young men were preparing for the priesthood for the Diocese of Little Rock and forty-two were studying for other dioceses. There were now 582 religious sisters, including novices and postulants, serving in the diocese. Twenty Catholic high schools with over 1,500 students were scattered around the state. There were sixty parochial elementary schools with more than six thousand pupils. The youth in Catholic schools in the state numbered 7,710. Catholic hospitals had a bed capacity of almost one thousand, and they treated more than 35,000 people during 1945. This was all from a Catholic population that was estimated at 35,196.[107]

Clearly, Morris had some setbacks; the Little Rock College closed and his black Catholic orphanage, St. Raphael's, near Pine Bluff failed, but his successes were monumental for a missionary diocese. The establishment of a Catholic seminary in Little Rock that served other missionary dioceses, an orphanage in North Little Rock, and a diocesan newspaper, were all significant milestones. This bishop had truly left a far greater number of institutions than any of his predecessors.

But who was to be his successor? Unlike forty years earlier when everyone knew by Morris' title as coadjutor that he would become the bishop at the death of Bishop Fitzgerald, Fletcher was an auxiliary bishop, a man who operated the diocese in the name of the bishop, but who had no intrinsic claim to the office upon the death of the ordinary. Pope Pius XII was free to name anyone he wanted, but, quite probably on the suggestion of the apostolic delegate, the Holy Father chose Fletcher as the fourth regular bishop. As Bishop Fletcher recounted it for the diocesan newspaper, at a little before midnight on Wednesday, December 11, 1946, the apostolic delegate informed him of his appointment. Fletcher passed the news to the faculty and seminarians at St. John's at early morning Mass the next day.[108] Seven years earlier to the very day, December 11, he had been informed that he was to be auxiliary bishop.

Albert Lewis Fletcher was formally enthroned at a 10 a.m. consecration on February 11, 1947. As the procession moved from the Lafayette Hotel and made its way to the cathedral, snow flurries fell on the mantles of the clergy as they made their way to the cathedral that Bishop Fitzgerald had built. Four archbishops and thirty bishops witnessed this impressive two-hour ceremony.

His mother, Helen Wehr Fletcher, the only surviving member of the new bishop's immediate family, was there. Bishop Jules Jeanmard of Lafayette, the senior bishop in the Province of New Orleans, delivered the sermon. Bishop Fletcher thanked his parents, friends, supporters, and the Catholic Church. He dedicated the diocese to the Sacred Heart of Jesus and the Immaculate Heart of Mary and mentioned that as the presiding bishop, he wore some marks of his predecessors. He had Bishop Byrne's episcopal ring, Bishop Fitzgerald's pectoral cross around his neck, and he carried the crozier or episcopal staff of Bishop Morris.[109] When the liturgy was over, there was a huge banquet for clergy, religious sisters, and some lay guests at the Hotel Marion a few blocks away.[110] For the next quarter-century, this native Arkansan would lead the Catholic Church in Arkansas. For a man of quiet disposition, the years of his rule would be anything but calm.

Pine Bluff, Colored Industrial School

Female Student Body, 1892

The School Building, 1890

Male Student Body, 1892

Motherhouses, Abbeys, Monasteries

(The dates refer to the use of the pictured building, not to the existence of the religious community.)

Mt. St. Mary's: Pulaski
Religious Sisters of Mercy
This was the Motherhouse from 1908-1929

Subiaco: Subiaco Abbey
Benedictine Monks, 1903-

Fort Smith: St. Scholastica Monastery
Benedictine Sisters, 1924-

Jonesboro: Holy Angels Convent
Olivetan Benedictine Sisters, 1974-
Courtesy Holy Angels Archives

Motherhouses, Abbeys, Monasteries

Hot Springs: Monastery of Our Lady of Charity of Refuge
Sisters of Our Lady of Charity of Refuge

Little Rock: Monastery of Marylake
Discalced Carmelite

Little Rock: Carmelite Monastery of St. Teresa of Jesus
Discalced Carmelite Nuns

Dedication in 1960 of the Carmelite Monastery in Little Rock

Hospitals

Little Rock: St. Vincent Infirmary Medical Center

Jonesboro: St. Bernard Regional Medical Center

Fort Smith: St. Edward Mercy Medical Center
Courtesy: St. Edward's Public Relations Office

Hot Springs: St. Joseph Regional Health Center
Courtesy: St. Joseph's P.R. Department

Rogers: St. Mary-Rogers Memorial Hospital

Texarkana: Michael Meagher Memorial Hospital
Courtesy: St. Michael Hospital of Texarkana

Morrilton: Conway County Hospital
Courtesy: St. Scholastica Monastery Archives

Orphanages

North Little Rock:
St. Joseph's Orphanage
1930

Children with Bp. Fletcher and Sister Thomas, O.S.B., in 1970 at St. Joseph's

Pine Bluff: St. Gabriel's Orphanage
Courtesy: St. Scholastica Monastery Archives

Children at St. Raphael's in 1934 with Sisters Josephine, Teresa Marie, and Wilhelmina, O.S.B.

Diocesan Council of Catholic Women

Setting the Convention program for the 1953 meeting
Seated: Bishop Fletcher, Dr. Frances Rothert.. Standing: Mrs. Reville Flannigan, Mrs. James Campbell, Mrs. John L. Sullivan, Mrs. Granville Sutton, Mrs. M.A. Biltz.
Courtesy: Little Rock Diocesan Council of Catholic Women

Dr. Frances Rothert, a native of Indiana, came to Arkansas in 1944. She was active in many phases of church work in the state and also on the national level. After serving as the Director of the Division of Maternal and Child Care in the Arkansas State Department of Health, she worked for many years in the medical missions in Latin America. She is now residing at Benedictine Manor Retirement Home in Hot Springs.

Marian Devotions

Jonesboro: Blessed Sacrament Church
Our Lady of Fatima Pilgrim Statue, May, 1948
Pastor, Msgr. Edwin Hemmen

Fort Smith: St. Anne's Academy
Living Rosary formed by the students

Little Rock: St. John's Seminary Oval
Closing of the Novena to Our Lady of Mount Carmel, July, 1955

CHAPTER X

Calm Equanimity Amidst Tumultuous Change

The Career of Bishop Fletcher, 1947-1972

ON FEBRUARY 11, 1947, Albert Lewis Fletcher was formally installed as Little Rock's fourth bishop, the first native Arkansan after a century of the diocese's history. In some ways, Fletcher presented a sharp contrast to his predecessor. Where Morris was brought in as an outsider from Tennessee in 1906, Fletcher was very much the insider. As the first Arkansan ever raised to the Roman Catholic hierarchy, he was a man whose whole education, except for a few summers at the University of Chicago, had been in Catholic schools, college, and seminary in Arkansas. Morris had been short and rotund, while Fletcher was over six feet tall and thin. Where Morris was known for his explosive temper, autocratic manner, and especially in his later years, crotchety disposition, Fletcher possessed a calm, soothing voice and courtly manners. Those who worked with him remember that he always called them Mr., Mrs., or Miss, never by their first names.[1] Quiet by nature, somewhat shy, Fletcher was a man of both extreme piety and parochial vision.

The similarities between Morris and Fletcher, however, were more substantive than their apparent differences. Both were reared in the segregated South. Neither was overtly racist or bigoted, and theologically, both would have rejected such views. Both generally accepted the segregated social norms that were prevalent throughout the South, but in this, they would be not very different from their fellow Southern Catholic prelates of the time. As with most white religious denominations in the South at the time, they were more shaped by their society than interested in shaping it. Black churches themselves offered little challenge, using the segregated religious society to fashion their own spiritual vision and autonomy. Sunday mornings in the South, the "Bible Belt" of America, remained one of the most segregated moments of the week. Fletcher had been trained in the college and seminary that Bishop Morris had both founded and staffed. Fletcher had been president of Little Rock College in the 1920s and had served as the bishop's chief assistant and vicar general since 1930. It was Bishop Morris who had recommended to Rome that Fletcher be made auxiliary bishop for the Diocese of Little Rock, and he was so named in 1940. Although in appearance, manners, and disposition, the two men were quite different, in their societal and intellectual upbringing, they had much in common.

Fletcher's career as bishop can easily be divided into three parts: a relatively placid decade between 1947-1957; an era of extreme social, racial, and theological controversy for the next 10 years, culminating in the closing of St. John's Home Missions Seminary in the summer of 1967; and five final years of uneasy peace after the storm. American society in that last era continued to deal with the Vietnam War and race relations after the civil rights movement; the Catholic Church, nationally and locally, attempted to deal with controversies of the post-Vatican II Church. While not a notable leader in an era of racial and theological change, it is certain that this tall, gentlemanly cleric meant well and tried his best. If Bishop Fitzgerald can be considered Arkansas' most historically significant bishop, Bishop Fletcher was the prelate during the most historically turbulent period.

In the first decade of his episcopacy, Fletcher continued to build Catholicism in a strongly Protestant state. While still an auxiliary bishop, seven months prior to the death of Bishop Morris, Fletcher received a letter from then Monsignor Fulton J. Sheen of New York, later a bishop and then archbishop. In 1946, he was merely a well-known Catholic radio personality; he would become even more famous with television programs beginning in 1951.[2] Sheen wrote Fletcher that James O'Brien of Rushing, a small hamlet in Stone County, wanted help in getting a church started in his area. Sheen asked if financial assistance would be needed to build a church.[3] In a long, revealing letter, Fletcher outlined what would be the policy for founding churches in rural Arkansas:

> What we try and do is to attend scattered Catholics as frequently as we can and say Mass in a centrally located Catholic home, where other Catholics can more conveniently attend. We do this until ten to fifteen people seem definitively located. After this point is reached, we try to build a little chapel for them . . . It is ordinarily unwise to build anything for a half dozen people when they are liable to pull up stakes and thus the building would be of no use for the church.[4]

This seems to have been the last correspondence between this famous Catholic evangelist and the fourth bishop of Little Rock, at least according to Bishop Fletcher's papers. These men died only three days apart in December 1979.[5]

One major style change from Morris to Fletcher was the way in which Fletcher traveled the state. In May 1948, Fletcher wrote Auxiliary Bishop William O'Brien of the Catholic Extension Society, "I don't expect to spend my years as a missionary Bishop in an office."[6] Indeed, the correspondence of Bishop Fletcher and the testimony of those who remember him, attest to his efforts to get around the diocese.[7] In November 1948, he once again wrote to Bishop O'Brien that of the seventy-five counties in the state, ten were without priests.[8] Since becoming auxiliary bishop, he had often traveled across the state administering the sacrament of confirmation for Bishop Morris, whose poor health had confined him to Little Rock. While Morris had lived at the old cathedral rectory and did much of his work at the building on Louisiana Street, Fletcher, in the summer of 1947, had a chancery office built on the southwest corner of Second Street, diagonally across from the original site of St. Andrew's Cathedral. There, the affairs of the diocese would be carried out for the next twenty years.[9] Bishop Fletcher continued to live at St. John's Seminary until 1949, when he purchased a home at 4605 Crestwood Drive in what was then western Little Rock. There, he lived with his mother, the only surviving member of his immediate family, until her death at the age of ninety in 1958. The bishop continued to live in that home until two months before his death in 1979.[10]

Very early in his episcopate, Fletcher dealt with the problem of displaced persons from the recently concluded war in Europe. This situation occurred in 1948, when the Federal government tried to distribute European war refugees from Poland and other parts of eastern Europe throughout the United States. Fletcher set up a Diocesan Resettlement Commission under the direction of Father Anthony Lachowsky, C.S.Sp., a Holy Ghost Father at St. Joseph's Church in Conway. Fletcher sent Lachowsky to Lafayette, Louisiana, to find out how many displaced persons would be coming into the state and when.[11] In a letter to Monsignor William Castel, New Orleans archdiocesan director of resettlement, in November 1948, Bishop Fletcher reported that one of his diocesan priests, Father Louis Janesko, had spoken with four to eight families from Slovakia, in West Memphis, in eastern Arkansas, who asked for more information and assistance for them.[12]

Five months later, Castel wrote that some fifteen families, a few Slovacs and Poles, would be coming to Arkansas, and he inquired about jobs for them. Bishop Fletcher wrote that until they learned the language better, or unless they had some education, the best he could offer was farm labor in the eastern Arkansas Delta. He knew a few planters who would be interested in their labor. A few families came and were hired as farm laborers for the spring planting in 1949, but they did not stay long. Father Janesko wrote the bishop on April 11, 1949, that of the three displaced families that came to his area of West

Memphis, two had already left because they told him that there was no Catholic school for their children, and that they could be with other Slovacs and get better-paying jobs in Chicago.[13] Father John M. Bann, another member of the Diocesan Resettlement Commission, wrote the bishop two days later that "unless we give reassurance that the displaced people will stay on the land and not try to migrate immediately to larger centers, we cannot afford to continue work on this resettlement program."[14]

Only a few would ever come to Arkansas, although there was some occasional comment about certain displaced persons in the state. For example, Bishop Fletcher wrote to Father George Carns, of Our Lady of the Lake parish in Lake Village, in early 1950 asking him to meet a German family living in McGehee, because the priest spoke German. Correspondence on this situation continued for another year with Father Lachowsky still in charge of the diocesan efforts for resettlement.[15] This small and feeble attempt to bring a few of the displaced persons from eastern Europe, many of whom were Catholic, into Arkansas seemed to dissipate after 1951. In a rural state like Arkansas, which could only offer agricultural jobs at low wages, and with few European immigrants present as support, there was nothing to keep the immigrants in the Diocese of Little Rock. As with the earlier tide of European immigration, the post-World War II flood of immigration barely trickled into Arkansas.

Bishop Fletcher had better luck attracting new religious orders to Arkansas. A group of cloistered Carmelites arrived in the summer of 1950. Led by Mother Prioress Mary of Jesus, six Carmelite nuns came from Loretto, Pennsylvania, and moved into an old frame house at 812 Louisiana Street, two blocks south of the cathedral.[16]

These female Carmelites would soon be joined by a male order of Carmelite monks who acquired a site south of Little Rock that would be designated Marylake. The monks' building rests beside a small lake on about 420 acres, fifteen miles south of the city. A stone building constructed in 1926 had served as a Shriners' country club from 1926 to 1936, when it was sold to a Dr. Brinkley, who used it as a private hospital from 1937 to 1941. From 1941 to 1948, it was an annex for the Arkansas Baptist Hospital. In February 1952, the Diocese of Little Rock bought the property and donated it to the Carmelite Order. According to the local diocesan paper, the group was led by their Provincial, Father Edward Soler, O.C.D., a seventy-two year old Spanish native who had long been a missionary in Mexico before being expelled in 1914. Father Felix Da Prato, who was elected the first prior at Marylake, said the first Mass there on May 4, 1952. The novices from San Antonio arrived on May 15 and the next day, Carmelite observance began. Bishop Fletcher formally blessed the chapel and the monastery on July 25, 1952. Fourteen years later, the bishop dedicated the provincial cemetery. Some reconstruction of the interior of the monastery was completed in 1977.[17]

As the new ordinary of the Diocese of Little Rock, Fletcher was to make his five-year *ad limina* visit to the Holy Father in 1949, but he delayed his visit one year to 1950, designated a Holy Year by Pope Pius XII. Fletcher had been to Rome only once, in 1934, when he traveled with Bishop Morris as his aide and secretary. Not yet thirty-eight at the time, the trip made an impression on the young cleric. His memoirs of the trip account for more than thirty-five pages in his "Reminiscences," which ran to 168 pages.[18] Bishop Fletcher made his trip across the Atlantic in 1950 a real pilgrimage; he went to the Holy Land that summer and was present at the canonization of St. Maria Goretti on June 24.[19] That Holy Year would be special in another sense as Pope Pius XII, in consultation with the bishops from around the world, issued an infallible declaration on the Assumption of the Blessed Mother Mary.[20]

In that year, Bishop Fletcher dedicated a shrine to Our Lady of the Ozarks near Winslow, in Washington County, just south of Fayetteville.[21] There was considerable Marian devotion in post-War American Catholicism between 1945 and 1960, and Bishop Fletcher, as well as many Arkansas Catholics, shared in that devotion.[22] In the spring of 1951, Bishop Fletcher called upon the Catholic clergy and people of Arkansas to dedicate themselves more to Jesus and His Blessed Mother through penance and daily recitation of the rosary.[23] For a week in January 1952, a Family Rosary Crusade was sponsored by the diocese and major rallies were held in Little Rock, Fort Smith, and Jonesboro. The major speaker for these large rallies was Father Patrick C. Peyton, C.S.C. (Confraternity of the Sacred Cross or Holy Cross Fathers). Father Peyton was actually founder of the national Rosary Crusade. At these large rallies, the laity was encouraged to pledge to pray the rosary daily, and all were to dedicate themselves more to Jesus and His Blessed Mother.[24]

From December 8, 1953, through December 8, 1954, Bishop Fletcher celebrated a Marian year throughout the diocese and special Catholic events were held to mark that special occasion. At Robinson Auditorium, a special Mass for Catholic youth was held on September 12, 1954. A month later at the same place, a Holy Hour Devotion was held, where Catholics came and prayed before Jesus present in the Holy Eucharist. This latter event was originally scheduled for Travelers Field, but inclement weather moved it to Robinson Auditorium. The speakers on hand for the Holy Hour included Auxiliary Bishop Maurice Schexnayder of Lafayette, Louisiana.[25] In the fall of 1959, Bishop Fletcher called upon Catholics in the state to remember their pledges some seven years earlier and renew their efforts to keep praying the rosary for world peace and the salvation of souls.[26]

Arkansas' first Catholic book and religious supply store also opened in 1950. During the Civil War, in 1862, R.A. Bakewell of Jacksonport, a Catholic lawyer and former Missouri newspaper editor, wrote to Bishop Byrne proposing a Catholic bookstore for Arkansas and seeking help for it.[27] There is no record of Byrne being able to consider the proposal. Almost a century later, Monsignor Thomas Prendergast opened a small Guardian Church Goods Store next to the

Guardian Press building on Second Street.[28] In July 1966, the diocese sold the store to a Little Rock Catholic couple, Edward and Madge Lipsmeyer, who kept the name and location for another two years. In 1968, the Lipsmeyers moved the location to Seventh Street, one-half block east of Broadway Avenue. Now under the proprietorship of their son Michael Lipsmeyer, the Guardian Church Goods Store is still the only Catholic book and church goods store in Arkansas.[29]

That a Catholic bookstore would be founded and survive during the last half of the twentieth century is a small indication of the growth, though still incremental, of Catholicism in Arkansas after World War II. In fact, for twenty years from 1940 to 1960, the growth of Catholicism in the United States was phenomenal. The number of Americans who identified themselves as Catholics jumped from twenty-one million in 1940 to forty-two million by 1960, and this was at a time when the U.S. population was under 180 million. Catholics were now 23 percent of the total population. Between 1912 and 1963, the number of Catholics in the United States had grown from 15,015,569 to 43,851,538; more than twelve million had been added just since 1954.[30] In the two decades after World War II, seminaries expanded all across the United States. Nearly a quarter of the world Jesuit Order was from the United States by 1965. In 1954, there were 158,069 religious sisters, and by 1965, there were 181,421. These women were the mainstays of service to the American Catholic Church, working in schools, hospitals, and other charitable institutions. Seminarians went from 32,344 in 1954 to 48,992 by 1964; the 48,970 priests in 1954 grew to 59,892 by 1966, the highest number of men in the Roman Catholic priesthood in history of the United States.[31]

Arkansas Catholicism and St. John's Home Missions Seminary shared in the numerical expansion. In 1947, the first year of Bishop Fletcher's reign, Arkansas Catholics were estimated at 35,502; by 1950, that number had reached 36,943. Given the state population of 1,909,511, Catholics now made up 1.9 percent of the population and 2.4 percent of the white population.[32] St. John's Seminary, in 1945, had 115 students from high school through theology, with sixty-three enrolled in the seminary. Five years later, there were 160 seminarians from Little Rock and other dioceses, and 240 men was the total enrolled.[33] There was little wonder, then, that a few additions were necessary. With the help of the Catholic Extension Society, a major addition was built onto the back of Morris Hall, providing room for a greatly enlarged chapel and library at a cost of $150,000.00. In the presence of twenty-two bishops and three archbishops, Cardinal Samuel Stritch of Chicago, head of the Catholic Extension Society, dedicated the addition, and Archbishop Joseph H. Rummel of New Orleans was the homilist. It had been twenty years since then-Archbishop Stritch of Milwaukee had visited Little Rock to celebrate the twenty-fifth anniversary of the episcopate of Bishop Morris at St. John's Seminary. That evening, Cardinal Stritch spoke at a special dinner at the

Lafayette Hotel.[34]

Another indication of growth was the establishment of a new parish in west Little Rock, Our Lady of the Holy Souls, in 1947, and one in south Little Rock, St. Theresa's, in 1951. With the erection of Immaculate Conception parish in the northern part of North Little Rock in 1956, the twin cities of central Arkansas would have ten Catholic parishes. While certain towns might have two Catholic churches, a white and a black parish, only one city outside Little Rock, Fort Smith, had a large enough Catholic population to have four Catholic parishes.[35] Unlike the ethnic division of an earlier day, the Irish and German parishes, these new churches were suburban churches. Bishop Fletcher established territorial boundaries for these city parishes in 1949, but the guidelines could never be totally enforced.[36] A unique parish was created in 1957, the university Catholic parish called St. Thomas Aquinas, established for the faculty and Catholic students associated with the University of Arkansas. It was to operate separately from the church serving the Catholics of Fayetteville, St. Joseph's.[37]

The Catholic population in Arkansas continued to increase during the 1950s, rising to 44,765 in 1960, while Arkansas' overall state population was declining 6.5 percent to 1,786,000. But this was a significant year for Arkansas Catholics. For the first time since the diocese's creation in 1843 and the beginning of the census surveys in 1850, Catholics made up more than two percent of the total population, up to 2.5 percent. The increase from 1.9 percent in 1950 represented one of the largest increases in Arkansas history. Catholics were 3.2 percent of the white population, an increase of eight-tenths of one percent.[38] Between 1920 and 1960, the number of Catholics in Arkansas almost doubled from 23,192 to 44,765, and likewise, the percentage of Catholics in the total population almost doubled, from 1.3 percent to 2.5 percent.[39]

But the real story was not that Catholicism had gained so much between 1940 and 1960; after all, the Catholic population stood at 33,374 in 1940. What had happened was that Catholic growth was constant while the overall population of the state declined, from 1,949,511 to 1,786,000.[40] Another lesson is to be learned from these statistics, and it corresponds with the overall history of the Church in Arkansas. While nationally the Catholic population was doubling between 1940 and 1960, Catholicism in Arkansas was merely holding to about the same level of growth it had enjoyed between 1920 and 1940. Just as the Catholic Church in Arkansas failed to share in the great immigrant expansion in the late nineteenth and early twentieth centuries, it also failed to share in a mid-century Catholic resurgence. It is an example of a separate diocesan experience within the general contours of American Catholicism.

Such small numbers in a strongly evangelical Protestant culture meant that Arkansas Catholics continued to be held suspect well into the 1950s. There are priests living today who have worked in rural Arkansas since the 1940s, who can recount some stories indicating a lingering suspicion of Catholics, yet all of them would readily attest that most Arkansans are genuinely friendly and hospitable. One priest from the Little Rock diocese has written of his experience, Father Joseph W. Lauro, who served as a priest in the Ozarks from 1949 to 1959, and as a pastor in Russellville from 1959 to 1962. Afterward, he joined Cardinal Richard J. Cushing of Boston's Society of St. James the Apostle, a group dedicated to work among the poor in Latin America. As Father Lauro's autobiography continues, he would be assigned for duty in the mountains of Ecuador. Before Father Lauro ministered in the Andes, however, he served in the Arkansas Ozarks.

Born in Chicago on July 13, 1911, of Croatian immigrant parents, Joseph W. Lauro felt the calling to be a priest early in life. After one year at St. John's Seminary, and after serving as a fighter pilot in Europe with the Canadian and then American Air Force from 1941 to 1945, Lauro reentered St. John's in 1945 as a seminarian for the missionary Diocese of Little Rock. Bishop Fletcher ordained this ex-G.I. on May 17, 1949, at St. Andrew's Cathedral.[41] Sent as an assistant at Harrison to Father Henry J. Chinery, a Philadelphian ordained for the Diocese of Little Rock in 1942,[42] Father Lauro was given the job of serving the few Catholics in Eureka Springs near the Missouri border. Using money from his Catholic friends in Chicago, Lauro rebuilt St. Elizabeth's Catholic Church in Eureka Springs, originally built in 1904. In 1958, he constructed St. Anne's Catholic Church in Berryville, another small town in Carroll County. He also built a five-room rectory for himself in Eureka Springs in 1954 and became the first resident Catholic priest in Carroll County.[43]

Fr. Lauro had a few interesting experiences being a Croatian Chicago native serving as a Catholic priest in the Arkansas Ozarks. Preparing for the marriage of a Catholic girl and a Baptist boy, Father Lauro conducted the necessary prenuptial interview with the groom's parents by shouting questions over a swollen creek to the parents while the father held a shotgun under his arm. They would not allow the priest to come any closer. When Father Lauro was called as a witness for the prosecution in a drugstore robbery in Eureka Springs, the defense attorney's judicial strategy consisted of cross-examining Father Lauro, not on the details of the crime, but on the theology of the Catholic Church.[44]

One touching story involved the priest's work of giving away food at Christmas to the very poor in Carroll County. He had given away fifty or so baskets, but one family misinterpreted his efforts and returned his Christmas basket with the message, "We're not Catholics!" Lauro sought out the family to let them know that he had no ulterior motive. Back in the hills, he found a poor family living in a broken-down cabin with dusty floors and broken window panes. The father still refused the basket because, "We ain't Kath-a-licks, and we ain't a'goin to jine yo church. We're good Baptists." Lauro replied, "You stay Baptist. But there's no reason why you can't accept something you need and that's freely given." The man agreed to take it, but he would have to consult with his preacher to see if he was allowed to accept gifts from a Catholic priest.

If not, they would return all the items. A few weeks later, the man showed up at the church, thanked Fr. Lauro for the groceries, and wanted to know what he could do for him in return. Knowing that a refusal to accept some kind of repayment would be judged an insult by this proud Ozark yeoman, the priest had him run a few errands and do odd jobs around the church.[45] In these and other small ways, relationships between Catholics and those of other faiths improved.

Another wall that had to be breached was the racial segregation that persisted in the South and that was reflected in the churches. When Bishop Fletcher became Arkansas' fourth bishop, nine Catholic churches were serving primarily black congregations: St. Peter's at Pine Bluff and St. Raphael's mission, south of the city; St. Bartholomew's at Little Rock; St. Augustine's at North Little Rock; St. John the Baptist at Fort Smith; St. Cyprian's at Helena; St. Gabriel's at Hot Springs; Holy Martyrs of Uganda at El Dorado; and St. John the Baptist at Lake Village. The four black Catholic parishes in the Little Rock and Pine Bluff areas were pastored by members of the Society of the Divine Word, while the Franciscans and the Holy Ghost Fathers had the other areas of the state. These latter religious communities expanded their work among black Catholics during the first five years of Bishop Fletcher's episcopate.

On September 30, 1948, McGehee would see its second Catholic parish, St. Anthony's. There had been a predominately white parish, St. Winand's, for some years, but now there would be a Franciscan parish for black Catholics headed by Father Philip Matusko, O.F.M. In 1950, Fr. Matusko was replaced by Father Joseph Moellman, O.F.M. As mentioned in the previous chapter, the Franciscans also took over the operation of Holy Martyrs of Uganda parish in El Dorado on January 24, 1952. By then, the Franciscans were operating three black parishes in Lake Village, McGehee, and El Dorado.[46]

The same year, 1952, that the Franciscans took over the black parish in El Dorado, the Holy Ghost Fathers founded another black church in Conway, The Good Shepherd Catholic Church. The Holy Ghost Congregation had been the first religious society to work among blacks in Arkansas and had founded the first Catholic school for blacks in Conway in the early 1880s. Some seventy years later, ironically, they would found what would be the eleventh black Catholic parish in the state.[47] The Holy Ghost Fathers already pastored black Catholic congregations in Fort Smith, Helena, and Hot Springs. By 1955, Good Shepherd parish had a school staffed by three Fort Smith Benedictine nuns with fifty students.[48] (It would be this parish and school, the last one set up in the diocese, that would eventually foster the first African-American to be ordained for the Catholic priesthood for the Diocese of Little Rock, Father L. Warren Harvey.)

Regarding these schools, Bishop Fletcher proudly wrote in 1952 that he had restarted an adult school at the St. Raphael's mission south of Pine Bluff. He aptly summarized the challenges of working with blacks and how he intended to bring them into the Catholic Church:

> It is pretty hard to teach religion and to attract people to the Church when their thoughts are particularly centered on where their next meal is coming from, or how they evade the collector . . . The greatest hope for the development of the Church among the colored people is to keep the youth constantly close to the church and the school.[49]

There is no mention by Bishop Fletcher of the adult school at St. Raphael's mission. Unfortunately, much of the old buildings and the old mission church were destroyed in a devastating fire on August 20, 1955.[50] Although the buildings would be rebuilt, by 1961, the Franciscans had abandoned St. Raphael's, making it a mission church pastored from St. Peter's in nearby Pine Bluff.[51] By 1960, there were seven black Catholic grade schools and two high schools, St. Bartholomew's in Little Rock and St. Peter's in Pine Bluff, the oldest of these minority-oriented parishes. The diocese itself had a total of seven high schools and fifty-seven elementary parochial schools.[52] Many of the black Catholic churches and schools were profoundly affected by the racial changes that swept Arkansas and the South between 1954 and 1966, and most would not last the decade.

Such changes became apparent after the U.S. Supreme Court on May 15, 1954, issued its landmark decision in *Brown vs. Board of Education of Topeka, Kansas,* outlawing segregation in the United States. On June 28, 1954, Bishop Fletcher wrote the American Board of Catholic Missions, "I believe that the recent Supreme Court decision on segregation makes it advisable, at the present time, to go slow on new building projects dedicated exclusively to colored work."[53] Months after the decision, Bishop Fletcher issued a pastoral letter to the diocese dated August 3, 1954, concerning race relations and the Catholic schools. Part of this work was a defense of the segregation of the Church and part of it showed a willingness to change whenever it became possible:

> The Church had never made any distinctions of race. In places where segregation is enforced by laws and customs, the Church simply does the best it can by trying to provide separate churches and schools for the different races. Such has been the case in our Southland and in our Diocese in regards the members of the Negro race. Such has been the accepted pattern of operations by the Church as the best possible situation given the circumstances . . . Persons of every race, creed, and national origin should always be made to feel at home in every Catholic Church.[54]

This letter, at the opening of what some historians refer to as the Second

Reconstruction, demonstrated the style with which Bishop Fletcher dealt with racial matters. Never wanting to alienate any side, he moved cautiously, realizing that only a few white Catholics in the state shared the opinion of other whites in the state on segregation. The bishop's critics, both then and later, contended that he moved too slowly, but nonetheless, he never wavered in his belief that racial separation and segregation were wrong and should be abolished in a peaceable and orderly manner. As a Southerner and a native Arkansan, he had grown up in the segregated South, and like many other southern Catholics prelates, he went along with the prevailing social pattern. As the head of a religious minority in Arkansas, Bishop Fletcher was concerned about stirring up religious and racial animosities and giving anti-Catholics in Arkansas more ammunition to attack the Church. Father Lauro mentioned that this was a major concern of the bishop during the 1950s.[55] To his credit, Bishop Fletcher understood that racial hatred and bigotry were contrary to Catholic doctrine, and even his most impatient critics never accused the bishop of being racially prejudiced.[56] Arkansas' fourth bishop desired peaceful change, and from that course, he would not be deterred. That stand would be severely tested during the Little Rock Crisis, 1957-1959.

Little Rock had a reputation for racial moderation, so both the federal government and the local authorities planned to have a peaceful experiment in racial integration. Such a plan was drawn up by Little Rock's school superintendent, Virgil Blossom. It consisted of three stages: a new black high school, Horace Mann, opened in 1956, and it was to remain all-black; Hall High School in the western part of the city would open in 1957 and remain all-white; and at the city's oldest high school, Central High School, nine black students were to be admitted to a school that enrolled more than one thousand students. The high schools were to be integrated first, and by 1960, the junior high schools would be included. Although the plan had been approved weeks after the *Brown* decision, integration was not to take place for three more years and only after the all-white school for upper-income whites opened in the western part of the city. Integration would first occur at a middle-to-lower income, working-class school. The three-year lapse gave white segregationists time to organize opposition. That opposition grew, as Arkansas easily passed a state constitutional amendment in 1956 defying and denouncing the *Brown* decision. This amendment remained a part of Arkansas' Constitution until it was declared unconstitutional by a Little Rock federal judge on March 31, 1989.[57]

The crisis was provoked in 1957 when Governor Orval Faubus ordered the Arkansas National Guard to block the black students from entering the school. This action drew national and international attention to Central High, and the television pictures of white students harassing and even attacking black students damaged Arkansas' image in the nation and the world. Eventually, President Dwight D. Eisenhower nationalized the state Guard and sent in federal troops to escort and protect the black students integrating the school;

all of these dramatic events took place in September 1957. In response to the federal action, segregationists on the Little Rock School Board closed the city's public schools during the academic year 1958-1959. In the spring of 1959, a group of parents called the Women's Emergency Committee to Open Our Schools circulated petitions for a special election on May 25, 1959. The special election removed the segregationists from the school board, and the schools were reopened in the fall of 1959, bringing an end to the crisis. One of the founders of the Women's Emergency Committee was the wife of the late Congressman David D. Terry, Mrs. Adolphine Fletcher Terry, who was also a cousin of Bishop Fletcher. Not all of the city's public schools would open for blacks until the beginning of the 1970s.[58]

Soon after the crisis broke, Bishop Fletcher stated in *The Guardian*, "Integration is the law, and it is wrong to interfere with its peaceful inauguration."[59] He criticized the actions of Governor Faubus and the local press for inciting hatred and taking action, "sadly enough, at the expense of both peaceful integration, and the good name of the state of Arkansas."[60] He later called for special prayers for peace, understanding, and charity to replace rancor and bitterness in the Little Rock community and the country.[61] In the middle of this controversy, Bishop Fletcher became the first Arkansas Catholic cleric to appear on local television on a program called "Quiz a Catholic," which was broadcast on Saturday, October 26, 1957, on Channel 11, KTHV, the local CBS affiliate. This apparently was a one-time broadcast as part of its public affairs programming.[62] A year later, in November 1958, the American Catholic bishops declared racism a sin; Bishop Fletcher concurred and wrote in the local diocesan paper that "as a Christian people, we are obliged not only in private but in our public life to follow the teachings of the Master in solving our race problems."[63] In the same letter, Fletcher maintained that Catholics had to follow the U.S. Supreme Court unless their decisions violated the Catholic faith or conscience. In moving toward peaceful racial integration, he steadfastly maintained that the U.S. Supreme Court decision was correct.[64]

As if these pastoral letters were not enough, both Bishop Fletcher and his new editor of *The Guardian* published small books addressing the race question and basically upholding the ideals of peaceful integration and brotherhood between the races. Editor William W. O'Donnell was a native of New Jersey who had come to Arkansas after leaving a newspaper position in Providence, Rhode Island. In 1954, he became the first layperson to edit the *Guardian* in its forty-three years of existence, one of the few lay editors in the Catholic press at the time.[65] He published in 1959 *America's Race Problem: A Catholic Editor's Analysis*. The next year, Bishop Fletcher wrote *An Elementary Catholic Catechism on the Morality of Segregation and Racial Discrimination*. Bishop Fletcher flatly stated in that work that racial segregation and discrimination were immoral, because they opposed two of the great demands of the Gospel, justice and charity to all.[66] Fletcher's small book appeared during Lent, in the spring of 1960, and Frank J. Duff, assistant publisher of the *Arkansas Gazette,* the Little Rock newspaper leading the fight for integration, wrote the bishop thanking him for his efforts to bring the teachings of the Catholic Church to bear on race relations in the state and nation.[67] By 1959, St. Vincent's Infirmary and all other Catholic hospitals had been integrated, according to Bishop Fletcher.[68]

Not all were pleased with the bishop's pronouncements. A fair number of hate messages and comments were mailed to the bishop, accusing both him and the Catholic Church of hypocrisy. After all, as one person wrote, "If Catholics believed so much in integration, why did they segregate themselves from Protestants and their schools?" Besides, there were still separate black Catholic schools. Many of these messages also claimed that the whole integration movement was either a Communist or Jewish conspiracy, or a little bit of both.[69] Racial prejudice was not manifested to non-Catholics alone; it existed some among Arkansas Catholics. When Father Lauro announced from the pulpit in St. John's Catholic Church in Russellville in the spring of 1960 that all people, white or black, were welcome to the Catholic church and school, two families walked out of the church. The Chicago-born priest said that 98 percent of the parish made no complaint about his talk, but few blacks sought to come to either the church or school. He did begin distributing food and other items to blacks as part of the social ministry of the church.[70]

All of this racial strife caused the relocation of the cloistered Carmelite sisters. According to Fr. Lauro, "dissidents" to the integration of the Little Rock schools placed ten sticks of dynamite in the school board building in September 1959, only eighty feet from the sisters' residence on Louisiana Street. Bishop Fletcher brought Father Lauro to Little Rock from Eureka Springs a month later to supervise the relocation of the sisters, as he had raised the funds to build a new convent which was to be located a few blocks west of University Avenue, not far from the University of Arkansas at Little Rock, then known as Little Rock University. The sisters moved in September 1961, and Bishop Fletcher made the formal enclosure ceremony on November 4.[71] Bishop Fletcher wrote the Vatican in his Quinquennial report two months after the dynamite incident that "Racial hatred has been increasing as a result of the last two years experience."[72]

While much of Arkansas was caught up in the racial turmoil from 1957 to 1960, the state, nation, and Church were undergoing transition in other ways. Since its debt had been retired, Subiaco saw new buildings in the postwar years. A new water-supply lake was built between 1946 and 1948, and a new classroom building was completed by February 5, 1952. Plans unfolded later that year for a new abbey church. This massive church rose slowly over the landscape of Subiaco. As Abbot Nahlen lay dying in a hospital, Bishop Fletcher arrived on June 29, 1957, to dedicate the new bells for the church. A few months later, the industrious Abbot Paul Nahlen died, and the church that he envisioned was not completed until February 8, 1959. The new church, which he considered his crowning achievement, was large; the nave seating six hundred and the transept seven hundred. On March 31, 1959, Bishop Fletcher dedicated this massive Gothic church. It is one of the most beautiful structures in Logan County.[73]

Another landmark event happened at the end of Abbot Nahlen's reign. Black students were admitted to Subiaco Academy in the fall of 1955. Few blacks lived in western Arkansas, and while the monks had voted to accept blacks several years earlier, none had applied. At the urging of Bishop Fletcher and with the overwhelming approval of the monks, black students started to attend. There were initial problems–insults to the black students, loss of a few white students, vexing moments in restaurants and theaters–but the incidents soon stopped.[74] The abbot lost a bout with cancer on August 31, 1957, at St. Vincent's Infirmary. Bishop Fletcher said the requiem Mass. Nahlen was the first abbot to die at Subiaco and the first to be buried there. (Abbot Ignatius Conrad had gone back to Switzerland to die and is buried there. Abbot Edward Burgert, the second abbot, would live until January 1968.)[75] Called the "Saviour of Subiaco" at his funeral on September 3, 1957, Nahlen could also be rightfully termed its second founder.

On September 23, 1957, the monks of Subiaco elected their fourth abbot, Michael Lensing. Born near the Arkansas monastery in Scranton, in 1916, he came to Subiaco as a high school student in 1928, and five years later, he entered the monastery. Ordained a priest in 1939, he did many different jobs around the abbey: editor of the *Abbey Message*, retreat master, and novice master. He also was involved in many activities far beyond the monastery. From 1945 to 1948, he was president of the National Catholic Rural Life Conference, and at the time of his election, he gave retreats and explained Catholic doctrine in pamphlets that were distributed to non-Catholics. (Despite all these activities, he had never been assigned outside Subiaco in his eighteen years as a priest.)[76]

In his seventeen years as abbot, missions of Subiaco expanded beyond the United States and the western hemisphere. One of his first actions was to elevate a Benedictine priory in Texas that had been erected from Subiaco in 1949. After ten years, it was ready to be independent and was given that status on September 29, 1959. The priory then applied to the Holy See to have its status raised to that of an abbey. That permission was forthcoming, and on September 12, 1961, Corpus Christi Abbey near Corpus Christi, Texas, elected its first abbot. It was the first such ecclesiastical structure to be formed from the Arkansas Benedictine community. The Arkansas Benedictines then established in eastern Nigeria a St. Mukasa Priory, named for one of the black African Catholic martyrs in Uganda in 1886. The cost of supporting this work, and the Nigerian-Biafran war that broke out on May 30, 1967, doomed this mission. The Arkansas Benedictines, caught in the middle of the bloody strife, barely made it out of the country with their lives the next year. The mission lasted from 1963 until 1968.[77] The Arkansas monks had more success in 1970 with a monastic community in British Honduras, to be known as Belize after independence in 1971. This mission, called *Santa Familia* monastery, is still a functioning outreach of Subiaco.[78] It seems ironic that these faraway missions would begin under the administration of an abbot whose whole career had been inside the walls of Subiaco.

During the early 1960s, buildings sprang up all over Subiaco. A large guest retreat house was completed and dedicated in 1963, the first and only such facility in the diocese. A gym-field house, football stadium, and residence building were built by 1967. The following year, an expanded library with archives was constructed.[79] But with so much expansion, some aspects of monastic life had to give. The Subiaco farm sold its dairy cows in 1964 with the announcement that it was auctioning off "the oldest herd of Holstein dairy cattle in the state of Arkansas."[80] After ninety years, Subiaco Abbey had certainly grown. From a small group of German and Swiss-German monks struggling on a plot of land in Logan County, Subiaco had become a major focus of Catholic education and presence in western Arkansas. The physical changes between 1950-1970 were nothing short of amazing.[81]

More tumult for American Catholics came with the election of the two Johns, John XXIII and John F. Kennedy. Cardinal Angelo Roncalli was elected Pope on October 28, 1958; the 78-year-old Pope chose the name John XXIII. Within a few months of his election, on January 25, 1959, the new pontiff called a second general church council to be held at the Vatican.[82] Before the council convened in 1962, United States Senator, John F. Kennedy of Massachusetts, became the first Roman Catholic to be elected as President of the United States. In Arkansas, and throughout the country, there was skepticism that America had become sufficiently tolerant to elect a Catholic president. Although Kennedy won the popular vote by the narrowest of margins, his electoral vote was solid, and he became the thirty-fifth president. Father Lauro remembered attempts by a few ministers in Arkansas to rally their congregations against the Catholic Democrat. A minister in Lauro's town of Russellville asked his congregation to swear that they were not going to vote for Kennedy. A few Catholics told their pastor that they had felt so much hostility toward them for being Catholic, that they had passed themselves off as Protestants. Lauro also remembered that he had received a number of harassing phone calls as the campaign drew to a close. The night of the election, he got a call from a man who had changed his mind at the last minute and voted for the Massachusetts Democrat.[83]

A major speaker from Protestants and Other Americans United for the Separation of Church and State rented Robinson Auditorium at Little Rock in the fall of 1960 to denounce the power and influence of the Catholic Church and the Kennedy candidacy. Reverend W.O. Vaught, Pastor of Immanuel Baptist Church in Little Rock, denounced Kennedy from the pulpit and called upon his congregation not to vote for a Catholic.[84] True to their Democratic loyalty, and just as they did for Al Smith in 1928, Arkansans gave their electoral votes to a Catholic presidential candidate. The Arkansas Catholic weekly almost ignored the Kennedy candidacy. Only after the election did it run his picture and ask the blessing of Almighty God to descend on him and bless him.[85]

The year that President Kennedy was elected was also the year that Catholic High School in Little Rock left its original location at Twenty-Fifth and Gaines Streets and moved to Lee Avenue west of University Avenue, then near the western edge of the city. Plans had been announced in 1958, but the new facility would not be occupied until the fall of 1960.[86] With the abandonment of the property at Twenty-Fifth and Gaines, an old connection with Little Rock College and St. John's Seminary had ceased. As with St. John's Seminary and Mount St. Mary's Academy, Catholic education facilities above the elementary school level for central Arkansas had moved to western Little Rock. Although St. Bartholomew's High School would not close until 1971, both Catholic High and St. Mount Mary's had begun accepting black students by 1962. Ms. Carol Blow integrated Mount St. Mary's in 1962 and graduated in 1966.[87] But people like Ms. Blow were exceptions. As black Catholic high schools closed in Little Rock, few blacks were willing to attend a predominantly white Catholic high school across town. Bishop Fletcher's reports to the American Board of Catholic Missions made evident throughout the 1960s, that as black Catholic schools closed and the diocese tried to end separate education for blacks and whites, few blacks were either able or willing to go to a predominantly white Catholic school.

This pattern repeated itself as black Catholic churches and schools closed during the last ten years of Bishop Fletcher's administration, 1962-1972. In 1961, there were eleven black Catholic churches and seven schools. St. Cyprian's school closed in the spring of 1963 and the parish followed a year later. The Franciscans, by 1965, had given up their parishes of St. Anthony's in McGehee and St. John the Baptist in Lake Village.[88] In the spring of 1965, Good Shepherd school closed, and Arkansas' first future black Catholic priest, L. Warren Harvey, finished his education through high school at the predominantly white St. Joseph's school in Conway.[89] Two years after the school closed, Good Shepherd parish closed, and the Franciscans also closed Holy Martyrs of Uganda parish in El Dorado. Thus, Bishop Fletcher reported to the American Board of Catholic Missions in August 1967 that only six black Catholic churches still operated; St. Bartholomew's in Little Rock, St. Augustine's in North Little Rock, St. John the Baptist in Fort Smith, St. Gabriel in Hot Springs, and the parish of St. Peter's in Pine Bluff with its rural mission church, St. Raphael's.[90] Two years later, the Holy Ghost Fathers closed their parish in Fort Smith, ending more than fifty years of serving blacks in that western Arkansas city.[91] By 1972, St. Gabriel's church and school and the high school department of St. Bartholomew's had all closed, leaving only three black churches in Little Rock, North Little Rock, and Pine Bluff with its mission church, St. Raphael's. These black Catholic parishes still operated their parochial schools by the end of Bishop Fletcher's administration.[92]

While many blacks, Catholics or Protestants, were hesitant to attend predominantly white Catholic schools, other reasons helped account for the rapid decline of separate black churches and schools. The vocations crisis, which came after the mid-1960s, affected the ability of religious communities, particularly sisterhoods, to maintain these small and expensive schools. With few nuns to teach, small black Catholic parishes found it difficult to maintain schools with lay teachers.

That vocations crisis was not as yet on the horizon and growth was everywhere in the early 1960s. In 1963 the Diocese of Little Rock reached an agreement with the Glenmary Home Missioners, a domestic missionary society of priest and brothers, to staff churches in the Ozarks and Southern Arkansas. The Ozark parishes of Huntsville and Winslow were given back to the Diocese in 1975, yet the Glenmary Fathers are now marking their third decade in Arkansas by serving in the churches at Crossett, Monticello, and Warren. Subiaco Abbey in 1920 had the most men entering the monastery in its history, and the growth had been consistent and showed no sign of abating. Observed Subiaco's historian, "The Seminary was bursting at the seams."[93] The diocesan seminary in Little Rock kept up its large enrollment, but it was not much larger than the 1950 enrollment. Total seminary enrollment had dropped from 240 to 217 in the previous ten years, but that was primarily due to the decrease in minor seminarians, those of high school age.[94] By the fall of 1962, the minor seminary had closed at St. John's, and the local Catholic weekly reported that the seminary would try to develop its college and theological programs.[95]

In line with this, the diocese, a few months later, announced a ground breaking ceremony for a new residence hall for seminary faculty and students. Fitzgerald Hall, the former residence for students and faculty, had been used primarily for students for many years, though a few of the faculty had stayed there; others were housed in Morris Hall. The need for more modern quarters for both faculty and students was acute.[96] The building was occupied in late April 1965. At that time, the Bishop blessed the new facility known as Fletcher Hall.[97] This would be the last major building constructed at the seminary and the first completely new building on the grounds in almost fifty years.

Fletcher also hoped to upgrade the faculty by sending various members to prestigious religious institutions in the United States and Europe to give professors a broader and more thorough education. Because most of the seminary students were studying for other dioceses, both Bishop Fletcher and the rector of St. John's, Monsignor James E. O'Connell, hoped to keep the Arkansas seminary attractive to other dioceses.[98] Father David Boileau, who was originally from Kalamazoo, Michigan, received his doctorate in Theology from the Catholic University of Louvain in Belgium. He returned to teach at St.

John's in January 1962, and rapidly made a name for himself in the community. A year after arriving in Arkansas, in 1963, Father Boileau became the first priest of the diocese to open a session of the Arkansas General Assembly with a prayer. The last time that a Catholic cleric had been invited to a legislative session in Arkansas was during the Civil War, when an Irish military chaplain with the invading Union army opened a session of the Reconstruction-era General Assembly in 1864.[99]

Civil rights issues remained paramount in the early 1960s. The Little Rock Crisis was one of the first battles; the front now shifted to other southern states. An indication of continued concern on this issue came as the local Catholic paper announced the formation of a group called S.U.R.E., Seminarians United for Racial Equality, in May 1965, with Fathers James Drane and Walter Clancy as the faculty sponsors.[100] There was pressure for change in the diocese from the Little Rock branch of the Catholic Interracial Council. The national C.I.C. had evolved from the Catholic Layman's Union organized by a New York Jesuit, John LaFarge, in 1928, to work for interracial justice in U.S. society and the American Catholic Church. In 1934, it changed its name to the Catholic Interracial Council.[101] By 1960, a Little Rock branch was organized with the blessing of Bishop Fletcher.[102]

At times, there was some tension between the bishop and the local branch; the group usually pushed for more change on the interracial front, while Bishop Fletcher favored caution, which he considered prudent given the volatile nature of the situation. A former president of the Little Rock C.I.C. remembered that the bishop was willing to listen and consider their opinions, but he also wanted to consider all the different angles to a situation before acting. While in Rome attending the third session of the Second Vatican Council in the fall of 1964, Bishop Fletcher was quoted in *The Guardian* as saying that he would support and even join the Catholic Interracial Council, yet he never did.[103] It was not Bishop Fletcher's style to join with any political cause or organization.

Racial issues still remained unsettled into the mid-1960s. When Mrs. Viola Gregg Liuzzo, a Catholic housewife from Michigan, was assassinated for transporting civil rights marchers in the Selma-to-Montgomery march on March 25, 1965, a Mass was said in her honor on April 3 at St. Andrew's Cathedral. The service, sponsored by the Little Rock branch of the C.I.C., was delayed thirty minutes to an hour because of a bomb threat. After the police searched the area, Father Clancy was allowed to conduct the service.[104] The Little Rock branch of the C.I.C. also invited Auxiliary Bishop Harold Perry of New Orleans to a reception at St. John's Seminary, and a Mass and prayer breakfast at the Cathedral of St. Andrew on January 28-29, 1967; at all the events, Bishop Fletcher hosted the distinguished guest. Bishop Harold Perry was the first full African-American to be raised to the rank of bishop in the American Catholic hierarchy. As a member of the Society of the Divine Word, he had also served for a few months as pastor of St. Peter's Catholic Church in 1949-1950.[105]

Many changes had been made around the cathedral parish in the ten years before the visit of Bishop Perry. Air-conditioning was installed in 1957.[106] The cathedral had a new floor, new pews, and a new crypt below the northern transept for the bishops. The previous bishops had been buried below the southwest corner of the church, making it difficult for people to visit their remains. The spires, which had been slightly damaged by a tornado in 1950, were repaired. These changes were completed by March 1962.[107] A sadder change came with the closing of the cathedral parish school in 1961.[108]

The year the cathedral was renovated, 1962, also witnessed the first session of the Second Vatican Council. The First Vatican Council had met in almost continuous session from December 1869 to July 1870, yet the Second Vatican Council met for about three months at four general fall sessions from 1962-1965. The first session of Vatican II opened on October 11, 1962; Bishop Fletcher returned to Little Rock by December 4. Even the death of Pope John XXIII on June 3, 1963, did not end the council as it continued under the newly elected pontiff, Paul VI. While the First Vatican Council had drawn most of its participants from Europe, especially from Catholic countries, the Second Vatican Council reflected the success of worldwide missionary work of the Catholic Church because bishops from outside Europe dominated. Only one American priest had served in the theological preparation for the First Vatican Council; forty-three helped in the preparations for the second.[109]

At this council, Protestants and Orthodox Christians were allowed to be observers. This helped diminish some of the longstanding hostility between Christian denominations. When he returned from the first session at the Vatican, Bishop Fletcher found this letter from a Protestant Arkansan: "I think it was a beautiful gesture on the part of the Roman Catholic Church to invite Protestants and other observers. It certainly will make for better understanding between Roman Catholics and Protestants, as well as Eastern Orthodox."[110]

The Second Vatican Council produced sixteen major documents, all basically in line with the theological and liturgical movements in the Church prior to the council. Sixteen documents were produced, but not a single dogma, just a different way of looking at issues. One of the guiding concepts of the council was *aggiornamento*, meaning "adaptation" to the outward contemporary life and an inward change regarding modernity.[111] Given the confusion that beset the Church after the council, it is striking how mild and orthodox were the actual tone and letter of the documents.

The American Catholic presence at the council would be influential in three important documents: the Decree on Ecumenism, the Declaration on the Relations of the Church to Non-Christian Religions, and the Declaration on Religious Liberty. Having worked out their faith as a religious minority, the bishops of the American Church had great experience in all these areas. They had long cooperated with non-Catholic Christians on many issues. They were interested in the section on non-Christian religions, particularly relations with Judaism, a faith with which they had much experience in the United States. But it was on religious liberty and freedom of conscience that the Americans had their greatest impact. The council virtually endorsed the theological views elucidated before the council by the American, John Courtney Murray, S.J.[112] The documents drew from the American Catholic experience, and Bishop Fletcher heartily endorsed the changes concerning non-Catholics, Jews, and religious liberty. This is confirmed by the bishop's "Reminiscences" and by the testimony of then Monsignor and later Auxiliary Bishop, Lawrence Graves. Monsignor Graves served as the bishop's secretary, aide, and according to Fletcher, his major translator because Graves' Latin and Italian were much better than the bishop's.[113]

With the bishop absent from the diocese for three to four months during the years 1962-1965, operation of the diocese fell to the chancellor, Monsignor Joseph A. Murray. To keep the Catholic reading public informed about the council, editor William O'Donnell ran special supplements weekly while the council was in session. The supplements were expensive because *The Guardian* usually ran on a shoestring budget.[114] According to Graves, Bishop Fletcher attended the sessions every day. He also wrote letters to Arkansas Catholics about his impressions. In one letter dated late September 1963 and published in the Catholic weekly in early October, the bishop reported, "this being in Rome for this ecumenical council is like a dream . . . It is a wonderful kind of dream for a short time, yet for a hillbilly like me, it takes some getting used to it."[115]

In his "Reminiscences," written more than a decade later, the prelate was less sanguine about the whole affair. He felt that the council was too big, and he found it "difficult . . . to understand even the essentials of what the different speakers said with their various kinds of Latin pronunciation."[116] He believed that the council had made so many pronouncements and decrees that it became difficult to implement them.[117] The bishop served with seven members of the American Catholic hierarchy to advise the council on questions of faith and morals, a cause dear to the bishop.[118] With annoyance, and even anger, Bishop Fletcher denounced misleading news reports in November 1963 claiming that the council planned to de-emphasize devotion to Mary, the Mother of Jesus.[119] In the fall of 1964, Bishop Fletcher announced the change in the language of the liturgy to the vernacular–in America's case, to English. It would begin the first Sunday of Advent in 1964, the start of the Church's liturgical year.[120] This was probably the most apparent change to Catholic parishioners. The Arkansas prelate never gave an address at the Second Vatican Council, although he attempted to address it at the last session, the busiest, on the permanence and sanctity of Catholic sacramental marriage. He never had that opportunity because of the press of time. He did make some thirteen written interventions during the council and nine were accepted.[121] Eleven of the sixteen documents were approved at the last session in the fall of 1965.[122]

In a document dated May 13, 1970, Bishop Fletcher outlined what he considered to be the nine important objectives of Vatican II. He supported efforts for a new and more readable interpretation of Scripture and felt that the recently issued New American Bible was an "acceptable translation." He agreed with the council's reconstituting the bishop's organization to the National Conference of Catholic Bishops, and he wanted the council to emphasize the sanctity and permanence of marriage. On the issue of war and peace, he worried that the initial drafts at the council might be interpreted as condemning all who resort to force to protect the rights of others. He was glad they were altered, because they might have been construed as an attack on military service or the right of a country to help another defend itself from external aggression. He also was glad that the council did not overturn the prohibition of artificial contraception and that it called for consulting with a confessor in forming a right and sincere conscience on this issue.[123]

About a week before the council ended, Bishop Fletcher was given a special privilege. He was the main celebrant at the daily Mass at the high altar at St. Peter's on the feast day of St. Andrew the Apostle, the patron saint of the Diocese of Little Rock.[124] Whether he had requested this, or that honor only happened to fall to him that day, is unclear. There is no doubt, however, that the bishop understood how significant it was to celebrate *that* particular Saint's feast day at St. Peter's Basilica in Rome. The Second Vatican Council ended on December 8, 1965, the ninety-sixth anniversary of the opening of the First Vatican Council. Fletcher was back in Little Rock by December 10.[125]

The year 1965 was a significant one in the life of Bishop Fletcher, his twenty-fifth anniversary as bishop. He marked this celebration with Masses at two ceremonies in Little Rock. On April 28, he held a Mass of thanksgiving at St. Andrew's Cathedral for the visiting members of the hierarchy, diocesan clergy, members of religious orders, and delegations from the religious sisters. At this Mass were seven archbishops, including Cardinal James F. A. McIntyre of Los Angeles and Archbishop John P. Cody of New Orleans, the future Cardinal at Chicago, and forty-two bishops. Bishop Maurice Schexnayder of Lafayette, Louisiana, was the homilist at the Mass, whose main celebrant was Cardinal McIntyre. A letter was read from Cardinal Ameto Giovanni Cicognani, then the papal secretary of state under Pope Paul VI. The Italian cardinal had been the first apostolic delegate to visit Arkansas when he came to Bishop Fletcher's consecration in 1940. After the Mass, there was a dinner at the Marion Hotel. The following Sunday, May 2, 1965, there was a Mass and reception for a large crowd at Barton Coliseum for all the clergy, religious sisters, and laity.[126]

A year later, in May 1966, Fletcher would win another distinct honor for an Arkansas bishop. The Arkansas Conference of the National Conference of Christians and Jews gave him its annual brotherhood award for supporting efforts at racial harmony and the documents on ecumenism and religious liberty at the Second Vatican Council. At the award ceremony, Fletcher attacked communism and denied that the West could live in peaceful coexistence with it, contending that either it or Christianity would triumph.[127]

The subject was not new to the bishop. When Soviet President Nikita Khrushchev visited the United States in the fall of 1959, Fletcher denounced the visit and the welcome shown the Russian leader because he was "an enemy of man and God." Later, the Arkansas bishop announced that church bells throughout the diocese would toll at 11:00 a.m. each day of the visit asking for Christ's help and Mary's prayers to deliver the country from godless communism and for divine assistance in restoring "all things to Christ."[128] Anti-communism had been a strong strain in American Catholicism since the end of World War I. Eager to prove their loyalty against a godless foe, Catholics were generally superpatriots in the two decades after World War II.[129] Bishop Fletcher shared these sentiments.

By 1965, the United States was involved in its second war to contain communism, this time in South Vietnam (the first was Korea, 1950-1953). The American bishops mostly supported the war, only allowing for conscientious objectors in 1968.[130] Because anti-communism was so strong among American Catholics, some joined the John Birch Society, an anti-communist, political group formed in 1958.[131]

A few Catholics were active in the Little Rock chapter of the Birch Society, and they invited Father Francis Fenton from the Diocese of Bridgeport, Connecticut, to come to Arkansas. His appearance at the Albert Pike Hotel on January 28, 1967, was heavily advertised in the local Catholic newspaper. Father Fenton asserted that 40 percent of Birchites nationwide were Catholics and that two to three hundred priests were in the movement, but he offered no proof.[132] It was clear that many local Catholics were part of the movement, and the strong advertisement for Father Fenton's visit seems to have given his appearance a semi-official diocesan endorsement. Some criticism appeared in letters to the editor in the secular press about too much "Birchite" influence around the bishop.[133] There is no evidence, however, that the bishop was ever a member of the John Birch Society. As earlier stated regarding the Catholic Interracial Council, Bishop Fletcher usually eschewed formal association with any political group.

Two days after Father Fenton arrived, Bishop Fletcher was host at an historical ecumenical religious service at the main chapel of St. John's Seminary. In attendance were the Episcopal and Methodist bishops of Arkansas, and representatives from the Arkansas Presbyterians, Baptists, and Disciples of Christ. As the reports indicated, the meeting was indeed a religious first for Arkansas and a fruit of the theological development at the Second Vatican Council.[134] Such ecumenical contacts would continue for the duration of Bishop Fletcher's episcopate.

In January 1967, another parish was created in Little Rock. By geographically dividing Holy Souls parish in northwestern Little Rock, a new

Christ the King parish was formed and announced in *The Guardian* on January 6. Since it had no church, the new parish held its Sunday Masses at the chapel of St. John's until a church was built at Rodney Parham Road and Highway 10 in October 1969.[135]

While things in the diocese appeared peaceful, below the surface, especially among certain members of the faculty at St. John's Home Missions Seminary, a real crisis was brewing. Bishop Fletcher had tried to widen the theological training of the priests to make his home mission seminary academically accredited and appealing to bishops from other dioceses. The Diocese of Little Rock never generated enough vocations to keep the institution alive. Merely to keep the doors open cost the diocese $75,000.00 a year. By August 1966, it had fifteen faculty members: ten priests and five lay professors.[136] The younger faculty was far more liberal on many theological and social questions than most Arkansas Catholics and the bishop, and on issues such as racial equality and integration, they had been the leaders for change. According to Monsignor O'Connell, the third and last rector of the seminary, several of the younger faculty members had great disagreements with the bishop and would be invited to his house to talk to him. While the younger faculty members maintained that the bishop did not listen, Monsignor O'Connell was sure that he did, but that he just did not agree with them.[137] Tensions had existed at the seminary for a couple of years, but a series of articles written by Father James F. Drane, and published in the *Gazette* in the summer, pushed them into the open. The result would be the closing of St. John's Seminary that summer.

A native of Philadelphia, born in 1930, Father Drane came from an Irish Catholic family of ten. He entered St. John's in 1948 after graduating from a high school in his native city. Ordained for the Diocese of Little Rock in 1956, he was sent to do graduate study at the Catholic University of Madrid, returning to St. John's in 1960 to teach and finish his doctoral dissertation. He was at St. John's continuously from 1960 until 1967 except for one year, 1963-1964, when he returned to Spain to complete his doctorate. He had been allowed that year to travel behind the Iron Curtain in eastern Europe, and he subsequently wrote a book, published in 1965, about his experiences and perceptions of that region. He had also been Newman chaplain at what was then Little Rock University, where he had invited major speakers. After he had invited speakers on the "Death of God" theology, a trendy theological theme at the time, Bishop Fletcher removed Drane as chaplain in November 1966, a position he had held for six years.[138]

It was the articles he wrote the following June that led to his suspension from St. John's and caused him to eventually leave the priesthood. The Church was studying revising its traditional ban on artificial birth control for married couples. A papal commission had been working on the issue, and it made its recommendation to the papacy in the early summer of 1966. In April 1967, the text of the report leaked to a national Catholic weekly newspaper. The commission apparently had advised the Pope to lift the ban for married couples. The Church had not lifted the ban, but there was speculation that it would be lifted soon.[139]

Perhaps emboldened by the leaked report, Father Drane submitted a series of articles to the *Gazette* entitled "Church Authority and Natural Law." Although he said that he wrote "in no official capacity," Drane concluded, "It is altogether possible that the papal myth, so overburdened with an infallibility syndrome, will finally be laid to rest, only by some obviously fallible solemn pronouncement. This could very well come from the Birth Control issue."[140] In a provocative tone, the professor said that as long as Pope Paul VI hesitated in his decision about artificial contraception, he was contributing to the "demythologizing" of the papal office.[141]

Father Drane did not have to wait long for Bishop Fletcher's response. Within two weeks, Fletcher suspended Drane from teaching at the seminary because "it would be inconsistent to use the services of a priest to represent the Church when he does not believe in what it teaches."[142] It was not merely that Drane had disagreed with the Church's teaching on artificial contraception in a public, secular newspaper–that could be considered imprudent–but Drane had gone beyond that. In a taunting, disrespectful tone, he had questioned the doctrine of papal infallibility, a defined dogma of the Church. Bishop Fletcher asserted in his "Reminiscences," "I would not violate the trust imposed on me by other Bishops, who were sending students to the seminary, by giving these students a questionable preparation and formation to the priesthood."[143]

A week after Drane's suspension, Fletcher announced that the seminary would close after fifty-six years of operation. This decision, he recalled in this memoirs, was the most "sorrowful" he made in his career as bishop. Bishop Graves remembers that Fletcher agonized over the decision, and he witnessed Fletcher actually weeping over its closing. The school had been his own and he dearly loved it. [144] A few days afterward, Fletcher wrote Monsignor Kenneth Stack of the Catholic Church Extension Society, a longtime supporter of St. John's Seminary, stressing the "impossibility of getting hold of an adequate teaching staff."[145]

In Bishop Fletcher's "Reminiscences," he maintained that he "harbors no ill will toward the priests who made it impossible for the seminary to continue." He nevertheless expressed his extreme disappointment that the diocese had spent much money placing many of these liberal priests in graduate study to bolster the seminary. He reported that in April 1967, about half of the priest faculty had passed a resolution that "seminary teaching had become irrelevant, and not effective in the rapidly changing world."[146] Monsignor O'Connell saw not only the turmoil in the seminary, but the cost of running it. For a year afterward, priests from Little Rock were sent to Notre Dame Seminary in New Orleans because the Arkansas diocese was still part of the Province of New

Orleans. Fletcher then began sending Arkansas priests to Holy Trinity Seminary in Dallas, which had been opened by Bishop Thomas Gorman of the Dallas-Ft. Worth diocese. Many of the faculty priests took other positions. A few, like Father Clancy, who worked for a few years in diocesan Social Services, eventually left the priesthood. Others, like Father Boileau, left Arkansas and were eventually incardinated into other dioceses. Since 1982, Fr. Boileau has been a priest in good standing with the Archdiocese of New Orleans.[147]

News of Drane's suspension spread. *Life* magazine, a national pictorial newsweekly, ran a sympathetic article on the priest in September 1967.[148] Drane explained his position in a 1969 anthology of twelve men who had left the priesthood. Drane maintained that while he had disagreed with the bishop on such issues as war, racism, and ecumenism, he never felt that their friendship had dissolved. He said that he was fired without due academic process, and he appealed his case to Rome that fall. While the case was on appeal, Drane attended Yale University to finish a book entitled *Authority and Institution: A Church in Crisis,* which was published in 1969. While at Yale, Father Drane learned in April 1968 that the Vatican backed Bishop Fletcher completely. Bishop Fletcher was advised to offer him his place back in the diocese if Drane was willing to publicly recant his views. According to Drane, Bishop Fletcher accepted this directive, and with all good will, invited him to return to Arkansas on the condition that he renounce the views he embraced in the *Gazette* articles. Drane felt in conscience he could not do this. Father Drane said that the bishop also would not allow him to leave the diocese, as the Arkansas bishop could not, in conscience, recommend him as a priest. As he could not serve in another diocese and would not recant his opinions, Drane felt that he had no choice but to leave the priesthood.[149] Months after Bishop Fletcher received word on the case of Father Drane, Pope Paul VI published the encyclical *Humanae Vitae* in July 1968, reaffirming the traditional ban on artificial contraception, a position that Bishop Fletcher roundly endorsed in a pastoral letter on September 1, 1968.[150]

After the seminary closed in the summer of 1967, the diocese scrapped plans for a downtown chancery building, and instead built a new pastoral center on the grounds of the former seminary. It opened in January 1968, and is still the main office building for the bishop and his diocesan staff. The diocesan newspaper also moved its main offices into Morris Hall, the former administration and classroom building for the seminary.[151] The new chancery building, together with the enlarged chapel and Fletcher Hall, are all part of the legacies of the Bishop Fletcher era, the last church structures placed on what was once the campus of Little Rock College and St. John's Home Mission Seminary. For years after the closing of the seminary, the building and grounds were managed by Monsignor O'Connell.[152]

Whether affected by the Drane affair, or the closing of the seminary, or his advancing age, Bishop Fletcher sought an assistant. In his "Reminiscences," he mentioned that he had asked for an auxiliary in late 1968 and had recommended his longtime vice chancellor, Monsignor Lawrence P. Graves. Early the next year, Pope Paul VI made the appointment.[153] Graves would be the second native Arkansan to be elevated to the Catholic hierarchy.

Born in Texarkana, Arkansas, on May 4, 1916, the son of a grocer, Graves was reared in St. Edward's parish. All twelve years of his education were at this parish school. He was part of the first graduating class from a high school taught by the Sisters of Divine Providence. He entered St. John's Seminary, and after two years was sent to Rome to study at the North American College in 1936. Graves returned to St. John's Seminary in 1940, when Italy entered World War II. Bishop Morris ordained him in June 1942. He was sent first to Immaculate Conception parish in Fort Smith, yet returned a year later to teach moral theology at the seminary. In 1945, he was sent to Catholic University of America where he earned a *licentiate*, or license, in a canon or Church law (comparable to a master's degree) two years later.[154] When Father Graves returned to Arkansas, the newly consecrated Bishop Fletcher made him vice-chancellor of the diocese, a position that he held for the next twenty-two years. After teaching at Catholic High for one semester, Graves went again to St. John's Seminary, where he taught until 1961, when he became a full-time assistant to Bishop Fletcher in the chancery and auditor for the diocese. Graves was the man Fletcher chose to travel with him to the Second Vatican Council and translate for him. In 1969, he was named auxiliary bishop.[155]

With thirty bishops attending, and Archbishop Philip M. Hannan of New Orleans, who had taken the place of John P. Cody in 1965, presiding, Graves was consecrated before the television cameras of KARK, the NBC affiliate in Little Rock. It was the first time that such an event had been televised. A banquet followed at the Marion Hotel. The consecration took place on April 25, 1969, thirty-nine years to the day after Bishop Fletcher had been made auxiliary to Bishop Morris.[156] Fletcher knew that he would soon have to vacate the office. The Pope had decreed that bishops after the age of seventy-five had to step down; he used his own experience to gain an auxiliary, and he hoped, name his successor. People, both inside and outside the chancery, maintain that this was his expectation for Graves.[157]

While Bishop Fletcher was anticipating the changes that might flow from his retirement, the diocese was already implementing changes flowing from the Second Vatican Council. Parish councils began forming in the late 1960s, and the new liturgy of the Eucharist was instituted throughout the Church by 1969. The first concelebrated Mass outside of priestly ordinations (meaning having more than one priest saying the Mass) was celebrated in the diocese in March 1965 at Subiaco Abbey. Since 1953, the monks at Subiaco had said their daily prayers in English, except for Matins, the early morning prayers. By 1967, the vernacular language was used in all the prayer services and songs at Subiaco.[158]

Bishop Fletcher, however, would not go along with every change. The

Second Vatican Council had allowed the creation of the office of permanent deacons, men who were ordained to participate in some of the sacramental affairs of priestly ministry. Jerry Heil and Barry Findley, lay leaders of the Serra Club, a Catholic men's organization dedicated to fostering priestly vocations, advised Bishop Fletcher in November 1971 to have a permanent diaconate program because "the future of the Church in Arkansas will be enhanced by the ordination of deacons, who may serve the Church on a part-time basis, including being assistants to the priests and pastors."[159] The program, however, would have to wait until after the bishop's retirement.

Like his predecessor, Bishop Fletcher was fortunate enough to celebrate his fiftieth anniversary as a priest while still serving as bishop. At a Mass of thanksgiving at St. Andrew's Cathedral on June 4, 1970, Bishop Victor J. Reed of Oklahoma City claimed to speak for all his neighboring Catholic shepherds in Louisiana, Mississippi, Oklahoma, and the whole New Orleans metropolitan province when he praised the Arkansas prelate for his "calm equanimity." "No matter what happens, his manner is always the same, marked by a distinct trust, an abiding trust in Almighty God," he said.[160] At the dinner at Robinson Auditorium that evening, Bishop Fletcher said he didn't worry so much about the bad things that he had done, but the good things that he should have done and did not do. He also described himself as a "plodder, I know that I do nothing big, but I stick to the work."[161]

In many ways, this Mass and dinner celebration reflected the personality of Bishop Fletcher. It was not nearly as grand and elaborate as Bishop Morris' fiftieth priestly ordination anniversary in 1942, which was attended by many prominent figures in the hierarchy. The only bishops attending Fletcher's were from his own province. This was in keeping with Bishop Fletcher's overall modesty.

In the final two years of his episcopacy, Bishop Fletcher would suffer major disappointments and personal pain. In October 1970, Fletcher witnessed the closing of another of Bishop Morris' early projects, St. Joseph's Orphanage, after sixty-one years of operation. It would be called the St. Joseph's Children's Home because, of the fifty-three children there, only five were orphans. It would become more of a group home for children and later a day-care center.[162] On January 10, 1971, his old and dear friend, Monsignor Joseph A. Murray died. His longtime chancellor, the man he had entrusted with the diocese while he was at the Second Vatican Council, Monsignor Murray was also serving as vicar general of the diocese.[163]

More bad news came with the notice of the death of Father Joseph W. Lauro in Chicago. Father Lauro had gone to Ecuador in 1962, where he founded a medical facility and orphanage for the poor, high in the Andes Mountains. Father Lauro was supposed to return to the diocese, as his five-year stint in South America was complete. He called Bishop Fletcher in the spring of 1968 asking to stay for another five years. Prophetically, Fletcher responded,

"Joe, you cannot take another five years. It will kill you." Lauro assured the bishop that he would stay one year, two at the most. Fletcher agreed.[164] Severely ill, Lauro had to return to the United States in January 1971; he had stayed in South America for nearly three more years. Father Lauro never recovered; he died in Chicago on April 20, a few months short of his sixtieth birthday. Bishop Fletcher said a requiem Mass in his honor.[165]

Another source of pain was the feeling that, more and more, his political views were not in harmony with his fellow Catholic bishops. Although he had condemned indiscriminate bombing in Vietnam as early as 1966 in a letter to U.S. Representative Wilbur Mills, and had supported some conscientious objectors in 1970,[166] he refused to vote for the resolution approved by the American Catholic bishops in November 1971. That resolution said in part:

> At this point in history, it seems clear to us that whatever good we hope to achieve through continued involvement in this war is now outweighed by the destruction of human life and of moral values which it inflicts. It is our firm conviction, therefore, that the speedy end of this war is a moral imperative of the highest priority.[167]

A year later, the bishops would ask for amnesty for war resisters and draft dodgers.[168] Although Fletcher was retired by the time of the November 1972 meeting, he did attend the one in 1971 and vigorously dissented. In the local Catholic paper, Fletcher pointed out that "the South Vietnamese have *not* attacked the North, but they are trying to prevent the northern communists from taking over their country."[169] While no one is for war he said, "We are permitted to defend ourselves and help others defend themselves from unjust aggression."[170] In February 1972, the twenty-fifth anniversary of his elevation as the fourth ordinary of the diocese, Fletcher called upon Arkansas Catholics to seek peace with God, the only one who could bring true and lasting peace.[171] Bishop Fletcher was seeking this peace himself, because he saw many priests and nuns, inside and outside the diocese, leave their positions in the Church. After the close of the Second Vatican Council in 1965, the Church would see the number of priests, sisters, and brothers plummet.[172] (This loss of vocations nationally and in Arkansas will be documented in the subsequent chapters.) To Bishop Fletcher, it was a mystery. It was little wonder that he referred to his last five years as bishop as "the most difficult of my episcopal life."[173]

Despite his sadness, the bishop did not really want to retire. After turning seventy-five on October 28, 1971, he thought that retirement was merely recommended by the Pope, not required. Once he looked at the document in January 1972, and realized that it was mandatory, he immediately submitted his resignation to Rome. He would not hear back from Rome until late June. He was ordered by Archbishop Luigi Raimondi, the apostolic delegate, not to tell anyone until the person selected was notified.[174] When he was notified by the apostolic delegate on the Fourth of July, Bishop Fletcher announced that Monsignor Andrew Joseph McDonald of the Diocese of Savannah, Georgia, would become the fifth Bishop of Little Rock.[175] If Fletcher was disappointed that his auxiliary bishop was not named his successor, he never revealed it in his correspondence or his "Reminiscences." In his announcement of retirement as bishop in July 1972, Bishop Fletcher reminded his Arkansas flock that while society and the culture might be in chaos, the Church and its authentic teaching on faith and morals did not change.[176] But the Diocese of Little Rock would undergo some alterations with the arrival of the man from Georgia in September 1972.

Before one can conclude with the administration of Arkansas' present Catholic bishop, no treatment of Arkansas Catholicism would be complete without mention of the religious women serving in monasteries, schools, hospitals, and other charitable services. Their important contribution must be recounted before this history of the Arkansas Catholic Church can conclude.

CHAPTER XI

Sisters, Schools and Service

Some Catholic Contributions to Arkansas, 1838-1992

A HISTORY OF Arkansas Catholicism must necessarily include the contributions of women, especially women religious, to the mission of the Church. Works of mercy, healing, and instruction were often performed by Catholic women. The oldest continuous school and hospital in Arkansas were founded by Roman Catholic sisters who still play a prominent role in their operation. With little or no financial reward, these sisters educated children and ministered healing long before the national or state government provided such services. The Roman Catholic Church is not only one of the oldest religious faiths, it is also one of the longest running charitable institutions in Western history. This chapter will provide a brief survey of women religious, especially focusing on those orders which have been longest in Arkansas: the Sisters of Mercy, the Fort Smith Benedictines, the Olivetan Benedictine, and the Sisters of Charity of Nazareth.

However, the Sisters of Loretto at the Foot of the Cross, the first Catholic religious order founded west of the Appalachian Mountains, was the first group of women religious to serve in Arkansas. Mother Agnes Hart arrived, accompanied by Sisters Eulalia Kelly, Louise Phillips, Teresa Mattingly, and Alodia Vessals. They opened the first Catholic school in Arkansas on November 19, 1838, on the southern shore of the Arkansas River, just downstream from Pine Bluff near the present day community of Plum Bayou. In 1841, they founded St. Joseph's Catholic school, the first parochial school in Little Rock, and operated it where the cathedral now stands. The school at Plum Bayou was abandoned in 1842 to open St. Ambrose Female Academy at the Arkansas Post. Both of these schools operated until 1845, when lack of funds forced them to close.[1]

The next group of religious sisters came a much greater distance and have stayed longer. The Religious Sisters of Mercy, the oldest Catholic religious order in Arkansas, would found Arkansas' oldest continuous educational institution, Mount St. Mary Academy in Little Rock. As recounted in an earlier chapter, Bishop Byrne journeyed to his native Ireland and successfully recruited these sisters for his frontier diocese in 1851. The Religious Sisters of Mercy were established just twenty years earlier by Mother Catherine McAuley, in Dublin on Baggott Street. Not from this original convent did Bishop Byrne recruit these early sisters for Arkansas, but from another house of sisters at Naas in County Kildare, thirty miles west of the Irish capital.[2]

A recent history of the Mercy sisters in Arkansas has provided more details about the women who accompanied Bishop Byrne to his frontier diocese. Alicia Farrell, who headed the Mercy sisters in Arkansas, was born in Naas to Christopher and Marianne Farrell. Entering the Mercy convent at Naas in 1841, the young novice had the opportunity to meet Mother Catherine McAuley shortly before the latter's death. With Daniel O'Connell, the great Irish patriot of political and religious liberty in attendance, Alicia made her formal profession on September 27, 1843, taking the name Sister Mary Teresa. She stayed in this Mercy convent in her home town for seven more years before departing for Arkansas. There is no exact date for her birth, but the historians for the Mercy sisters in Arkansas maintain that she probably entered the order in her early twenties, which would have made her approximately thirty years of age at the time of her departure for Little Rock.[3] In leaving Ireland, Sister Mary Teresa was well aware that she would probably never return again, and was leaving family and homeland forever. "Travel was too complicated, too costly and too long. Very few religious orders had the surplus time or money to spare to send their immigrant members home for visits."[4] A new religious society like the Mercy sisters, founded in a poor country like Ireland, certainly had no excess funds for such amenities.

The other professed sisters willing to venture to the "wilds of Arkansas" included Rebecca Greene, who is thought to be the oldest in the group. Her exact date and place of birth is unknown, yet she entered the Dublin Mercy convent in 1837 and made her profession of vows on June 11, 1839, at the new convent in Carlow; she received the religious name of Mary Agnes. In September, 1839, she was sent as one of the founding sisters to the convent in Naas. Eliza O'Keefe, born in Carlow in the county of the same name, entered the Mercy convent at Naas when it opened on September 24, 1839. She made her profession two years later under Mother Catherine McAuley taking the name Sister Mary deSales. The last professed sister of the original group was Catherine Farrell, the cousin of Alicia Farrell, who entered the Naas convent in

1846 and took final vows on November 11, 1848, as Sister Mary Stanislaus.[5]

It is believed eight postulants left Ireland in the company of these four professed sisters. On June 22, 1851, at the first St. Andrew's Cathedral, five of these women become the first novices in the Diocese of Little Rock. The speaker for the occasion was Martin J. Spalding, then Bishop of Louisville and later Archbishop of Baltimore.[6] It is interesting that a churchman of his stature would be present at this historic event in Arkansas Catholicism.

Of these five novices, Mrs. Anne Healy was probably the oldest and the most notable. Born in Dublin in 1812, she was the cousin of Bishop Byrne, and a widow. From her deceased husband, she inherited some funds which were used to assist the early Mercy community in Arkansas. Her religious name would be Sister Mary Vincent. Charlotte and Jane Nolan were sisters from Teneelash in County Carlow, yet little is known of their background. Charlotte became Sister Mary Ignatius, while Jane became Sister Mary Xavier. Mary Farrell was the younger sister to Alicia Farrell, the leader of the Arkansas Mercy sisters, and she too was from Naas. She assumed the name Sister Mary Baptist. The last of the five was Alicia Carton of Dublin whose religious name was Sister Mary Alphonsus. She "may have been a close friend or relation to Bishop Byrne, who had many connections in Dublin."[7] These nine women would form the basis for the oldest Catholic religious community in Arkansas.

This Mercy community in Little Rock, established in 1851, was only the third established this side of the Atlantic and the first from the convent in Naas in County Kildare, Ireland. The only two American houses which preceded that of St. Mary's convent were in Pittsburgh, founded from the Carlow house in 1843, and in New York, founded from the Baggott street convent in Dublin in 1846.[8]

Their first decade within the state was a busy time for these Irish missionaries. From their arrival in Little Rock in mid-February 1851, until the following November, they lived in the bishop's residence behind the first St. Andrew's Cathedral at Second and Center Streets. They moved into their first convent in the city at Seventh and Louisiana Streets.[9] They called their school St. Mary's after their convent in Naas. Bishop Byrne brought back some boarding students with him after a trip to New Orleans in early 1852, the first such students for the Little Rock academy. This boarding school tradition would endure for over a century.[10] On June 10, 1852, the Mercy community in Little Rock received their first postulant, Margaret Fitzpatrick, who hailed originally from Portarlington, a town about forty miles west of Naas. When this Irish colleen came to Arkansas is unknown, but in December 1852, she assumed the religious name of Sister Mary Aloysius during her reception ceremony. That same event witnessed the reception of the second person to join the Arkansas Mercy sisters, Hanna Kean, from County Cork, Ireland. Her religious name would be Sister Mary Michael.[11]

By the end of 1852, the Mercy community consisted of four professed sisters, six novices, and one postulant. Despite their small numbers, Bishop Byrne wanted the community to divide in early 1853 so a second convent could be established in Fort Smith. Arkansas' first bishop had already purchased a great deal of property near this western Arkansas river town, where he established the state's first Catholic college. Once it was decided that the community would divide, the question then became who would go and who would stay. Eventually, it was decided that Mother Teresa Farrell and Sister Mary deSales O'Keefe, together with novices Mary Alphonsus Carton, Mary Xavier Nolan, and Mary Aloysius Fitzpatrick, would depart for Fort Smith. On January 19, 1853, these five women, Bishop Byrne, and his cousin Marianne Byrne, boarded a steamboat to travel up the Arkansas River to Fort Smith. Marianne Byrne eventually became a Mercy sister and entered the Mercy convent in Fort Smith in late 1854 or early 1855. The actual date of the arrival of the Mercy sisters and the founding of their new convent in Fort Smith is January 23, 1853. Bishop Byrne proudly reported later to Archbishop Anthony Blanc of New Orleans that St. Anne's Academy had thirty-six students enrolled.[12] It was at Fort Smith, on April 4, 1853, that three novices made their final profession as Mercy sisters, the first time final religious vows were taken in Arkansas. Those becoming full members of the Mercy community were Sister Alphonsus Carton, Sister Xavier Nolan, and Sister Mary Vincent Healy, who had just come from the Little Rock convent. On November 30, 1853, the feast day of St. Andrew the Apostle, the first full profession of sisters in Little Rock occurred with Sisters M. Ignatius Nolan and M. Baptist Farrell taking final vows. All of the five original postulants who had come to Arkansas in 1851 were now professed members of the Mercy sisters.[13]

Until 1856, Mother Teresa Farrell served as Superior for both convents of Arkansas Mercy sisters. This is reflected in the Catholic almanacs from this period. This arrangement was altered by Bishop Byrne. "From then on, each convent would elect superior and council and maintain its own novitiate."[14]

Although the convent in Little Rock accepted two Irish immigrants, Mary Brereton and Mary Higgins, as postulants in 1854 and 1855, the small number of Catholics in the state could not really sustain their membership. To survive in the state, they needed more recruits from Ireland. In 1856, Mother Teresa Farrell, along with Sister Mary Vincent Healy, left for the British Isles seeking more female religious missionaries. Apparently, the state's reputation as a wild and unruly place must have hurt their recruitment efforts, as they could only coax three women to Arkansas. On their return, the five sisters stopped at the newly established Mercy convent in Chicago and gathered two more sisters. In June 1857, a major reception ceremony was held in Little Rock with four Irish women receiving religious names. Two years later, Bishop Byrne returned from his native land with three postulants for his beloved Sisters of Mercy.[15]

In 1857, Bishop Byrne purchased a plantation near Helena, Arkansas. This elegant mansion would become a new Mercy convent for four Mercy sisters from St. Anne's convent at Fort Smith in January 1858. They opened St. Catherine's Academy the next fall. This school would soon become the largest one in Arkansas, as it was located in the wealthy and populous delta area. Sister Mary Aloysius Fitzpatrick, the first person to join the Mercy sisters after they became established in Arkansas, was the first Mercy sister to die in this missionary diocese, at St. Catherine's convent on October 2, 1859.[16] This convent would also serve as the final resting place for Arkansas' first Catholic bishop less than three years later.

The Civil War devastated the state and hampered the Mercy sisters' educational work. By the end of 1861, the women continued to teach their classes even with reduced enrollments.[17] The three convents were close to the site of battles. Even before Arkansas seceded on May 6, 1861, the state government sent Colonel Solon Borland of the Arkansas militia to attack Fort Smith. St. Anne's was close by.[18] St. Mary's convent was turned into a Confederate hospital during the siege at Little Rock in 1863. On July 4, 1863, the sisters at St. Catherine's witnessed the Confederates' unsuccessful attempt to retake Helena. In the final year of the war, the small number of boarders at the three Mercy academies were joined by homeless children seeking the protection and care of the religious women. "With these children dependent on them and their own survival at stake, the Sisters were challenged every day just to keep food on the table."[19] Although they did survive, the sisters could not keep St. Catherine's Academy in Helena open; both school and convent closed on January 23, 1868.[20]

There were some glimmers of light. Mary Agnes Burke, a native of New Orleans, became the first American-born postulant to enter the Arkansas Sisters of Mercy. She took the religious name of Sister Mary Antonia and was professed into the Mercy community on June 1, 1868. In 1872, Augusta Fischer of Little Rock became the first native Arkansan to enter the Sisters of Mercy, taking the name Sr. Francis in 1873 and making her final vows in 1875. After almost a quarter-century of work in Arkansas by the Sisters of Mercy, a native of the state had entered the order. The order started slowly to Americanize, yet for decades it depended on postulants from Ireland to fill its ranks, giving it a decidedly Hibernian flavor for much of the nineteenth century.[21]

The last quarter of that century saw many changes for the Arkansas Mercy community. On December 8, 1875, a fire destroyed the original convent in Fort Smith. A year later, the sisters moved into a new facility on the same site and stayed there for another thirty years.[22] Mother Teresa Farrell, now around sixty years of age, witnessed the moving of Bishop Byrne's body to the new cathedral in late November 1881. Her sight soon began to fail, and by the last time Bishop Fitzgerald visited her in Fort Smith in 1891, she was almost blind. On January 12, 1892, the foundress of the Arkansas Mercy sisters died in the fiftieth year of her life as a Sister of Mercy and in the fortieth year of her service in Arkansas.[23] Just before she died, the Mercy sisters opened a school for whites and one for blacks at Hot Springs, a growing resort town. The school for black children, however, would not survive.[24] On September 29, 1892, just months after Mother Farrell's death, the Mercy convent in Fort Smith accepted Alice O'Deady, the first candidate from Newfoundland. She would not be the last Canadian woman to serve in Arkansas as part of the Mercy community; many more would serve in the following years. As the chroniclers of the order have demonstrated, for the first seventy-eight years of their existence in Arkansas, from 1851-1929, the Mercy sisters drew over two-thirds of its members from either Ireland or Newfoundland, with the former island contributing almost half of all their members.[25]

In 1888, shortly after St. Vincent's opened in Little Rock, and just prior to the death of Mother Farrell, the Mercy sisters, on September 14, opened their first Arkansas hospital in Hot Springs, St. Joseph's. During the last decade of the nineteenth century, the Mercy sisters staffed the schools at Our Lady of Good Counsel in Little Rock, and St. Patrick's and St. Mary's in North Little Rock. Some sisters from the Little Rock convent also served the Italian Catholics at Sunny Side Plantation in Chicot County, in southeast Arkansas. The sisters from St. Anne's convent operated parochial schools in Van Buren and Mena by 1897.[26]

By 1900, after almost a half-century in the state, the Mercy sisters were no longer the only women religious in Arkansas, as other orders also arrived. Significantly, the Sisters of Mercy were the *only* Catholic women religious order present between 1851-1878, one of the most difficult periods in state history.

If the Mercy sisters had an Irish and Canadian flavor, the next two orders to grow and blossom in Arkansas were primarily Germanic. On September 16, 1878, four sisters left the convent in Ferdinand, Indiana, for the western part of Arkansas. They were sent by their Superior, Mother Agatha Werb, to occupy land granted to Bishop Fitzgerald by the Little Rock and Fort Smith Railroad. These women were: Sister Xaviera Schroeder, age thirty-four, the leader of the group; Sister Josepha Schmidt, age twenty-one; Sister Bonaventura Wagner, age twenty-three; and Sister Isidora Luebberman, age twenty-one. These four women would be the foundation of the mainly German-speaking order now known as the Fort Smith Benedictines based at St. Scholastica's Monastery. They first arrived at the Benedictine male community in Logan County which was also just starting at that time. Two of the sisters opened St. Benedict's school, the first parochial school in Logan County. Sisters Xaviera Schroeder and Bonaventura Wagner moved into a small cabin at Shoal Creek, about ten miles east of the men's Benedictine community on January 23, 1879. This date marks the official opening of the St. Scholastica convent.[27]

Despite the early struggles of this community, it managed to attract candidates in the spring of 1882. From March through June, three women entered: Christina Schuler and Apollonia Ehalt from Fort Smith and Katharina Hawerott from Shoal Creek.[28] Mother Agatha Werb visited the community that year and agreed to have a novitiate there at Shoal Creek rather than send candidates to Ferdinand, Indiana. The three young women were invested into the order on October 30, 1882. Mother Werb also appointed a Superior, Sister Meinrada Lex, one of the sisters she had brought with her from Indiana. When Mother Werb visited the community five years later, there were fourteen members, from postulants to professed sisters, who were operating three schools and farming the land. Mother Agatha Werb decided to allow the community to become an independent motherhouse. On May 20, 1887, the St. Scholastica Community held its first election and selected Mother Meinrada Lex as the first prioress. She would be its leader for the next twenty-one years.[29]

There is little known about this determined woman who was the first prioress of the Fort Smith Benedictines. She was born at sea on March 1, 1856. Her parents settled in Fulda, Indiana, which is listed as her birthplace. Baptized Balbina Lex, she entered the Convent of the Immaculate Conception in Ferdinand on January 15, 1872. Ten years later, she became the superior at Shoal Creek community in rural Logan County. The convent was enlarged by 1898, becoming a two-story building forming an enclosed courtyard. Under the leadership of Mother Meinrada Lex, the sisters expanded their operations into other areas; St. Boniface School in Fort Smith in 1887, Paris (Logan County) in 1889, Dixie and Altus by 1890, and Marche in 1891. By the time Mother Meinrada resigned as prioress in 1908, her sisters were staffing twenty-six schools, most of them in Arkansas from Little Rock to Fort Smith, in the German or German-speaking parishes. It was from these sisters that Bishop Albert L. Fletcher received his Catholic education while living in Paris, Arkansas, in the first decade of this century. The sisters also operated schools in Oklahoma, Missouri, and Texas.[30] On June 30, 1908, an election was held, and Sister Agatha (formerly Apollonia) Ehalt, the third person in Arkansas to join the community in 1882, became the second prioress and governed the community for the next twelve years (1908-1920). Mother Meinrada Lex returned to her home community in Ferdinand, Indiana, in 1909. She died there five years later.[31]

One of the new activities for these Benedictines after the turn of the century was taking charge of St. Joseph's Orphanage in North Little Rock. The first sister that Mother Meinrada Lex sent to college, Sr. Anne Grondkoski, served as administrator at the orphanage for forty years, 1910-1950. At her death on November 15, 1971, she had served a record of seventy-five years in the Benedictine community. In 1915, the Sisters of St. Joseph in Pilot Grove, Missouri, a struggling community, amalgamated with the St. Scholastica Community. As the Pilot Grove sisters operated a hospital in Booneville, Missouri, the Fort Smith Benedictines now added health care as part of their community ministry.[32]

By the early 1920s, the sisters had clearly outgrown the facilities at Shoal Creek which, because of its isolation and lack of water, was not the best place for a motherhouse of an order which had grown to over two hundred sisters. Under the leadership of its third prioress, Mother Perpetua Gerard (1920-1947), the community voted to move to Fort Smith in September 1922. Bishop Morris, however, did not actually give his consent until the following July.[33]

On November 30, 1923, the feast day of St. Andrew the Apostle, long recognized as an important date in Arkansas Catholic history, Mother Perpetua signed the contract for building the new convent in Fort Smith. The first wing of the proposed three-part structure was completed the next year and dedicated by the bishop on September 14, 1924. At the same time, St. Joseph's Academy at Shoal Creek was moved to Fort Smith and renamed St. Scholastica's Academy. On May 17, 1925, the community officially transferred their motherhouse from Shoal Creek to Fort Smith, marking a real turning point in the history of the community.[34]

Across the state, another Benedictine community with a teutonic flavor was being formed. Father Eugene John Weibel at Pocahontas, Arkansas, had asked for sisters to continue his school. Four nuns from southeastern Missouri answered the call in September, 1887; Sisters Mary Frances Metzler, Mary Walburga McFadden, and Mary Agnes Dali were led by Mother Mary Beatrice Renggli. Just before they left Maryville for Pocahontas, Arkansas, they heard a mission preached by the Redemptorist Fathers. One of them, a Father Enright, "cautioned them to take their coffins with them. In Arkansas the sisters would encounter intense heat and swarms of mosquitoes."[35] They arrived at Pocahontas, Arkansas, on December 13, 1887.[36]

The woman who led this group into Arkansas was born Rose Renggli on January 1, 1848, at Entlebuch, Canton Lucerne, Switzerland. The exact date of her entry into religious life is not clear. She crossed the Atlantic at the age of twenty-six to her destination in Missouri. Now almost forty years of age, she would become the leader of a new community of women in northeastern Arkansas. The women had a cash fund of eighty-three cents when they arrived at Pocahontas.[37] The historian of this community described Mother Mary Beatrice as "a model religious, endowed with great intellectual gifts, deep spirituality, a profound insight and depth in religious life."[38] The sisters soon opened two Catholic schools in Pocahontas, one for whites and one for blacks. The latter institution was staffed by Sister Mary Agnes Dali who had taught Indian children as a missionary in Oregon. Fr. Weibel received threats that the school for blacks would be burned down, which he ignored.[39]

On June 24, 1888, Bishop Fitzgerald dedicated the new convent in Pocahontas called Maria Stein, after Father Weibel's former monastery in Switzerland. In the fall of 1889, they opened a Catholic school in Jonesboro. Real growth came, however, after Mother Beatrice Renglli visited Europe in 1889 and returned with five young women from Germany and eleven from Switzerland.[40] Sixteen women responded to the call to serve Christ and his Gospel in faraway America, marking a real turning point for these sisters in

Pocahontas. When three more women came from Maryville, Mother Renggli's community now numbered four professed sisters, four novices, and eighteen postulants. Sister Mary Francis Metzler, one of the original four who came to Arkansas, became the first one of the group to die on March 24, 1890.[41] In these early years, nuns from this order staffed the Catholic schools in Paragould, Engelberg, and the two schools in Pocahontas, along with two more schools in Jonesboro. They also began working at St. Edward's school in Little Rock.[42]

Despite this success, Mother Renggli and Fr. Weibel had personality conflicts, and she resigned in 1892. She continued in the order and lived another fifty years, dying at the age ninety-four on September 6, 1942, at Holy Angels convent in Jonesboro. Auxiliary Bishop Albert L. Fletcher conducted her funeral.[43]

The first novice to be received into the new community from the local Arkansas area was an immigrant woman from Switzerland, Christine Unterberger, who took the religious name Sr. Mary Aloysia; she made her final vows on February 28, 1890.[44] The community at Maria Stein operated under the authority of Bishop Fitzgerald. Against the wishes of Father Weibel, the second Arkansas Catholic prelate wanted the community to become affiliated with a larger religious society outside the diocese. Bishop Fitzgerald commissioned Father Weibel to go Europe to obtain such a connection, and the Swiss German priest successfully aligned this order with the Olivetan Benedictines, an order which dates back to the fourteenth century. The actual date of the transfer was January 15, 1893. This would be the first daughter house of the Olivetan Benedictines in the United States.[45]

In the spring of 1894, the sisters held their first election for a superior under the Olivetan rules, and Sister Mary Agnes Dali became the first superior. Born Anna Dali in 1839, in Neudorf, Caton Lucerne, Switzerland, she entered Convent Maria Rickenbach in May 1862 at the age of twenty-one. She came to America in 1874 and settled at the Maryville convent in southeast Missouri. After working in Missouri and at Indian missions in Oregon, Sister Dali was one of the first group who answered the call to come to Arkansas. Like Mother Mary Beatrice, she had her disagreements with Father Weibel and stayed as prioress for only two years. She continued working as a sister until her death in June 1915.[46]

In the last decade of the nineteenth century, the Olivetan Benedictines expanded their work in northeastern and eastern Arkansas as far south as Forrest City and Stuttgart. They also staffed a school in Muenster, Texas. In 1898, they moved their main convent headquarters from Pocahontas to Jonesboro which had become the railroad hub for northeast Arkansas. This new motherhouse would be called Holy Angels Convent. The Olivetan Benedictines opened St. Bernard's Hospital in Jonesboro on July 5, 1900, Arkansas' third Catholic hospital. In the first years of the new century, they expanded their educational work not only in Arkansas, but also in southeastern Missouri and into Cairo, Illinois.[47]

The Sisters of Charity of Nazareth, another major women's order important in Arkansas' Catholic history, was founded in Kentucky just a few months after the Sisters of Loretto. Like the other Kentucky religious order, the Sisters of Charity would not set up a special convent, priory, or motherhouse in Arkansas. Their work in schools and hospitals would primarily be in Kentucky. These sisters still labor in eight other states, including Arkansas.[48]

Alexander Hager's Will financed the creation of St. Vincent's Infirmary (covered in an earlier chapter), and also stipulated that Bishop Fitzgerald should choose the particular order to operate the hospital. He chose the Sisters of Charity of Nazareth. The first St. Vincent's opened on July 14, 1888, in an antebellum mansion built in 1858 or 1859 by Mr. Alexander George, a German immigrant and one of the founders of the Lutheran church in Little Rock. Located at Second and McClean Streets, it had lawns and gardens which once stretched to the Arkansas River. It was described as "solid but in disrepair."[49] This institution was Arkansas' first Catholic hospital and the oldest continuous health facility in the state.

Sister Hortense Gillfoyle, with four other sisters from Kentucky, founded St. Vincent's Infirmary. It started as a ten bed facility, but soon expanded to a twenty-six bed unit. Within a decade, the hospital outgrew its space at the old George home, and plans were made for a new building by the turn of the century. A granite, four-story, fifty bed hospital opened at the corner of Tenth and High Streets, equipped with an operating room and a facility for obstetrics and pediatrics.[50] They would occupy this location for over a half-century.

While the Sisters of Charity would make St. Vincent's Infirmary one of their central ministries in the diocese, they had actually been in the state for almost a decade before 1888. In August 1879, they opened Sacred Heart Academy in Helena. Located in an historic private home on a hill overlooking the Mississippi River, this structure was turned into an eight room convent and boarding school for a hundred girls. A year later, Annunciation Academy started in Pine Bluff. In 1889, these sisters began instructing blacks at Father Lucey's Colored Industrial School. They stayed at the latter school until replaced by the black religious Sisters of the Holy Family in 1901. The sisters did not totally abandon teaching African American students in Arkansas, as they would begin teaching catechism at St. Cyprian's parish in Helena and would later staff the parish school there when it opened in the 1930s.[51] They would be staffing St. Cyprian's school, Annunciation Academy, and Sacred Heart Academy through World War II and after.[52]

By the turn of the twentieth century, there was real progress in the number of sisters and religious schools operating in the state. There were nine Sisters of Mercy in 1851, four sisters and five postulants. By 1900, the *Official*

Catholic Directory listed 150 women religious in the state, with five academies, thirty-two parishes with schools, and one black industrial college in Pine Bluff. In addition to the four orders mentioned above, the School Sisters of Notre Dame would be invited to take over St. Joseph's school in Conway in 1898 and Sacred Heart school in Morrilton in 1899. They would stay at St. Joseph's in Conway until 1971 and at Sacred Heart until 1984. Since that date, they have concentrated their work at black parishes; St. Peter's Catholic school in Pine Bluff and at an early childhood education center at St. Augustine's parish in North Little Rock.[53]

The work of the sisters flourished in Arkansas over the next forty years. The Sisters of Mercy founded their second and Arkansas' fourth Catholic hospital, St. Edward's in Fort Smith, on November 27, 1905. The institution was named in honor of the sick and partially paralyzed Bishop Edward M. Fitzgerald.[54]

The name choice is interesting since the ill bishop, the year before, had blocked the Mercy sisters from moving out of downtown Little Rock. By the time Bishop Fitzgerald had laid the cornerstone for his new cathedral in 1878, a newspaper account mentions that the edifice would be directly across the street from St. Mary's convent and academy.[55] This imposing Victorian style structure in downtown Little Rock was probably built in the late 1860s or early 1870s, yet the sisters desired a new location as early as 1883. When the old and infirm bishop read in the summer of 1904 that the sisters had purchased land in Pulaski Heights, he uncharacteristically penned an angry and bitter letter to the Superior of St. Mary's prohibiting her from erecting any buildings on the land they purchased. He wrote that he always opposed their moving out of downtown. If they had not yet purchased the land, he now prohibited them from doing so.[56] After Bishop Fitzgerald's death in 1907, and with the assistance of the new prelate John B. Morris, the Sisters of Mercy purchased a ten-acre plot in Pulaski Heights on which they erected a five-story Gothic style building which served as a landmark in western Little Rock after 1908. It was dedicated on June 11, 1908, on the second anniversary of Bishop Morris' installation.[57]

While the new bishop was quite generous with the Mercy sisters based in Little Rock, his relations with the Mercy community in Fort Smith were stormy. Beginning in 1906, he asked them to consider amalgamation with the community in Little Rock. The two Mercy communities had maintained a cordial relationship since their separation some fifty years earlier. Bishop Morris, however, was determined, against the wishes of the Fort Smith sisters, to merge them. The prelate kept up constant pressure to affect his demands. He even wrote the apostolic delegate complaining of their irreligious and incompetent behavior. Finally, in a letter dated January 23, 1915, the members of the St. Anne community agreed to merge with the St. Mary's Mercy sisters, and thus closed their novitiate after almost sixty years.[58]

The Mercy sisters in western Arkansas had not been confined just to Fort Smith. In 1906, the Mercy sisters from Fort Smith staffed the Catholic school at Tontitown; yet, they left in 1912 to enable the Congregation of the Incarnate Word of the Blessed Sacrament, a refugee religious order from Mexico, to work there. Later, the Ursulines came to Tontitown in 1914, and then the Mercy sisters returned a decade later.[59]

In 1929, many of the Sisters of Mercy communities merged into the Sisters of Mercy of the Union which was divided into six provinces. Since 1929, the Mercy sisters in Arkansas have been a part of the St. Louis province; the headquarters for the Sisters of Mercy of the Union was located in Maryland.[60] As the Mercy sisters merged nationally, Mount St. Mary's Academy in Little Rock experienced some real growth. An annex was added to the main building in 1924 and a gymnasium-auditorium and pool were completed by 1930.[61] In 1926, St. Anne's Academy in Fort Smith became a co-educational high school.[62]

Inasmuch as the Mercy sisters had moved their school to Pulaski Heights, Bishop Morris invited the Olivetan Benedictines in 1908 to take over the cathedral school, their first parish school in central Arkansas. Some twenty years later, they would take over a school in western Little Rock which would eventually become Our Lady of Holy Souls School.[63] Two more landmarks came early in the century for the Jonesboro-based Benedictines. Christine Unterberger, now Sister Mary Aloysia, became prioress between 1909-1915, and one of their pupils, Walter J. Tynin, in 1911, became the first native-born Arkansan to be ordained a priest for the Diocese of Little Rock.[64] More changes and progress would take place with the building of a convent annex and the opening of Holy Angels girls' academy in Jonesboro in the fall of 1930. This educational institution would serve northeastern Arkansas for the next thirty-two years.[65] In 1915, the Olivetan Benedictines, at the behest of Father Weibel who was then located in Hot Springs, began staffing St. John's Hospice or Sanatorium. After some fifty years of operation, a new building was constructed in 1968 at Second and Grand Avenue in Hot Springs, and the facility was renamed Benedictine Manor, a retirement home. It was still in operation by the early 1990s.[66]

The Olivetan Benedictines also taught at a Catholic school and hospice at Armstrong Springs in White County founded in 1908 by Bishop Morris. First staffed by the Brothers of St. Paul, a religious order Father Fintan Kraemer attempted to form as a new community with some diocesan priests who had fled France, this particular order did not work out. These French priests abandoned the school by 1911.[67] Their place was taken by Olivetan Benedictines who stayed until 1915. The school continued to operate, but in 1921 at the invitation of Bishop Morris, the Franciscan Brothers from Mt. Alverno in Cincinnati came to staff the institution. The school was renamed the Morris School for Boys in 1922, and the bishop dedicated the new facility that fall. The school continued during the depression and the war years. By the

1960s, it had modern school buildings, a new St. Anthony's Friary, and a newly constructed Our Lady of Guadalupe Chapel. By the early 1990s, these Franciscan brothers were marking more than seven decades of service at this particular school.[68]

Although this chapter focuses primarily upon the oldest religious orders in the state, other important educational and social services were performed by various religious societies in the early part of the twentieth century. At the request of Bishop Morris, the Sisters of Our Lady of Charity of Refuge, a French religious society founded by St. John Eudes in 1641, came to Hot Springs, Arkansas, from Ottawa, Canada, in 1908. This order is sometimes known as the Sisters of the Good Shepherd. They opened St. Michael's school in Hot Springs in the same year they arrived at Arkansas' premier resort city. Since the convent there was completely autonomous, it established its own novitiate in the diocese. The school had two departments, one for younger girls given to the care of the sisters by their parents, and the other for older girls put there by the courts or the Arkansas Department of Welfare. In 1960, the department for older girls was discontinued, and St. Michael's became a day school. At present, the Sisters of Our Lady of Charity operate a preschool program for children from six weeks of age to kindergarten. They also operate a day school for students from kindergarten through the sixth grade.[69]

A major change took place in education when Bishop Morris created the position of Superintendent for the Catholic schools. This position was created by 1909, as the *Official Catholic Directory* that year listed Father Denis W. O'Hern as the first Superintendent of Catholic Schools.[70] Yet, significant change came when Bishop Morris appointed the young priest, John J. Healy, as Superintendent of Diocesan Schools in 1930. He held that position for twenty-two years and would help modernize and standardize the schools throughout the diocese. Born in Little Rock in 1903, and educated in parochial schools before entering St. John's Seminary, he was ordained for the priesthood in 1927.[71] This Little Rock priest created a more systematic Catholic school system; he organized teacher certification records, maintained student records, conducted a yearly census of Catholic schools, and instituted annual teachers' meetings. He appointed textbook and curriculum committees, developed a school manual for Catholic schools, and made great efforts toward the certification of Catholic schools by the Arkansas Department of Education.[72]

Catholic education had grown substantially by 1940. Ten academies, double the number forty years earlier, and fifty-five parochial schools were instructing 7,136 students. In addition, there were now 120 children in St. Joseph's Orphanage. There were then 664 postulants, novices, and professed sisters working in the Little Rock diocese.[73] There were also an increased number of different orders of women religious working in Arkansas by the end of World War II; the directory in 1945 now listed eleven.[74]

From the time Albert L. Fletcher became auxiliary bishop in 1940, until the close of the Second Vatican Council a quarter-century later, the number of Catholic sisters and Catholic schools grew unevenly. The number of sisters in the diocese increased slightly from 664 to 693; the number of pupils in Catholic schools increased to 10,980; however, only 246 sisters were involved directly in education, about thirty-five percent of the total number.[75] While the number of sisters listed would be the highest in diocesan history, about two-thirds of the sisters were not involved in education.

Outside of education, most were involved in hospital work. Four hospitals had been founded between 1888-1905 in Little Rock, Hot Springs, Jonesboro, and Fort Smith. Over the next forty years, the number of Catholic hospitals would increase to nine with these additions: St. Mary's in Dermott, St. Hildegarde's in Clarksville, and St. Anthony's in Morrilton, all of them operated by the Fort Smith Benedictines. Two others were also opened between 1905-1945: Warner-Brown Hospital in El Dorado, operated by the Sisters of Mercy, and the Michael Meagher Hospital (later St. Michael's) in Texarkana, conducted by the Sisters of Charity of the Incarnate Word from Houston, Texas.[76] (This latter facility and its history will be outlined later in this chapter.)

Some of this new growth must be attributed to the work of Father Healy, who served as the director of Catholic hospitals for the diocese from 1931-1952. Hannah Peck, the historian for St. Vincent's hospital, claims that the Little Rock priest "played a major role in the growth of St. Vincent's in the 1940s and the 1950s."[77] His achievements were noted by Church authorities. He was given the title Monsignor in 1942 and was designated as Bishop Albert L. Fletcher's first vicar general in July 1947, a position he held for the rest of his life.[78] National and international recognition came to the Arkansas cleric with his election as President of the North American Catholic Hospital Association in June 1951, the official representative of thousands of Catholic hospitals in both the United States and Canada.[79] Six months after completing his one year term, Monsignor Healy would die on December 6, 1952.[80] Interestingly, Bishop Fletcher himself died exactly twenty-seven years to the day after the death of his friend and first vicar general.

Monsignor Healy had indeed made his impact in his work on Catholic hospitals and diocesan schools. He would not be an easy person to replace. Over the next two decades, the duration of Bishop Fletcher's tenure as bishop, two priests would serve as his successor. Father John Kordsmeier served from 1952 until 1962. He published the first *Diocesan* Handbook for Catholic schools and introduced more standardized tests for both teachers and students within the parochial system. Father William Beck served as the superintendent for the next eleven years and under his direction, Catholic school boards were initiated.[81]

Another legacy from Monsignor Healy's era was the creation of the Arkansas Conference of Catholic Hospitals, organized in May 1955. In addition to the nine hospitals already mentioned, two more had been added over the previous decade. In 1953, the Mercy sisters opened Mercy-Gazzola Memorial hospital in Brinkley. The building for this hospital was provided by the Will of John Gazzola, a Brinkley merchant, planter, and cotton buyer.[82] Two years earlier on January 15, 1951, five Dominican sisters from Springfield, Illinois, arrived to take charge of the Rogers Memorial Hospital which had opened the previous September. The sisters were led by Sister Rita Rose, who would become the new administrator for the hospital which maintained its previous name.[83] Sister Rita Rose, head of the Rogers facility, was elected the first president of this new association of Arkansas Catholic hospitals.[84] Within another decade, two more Catholic hospitals would be founded. Van Buren's Crawford County Hospital was staffed by the Fort Smith Benedictines, and the Carroll County Hospital in Eureka Springs was operated by the Olivetan Benedictines from Jonesboro. A prominent figure in the origin of the latter institution was an enterprising priest, the ex-fighter pilot, Father Joseph Lauro.[85] In sixty years, from 1905-1965, the number of Catholic hospitals in Arkansas went from four to thirteen.

New hospitals were not the only changes as far as the women's communities were concerned. In 1950, the Discalced Carmelite nuns of Loretto, Pennsylvania, one of the contemplative orders in the Catholic Church, had such a plethora of vocations that is seemed right to set up a new foundation. The prioress had written various bishops about having a cloistered convent in their dioceses, yet none seemed interested. She noticed in the *Official Catholic Directory* that the motto for the Diocese of Little Rock, *Pax Christi,* was the same for her religious order. Mother Mary of Jesus contacted Bishop Fletcher, who was both willing and even eager to have these sisters in Arkansas. She visited with the bishop in February, and after receiving the necessary papers from Rome, these new sisters came that summer. They stayed for a while with the Benedictines sisters at St. Joseph's Orphanage until they moved into their new home, a frame house at 812 Louisiana Street. Their first community Mass was celebrated on August 22, and cloister was established on September 12, 1950.[86]

As mentioned in the previous chapter, the racial strife in Little Rock caused the nearby headquarters of the Little Rock School Board to be bombed at 11:00 a.m., September 7, 1959. Since this explosion was quite close to the sisters, Bishop Fletcher, with the aid of Father Joseph Lauro, procured the funds necessary to build a new monastery. On September 12, 1961, the first Mass was celebrated in the new facility located at 7201 West Thirty-Second Street. The new structure is a simple, one-story stucco building containing a large chapel, which has a high pointed roof with a long skylight at its peak. These particular sisters make altar bread for almost all the Catholic churches in Arkansas, as well as quite a few Episcopal and Methodist churches. This community was quite close to the heart of Bishop Fletcher and also to his successor, Bishop Andrew J. McDonald. The latter prelate usually says Mass for them about once a month, committing to their prayers the special needs of the diocese.[87]

The last half-century has been a time in which many of the religious communities experienced a great amount of recognition, maturation, and change. For example, thirteen years after joining the national union of Mercy communities and belonging to the St. Louis province, a sister from St. Mary's convent in Little Rock, Sister Mary Fidelius Maher, became Mother Provincial in 1942. Born in Ottawa, Illinois, her family moved to Little Rock, where she entered the Mercy convent in 1895 at the age of sixteen. As a professed sister, she taught for decades at the Mercy academies in Little Rock and Hot Springs. After serving on the provincial council for nine years, she was elected as Assistant Mother Provincial in 1939 and then Mother Provincial three years later. This position she held for the next six years.[88]

New growth would come to other Mercy facilities. St. Edward's Hospital in Fort Smith had moved into its second home in 1922 and a 1953 annex expanded it into a 150 bed facility. The sisters opened a nursing home for elderly women in Fort Smith known as Mercy Villa in 1942, but it was forced to close thirteen years later due to overwhelming operating costs.[89] Mount St. Mary's in Little Rock grew so much that a new building was built and dedicated in 1954 as Marian Hall. During this time, vocations from Mount St. Mary's were quite numerous. Sister Werner Keith, a 1944 graduate of Mount St. Mary's, remembers that "St. Mary's was a powerhouse of vocations and the Sisters had a beautiful spirit." The example of these women greatly influenced her decision to enter religious life.[90] St. Anne's Academy in Fort Smith added a new building; the only closing was the school in Mena, in 1960.[91]

Other signs of maturity and change would come to other longstanding Arkansas women religious orders. The Olivetan Benedictines elected their first American-born prioress in Sister Perpetua Reinhart. Born Susan Reinart in Iowa, in 1896, her family was in Texas when she first came into contact with the Olivetan Benedictines in Muenster. She entered Holy Angels convent in 1909, took the religious name of Perpetua, and after many years of service to her community, she was elected prioress on July 2, 1945.[92] Under her direction, a major annex was built at St. Bernard's Hospital and dedicated on July 11, 1952. At the time of the dedication, Bishop Fletcher remarked that "this annex could not have been built without God's blessing."[93] After nine years as prioress, Mother Reinart turned her position over to another American-born sister, Mother Philippa Wavrick.[94] Another addition to their ministry came on January 1, 1964, when the Mercy sisters handed over control of the Catholic hospital in Brinkley to these Olivetan Benedictines.[95]

St. Scholastica's had to endure the worst fire in its history on November 20, 1940. The original convent at Shoal Creek was completely destroyed as the "convent, church, rectory, school, and laundry were a smoldering heap of ruins."[96] Mother Perpetua Gerard governed the community from 1920-1947 and saw it through the difficult depression which put tremendous financial strain upon the community. Mother Gerard and the sisters spent long nights in prayer before the Blessed Sacrament asking God and the prayers of St. Joseph to assist them in keeping them from bankruptcy. The earnest prayers, hard work, and leadership of their determined superior, kept St. Scholastica's from total financial collapse. Much of the church was rebuilt and the Fort Smith Benedictines were out of debt by the time she ended her term as superior in 1947.[97] Under the new superior, Mother Jane Frances Brockman, a major new building was added to the community. On October 18, 1958, Bishop Fletcher dedicated a new academy building with a dormitory which could house 120 boarders and a classroom building for 450 students. There was growth during those years–in 1929, the convent had 125 sisters and seventy students; by 1950 the numbers stood at three hundred sisters with 150 students.[98]

Buildings and statistics, however, do not tell the full story of a community. The Fort Smith Benedictines were real pioneers in liturgical renewal within the Little Rock diocese. Sister Innocence Wallmeier had taught Gregorian chant in the community since the late 1930s and would be praised by Bishop Fletcher in 1950 for "executing this pioneer plan for developing Gregorian Chant for the Diocese."[99] Mother Jane Frances Brockman, superior of the order from 1947 to 1959 and from 1963 to 1967, was a strong promoter of liturgical renewal. In 1949, the community in Chapter overwhelmingly voted to have their Divine Office sung and recited *in English*, long before such adaptations were conducted in other communities. Sister Clarine Rockenhaus of the Fort Smith Benedictines and Father Raban Hathorn from St. Meinrad's Benedictine Abbey, helped the sisters adopt this new vernacular chant for their daily community prayers.[100]

In 1964, the community became a member of the Religious Federation of St. Gertrude, and thus came under pontifical jurisdiction rather than diocesan. In 1969, its convent in Columbia, Missouri, became an independent daughterhouse, and two years later, St. Gertrude convent in Ramsey, Louisiana, amalgamated with the St. Scholastica Benedictines. St. Benedict Priory in Canyon, Texas, became a dependent priory with the Fort Smith order a decade later. Hesychia House of Prayer was begun during the era of their community's prioress, Sister Mary Hawkins (1981-1985). Since 1985, Sr. Louise Sharum, author of the community's centennial history *Write the Vision Down*, has been serving as the ninth prioress for these Benedictine sisters of western Arkansas.[101]

The Sisters of Charity of Nazareth would also make some real alterations and changes in their ministry after World War II. While their teaching ministry in the diocese declined, they witnessed a major expanse of their main hospital facility in the state, St. Vincent's. In 1961, the high school department of Sacred Heart Academy in Helena closed, and seven years later, the whole historic institution closed. Also in 1968, the Kentucky-based religious order closed Annunciation Academy in Pine Bluff. This did not mean they completely abandoned Catholic education in either Helena or Pine Bluff. They continued to teach in St. Mary's parish school in Helena until 1974 and at St. Joseph's Catholic school in Pine Bluff until 1971.[102]

As their teaching commitment in Arkansas shrank, their hospital in Little Rock was about to undergo tremendous growth over a forty year period. The hospital at Tenth and High Streets moved to a new location, what was the western boundary of the city, the corner of Markham and Hayes Streets, now University Avenue. The new facility opened in December 1954, and the old St. Vincent's became a medical nursing home known as Our Lady of Nazareth Home. This latter institution stayed in downtown Little Rock for ten years before closing in July 1964. For the first time since 1888, there was no longer a Catholic medical or nursing facility in downtown Little Rock. The nursing home, Our Lady of Nazareth, moved out near St. Vincent's on Lee Avenue, but eventually closed in 1968.[103]

One of the major figures of this new St. Vincent's was Sister Margaret Vincent Blandford, who served as administrator of the new facility from 1955-1961. Under her leadership, the hospital was fully integrated and her talents were locally recognized. The *Arkansas Democrat* named her "Woman of the Year" in 1960.[104] Six years after Sr. Blandford left her post, St. Vincent's hired its first lay person to operate the facility in eighty years. Mr. Allen Weintraub became, in the opinion of the historian of St. Vincent's hospital, the first person of Jewish faith to direct an American Catholic hospital. In 1971, after four years at St. Vincent's, Mr. Weintraub died of a heart attack.[105]

Sister Blandford returned as administrator in 1971, after serving as President of the Catholic Hospital Association of the United States and Canada, the same position Monsignor Healy held some two decades earlier. She continued to serve as administrator until she retired at the age of seventy in 1988, St. Vincent's centennial year. Under her administration, the physical facility of St. Vincent's grew tremendously. Parkview Medical Office Building was constructed in 1975 and the Blandford Physicians Center completed in 1984; The Guesthouse opened two years later. The Guesthouse is independently owned and operated apart from St. Vincent's, but it shares in the ministry of St. Vincent's in the care it gives to the families of patients. A lay board also took over control of St. Vincent's in the 1970s, yet one-third of the board would still be members of the Sisters of Charity of Nazareth.[106] Now known as St. Vincent's Infirmary Medical Center, it is in its second century as Arkansas' oldest health care unit.

St. Vincent's was not the only Catholic hospital undergoing growth over the previous few decades. In 1966, St. Joseph's Infirmary in Hot Springs opened Arkansas' first coronary care unit. Sister Mary Werner Keith was appointed administrator of this facility, and under her tenure, a new building project enlarged the east and west wings of the main building, increasing its bed capacity to 250. More additions under other administrators added another new wing to the building in 1980, and four years later, Medical Resources Center was opened. St. Joseph's Ambulatory Care Center was also added in 1986. In mid-December 1991, it moved into a completely new hospital.[107]

The other Mercy hospital in the state, St. Edward's in Fort Smith, matched the growth of its sister institution in Hot Springs. Under the leadership of Sister Mary Kieran Moloney, St. Edward's added an intensive care unit in 1966. Her place was then taken after 1970 by Sister Judith Marie Keith, the natural sister of Sister Mary Werner Keith. Soon after she became administrator, the decision was made to abandon the old site and move to a new facility at Rogers Avenue and Wildcat Mountain Road in Fort Smith. Governor Dale L. Bumpers was present at the ground breaking ceremony in 1973. When the building was completed, Arkansas' fifth Catholic bishop, Andrew J. McDonald, was on hand to dedicate the facility on August 10, 1975. Among the dignitaries who came to this event was the President of the United States, Gerald R. Ford. Other important public figures attending included Arkansas Governor David H. Pryor, U.S. Senators John L. McClellan and Dale L. Bumpers, along with U.S. Representative John Paul Hammerschmidt. In his comments, President Ford praised the work of the Sisters of Mercy in a state long outside the mainstream of the U.S. Catholic population. The chronicles of the Mercy sisters in Arkansas rightly point out that Mother Teresa Farrell and Bishop Andrew Byrne would never have dreamed that after the order had worked here for almost 125 years, the President of the United States would come to help dedicate one of their facilities and recognize their contribution to Arkansas.[108]

That same year, 1975, the Mercy sisters of Fort Smith moved into their new convent near the hospital. St. Edward's Mercy Medical Center has provided, and continues to provide, real leadership in bringing health care to the rural areas of western Arkansas. In 1978, they opened the North Logan Memorial Hospital in Paris, Arkansas; four years later, a new Mercy hospital and nursing home started in Waldron, in Scott County. As part of St. Edward's concern for health needs of the community, Harbor View Mercy Hospital was inaugurated in 1984, an eighty bed all private hospital which is the first church-sponsored psychiatric facility in the state.[109]

While the Mercy sisters' health facilities were growing in western Arkansas, there were other changes in the Catholic Church which affected religious orders of women. The loss of religious vocations after the Second Vatican Council and the expense of hiring lay teachers, greatly impacted all religious orders and affected their ability to maintain their educational and health facilities. In 1965, for example, there were 693 religious sisters in Arkansas and 286 were engaged in teaching school. By 1980, there were 534 sisters in the state, with 103 engaged in teaching.[110] In only fifteen years, the number of sisters teaching in Catholic schools dropped by almost two-thirds.

Over the next ten years, the situation worsened. The number of sisters in the diocese fell to 393, but only fifty-nine were still in teaching.[111] In the quarter-century after the end of the Second Vatican Council in 1965, the number of religious sisters in Arkansas declined forty-three percent, the same as the national average,[112] but the number of teaching sisters fell about eighty percent.

Due to their reduced numbers, the Sisters of Mercy were forced to abandon some of their institutions and ministries. They withdrew from schools in Camden in 1962 and in El Dorado in 1971. In 1973, St. Anne's Academy in Fort Smith closed after operating for 120 years. The Mercy sisters still staff, however, Catholic schools in Little Rock, North Little Rock, Hot Springs, and Fort Smith.[113] In the same year, they closed St. Anne's; the Mercy religious order had to close Warner-Brown hospital in El Dorado.[114] Mount St. Mary's in Little Rock was unable to accept boarding students after 1970 and was forced to eliminate grades one through three for the first time in its 119 year history. In 1975, it graduated its last student who would have attended St. Mary's for all eight grades. Those girls, who continued through four years of high school, would be the last to obtain twelve years of education at St. Mary's.[115]

Despite such difficulties, Mount St. Mary's Academy has not only survived, but has undergone a total restoration at its Pulaski Heights location. On September 22, 1977, Bishop McDonald dedicated a new classroom and library building for St. Mary's, which by then enrolled a total of 750 students.[116] The main building, however, had grown too expensive to maintain, as it needed extensive structural repairs. This Gothic structure had long been a landmark in the city. It served as a good backdrop to nationally televised football games at nearby War Memorial Stadium. There was a strong local effort to save it, but there was not enough money available for restoration. In the summer of 1983 it was demolished, leaving only a marker recounting the history of this building which educated and housed so many Catholic and non-Catholic women for three-quarters of a century. Construction on a new convent began in 1981; the sisters moved into their new home on June 7, 1982.[117] Sister Deborah R. Troillett, a Little Rock native and 1973 graduate of Mount St. Mary's, is currently serving as principal of Arkansas' oldest educational institution which celebrated its 140th anniversary in 1991.[118]

The other women's religious orders were also affected by the decline in religious vocations after 1965. As mentioned in an earlier chapter, St. Joseph's Orphanage, long staffed by the Fort Smith Benedictines, had to close as an orphanage in 1970. It continues as a day-care center into the early 1990s. In 1968, St. Scholastica's Academy had to close its doors, and four years later, they were forced to withdrawal from staffing and operating the Crawford County Hospital in Van Buren.[119] The Olivetan Benedictines, who had accepted the hospital in Brinkley from the Mercy sisters in 1964, had to abandon that health care unit twelve years later.[120]

Although Olivetan Benedictines had to abandon the Brinkley facility, their main hospital in Jonesboro underwent some significant growth. On June 2, 1962, there was a legal separation between St. Bernard's Hospital and the Olivetan Benedictines. This meant that while the sisters still work and serve in the institution, they are no longer in complete charge of it. St. Bernard's was also enlarged and expanded into St. Bernard's Regional Medical Center in 1964. A new motherhouse, Holy Angels convent in Jonesboro, was opened and dedicated by Bishop McDonald on October 12, 1974.[121] St. Bernard's remains the main medical facility partially staffed by the Olivetan Benedictine Sisters, a religious order which is now in its second century of service in the Diocese of Little Rock.

At the other end of the state diagonally, the Sisters of Charity of the Incarnate Word, as of 1991, were celebrating seventy-five years of service in Texarkana, Arkansas. Like St. Vincent's, this unit was founded from the Will of a certain individual, Michael Meagher, an Irish immigrant and civil engineer in San Antonio who was found murdered in 1909. Although the culprit was never discovered, his Will called for the creation of a medical hospital with a board of trustees named in the Will. These trustees turned to the Sisters of Charity of the Incarnate Word in Houston, Texas, for its administration and staffing. After seeking several different sites, they decided to locate the new medical facility at Fifth and Walnut Streets in Texarkana, Arkansas. Called the Michael Meagher Memorial Hospital, it opened on September 14, 1916, with ten physicians, ten nurses, one dentist, and six sisters from the Houston-based religious order. By 1948, it moved into a new 127 bed facility and it changed its name to St. Michael's Hospital of Texarkana. After sixty-seven years of operation, Mr. Tom Byrne became its first lay administrator in 1983. As of 1991, its seventy-fifth anniversary, St. Michael's is now a 253 bed facility with Air Life helicopter, Physical Medicine and Rehab Care unit, and a cancer treatment center. At present, there are plans to build a new St. Michael's Hospital; a 354 bed, 400,000 square feet facility on the Texas side of Texarkana by 1995. What will become of the older building still located in the Diocese of Little Rock, is still unclear.[122]

In northwestern Arkansas, the Catholic hospital in Rogers has undergone change and growth over the past forty years. Expansions in 1956 and 1964 brought the facility up to a 105 bed unit. In 1963, the Dominican sisters were given full title to the facility and renamed it St. Mary-Rogers Memorial Hospital, although it is usually referred to as St. Mary's Hospital. Since the 1960s, more additions have been made to the facility: a coronary care unit, nuclear medicine department, and an intensive care nursery. It was the first hospital in the state to use Yag Lasar in 1976. In 1982, it became the second health facility in the state to have a certified cancer treatment center. A new building project launched in October 1991 includes plans for an enlarged maternity department, increased Imaging Services, Cardiac Catheterizations unit, an education center, and a new emergency department.[123]

Catholic religious orders minister within fourteen medical, nursing, and psychiatric facilities throughout the state of Arkansas. In addition to the four religious orders in the state which have ministered here for more than a century, the Sisters of Mercy, Ft. Smith Benedictines, the Olivetan Benedictines, and the Sisters of Charity of Nazareth, there are members of sixteen other women's religious communities providing ministry and service to all Arkansans, regardless of their race or creed.[124]

The last quarter-century has been difficult for Catholic schools throughout the United States, and the Diocese of Little Rock has not been exempt from this overall trend. The number of Catholic schools went from sixty, including ten high schools in 1965, to forty with six high schools fifteen years later. The number of students enrolled in the same period dropped from an historical high of 10,980 to 7,647.[125] In these challenging times, Bishop Andrew J. McDonald has appointed women religious to head diocesan schools.

In the summer of 1973, Bishop McDonald appointed Sr. Consuella Bauer, a member of the Fort Smith Benedictines, to become the first woman Superintendent of Schools. Born on July 29, 1916, in Morrison Bluff, in Logan County, she entered the convent in 1934 and received her undergraduate degree in Education from Marymount College in Salina, Kansas, in 1942. She eventually earned her advanced degree in Education at Catholic University of America in 1956. She taught in schools in both Arkansas and Missouri, yet she also served as principal at St. Scholastica's Academy in Fort Smith in the 1960s. In her four-year tenure as Superintendent of Catholic Schools, she initiated and organized annual spring meetings for Catholic school principals. The annual Diocesan Teachers Institute was reactivated by Sr. Bauer, and she inaugurated a much needed life and health insurance program for lay teachers.[126]

For the past fifteen years, the Superintendent of Schools for the diocese has been Sister Henrietta Hockle, a member of the Olivetan Benedictines. Born in Jonesboro on April 8, 1927, she entered the convent in 1945 and graduated from St. Scholastica College in Duluth, Minnesota, in 1959. She had been both a teacher and principal for many years. She earned a Master's degree in Education and an Education Specialist degree from Arkansas State University in 1965 and 1977. The thesis for her final education degree was a history of the Catholic schools in Arkansas.[127]

During the last decade, there has been a real effort to sustain Catholic education in Arkansas. Sister Hockle states that when she became superintendent in 1977, there was only one lay principal in the state; now, there are twenty-two. With the joint cooperation of both the clergy and laity, Catholic schools are being maintained in the diocese. Sister Hockle recalls that when she was first brought in as superintendent, Bishop McDonald commissioned the Diocesan Board of Education to do their best to "keep our Catholic schools open."[128] Since 1978, twelve schools have added more classrooms and grades. In

1985, the three parishes in Fort Smith opened Trinity Junior High School which is housed in the classroom building of St. Scholastica's. A completely new Catholic grade school, Christ the King parochial school, opened in Little Rock in 1986. There have, of course, been some losses during this time. St. Paul's Catholic High School in Pocahontas (1989) and Holy Redeemer grade school in Clarksville (1990) were closed. Between 1983-1991, ninety-one classrooms have been constructed in the diocese. Since 1977, twelve parishes have added licensed day-care and early child care programs.[129]

Sister Hockle was also instrumental in starting an Arkansas chapter of the National Federation of Nonpublic School State Accrediting Associations in the fall of 1989. She became the first Executive Director of the Arkansas Nonpublic School Accrediting Association.[130]

Due to this hard work, the decline of students enrolled in Catholic schools has been stemmed, but not entirely halted. By 1991 there were thirty-seven Catholic schools in the state, including five high schools. The number of students in Catholic schools was 6,357. Thus, the number of Catholic children receiving religious instruction outside of their regular school classes has increased to a point where their number is 5,413, almost equal to those enrolled in the diocesan Catholic schools.[131] As such, "out of regular school" religious instruction becomes more common. The Office of Religious Education has become more of an integral part of the Church's religious instruction.

Religious instruction is as old as organized Christianity, yet a more formal organization for that purpose came out of the Council of Trent during the sixteenth century. In addition to such changes as an educated clergy and a Catholic schools program, the fathers at that Council recognized the overwhelming need for better religious instruction for the laity. To a large degree, this change was brought about by the innovative and saintly Archbishop Charles Borromeo of Milan. The Council of Trent and Pope St. Pius V mandated that each diocese have a program of religious instruction for the laity and the children. Catholic schools are really a part of that commission, but it has never been feasible to put every baptized Catholic in a parochial school. For this reason, St. Charles Borromeo would institute what became known as the Confraternity of Christian Doctrine. A national office for this C.C.D. was created within the American Catholic Bishops' Conference in 1933.[132]

In this missionary diocese, with only a small and widely scattered Catholic population, much of the religious instruction had traditionally been given in some type of catechism class or C.C.D. program outside of the normal school day. In 1963, a time when Catholic schools were at their zenith, it was estimated that five million children were in Catholic schools and four million in C.C.D. programs.[133]

For the Little Rock diocese, each parish is mandated to have some type of religious instruction program. The diocese has always provided for religious instruction for children who do not attend Catholic schools. Since 1977, this effort has been more focused with the creation of the diocesan Office of Religious Education. For the past fifteen years, it has been led primarily by religious sisters. All Catholic parishes and missions operate their religious education programs under the leadership of the diocesan office. Since 1985, that office has been headed by Sister Maria Kleinschmidt, a member of the Daughters of Charity.[134]

Since the Second Vatican Council, many women's religious orders have shifted the focus of their ministry from Catholic education or health care, to ministry to the poor. An example of such new directions is the work of the Daughters of Charity of St. Vincent De Paul, Sister Kleinschmidt's order, which has been in the diocese since 1973. For their first fifteen years, the Daughters of Charity centered their work on providing needed social and health care services to the poor, predominately in black areas of Fort Smith and Pine Bluff. Since 1988, they focused their work in central Arkansas, serving at Little Rock's black Catholic parish of St. Bartholomew and working with hispanics at Our Lady of Good Counsel parish. By 1992, one of their own sisters assumed the role of director at Helping Hand, a food and clothing distribution center operating out of St. Bartholomew's parish. They also minister in the black communities in Hamburg and Gould, in southeast Arkansas, and work with Hispanics in Hope, in southwest Arkansas.[135]

In the last quarter-century, the laity has been performing more of the traditional charitable works of the Church. This is the result of two factors, the call of the Second Vatican Council for more lay participation in the Church and the loss of membership in religious communities. Catholic education, for example, was once almost exclusively the work of the female orders; now, the laity provides many teachers and administrators. The laity has also been more active in the works of mercy of the Church, in actions associated with Catholic Social Services.

The Office of Social Services in the diocese was formally established in 1940 as a branch of the Department of Schools, Hospitals, and Charities. This was under the direction of Monsignor Healy until his death in December 1952. Bishop Fletcher then appointed Father John Kordsmeier to his position and changed the title of the agency to the Department of Education, Hospitals, and Catholic Welfare. In 1962, Bishop Fletcher separated the education office. The department became the diocesan Department of Hospitals and Social Services, still under the direction of Father John Kordsmeier. In 1967, Father Walter J. Clancy became Fr. Kordsmeier's assistant with the main responsibility for social services, while the director focused his attention to hospital work. With Father Clancy's appointment, for the first time in its history, the Little Rock diocese had assigned a person to work exclusively in the area of social service. A year later, Father Clancy became the Director of Catholic Hospitals and Social Services.[136]

Under Father Clancy's leadership, the first food bank centers were established in 1970 under the day-to-day operation of Sister Annella Willett, an Olivetan Benedictine who only recently resigned from this activity in December 1991. Her place has since been taken by Sr. Joan Pytlik, a member of the Daughters of Charity.[137] In 1970, Father James R. Savary became the Director of Catholic Hospitals and Social Services and under his direction, a free medical clinic opened in west Little Rock on February 16, 1971.[138] In 1973, Sister Leona Hoelting, a Fort Smith Benedictine, was made Associate Director for Social Services. Sister Hoelting instituted a lay board with Mr. Bill Waters as the first elected head of the Board for Catholic Social Services on November 30, 1974. Bishop McDonald separated the diocesan Department of Hospitals and Social Services in 1974 and made Father Savary the first Director of Catholic Social Services. Father Savary then chose Father Joseph M. Biltz as his associate director.[139] Father Biltz became the Director of the Office of Justice and Peace in 1978, while Father Savary continued as Director of Catholic Social Services.[140]

In January 1985, Bishop McDonald appointed Mr. Dennis C. Lee of Little Rock as the first layperson to head the Catholic Social Services Department. Born in the Arkansas capital in 1959, Mr. Lee attended Catholic schools through high school and then graduated from St. Benedict's College, in Louisiana, in 1982. He earned a Master's degree in Social Work from the University of Arkansas in 1984 and came to work for the diocese shortly after gaining that degree.[141] His agency is one of the largest in the diocese. Ms. Antje Harris, a Licensed Social Worker, heads the Adoption Services which is an ecumenical, non-discriminatory adoption ministry operating in the diocese since May 1984. A comprehensive and professional program of counseling, casework, medical assistance, and education is provided at no cost to the birth parents. Ms. Harris points out that the Catholic Church in Arkansas has had a long history of trying to find homes for children before her agency was created.[142] Other major agencies operating under the Department of Catholic Social Services include the Respect Life Office, directed by Mrs. Anne Dierks, and the Westside Medical Clinic, directed by Ms. Karen DiPippa. Mrs. Jo Ann Bemrich heads the area of Social Action, which works with the St. Vincent DePaul Society and directs Arkansas' part of the National Catholic Bishop's Campaign for Human Development. It has recently absorbed the Office of Justice and Peace.[143]

Under Mr. Lee's direct concern is the Catholic Relief Service and the activities for the Society for the Propagation of the Faith. He works closely with the Christopher Homes program, which provides low income housing for the elderly. Mr. James T. Davis serves as the executive director of the program. In addition to overseeing these programs, Mr. Lee writes proposals for government grants and coordinates the overall diocesan concerns for the poor and needy. The diocese also participates in other social programs such as the St. John's Community Center in Fort Smith and the ecumenically-based outreach to the homeless called "Our House" at the old parish hall at St. Andrew's Cathedral in downtown Little Rock. The 1991 diocesan directory lists Mr. Heine Upchurch and Ms. Patricia Reed as working at St. John's and Mr. Joe Flaherty as the executive director for "Our House."[144]

No treatment of Catholic social services would be complete without some mention of diocesan outreach to the Hispanic people. This concern dates back seventy years. In 1921, Fr. John P. Fisher, then secretary to Bishop Morris, wrote Mr. J. J. Fuller of the American Bauxite Company in Bauxite, Arkansas, about allowing the diocese to provide a priest to work among the Mexican workers in the mines.[145] Some three decades later, Bishop Fletcher sought to bring in a priest from Mexico to minister to the migrant farm workers laboring in the fields of eastern and southern Arkansas. Chancellor Monsignor Joseph A. Murray, in 1965, directed Father John B. Manchino to minister to these Spanish-speaking Catholics. Father Manchino opened Our Lady of Guadalupe mission church near Elaine, Arkansas, in December 1965. Their poverty and the transitory nature of their work made it difficult to minister to them in a traditional parish.[146]

In 1976, Bishop McDonald appointed Father Robert A. Torres as director of the Mexican-American-Spanish ministry.[147] More than fifteen years later, Father Scott A. Friend, pastor at St. Louis Catholic Church in Camden, was assigned to work among the Hispanic missions and for the Diocesan Council for Hispanics. Spanish-speaking Catholics are increasingly coming to Arkansas to work in farming and other industries. In certain parishes in Little Rock, Spanish Masses are being celebrated on a monthly basis. Such Masses will probably increase as the Hispanic population in the diocese continues to grow.[148] This minority will, no doubt, make its impact on the future Catholic Church in Arkansas.

Over the past 150 years of diocesan history, the women's religious communities–the Sisters of Mercy, the Ft. Smith Benedictines, the Olivetan Benedictines, and the Sisters of Charity of Nazareth, along with many others–have performed great service to the people of all faiths in Arkansas. Together with the Catholic laity, they are making contributions in Arkansas that often go unnoticed and unrewarded. That story is much larger than this chapter or even this book can recount.

As the diocese approaches its sesquicentennial, it has also been affected by the presence and activity of its present bishop, Andrew Joseph McDonald. For the last two decades, this native Georgian would help shape Arkansas Catholicism to meet the challenges and opportunities of the post-conciliar Church.

CHAPTER XII

"To Prove That I Love"

Bishop McDonald and the Post-Conciliar Church, 1972-1992

THE REVEREND MONSIGNOR Andrew Joseph McDonald, a forty-nine year old pastor from Savannah, Georgia, succeeded Bishop Fletcher in 1972, becoming the fifth ordinary in the 129-year history of the Catholic Diocese of Little Rock. The new bishop had something in common with at least three of his predecessors. Like Bishop Byrne, he had worked in a diocese that once encompassed the Carolinas and Georgia, although Byrne had served his priesthood only in the Carolinas. Like Bishop Morris, he was a native southerner of Irish ancestry; and like Bishop Fletcher, the first native Arkansan raised to the hierarchy, Bishop McDonald was the first native of Savannah, Georgia, appointed to the episcopacy.[1] Bishop McDonald would be coming to a diocese with a Catholic population, in 1970, of 55,283 in a total population of 1,923,000, and Catholics were 2.8 percent of the population.[2]

Andrew Joseph McDonald was the eleventh of twelve children born to James Bernard McDonald and Theresa McGreal. James B. McDonald's brothers and sisters died in the terrible yellow fever epidemic of 1886, so young Andrew had few relatives on his father's side. His parents were married in 1901 and their children, four sons and eight daughters, were born between 1902 and 1926. The future bishop was born on October 24, 1923. His was a devout Irish Catholic family, and he was imbued with a strong respect for the Church, priests, and nuns. Four of the bishop's sisters entered religious life, and young

Andrew followed a call to the priesthood; the other three brothers and four sisters married. As of 1992, two of the religious sisters, three of his married sisters, and his younger brother Richard were the only members of the McDonald family still living.[3]

The bishop's father possessed clerical skills that enabled him to serve as a secretary for the attorneys who represented the Central Georgia Railroad based in Savannah. Because of his father's position, the future bishop and his large family were allowed to travel on railroad passes to visit members of the family living in other areas of the United States. The railroad passes also would be important for Bishop McDonald's education, using them to travel to and from his major and minor seminary.[4]

Bishop McDonald received his early education with the Marist Brothers of Poughkeepsie, New York, who operated a boys' grammar school at the St. John the Baptist Cathedral parish in Savannah until 1939. The Diocese of Savannah had been erected in 1850, and after almost a century, it still encompassed the whole state of Georgia. As a member of the cathedral parish, young Andrew served at the altar of Bishop Michael J. Keyes, an Irish immigrant and a member of the Marist order of priests, who was Bishop of Savannah from 1921 to 1935. With his retirement, came Bishop Gerald P. O'Hara from the Archdiocese of Philadelphia, 1935-1959.[5]

The young man first mentioned his desire to become a priest to his parents, and because they lived in the cathedral parish, they consulted Bishop O'Hara. Later, Bishop O'Hara interviewed the prospective seminarian and informed him he would be sent to a minor seminary in Maryland. Not yet fourteen years old, young Andrew left Savannah on a railroad pass in September 1937 for St. Charles Minor Seminary in Catonsville, Maryland.[6]

Bishop McDonald recalls his six years at St. Charles as happy ones, but he readily admits being terrified about leaving home at such a tender age. He remembers fondly two priest-teachers during his first year at St. Charles, which was operated by the Society of St. Sulpice: Father Jack Franey, S.S., who taught him his first-year English and Father Fred Chudzinski, S.S. Father Franey's aunt would later grant a scholarship at St. Mary's for a student from a Southern diocese, and Father Franey saw that this seminarian from Savannah received the scholarships which paid for his four years of theology at St. Mary's Seminary in Baltimore. After graduating from St. Charles, he completed his philosophy studies at the old St. Mary's on Paca Street from 1943 to 1945, and then he finished his theological training at the new St. Mary's facilities at Roland Park from 1945 to 1948.[7]

While the young seminarian was completing his theological training in Maryland, Bishop O'Hara left the Diocese of Savannah for Rome, where he entered the diplomatic service for the Vatican and was given the title Archbishop O'Hara. From 1945 until 1957, Savannah had no resident bishop. Archbishop O'Hara only returned for a few periodic visits. Monsignor Joseph E.

Weyland, V.G., administered the diocese. On May 8, 1948, Andrew J. McDonald became a priest for the Diocese of Savannah, ordained by Bishop Emmet Walsh of Charleston, South Carolina. All of his brothers and sisters were present together for the first time since 1926. Her religious superiors allowed his sister Josephine, Sister Celine of St. Rose, a Little Sister of the Poor, to come home for the ordination.[8]

The newly ordained Father Andrew J. McDonald spent his first months as a priest as an assistant at the cathedral. During the academic year 1948-1949, he was sent to study canon law at Catholic University of America in Washington, D.C. In August 1949, from his diplomatic position in Romania, Archbishop O'Hara sent the young priest to the Lateran University in Rome.[9]

Bishop McDonald spent two years in the Eternal City. In the summer of 1950 he went to Perugia, a city between Rome and Florence, to study Italian at a state university. He recalls that he did moderately well in grasping the language. While in Perugia, he lived with some poor and simple priests and gained considerable inspiration from them. They allowed him to accompany them to their various missions, including Catholic orphanages, where the Catholic sisters also provided a strong Christian witness. In June 1951, Father McDonald received his doctorate in canon law from the Lateran University in Rome. After a few weeks of European travel, he returned to Savannah in August 1951. That fall, he journeyed to Chicago to work in the Chancery and Marriage Tribunal Office of the archdiocese. In early January 1952, Father McDonald returned again to Savannah. He was assigned to Our Lady of Lourdes parish in Port Wentworth, about seven miles from Savannah.[10]

A Catholic parish had been created there in 1940, and Father McDonald worked as an assistant to Father Daniel McCarthy, who was in his mid-sixties and not in the best of health. In these same years, the young priest also served in the Savannah Chancery and on the Marriage Tribunal. This was his position for five years.[11]

Changes would come to the Catholic Church in Georgia by the late 1950s. In 1956, the Diocese of Atlanta was created, cutting off northern Georgia and creating the first new ecclesiastical jurisdiction in the state in more than a century. Archbishop O'Hara, essentially absent from Savannah since 1945, received a new auxiliary bishop in 1957, Thomas J. McDonough, who came to the diocese from St. Augustine, Florida. Archbishop O'Hara formally resigned as the Bishop of Savannah in 1959; in March 1960, Bishop McDonough was installed as the tenth Bishop of Savannah. He represented the Diocese of Savannah at the Second Vatican Council.[12]

Auxiliary Bishop McDonough appointed Father McDonald his chancellor in 1957, and soon thereafter, the priest received the title of Monsignor. In September 1963, Monsignor McDonald became the pastor of Blessed Sacrament parish, one of the largest parishes in the city. There, he would stay for nine years. The Diocese of Savannah would soon receive yet another bishop,

Gerald P. Frey, in 1967. The new prelate left Monsignor McDonald at Blessed Sacrament and appointed him vicar general for the Savannah diocese.[13]

Bishop Frey instituted a presbyterial council, a clergy personnel board, and other structures inspired by the Second Vatican Council. These changes reduced Monsignor McDonald's responsibilities somewhat, but he did not mind, because his duties as pastor at Blessed Sacrament kept him busy. In years to come, as Bishop of Little Rock, McDonald would make many of the same diocesan structural changes he helped implement in Savannah.[14] As pastor of one of the major parishes in his native city and as vicar general for the diocese, Monsignor McDonald had no reason to suspect that he was going to leave either his parish or the diocese.[15] In the two decades since his return from Rome and the Chicago archdiocese, Msgr. McDonald had never served in a parish outside the Savannah vicinity. After June 11, 1972, his life would never be the same.

It was a Sunday, and Bishop Frey had been out of town for a few weeks and had returned to bless a new Catholic retirement home in Savannah. At 8:00 p.m., Monsignor McDonald received a call from Bishop Frey announcing that he was coming for a visit. When Bishop Frey arrived, he showed Monsignor McDonald a letter he had received from the apostolic delegate in the United States, Archbishop Luigi Raimondi. The letter stated that His Holiness Paul VI was asking the Savannah priest to become Bishop of the Diocese of Little Rock. Taken aback, Monsignor McDonald went over to the Church to pray before the Blessed Sacrament. Andrew J. McDonald was notified of his appointment on the anniversary of his father's death, which had come on June 11, 1943. He was not allowed to make this selection public until July 4, 1972, the thirty-second anniversary of his mother's death.[16] These coincidences seem fitting, since neither parent had been alive on his ordination day.

Andrew J. McDonald had visited Arkansas twice, both times to encourage Savannah seminarians at St. John's Home Missions Seminary. The visits occurred in 1964 and 1965. Bishop McDonald now recalls seeing the grounds and having lunch with Monsignor James O'Connell, the rector. Monsignor McDonald interviewed the few Savannah seminarians and dined with them that evening. He remembers that on one of his visits, an informal discussion took place among the seminary professors about the possibility of a new diocese for eastern Arkansas and western Tennessee. Memphis would be made a diocese in 1970, yet all of Arkansas would remain part of the Little Rock See.[17]

On September 5, 1972, the day following Labor Day, Andrew J. McDonald was ordained a bishop at St. John the Baptist Cathedral in Savannah. In addition to the large and enthusiastic crowd attending the ordination, there were in attendance five archbishops and twenty-four bishops. Among them was Bishop Frey, who wished the new prelate well in his diocese to the west. The homilist, and principal consecrator, was Thomas McDonough, the former Bishop of Savannah who had become Archbishop of Louisville, Kentucky. The co-consecrators were Bishop Frey and Archbishop Hannon of New Orleans. Also present were Arkansas Bishops Fletcher and Graves, and all the new bishop's brothers and sisters except Josephine, who had died in 1965.[18] Bishop McDonald arrived at the newly expanded and enlarged Little Rock municipal airport late in the afternoon of September 6, 1972. That evening, Bishop McDonald met with the consulters of the diocese. The new bishop then presented his original documents from the Vatican, and Chancellor Father Charles Kordsmier read the papal documents.[19]

Like three of his predecessors, Bishop McDonald would arrive as an unknown. Bishop Byrne rode into Little Rock from New York on a horse with two priests in tow, in June 1844. Bishop Fitzgerald arrived on a steamboat from Columbus, Ohio, in 1867, to find only six priests in a diocese that had endured a civil war and no bishop for five years. Bishop Morris had visited an ill Bishop Fitzgerald in Hot Springs in May, but came as bishop in 1906 on a train from Nashville, Tennessee. As with the others, Bishop McDonald came from east of the Mississippi River, and two bishops had even been born east of the Atlantic Ocean in Ireland. Arkansas' fifth bishop arrived on an airplane from Georgia. As with the other three bishops who came from outside the state, Bishop McDonald was ordained bishop in the diocese he was departing. At the installation ceremony at the Cathedral of St. Andrew on Thursday morning, September 7, 1972, one of the presiding dignitaries would be Archbishop Philip Hannan of New Orleans, one of the co-consecrators in Savannah, who now welcomed Bishop McDonald into the New Orleans Metropolitan Province. Apostolic Delegate Archbishop Raimondi was on hand to present greetings from the Holy Father, and Bishop Fletcher warmly welcomed the Georgian to the Arkansas diocese. Governor Dale Bumpers of Arkansas attended the ceremony, and President Richard M. Nixon sent his felicitations.[20] A Little Rock newspaper quoted the new bishop as saying, "With God's help, and the guidance of the Holy Spirit, I will live and, if necessary, I will die to prove that I care, to prove that I love."[21]

Only three months later, Pope Paul VI ordered a major change for the diocese. In the first six years of its existence, the Arkansas diocese had been part of the Province of Baltimore. In 1850, Pope Pius IX created New Orleans as an archdiocese and made Little Rock part of that ecclesiastical province. On December 19, 1972, word came that the Oklahoma City diocese would become a diocese with two suffragan Sees, Little Rock and the newly created Diocese of Tulsa. Bishop John R. Quinn of Oklahoma City became the first Archbishop of Oklahoma City. The first bishop of the See at Tulsa was Bernard Ganter. For the first time in 122 years, the Arkansas diocese would no longer be connected ecclesiastically with the Archdiocese of New Orleans. At the news of this announcement, Bishop McDonald wrote in *The Guardian*, "The Holy Father has directed us in Arkansas to turn our eyes from the South to the West . . . We extend thanks to all of you down South for all you have meant to us over the years."[22]

The new arrangement was filled with historical irony. While the boundaries of the Diocese of Little Rock have always been congruent with those of the state, Bishop Byrne, at some unknown time of his episcopacy, was given supervision over what was then the Indian Territory, just to the west of the state and the diocese. In January 1873, during a meeting in New Orleans with the other members of the province, Bishop Fitzgerald had asked that the Indian Territory be separated from the Diocese of Little Rock. Three years later, the Holy See complied and provided for that area a prefect apostolic, an ecclesiastical term applied to one overseeing a missionary area. In 1891, only two years after the famous Sooner land rush, the papacy provided the new Territory of Oklahoma with a vicar apostolic, a person who holds the rank of a bishop, yet does not have the title and does not govern, as yet, a diocese.[23] In 1905, two years before Oklahoma became the forty-sixth state, Pope Pius X gave the area a bishop and erected the Diocese of Oklahoma City. Now, sixty-seven years later, the state would have its own archdiocese and a newly created See for its northeastern section.[24]

Almost a century after Bishop Fitzgerald had suggested the separation, Catholic growth in what was once known as the Indian Territory would so far exceed that of the older state, that the Holy See would create an archbishopric, not in Arkansas, but in Oklahoma. The decision was a triumph of numbers over history. While Oklahoma had by 1970 twice the Catholics of Arkansas, its overall percentage of Catholics was not much greater. Oklahoma Catholics made up 4.4 percent of their state's population compared with Arkansas' 2.8 percent.[25]

On February 6, 1973, Bishop McDonald attended the ceremonies elevating John R. Quinn as the first Archbishop of Oklahoma City. The next day, he participated in the installation of Bernard Ganter as the first Bishop of Tulsa.[26] Within days, Archbishop Quinn would invite Bishop McDonald to the first meeting of the Oklahoma City Province to be held in his home on March 23, 1973.[27]

Only months after Arkansas' transfer to the new province, Auxiliary Bishop Lawrence P. Graves was named Bishop of Alexandria, Louisiana. Since 1969, he had served as auxiliary bishop to help an aging Bishop Fletcher. Bishop Graves was reappointed by the Pope as auxiliary bishop on October 7, 1972. Bishop McDonald immediately appointed him vicar general.[28] By December, Bishop Graves became pastor at St. Joseph's Church in Pine Bluff. He soon found himself in the middle of a difficult struggle over the integration of the predominantly white St. Joseph's school and the predominantly black St. Peter's school. The goal of both Bishop McDonald and Bishop Graves was to integrate the two schools with some grades to be taught at one school and the rest at the other school.[29]

Bishop Graves stayed in Pine Bluff for only three months, during which time he strove diligently to facilitate the integration of the two schools, despite community resistance. On May 4, 1973, Bishop Graves was appointed Bishop of Alexandria, the diocese for northern Louisiana. The public announcement came later that month.[30] He would govern a diocese that bordered Arkansas and that was close to his birthplace, Texarkana.

Bishop Graves was supposed to be installed in July 1973, but the ceremony was postponed for two months, because the bishop had contracted pneumonia. On September 18, 1973, in the Cathedral of St. Francis in Alexandria, Lawrence Graves became the second native Arkansan to be elevated to the episcopate. The ceremony included Archbishop Philip Hannan of New Orleans and Bishops Fletcher and McDonald.[31] Bishop McDonald congratulated Bishop Graves and wished him well in his new diocese.[32] The fifty-seven year old Bishop Graves served in Alexandria for nine years. Poor health forced his resignation in November 1982. In 1992, he was still living in retirement in Alexandria, Louisiana.[33]

In the fall of 1972, Bishop McDonald made a major tour of the state to get acquainted with Arkansas Catholics. A month after he arrived, the local Catholic paper wrote that the bishop was still touring the state. As late as March 1973, and for some years later, McDonald was publishing a column in the paper entitled "Getting to Know You."[34]

The changes brought in by the new bishop have often masked the tremendous continuity from Bishop Fletcher to Bishop McDonald. For example, Bishop McDonald's office would be in the Chancery built by Bishop Fletcher on the grounds of the old seminary. Under Bishop McDonald, the old grounds were not to be abandoned, but utilized as the new hub of diocesan ministries and retreats. Like his predecessor, Bishop McDonald would not live downtown, but in a home at 30 Sherrill Road, not more than a mile from the former bishop's home on Crestwood Drive.[35] Parish councils, begun under Bishop Fletcher, continued under Bishop McDonald. Bishop Fletcher was instrumental in beginning a major outreach for the diocese, social-service retirement homes for low-income families called the Christopher Homes, in 1970. This program would be greatly expanded by Bishop McDonald, and over the next two decades, fourteen cities would have housing for the poor sponsored by Christopher Homes.[37]

Ecumenical relationships, initiated by Bishop Fletcher, were also expanded. Religious conferences between representatives of different faiths, which had begun in January 1967, would continue and even broaden under Bishop McDonald. Without exaggeration, cooperation between Catholics and people of other faiths in the last two decades has been stronger and at more levels than at any time in Arkansas history. This has been especially true between the Catholic diocese and three mainline Protestant denominations, the Episcopalian, Methodist, and Presbyterian. This cooperation had mainly, but not exclusively, been in caring for the poor and other forms of organized charity. Examples of these are the following:

Helping Hand–This ministry has its roots during the Bishop Fletcher era. It began in June 1970 as Catholic Social Services Center of Pulaski County, a food and clothing center. It started with just one center in Little Rock, and then it moved across the river to North Little Rock, where it eventually opened a fairly large center on Main Street. To make it more attractive for other churches to support it, the name was changed, in 1983, to "Helping Hand." In 1991, the Helping Hand facility moved to the school building on the grounds of St. Bartholomew parish in Little Rock. For more than two decades, thousands have received help from this center.[38]
Interfaith Hunger Task Force–This is a statewide, inter-denominational project, in which the Catholic Diocese of Little Rock joined with other churches to fight hunger in Arkansas and around the world.[39]
Good Shepherd Retirement Center–This housing complex for the elderly in Little Rock resulted from inter-denominational cooperation on social services that began in 1976 through the collaboration of Bishop McDonald, Episcopal Bishop Christopher Keller, and Methodist Bishop Eugene Frank. This center opened in early 1979.[40]
Arkansas Interfaith Conference of Churches and Synagogues–In November 1982, Bishop McDonald appointed Father Albert J. Schneider as diocesan Director of Ecumenical and Interreligious Affairs. The next year, the predominately Protestant Arkansas Council of Churches admitted Roman Catholic and Jewish congregations to its membership and altered its title to reflect this change.[41]
Catholic-Episcopal Covenant–On April 30, 1985, a year and a half after the Little Rock Catholic diocese became a member of the Arkansas Ecumenical Conference, Bishop McDonald and Episcopal Bishop Herbert Donovan signed an historical covenant, pledging mutual cooperation and support. The covenant signing ceremony began at the Cathedral of St. Andrew and proceeded to the nearby Trinity Episcopal Cathedral.[42]
Billy Graham Crusade–In 1989, the Catholic diocese cooperated in promoting an evangelical crusade in Little Rock by the famous Southern Baptist minister, the Reverend Billy Graham. Catholic participation was directed by Monsignor John F. O'Donnell, pastor of Immaculate Conception parish in North Little Rock.[43]

Unhappily, other events representing continuity from Bishop Fletcher to Bishop McDonald included the closing of black Catholic schools. As outlined in a previous chapter, black Catholic schools had reached their height in the diocese in the early 1960s and then suffered a decade of decline. By 1976, for the first time in ninety-five years, the Little Rock diocese had no schools exclusively for the education of black children. In Pine Bluff, St. Peter's black Catholic school merged with the predominant St. Joseph's Catholic school. The integration effort, begun in 1972 under Bishop Lawrence Graves, continued under Father (now Monsignor) John F. O'Donnell, pastor of St. Joseph's parish, with the support of Father Francis J. Ecimovich, S.V.D., pastor of St. Peter's parish. The merger lasted for only a few years, as both schools closed by 1975.[44] The two remaining Catholic schools which had been historically known for African-Americans, St. Augustine's in North Little Rock and St. Bartholomew's in Little Rock, continued for another academic year, yet both closed by the spring of 1976.[45]

The void resulting from these closings lasted for eight years. In 1984, Divine Word Father Clem Mathis reopened a kindergarten through sixth grade school at St. Peter's parish in Pine Bluff. He managed to have the school staffed by the School Sisters of Notre Dame. It is now the only Catholic school in Pine Bluff, and it is predominately, though not exclusively, made up of African-American children. The year 1989 marked the centennial year of efforts of black Catholic education in Pine Bluff.[46]

A major reason for the closing of black Catholic schools after the 1960s is due to the increase in costs of maintaining such institutions due to the decline in religious vocations. The decline in the United States and in other parts of the world started shortly after the closing of the Second Vatican Council and has continued over the last quarter-century. This downturn in religious vocations had started during the latter years of Bishop Fletcher and continued into the era of Arkansas' present prelate. This has had a major impact on religious sisters and on Catholic schools. (This decline and its impact on Catholic schools was covered in the previous chapter.)

The number of men who left the American Catholic priesthood between 1966 and 1978 is estimated at 10,000; but the actual number of priests did not decline greatly. The number of priests nationally fell from a high of 59,892 in 1966, to 53,088 a quarter-century later.[47] In 1965, 190 priests were working in the Diocese of Little Rock, an all-time high and a remarkable figure when you consider that Fitzgerald found only six priests in Arkansas about a century earlier. Over the next fifteen years, those numbers did not decline sharply, down only to 174. By 1990, that number had declined to 147.[48] Between 1966 and 1991, the number of priests declined nationally by 11 percent; in Arkansas, the decrease between 1965 to 1990, roughly the same period, was 22 percent.

The decline in the number of seminarians was even more marked. In 1964, 47,500 young men were preparing for the priesthood; by 1984, that number had dropped to about 12,000. Between 1965-1985, 241 American Catholic seminaries closed.[49] The closing of St. John's Home Missions Seminary, in 1967, was apparently at the start of this national trend. In 1965, fifty-five men were preparing for the priesthood for the Diocese of Little Rock; fifteen years later, that number was down to twenty-three. In addition, the 1990 *Official Catholic Directory* lists two Arkansas parishes with deacon administrators and one religious sister administrator.[50] Bishop McDonald calls the lack of religious vocations the greatest challenge of his episcopacy.[51]

With the departure of Bishop Graves in September 1973, Bishop McDonald named Monsignor Francis A. Allen vicar general. He was the founding pastor of Our Lady of the Holy Souls parish in Little Rock, a position he held for forty years until June 1987. Six months prior to his retirement, his position as vicar general was given to Father (now Monsignor) Royce Thomas. Monsignor Allen did not live long after his retirement. The eighty year old priest died October 11, 1988.[52]

While the office of vicar general is still held in high esteem, the day-to-day operations of the diocese is done more through the various departments of the diocese. An example is the Priest Synod, Presbyterial Council, and the Diocesan Council of Women Religious. Bishop McDonald asserted in his first Quinquennial Report to Rome, on August 15, 1974, that while many diocesan departments had existed under his predecessor, he had created a Personnel Board, a Clergy Welfare Board, and new ministries like those to Hispanics in his first years as bishop. He also mentioned that he had added qualified lay people to certain boards like Building and Finance.[53]

In 1973-1974, a misunderstanding arose concerning secondary Catholic education in Little Rock. It was rooted in a fear that Catholic High School, headed by Father George W. Tribou, and Mount St. Mary's, then headed by Sister Elisa Bauman, were about to be merged. A native of Pennsylvania, Father Tribou was trained at St. John's Seminary and ordained for the Arkansas diocese in 1949. A year later, he was brought to Catholic High by Assistant Principal, Father William E. Galvin. A decade later, Father Galvin became Principal and Father Tribou assumed his former position. In 1966, Monsignor Galvin became pastor at Immaculate Conception parish in Fort Smith and Father Tribou became the Principal at Catholic High, which had been located since 1960 in west Little Rock. The school became known for its strict personal and academic standards, and for a policy of strict discipline during the permissive era of the 1960s.[54] There have been some major changes at the school. Fr. Tribou recalled that when he arrived at Catholic High in 1950, all the faculty were priests; two decades later, only ten of the twenty-three faculty members were priests. After more than a quarter century, Father Tribou still serves as Principal of Catholic High School and is one of the two remaining clerics on the faculty.[55]

In 1973, Bishop McDonald proposed, in an address to the male student body of Little Rock's Catholic High School, that more personal responsibility be required of students, that students be warned if they were failing, and that religious instruction include some material about faiths other than just

Catholicism. From these comments, it was erroneously deduced that the bishop had called for the "diminution of discipline" at Catholic High.[56] In March 1974, the bishop temporarily suspended a fund appeal to finance new construction at Mount St. Mary's Academy; this made front page news in the *Arkansas Gazette* and fueled fears that he intended to merge Catholic High and Mount St. Mary's.[57] He soon allowed the new construction at Mount St. Mary's and dedicated that facility in September 1977.[58] Bishop McDonald subsequently attributed some of the misunderstanding to poor communications.[59]

Soon after this controversy, Bishop McDonald turned his attention to redecorating the Cathedral of St. Andrew. The sanctuary was enlarged to allow the use of an altar that faced the congregation. The rear wall of the church was replaced with a back window and glass door into the vestibule. One small stained glass window was moved from the front to the back of the church, but the beautiful stained glass side windows in the nave were retained. Also kept was the burial crypt installed by Bishop Fletcher and the beautiful main altar donated by the Hager family whose Will helped to found St. Vincent Infirmary Medical Center. Most of the changes were made to conform to the liturgical reforms promulgated by the Second Vatican Council. The alterations added to the quiet, reverential ambience of the cathedral's interior.[60] In August 1979, a large marble statue of St. Andrew the Apostle, the patron saint of the diocese, was erected to the immediate left of the front entrance. A gift from many families in the parish, the sculpture has the apostle embracing an X-shaped cross which tradition holds was the instrument of his martyrdom.[61]

Other changes would also come to the diocese. In 1978, Bishop McDonald instituted a permanent diaconate program, another recommendation from the Second Vatican Council.[62] On November 7, 1981, twenty-one men were ordained for the diaconate. Ten years later, the *Official Catholic Directory* recorded forty-eight permanent deacons in the diocese out of a total of about 11,000 throughout the nation.[63]

Just as the diaconate program got underway, Bishop McDonald named James T. Davis as comptroller for the diocese. This was the first time a layperson had been given such a responsibility in diocesan administration. Mr. Davis continued in that position through 1989 and is now the Executive Director of the diocese's fourteen Christopher Homes. He also serves as Executive Director of the Diocesan Building Commission.[64] In 1983, Deacon William Hartmann was appointed Director of Finance and Administration. As a CPA and former financial officer for a multi-national corporation, and as one who had served the previous seven years as Chairman of the Diocesan Finance Board, Deacon Hartmann was most qualified for this position. In 1990, his title was shortened to Director of Finance, yet he retained his overall duty as fiscal director for the diocese.[65]

Deacon Hartmann's change in title allowed Mr. Gregory C. Wolfe to be given the new position of Director of Administration in May 1990. A Little Rock native, Mr. Wolfe earned a BA in theology from the University of Dallas in 1977 and his MA in formative spirituality two years later from Duquesne University in Pittsburgh. First employed by the diocese as Director of Lay Ministry, in January 1989, he became the first layman in diocesan history to be named vice-chancellor. This title allowed him to assume responsibility for directing the work and personnel of the diocesan offices. When Father Scott Marczuk returned from his studies at Catholic University and was named vice-chancellor, Mr. Wolfe's title was changed to diocesan Director of Administration, with the same overall responsibilities. Both Father Marczuk and Mr. Wolfe still retain those positions as of 1992.[66]

Among the more profound contributions of the Catholic laity in Arkansas has been in the development of the now-famous Little Rock Scripture Study. Fred and Tammy Woell of Little Rock launched a Scripture study program in the summer of 1974 with the theological assistance of several diocesan priests and Father (now Abbot) Jerome Kodell, O.S.B., a Benedictine Scripture scholar who authored much of the printed material for the program. Initially held in Fitzgerald Hall at St. John's Catholic Center (the old seminary grounds), the program grew rapidly, and the materials were sent around the country from the Woell's home. By the summer of 1977, Bishop McDonald gave his official approval and diocesan backing to the program, and its offices were moved to St. John's Center.[67]

In 1986, Little Rock Scripture Study entered into a partnership with The Liturgical Press of Collegeville, Minnesota. Its materials are still developed in the diocese; they are published and distributed by The Liturgical Press. Supplemental audio- and video-tapes are also produced for the program. Father Richard Oswald and Deacon Johnson S. Mattingly directed the program in the 1980s and early 1990s. They oversaw the revision of existing materials and the development of a new line of materials for Young Adults authored in 1991 by Father Stephen Binz of Little Rock.[68] The first annual Bible Institute was held in Little Rock on June 1-3, 1990, attracting participants from around the United States.[69] On June 1, 1992, Father Binz became the overall Director of Little Rock Scripture Study.[70]

Arkansas Catholicism has not only provided much to the larger Church, but has received as well. Renewal movements have spread into the diocese and have thrived in the Bishop McDonald era. Among these are:

> *The Cursillo*—Begun in Spain, in 1949, and introduced into the United States by Hispanic Catholics in 1957, the Cursillo movement brings together priests and laity to stress reliance on the Holy Spirit in personal and societal renewal.[71] The first Cursillo weekend in Little Rock was from November 30 to December 3, 1967. Monsignor B. Francis McDevitt, longtime rector at St. Andrew's Cathedral, was one of the priests who led the Cursillo movement through the early years.

After his death in 1981, his place was taken by Father Michael Aureli and then by Father Francis I. Malone. By 1991, the Cursillo movement would have an overall moderator in Father John Marconi and an executive lay director in Mr. John Sweeney.[72]

Marriage Encounter–This is another renewal movement imported from Spain. It is designed to strengthen the bond between husband and wife. It came to the United States in 1967, and the first Marriage Encounter weekend in Arkansas was held in late March 1973, with a team brought in from the national headquarters in Chicago. Since then, Marriage Encounter has become an integral part of the Family Life Ministry.[73]

Pre-Cana–A marriage preparation program for engaged couples, Pre-Cana was the movement undertaken by the diocese for its Family Life Ministry.[74]

Retrouvaille–(pronounced Re-tro-vi) is a ministry for troubled marriages. This ministry was introduced into the Diocese of Little Rock in October 1989 by Father Walter Bracken, a Divine Word Missionary. Retrouvaille is a couple-to-couple ministry which begins with a weekend retreat and continues with six follow-up sessions of four hours each. Couples who have experienced Retrouvaille and have made progress in their own relationships, sometimes choose to minister to other couples.[75]

The charismatic movement, which originated at Duquesne University in 1967, spread throughout the United States and in other parts of the world. By 1974, Catholic charismatic prayer groups were in Little Rock, Fort Smith, and Fayetteville. Father James E. Mancini, then associate pastor at Our Lady of Good Counsel Church in Little Rock, was named official charismatic liaison with the bishop. Although the movement was expressed in many ways throughout the country, from covenant communities to very small prayer groups, the smaller groups were prevalent in Arkansas. The movement called for an intense personal commitment to Jesus Christ, who not only fills the individual with the personal gifts of the Spirit, but also the "charismatic" gifts of the early Church; for example, words of knowledge, tongues, and the gift of healing. Charismatics see Catholic participation as part of the Pentecostal movement begun early this century in other Christian denominations. Since 1980, the three main prayer groups have been largely replaced with scattered prayer groups in various parts of Arkansas.[76]

Nationally known charismatic healers and preachers came to the diocese in the middle of the 1980s. These included Father Ralph DiOrio from Worcester, Massachusetts, a priest nationally known for his gift of healing. He visited the Fort Smith Civic Center, and filled Barton Coliseum in Little Rock on March 2, 1986, with 12,000 people. Later that year, Father John Bertolucci, a nationally known charismatic preacher, spoke to about a thousand people at

Our Lady of Good Counsel Church.[77]

Father Mancini was also linked with another movement known as RENEW, which began in 1978 in the Archdiocese of Newark. RENEW is similar to the charismatic movement in that it uses small group sharing, but its object is parish renewal rather than the personalistic approach of Catholic pentecostalism. Within five years, RENEW had spread to more than four thousand Catholic parishes. In 1984, Bishop McDonald named Father Mancini Director of diocesan RENEW. Deacon Edwin Read of St. Elizabeth's, in Oppelo, was Associate Director. They were later joined by Deacon Johnson S. Mattingly who also served as Associate Director. The Arkansas RENEW program was begun by the bishop at a special Mass at the Little Rock Convention Center on October 6, 1985. Music was provided by John Michael Talbot and the state Catholic choir, and orchestra under the direction of Fabian Yanez. The second year, 1986, was begun in Little Rock with a commissionary ceremony and a blessing of oils. The speaker for this occasion was Father David Knight from Memphis, Tennessee. Its final season inaugurated a year later on September 27, 1987, at a special Mass for three thousand people at the Pine Bluff Convention Center. Father John Bertolucci served as the principal homilist. The Catholic state choir and orchestra was under the direction Mrs. Rita Wells. The close of RENEW featured a concert of sacred music performed by John Michael Talbot on November 15, 1987, at the Little Rock Convention Center.[78]

As important as these renewal ministries were to both the laity and clergy, Bishop McDonald developed his own style of administration which often reflected the changes that came to the Church after 1970. One major change had been the growth of pastoral planning at the diocesan level. Under the fifth bishop, diocesan administration has spread far beyond the chancery building. Many new departments and agencies now occupy the offices of Morris Hall, joining the diocesan newspaper which has been there since the late 1960s.

During the 1970s, American Catholic bishops approved such liturgical changes as communion in the hand and the rite of penance.[79] With these actions, the bishops felt they were fully participating in the renewal of the sacraments mandated by the recent Vatican council.

During the same decade, the bishops began to take more public stands on the moral implications of political issues. In November 1972, the bishops called for amnesty for draft dodgers and resisters. Bishop McDonald endorsed this position. The national Catholic hierarchy also endorsed a boycott to help farm workers win recognition for their union. Bishop McDonald received some local criticism for his stand on the boycott in behalf of California farm workers. The *Arkansas Democrat* quoted him as saying, "The Church ought to be associated with the poor."[80]

While Bishop McDonald has refrained from endorsing specific candidates, he has demonstrated a greater willingness than previous bishops to take public stands on different issues. This is perhaps his greatest difference from Bishop

Fletcher, who took a more cautious approach to the moral implications of different political issues.

In contrast to his predecessor's position, Bishop McDonald wrote newly elected Senator Dale Bumpers in 1975 asking that all military aid to South Vietnam be cut off to end our involvement in that war. "For two decades," the Bishop wrote, "we have tried to impose a political decision on Indo-China by the weight of our military presence. It has only brought slaughter and devastation. A sense of morality demands the cessation of hostilities."[81] The senator agreed and said that he would indeed vote that way. Bumpers ended his letter to the bishop this way, "There have been few chapters in America's history as devastating to this country's morale and general well-being as our experience in South Vietnam."[82]

When South Vietnam did fall to communism, thousands of refugees came to the United States. Many were housed at Fort Chaffee near Fort Smith. First under the direction of Fr. Joseph Biltz, and then later under Retired United States Army Colonel "Dutch" Dorsch, who became Refugee Director in 1979, the diocese helped thousands of Asian refugees between 1975-1980. In 1980, hundreds more Cubans would come to the camp. Colonel Dorsch maintained that refugee aid leveled off in the early 1980s, but after 1987, the diocese saw more and more refugees from Central and South America, Hong Kong, and Singapore. On October 16, 1981, the Diocese of Little Rock hired Somphone Vongsaravane to help in Asian relief work. A refugee herself from Laos, she arrived in the United States in February 1980, about a year and half before working at the diocesan center. Colonel Dorsch estimated that between 1975 and 1991, the diocese has helped more than twelve thousand refugees.[83]

In 1976, Bishop McDonald made another controversial stand in favor of repealing Arkansas' Right to Work Amendment. Since 1944, the state Constitution had allowed one the right to join a union, but no one could be compelled to join a union to hold a job, which effectively prohibited "union" or "closed" shop labor contracts. This had stifled the growth of unions in the state; the Arkansas State AFL-CIO put a repeal amendment on the ballot in 1976. Bishop McDonald endorsed the repeal. His reasons were based on the Catholic Church's traditional support for labor unions since the papal document *Rerum Novarum* in 1891.[84] By this position, Bishop McDonald demonstrated that he had much in common with the second Bishop of Little Rock, Edward M. Fitzgerald, who had supported the Knights of Labor and unionization in his day. It was also consistent with his position on the farm boycott.

A storm of criticism followed. One lay Catholic angrily wrote the bishop, "Your feeling, because of your position, should remain yours, and should never have been permitted to be used as an issue in the upcoming election campaign."[85] The right-to-work-repeal effort failed dismally.[86]

That same year, Bishop McDonald attended the Call to Action conference in Detroit, sponsored by the bishops of the United States, which was criticized for being manipulated by the most liberal elements of the Catholic Church. Fifteen years later, the bishop would still be proud of the way the Arkansas Call to Action developed, yet he thought that the national meeting was not free, but set up to satisfy a pre-arranged agenda.[87]

The transition of the diocese from the fourth to the fifth bishop paralleled changes at the Benedictine Subiaco Abbey, which elected its fifth abbot two years after Bishop McDonald arrived. Abbot Michael Lensing announced his resignation to the community on August 29, 1974. Although he was only fifty-eight years old, the abbot was having serious health problems and had been contemplating retirement for a year and a half.[88] He had been abbot for seventeen years and had accomplished much, including the completion of the abbey church and overseeing the continued physical growth at Subiaco. In the last years of his service, Abbot Lensing had promoted the building of the Arkansas River Lock and Dam System. He was constantly called upon to give the invocation at ground-breaking and dedication ceremonies. It was, it is said, "the abbot's prayers and blessings that opened the river to navigation."[89]

After attending a special Mass of the Holy Spirit, the monks met October 30, 1974, and chose a new abbot, Raphael DeSalvo, the first person not of Germanic ancestry to be elected abbot. On December 11, he received a blessing for abbots from Bishop McDonald.[90]

Abbot Raphael was one of nineteen children of an Italian family from Center Ridge. He was born October 7, 1919, attended Subiaco Academy during his high school years, and graduated in 1938. In the fall of 1939, he entered Subiaco Monastery and was ordained a priest by Auxiliary Bishop Albert L. Fletcher on May 31, 1945, at St. Andrew's Cathedral in Little Rock. He was immediately sent for advance theological studies at Catholic University of America, where he received a doctorate in Theology in 1948. He returned to his monastic community to teach theology, first at the academy and then at the monastic seminary. In 1959 he became novice master, a position he held until he was selected to head the St. Mukusa Benedictine mission in Nigeria, in 1964.

After the civil war in Nigeria destroyed the mission, Father DeSalvo left Africa in the summer of 1967. Upon his return, Abbot Lensing appointed him pastor at St. Joseph's Church in nearby Paris, and a year later, he became prior for the abbey, which was his position at the time of his election as abbot six years later. At fifty-five years of age, he was not much younger than his predecessor, but the community was confident that it had the right man. He assumed leadership of an abbey that had fifty-eight priests, twenty-seven of whom were stationed at parishes in Arkansas and Texas. Four were in Belize, in Central America, at the Santa Familia Priory. There were also twenty-two brothers in the community.[91]

During his fifteen year tenure, Abbot Raphael opened the abbey for more outside activities and ministries. For example, a Marriage Encounter weekend was held there in 1975. He also invited a Vietnamese refugee family to stay and work at the abbey. A performing arts center was begun in 1977, and the eighty year old retired bishop, Albert L. Fletcher, was present to participate in the ground breaking. This would give the abbey's academy a new auditorium and new classrooms for instruction in speech, drama, and music. The new building was dedicated on March 21, 1979, and given the title Centenary Hall, in honor of the more than one hundred years since the first group of Swiss-German monks appeared in Logan County. On hand to bless the new building was Bishop McDonald and the new Bishop of Tulsa, Eusebius Beltran. As an additional way to remember the abbey's centenary, Abbot Raphael commissioned Father Hugh Assenmacher, O.S.B., to write a history of Subiaco and the Arkansas Benedictines. The book was published in 1977.[92]

Honors flowed to the new abbot, including his election in 1978 as president of the Swiss-American Federation of Benedictine monasteries. Abbot Raphael could rightly be termed the "traveling abbot" for all his trips to Europe and Central America. In 1980, he visited the mother monastery for Arkansas Benedictines, Einsiedeln, in Switzerland. A year later, he journeyed to Hungary for a meeting with other Benedictine Federation leaders. Three years later, he was in Belize to dedicate the new priory building at *Santa Familia Priory*, a building constructed by the monks themselves.[93] He made another trip to Central America three years later, but this sojourning abbot had to curtail his activities after suffering a heart attack on November 17, 1987. A year later on December 30, 1988, came the news of the death of former Abbot Michael Lensing, who was just short of his seventy-third birthday, after suffering illness for many years. Ten months later, on September 11, 1989, Abbot DeSalvo offered his own resignation as abbot, because of the stress on his heart from his many duties as leader at Subiaco.[94]

On November 8, 1989, the Arkansas Benedictine community elected Father Jerome Kodell, O.S.B., as abbot. A week later, Bishop McDonald gave the traditional abbatial blessing to the forty-nine year old Benedictine.[95]

Born on January 19, 1940, in Clarksville, Arkansas, the son of Frank and Clara Spanke Kodell, Abbot Jerome attended grade school at Holy Redeemer School and then enrolled at Subiaco Academy where he graduated in 1958. He then entered the monastery, where he was ordained to the priesthood by Bishop Fletcher on May 29, 1965. Sent to Collegio Sant Anselmo, the Benedictine Theological Institute in Rome, Father Jerome earned advanced degrees both in Theology and Scripture. He returned to Subiaco to teach sacred Scripture, Theology, and English at the Academy; this position he held between 1969-1987. In addition to his teaching duties, he formed and coached Subiaco's first soccer team, which won state championships under Father Kodell's guidance. He served as subprior of the abbey from 1974-1978 and as Director of formation for twelve years.[96]

Father Jerome's reputation as a Scripture scholar, linguist, and lecturer brought him fame far beyond his Benedictine base at Subiaco. He was the chief consultant to Little Rock Scripture Study program. From this activity, he earned a well-deserved international reputation as a scholar and teacher. He has written several books: *Responding to the Word: A Biblical Spirituality,* (1978); *Commentary on the Minor Prophets,* (1982); *The Catholic Bible Study Handbook,* (1985); *Eucharist in the New Testament,* (1987).[97] In 1987, he abandoned teaching and writing to become prior at *Santa Familia* priory in Belize, Central America. Upon the suggestion of Bishop O.P. Martin of Belize, Father Kodell composed leaflets in both Spanish and English explaining Catholic doctrine. After his election and his blessing, he returned to Belize to take care of unfinished business at the priory. He was back at the monastery by late November 1989, to take up his duties as Subiaco's sixth abbot. As New Subiaco Abbey moved into its second century in 1991 (it had been designated as an abbey in 1891), it had a well-qualified leader at the helm.[98]

The decade of the 1970s ended with the passing of a major figure of Arkansas Catholicism, Bishop Albert L. Fletcher. The retired bishop had continued to live at his home on Crestwood Drive until his health began to fail. In the fall of 1979, he moved to the rectory alongside St. Andrew's Cathedral. He continued to attend functions like the ground breaking for the new building at Subiaco in 1977. On December 6, 1979, he traveled to Our Lady of Holy Souls parish in Little Rock to participate in a funeral Mass for his longtime friend, Thomas Morrissey, a retired musician. After attending the grave side ceremony, he went to the chancery to look at his mail and pick up a few gifts he had ordered for Christmas. After talking for some twenty minutes with Monsignor Francis X. Murphy, then vice-chancellor for the diocese, the bishop drove off in his car to return to the cathedral for lunch.

Perhaps not feeling well, he stopped at the foot of Cantrell hill and entered the Steak and Egg restaurant to have coffee. After sitting several minutes without picking up his drink, he collapsed, and the patrons and workers at the restaurant tried to revive him. He was rushed by ambulance to St. Vincent's Infirmary, where Father Patrick Walsh administered the last rites of the Church. He was pronounced dead at 2:13 p.m. of a heart attack.[99]

He died on the feast day of St. Nicholas. He was the second bishop to die in Little Rock; the first was Bishop John B. Morris in 1946. (Arkansas' first two bishops had passed away in Helena and Hot Springs.) On December 11, 1979, Bishop McDonald blessed the body of his predecessor as it lay in the chapel of the Carmelite Sisters Monastery in Little Rock, a community the bishop had invited into the diocese in 1950. At 3:00 p.m., Bishop McDonald, thirteen other bishops, and two abbots conducted the funeral of Arkansas' fourth bishop. Bishop Fletcher was put in the crypt that he had built beneath the cathedral as the final earthly home for the Catholic bishops of Arkansas.[100] A profound chapter in Arkansas Catholic history had ended with the death of the state's first native bishop.

By 1980, Catholics in Arkansas numbered 56,911, in a total state population of 2,286,000. This was the smallest numerical increase of Catholics in the state in the twentieth century. In fact, between 1940 and 1970, Catholic population increases had been roughly 11,000 every ten years; during the 1970s, that increase had been only 1,618.[101] The small increase meant that Catholics fell from 2.8 percent of the population in 1970 to 2.4 percent. While the percentage decrease was marginal, it was the first such percentage decrease of Catholics in the overall Arkansas population in the twentieth century.[102] The next ten years did see a return to the previous pattern of increases. By 1990, Catholics in Arkansas numbered 62,032 in a total state population of 2,427,000; 2.5 percent, which basically was the same percentage as in 1960.[103]

This was conservative Catholic growth in a politically conservative decade–the years of the administration of President Ronald Reagan. In the Diocese of Little Rock, however, especially in the newly created Office of Justice and Peace, spokespersons like Father Joseph M. Biltz took increasingly liberal political and social positions, often at variance not only with the views of most Arkansans, but with many Catholics as well. To Father Biltz, however, such positions were mandated by Catholic social teaching and the Church's overall concern for justice.

Father Biltz was born in Little Rock in 1930 and attended the cathedral school and Catholic High School before entering St. John's Seminary in 1948. Ordained to the priesthood in 1955, Father Biltz attended Catholic University of America, where he earned a doctorate in Theology. He returned to teach moral theology at St. John's Seminary, where he became the Dean of students in 1961. Father Biltz was one of the group of younger, more liberal professors at the seminary. Just before the closing of St. John's Seminary, Bishop Fletcher assigned the priest to Forrest City, where he became heavily involved in race relations and the local Head Start program. He left Arkansas in 1968 to teach theology at Mount Angel College in Oregon. He returned to Arkansas in 1972 and worked with the southeast Asian refugees and Catholic Social Services. In an article in *The Guardian* some years later, he said that in the issues of social justice "the promotion of human rights and human dignity through structural change become the new priorities in the church mission in the modern world."[104] In August 1978, Bishop McDonald appointed Father Biltz head of the Office of Justice and Peace, under the department of Social Services. In 1980, the Office of Justice and Peace became a separate department.[105]

Over the next several years, the Office of Justice and Peace under Father Biltz adopted liberal positions on many issues. It opposed registration for the draft, supported the nuclear freeze movement, and condemned the United States intervention in Grenada in 1983. Father Blitz introduced the Catholic pacifist organization *Pax Christi* to the diocese in February 1983. That year, the office of Justice and Peace also vigorously supported the bishops' letter on war and peace which came out in May.[106] These positions angered people, including some Catholics. Don Curdie, a Catholic attorney in Little Rock, wrote to the local diocesan weekly attacking religious leaders "who use their positions in the church to force their political leanings on the flock and doing so in the name of religious dogma."[107]

Although he may not have always agreed with everything Father Biltz stood for, Bishop McDonald tended to adopt a "laid-back" attitude about these positions. Although the bishop's political views may have been more to the left, his theological opinions were orthodox. In response to an irate Catholic woman who was upset by a political statement made by a religious sister in 1976, the bishop wrote, "In days gone by when our church was a more authoritarian posture, it was customary to look to the Bishop for complete control for these judgements. While the Bishop retains his authority in the church, . . . , individuals are given more freedom to probe and take stands."[108] On November 29, 1987, while walking on the grounds of St. John's, Father Biltz suffered a fatal heart attack.[109]

Father Biltz's position was taken over by Sr. Catherine Markey, M.H.S., who had come to the diocese September 1, 1979, as diocesan archivist. Sister Markey did a splendid job organizing and setting up the archives after many years of neglect.[110] Sister Markey would continue as both archivist and activist in the Office of Justice and Peace, although her style was more low-key than her predecessor's. She still concentrated on peace issues, yet it was capital punishment that often preoccupied her office. Even before Father Biltz had died, Bishop McDonald had come out against capital punishment.[111] Sister Markey, Bishop McDonald, Monsignor John O'Donnell, and Father Louis J. Franz, C.M., a priest stationed at Star City near the Cummins prison facility, were leading opponents of the execution of convicted multiple murderer John Edward Swindler in June 1990. Ultimately, they were unsuccessful, because Swindler became the first person executed in Arkansas in more than a quarter-century.[112] Sister Markey also served as Director of Ecumenical and Inter-Religious Affairs after 1988. After three years at her various positions, Sister Markey joined the Fort Smith Benedictines and resigned from all her offices except that of diocesan archivist in 1991. That year, the Office of Justice and Peace was combined with the Office of Parish Social Ministry to become the Diocesan Social Action Office under the direction of Mrs. Jo Ann Bemrich of Little Rock. John Marschewski, a parishioner at Little Rock Christ the King parish, became the new Ecumenical and Interreligious Officer.[113]

One issue on which Bishop McDonald has taken the lead throughout his episcopacy is the protection of innocent, unborn life. A few months after his arrival in Arkansas, the United States Supreme Court legalized abortion with the decision in *Roe vs. Wade*, January 22, 1973. Bishop McDonald attacked the decision in the local Catholic paper, "Of those who voted yes, it is better if they had never been born. Those who voted nay, well done, good and faithful servant."[114] In response to an editorial attacking the pro-life movement in the *Arkansas Gazette* in 1976, the bishop wrote in *The Guardian*, "Pro-life citizens believe that the Supreme Court decision is immoral and is not in accord with human dignity and the right to life proclaimed in the Declaration of Independence and the Constitution of the United States."[115] A decade later, Father Biltz attacked abortion as a violation of human dignity in a column in the Catholic paper.[116]

Bishop McDonald and other pro-life leaders recognized that opposition to abortion was not enough. One had to offer alternatives, providing women with places to live while they are pregnant. The diocese backed the local chapter of Birthright, a national organization dedicated to persuading women to give birth and helping facilitate adoptions.[117]

The bishop, however, wanted to do more, so he personally invited Mother Teresa of Calcutta to send members of her Missionaries of Charity Order to Arkansas to staff a home for unwed mothers. The home they staffed on Oak Street in Little Rock is called Abba House, and Mother Teresa herself came to Arkansas to see the facility. Addressing the crowd on the lawn from the second story porch at Abba House, Mother Teresa said, "I don't have silver or gold to give you, but I give you my sisters . . . I hope together we can do something beautiful for God."[118] After inspecting the home, Mother Teresa and the bishop appeared at a major rally on June 2, 1982, at Ray Winder Field, the home of the Arkansas Travelers, the local minor league professional team. The crowd was large, 5,429, and according to Bill Valentine, the general manager for the Travelers, the largest group at Ray Winder Field for a non-baseball event.[119] Bishop McDonald termed the event "historic," and indeed, it was rare to see someone of Mother Teresa's stature, a winner of the Nobel Peace Prize, come to Arkansas.[120] At the ballpark rally she made a plea for the unborn, "It is clearly murder when a mother kills her unborn child. They are so innocent and helpless, . . . these little human beings should have the joy of recognizing Christ."[121] No doubt, Bishop McDonald was happy to serve as Arkansas' host for this world-renowned servant of the poor and helpless.

The diocese has a long history in the pro-life cause. Jacki Ragan started as a volunteer for the right-to-life movement in the diocese in 1975, before she was hired in 1980 as Respect Life Director. She held this position for five years before assuming a position with the National Right-to-Life Office in Washington, D.C.[122] Many Catholics and members of other faith traditions helped ratify an Arkansas constitutional amendment in November 1988 banning state funds for abortion.[123] In December 1989, Bishop McDonald appointed Mrs. Anne Dierks of Hot Springs, Director of the diocesan Respect Life office.[124] In January 1991, he issued a policy which said that as of that date, "no person in public life who states publicly that he or she is for a pro-choice position on the abortion question may serve on any parish councils, boards of Catholic institutions, or may serve as Eucharistic ministers or lecturers."[125] He was joined in that statement by Archbishop Charles Salatka of Oklahoma City and Bishop Eusebius Beltram of Tulsa. The policy would take effect throughout the province, which included Oklahoma and Arkansas.[126] It was one of the strongest positions on abortion ever taken by members of the Catholic hierarchy.

Because of his long and enduring efforts to protect innocent human life, especially unborn children, the Arkansas chapter of National Right-to-Life featured the bishop as the keynote speaker at its state convention October 26, 1991. Bishop McDonald and Anne Dierks were honored with the special Mary Rose Doe award "for their dedication and tireless efforts on behalf of the unborn."[127]

In addition to supporting Abba House, Birthright, and other pro-life organizations, the diocese has had, since 1984, an Adoption Service as part of its department of Catholic Social Services. Bishop McDonald was instrumental in developing and expanding this diocesan adoption program and continues to serve on its board of directors. As of 1992, Ms. Antje Harris, L.S.W., serves as its Director.[128]

Mother Teresa was not the only famous Catholic to come to Arkansas during the 1980s. John Michael Talbot, a nationally known singer, songwriter, and guitarist, put down roots in the Arkansas Ozarks. He was born in 1954, in Oklahoma, and spent a few years as a child in Little Rock before moving to Indiana with his family. He achieved fame as a guitarist and singer with country-folk-rock star Mason Profitt before turning his life to Christ and becoming a major figure in contemporary Christian music. Talbot converted to Catholicism in 1978 and dropped out of professional entertainment to produce mainly liturgical and sacred music. In 1982, he moved to land he had purchased near Eureka Springs, the same Ozark community that Father Joseph Lauro had pastored some thirty years earlier. Talbot formed a small Franciscan-style community based on the radical call of the Gospel to live in simplicity and poverty. He formed a close friendship with Bishop McDonald, who witnessed the marriage of John Michael and Viola Talbot on February 17, 1989. Later that spring, Talbot sought to start a lay religious community of both married and single people committed to a life of simplicity and poverty. On December 6, 1990, they became a private religious association under the direct supervision of Bishop McDonald. A year later, the community had about thirty people living at a place they call Little Portion near Eureka Springs.[129]

Small, but evident, changes would take place at the Little Rock Catholic diocese in administration and publications. In the summer of 1983, computers were introduced into the diocese, yet adapting all the administration into the new technology has been slow. According to the bishop's report to Rome on March 30, 1988, with the help of Father Thomas Sebaugh and Joey Halinski, the diocesan offices had computerized twenty-one parishes. The same document reported a stewardship program to remind Catholics of the importance of supporting the work of Christ and his Church.[130] In 1989, the

Bishop's Special Projects Appeal was changed to Catholic Arkansas Sharing Appeal or CASA. This program is to provide more permanent funding for some of the diocese's special needs and ministries.[131] In the summer of 1987, a major renovation project began. Over the next four years, what was once St. John's Woods became new homes. Another project recently completed was the renovation of Fitzgerald Hall, transforming it into a home for retired priests. On August 18, 1991, the newly remodeled Fitzgerald Hall had an open house, tour, and dedication by the bishop.[132]

Other changes would come to the diocese in the area of communications and publications. Father Albert J. Schneider, in 1988, became Director of Communications, a department overseeing relations with the press, radio, television, and video production.[133] The diocesan paper underwent a major metamorphosis. In January 1985, Managing Editor William O'Donnell, K.S.G., retired and Father Joseph Conyard, S.J., took his place. In actuality, O'Donnell was replaced by two persons, Father Conyard as Managing Editor and Karl Christ as Editor. The name of the newspaper also changed from *The Guardian* to the *Arkansas Catholic* after the completion of its 75th volume on March 21, 1986.[134] Father Conyard left the paper in 1988, and Father Schneider's appointment followed. Editing duties were still with Karl Christ, with Deborah Halter hired to assist him in 1987. In 1989, Ms. Halter became the first woman editor of the diocesan paper. Father Schneider, as Communications Director, is the paper's Managing Editor.[135]

Arkansas marked its 150th anniversary as a state on June 15, 1986. Pope John Paul II sent a piece of marble from the fourth-century Constantine Basilica as the Holy Father's gift to the state. Bishop McDonald presented it to the state government in the name of the Holy Father.[136]

Two years later, on May 28, 1988, the bishop ordained three young men to the priesthood at St. Andrew's Cathedral: Paul Worm, Charles Thessing, and L. Warren Harvey, the latter being the first native African-American Arkansan to be ordained to the Roman Catholic priesthood.

The youngest of fourteen children, Father Harvey was born March 3, 1954, in Conway, the site of the first black Catholic school in Arkansas. He attended Good Shepherd Catholic School until 1965 and then attended St. Joseph's Elementary school, later graduating from St. Joseph's High School in 1972. After studying at the University of Central Arkansas, where he earned various nursing degrees, he worked at Conway Memorial Hospital. In January 1982, he entered St. Joseph's Seminary in Covington, Louisiana, where he gained an undergraduate degree in Philosophy two years later. Father Harvey did his graduate theological studies at Notre Dame Seminary, in New Orleans, where he obtained his Masters of Divinity degree in 1988, graduating *cum laude*.[137]

Named as associate pastor at Our Lady of Good Counsel Church in Little Rock, in June 1988, Father Harvey was given additional responsibility as administrator of St. Augustine's Church in North Little Rock. He also serves as the bishop's liaison for the Diocesan Council for Black Catholics and as the state chaplain and regional chaplain for the Knights of St. Peter Claver, a black Catholic lay organization. In January 1992, he began serving a three-year term on Presbyterial Council for the Diocese of Little Rock.[138] A dynamic preacher and singer, Father Harvey contributes much to the life and liturgy of the churches he pastors.

The month in which Bishop McDonald ordained Frs. Harvey, Thessing, and Worm, also marked the bishop's fortieth anniversary of ordination to the priesthood. A long article in the diocesan paper marked the occasion.[139] A few months after his anniversary and the ordinations, Bishop McDonald named a new vicar general. Monsignor Royce Thomas had served from January 1987 to September 1988, when Bishop McDonald named Father J. Gaston Hebert, pastor of Christ the King Church in Little Rock, to the position. Nine months later, in 1989, the Holy Father designated Father Hebert the title of Monsignor. Monsignor Hebert still held the position of vicar general as of 1992.[140]

In early September 1992, Bishop McDonald marked the twentieth anniversary of his episcopacy with two major liturgies. One was held at St. Andrew's Cathedral on Friday, September 4, at 5:30 p.m. for priests of the diocese. Two days later, on Sunday afternoon, a 2:00 p.m. Mass was held for the public at the newly renovated and expanded Christ the King Church in west Little Rock.[141]

The years of Bishop McDonald are not complete. Like his predecessor, the Arkansas bishop must submit his resignation to Rome when he turns seventy-five years of age. Obviously, one cannot totally evaluate his ministry until it is finished. Over the past two decades, however, there has been both continuity and change. Building upon Bishop Fletcher's earlier initiatives, Bishop McDonald has greatly expanded the Church's ecumenical efforts and its work among the poor. There have, of course, been changes. Bishop McDonald has his own administrative style; he launched the permanent diaconate, and he further implemented the liturgical renewal mandated by the Second Vatican Council. Arkansas Catholics have also participated in, and contributed to, the various renewal movements which came to the Catholic Church after the Second Vatican Council.

At present, Bishop McDonald spends much of his time in a truly pastoral fashion: visiting the hospitals, witnessing marriages, conducting baptisms and funerals. By these and other ways, Bishop McDonald continues to try to achieve one goal. He tries daily to fulfill the commitment he made when he first came as bishop in 1972, to prove that he loves–that he cares.

EPILOGUE

THE MEMORY – THE MOMENT – THE MISSION ONE PLANTS, ANOTHER WATERS, GOD GIVES THE GROWTH

MEMORY is an essential part of the Christian experience. So it was, that the early Church came to fully recognize who Jesus was only as they reflected after the resurrection on his life among them.

It is appropriate, therefore, that we begin our sesquicentennial celebration by first recalling how Jesus has been at work among us in Arkansas over the last century and a half. That reflection is set forth in rich detail in the history you have just read.

The saving work of Jesus among us came to a glorious climax in the graced MOMENT of the Second Vatican Council whose influence and vitality we have all experienced over the past thirty years.

Those years have seen the Church in Arkansas rejuvenated and re-energized. A renewed liturgy has allowed us to experience Jesus anew in the Breaking of the Bread as a model of selfless service to all, especially the poor. In this effort, we have gladly joined hands with our separated brethren and found added strength in doing so.

But, above all, our renewed Catholic community has found a special vitality because of a challenged and responsive laity working with me as well as the priests, deacons, sisters, and religious brothers of our diocese.

As this moment ushered in by Vatican II comes to a close, our vision is drawn to the MISSION that lies ahead, the great task that has faced the Church from the beginning, claiming Jesus more fully as the center of our lives in an on-going conversion and proclaiming him as saving Lord to others.

Our unique mission as the years unfold will be to see his face in those of many different cultures: Hispanic, African-American, and Asian. Like the woman at the well, a Samaritan, they come thirsty, not only to satisfy their material needs, but for the fullness of life Jesus promised. It will be our privilege and challenge to meet their needs, and in so doing, our own.

As exciting as the history of the Catholic Church in Arkansas has been since 1843, as rejuvenating as the experience of the graced moment in that history provided by Vatican II, it is only prelude to the exciting vision that lies ahead. Truly, we have only just begun!

NOTES

Abbreviations in the Reference Notes

AAB	Archives of the Archdiocese of Baltimore
AANO	Archives of the Archdiocese of New Orleans
AASL	Archives of the Archdiocese of St. Louis
ADLR	Archives of the Diocese of Little Rock
AUND	Archives of the University of Notre Dame
SAB	Sulpician Archives, Baltimore

Some of the material utilized in the Archives of the Archdiocese of New Orleans were copies of material found in the Archives of the University of Notre Dame. Regretfully, I did not make that distinction in my notes. All the material cited in the notes from the Archives of the Archdiocese of New Orleans was material I used while I was there; just some of the original material is also in the Archives of the University of Notre Dame.

The Arkansas History Commission in Little Rock and the Special Collections Department of the University of Arkansas at Little Rock were also used as a source for such primary printed material as newspapers and books and for secondary sources such as theses and dissertations.

To assist the reader, a full bibliographical entry is provided with each initial citation in every chapter.

NOTES

CHAPTER I

[1]Benjamin F. French claims that De Soto was 42 in 1542, but he does not give the birth date, which means he was born in 1500 or 1499. Benjamin F. French, *Historical Collection of Louisiana, Embracing Translations of Many Rare and Valuable Documents Relating to the Natural, Civil, and Political History of that State, compiled Historical and Biographical Notes, and an Introduction* 5 vols. (Philadelphia, PA: Daniels & Smith, 1850) 2:107, note 4. On the sighting of the Mississippi River on May 21, 1541, see Edward Gaylord Bourne, *Narratives of the De Soto Expedition,* 2 vols. (New York: Allerton Company, 1922) 2:137. Cabeza De Vaca felt the fresh waters of the Mississippi flowing into the Gulf of Mexico during his unique journey across the southern United States from 1528-1536; see Morris Bishop, *The Odyssey of the Cabeza De Vaca* (New York: Century Company, 1933) 56-59. There is presently strong debate about the exact route of De Soto. I have followed some of the newer studies on this route through Arkansas and they are presented recently in a school textbook on Arkansas history; see T. Harri Baker and Jane Browning, *An Arkansas History for Young People* (Fayetteville, AR: University of Arkansas Press, 1991) 34-42. They do provide a map of the older route approved by a government study in the 1930s, 36.

[2]The diocesan priests whom we know are as follows: Rodrigo de Gallegos, Dionisio de Paris, Francisco de Pozo, Diego de Bannuelos. The Trinitarian priest was Francisco de la Rocha, the Franciscan was Juan de Torres, and the two Dominicans were Juan de Gallegos and Luis de Soto. There is no evidence that the two priests Gallegos were related or that De Soto was related to the Dominican, but it is possible. The names taken from Roger Baudier, *The Catholic Church in Louisiana* (New Orleans, LA: Private Printing, 1939) 14; John R. Swanton, *Final Report of the United States De Soto Expedition Commission 76 Congress 1st Session, House Document no. 71* (Washington, D.C.: Government Printing Office, 1939) 88.

[3]Woodbury Lowery, *Spanish Settlements Within the Present Limits of the United States* (New York: G.P. Putnam & Sons, 1901) 214-217. For a more complete account of the expedition with a map of the route see, Swanton, *Final Report of the United States De Soto Expedition,* passim, map between pp. 348-349. For a recent biography of this Spanish explorer see Miguel Alboroz, *Hernando De Soto: Knight of the Americas,* translated from the Spanish by Bruce Boeglin (New York: Franklin Watts, 1986).

[4]Francis Shaw Guy, "The Catholic Church in Arkansas," typescript copy in the Francis S. Guy Papers, Arkansas History Commission, p. 4. This manuscript is partly based on his Masters thesis, "The Catholic Church in Arkansas, 1541-1843" (M.A. thesis, Catholic University of America, 1932).

[5]Fidalgo de Elvas was the Portuguese gentleman who wrote the most extensive account of De Soto's expedition; see Bourne, *Narratives of the De Soto Expedition,* 1:115.

[6]Ibid., 2:137.

[7]Ibid., 2:138. For another look at the crossing see Charles McGimsey, *Indians of Arkansas* (Fayetteville, AR: Arkansas Archeological Survey, 1969) 30, 31.

[8]Rev. John Rothensteiner, *History of the Archdiocese of St. Louis: In Its Various Stages of Development from A.D. 1673 to A.D. 1928,* 2 vols. (St. Louis, MO: Blackwell Wielandy Company Press, 1928) 1:3. For an account of the history of Quapaws and their background and location in early Arkansas consult W. David Baird, *The Quapaw Indians: A History of the Downstream People* (Norman, OK: University of Oklahoma Press, 1980) 1-38.

[9]Rothensteiner, *History of the Archdiocese of St. Louis,* 1:3.

[10]Ibid.

[11]Bourne, *Narratives of the De Soto Expedition,* 2:27-28; Alboroz, *De Soto,* 324; Swanton, *Final Report of the De Soto Expedition,* 230. There is an artistic reproduction of DeSoto's cross at Casqui in Baker and Browning, *An Arkansas History for Young People,* 38.

[12]Guy, "Catholic Church in Arkansas," 6.

[13]Bourne, *Narratives of the De Soto Expedition,* 1:136.

[14]Guy, "Catholic Church in Arkansas," 7.

[15]Baker and Browning, *An Arkansas History for Young People,* 40.

[16]Bourne, *Narratives of the De Soto Expedition,* 1:161-162; Alboroz, *De Soto,* 329-345.

[17]Bourne, *Narratives of the De Soto Expedition,* 1:213, 215; Alboroz, *De Soto,* 347-350; Baker and Browing, *An Arkansas History for Young People,* 40-42.

[18]Swanton, *Final Report of the De Soto Expedition,* 87.

[19]Guy, "Catholic Church in Arkansas," 11; Alboroz, *De Soto,* 348.

[20]For a history of the French role in early European colonization in North America vis-a-vis the British colonies see the classic, yet dated work by Francis S. Parkman. This New England aristocrat saw the whole history of this event as the forces of political and religious oppression, France and the Catholic Church versus political and religious liberty, Britain and the Protestant colonies. Francis S. Parkman, *France and England in the New World,* 7 vols. (Boston, MA: Little Brown & Co., 1864-1892). A little less biased, yet much in the same vein, is Rueben Gold Thwaities, *France in America, 1597-1763* (New York: Harper & Brothers, 1905). A better balanced and updated treatment of France in the New World is William Eccles, *France in America* (New York: Harper & Row, 1972).

[21]Rueben Gold Thwaities, editor, *Jesuit Relations and Other Allied Documents,* 75 volumes (Cleveland, OH: Barrows Brothers, 1895-1909) 59:93.

[22]Guy, "Catholic Church in Arkansas," 14.

[23]Rothensteiner, *History of the Archdiocese of St. Louis,* 1:8-9; for a recent and welcome biography of Fr. Marquette which covers his background and career up to his voyage down the Mississippi River see Fr. Joseph P. Donnelly, S.J., *Jacques Marquette, S.J., 1637-1675* (Chicago, Ill: Loyola University Press, 1985) 1-204

[24]Thwaities, *Jesuit Relations,* 59:151; Donnelly, *Jacques Marquette,* 209-223.

[25]Thwaities, *Jesuit Relations,* 59:151, 153.

[26]Ibid., 59:153; same report of his speech and the same quote in Donnelly, *Jacques Marquette,* 224.

[27]Thwaities, *Jesuit Relations,* 59:153.

[28]Guy, "Catholic Church in Arkansas," 16; Thwaities, *Jesuit Relations,* 59:153, 155, 157, 159.

[29]Thwaities, *Jesuit Relations,* 59:155.

[30]Ibid., 59:155, 159. They left on July 17 according to Fr. Marquette, 59:161. This reported by Marquette's recent biographer who also supplied the exact day of the week, Donnelly, *Jacques Marquette,* 226.

[31]Rothensteiner, *History of the Archdiocese of St. Louis,* 1:15; for a more recent account of his voyage up the river see Donnelly, *Jacques Marquette,* 226-228.

[32]Rothensteiner, *History of the Archdiocese of St. Louis,* 1:15-17. For an account of Fr. Marquette's last few months consult, Donnelly, *Jacques Marquette,* 230-266.

[33]Morris, S. Arnold, *Unequal Laws Unto a Savage Race: European Legal Traditions in Arkansas, 1686-1836* (Fayetteville, AR: University of Arkansas Press, 1985) 1-3. There were about 6,000 Quapaw Indians in eastern Arkansas in 1681. Stanley Faye, "The Arkansas Post of Louisiana: French Domination," *Louisiana Historical Quarterly* 26 (July 1943) 635.

[34]Guy, "Catholic Church in Arkansas," 21.

[35]Ibid.

[36]For Tonti's (or Tonty's) background see Edmund Robert Murphy, *Henri de Tonty: Fur Trader of the Mississippi* (Baltimore, MD: Johns Hopkins University Press, 1941) 1-42; French, *Historical Collection of Louisiana,* 1:86; Arnold, *Unequal Laws.* 5-6. That this was the only European settlement west of the Mississippi River in what is now the United States; see Morris J. Arnold, *Colonial Arkansas, 1686-1804: A Social and Cultural History* (Fayetteville, AR: University of Arkansas, 1991) 5-7.

[37]Arnold, *Unequal Laws,* 5-6.

[38]Henry Joutel and Fr. Louis Cavalier, La Salle's brother made it from southeast Texas to Arkansas on July 24-29, 1687. They found only Messrs. Couture and De Launay, who told them there had been originally six, the others had all left. French, *Historical Collection of Louisiana,* 1:173-178; Henri Joutel, *Journal of La Salle's Last Voyage, 1685-1687* (New York: Burt Franklin Reprint, 1968, Original Edition 1866) 151-159. Guy claims that Fr. Cavalier said Mass, but no real evidence for this from Joutel's journal. Guy, "Catholic Church in Arkansas," 24.

[39]Guy, "Catholic Church in Arkansas," 23.

[40]William Eccles gives a brief account of this war. Eccles, *France in America,* 95-99.

[41]Arnold, *Unequal Laws,* 6.

[42]Guy, "Catholic Church in Arkansas," 25; Murray, *Henri de Tonty,* 39, 42-94.

[43]Fr. Jean Delanglez, S.J., *The French Jesuits of Lower Louisiana, 1700-1763.* (Washington, D.C.: Catholic University of America Press, 1935) 433.

[44]Roger Baudier claims that Fr. St. Cosme stationed himself among the Tamarois Indians at the mouth of the Arkansas River. St. Cosme did establish his mission among the Tamarois, but that Indian tribe was further up the Mississippi River in what is now southern Illinois and eastern Missouri. Baudier, *Catholic Church in Louisiana,* 19. For the location of the Tamarois, see H.R. Schoolcraft, *Historical and Statistical Information Respecting the History, Condition, and Prospects, of the Indian Tribes in the United States,* 6 vols. (Philadelphia, PA: Lippincott & Co., 1851-1857) 2:588. For the location of the Tunicas and Tensas Indian tribes see Carl Waldman, *Atlas of the North American Indians* (New York: Facts on File Publication, 1985) 32, 33, 39; Baird, *Quapaw Indians,* 1-38.

[45]Thwaities, *Jesuit Relations,* 65:163; Guy, "Catholic Church in Arkansas," 32.

[46]Thwaities, *Jesuit Relations,* 65:163; Delanglez, *French Jesuits in Louisiana,* 28-29.

[47]Thwaities, *Jesuit Relations,* 65:121; Delanglez, *French Jesuits in Louisiana,* 433-434.

[48]Foucault had complained in a letter that the Quapaws had mistreated him in unspecified ways. Delanglez, *French Jesuits in Louisiana,* 434; Arnold, *Unequal Laws,* 115, n. 8.

[49]Delanglez, *French Jesuits in Louisiana,* 33-34; Baudier, *Catholic Church in Louisiana,* 21; Arnold, *Colonial Arkansas,* 88.

[50]Fr. Antoine Davion's letter of February 14, 1703, quoted in Delanglez, *French Jesuits in Louisiana,* 34, n. 23.

[51]John Gilmary Shea, *The Catholic Church in Colonial Days: The Thirteen Colonies, The Ottawa and Illinois Country, Louisiana, Florida, Texas, New Mexico and Arizona.* (New York: John G. Shea, Private Printing, 1886) 545.

[52]Fr. Davion quoted in Delanglez, *French Jesuits in Louisiana,* 34.

[53]For the early history of Louisiana consult Charles Gayarre, *The History of Louisiana,* 4 vols. (New Orleans, LA: James Gresham Publishers, 2nd Edition, 1879, 1st Edition, 1854) 1:1-115; Marcel Giraud, *A History of French Louisiana: Volume I: The Reign of Louis XIV, 1698-1715* (Baton Rouge, LA: Louisiana State University Press, 1974).

[54]Faye, "Arkansas Post of Louisiana: French Domination," 650-653; Arnold, *Unequal Laws,* 6-8. In March, 1722, 200 Germans had arrived, but when they found out about the bubble bursting they wanted to go home. The officials finally persuaded them to stay by giving them some land along the Mississippi River, and this part of the country became known as the German Coast. Les Allemande, Baudier, *Catholic Church in Louisiana,* 71, 192. There is a persistent and popular legend that these Germans first went up the Mississippi River to Arkansas Post, but this story has no basis in fact; Arnold, *Colonial Arkansas,* 9-17.

[55]Arnold, *Colonial Arkansas,* 12; Le Harpe's journal of his trip up the Arkansas translated and printed in Anna Lewis, *Along the Arkansas* (Dallas, TX: Southwest Press, 1932) 61-85, his discovery of the "Big Rock" and the "Little Rock" on 76-77.

[56]Faye, "Arkansas Post of Louisiana: French Domination," 667; Arnold, *Unequal Laws,* 8; Arnold, *Colonial Arkansas,* 12.

[57]Arnold, *Colonial Arkansas,* 12. Charlevoix did not stay long for he celebrated New Years Day Mass in 1722 in Baton Rouge; he returned to France by 1723 where he made his report. Baudier, *Catholic Church in Louisiana,* 45, 46, 78, 220; Guy, "Catholic Church in Arkansas," 38;

French, *Historical Collection of Louisiana*, 3:128.

[58]Delanglez, *French Jesuits in Louisiana*, 91; Guy, "Catholic Church in Arkansas," 39.

[59]This dispute reported in various works, see Rothensteiner, *History of the Archdiocese of St. Louis*, 1:75; Baudier, *Catholic Church in Louisiana*, 64-66; Delanglez, *French Jesuits in Louisiana*, 92-137. Delanglez, as a Jesuit, takes the Jesuit side in this dispute, for the Capuchin view see Rev. Claude L. Vogel, O.F.M., Cap. *The Capuchins in French Louisiana, 1722-1766* (Washington, D.D.: Catholic University of America Press, 1928). Quote from Arnold, *Colonial Arkansas*, 88-89.

[60]That the first Jesuit priest died en route to Arkansas see Arnold, *Colonial Arkansas*, 89. The other two French Jesuits traveling upriver were Fr. Jean Souel, who went to serve among the Yazoo in what is now Mississippi, and Fr. Jean Dumas, who went among the Illinois Indians in the state later named for that tribe. Delanglez, *French Jesuits in Louisiana*, 430, 431.

[61]Guy, "Catholic Church in Arkansas," 40.

[62]Fr. du Poisson to Fr. Patouilet, December, 1727, letter translated and printed in W.A. Falconer, "Arkansas and the Jesuits in 1727: A Translation," *Publications of the Arkansas Historical Association*, 4 vols. (Little Rock: Democrat Printing and Lithograph Co., 1905-1917), 4:371.

[63]Fr. du Poisson to Fr. (?), October 9, 1727 in Falconer, "Arkansas and the Jesuits," 4:369.

[64]Fr. du Poisson to Fr. Patouilet, December, 1727 in Falconer, "Arkansas and the Jesuits," 4:375.

[65]Arnold, *Unequal Laws*, 15.

[66]Delanglez, *French Jesuits in Louisiana*, 437. Brother Philip Crucy came to New Orleans with the original group of Ursulines in August of 1727, Baudier, *Catholic Church in Louisiana*, 104. Judge Arnold maintains that Crucy came in 1729, but this is contradicted by Fr. Delanglez in the above citation. Arnold, *Colonial Arkansas*, 89.

[67]Fr. Le Petit to Fr. Avagour, July 12, 1730, in Falconer, "Arkansas and the Jesuits," 4:376-377; Delanglez, *French Jesuits in Louisiana*, 251-252. This account of Fr. du Poisson's death does not exactly follow that presented by Judge Morris Arnold. Arnold, *Colonial Arkansas*, 89.

[68]The official date of the papal proclamation erecting the Catholic Diocese of Little Rock for the whole state of Arkansas is dated Nov. 28, 1843. This original Latin document in the ADLR.

[69]Faye, "Arkansas Post of Louisiana: French Domination," 672; Arnold, *Unequal Laws*, 16.

[70]Delanglez, *French Jesuits in Louisiana*, 437.

[71]Fr. Vitry quoted in Ibid., 438. Fr. Delanglez is also the source of his birth date of May 11, 1701, 438, n. 54.

[72]Ibid., 439. Arnold also reports no priest in the Arkansas Post in 1743 to help settle a major legal dispute over property and inheritance, Arnold, *Unequal Laws*, 18-22. Fr. Guy obviously made an error when he reported that Fr. Avond came in 1747 and left in 1745, Guy, "Catholic Church in Arkansas," 46, 47.

[73]Guy, "Catholic Church in Arkansas," 47; Delanglez, *French Jesuits in Louisiana*, 439.

[74]Arnold estimated his families as an average of four for 18th century Arkansas. Arnold, *Unequal Laws*, 21, n. 61.

[75]Ibid., 22-23, n. 65; Faye, "Arkansas Post of Louisiana: French Domination," 684.

[76]This would be the location of the Post until 1756. Arnold, *Unequal Laws*, 4.

[77]Ibid., 23.

[78]Ibid., 28; Guy "Catholic Church in Arkansas," 47; Delanglez, *French Jesuits in Louisiana*, 443, n. 86. Although Fr. Delanglez provides Fr. Carette's date of birth and when he entered the Society of Jesus, yet he does tell us where he was born. Fr. Carette would eventually leave America and return to Lille, France, p. 523.

[79]Shea, *Catholic Church in Colonial Days*, 576; Arnold, *Unequal Laws*, 28-32. Judge Arnold writes that while there is no evidence that Fr. Carette had any legal training, "he was a Jesuit, and thus a learned man, one of a handful of such who made their residence in eighteenth century Arkansas." 28.

[80]The "chicken and chalice" story in various sources see Shea, *Catholic Church in Colonial Days*, 576; Rothensteiner, *History of the Archdiocese of St. Louis*, 1:93; Delanglez, *French Jesuits in Louisiana*, 443-444; Guy, "Catholic Church in Arkansas," 48. By this time, 1758, Arkansas Post moved to its third location. Arnold, *Unequal Laws*, 4; Arnold, *Colonial Arkansas*, 89.

[81]Fr. Carette became superior of the Jesuits, Louisiana Mission from 1759-1762 and he became chaplain at the Royal Hospital in New Orleans from 1762 until he left in December, 1763. On when he left Arkansas see Faye, "Arkansas Post of Louisiana: French Domination," 719; Guy, "Catholic Church in Arkansas," 49. On his career in Louisiana after that see Delanglez, *French Jesuits in Louisiana*, 443, n. 88, 446, 527. Eighteenth century French Jesuit Father Watrin quoted in Arnold, *Colonial Arkansas*, 89.

[82]For a good general study of this controversy and the whole Catholic Church during this period see Henri Daniel-Rops, *The Church in the Eighteenth Century* (New York: E.P. Hutton, 1964) 218-227.

[83]Fr. Meurin departed New Orleans in February, 1764 and came to Arkansas Post by March. By July he was far up the river and then crossed the Mississippi into the now English-controlled Illinois country. Baudier, *Catholic Church in Louisiana*, 166-167; Rothensteiner, *History of the Archdiocese of St. Louis*, 1:101-102. Guy claims that Fr. Meurin said Mass and performed baptisms in the new Church of St. Stephens, actually no church according to the Spanish commander in 1770, and no church built in Arkansas for almost another three decades. Guy, "Catholic Church in Arkansas," 53; Arnold, *Unequal Laws*, 117-118, n. 21.

[84]Baudier, *Catholic Church in Louisiana*, 168. For the number of Jesuits departing Louisiana see Delanglez, *French Jesuits in Louisiana*, 526-527.

[85]Eccles, *France in America*, 228-230; for the best overall treatment of this revolt consult John B. Moore, *Revolt in Louisiana: The Spanish Occupation, 1766-1770* (Baton Rouge, LA: Louisiana State University Press, 1976). Arkansas did not participate in the revolt for the Spanish peacefully assumed control over Arkansas in 1768. Faye, "Arkansas Post of Louisiana: French Domination," 721.

[86]Arnold, *Unequal Laws*, 117, 118; Arnold, *Colonial Arkansas*, 90.

[87]Fr. P. Valentin stayed behind with the Spanish and his work in Arkansas see Baudier, *Catholic Church in Louisiana*, 183; Rothensteiner, *History of the Archdiocese of St. Louis*, 1:106; Guy, "Catholic Church in Arkansas," 53. According to Rothensteiner, Fr. Valentin stayed in St. Louis for three years, 106, 108. For Fr. Guignes' work in Louisiana and Arkansas see Baudier, *Catholic Church in Louisiana*, 196; Guy, "Catholic Church in Arkansas," 53.

[88]Samuel F. Bemis, *The Diplomacy of the American Revolution* (New York: Appleton Company, 1935) 81-112, Spanish declaration of war on England on June 21, 1779, 87; Jonathon R. Dull, *A Diplomatic History of the American Revolution* (New Haven, CN: Yale University Press, 1985) 107-127.

[89]Arnold, *Unequal Laws*, 4, 86-89.

[90]Ibid., 91.

[91]Ibid.

[92]Duvon C. Corbett, "Arkansas in the American Revolution," *Arkansas Historical Quarterly* 1 (December 1942): 290-306; Gilbert C. Din, "The Arkansas Post in the American Revolution," *Arkansas Historical Quarterly* 40 (Spring 1981):3-30. For another account of the conflict see Stanley Faye, "The Arkansas Post of Louisiana: Spanish Domination," *Louisiana Historical Quarterly* 27 (July 1944): 684-685.

[93]Bemis, *Diplomacy of the American Revolution*, 243-256, text of treaty, 259-2264; Dull, *Diplomatic History of the American Revolution*, 137-163, text of treaty, 170-174.

[94]Arthur Whitaker, *The Spanish-American Frontier, 1783-1795* (Gloucester, MA: Peter Smith Company Reprint Edition, 1962, 1st edition, 1927), 54-56.

[95]Arnold, *Unequal Laws*, 21, n. 61, 85, 95-96.

[96]Ibid., 98-100.

[97]Ibid., 118, n. 21; Arnold, *Colonial Arkansas*, 90.

[98]Rothensteiner, *History of Archdiocese of St. Louis,* 1:124, 132-139; Fr. Joseph P. Donnelly, S.J., *Pierre Gibault, Missionary, 1737-1802* (Chicago, IL: Loyola University Press, 1971) 33-85.

[99]Donnelly, *Pierre Gibault,* 86-148; the exact number of persons baptized given on p. 137. An earlier historian of the Archdiocese of St. Louis presented the number of times Fr. Gibault visited the Arkansas Post from 1792-1793, and put the number of baptized children at fifty-nine adults and children and burying five persons. Both secondary sources agree as to the number of marriages given in the text, twenty. Rothensteiner, *History of the Archdiocese of St. Louis,* 1:179-180, 183.

[100]Baudier, *Catholic Church in Louisiana,* 224; Arnold, *Colonial Arkansas,* 90.

[101]Baudier, *Catholic Church in Louisiana,* 224, 235.

[102]Rothensteiner, *History of the Archdiocese of St. Louis,* 1:184, 186.

[103]Ibid., 1:213.

[104]Baudier, *Catholic Church in Louisiana,* 223-224. Bishop Penalver y Cardenas was the Louisiana and Florida prelate stationed in New Orleans from 1795-1801. For his career see Baudier's above cited work, 223-246.

[105]The documents on the appointment of Fr. Janin to the parish *de Arcanzas* are in the Penalver y Cardenas papers, AANO. These documents contain Janin's acceptance of the position dated May 17, 1796, from Natchez, and Governor Carondelet's letter approving it on May 31, 1796, and the bishop's formal appointment of Janin to *Arcanzas.* That Fr. Janin arrived on August 5, 1796 see Arnold, *Unequal Laws,* 119.

[106]Historian Faye states his belief that the church may have been built by late 1797. Faye, "Arkansas Post of Louisiana: Spanish Domination," 714; but this is not correct according to a most recent account using the primary documents, Arnold, *Colonial Arkansas,* 91-92. From the just cited work is a brief description of Janin's career as Arkansas's resident Catholic priest, 1796-1799, 90-93.

[107]Guy, "Catholic Church in Arkansas," 54; David Wallis and Frank Williamson, *A Baptismal Record of the Parish Along the Arkansas River* (Pine Bluff, AR: n.p., 1977) 1-39.

[108]Rothensteiner, *History of the Archdiocese of St. Louis,* 1:214; Arnold, *Colonial Arkansas,* 92.

[109]Wallis and Williamson, *A Baptismal Record,* 40-62; Dorothy Jones Core, *Abstract of the Catholic Register of Arkansas, 1764-1858* (DeWitt, AR: DeWitt Publishing Company, 1976) 80-81. Fr. Juan Brady post in Avoyelles Our Lady of Mt. Carmel parish in Baudier, *Catholic Church in Louisiana,* 253.

[110]Herbert E. Bolton, editor, *Athanase de Mezieres and the Louisiana-Texas Frontier, 1768-1780* 2 vols. (Cleveland, OH: Arthur Clarke Company, 1914) 1:166.

[111]Arnold, *Unequal Laws,* 82, 83. For a look at this Frenchman's career working for the Spanish at Ouachita Post, what is now Monroe, LA, see Samuel Dorris Dickinson, "Don Juan Filhiol at Ecore a Fabri," *Arkansas Historical Quarterly* 46 (Summer 1987): 133-155.

[112]Arnold, *Unequal Laws,* 122-123.

[113]Ibid., 124.

[114]Ibid., 28.

[115]Ibid., 124-125.

[116]Ibid., 124.

[11]Arnold, *Colonial Arkansas,* 94.

[118]For the dates on the transfer at New Orleans see David Y. Thomas, *Arkansas and Its People,* 4 vols. (New York: American Historical Association, 1930) 1:57; for the exact date and the people who exchanged command of Arkansas Post see Arnold, *Unequal Laws,* 110; the material quoted in the text from Arnold, *Colonial Arkansas,* 174.

[119]Samuel D. Dickinson, "Colonial Arkansas Place Names" *Arkansas Historical Quarterly* 48 (Summer 1989): 137-168.

[120]Arnold, *Unequal Laws,* 128.

CHAPTER II

[1]Francis Shaw Guy, "The Catholic Church in Arkansas", 57-76. Typescript copy in the Francis Shaw Guy Papers, Arkansas History Commission. This manuscript is partly based on his Master's thesis "The Catholic Church in Arkansas, 1541-1843." (M.A. thesis, Catholic University of America, 1932) 42-31.

[2]D.Y. Thomas, *Arkansas and Its People* 4 vols. (New York: American Historical Association, 1930) 1:57. For a good one-volume history of Arkansas from the Louisiana Purchase through the territorial period up to statehood in 1836, see Lonnie J. White, *Politics on the Southwestern Frontier: Arkansas Territory, 1819-1836* (Memphis, TN: Memphis State University Press, 1964).

[3]Morris S. Arnold, *Unequal Laws Unto a Savage Race: European Legal Traditions in Arkansas, 1686-1836* (Fayetteville, AR: University of Arkansas Press, 1985) 130-202.

[4]Arnold, *Unequal Laws*, 95-96, 126, 128.

[5]U.S. Department of State, *The Third Census of the United States*, (Washington, D.C.: Government Printing Office, 1811) 84. For the records from 1820 through 1860 the best one source reference for this information, see U.S. Department of the Interior, *The Eighth Census of the United States*, 4 vols. (Washington, D.C.: Government Printing Office, 1864-1866) 1:598-599. For a more accessible source for this same information, see James M. Woods, *Rebellion and Realignment: Arkansas' Road to Secession* (Fayetteville, AR: University of Arkansas Press, 1987) 171, 180.

[6]Robert Walz, "Migration into Arkansas, 1834-1880," (Ph.D. dissertation, University of Texas, 1958) 115; Woods, *Rebellion and Realignment*, 17-21.

[7]U.S. Department of the Interior, *The Seventh Census of the United States* (Washington, D.C.: Robert Armstrong, Public Printer, 1853) 560-561.

[8]The details of this whole affair can be found in Roger Baudier, *The Catholic Church in Louisiana* (New Orleans, LA: n.p. 1939) 247-267; the schism not ended until 1844, 344. See also Stanley Faye, "The Schism of 1805 in New Orleans," *Louisiana Historical Quarterly* 22 (January, 1939) 98-141.

[9]Baudier, *Catholic Church in Louisiana*, 260.

[10]Louis William Dubourg was born in Cape Francais in what is now Haiti in January, 1766. He was educated and ordained for the Sulpician Order in France until the French Revolution drove him to the United States in 1794. He served at St. Mary's Seminary in Baltimore for many years until he was made Rector of the Seminary in 1806. In 1812, John Carroll, who was elevated from bishop to archbishop in 1808, appointed Dubourg as Apostolic Administrator for the New Orleans diocese in 1812. He was made Bishop of New Orleans by Pope Pius VII in 1815 while visiting in Rome. For a recent full length biography of this important Catholic prelate see Annabelle M. Melville, *Louis William Dubourg: Bishop of Louisiana and the Floridas, Bishop of Montauban and Archbishop of Besancon, 1766-1833* 2 vols. (Chicago, IL: Loyola University Press, 1986).

[11]Rev. John Rothensteiner, *History of the Archdiocese of St. Louis: In Its Various Stages of Development from A.D. 1673 to A.D. 1928*, 2 vols. (St. Louis, MO: Blackwell, Wielandy Company Press, 1928) 1:470; Guy, "Catholic Church in Arkansas," 71-72.

[12]Father Ennemond Dupuy to Bishop Joseph Rosati, 7 January 1833, Rosati Papers, AASL.

[13]Rev. Msgr. F.C. Holweck, "The Arkansas Mission Under Rosati," *St. Louis Catholic Historical Review*, 1 (July-October, 1919): 243-267. Article reprinted completely under the same title in *Jefferson County Historical Quarterly* 5 (no. 3, 1974): 11-37. I will be quoting from the *Jefferson County Historical Quarterly* reprint, 30.

[14]Thomas Nuttall quoted in Arnold, *Unequal Laws*, 189.

[15]Rothensteiner, *History of the Archdiocese of St. Louis*, 1:402-403.

[16]Ibid., 1:416-417. This is a map of the original boundaries of the Diocese of St. Louis.

[17]Ibid., 1:245, 292-299. For another biography of Rosati see Richard N. Clarke, *Lives of the Deceased Bishops of the Catholic Church in the United States, With an Appendix and Analytical Index*, 2 vols. (New York: P.V. Shea, 1872): 353-373.

[18]S.H. Long's travel guide quoted in Arnold, *Unequal Laws*, 187.

[19]Clarke, *Lives of the Deceased Bishops,* 2:203-206, 337-340; James Talmadge Moore, *Through Fire and Flood: The Catholic Church in Frontier Texas, 1836-1900* (College Station, TX: Texas A & M University Press, 1992) 36.

[20]Father Jean Marie Odin to Father Cholleton, After 31 October 1824 Propagation of the Faith, Tome 11, no. 12, Nov. 1827, pp. 374-389, English translation in typescript, 1-12, Odin Papers, AANO. I will be quoting from the English translation found in the AANO. Other accounts of this journey can be found in the secondary literature; see Holweck, "Arkansas Missions," 12-13; Rev. Msgr. Holweck, "The Beginnings of the Church in Little Rock" *Catholic Historical Review* 6 (July, 1920): 156-157.

[21]Father Odin to Father Cholleton, after 31 October 1824. 2, AANO.

[22]Ibid.

[23]Sarasin, a half-blooded Indian chief of the Quapaws, W. David Baird, *The Quapaws: A History of the Downstream People* (Norman, OK: University of Oklahoma Press, 1980) 72, 79, 84, 89.

[24]Ibid., 8, 11, 12. Holweck, "Arkansas Mission," 13; Holweck "Beginnings of the Church," 157; Guy, "Catholic Church in Arkansas," 75.

[25]Bishop Rosati to Mother Phillippine Duchesne, 28 September 1824, quoted in Melville, *Dubourg,* 2:733.

[26]Bishop Rosati to Fr. Peter Caprano, 1 November 1825, quoted in Ibid. That Peter Caprano was the Secretary for the Office of Propaganda, see Ibid., 2:602.

[27]Bishop Rosati quoted in Ibid., 2:733.

[28]Clarke, *Lives of the Deceased Bishops,* 2:206-239.

[29]Ibid., 2:340-369.

[30]Holweck, "Arkansas Mission," 13.

[31]Ibid., Holweck, "Beginnings of the Church," 157. That Father Martin did visit Little Rock during his stay in Arkansas, see Fr. Ennemond Dupuy to Bishop Joseph Rosati, 7 August 1834, Rosati Papers, AASL. This letter was translated and printed in Holweck, "Beginnings of the Church," 160-161.

[32]Holweck, "Arkansas Mission," 13. He makes the same point in another article, Holweck, "Beginnings of the Church," 157.

[33]Rosati's appeal translated and printed in Rothensteiner, *History of the Archdiocese of St. Louis,* 1:471. The Leopoldine Society was based in Vienna, Austria and founded in 1828-1829. This group would give help to establish the Catholic Church in the United States. James J. Hennesey, S.J., *American Catholics: A History of the Roman Catholic Community in the United States* (New York: Oxford University Press, 1982) 112.

[34]Rothensteiner, *History of the Archdiocese of St. Louis,* 1:472.

[35]Ibid., 1:441. For Saulnier's background, see 276, 283, 298, 406, 408, 439.

[36]Ibid., 1:472. That Beauprez was ordained on November 20, 1831, see Rev. Msgr. Holweck, "Father Beauptez's Letters," *St. Louis Catholic Historical Review* 5 (January, 1923): 40-53. This article was reprinted completely under the same title in the *Jefferson County Historical Quarterly* 5 (no. 2, 1974): 1937. I will quote from the *Jefferson County Historical Quarterly* reprint, 20.

[37]Rothensteiner, *History of the Archdiocese of St. Louis,* 1:472. For a description of their trip south, see Saulnier to Rosati, 24 December 1831, Rosati Papers, AASL. This letter was translated and published in Holweck, "Arkansas Mission," 14, 16-17.

[38]Ibid., Holweck, "Arkansas Mission," 18; also in Rothensteiner, *History of the Archdiocese of St. Louis,* 1:472-473.

[39]Ibid., Holweck, "Arkansas Mission," 17.

[40]Ibid., Holweck, "Arkansas Mission," 18.

[41]Ibid., Saulnier to Rosati, 7 January 1832, Rosati Papers, AASL; translated and printed in Holweck, "Arkansas Mission," 18-19.

[42]Saulnier to Rosati, 7 January 1832; Holweck, "Arkansas Mission," 18.

[43]Saulnier to Rosati, 13 January 1832, Rosati Papers, AASL; translated and printed in

Holweck, "Arkansas Mission," 19-20.

[44]Saulnier to Rosati, 27 February 1832, Rosati Papers, AASL; translated and printed in Holweck, "Arkansas Mission," 22.

[45]Beauprez to Rosati, 15 March 1832, 5 April 1832, Rosati Papers, AASL; translated and reprinted in Holweck, "Beauprez's Letters," 21-24. In the second letter, Beauprez wanted to stay with Saulnier since he has a "beautiful house," while he must stay with Jacques and Pierre Landesque.

[46]Beauprez to Rosati, 15 March 1832; Holweck, "Beauprez's Letters," 21, 23. Holweck, "Arkansas Mission," 23.

[47]Saulnier to Rosati, 19 March 1832, Rosati Papers, AASL; translated and printed in Holweck, "Arkansas Mission," 23.

[48]Saulnier to Rosati, 9 April 1832, Rosati Papers, AASL; translated and printed in Holweck, "Beginnings of the Church," 158.

[49]Saulnier to Rosati, 10 April 1832, Rosati Papers, AASL; translated and printed in Holweck, "Arkansas Mission," 24.

[50]Saulnier to Rosati, 7 May 1832, Rosati Papers, AASL; translated and printed in Holweck, "Arkansas Mission," 24.

[51]Saulnier to Rosati, 4 July 1832, Rosati Papers, AASL; translated and printed in Holweck, "Arkansas Mission," 24-25. Both Holweck and Rothensteiner incorrectly date the letter on June 4th but the incident happened according to the letter on June 28. Rothernsteiner, *History of the Archdiocese of St. Louis,* 1:475-476.

[52]Beauprez to Rosati, 12 July 1832, Rosati Papers, AASL; translated and printed in Holweck, "Beauprez's Letters," 26. In his earlier article Msgr. Holweck incorrectly listed the date as June 12. Holweck, "Arkansas Mission," 25.

[53]That Saulnier left on July 14, see Beauprez to Rosati, 23 July 1832, Rosati Papers, AASL; translated and printed in Holweck, "Beauprez's Letters" 27; Holweck, "Arkansas Mission," 26.

[54]Holweck, "Arkansas Mission," 26; Rothensteiner, *History of the Archdiocese of St. Louis,* 1:477.

[55]Beauprez to Rosati, 1 October 1832, Rosati Papers, AASL; translated and printed in Holweck, "Beauprez's Letters," 32.

[56]Rosati to Beauprez, 7 October 1832, Rosati Papers, AASL; translated and printed in Holweck, "Arkansas Mission," 27; Rothensteiner, *History of the Archdiocese of St. Louis,* 1:478.

[57]Holweck, "Arkansas Mission," 27, 27 n. 8.

[58]Holweck, "Beginnings of the Church," 159; Rothensteiner, *History of the Archdiocese of St. Louis,* 1:478.

[59]Holweck, "Bauprez's Letters," 36; Holweck, "Arkansas Mission," 27 n. 9.

[60]Holweck, "Beauprez's Letters," 27; Rothernsteiner, *History of the Archdiocese of St. Louis,* 1:479; Holweck, "Beginnings of the Church," 159.

[61]Dupuy to Rosati, 29 October 1832, Rosati Papers, AASL; translated and printed in Holweck, "Arkansas Mission," 27-28.

[62]Dupuy to Rosati, 12 November 1832, Rosati Papers, AASL; translated and printed in Holweck, "Arkansas Mission," 28-30, quote on p. 28.

[63]Ibid., Holweck, "Arkansas Mission," 29.

[64]Ibid.

[65]Dupuy to Rosati, 7 January 1833, Rosati Papers, AASL; translated and printed in Holweck, "Arkansas Mission," 30.

[66]Dupuy to Rosati, 12 April 1833, Rosati Papers, AASL. Portions of this letter cited in Rothernsteiner, *History of the Archdiocese of St. Louis,* 1:481.

[67]Holweck, "Arkansas Mission," 30.

[68]Dupuy to Rosati, 26 December 1833, Rosati Papers, AASL. Also see Holweck, "Arkansas Mission," 31; Rothensteiner, *History of the Archdiocese of St. Louis,* 1:481.

[69]Dupuy to Rosati, 29 April 1834, Rosati Papers, AASL. Holweck, "Arkansas Mission," 31; Rothernsteiner, *History of the Archdiocese of St. Louis,* 1:481-482. The exact location of the

church given in a letter three years later, Dupuy to Rosati, 6 April 1837, Rosati Papers, AASL. Letter translated and printed in Holweck, "Arkansas Mission," 33-34.

[70]Dupuy to Rosati, 9 July 1834, Rosati Papers, AASL; translated and printed in Holweck, "Beginnings of the Church," 160.

[71]Ibid.

[72]Dupuy to Rosati, 7 August 1834, Rosati Papers, AASL; translated and printed in Holweck, "Beginnings of the Church," 160-161, quote on p. 161.

[73]Ibid., Holweck, "Beginnings of the Church," 161.

[74]Rothensteiner, *History of the Archdiocese of St. Louis,* 1:483.

[75]Ibid., Holweck, "Arkansas Mission," 31-32.

[76]Dupuy to Rosati, 2 July 1835, Rosati Papers, AASL. This Latin phrase cited and translated in Rothensteiner, *History of the Archdiocese of St. Louis,* 1:483.

[77]Dupuy to Rosati, 24 July 1835, Rosati Papers, AASL. Portions of this letter were translated and cited in Holweck, "Arkansas Mission," 32.

[78]Dupuy to Rosati, 31 August 1835, Rosati Papers, AASL; portions cited in Holweck, "Arkansas Mission." 32.

[79]Dupuy to Rosati, 11 August 1835, Rosati Papers, AASL; letter translated and printed in Holweck, "Beginnings of the Church," 161162. Chester Ashley would later be a U.S. Senator from Arkansas and play a major role in Arkansas politics in the territorial period and the early years of statehood. See Susan H. Ruple, "The Life and Times of Chester Ashley, 1791-1848" (M.A. thesis, University of Arkansas, 1983).

[80]Holweck, "Beginnings of the Church," 162.

[81]Ibid.

[82]Dupuy to Rosati, 7 December 1835, 8 December 1835, Rosati Papers, AASL. Portions of these letters translated and cited in Holweck, "Arkansas Mission," 32.

[83]Dupuy to Rosati, 19 January 1836, Rosati Papers, AASL; portions of this letter translated and cited in Holweck, "Beginnings of the Church," 161-162.

[84]Dupuy to Rosati, 19 January 1836, Rosati Papers, AASL; portions of this letter translated and cited in Holweck, "Beginnings of the Church," 161-162. For the convention which drew up Arkansas' first state constitution see Lonnie J. White, *Politics on the Southwestern Frontier: Arkansas Territory, 1819-1836* (Memphis, TN: Memphis State University Press, 1964) 184-191.

[85]Little Rock *Old Line Democrat,* 15 September 1859, 2; Woods, *Rebellion and Realignment,* 92.

[86]Dupuy to Rosati, 4 May 1836, Rosati Papers, AASL. Letter cited in Rothernsteiner, *History of the Archdiocese of St. Louis,* 1:483-484.

[87]Holweck, "Arkansas Mission," 32; Rothernsteiner, *History of the Archdiocese of St. Louis,* 1:484.

[88]Dupuy to Rosati, 9 January 1837, Rosati Papers, AASL; letter translated and printed in Rothensteiner, *History of the Archdiocese of St. Louis,* 1:484.

[89]Donnelly to Rosati, 23 March 1837, Rosati Papers, AASL. Donnelly wrote in English, but he wrote in an Irish brogue, for example "lait" for "late". His spelling is corrected and his letter printed in Holweck, "Arkansas Missions," 33.

[90]Dupuy to Rosati, 6 April 1837, Rosati Papers, AASL. Letter translated and printed in Holweck, "Arkansas Mission," 33-34.

[91]Ibid., Holweck, "Arkansas Mission," 34.

[92]Antoine Barraque to Bishop Rosati, 13 April 1837, letter cited in Rothensteiner, *History of the Archdiocese of St. Louis,* 1:485; Holweck, "Arkansas Mission," 34.

[93]Dupuy to Rosati, 28 August 1837, 2 September 1837, 5 October 1837; Rosati to Donnelly, 2 September 1837, Rosati Papers, AASL. Events also in Holweck, "Arkansas Mission," 34; Holweck, "Beginnings of the Church," 163; Rothensteiner, *History of the Archdiocese of St. Louis,* 1:485.

[94]Dupuy to Rosati, 16 October 1837, Rosati Papers, AASL. Letter also cited in Holweck,

"Arkansas Mission," 34. This would be Dupuy's last letter from Arkansas.

[95]Donnelly to Rosati, 31 October 1837, Rosati Papers, AASL; Holweck, "Arkansas Mission," 34.

[96]Barraque's faction supported Donnelly and another faction led by a man named John Dodge supported the ousted Father Dupuy, AASL. See also, Holweck, "Beginnings of the Church," 163 n. 17.

[97]Baudier, *Catholic Church in Louisiana,* 350.

[98]Donnelly to Rosati, 31 October 1837; Barraque to Rosati, 9 November 1837, Rosati Papers, AASL; Rothensteiner, *History of the Archdiocese of St. Louis,* 1:485.

[99]Donnelly to Rosati, 20 January 1838, Rosati Papers, AASL; also see Holweck, "Arkansas Mission," 35.

[100]Donnelly to Rosati, 19 February 1838, Rosati Papers, AASL. Portions of this letter can be found in Holweck, "Arkansas Mission," 35; Holweck, "Beginnings of the Church," 163; Rothensteiner, *History of the Archdiocese of St. Louis,* 1:486.

[101]Donnelly to Rosati, 26 March 1838, Rosati Papers, AASL. This letter printed in Holweck, "Beginnings of the Church," 163-164. Prominent Protestants included men like Chester Ashley, later U.S. Senator from Arkansas in the 1840s; Edward Cross, a Territorial Judge and the second Congressman Arkansas sent to the U.S. House of Representatives, 1838-1844; William Woodruff, founder and editor of the Little Rock *Arkansas Gazette,* the state's oldest newspaper; Benjamin Johnson, First Federal District Judge for the state. Johnson's son Robert Ward Johnson would be Arkansas' first Attorney General and later a Representative and U.S. Senator from Arkansas from 1846-1861. For the day of the first Catholic Mass in Colonial English America March 25, 1634, see Hennesey, *American Catholics,* 39. For the location of Dugan's store, see Diocesan Historical Commission, *The History of Catholicity in Arkansas* (Little Rock, AR: Guardian Press, 1927) n.p. (34).

[102]The Nuns arrived on October 11, 1838, but the school formally opened on November 19, 1838. Sr. Matilda Bennett, S.L. "Sisters of Loretto: One Hundred and Fifty Years." (Unpublished typed manuscript, Loretto Motherhouse, Nerinckx, Kentucky, n.d.) 96; Little Rock *Arkansas Gazette,* 14 November 1838, 3.

[103]Donnelly to Rosati, 28 November 1838, Rosati Papers, AASL; Holweck, "Beginnings of the Church," 165.

[104]Donnelly to Rosati, 12 December 1838, Rosati Papers, AASL; Holweck, "Beginnings of the Church," 165.

[105]Donnelly to Rosati, 2 January 1839, Rosati to Donnelly, 21 May 1839. On the same day Rosati chose Donnelly's replacement; Rosati to Fr. Joseph Richard-Bole, 21 May 1839. All of the letters are in the Rosati Papers, AASL. These documents also cited in Holweck, "Beginnings of the Church," 166; Holweck, "Arkansas Mission," 35.

[106]Donnelly to Rosati, 26 May 1839, Rosati Papers, AASL; Letter printed in Holweck, "Beginnings of the Church," 165-166.

[107]Holweck, "Beginnings of the Church," 166. Rothensteiner, *History of the Archdiocese of St. Louis,* 1:485. For an account of their journey to Arkansas including saying the first Catholic Mass in Napoleon, see Richard-Bole to Rosati, 13 June 1839, Rosati Papers, AASL. A portion of this letter was translated and printed in Holweck, "Beginnings of the Church," 166.

[108]Richard-Bole to Rosati, 29 October 1839, Rosati Papers, AASL. This letter was translated and printed in Holweck, "Beginnings of the Church," 167.

[109]Ibid.

[110]Richard-Bole to Rosati, 19 November 1839, Rosati Papers, AASL. Portions of this letter was translated and printed in Holweck, "Beginnings of the Church," 168.

[111]Holweck, "Arkansas Mission," 37; Father August Simon Paris to Bishop Antoine Blanc of New Orleans, 1 December 1840, Blanc Papers, AANO. This letter by Fr. Paris indicates that a church will be finished finally at the Post by March 1841. He also hopes that Fr. Richard-Bole will be able to finish a church in Little Rock by 1841.

[112]Richard-Bole to Rosati, 29 January 1840, Rosati Papers, AASL. Letter translated and

printed in Holweck, "Beginnings of the Church," 169.

[113]Richard-Bole to Rosati, 21 April 1840, Rosati Papers, AASL. Portions of this letter were translated and printed in Holweck, "Beginnings of the Church," 170. In an earlier letter Richard-Bole had a very low perception of the Catholics in the Arkansas capital. He writes: "You know here everybody is Protestant–there are some Catholics, but in the case of a great number of them, I would wish they were Protestants." Richard-Bole to Rosati, 15 February 1840, Rosati Papers, AASL; translated and quoted in Holweck, "Beginnings of the Church," 169.

[114]Fr. Paris to Bishop Blanc, 1 December 1840.

[115]Ibid.

[116]Little Rock *Arkansas Gazette,* 14 November 1838, 3.

[117]Bennett, "Sisters of Loretto," 86-88; Sr. Henrietta Hockle, O.S.B., "Catholic Schools in Arkansas: An Historical Perspective, 1838-1977." (Ed. S. thesis, Arkansas State University, 1977), 3.

[118]Bennett, "Sisters of Loretto," 90; Rothensteiner, *History of the Archdiocese of St. Louis,* 1:859.

[119]Ibid. That Fr. A. Simon Paris moved to the Arkansas Post, see the bill for the cost of his house, dated 13 April, 1842. Also see the letter of Mother Superior Teresa Mattingly to "?," 5 November 1844; both documents in ADLR. The school St. Ambrose Female Academy at the Arkansas Post was advertised in the Louisville *Catholic Advocate,* 8 October 1842, n.p., newspaper clipping in ADLR.

[120]Bennett, "Sisters of Loretto," 90; Rothensteiner, *History of the Archdiocese of St. Louis,* 1:859.

[121]There is considerable confusion in the secondary literature over whether a church was ever built in Little Rock prior to the creation of the diocese. Msgr. Holweck claims no church was built there and he is echoed by Rothernsteiner. Holweck, "Beginnings of the Church," 170. A 1925 history of Arkansas Catholicism stated that a church was built by Donnelly and Richard-Bole in 1843 at the northwest corner of Louisiana and Seventh Streets, D.H.C., *History of Catholicity in Arkansas,* n.p. (6, 34). The location is correct, and date of completion is probably correct. Fr. Richard-Bole bought the property from William and Deborah Brown on September 10, 1842. That property was then sold to Fr. Constantine Maenhaut on October 11, 1845. Maenhaut had a Little Rock lawyer Lemuel R. Lincoln act as his agent for the property, and in a letter Lincoln describes it as being a brick church with a two story house next to it and a fence around it. Lincoln asked Maenhaut whether he would like to rent the church out as a school in 1847. This information from Property Abstract Deed, #6, Pulaski County, Diocese of Little Rock, pp. 52, 53; Lemuel R. Lincoln to Fr. Constantine Maenhaut 8 November 1847. John Davis and John Walker of Little Rock appear before a Justice of the Peace, David Carroll, in late 1847 and describe it as a two-story frame house and brick building, formerly used by the Sisters of Loretto, statement dated 27 December 1847. All of the above documents in the ADLR.

[122]Guy, "Catholic Church in Arkansas," 106.

[123]Papal Bull, 28 November 1843, Pope Gregory XVI. Original document in the ADLR. Translation taken from Guy, "Catholic Church in Arkansas," 106-107.

[124]Guy, "Catholic Church in Arkansas," 107-108; Rothensteiner, *History of the Archdiocese of St. Louis,* 1:489. Superior of the Sisters of Loretto at the Arkansas Post writes that Fr. Richard-Bole came through there on July 20, 1844 on his way out of the diocese. She also complains that he had overcharged them for some materials. Sr. Teresa Mattingly to '?", 5 November 1844. ADLR.

CHAPTER III

[1]Certificate of Consecration, 11 March 1844, Byrne Papers, ADLR.

[2]The other men consecrated that day was William Quarter, first Bishop of Chicago, and John McCloskey made coadjutor to New York Bishop John Hughes. Of the three men elevated to the episcopacy that day, John McCloskey would be the most outstanding. He became the first Bishop of Albany, New York in 1847 and succeeded Archbishop Hughes of New York when that prelate died in 1864. In 1875, Pope Pius IX chose to make McCloskey the first American

Cardinal. For the careers of these men see Richard N. Clarke, *Lives of the Deceased Bishops of the Catholic Church in the United States: With an Appendix and Analytical Index,* 2 vols. (New York: P. O'Shea, 1872) 2:267; James Hennesey, S.J., *American Catholics: A History of the Roman Catholic Community in the United States* (New York: Oxford University, 1981) 176.

[3]Both Clarke and Francis Shaw Guy give December 5, 1802, as the incorrect date of Byrne's birth. Clarke, *Lives of the Deceased Bishops,* 2:264; Francis S. Guy, "The Catholic Church in Arkansas." (Unpublished typescript history, ADLR.), 110. A copy of Byrne's baptismal certificate found Byrne Papers, ADLR.

[4]Both Clarke and Guy claim Byrne came over in 1820, yet no confirmation of this either in Bp. England's biography or within the records of the Diocese of Charleston. Clarke, *Lives of the Deceased Bishops,* 2:265; Guy, "Catholic Church in Arkansas," 110; Msgr. Peter Guilday, *The Life and Times of John England: First Bishop of Charleston,* 2 vols. (New York: America Press, 1927) 296, 299-300.

[5]Clarke, *Lives of the Deceased Bishops,* 2:264. Guilday mentions England ordaining men around the time Clarke gives for Byrne's ordination, yet he does not name him directly. Guilday, *John England,* 1:503.

[6]In March, 1827 England promised Gaston to send one or two priests up to North Carolina. England to Gaston, 22 March 1827, quoted in Guilday, *John England,* 1:498. For the statement that Byrne worked in North Carolina and Georgia, consult Clarke, *Lives of the Deceased Bishops,* 2:265; John G. Shea, *History of the Catholic Church in the United States,* 4 vols. (New York: J. G. Shea Publishers, 1886-1892) 3:328.

[7]Clarke, *Lives of the Deceased Bishops,* 2:265; Guilday, *John England,* 2:260. England mentions that Byrne is the Keeper of the Seal of the Diocese in a letter to the New Orleans Bishop. England to Leo Raymond de Neckers, 4 July 1832. De Neckers Papers, AANO.

[8]An older diocesan history says that Fr. Byrne and Bishop England broke over "a detail of the Sunday School." Diocesan Historical Commission, *The History of Catholicity in Arkansas* (Little Rock, AR: Guardian Press, 1925) n.p. (9). A more realistic reason is that Baker replaced Byrne as vicar general. Guilday, *John England,* 2:534. Byrne's exeat from the diocese in ADLR.

[9]Clarke, *Lives of the Deceased Bishops,* 2:265; Bishop Byrne's consecration certificate, 11 March 1844, ADLR.

[10]Bishop John Hughes to the Archbishops and Bishops of Ireland, 30 April 1842, ADLR.

[11]Clarke, *Lives of the Deceased Bishops,* 2:266; Byrne's letter proved instrumental in blocking Fr. Richard S. Baker from being the successor to Bishop England in the Diocese of Charleston. Guilday, *John England,* 2:549-550.

[12]Guy, "Catholic Church in Arkansas," 112; The Register of Bishop Byrne, 4 June 1844, in manuscript, Byrne's Papers, ADLR. Hereafter cited as Byrne's Register.

[13]Byrne's Register, 14 June 1844.

[14]Sr. Teresa Mattingly, S.L. to (?), 5 November 1844, ADLR; Sr. Eulalia Kelly to Bishop Antoine Blanc, 8 March 1845, Blanc Papers, AANO.

[15]Sr. Matilda Bennett, S.L. "Sisters of Loretto: One Hundred and Fifty Years (Unpublished Manuscript, Loretto Motherhouse, Nerinckx, Kentucky, n.d.) 98; Sr. Henrietta Hockle, O.S.B., "Catholic Schools in Arkansas: An Historical Perspective." (Ed. S. thesis, Arkansas State University, 1977) 4-5.

[16]Guy, "Catholic Church in Arkansas," 112; D.H.C., *History of Catholicity in Arkansas,* n.p. (9). As early as December, 1844, Bishop Byrne thought Father Corry would leave Arkansas, Byrne to Blanc, 5 December 1844, Blanc Papers, AANO.

[17]Byrne to Blanc, 11 July 1844, Blanc Papers, AANO.

[18]Byrne's Register, 28 September 1844. Byrne described it to Blanc as a "bilious fever." Byrne to Blanc, 5 December 1844, Blanc Papers, AANO.

[19]Byrne writes that just after arriving back in Little Rock, "Providence sent to my aid, Rev. Peter M. Walsh." Byrne's Register, 28 September, 1844. Guy mistakenly claims a Fr. "P.W. Walsh arrived in 1845". Guy, "Catholic Church in Arkansas," 113.

[20]Byrne's Register, 23 October 1844.

[21]Byrne's Register, 24 October 1844. This date in the Register is incorrect for the in previous inscription he claims to be in the Arkansas Post on October 24 and this Register insertion has him back in Little Rock. I doubt that the good bishop could bi-locate. He could well have meant November 24 or December 24. That Byrne's cathedral would be at the southeast corner of Second and Center Streets, see the newspaper article about its history and about its being torn down in 1889. Little Rock *Arkansas Gazette* 30 June 1889, p. 5.

[22]Byrne's Register, 29 June 1844, D.H.C., *History of Catholicity in Arkansas,* n.p. (34).

[23]Byrne's Register, 1 January; 2 and 12 February; 26, 27, 30 March; 4, 13, 30, April; 6, 10 May; 30 November; 1, 20 December 1845. On Arkansas' poor transportation during the antebellum period, see Walter Moffatt, "Transportation in Arkansas, 1819-1840" *Arkansas Historical Quarterly* 15 (Autumn 1956) 187-201; James M. Woods, *Rebellion and Realignment: Arkansas's Road to Secession* (Fayetteville, AR: University of Arkansas Press, 1987) 9-11.

[24]Byrne's Register, 20 May 1845; Hockle "Catholic Schools in Arkansas," 5; Bennett "Sisters of Loretto," 90.

[25]Byrne's Register, 1 December 1845.

[26]Byrne to Archbishop Eccleston, 5 December 1845, quoted in Shea, *History of the Catholic Church,* 4:285.

[27]Byrne to Choiselat Gallien, 28 December 1847, Byrne Papers, ADLR. A recent historian for the Archdiocese of Baltimore termed the sixth provincial council of 1846 as "singularly unproductive." Thomas W. Spalding, *The Premier See: A History of the Archdiocese of Baltimore, 1789-1989* (Baltimore, MD: Johns Hopkins University Press, 1989) 148.

[28]Bishop John Joseph Chanche to Bishop Blanc, 29 August 1847, Blanc Papers, AANO.

[29]Byrne to Blanc, 12 October 1846, Blanc Papers, AANO.

[30]Byrne to Fr. Peter McMahon, 7 November 1846, AANO.

[31]Byrne's Register, 18 September, 19 October, 1846. This Mass recorded in the first chapter of this book.

[32]Little Rock *State Democrat,* 2 November 1846, 2.

[33]Byrne's Register, 7, 23, 27 November; 24, 27, 28 December, 1846.

[34]Little Rock *Arkansas Gazette,* 19 January 1847, 3. The advertisement actually stated that school had begun on January 5, 1846.

[35]*Metropolitan Catholic Almanac, 1850.* (Baltimore, MD: John Murphy Co., 1850) 153-154.

[36]Citizens to Bishop Andrew Byrne, 5 December 1845, Byrne Papers, ADLR. Prominent individuals included J.L. Dickson, Alfred Wilson, James Neal, John L. Stirman, elected Secretary of State in 1860, and Alfred Burton, Greenwood, U.S. Representative to Congress, 1853-1859, Woods, *Rebellion and Realignment* 62, 117, 183.

[37]Byrne's Register, 28 November 1847; Byrne to Blanc, 20 December 1847, Blanc Papers, ANNO. Byrne to Msgr. Gallien, 28 December 1847, Byrne Papers, ADLR; Guy, "Catholic Church in Arkansas," 122-123.

[38]Receipts of the Propagation of the Faith to Byrne during the years, 1844, 1848, 1854, 1861; Leopoldine Society to Byrne with check receipts 1845-1855, Byrne Papers, ADLR. The French Society began in Lyon, France in 1822 and Leopoldine Society began in 1829, sent money to Catholic dioceses in l9th century. Hennesey, S.J. *American Catholics,* 112.

[39]Byrne to Eccleston, 5 December 1845, quoted in Shea, *History of the Catholic Church,* 4:285.

[40]Byrne's Register, 1, 10 January; 28 February; 7 March; 4, 25 April; 5 June; 28 July; 22 August; 21, 28 November, 1847.

[41]Byrne to Blanc, 6 May 1846, Blanc Papers, AANO. For Rocky Comfort as an Irish settlement and its place near present day Foreman in Little River County, see Guy "Catholic Church in Arkansas," 116.

[42]Byrne to Blanc, 6 May 1847.

[43]Bishop Odin to Blanc, 21 September 1847, Blanc Papers, AANO.

[44]Clarke, *Lives of the Deceased Bishops* 2:352. On Timon's and Odin's 1824 missionary tour in Arkansas, see the previous chapter or James M. Woods: "To the Suburb of Hell: Catholic

Missionaries in Arkansas, 1803-1843." *Arkansas Historical Quarterly* 48 (Autumn, 1989): 221-223.

[45]Byrne to Msgr. Gallien, 28 December 1847. Bishop Edward Purcell of Cincinnati wrote the Archbishop of New Orleans almost a year later: "Nothing more is said of late of Bishop Byrne wanting to leave Little Rock. He should stay there." Purcell to Blanc, 7 November 1848, Blanc Papers, AANO.

[46]Guy, "Catholic Church in Arkansas," 113; Byrne's Register, 25 April 1848.

[47]Byrne's Register, 5 May 1848; 4, 25 April 1849.

[48]Monsignor John Michael Lucey, "Souvenir of a Silver Jubilee, February 5, 1892" (Typescript from the original found in ADLR), 9. This story repeated in D.H.C., *History of Catholicity in Arkansas,* n.d. (9); Guy, "Catholic Church in Arkansas," 112. These accounts do not give the approximate date; that can be obtained from an address given by Fr. Theobald Matthew, an internationally known Irish advocate of Temperance. He spoke in Little Rock in August 1850, and he mentions the recent death of Fr. Donohoe. Little Rock *Arkansas Gazette,* 30 August 1850, 2.

[49]*Journal of the Senate for the Seventh Session of the General Assembly of the State of Arkansas,* (Little Rock, AR: Arkansas Gazette Printing Office, 1849) 171-174, 184-186. *Journal of the House of Representatives for the Seventh Session of the General Assembly of the State of Arkansas* (Little Rock, AR: Arkansas Gazette Printing Office, 1849) 191, 289.

[50]I could find no record of this bill or of its defeat in the *Journal* for the state House of Representatives, yet the bill was openly cited, discussed and the roll call vote provided in letters which appeared in the local press. Little Rock *Arkansas Gazette* 2 August 1850, 2; 9 August 1850, 2.

[51]Little Rock *Arkansas Gazette,* 22 March 1849, 2. For the work Byrne did with the college and his pride in seeing it open, see Byrne's Register, 1 January, 7 February, 12 March, 15 October, 1849.

[52]Byrne's Register, 5 March 1848. Sometime after the Civil War it became the Church of the Immaculate Conception, Parish Records, Immaculate Conception, Fort Smith, ADLR.

[53]*Metropolitan Catholic Almanac, 1850,* 153.

[54]Shea, *History of the Catholic Church,* 4:32; Byrne's Register, 24 April 1849.

[55]Odin to Blanc, 29 June 1849, Blanc Papers, AANO.

[56]Byrne's Register, 24 April; 4 November, 1849.

[57]Byrne's Register, 10 March; 11 June 1850. This is unfortunately the last date we have in the bishop's official Register.

[58]Little Rock *Arkansas Banner,* 2 July 1850, 2.

[59]Little Rock *Arkansas Gazette,* 5 July 1850, 2.

[60]Ibid., 12 July 1850, 2.

[61]Ibid., 2 August 1850, 2.

[62]On the background to anti-Catholicism in early America, see Sr. Mary Augustine Ray, *American Opinion of Roman Catholicism in the Eighteenth Century* (New York: Columbia University Press, 1936); Ray Allen Billington, *The Protestant Crusade, 1800-1860: A Study of the Origins of American Nativism* (New York: MacMillan, 1838).

[63]The creation of the St. Louis Province with its Dioceses of Nashville, Dubuque, Milwaukee, Chicago, and the new Diocese of St. Paul found in Rev. John Rothensteiner, *History of the Archdiocese of St. Louis: In Its Various Stages of Development from A.D. 1673 to A.D. 1928.* 2 vols. (St. Louis, MO: Blackwell, Wielandry & Co., 1928) 2:1-5. For the creation of the southern province out of New Orleans, see Roger Baudier, *The Catholic Church in Louisiana* (New Orleans, LA: Private Printing, 1939) 374.

[64]Sisters of Mercy, editors, *Popular Life of Catherine McAuley: Foundress of the Institute of the Religious Sisters of Mercy, Dublin, Ireland.* (New York: P.J. Kenedy, 1893).

[65]Sr. Mary Teresa Carroll, R.S.M. *Leaves from the Annals of the Sisters of Mercy* (New York: Catholic Publication Society, 1889) 328.

[66]Ibid., 329.

[67]Ibid., 329-330. Sr. Carroll work written more than a century ago claims eight postulants accompanied the four professed sisters. A later writer claims that only five came although there may have been eight originally, but only five would join the Arkansas Mercy community. Jane Ramos and the Sisters of Mercy of Arkansas, *Arkansas Frontiers of Mercy* (Fort Smith, AR: St. Edward Press, 1989) 55. For Arkansas' wild and unsettled reputation, see Woods, *Rebellion and Realignment,* 12-16, 201 n. 60.

[68]Carroll, *Leaves from the Annals,* 330.

[69]Byrne to Blanc 30 November 1850, Blanc Papers, AANO. In this letter, Byrne mentions that he has a priest with him for the Diocese of Galveston but does not give his name. He does not mention any priests who might be with him, yet since he had three more traveling with him by spring, it seems quite plausible that he had some priests with him for his diocese as well.

[70]Carroll, *Leaves From the Annals,* 330. Sr. Carroll describes how heartrending this trip was for "when the long, narrow vessel began to move out of sight of motherland that some of the Sisters realized what the sacrifice involved. One of them exclaimed with a burst of anguish, 'O Father! I cannot, cannot go!' The bishop, whose own eyes were swimming, affected to be amused, and to distract them from their grief called out, 'Halloo, captain, turn back. Here are people who declare they cannot go on. Stop the vessel.' This made everyone laugh. After a while the grief was abated and all renewed the sacrifice of themselves to God." p. 331. For the number of Sisters and postulants, see Guy, "Catholic Church in Arkansas," 124.

[71]Carroll, *Leaves from the Annals,* 331-333. Sr. Carroll claims that they arrived in Little Rock on February 6, 1851, but local papers maintain they arrived on Wednesday, February 5, 1851. Little Rock *Arkansas Gazette,* 7 February 1851, 2. Fr. Guy lists the correct date. Guy, "Catholic Church in Arkansas," 125.

[72]Little Rock *Arkansas Banner,* 12 February 1851, 2.

[73]Little Rock *Arkansas Gazette,* 14 February 1851, 2. "Fellow Citizen" made another attack on the sisters in a letter which appeared in the next issue of the *Gazette,* 21 February 1851, 2. Rev. Joshua Green of the Presbyterian Church wrote a letter that summer stating that the Sisters of Mercy should have stayed back in Ireland where they are really needed. *Arkansas Gazette,* 11 July 1851, 2.

[74]Information that the property was rented and a good description of the old church and convent can be found in Lemuel R. Lincoln to Fr. Constantine Maenhaut, 8 November, 1847, ADLR.

[75]Lincoln asks for Fr. Maenhaut's price and tells of Bishop Byrne's interest in the place. Lincoln to Maenhaut, 15 January, 1850, ADLR. Byrne's counter-offer is mentioned in a letter to Blanc. Byrne to Blanc, 2 May 1850. There is more discussion of it in another letter about a year later. Byrne to Blanc, 27 April 1851. Both of these letters are in Blanc Papers, AANO. There seems to be a meeting of the minds by the summer. Byrne to Fr. Maenhaut, 28 July 1851, Byrne Papers, ADLR. For the actual date of the sale on August 13, 1851, see Property Abstracts, Pulaski County, Deed Book #6, p. 54, Chancery, Diocese of Little Rock.

[76]Newspaper clipping, undated and no publication listed. Clipping signed by Mother Teresa Farrell. Clipping in AANO.

[77]Guy, "Catholic Church in Arkansas," 127-128.

[78]Little Rock *Arkansas Gazette,* 27 June 1851, 3. The names of the postulants listed: Miss Anne Healey (Sr. Mary Vincent, R.S.M.), Miss Charlotte Nolan, (Sr. Mary Ignatius, R.S.M.), Miss Jane Nolan (Sr. Mary Xavier, R.S.M.), Miss Teresa Farrell (Sr. Mary Baptist, R.S.M.), Miss Alice Carton (Sr. Mary Alphonsus, R.S.M.).

[79]Fr. Patrick Martin, b. 1825 from Byrne's county of Meath, Ireland. He studied at All Hallows Seminary in Ireland. Kevin Condon, C.M. *The Missionary College of All Hollows, 1842-1891* (Dublin, Ireland: All Hallows College Press, 1986) 294. Fr. Patrick Reilly, b. 1817 from Kilmassen, County Meath, Ireland. He studied at Maynooth Seminary. Obituary gives his death on April 29, 1882. Irish newspaper, no name or date given, clipping in ADLR. Fr. Patrick Behan's birth and training I have not been able to ascertain. Sr. Carroll claims that all three men were ordained in Little Rock on St. Patrick's Day, 1851. I could find no confirmation of this in the

primary sources. Carroll, *Leaves from the Annals*, 356.

[80]Little Rock *Arkansas Gazette,* 7 January 1852, 3. Later Catholic Almanacs will call it St. Patrick's Male Academy, 1852, 1855-1858. For two years, 1853, 1854, it is called St. John's Male Academy. *Metropolitan Catholic Almanac 1852,* 166, *1853,* 200, *1854,* 227, *1855,* 206, *1856,* 220, *1857,* 252, *1858,* 163. There is no mention of the school in the issues of *1858,* 124, *1860,* 128. All of these *Almanacs* (Baltimore, MD: John Murphy, 1852-1860).

[81]Guy, "Catholic Church in Arkansas," 122; Amelia Martin, "Migration: Ireland, Fort Smith and Points West" *The Journal of the Fort Smith Historical Society* 2 (September 1978): 43.

[82]Little Rock *Arkansas Gazette,* 20 December 1850, 2.

[83]*Arkansas Gazette,* 14 February 1851, 3.

[84]Ibid.

[85]Ibid.

[86]Martin, "Migration," 43; Guy, "Catholic Church in Arkansas," 123.

[87]This attack filled two lengthy columns in the newspaper, Little Rock *Arkansas Gazette,* 4 July 1851, 2, 3.

[88]Ibid., 29 August 1851, 2.

[89]Rev. Green wrote an article declaring that neither Byrne nor Behan would accept his challenge to a debate, Little Rock *Arkansas Gazette* 6 February 1852, 2.

[90]Lincoln's religious beliefs outlined in his letter to Fr. Meanhaut, in this document he mentions that he is often called "an aristocratic Protestant." Lincoln to Maenhaut, 15 January 1850. On the controversy around his death and funeral see Little Rock *Arkansas Gazette,* 7 October 1851, 3; 154 October 1851, 3. Byrne wrote Blanc that he was happy that Lincoln died a Catholic. Byrne to Blanc, 20 November 1851, Blanc Papers, AANO.

[91]Rev. Green spoke in Fayetteville that the Pope of Rome is the Whore of Babylon talked about in the 17th chapter of the Book of Revelation. Fayetteville *Southwest Independent,* n.d. cited in Little Rock *Arkansas Gazette,* 4 November 1853, 2. Rev. Green died in Memphis on August 1, 1854 from cholera. *Arkansas Gazette* 11 August 1854, 2.

[92]Byrne's letter and Rome's feelings about Byrne's real intention are presented in Fr. Finbar Kenneally, O.F.M., *U.S. Documents in the Propaganda Fide Archives: A Calendar,* 1st Series, 7 vols. (Washington, D.C.: Academy of Franciscan History, 1966-1977) 4:258; 6:63. These volumes supply an annotated and paraphrased translation of the documents.

[93]Guy claims that St. Anne's was founded on January, 1852. This may be true, but Byrne only mentions in May, 1853 that St. Anne's Academy in Fort Smith is growing and had thirty-six students. Guy, "Catholic Church in Arkansas," 128; Byrne to Blanc, 22 May 1853. Bp. Byrne maintains in the late summer of 1854 there are still things that need to be finished at the convent in Fort Smith. Byrne to Blanc, 14 August 1854. Both of these letters just mentioned in the Blanc Papers, AANO.

[94]Nagle's ordination listed in *Metropolitan: A Monthly Review Dedicated to Religious Education,* 7 (October 1853): 478. Byrne to Blanc 30 March 1854, AANO.

[95]Little Rock *Arkansas Gazette,* 11 August 1854, 2.

[96]Byrne writes that Fr. O'Reilly thinks "Arkansas too small for his importance . . . He went to Ft. Smith after being ordered not to." Byrne to Blanc, 30 March 1854, Blanc Papers, AANO.

[97]Behan to Blanc, 14 July 1854, Blanc Papers, AANO. Behan signed his name as Vicar General, but the following year's Almanac lists Fr. Reilly as vicar general. Then no one is listed in 1856, 1857, and then Reilly is once again listed as vicar general in 1858. *Metropolitan Catholic Almanac 1855,* 206, *1856,* 220, *1857,* 252, *1858,* 162. By 1855 there were now eight Catholic priests in the Diocese; Byrne, Reilly and Walsh in Little Rock and going to missions around central Arkansas; Behan at Pine Bluff, New Gascony with a mission in Helena; McGowan at Napoleon and Arkansas Post; Nagle and Martin working at Camden and Rocky Comfort in southwestern Arkansas; Monaghan at Fort Smith and Van Buren with a mission to Fayetteville. Fr. John Miege, S.J. is listed in Fort Smith, yet really as a missionary to the Indians. *Metropolitan Catholic Almanac, 1855,* 206; Guy, "Catholic Church in Arkansas," 130, no. 28.

[98]The actual number of immigrants is larger in the 1905-1914 period, yet the number of

immigrants coming in proportion to the existing population was larger in 1845-1854. David Potter, *The Impending Crisis, 1848-1861* (New York: Harper & Row, 1976) 220.

[99]Billington, *The Protestant Crusade*, 53-90, 196-198, 220-236, 302-340. He has an excellent chapter on the literature of anti-Catholicism in the first sixty years of the nineteenth century, 344-370.

[100]James D. B. DeBow, *Statistical View of the United States: A Compendium to the Seventh Census, 1850* (Washington, D.C.: Government Printing Office, 1853) 118, 399.

[101]Ibid., 118.

[102]Ibid., U.S. Department of the Interior, *The Seventh Census of the United States, 1850* (Washington, D.C.: A.O.P. Nicholson, Public Printer, 1853) 535, 560-561.

[103]Arthur C. Cole, *The Whig Party in the South* (Washington, D.C.: American Historical Association, 1913); W. Darrell Overdyke, *The Know Nothing Party in the South* (Baton Rouge, LA: Louisiana State University Press, 1950).

[104]Walter L. Brown, "Albert Pike, 1809-1891" (Ph.D. dissertation, University of Texas, 1955) 449-493. For a look at the *Arkansas Gazette* and the Know Nothing cause, see Margaret Ross, *The Arkansas Gazette: The Early Years, 1810-1866* (Little Rock, AR: Arkansas Gazette Foundation Library, 1969) 299, 316-317. For Woodruff's earlier remarks and Danley's comment on the Know Nothings, see Little Rock's *Arkansas Gazette*, 29 August 1851, 2; 25 August 1854, 2.

[105]Harold T. Smith, "The Know Nothing Party in Arkansas", *Arkansas Historical Quarterly* 34 (Winter 1975): 291-303; Woods, *Rebellion and Realignment*, 60-63. For a look at Borland's career in Central America, see "Expansionism as Diplomacy: The Career of Solon Borland in Central America, 1853-1854," *The Americas: A Quarterly Review of Inter-American Cultural History* 40 (January 1984): 399-417. Borland joins the staff as editor, Little Rock *Arkansas Gazette* 31 August 1855, 3

[106]Catholics as enemies of the Republic, Little Rock *Arkansas Gazette* 7 September 1855, 2; Catholics hate Protestants, 19 October 1855, 2; cheat at poker, 5 October 1855, 2; Catholics disloyal to slavery and to the U.S. in the war with Mexico, 19 October 1855, 2, 3; no Bible reading, 31 August 1855, 2; Pope is the Anti-Christ 9 November 1855, 2; Catholics are subversives, tools of the Pope, 26 October 1855, 2.

[107]Ibid., 28 September, 1885, 1.

[108]Ibid., 9 November 1855, 3.

[109]Moore's pamphlet appeared as series in these issues of the *Arkansas Gazette* 23 November 1855, 3; 30 November 1855, 3; 14 December 1855, 3; 28 December 1855, 3; 2 February 1856, 2; 23 February 1856, 3; 29 March 1855, 2. Saunders work appeared 12 July 1856, 3; 19 July 1856, 3; 2 August 1856, 3; 9 August 1855, 2; 16 August 1855, 2; 23 August 1855, 3; 30 August 1855, 3.

[110]Ibid., 17 August 1855, 2; 5 October 1855, 2; 2 November 1855, 2; 2 February 1856, 2. The "connubial felicity" quote from 14 December 1855, 3.

[111]"Backslidden Baptist" Little Rock *True Democrat*, 1 January 1856, 2. Editor Richard H. Johnson brought up this charge against Borland in early December and apparently it had some truth for Borland refused to talk about it. Johnson later taunted him for not discussing it. 11 December 1855, 2; 18 December 1855, 2. Borland said the charge was indecent and would not talk about it. Given his temper and his past outbursts, if the charge was not true, Borland would have probably shot Johnson. Borland's views, Little Rock *Arkansas Gazette*, 14 December 1855, 2; 28 December 1855, 2.

[112]Little Rock *Arkansas Gazette*, 26 April 1856, 2.

[113]Little Rock *True Democrat*, 14 August 1855, 2; 21 August 1855, 2; 11 September 1855, 2.

[114]Ibid., 4 March 1856, 2.

[115]For Carroll's successful election to the state House of Representatives, see Little Rock Arkansas Gazette, 9 August 1850, 2. Concerning Creed Taylor, the Know Nothing organ, *Gazette*, relished telling its readers that the chairman of the state Democratic convention, "is a firm believer in, and an adherent to, the Roman Catholic Faith." Little Rock *Arkansas Gazette* 10 May

1856, 2. Taylor had been the one to donate some land to the Sisters of Loretto to build the first Catholic school in Arkansas. Hockle, "Catholic Schools", 4.

[116]Woods, *Rebellion and Realignment,* 63, 222, n. 84, n. 85, n. 87.

[117]Both quotes from Little Rock *Arkansas Gazette,* 13 June 1857, 2.

[118]Little Rock *Arkansas Gazette,* 11 December 1858, 2.

[119]Baudier, *Catholic Church in Louisiana,* 377. For a fuller treatment of the First Plenary Council of the American Catholic Bishops in May, 1852 and what it stated see Hennesey, *American Catholics,* 109, 114; Spalding, *The Premier See,* 154-155.

[120]Blanc to Byrne, 25 April 1855, Byrne Papers, ADLR.

[121]Baudier, *Catholic Church in Louisiana,* 377-378.

[122]Byrne to Blanc, 17 January 1857, Blanc Papers, AANO.

[123]Byrne to Nagle, 14 October 1858, 20 May 1859, Byrne Papers, ADLR. Kenneally, *U.S. Documents in the Propaganda Fide Archives,* 4:351; 7:41, 58.

[124]Fr. Patrick Behan to Fr. Napoleon Joseph Perche, 14 July 1856, AANO.

[125]Behan to Blanc, 3 November 1856; Reilly to Blanc, 17 November 1856, Blanc Papers, AANO.

[126]Fr. Philip Shanahan to Blanc, 17 November 1856, Blanc Papers, AANO.

[127]Byrne to Blanc, 17 January 1857; 2 April 1857, Blanc Papers, AANO.

[128]Byrne to Blanc, 3 December 1857, 14 December 1857, Blanc Papers, AANO. The two men were Henry Biscoe and Thomas Hanly. For Biscoe's position, see Woods, *Rebellion and Realignment,* 72; Hanly later a Confederate Congressman, James M. Woods, "Devotees and Dissenters: Arkansans in the Confederate Congress, 1861-1865" *Arkansas Historical Quarterly* 38 (Autumn 1979): 235-236, 246.

[129]Carroll, Leaves from the Annals, 343; *Metropolitan Catholic Almanac,* 1859, 124.

[130]Byrne to Blanc, 7 April 1859, Blanc Papers, AANO.

[131]*Metropolitan Catholic Almanac,* 1859, 124.

[132]Byrne to Blanc, 8 November 1858, 22 November 1858, 7 April 1859, Blanc Papers, AANO.

[133]Byrne to Blanc, 12 November 1859, Blanc Papers, AANO.

[134]Byrne to Blanc, 3 November 1859, Blanc Papers, AANO.

[135]Guy, "Catholic Church in Arkansas," 113.

[136]Behan to Byrne, 22 December 1858. An earlier letter also mentions some strange things which Fr. Clarke had done, 1 November 1858. Both letters are in Byrne Papers, ADLR.

[137]Byrne to Smyth, 15 March 1860; Byrne to Clarke, 21 May 1860, 30 June 1860; Byrne to Smyth, 30 June 1860, all letters in Byrne Papers, ADLR.

[138]The circumstances surrounding the death of the black man are rather vaguely mentioned in Byrne to Clarke, 30 June 1860.

[139]Ibid., Byrne to Smyth, 30 June 1860.

[140]Baudier, *Catholic Church in Louisiana,* 378.

[141]*Metropolitan Catholic Almanac,* 1860, 128.

[142]U.S. Department of the Interior, *The Eighth Census of the United States,* 4 vols. (Washington, D.C.: Government Printing Office, 1864-1866) 1:18, 356.

[143]*Metropolitan Catholic Almanac,* 1861, (Baltimore, MD: John Murphy Co., 1861) 114-116.

[144]Property Abstracts, Pulaski County, Deed Book #6, p. 55. Diocese of Little Rock. Copy of the act incorporating the Sisters of Mercy, certified as law, January 2, 1861, copy in ADLR.

[145]Archbishop Blanc died on June 20, 1860. His successor was not put into office until the following May. Baudier, *Catholic Church in Louisiana,* 401, 412. For Byrne's letter, see Byrne to Odin, 23 May 1861, Odin Papers, AANO.

[146]Guy, "Catholic Church in Arkansas," 136.

[147]Byrne to Odin, 4 December 1861, Odin Papers, AANO.

[148]Bakewell to Byrne, 12 March 1862, Byrne Papers, ADLR.

[149]The Will of Rt. Reverend Andrew Byrne, dated 20 June 1859. Copy in Byrne Papers, ADLR.

[150]Lucey, "Souvenir of a Silver Jubilee", 19; Guy, "Catholic Church in Arkansas", 136-137; Little Rock Arkansas Gazette, 1 December 1881, 1.

[151]Guy, "Catholic Church in Arkansas," 137.

[152]Little Rock *Arkansas Gazette,* 28 June 1862, 2.

[153]Allen W. Jones and Virginia Ann Buttry, "Military Events in Arkansas During the Civil War, 1861-1865", *Arkansas Historical Quarterly* 22 (Summer 1963): 146-147.

CHAPTER IV

[1]John Gilmary Shea, *History of the Catholic Church in the United States,* 4 vols. (New York: J.G. Shea, Publishing, 18861892) 4:679.

[2]Fr. Lawrence Smyth to Archbishop Odin, 7 July 1862, Odin Papers, AANO.

[3]That Odin was absent during the latter half of 1862 until early 1863 and in Rome see Roger Baudier, *The Catholic Church in Louisiana* (New Orleans, LA: Private Printing, 1939) 414. Bishop Augustin Martin to Vicar General Patrick Reilly, 12 October 1862, Reilly Papers, ADLR. Bishop Martin informed the New Orleans Archdiocese of his action, see Martin to Vicar General Msgr. Etienne Rousselon, 4 November 1862, Rousselon Papers, AANO.

[4]"Death of the Vicar General of the Diocese of Little Rock." newspaper clipping, unnamed Irish paper, n.d., (1882), n.p. Clipping found in ADLR.

[5]Ibid., Reilly's ordination date was also confirmed by a later source which reported the celebration of his twenty-fifth anniversary on March 17, 1876. Little Rock *Arkansas Gazette,* 18 March 1876, 4. For Reilly's first assignment as priest see statement by Bishop Byrne that Reilly is a priest in good standing, assigned to the cathedral and will work at the boys' school, Statement by Bishop Byrne, 17 May 1851, ADLR. He was also assigned as chaplain for the Sisters of Mercy in Little Rock, see Sr. Teresa Carroll, R.S.M., *Leaves from the Annals of the Sisters of Mercy* (New York: Catholic Publication Society, 1889) 348.

[6]*Metropolitan Catholic Almanac, 1852* (Baltimore, MD: John Murphy, 1852) 166; *Metropolitan Catholic Almanac, 1953,* (Baltimore, MD: John Murphy, 1853) 200; *Metropolitan Catholic Almanac, 1854* (Baltimore, MD: John Murphy, 1854) 226; *Metropolitan Catholic Almanac, 1855* (Baltimore, MD: John Murphy, 1855) 204; *Metropolitan Catholic Almanac, 1856* (Baltimore, MD: John Murphy, 1856) 220; *Metropolitan Catholic Almanac, 1857* (Baltimore, MD: John Murphy, 1857) 252; *Metropolitan Catholic Almanac, 1858* (Baltimore, MD: John Murphy, 1858) 163; *Metropolitan Catholic Almanac, 1859* (Baltimore, MD: John Murphy, 1859) 133; *Metropolitan Catholic Almanac, 1860* (Baltimore, MD: John Murphy, 1860) 127; *Metropolitan Catholic Almanac, 1861* (Baltimore, MD: John Murphy, 1861) 114.

[7]Bishop Martin to Fr. Reilly, 7 December 1862, Reilly Papers, ADLR.

[8]Ibid.

[9]Ibid.

[10]Bishop Martin to Fr. Reilly, 9 June 1863, Reilly Papers, ADLR.

[11]There is at present no real updated story of Arkansas during the Civil War that contains both a military, political, and economic look at the state during wartime. For an early yet very dated look at war, see David Y. Thomas, *Arkansas in War and Reconstruction* (Little Rock, AR: United Daughters of the Confederacy, 1926). Some more recent studies of the war included Michael Dougan, *Confederate Arkansas: The People and Politics of a Frontier State in Wartime* (University, AL: University of Alabama Press, 1976); Bobby Roberts and Carl Moneyhon, *Portraits of Conflict: A Photographic History of Arkansas in the Civil War* (Fayetteville, AR: University of Arkansas Press, 1987). This is perhaps the best book on the subject at present. For a listing of the military events only, see Allen Jones and Virginia Bettry, "Military Events in Arkansas During the Civil War, 1861-1865" *Arkansas Historical Quarterly* 23 (Summer 1963) 124-170. For a very good brief survey of the war consult Margaret Ross, *The Arkansas Gazette: The Early Years, 1819-1866* (Little Rock, AR: Arkansas Gazette Foundation Library, 1969) 357-394.

[12]James M. Woods, "Devotees and Dissenters: Arkansans in the Confederate Congress, 1861-1865" *Arkansas Historical Quarterly* 38 (Autumn 1979): 241-242.

[13]Carroll, *Leaves from the Annals,* 369.

[14]Little Rock *Arkansas Gazette,* 22 August 1863, 2. This is one of the last issues of the *Arkansas Gazette* during the war. Danley was getting the September 13, 1863 issue printed when the Federal troops arrived in the city. Not another issue until May 10, 1865. Ross, *Arkansas Gazette,* 386, 394.

[15]Carroll, *Leaves from the Annals,* 368.

[16]Ibid.; Baudier, *Catholic Church in Louisiana,* 426, 436.

[17]Carroll, *Leaves from the Annals,* 368.

[18]Ibid.

[19]Father John Dunne to Msgr. Reilly, 23 April 1863, Reilly Papers, ADLR.

[20]Dunne to Reilly, 12 June 1863; undated letter, c. late 1863, Reilly Papers, ADLR.

[21]Fr. Dunne to Fr. Reilly, 4 May 1864, 18 May 1864, Reilly Papers, ADLR.

[22]Content of the letter and the quote from Fr. Dunne to Fr. Reilly, 20 June 1864, Reilly Papers, ADLR.

[23]Carroll, *Leaves from the Annals,* 363.

[24]Mr. L. F. Kavanaugh to Fr. Reilly, Administrator, 11 March, (?) May, 1864, 13 June 1865, 14 November 1865, 31 May 1866, Reilly Papers, ADLR.

[25]Society for the Propagation of the Faith, Lyon and Paris, France to Fr. Reilly, Administrator, 26 January 1864, 31 May 1864, 15 January 1865,m 17 June 1865, 14 November 1865, 30 May 1866, Reilly Papers, ADLR. Hereafter the Propagation of the Faith will be abbreviated to POF.

[26]POF to Fr. Reilly, 31 October 1866, Reilly Papers, ADLR.

[27]*Metropolitan Catholic Almanac, 1865,* (New York: J. D. Sadlier, 1865) 204; *Metropolitan Catholic Almanac, 1866,* (New York: J. D. Sadlier, 1866) 229. For my claim that no *Catholic Almanacs* were published in 1862 and 1863 not being published comes from the Sulpician Archivist Fr. John W. Bowen, S.S., in Baltimore, Maryland. At these Sulpician archives, they have a copy of all the Catholic *Almanacs* and *Directories* in print.

[28]*Metropolitan Catholic Almanac, 1864* (New York: J.D. Sadlier, 1864) 196.

[29]Fr. Reilly to Archbishop Jean Marie Odin, 23 April 1865, Odin Papers, AANO.

[30]*Metropolitan Catholic Almanac, 1867* (New york: J.D. Sadlier, 1867) 150.

[31]Dunne on Langhran, see Fr. Dunne to Fr. Reilly, 18 May 1864; Dunne on Cogan, see Fr. Dunne to Fr. Reilly, 4 May 1864. Both letters in Reilly Papers, ADLR.

[32]Fr. D.J. Cogan to Archbishop Jean Odin, 1 October 1864, Odin Papers, AANO. Letter written from Helena. For another source on Cogan at Helena, see Diocesan Historical Commission, *The History of Catholicity in Arkansas* (Little Rock: AR: Guardian Press, 1925) n.p. (p. 105).

[33]Fr. Reilly to Archbishop Odin, 23 April 1865, Odin Papers, AANO.

[34]Fr. Cogan to Archbishop Odin, 9 June 1865, 6 July 1865, 25 July 1865, 28 July 1865, Fr. Reilly to Archbishop Odin, 21 October 1865, 1 March 1866, all letters in Odin Papers, AANO.

[35]Petition to Fr. Reilly, Administrator, from the Catholic Congregation of Helena, 14 July 1866, petition in Reilly Papers, ADLR.

[36]*Metropolitan Catholic Almanac, 1867,* 150; *Metropolitan Catholic Almanac, 1868,* (New York: J.D. Sadlier, 1868) 177; D.H.C., *History of Catholicity in Arkansas,* n.p. (105).

[37]Little Rock *Arkansas Gazette,* 14 July 1866, 1.

[38]For the date of the October 13, 1833, see J. G. Shea, *The Hierarchy of the Catholic Church in the United States Embracing Sketches of All the Archbishops and Bishops From the Establishment of the See at Baltimore to the Present Time.* (New York: Catholic Publishing Society, 1886) 275; for the date October 16, 1866, Rev. John H. Lamott, *A History of the Archdiocese of Cincinnati, 1821-1921* (New York: Frederick Puster, 1921) 353; for the date of 26th, see Svend Petersen, "The Little Rock Against the Big Rock," *Arkansas Historical quarterly* 2 (June 1943) 2:165; for the date of the 28th, see Msgr. James E. O'Connell, "Fitzgerald, Edward" *New Catholic Encyclopedia* 15 vols. (New York: McGraw-Hill, 1966-1967) 5:950. Fitzgerald's baptismal certificate from Ireland sent from the Diocese of Limerick on 20 July 1962. Fitzgerald apparently believed his birth date to be October 28, see Fr. Fintan Kraemer, O.S.B., to Bishop

Fitzgerald, 26 October 1903, 28 October 1904. That his feast day fell on October 13, see Kraemer to Fitzgerald, 12 October 1905. All documents found Fitzgerald Papers, ADLR.

[39]Peterson, "Little Rock Against the Big Rock," 165-166; Lamott, History of the Archdiocese of Cincinnati, 353i Shea, *History of the Hierarchy of the United States*, 275.

[40]Sr. Ann Feth. S.N.D. de N. "Early Years in Columbus of the Sisters of Notre Dame: The Interdict at St. Patrick's, 1857," *Bulletin of the Catholic Record Society, Diocese of Columbus*, 5 (August 1980) 532-534, quote on p. 533.

[41]Certificate of Naturalization, 11 October 1859, Fitzgerald Papers, ADLR.

[42]D.H.C., *History of Catholicity in Arkansas*, n.p. (p. 15). Petersen, "Little Rock Against the Big Rock," 166; Francis Shaw Guy, "The Catholic Church in Arkansas," 143. Papal Bull of appointment, 24 April 1866, Fitzgerald Papers, ADLR.

[43]The Register of Bishop Fitzgerald, 1 September 1866, manuscript in Fitzgerald Papers, ADLR. Hereafter this document will be cited as merely Fitzgerald's Register. Also see letter Fr. Fitzgerald to Archbishop Odin, who mentions that he is turning down the position after spending an eight-day retreat. Fr. Fitzgerald to Archbishop Odin, 31 August 1866, Odin Papers, AANO.

[44]Fr. Reilly to Archbishop Odin, 6 September 1866, Odin Papers, AANO.

[45]Fr. Smyth to Archbishop Odin, 1 September 1866, Odin Papers, AANO.

[46]Ibid.

[47]Fr. Smyth to Archbishop Odin, 6 September 1866, Odin Papers, AANO.

[48]Ibid.

[49]Ibid.

[50]Fitzgerald's Register, (n.d.) October 1866.

[51]Rev. Thomas T. McAvoy, C.S.C. *History of the Catholic Church in the United States*, (Notre Dame, IN: University of Notre Dame, 1969) 199-204.

[52]Fr. Edward Fitzgerald to Archbishop Odin, 7 December 1866, Odin Papers, AANO.

[53]Fitzgerald's Register, October 1866, (n.d.) December 1866; Fitzgerald received the *mandamus* by mid-December, see Bishop William Henry Elder to Archbishop Odin, 22 December 1866, Archbishop Purcell to Archbishop Odin, 27 December 1866, these two letters in Odin Papers, AANO. For the route of the *mandamus* from Odin to Purcell to Fitzgerald, see Odin to Fitzgerald, 15 December 1866. Archbishop Purcell gave him the command from Rome and sent his note with it, Purcell to Fitzgerald, 10 December 1866, last two letters in Fitzgerald Papers, ADLR.

[54]Bishop John Lynch to Fr. Fitzgerald, 24 December 1866, Fitzgerald Papers, ADLR.

[55]Brother Chrysostom, Cistercian Abbey of St. Bernard's Leicestershire, England, to Fr. Fitzgerald, 1 January 1867, Fitzgerald Papers, ADLR.

[56]Guy, "Catholic Church in Arkansas," 144; Fitzgerald's Register, 3 February 1867.

[57]Bp. Fitzgerald to Archbishop Odin, 5 February 1867, Odin Papers, AANO.

[58]Fitzgerald's Register, 27 February 1867, 3, 4, 12, 13, 14, March 1867.

[59]Fitzgerald's Register, 14, 15, 16, March 1867. Arkansas Post was captured and destroyed in January 1863, Dougan, *Confederate Arkansas*, 102.

[60]Fitzgerald's Register, 16, 17 March 1867.

[61]*Metropolitan Catholic Almanac, 1867*, 150.

[62]U.S. Department of the Interior, *The Eighth Census of the United States* 4 vols. (Washington, D.C.: Government Printing Office, 1864-1866) 1:18, 356; Bp. Fitzgerald to Archbishop Purcell of Cincinnati, 31 March 1868, Purcell Papers, AUND.

[63]Fitzgerald's Register, 18 March 1867; Bishop Fitzgerald to Propagation of the Faith, Lyon & Paris, France, 27 March 1867, hereafter cited as POF. The letters of the Diocese of Little Rock are on microfilm at AUND.

[64]Fr. Philip Shanahan left the Diocese in 1866, see Fr. Reilly to Archbishop Odin, 29 June 1866, Odin Papers, AANO. In 1868 Cogan in Helena and Shanahan in Monticello, Iowa. A year later Cogan in Mount Pleasant, Iowa and Shanahan in Pine Bluff, *Metropolitan Catholic Almanac, 1868* (New York: J.D. Sadlier, 1868) 157, 177; *Metropolitan Catholic Almanac, 1869* (New York: J. D. Sadlier, 1869) 171, 203.

[65]Fr. D.J. Cogan to Bishop Fitzgerald, 2 July 1886, 26 September 1866, both letters in ADLR. Fitzgerald and Cogan's differences, see Cogan to Odin, 7 December 1867; Fitzgerald to Cogan 17 December 1867, 3 January 1868, Cogan to Odin 16 January, 10 February, 19 March 1868. In the last three letters, Cogan begged Odin to overrule Fitzgerald, yet the New Orleans archbishop was not willing to intervene in what appeared to be a domestic matter between the priest and his bishop. All letters in Odin Papers, AANO.

[66]Fitzgerald's Register, 18 April 1867, (n.d.) January 1868.

[67]Ibid., 27, 31 March 1867, 6, 10 April 1867.

[68]Fitzgerald dedicated it on August 18, 1867, and the Fort Smith paper called it the Church of the Assumption. Fort Smith *Herald,* n.d., quoted in the Little Rock *Arkansas Gazette,* 3 September 1867, 3. Church completed, *Arkansas Gazette,* 3 November 1867, 3.

[69]Fitzgerald's Register, 18 May 1867.

[70]Washington *Telegraph,* n.d., quoted in the Little Rock *Arkansas Gazette,* 21 May 1867, 2.

[71]Fitzgerald's Register, 18, 25 May 1867, 2 June, 1867.

[72]Ibid., 9, 27 June, 1867, 3, 5, 8, 10 July 1867.

[73]Ibid., 29-31 July 1867.

[74]Ibid., (n.d.) January, 1868, 23 March, 1868; Little Rock *Arkansas Gazette,* 14 April 1868, 3.

[75]Little Rock *Arkansas Gazette,* 21 July 1868, 2. On Fr. James S. O'Kean there is little to his background, except that a German missionary who later followed Fr. O'Kean in Pocahontas maintained that he had come from to Arkansas after first working in the Memphis diocese. This same missionary claims that the O'Kean was a distant relative of Bishop John B. Morris, Fr. Eugene John Weibel, *Forty Years Missionary in Arkansas,* translated by Sr. Mary Agnes Voth, O.S.B. (St. Meinrad, IN: Abbey Press, 1968) 51. Fr. Weibel 1853-1934, served as a Missionary in Arkansas 1879-1919.

[76]Pocahontas *Black River Standard,* n.d., quoted in the Little Rock *Arkansas Gazette,* 20 October 1868, 2.

[77]Ibid.

[78]Little Rock *Arkansas Gazette,* 10 January 1869, 3.

[79]Fr. Cogan to Archbishop Odin, 10 February 1868, Odin Papers, AANO; Msgr. John M. Lucey, *The Catholic Church in Arkansas* (Little Rock, AR: Little Rock Board of Trade, 1906) 22; Guy, "Catholic Church in Arkansas," 145.

[80]*Metropolitan Catholic Almanac, 1869,* 203.

[81]Little Rock *Arkansas Gazette,* 21 August 1869, 3.

[82]*Metropolitan Catholic Almanac 1870* (New York: J.D. Sadlier, 1870) 207-208; Reilly's name listed quite prominently below that of Fitzgerald's name, and the vicar general usually conducts the responsibilities of the diocese in the absence of the bishop.

[83]McAvoy, *Catholic Church in the United States,* 210-211, Fr. McAvoy lists the names of the archbishops and bishops who were there, p. 211.

[84]James Hennesey, S.J., *American Catholic: A History of the Roman Catholic Community in the United States* (New York: Oxford University Press, 1981) 168.

[85]McAvoy, *Catholic Church in the United States,* 211. For this description of the council I have leaned on the brief accounts recorded in Fr. McAvoy's book, pp. 211-217; Hennessey, *American Catholics,* 168-171. and the most complete book-length account of the council from the experience of American Catholic archbishops and bishops, see James Hennessey, S.J., *The First Council of the Vatican: The American Experience* (New York: Herder & Herder, 1963).

[86]Henri Daniel-Rops, *The Church in the Age of Revolution, 1789-1870* (New York: E.P. Dutton & Company, 1965) 293. For an important new book on the French minority bishops see Margaret O'Gara, *Triumph in Defeat: Infallibility, Vatican I, and the French Minority Bishops* (Washington, D.C.: Catholic University of America Press, 1988); also see Hennesey, *The First Council of the Vatican,* passim.

[87]Hennesey, *American Catholics,* 169; McAvoy, *Catholic Church in the United States,* 213.

[88]McAvoy, *Catholic Church in the United States,* 213. Fr. McAvoy provides all the names of seventeen bishops on the same page. Hennessey, *The First Council of the Vatican,* 101, 124.

[89]Petersen, "Little Rock Against the Big Rock," 166; for Gibbons' age and his position at the time of the council, Hennesey, *American Catholics*, 179; for a fuller account of the life of Cardinal James Gibbons of Baltimore with particular attention to his early life and career through the First Vatican Council see Monsignor John Tracy Ellis, *The Life of James Cardinal Gibbons: Archbishop of Baltimore, 1834-1921*, 2 vols. (Milwaukee, WI: Bruce Publishing Co., 1952) 1:1-100. Msgr. Ellis records that Gibbons was born on July 23, 1834, about nine months after Fitzgerald, p. 3.

[90]For Kenrick's role, see Fr. John Rothensteiner, *History of the Archdiocese of St. Louis: In Its Various Stages of Development From A.D. 1673 to A.D. 1928* 2 vols (St. Louis, MO: Blackwell, Wielandy & Co., 1928) 303-311. For Bishop Verot's activities at the Council see Fr. Michael V. Gannon, *Rebel Bishop: The Life and Era of Augustin Verot, Confederate Bishop and 'Enfant Terrible' of the First Vatican Council* (Milwaukee, WI: Bruce Publishing Company, 1964) 192-227; Hennessey, *The First Council of the Vatican*, passim.

[91]McAvoy, *History of the Catholic Church in the United States*, 214; Hennessey, *The First Council of the Vatican*, 177-178.

[92]McAvoy, *History of the Catholic Church in the United States*, 214-215; Hennessey, *American Catholics*, 169170; Rothensteiner, *History of the Archdiocese of St. Louis*, 2:309.

[93]Hennesey, *American Catholics*, 169; Rothensteiner, *History of the Archdiocese of St. Louis*, 2:310-311. For a brief presentation and discussion of Archbishop Kenrick's treatise see Hennesey, *The First Council of the Vatican*, 244-250.

[94]Bishop Fitzgerald to Mother Alphonsus Carton, 25 April 1870. The last name of Mother Alphonsus given in a later letter to her from Fitzgerald, Fitzgerald to Mother Alphonsus Carton 22 September 1873, letters in Fitzgerald Papers, ADLR.

[95]Fitzgerald to Mother Alphonsus Carton, 25 April 1870, Fitzgerald Papers, ADLR.

[96]Ibid.

[97]Ibid.

[98]Bishop Fitzgerald to Mother Mary Alphonsus Carton, 17 June 1870, Fitzgerald Papers, ADLR.

[99]Hubert Larkin, "The Late Bishop Fitzgerald at the Vatican Council," newspaper clipping, John Joyce scrapbook, ADLR.

[100]Ibid.

[101]Ibid.

[102]Ibid.

[103]Ibid.

[104]Fr. Joseph McHugh, "Papal Infallibility," *God's Word Today*, 10 (July 1988): 47, 48; that the minority position did win some major concessions from the papacy is spelled even more in O'Gara, *Triumph in Defeat*, 89-269.

[105]McHugh, "Papal Infallibility," 48. For a fuller text of the document as it was first proposed and what was finally approved see O'Gara, *Triumph in Defeat*, 257-269.

[106]McAvoy, *History of the Catholic Church in the United States*, 215; Petersen, "Little Rock Against the Big Rock," 167. Fr. Hennessey lists all the American prelates and how they voted, Hennessey, *The First Council of the Vatican*, 274, n. #3; yet he inadvertently left out Bishop Verot in his count. For the vote of the Savannah bishop and the fact that Purcell and Whelan did not participate see Gannon, *Rebel Bishop*, 219, 219 n. 77.

[107]Hennessey, *First Council of the Vatican*, 279-280.

[108]Ibid., 281.

[109]The twenty-five who voted *placet* listed in Hennesey, *The First Council of the Vatican*, 281-282. From that list one can ascertain those who did not vote for or against the declaration. Gibbons is not in the initial list of those who voted *placet* on July 13th, but the future prominent churchman was there for the final vote, see Ibid., 274 n. 3; 281-282; Ellis, *Life of James Cardinal Gibbons*, 1:99-100.

[110]Larkin, "Late Bishop Fitzgerald at the Vatican Council," n.d., n.p.

[111]McAvoy, *History of the Catholic Church in the United States*, 215-216; Petersen, "Little

Rock Against the Big Rock," 167; Gannon, *Rebel Bishop*, 219; Guy, "Catholic Church in Arkansas," 149-150; Hennesey, *The First Council of the Vatican*, 281, the vote of all the American archbishops and bishops on pp. 281-282.

[112]Guy, "Catholic Church in Arkansas," 150; Petersen, "Little Rock Against the Big Rock," 168; Rothensteiner, *History of the Archdiocese of St. Louis*, 2:311, note #10; Hennesey, *The First Council of the Vatican*, 281.

[113]Petersen, "Little Rock Against the Big Rock," 170.

[114]Fitzgerald had just left on October 27, 1869, and arrived back the same day, Little Rock *Arkansas Gazette*, 27 October 1869, 4; 28 October 1870, 4.

[115]Ibid., 30 October 1870, 4.

[116]Ibid.

[117]Ibid.

[118]Ibid.

[119]Rothensteiner, *History of the Archdiocese of St. Louis*, 2: 312-318; Gannon, Rebel Bishop, 223-224; McAvoy, *History of the Catholic Church in the United States*, 216; Gerland P. Fogarty, D.J., *The Vatican and the American Hierarchy from 1870 to 1965* (Wilmington, DE: Michael Glazier, 1985) 1-9; Hennesey, *The First Council of the Vatican*, 294-327.

[120]Little Rock *Arkansas Gazette*, 19 May 1871, 4.

[121]Bishop Edward M. Fitzgerald, "The Vatican Council: Ten Years After," address in manuscript, Fitzgerald Papers, ADLR.

[122]Ibid.

[123]Ibid.

[124]Ibid.

[125]Ibid.

[126]Ibid.

[127]Hennesey, *The First Council of the Vatican*, 161.

[128]Diary of Fr. Peter Benoit, S.S.J, 18 April 1875, transcript p. 235. This transcript in the Archives of the Society of St. Joseph, Baltimore, Maryland. A portion of that transcript that pertains to Benoit's visit with Fitzgerald is in the ADLR, and I have used that document for my citation.

[129]Ibid.

[130]Ibid.

CHAPTER V

[1]*Catholic Directory, 1870* (New York: J.D. Sadlier, 1870) 207-208; *Catholic Directory, 1871* (New York: J.D. Sadlier, 1871) 202-203.

[2]Fr. John M. Lucey, "Souvenir of a Silver Jubilee, February 3, 1892," typescript copy in ADLR.

[3]Bishop Fitzgerald to Propagation of the Faith, Lyon, France, 13 November 1874, microfilm copy of this letter found in AUND. Hereafter, all references to French missionary society, Propagation of the Faith will be referred to simply as POF.

[4]Fitzgerald to POF, 21 August 1871, AUND. This was a French Missionary Society which gave money to the American Catholic Church. See *New Catholic Encyclopedia* 15 vols. (New York: McGraw-Hill, 1967) 11:844-846.

[5]Roger Baudier, The Catholic Church in Louisiana (New Orleans, La: Private Printing, 1939) 445.

[6]*Catholic Directory,* 1873 (New York: J.D. Sadlier, 1873), 212-213. On Lucey ordination and assignment see Lucey papers, Deceased Priest File, ADLR. In a parish history of Immaculate Conception Church in Fort Smith, Fr. Lawrence Smyth's first name is spelled "Laurence." No author listed, *Church of the Immaculate Conception: Fort Smith, Arkansas, 1868-1968* (Fort Smith, AR: Private Printing, 1969) n.p. (p. 8.)

[7]Camden *Journal* n.d., quoted in the Little Rock *Arkansas Gazette*, 27 May 1873, 2.

[8]Fitzgerald to POF, 13 November 1874, AUND.

[9]Fitzgerald to POF, 3 December 1872, AUND. For the material on Fr. Marivault and Fr. Miege and the Indian Territory see *Metropolitan Catholic Almanac, 1850* (Baltimore, Md: John Murphy & Co., 1850) 153; *Metropolitan Catholic Almanac, 1852* (Baltimore, Md.: John Murphy & Co., 1852) 165; *Metropolitan Catholic Almanac, 1857* (Baltimore, Md.: John Murphy & Co., 1857) 252; *Metropolitan Catholic Almanac, 1858* (Baltimore, Md.: John Murphy & Co., 1858) 163; *Metropolitan Catholic Almanac, 1859* (Baltimore, Md., John Murphy & Co., 1859) 124.

[10]Fr. Jean B. Miege, S.J., to Bishop Byrne, 18 September 1860, Byrne Papers, ADLR.

[11]Fitzgerald to POF, 12 January 1873, AUND. In his letter to Archbishop Purcell, Fitzgerald revealed that he asked to be relieved of the Indian Territory at the meeting of bishops in New Orleans in January, 1873. Fitzgerald to Purcell, 6 March 1873, Purcell Papers, AUND.

[12]Fitzgerald to POF, 11 November 1875, AUND. That Robot arrived in the fall of 1875, see Fr. James White, historian of the Diocese of Tulsa, letter to Mr. Dorothy Mulvey, 21 October 1988. This letter in possession of the author.

[13]This question as to when the Indian Territory became assigned to Little Rock and when it was separated has not been easy to settle. Much of the information in the text has been discovered by Fr. James D. White, historian for the Diocese of Tulsa. Fitzgerald to Fr. Charles Ewing, 12 February 1875, Fitzgerald to Ewing 7 May 1879; Fr. Isidore Robot to Mary Elizabeth Rex, 17 December 1875, letter in French. These letters are in the Archives of the Bureau of Catholic Indian Missions, Marquette University, Milwaukee, Wisconsin. Copies of these documents, and the translation of Robot letter to Mrs. Rex provided to the author by Fr. James D. White, historian of the Diocese of Tulsa. I am greatly in his debt.

[14]The date of the Indian Territory's separation is revealed in a letter from Archbishop Francis Janssens of New Orleans to Cardinal Giovanni Simeoni, Prefect of the Propagation of the Faith office in Rome, Italy, 20 November 1889, letter in Latin found in the AANO. This letter discovered by Fr. James D. White of the Diocese of Tulsa and who graciously provided me a copy of this document as well as a translation. From this translation, Archbishop Janssens wrote the Vatican official that the Indian "territory that was erected into a Prefecture Apostolic in 1876 had been contained in the Diocese of Little Rock."

[15]Fitzgerald to Purcell, 8 December 1873, Purcell Papers, AUND.

[16]Ibid.

[17]Ibid.

[18]Ibid.

[19]Ibid.

[20]Ibid.

[21]Bishop Joseph Durenger to Archbishop Purcell, 11 September 1873, Purcell Papers, AUND.

[22]Archbishop Perche to Bishop Fitzgerald, 2 February 1874, Fitzgerald Papers, ADLR.

[23]Ibid.

[24]Ibid.

[25]Fitzgerald to POF, 12 January 1873, AUND.

[26]Fitzgerald to POF, 16 October 1873, AUND.

[27]Fitzgerald to POF, 13 November 1874, AUND.

[28]*Catholic Directory, 1875* (New York: J.D. Sadlier & Co. 1875) 218-219. Fr. Quinn was first mentioned as working in eastern Arkansas in the directory in the previous year. *Catholic Directory, 1874* (New York: J.D. Sadlier, 1874) 218-219. The pagination is the same in the *Directory* for both of these years.

[29]Rev. D.A. Quinn, *Heroes and Heroines of Memphis: or Reminiscences of the Yellow Fever That Afflicted the City of Memphis During the Autumn Months of 1873, 1878, 1879, To Which is Addended a Graphic Description of Missionary Life in Eastern Arkansas* (Providence, RI: R.L. Reeman and Son, State Printers, 1887). That Quinn served at St. Brigid's Parish at the start of the epidemic see Thomas L. Stritch, *The Catholic Church in Tennessee: The Sesquicentennial Story* (Nashville, TN: The Catholic Center, 1987) 196. For a general account of the yellow fever epidemic see the early work of Gerald M. Capers, "The Yellow Fever Epidemics in

Memphis in the 1870s'," *Mississippi Valley Historical Review* 24 (March, 1938): 483-502. Gerald M. Capers, *The Biography of a Rivertown, Memphis: Its Heroic Age* (Chapel Hill, NC: University of North Carolina Press, 1939) 67-94. For more recent works see John H. Ellis, "Yellow Fever and the Origins of Modern Public Health in Memphis, 1870-1900." (Ph.D. dissertation, Tulane University, 1962); Harold T. Smith, *The Commercial Appeal: A History of a Southern Newspaper* (Baton Rouge, LA: Louisiana State University Press, 1971) 131-134; Dennis Rousey, "Yellow Fever and Black Policemen: A Post-Reconstruction Anomaly," *The Journal of Southern History* 51 (August, 1985): 357-374

[30]Quinn, *Heroes and Heroines, A Graphic Description*, 235.

[31]Ibid., 236-237.

[32]Ibid., 237.

[33]Ibid., 237-238.

[34]Ibid., 238.

[35]Ibid., 238.

[36]Ibid., 246.

[37]Ibid.

[38]Ibid., 247-249; comment on the weather and the railroad schedule, p. 248.

[39]Ibid., 250.

[40]Ibid., 252-253.

[41]Ibid., 266-271, quote on "dreary wilderness" on p. 270.

[42]Ibid., 271-272.

[43]Ibid., 266-268, 275-276, 282.

[44]Ibid., 289.

[45]Ibid., 291.

[46]Ibid., 294.

[47]Ibid., 296.

[48]Ibid., 299.

[49]Ibid., 300.

[50]Ibid., 301-302.

[51]Ibid., 303.

[52]Fr. John M. Lucey, "Souvenir of a Silver Jubilee, February 3, 1892," n.p., p. 34. *Catholic Directory, 1875* (New York: J.D. Sadlier, 1875) 219; *Catholic Directory, 1876* (New York: J.D. Sadlier, 1876) 293.

[53]Little Rock *Arkansas Gazette,* 11 December 1875, 4.

[54]Ibid., 18 March 1876, 4; Bishop Fitzgerald, it was reported, said a memorial Mass on the third anniversary of the death of Fr. James O'Kean in Little Rock in late July 1877. *Arkansas Gazette*, 28 July 1877, 4. For Fr. O'Kean's death and the town being named for him see Fr. E.J. Weibel, *Forty Years Missionary in Arkansas* translated by Sr. Mary Agnus Voth, O.S.B. (St. Meinrad, IN: Abbey Press, 1968) 53, 71, 86, 87.

[55]Fitzgerald to POF, 24 October 1876, AUND.

[56]Little Rock *Arkansas Gazette*, 7 January 1877, 4.

[57]*Catholic Directory, 1878* (New York: J.D. Sadlier, 1878) 295. This institution not listed a year later, though in some later directories it did mention a few orphans still being cared for. *Catholic Directory, 1879* (New York: J.D. Sadlier, 1879) 298; *Catholic Directory, 1880* (New York: J.D. Sadlier, 1880) 297.

[58]Little Rock *Arkansas Gazette*, 9 December 1877, 4.

[59]Fitzgerald to POF, 1 December 1877, 12 November 1881, AUND.

[60]Lucey, "Souvenir of a Silver Jubilee," 30.

[61]Memphis *Herald*, n.d., quoted in the Little Rock *Arkansas Gazette*, 5 April 1878, 4. Fr. Quinn recorded his opinion that at that time, in this church just across the river from Memphis, Tennessee, Bishop Fitzgerald "delivered one of his finest lectures on the occasion. Indeed, myself and many others who could hear him through the open doors and windows, felt mortified that such beautiful thoughts, choice language and zealous efforts should be lost with luke-warm

pagans and semi-civilized natives, incapable of appreciating his eloquence or estimating the spiritual import and depth of his discourse." Quinn, *Heroes and Heroines: A Graphic Description*, 303.

[62]The whole ceremony described in Little Rock *Arkansas Gazette*, 9 July 1878, 4.

[63]Little Rock *Arkansas Gazette*, 17 August 1879, 2.

[64]*New Catholic Encyclopedia* 15 vols. (New York: McGraw-Hill, 1967) 3:876.

[65]Bishop William McCloskey to Bishop Fitzgerald, 23 October 1879, Fitzgerald Papers, ADLR.

[66]That Fitzgerald was the choice of the Cincinnati Province and that he withdrew his name from consideration is from Fr. Gerald P. Fogarty, S.J., see *The Vatican and the American Hierarchy From 1870 to 1965* (Wilmington, DE: Michael Glazier, 1985) 21.

[67]Lucey, "Souvenir of a Silver Jubilee," p. 32.

[68]Ibid., Diocesan Historical Commission, *The History of Catholicity in Arkansas* (Little Rock, AR: Guardian Press, 1924) n.p., 32. Their names are on the high altar at the Cathedral.

[69]D.H.C., *History of Catholicity in Arkansas*, n.p., (32).

[70]For a full description of the ceremony, see Little Rock *Arkansas Gazette*, 29 November 1881, 4.

[71]D.H.C. *History of Catholicity in Arkansas*, n.p. (32); *Catholic Directory, 1890*, (New York: J.D. Sadlier, 1890) 282; *Catholic Directory, 1899*, (New York: J.D. Sadlier, 1899) 347

[72]Obituary, newspaper clipping, unnamed Irish newspaper, n.d., n.p., clipping found in ADLR.

[73]D.H.C., *History of Catholicity in Arkansas*, n.p., (32); *Catholic Directory, 1881*, (New York: J.D. Sadlier, 1881) 325; *Catholic Directory, 1883* (New York: J.D. Sadlier, 1883) 356; *Catholic Directory, 1884*, (New York: J.D. Sadlier, 1884) 343; *Catholic Directory, 1890* (New York: J.D. Sadlier, 1890) 281.

[74]Little Rock *Arkansas Gazette*, 1 December 1882, 4.

[75]Archbishop William Elder to Bishop Fitzgerald, 4 December 1882, Fitzgerald Papers, ADLR.

[76]Fitzgerald to POF, 1 November 1880, AUND.

[77]Fitzgerald to POF, 12 November 1881, AUND; U.S. Department of the Interior, *The Tenth Census of the United States*, 3 vols. (Washington, D.C: Government Printing Office, 1883-1885) 1:378. On the white population in Arkansas in 1880, see U.S. Department of the Interior, *Compendium of the Tenth Census* (Washington, D.C.: Government Printing Office, 1886) 2. For the Catholics in Arkansas of the free, mostly white population in Arkansas in 1850 see James M. Woods, *Rebellion & Realignment: Arkansas' Road to Secession*, (Fayetteville, AR: University of Arkansas Press, 1987) 64, 223.

[78]Fitzgerald to POF, 19 January 1882, AUND.

[79]Fitzgerald to POF, 18 November 1882, AUND.

[80]*Catholic Directory, 1885*, (New York: J.D. Sadlier, 1885) 240-241.

[81]Archbishop Perche was near death by the fall of 1883, and he would die by January 2, 1884; Baudier, *Catholic Church in Louisiana*, 463. Fitzgerald trip to Rome was covered in Little Rock *Arkansas Gazette*, 4 October 1883, 2; Halliman served as vicar general while Fitzgerald was out of Arkansas, Lucey, "Souvenir of a Silver Jubilee," 40.

[82]Fitzgerald informed in early 1884, Fitzgerald accepted the invitation in March, Fitzgerald to Monsignor Foley, 20 March 1884, Foley Papers, AAB. That Fitzgerald was given the invitation, see Rev. Msgr. Peter Guilday, *A History of the Councils of Baltimore, 1784-1884* (New York: MacMillen Press, 1932) 140.

[83]*Memorial Volume of the Third Plenary Council*, (Baltimore, MD: Baltimore Publishing Company, 1885) 177-184. A very youthful looking picture of Bishop Fitzgerald appears on p. 185.

[84]Fitzgerald quoted in Jay P. Dolan, *The American Catholic Experience: From Colonial Times to the Present*, (Garden City, NY: Doubleday & Co., 1985) 272.

[85]Ibid., 291-292; James Hennesey, S.J., *American Catholics: A History of the Roman Catholic Community in the United States*, (New York: Oxford University Press, 1981) 107, 182.

[86]Bishop Fitzgerald to Archbishop Gibbons, 14 February 1887, Gibbons Papers, AAB.

[87]Ibid.

[88]Ibid.

[89]Ibid. Bishop Janssens was born in Holland in 1843. Baudier, *Catholic Church in Louisiana*, 473.

[90]Leray died in Chateau Giron in France and Janssens was appointed in August 7, 1888 and he took charge of the Archdiocese on September 13, 1888. Baudier, *Catholic Church in Louisiana*, 467, 473.

[91]Cardinal Gibbons to Bishop Fitzgerald, 1 March 1887, Fitzgerald Papers, ADLR. For the role Cardinal Gibbons would play in halting a Vatican condemnation of labor unions in general and the Knights of Labor in particular see Monsignor John Tracy Ellis, *The Life of James Cardinal Gibbons: The Archbishop of Baltimore, 1934-1921*, 2 vols. (Milwaukee, WI: Bruce Publishing Co., 1952) 1: 486-594.

[92]Cardinal Gibbons to Bishop Fitzgerald, 1 March 1887, Fitzgerald Papers, ADLR.

[93]Bishop Fitzgerald to Cardinal Gibbons, 19 March 1887, Gibbons Papers, AAB.

[94]Bishop Fitzgerald to Cardinal Gibbons, 20 March 1887, Gibbons Papers, AAB.

[95]Archbishop Patrick John Ryan of Philadelphia to Fitzgerald, 17 July 1887, Fitzgerald Papers, ADLR.

[96]Little Rock *Arkansas Gazette*, 13 March 1886, 8. This article contains the whole will of Mr. Alexander Hager.

[97]Ibid., 18 May 1888, 5. The *Arkansas Gazette* would later report that "one year ago today, the Little Rock Infirmary opened" 14 July 1889, 5.

[98]Ibid, 14 July 1889, 5. For the name change by 1890, see *Catholic Directory, 1890* (New York: J.D. Sadlier, 1890) 278. This directory also lists the new hospital in Hot Springs.

[99]Little Rock *Arkansas Gazette*, 25 August 1888, n.p.; 28 November 1889, n.p., both newspaper clippings found in Lucey scrapbooks, ADLR.

[100]*Catholic Directory, 1890*, 283.

[101]Fitzgerald to POF, 19 November 1890, AUND.

[102]The number of Catholics in Arkansas 1890 taken from U.S. Department of Commerce and Labor, *Special Report: Religious Bodies in the United States*, 2 vols. (Washington, D.C.: Government Printing Office, 1907) 1:49; the total population in 1890 in Arkansas was 1,128,179, the total white population was 804,658, both numbers from U.S. Department of the Interior, *Abstract to the Eleventh Census, 1890* (Washington, D.C.: Government Printing Office, 1896) 10, 11.

[103]The figures reported in the text came from the number of religious members or communicants reported nationally and by each state reported by the Census in 1890. The author then that number and divided by the total population listed for that year to arrive at the percentages given. This from U.S. Dept of Commerce and Labor, Religious Bodies in the United States, 1: 48-49; U.S. Dept of Interior, *Abstract of the Eleventh Census*, 10.

[104]Terry's campaign coverage can be followed in the *Arkansas Gazette*. He announced in March, secured the *Gazette*'s endorsement the next month, and was nominated by the Democratic party convention in June. The election was in November. Little Rock *Arkansas Gazette*, 6 March 1890, 8; 4 April 1890, 4; 18 June 1890, 1; 8 November 1890, 1; counties he won, 9 November 1890, 1. The Terry family in Little Rock has long been active in politics; One member of the family, Francis Terry, was one of the members of the state Democratic party who walked out of the Democratic convention in 1860 and was a state senator in the Arkansas legislature 1860-61 and a supporter of secession, Woods, *Rebellion and Realignment*, 117, 130, 234 n. 59. William L. Terry's background in U.S. Congress, *Biographical Directory of the United States Congress, 1774-1971* (Washington, D.C.: Government Printing Office, 1971) 1801.

[105]U.S. Congress, *Biographical Directory of the United States Congress, 1774-1971*, 1801.

[106]That Parker converted to Catholicism on November 15, 1896 just two days before his death is in a parish history of Immaculate Conception Church, *Church of the Immaculate*

Conception, Fort Smith, Arkansas, n.p. (p. 9.) That Parker's wife was Mary O'Toole and a fervent Catholic and that Fr. Smyth conducted the funeral services at Immaculate Conception Church and sprinkled holy water upon his grave the next day is all in Glenn Shirley, *Law West of Fort Smith: A History of Frontier Justice in the Indian Territory, 1834-1896* (Lincoln, NE: University of Nebraska Press, 1957, Paperback Edition, 1968) 26, 205. Shirley's book a classic account of frontier justice in Judge Parker's court. There is also a record of his baptism in the baptismal register for the parish of Immaculate Conception, Fort Smith, Arkansas. Parish Records, ADLR.

[107]This story had been told to me quite often by people who have had long careers in the Diocese and who grew up Catholic in Fort Smith. This story mainly taken from taped interview with Msgr. James O'Connell with James M. Woods, 14 August 1989, copy of tape in ADLR. A Mr. Thomas J. Sexton of Little Rock grew up in Fort Smith and his family were long-time church members. He also has a version of this story that differs only slightly from Msgr. O'Connell's.

[108]Little Rock *Arkansas Gazette,* 4 February 1892, 5.

[109]Ibid., 3 February 1890, 2.

[110]Ibid., 4 February 1892, 5.

[111]The whole ceremony described in Ibid., 4 February 1892, 4-5.

[112]All quotes from Little Rock *Arkansas Gazette,* 4 February 1892, 6. This article first appeared in the *Gazette,* but a typescript copy of this article called "Souvenir of a Silver Jubilee, February 3, 1892" was written later by Fr. John M. Lucey, and this comment is repeated there on p. 40.

[113]Little Rock *Arkansas Gazette,* 4 February 1892, 5.

[114]Cardinal Miecislaus H. Ledochowski, 1822-1902, was by 1892 prefect of the Propaganda Office, which meant that he oversaw developments in missionary lands, and that included the United States until 1908. This position he held from 1892 until his death a decade later. Cardinal Ledochowski had Archbishop Janssens send Bishop Fitzgerald to assume control of the Diocese of Dallas. Archbishop Janssens to Fitzgerald, 2 December 1892, ADLR. That Fitzgerald arrived there by New Year's Day, said Mass in the Dallas Catholic Church where he introduced himself and told the congregation that he had come to assume control of the diocese as ordered by the Vatican, see Dallas *Morning News,* 2 January 1893, n.p., newspaper clipping, Lucey scrapbook, ADLR. A recent book on the history of the Catholic Church in Texas from 1836-1900 provides an account of Bishop Brennan and his administration at Dallas. James Talmadge Moore, *Through Fire and Flood: The Catholic Church in Frontier Texas, 1836-1900* (College Station, TX: Texas A & M University Press, 1992) 222-236.

[115]That Dunne arrived in Dallas in December and that he generally approved of the way things were handled by Fitzgerald, see his letters to Fitzgerald, 20 January 1894, 1 March 1894, 20 March 1894, 30 September 1894, all in Fitzgerald Papers, ADLR. A petition praising Fitzgerald was signed by 25 citizens and sent to Rome, dated 9 February 1893, Propaganda Fide microfilm, Dallas Diocese, AUND.

[116]John Moore to Propaganda Fide Office, 19 April 1893, Propaganda Fide microfilm collection, Dallas Diocese, AUND.

[117]Bishop Fitzgerald to Propaganda Fide office, 15 September 1893, Propaganda Fide microfilm collection, Dallas Diocese, AUND.

[118]Fitzgerald to POF, 13 November 1893, AUND.

[119]Fitzgerald to POF, 30 November 1894, AUND.

[120]The New Orleans Provincial meeting described in Baudier, *Church in Louisiana,* 476, newspaper clipping, n.d., n.p., Lucey scrapbook, ADLR.

[121]Pine Bluff *Press Eagle,* n.d., n.p., Lucey scrapbook, ADLR. Within the archives there are some 90 to 100 manuscript copies of his sermons. These sources could be quite useful for a future biography of Bishop Fitzgerald.

[122]Minutes of the Meeting of the Archbishops, Philadelphia, 10 October 1894, Fitzgerald Papers, ADLR.

[123]Fitzgerald to Gibbons 20 June 1897 Gibbons Papers, AAB; Bishop Edward Allen of Mobile to Bishop Fitzgerald 3 August 1897; Bishop Edward Dunne of Dallas to Bishop Fitzgerald

1 July 1897, Fitzgerald Papers, ADLR.

[124]The figures came from the Directory of 1868, the first one prepared by Fitzgerald when he came in Arkansas in the spring of 1867. They reflected the condition of the Church in the fall of 1867. Also for the description of the Church in 1900 it usually reflected the condition of the Church in the fall of 1899. *Catholic Directory, 1868* (New York: J.D. Sadlier, 1868) 177-178; *Catholic Directory, 1900* (New York: J.D. Sadlier, 1900) 358-361.

[125]*Catholic Directory,* 1900, 361.

[126]Ibid., regarding Fitzgerald's estimate of Catholics. For the total population of the state of Arkansas in 1900 see U.S. Department of Commerce, *Historical Statistics of the United States* 2 vols (Washington, D.C.: Government Printing Office, 1975) 1:24.

[127]Weibel, *Forty Years Missionary in Arkansas,* 147.

[128]Ibid., 147-148; Little Rock *Arkansas Gazette,* February 1900, n.p.; 10 February 1900, n.p. Lucey scrapbook, ADLR.

[129]Fr. Callaghan is supposed to have died in New York City in December 1900, according to one early account of Arkansas Catholicism. D.H.C., *History of Catholicity in Arkansas,* n.p. (32). This information contradicted by a more reliable source. This source from May, 1900 reports on the death of Callaghan in December 1899 and mentions Fr. Fintan Kraemer was offered the position of Vicar General after Fr. Callahan's death. Fr. Eugene J. Weibel et. al., "Memorial of the Priests of Northeast Arkansas to the Right Reverend Bishops of the Province of New Orleans, 22 May 1900, 1, 3. This four page printed document found in Fitzgerald Papers, ADLR. For another source on Callaghan's death in December 1899, see Fr. Michael McGill to Cardinal Ledowchowski, 23 February 1900, McGill Papers, Deceased Priests File, ADLR. Fr. Fintan Kraemer was born on April 18, 1868, see his obituary in Little Rock *Arkansas Gazette,* 19 April 1935, 18.

[130]Little Rock *Arkansas Gazette,* 15 February 1900, n.p., Lucey scrapbook, ADLR; Weibel et.al., "Memorial of the Priests," 3.

[131]Fr. Michael McGill, pastor at the Catholic Church in Hot Springs, to Cardinal Miecislaus H. Ledochowski, Prefect of Propaganda, 23 February 1900.

[132]This letter from Bishop Fitzgerald to Priest of his Diocese in the Fitzgerald Papers, ADLR. For a newspaper source see Pine Bluff *Commercial* 3 May 1900, n.p., clipping in the Lucey scrapbook, ADLR.

[133]Weibel, "Memorial of the Priests," 3.

[134]Ibid.

[135]Boston *Pilot* 14 June 1900, n.p., newspaper clipping. Lucey scrapbook, ADLR.

[136]Weibel et.al., "Memorial of the Priests," quotes from pp. 4,3.

[137]That the Smyth brothers had served in Fort Smith since the early 1870s. *Catholic Directory, 1872* (New York: J.D. Sadlier, 1872) 208. Fr. Michael Smyth died in mid-June, Fort Smith *Times,* 18 June 1900, n.p., newspaper clipping, Lucey scrapbook, ADLR. That these differences in loyalty existed, see the various articles in Fort Smith paper, 3 June 1900, n.p., 17 June 1900, n.p., 18 June 1900, n.p., newspaper clippings, Lucey scrapbook, ADLR.

[138]*Catholic Directory, 1901* (Milwaukee, WI: M.H. Wiltzius, 1901) 864; *Catholic Directory, 1902* (Milwaukee, WI: M.H. Wiltzius, 1902) 375; *Catholic Directory, 1903* (Milwaukee, WI: M.H. Wiltzius, 1903) 386; *Catholic Directory, 1904* (Milwaukee, WI: M.H. Wiltzius, 1904) 396; *Catholic Directory, 1905* (Milwaukee, WI: M.H. Wiltzius, 1905) 412; *Catholic Directory, 1906* (Milwaukee, WI: M.H. Wiltzius, 1906) 411.

[139]The file in the Archives from 1900 contains about 50 letters of Fr. Kraemer who signed his name as vicar general to Bishop Fitzgerald, Fitzgerald Papers, ADLR.

[140]Weibel, *Forty Years Missionary in Arkansas,* 177.

[141]Lucey, "Souvenir of a Silver Jubilee," 40.

CHAPTER VI

[1]Bishop Fitzgerald to Society of the Propagation of the Faith, Lyon & Paris, France, 12 January 1873, microfilm copy of letter, AUND. Hereafter the Society for the Propagation of the

Faith in France will be abbreviated to POF.

[2]The Oregon Territory had 1,115 foreign born out of population of 13,087 or 8.5 percent. In the South, total foreign-born was 145, 124 out of total white population of 4,188,244. Louisiana had 66,413 or 45 percent of the total in the South and Texas had 16,774 or 11.5 percent of the total in the South. The number of Germans in Arkansas was 616, the number of Irish, 514. These statistics for 1850 taken from J.D.B. DeBow, *Statistical View of the United States: A Compendium to the Seventh Census, 1850* (Washington, D.C.: Beverly Tucker, 1854) 45, 117-118. Computations by the author.

[3]Much of this information from Francis S. Guy, "The Catholic Church in Arkansas." Unpublished typewritten manuscript, ADLR, 122123; Sarah Fitzjarrold, "A Street By Any Other Name," *The Journal of the Fort Smith Historical Society,* 13 (April 1989): 19-20.

[4]Fr. John M. Lucey, "Souvenir of a Silver Jubilee, February 4, 1892," 5, Unpublished typewritten manuscript in ADLR; Guy, "Catholic Church in Arkansas," Fitzjarrold, "A Street by Any Other Name," 20-21.

[5]Fitzjarrold, "A Street By Any Other Name," 21. On the same page, Ms. Fitzjarrold outlines the present boundaries of this property in today's Fort Smith: "The Catholic Mile is roughly measured as being bordered on the west by Towson Avenue (extended north three blocks), on the north by Grand Avenue (formerly Catholic Avenue), on the east by Greenwood Avenue (not to be confused with Old Greenwood Road), and on the south by Dodson Avenue." The map is presented on p. 20.

[6]North Carolina's white population in 1860 was 629,942, its foreign-born was 3,290. Florida's whites amounted to 77,747, its foreign-born, 3,280. The four territories with fewer foreign-born yet with higher percentages of foreign-born than Arkansas were as follows: Colorado 2,666 or 7.7, Dakota 1,774 or 68.8, Nevada 2,000 or 29.3, and Washington 3,141 or 28.2. Of the future 11 Confederate states there were 233,124 foreign-born out of a total white population of 5,451,220. Of the 233,124, Louisiana had foreign population of 80,603 or 34.5 percent of the total in the whole Confederacy; Texas had 43,401 or 18.6 percent of the whole Confederacy. When you combine these two states' amounts, they contained 53.1 percent of the foreign-born in the 11 Confederate states. Author compiled and computed these figures from U.S. Department of the Interior, *The Eighth Census of the United States, 1860* 4 vols. (Washington, D.C.: Government Printing Office, 1864) 1:18-20, 592-593, 606-607.

[7]The Irish-born now numbered 1,312 to the German-born, 1,143. Ibid., 1:20.

[8]Jonathan J. Wolfe, "Background of German Immigration: Part I," *Arkansas Historical Quarterly* 25 (Summer 1966): 163-165.

[9]Frederick Allsopp, *History of the Arkansas Press for the First Hundred Years and More* (Little Rock, AR: Parke-Harper, 1922) 22.

[10]Wolfe, "German Immigration: Part I," 167-169. For a look at the history of the German Lutheran Church in Little Rock see Delbert Adolph Schmand, *Heritage of the First Lutheran Church, Little Rock, Arkansas, 1868-1988* (North Little Rock, AR: Horton Brothers Printing, 1988.)

[11]Wolfe, "German Immigration: Part I," 166.

[12]Little Rock *Arkansas Gazette,* 10 March 1871, 4.

[13]Wolfe, "German Immigration: Part I," 170.

[14]The North Carolina white population total in 1870 was 678,470, its foreign-born, 3,089. The Florida white population was 96,057, foreign-born, 4,967. Dakota had 4,815, Washington, 5,024, Wyoming, 3,513. The foreign-born percentage in each of the three territories was, respectively, 37.5%, 22.6%, 40.2%. Louisiana and Texas still contained 58.9 percent of the total foreign-born population of the 11 former Confederate states. The Germans in Arkansas numbered 1,526 to the Irish 1,428.U.S. Department of the Interior, *The Ninth Census of the United States, 1870* 3 vols. (Washington, D.C.: Government Printing Office, 1872) 1:4, 299, 338-340.

[15]Ibid., 1:4-5. South Carolina had a greater overall population than Arkansas, but its white population was only 289,667; South Carolina's large black population made up the difference. The Palmetto state was the only one in the South with a majority black population.

[16]Wolfe, "German Immigration: Part I," 158, 171-172. The text of the law quoted by Msgr. John M. Lucey, "History of Immigration to Arkansas," *Publications of the Arkansas Historical Association* 4 vols. (Little Rock, AR: Democratic Printing and Lithograph Company, 1906-1917): 3 (1911), 207-208.

[17]Wolfe, "German Immigration: Part I," 158-159.

[18]Jonathan J. Wolfe, "Background of German Immigration: Part III," *Arkansas Historical Quarterly* 25 (Winter 1966): 381383.

[19]Stephen Wood, "The Development of the Arkansas Railroads: Periods of Land Grants and the Civil War," *Arkansas Historical Quarterly* 7 (Summer 1948): 119-131; Leo Huff, "The Memphis to Little Rock Railroad During the Civil War," *Arkansas Historical Quarterly* 23 (Autumn 1964): 260-262; James M. Woods, *Rebellion and Realignment: Arkansas's Road to Secession* (Fayetteville, AR: University of Arkansas Press, 1987) 96, 122.

[20]George H. Thompson, *Arkansas and Reconstruction: The Influence of Geography, Economics, and Personality* (Port Washington, NY: Kennikat Press, 1976) 120.

[21]Ibid.

[22]Ibid., 187-230.

[23]Wolfe, "German Immigration: Part I," 161-162; Lucey, "Immigration to Arkansas," 211-212.

[24]T.B. Mills *A History of the Northwestern Editorial Exposition to Arkansas* (Little Rock, AR: T.B. Mills & Company, 1876.) A copy in the Arkansas History Commission, Little Rock, Arkansas.

[25]Wood, "Development of the Arkansas Railroads," 138.

[26]Jonathan J. Wolfe, "Background to German Immigration: Part II," *Arkansas Historical Quarterly* 25 (Autumn 1966): 256-258.

[27]Ibid., 258.

[28]Lucey, "Immigration to Arkansas," 214-215.

[29]Wolfe, "German Immigration: Part II," 249-254.

[30]The story Fr. Lawrence Maus relates presented in Wolfe," German Migration: Part II," 254.

[31]Koppel S. Pinson, *Modern Germany: Its History and Civilization*, 2nd Edition. (New York: MacMillan Press, 1966) 187-189.

[32]Lucey, "Immigration to Arkansas," 215; Wolfe, "German Immigration: Part II," 265-266.

[33]The information on the foundation of Abbey Maria Einsiedeln in Switzerland in Fr. Hugh Assenmacher, O.S.B., *A Place Called Subiaco: A History of the Benedictine Monks in Arkansas* (Little Rock, AR: Rose Publishing Company, 1977) 25; for the foundation of St. Meinrad's Abbey from this Swiss Benedictine Abbey see Wolfe, "German Immigration: Part II," 262.

[34]Assenmacher, *A Place Called Subiaco*, 5, 8.

[35]Ibid., 9, 14.

[36]Ibid., 9-11.

[37]Ibid., 11.

[38]Ibid., 11-12, "Paradise Fallen from Heaven," quoted on p. 12.

[39]Ibid., 17-21. Fr. Assenmacher quotes Abbot Martin Marty of St. Meinrad's, who referred to Fr. Wolfgang Schlumpf as "a rigorous gentleman." p. 12.

[40]Ibid., 21-23; the two quotes come from p. 23.

[41]Ibid., 32, 36, 41, 55.

[42]Ibid., 56-57.

[43]Ibid., 58-59; same story recounted also in Wolfe, "German Immigration: Part III," 366.

[44]Table 6A material from U.S. Department of the Interior, *Compendium to the Eleventh Census of the United States, 1890* 2 volumes. (Washington, D.C.: Government Printing Office, 1892, 1894) 1:476-477; 2:613-614.

[45]Assenmacher, *A Place Called Subiaco*, 65.

[46]Ibid., 65-66; Wolfe, "German Immigration: Part III," 373-374.

[47]Assenmacher, *A Place Called Subiaco*, 66; Wolfe, "German Immigration: Part III," 373.

[48]Wolfe, "German Immigration: Part III," 373.

[49]Ibid., 374.

[50]Ibid., 365; Assenmacher, *A Place Called Subiaco,* 66.

[51]Wolfe, "German Immigration: Part III," 357.

[52]Ibid., 365-366. Wolfe quotes a Fr. Ludwig Stutzer, O.S.B., in a letter, to whom he does not say, letter dated 20 December 1885.

[53]Assenmacher, *A Place Called Subiaco,* 83, 95, 475, 480481.

[54]Ibid., 115-124.

[55]Ibid., 128.

[56]Ibid., 146-149.

[57]Ibid., 124, 191-192, 206.

[58]Ibid., 135, 165.

[59]Ibid., 120-124.

[60]Ibid., 38-40, 100.

[61]Ibid., 61-62, 100-102.

[62]Ibid., 170-171.

[63]Ibid., 100-102. Some of these later missionary places of the monks of Subiaco Abbey were also outlined in 1911 in a long handwritten document by Fr. Matthew Saettele, O.S.B. called "A Missionary Journey in Arkansas," document in the Leopoldine Microfilm collection, Reel #6, frame 280-282. This collection and all subsequent quotations from the Leopoldine collection came from an annotated translation of the microfilm collection. Both the microfilm and the annotated translation are in AUND.

[64]For the background on the Holy Spirit Order and Fr. Joseph Strub and his career see Fr. Henry J. Koren, C.S.Sp., *The Serpent and the Dove: A History of the Congregation of the Holy Ghost in the United States* (Pittsburgh, PA: Spiritus Press, 1985) 44-47, 83-95; Fr. Henry J. Koren, C.S.Sp., *A Spiritan Who Was Who: In North America and Trinidad, 1732-1981* (Pittsburgh, PA: Duquesne University Press, 1983) 36-37.

[65]Koren, *Serpent and the Dove,* 105-107.

[66]Ibid., p. 108. For the early beginnings of Conway and its connection to the Little Rock and Fort Smith railroad see Thompson, *Arkansas and Reconstruction,* 218.

[67]Koren, *Serpent and the Dove,* 108; Wolfe, "German Immigration: Part II," 264.

[68]Koren, *Serpent and the Dove,* 108.

[69]Ibid.

[70]Wolfe, "German Immigration: Part II," 264.

[71]The information about the Polish settlement at Marche came from Jan Sarna, editor, "Marche, Arkansas: A Personal Reminiscence of Life and Customs," *Arkansas Historical Quarterly* 26 (Spring 1977): 31, 33-36; Koren, *Serpent and the Dove,* 108-109; *Centennial Booklet: Immaculate Heart of Mary Church, Marche, Arkansas* (n.p., n. publ., 1978) n.p. (p. 19).

[72]Koren, *Serpent and Dove,* 109; Wolfe, "German Immigration: Part II," 265. According to Fr. Koren, in 1881 Bishop Fitzgerald set aside some 50,000 acres of land for some Irish migrants from southern Illinois, yet nothing apparently came of this venture. p. 112.

[73]Koren, *Serpent and the Dove,* 110.

[74]Ibid., 109, 109 n. 14.

[75]Ibid., 109, 114.

[76]Pinson, *Modern Germany,* 182.

[77]Wolfe, "German Immigration: Part III," 369-370.

[78]Ibid., 370.

[79]The dedication of the church in Conway announced in a Little Rock newspaper, Little Rock *Arkansas Gazette* 21 February 1879, 4; and the same was true regarding the event at Marche, Little Rock *Arkansas Gazette* 23 May 1880, 8. For a secondary source for these events see Koren, *Serpent and the Dove,* 110. Koren still terms the town, Warren, before the name changed to Marche.

[80]This whole event described in Koren, *Serpent and the Dove,* 111.

[81]Ibid.

[82]The Catholic Center party formed on December 13, 1870, to protect Catholic interests in a new Prussian and Protestantdominated Germany. Pinson, *Modern Germany,* 187. Fr. Koren quoted an unnamed member of the party and does not provide the date of this exchange. Koren, *Serpent and the Dove,* 112.

[83]Koren, *Serpent and the Dove,* 112.

[84]Ibid., 113. Fr. Charles Steurer, C.S.Sp., to Leopoldine Society, 29 August 1883, Leopoldine Society Microfilm collection, Reel #6, frame 256, AUND.

[85]Fr. Frederick Bosch C.S.Sp. to Leopoldine Society, 11 March 1884, Leopoldine Microfilm collection, Reel #6, frame 247, AUND.

[86]Fr. Charles Steurer, C.S.Sp. to Leopoldine Society, 29 July 1884, Leopoldine Microfilm collection, Reel #6, frame 248-249, AUND.

[87]Ibid.

[88]Ibid.

[89]Disease killed Brothers Wenceslaus Senger and Clemens Beckers, and the numbers in the different areas all contained in Koren, *Serpent and the Dove,* 113, 115. Fr. Eugene Schmidt, the successor to Fr. Steurer as pastor at Conway thought the numbers closer to 80 in his parish. Fr. Eugene Schmidt, C.S.Sp., to Leopoldine Society, 18 September 1889, Leopoldine Microfilm collection, Reel #6, frame 253. Another priest near Morrilton at Marienstaat reported a severe drought that year, which hurt the colony. Fr. Matthew Heizmann, C.S.Sp., to Leopoldine Society, 14 December 1887, Leopoldine Microfilm collection, Reel #6, frame 253, AUND.

[90]Little Rock *Arkansas Gazette,* 10 May 1892, 1; Koren, *Serpent and the Dove,* 116.

[91]Wolfe, "German Immigration: Part II," 265.

[92]On the land grants and where they were, see the map on the inside covers of Professor Thompson's book, *Arkansas and Reconstruction.* For the coming of the German migrants into this area, see Lucey, "Immigration to Arkansas," 215. Fr. Eugene Weibel gives the date about 1880 for the beginning of the influx of Germans into northeastern Arkansas. Fr. Eugene John Weibel, O.S.B., *Forty Years Missionary in Arkansas* translated from German by Sr. Mary Agnes, O.S.B. (St. Meinrad, ID: Abbey Press, 1968) 59.

[93]Table 6B taken from U.S. Department of the Interior, *The Eleventh Census, 1890,* 2:600-601.

[94]Information on the early life and career of Fr. Weibel taken from his *Forty Years Missionary,* 1-49. For another survey of his career see Assenmacher, *A Place Called Subiaco,* 4244.

[95]For a look at Fr. Weibel's career in northeastern Arkansas see Weibel, *Forty Years Missionary,* 49-186. On his new religious order and the Holy Angels Convent he built in Jonesboro and St. Bernard's hospital in 1900 see pp. 92-94, 127, 141-143, 150. Fr. Eugene Weibel, O.S.B., to the Leopoldine Society, 30 November 1898, Leopoldine Microfilm collection, Supplemental Reel #2, frame 231, AUND.

[96]Weibel, *Forty Years Missionary,* 212.

[97]Ibid., 193. On the same page Weibel commented favorably: "He spoke fluent German seldom found in an American, and this fact arouses admiration."

[98]Ibid., 187-217.

[99]Ibid., 217-239; his date of death on the title page.

[100]Assenmacher, *A Place Called Subiaco,* 239. Fr. Hugh termed his chapter on Fr. Matthew Saettele, O.S.B., "Arkansas' Greatest Missionary," he maintains that the term did not originate with him.

[101]Ibid.

[102]Ibid., 239-240. On Coal Hill and his pastorate at Dixie, see the letter he wrote from Altus, Fr. Matthew Saettele to Leopoldine Society 6 December 1893, Leopoldine Microfilm collection, Reel #6, frame 265; Fr. Matthew Saettele to Leopoldine Society, 17 November 1897, Leopoldine Microfilm collection, Supplemental Reel #2, frame 215, AUND.

[103]Assenmacher, *A Place Called Subiaco* 241; Weibel, *Forty Years Missionary,* 162-163.

Weibel calls the church of St. Paul's in Pocahontas his "grateful monument." p. 163. Fr. Weibel's comment about going back to Switzerland and Fr. Saettele being offered the coadjutorship, Fr. Eugene Weibel, O.S.B., to Leopoldine Society, 23 November 1900, Leopoldine Microfilm collection, Supplemental Reel #2, frame 245, AUND.

[104]Assenmacher, *A Place Called Subiaco,* 241. Fr. Matthew Saettele, O.S.B., to Leopoldine Society, 5 October 1911, Leopoldine Microfilm collection, Reel #6, frame 279, AUND.

[105]Fr. Matthew Saettele, O.S.B., to Leopoldine Society, 1 July 1913, Leopoldine Microfilm collection, Supplemental Reel #2, frame 303, AUND.

[106]Assenmacher, *A Place Called Subiaco,* 242; Weibel, *Forty Years Missionary,* 163.

[107]The details of Fr. Fintan Kraemer's early life are contained in his obituary in Little Rock *Arkansas Gazette* 19 April 1935, 18; Paris (AR) *Express,* 18 April 1935, newspaper clipping, Kraemer Papers, Deceased Priests File, ADLR.

[108]*Catholic Directory, 1902* (Milwaukee, WI: Wiltzius, 1902) 375; *Catholic Directory, 1903* (Milwaukee, WI: Wiltzius, 1903) 386; *Catholic Directory, 1904* (Milwaukee, WI: Wiltzius, 1904) 396; *Catholic Directory, 1905* (Milwaukee, WI: Wiltzius, 1905) 412; *Catholic Directory, 1906* (Milwaukee, WI: Wiltzius, 1906) 411; Fr. Maurus Rohner, O.S.B., to Leopoldine Society, 7 December 1907 Leopoldine Microfilm collection, Supplemental Reel #2, frame 290; Fr. Maurus Rohner, O.S.B. to Leopoldine Society, 20 September 1911, Leopoldine Microfilm collection, Reel #6, frame 278, AUND.

[109]*Catholic Directory, 1901* (New York: J.D. Sadlier, 1901) 364. For a look at Fr. Patrick Enright's position at the Cathedral during Kraemer's rule see the Directories quoted in the previous footnote, the very same pages cited.

[110]Fr. Fintan Kraemer, O.S.B., to Leopoldine Society, 22 November 1900, Leopoldine Microfilm collection, Supplemental Reel #2, frame 244, Kraemer to Leopoldine Society, 28 April 1901, Supplemental Reel #2, frame 150, Kraemer to Leopoldine Society, 1 November 1901, Supplemental Reel #2, frame 254, Kraemer to Leopoldine Society, 4 November 1904, Supplemental Reel #2, frame 275, Kraemer to Leopoldine Society, 18 July 1905, Supplemental Reel #2, frame 276, Kraemer to Leopoldine Society, 21 November 1905, Supplemental Reel #2, frame 278, Kraemer to Leopoldine Society, 16 May 1906, Supplemental Reel #2, frame 280, AUND.

[111]There are about fifty letters from Fr. Kraemer to Bishop Fitzgerald dating from the 1 July 1901 to 21 October 1906, Fitzgerald Papers, ADLR.

[112]At the end of the Kraemer letters to Bp. Fitzgerald within the Bp. Fitzgerald papers there is a typewritten letter not signed but purportedly from Bishop Fitzgerald and written to Dear Bishop and left blank. There is no date to the letter or signature. The contents claim that in the past six years Fitzgerald has not liked Kraemer's judgment about the type of priest he has allowed in the diocese. The letter also states that the German Benedictine is not liked by the diocesan priests The letter ends by saying that while Kraemer is an honorable man, Bishop Fitzgerald asked Rome to appoint Fr. Patrick Horan as bishop because he did not want a Benedictine bishop when a majority of the priests in the diocese belonged to either the Benedictines or other religious orders. What makes this letter suspect, other than the fact that it is not signed, is that Fitzgerald was by that time so ill he had to sign things in 1906 with an X, which witnesses verified. This is clear when you examine his will dated that year. Fitzgerald's will is in the Fitzgerald Papers, ADLR. This may have been some type of ploy by those still angry over the Kraemer appointment. What the letter demonstrates is that the some portion of the Arkansas Catholic clergy were still ethnically divided.

[113]From the *Catholic Directories* it appears that Kraemer appears to be vicar general, but other material has John Michael Lucey being named vicar general on June 18, 1907. *Catholic Directory, 1907* (Milwaukee, WI: Wiltzius, 1907) 430; *Catholic Directory, 1908* (Milwaukee, WI: Wiltzius, 1908) 433; *Catholic Directory, 1909* (Milwaukee, WI: Wiltzius, 1909) 436; *Catholic Directory, 1910* (Milwaukee, WI: Wiltzius, 1910) 448; *Catholic Directory, 1911* (Milwaukee, WI: Wiltzius, 1911) 172; on Lucey appointment see the document of his appointment, 18 June 1907 in Lucey papers, Deceased Priests File, Set I, Box 7. There is also a lot of material on Kraemer's

attempt to form the Brothers of St. Paul in Kraemer's papers, together with a newspaper clipping from the Paris (AR) *Express,* 18 April 1935, Kraemer's Papers, Deceased Priests File, ADLR. Also see Little Rock *Arkansas Gazette,* 19 April 1935, 18.

[114]Allsopp, *History of the Arkansas Press,* 363.

[115]Ibid., 382, quote on p. 383.

[116]Wolfe, "German Immigration: Part II," 255-256.

[117]Ibid., 256.

[118]Wolfe, "German Immigration: Part III," 385.

[119]For a look at these Austrians working at Coal Hill see the reports about who worked in Altus and ministered to these priests five miles east of them in Johnson County. Fr. Matthew Saettele, O.S.B. to Leopoldine Society, 6 December 1893, Leopoldine Microfilm collection, Reel #6, frame 265, Fr. Donatus Schloessner, O.S.B. to Leopoldine Society, 25 October 1898, Leopoldine Microfilm collection, Supplemental Reel, #2, Frame 225, AUND. For the founding of St. Wenceslaus for about 80 families of Bohemians see Diocesan Historical Commission, *The History of Catholicity in Arkansas* (Little Rock, AR: The Guardian Press, 1925) n.p., (p. 181); Assenmacher, *A Place Called Subiaco,* 240.

[120]Fr. Placidus Oechsle, O.S.B. to Leopoldine Society, 1 December 1898, Leopoldine Microfilm collection, Supplemental Reel #2, frame 233, AUND.

[121]Fr. Placidus Oechsle, O.S.B., to Leopoldine Society, 7 December 1901, Leopoldine Microfilm collection, Supplemental Reel #2, frame 261, AUND. For other information about this long and bitter strike, how it lasted from 1899 to 1901 and how these priests looked at it see Fr. Othmar Wehrle, O.S.B., to Leopoldine Society, no day or month, 1899, Leopoldine Microfilm collection, Reel #6, frame 270; Fr. Thomas Keller, O.S.B., to Leopoldine Society, 10 December 1900, Leopoldine Microfilm collection, Supplemental Reel, #2, frame 246, AUND. All these priests writing from Altus with a mission at St. Matthew's church at Coal Hill.

[122]Fr. Placidus Oechsle, O.S.B., to Leopoldine Society, 12 October 1908, Leopoldine Microfilm collection, Supplemental Reel #2, frame 296, AUND.

[123]Fr. J. Simonik to Leopoldine Society, 27 June 1895, Slovactown, AR. Leopoldine Microfilm collection, Supplemental Reel #2, frame 197, AUND. There is no further correspondence from this priest and the Catholic Directories of this era do not identify a priest by that name except one who seems to be in Minnesota and never came to Arkansas. He may have returned to Minnesota. The quote came from John Adelsponger to Bishop Fitzgerald, 13 April 1897, Stuttgart, Parish Records, ADLR.

[124]D.H.C., *History of Catholicity in Arkansas,* n.p., (p. 73). Fr. Joseph McQuaid listed as pastor there at Stuttgart serving Slovac *Catholic Directory* (Milwaukee, WI: Wiltzius, 1900), 300, 652. Fr. Matthew Saettele, Lake Village, to Leopoldine Society, 5 October 1911, Leopoldine Microfilm collection, Reel #6, frame 279, AUND. One curious feature is that also in Prairie County near Hazen, a Fr. John Balciewickz is listed as priest for a Lithuanian settlement in the 1895 *Catholic Directory,* yet neither this priest or this settlement is listed again in subsequent directories. *Catholic Directory, 1895* (New York: J.D. Sadlier, 1895) 363.

[125]Fr. Hippolytus Orlowski, C.S.Sp., to Leopoldine Society, 30 November 1896, Leopoldine Microfilm collection, Supplemental Reel #2, frame 209, AUND; *Centennial Booklet, Immaculate Heart of Mary Church,* n.p. (p. 9).

[126]Between 1901-1908 the number of Italians coming to America annually was 211,294, and of these 2,172 settled in the south central states. The south central states referred to included Arkansas, Kentucky, Tennessee, Alabama, Mississippi, Louisiana, Texas, Oklahoma. Louisiana drew 1,318 a year, while Texas attracted 211. Arkansas by contrast drew only 45 a year. These statistics taken from Ernesto Milani, "Marchigiani and Veneti on Sunny Side Plantation," in *Italian Immigrants in Rural and Small Town America* edited by Rudolph J. Vecoli (Staten Island, NY: American Italian Historian Association, 1987) 18-19.

[127]Ibid., 19-20.

[128]Ibid., 20-21; Jeffrey Lewellen, "'Sheep Amidst the Wolves': Father Bandini and the Colony at Tontitown, 1897-1917," *Arkansas Historical Quarterly* 45 (Spring 1986): 26-27, quote

on p. 27. For a complete history of Sunny Side Plantation, one of the largest in Arkansas history see Willard B. Gatewood, Jr., "Sunnyside: The Evolution of an Arkansas Plantation, 1840-1945," *Arkansas Historical Quarterly* 50 (Spring 1991): 529. For a look at the planters in the Mississippi delta and how they viewed Italian labor see Bertram Wyatt-Brown, "Leroy Percy and Sunnyside: Planter Mentality and Italian Peonage in the Mississippi Delta," *Arkansas Historical Quarterly* 50 (Spring 1991): 6084.

[129]Whites in Chicot County were 1,393 and blacks were 10,023, total population in the county 11,415. U.S. Dept. of the Interior, *Compendium to the Eleventh Census, 1890,* 1:476. That blacks in the county were unwilling to work at a large plantation like Sunny Side greatly owned by a New York businessman, see Milani, "Sunny Side Plantation," 21; Gatewood, "Sunnyside: The Evolution of an Arkansas Plantation," 22.

[130]For a discussion of the terms of the contract see Milani, "Sunny Side Plantation," 22-23. See the author's more recent article on this topic Ernesto Milani, "Peonage at Sunny Side and the Reaction of the Italian Government," *Arkansas Historical Quarterly* 50 (Spring 1991): 30-39.

[131]Milani, "Sunny Side Plantation," 23.

[132]Ibid., 23, 27.

[133]The conditions provoking immigration in Italy, Bishop Scalabrini and his religious society, plus Bandini's early lives and careers found in Lewellen, "Bandini and Tontitown," 22-24.

[134]Ibid., 24-25, 30.

[135]Ibid., 28-29; Milani, "Sunny Side Plantation," 24-27. Milani provides more detail as to what part of Italy these immigrants came from, the number coming, and the conditions of their travel to America, pp. 24-26.

[136]Milani, "Sunny Side Plantation," 26-27; that Bandini criticized the Italian government for not doing more, see Milani, "Peonage at Sunny Side and the Italian Government," 33. For Bandini's decision to move, see Lewellen, "Bandini and Tontitown," 29-30; W. J. Lemke, editor, *The Story of Tontitown* (Fayetteville, AR: Washington County Historical Society, 1963) 5.

[137]Lewellen, "Bandini and Tontitown," 30-37; Thomas Rothrock, "The Story of Tontitown, Arkansas," *Arkansas Historical Quarterly* 16 (Spring 1957): 85-87.

[138]Milani, "Sunny Side Plantation," 28.

[139]Milani, "Sunny Side Plantation," 28-30 for the fact that only two Italian families were still working there by the late 1930s see Gatewood, "Sunny Side: The Evolution of an Arkansas Plantation," 28. The other owners were investigated, see Randolph H. Boehm, "Mary Grace Quackenbos and the Federal Campaign Against Peonage: The Case of Sunnyside Plantation," *Arkansas Historical Quarterly* 50 (Spring 1991): 40-59.

[140]Lewellen, "Bandini and Tontitown," 33-34, 36, 40. That Bandini named the place "Tontitown" in Lemke, *Story of Tontitown,* 6; on the Sisters of Tontitown, see Jane Ramos and Sisters of Mercy in Arkansas, *Arkansas Frontiers of Mercy: A History of the Sisters of Mercy in the Diocese of Little Rock* (Fort Smith, AR: St. Edward Press, 1989) 146.

[141]Lewellen, "Bandini and Tontitown," 38-39.

[142]Fr. Daniel E. Hudson, C.S.C., "Tontitown, Arkansas," *Ave Maria* 68 (January 9, 1909): 55.

[143]Fr. Peter Bandini to Fr. Daniel E. Hudson, 7 January 1909; John Mathews to Fr. Daniel E. Hudson, 10 January 1909, Hudson Papers, AUND.

[144]Lewellen, "Bandini and Tontitown," 38. Lewellen does not provide the date for the gift from Italy; just that of his pontifical award.

[145]Ibid., 39.

[146]Bishop John Morris quoted in Lewellen, "Bandini and Tontitown," 39. Lewellen points out that while Bandini had a close relationship with Bishop Fitzgerald, he did not get along well with Bishop Morris. Morris had even recommended that the Pope not give him an award, a recommendation the Pontiff apparently ignored, pp. 35, 38.

[147]The material on Little Italy taken from a booklet, Patsy Womack, editor, *Living the Times: A Bicentennial History of Perry County, 1776-1976.* (n.p., n. publ., n.d., c. 1976), 5355. Also information from author's interview with Mr. Louis Belotti, 25 July 1990, Little Italy,

Arkansas. A copy of the audio tape interview in ADLR.

[148]In Arkansas, the foreign born amounted 10,350 out of white population of 591,531. U.S. Department of the Interior, *Compendium to the Tenth Census of the United States, 1880* 2 Vols. (Washington, D.C.: Government Printing Office, 1883) 1:2-3.

[149]Arkansas' foreign born population in 1890 was 14,264 out of white population of 818,752. The number in the whole southern confederacy was 323,140 out of white population 9,579,106 Texas and Louisiana had 62.7% of the foreign born to white population. The author compiled the numbers from U.S. Dept. of Interior, *Census of 1890,* 1:469, 472. Computations of numbers and percentages performed by the author.

[150]For 1900, 14,289 foreign born out of state white population of 944,580. U.S. Dept of the Interior, *The Twelfth Census of the United States, 1900* 12 vols. (Washington, D.C.: Government Printing Office, 1901-1904) l:cx, cxii; for 1910, there were 17,046 out of state white population of l,131,026.U.S. Department of Commerce, *The Thirteenth Census of the United States, 1910* 10 volumes (Washington, D.C.: Government Printing Office, 1913-1915) 1:143, 162.

[151]In 1890, 9,249,547 foreign-born out of a total national white population of 54,983,890. The total national population white and black in 1890 was 62,622,250. U.S. Dept. of Interior, *Census of 1890,* 1:468,469. In 1920 there was 13,920,692 foreign-born out of a total white population of 94,820,915. The total population white and black was 105,710,620. U.S. Department of Commerce, *The Fourteenth Census of the United States, 1920* 11 volumes (Washington, D.C.: Government Printing Office, 1922-1923) 2:31.

[152]The number of foreign-born in the South was 564,003 out of white population of 16,465,010. All the numbers in Table 6D on foreign-born to white population from U.S. Dept. of Commerce, *Census of 1920,* 2:1328, 1329, 1332, 1333, 1342, 1353, 1360, 1361, 1363, 1367. Texas and Louisiana together contained 71.8% of the total foreign-born in the South; Texas alone accounted for 63.9%.

CHAPTER VII

[1]On the meeting of the three bishops, announcement in San Antonio *Southern News* 29 August 1905. That the meeting was held in Hot Springs, San Antonio *Southern Messenger* 28 September 1905 n.p., 6 September 1905; both clippings in Msgr. John M. Lucey, scrapbook, ADLR. Dunne and Allen informed Fitzgerald they would come on September 20, Allen to Fitzgerald, 9 September 1905, Dunne to Fitzgerald, 17 September 1905, letters in Fitzgerald Papers, ADLR. For Chappelle's career and other duties which kept him out of New Orleans and an account of his death see Roger Baudier, *The Catholic Church in Louisiana* (New Orleans, La.: Private Printing, 1939) 493, 495, 499-500 Bishop Gustave Rouxel to Bishop Fitzgerald, 18 August 1905, Fitzgerald Papers, ADLR.

[2]San Antonio *Southern News,* 30 November 1905, n.p. newspaper clipping, Lucey scrapbook, ADLR.

[3]San Antonio *Southern Messenger,* 8 September 1905, Lucey scrapbook, ADLR.

[4]Apparently responding to a note sent by Fitzgerald, or possibly by someone acting in Fitzgerald's name, dated October 30, 1905, he asked the various bishops to meet in Hot Springs in late November 1905. Bishop Thomas Heslin of Natchez suggested that the meeting in November be held in New Orleans, not Hot Springs. It was apparently Bishop Nicholas Gallagher of Galveston, the senior bishop in the Province after Fitzgerald who set the date of meeting December 13 and put it in New Orleans and he informed Fitzgerald of this decision. On Fitzgerald's real or alleged correspondence on October 30 see the letter of Auxiliary Bishop Rouxel to Fitzgerald, 1 November 1905; Heslin's suggestion of New Orleans contained in his letter that same day to Fitzgerald, Heslin to Fitzgerald, 1 November 1905. Bishop Allen of Mobile also wrote a letter that day claiming that he would come. Bishop Gallagher's decision, Gallagher to Fitzgerald, 20 November 1905. All correspondence cited in Fitzgerald Papers, ADLR.

[5]Little Rock *Arkansas Gazette,* 14 December 1905, p. 4, also see the same newspaper clipping in Lucey scrapbook, ADLR. Verdaguer was listed as Bishop of Brownsville, Texas, but he served as vicar apostolic of Brownsville, an area of ecclesiastical jurisdiction separated from the

Diocese of Galveston in 1874. Located in Brownsville, Verdaguer, vicar since 1890, located his operations in Loredo, Texas. In 1912, the Pope set up from this area the Diocese of Corpus Christi, not until 1963 would a separate diocese of Brownsville be established. *New Catholic Encyclopedia* 15 volumes (New York: McGraw-Hill, 1967) 2:829; 4:347. On the policy sanctioned by the Third Plenary Council in 1884 see Fr. Gerald P. Fogarty, S.J., *The Vatican and the American Hierarchy From 1870 to 1965* (Wilmington, DE.: Michael Glazier, 1985) 33.

[6]Little Rock *Arkansas Gazette*, 29 December 1905, p. 5, also see Msgr. Lucey's scrapbook in ADLR. The article gave no particular order for the priests' list, just for the bishops' list. Horan was born in Birr, Ireland, December 2, 1866, his doctorate from Propaganda Fide on June 11, 1892. He came from a large family in Ireland for he had 10 brothers and two sisters. The fact that he was often referred to as "Dr." Horan can be gathered from his file and from priests who still remember him. For his personal information, see Deceased Priests, Box 4, ADLR; author's taped interview with Msgr. James O'Connell, 14 August 1989, tape in ADLR. On the college in Rome see *Catholic Encyclopedia*, 11:840.

[7]Bishop Dunne to Bishop Fitzgerald, 30 December 1905, Fitzgerald Papers, ADLR.

[8]Ibid. On the creation of the Archdiocese of San Antonio and the Texas province see *Catholic Encyclopedia*, 12:1016,1018.

[9]Baudier, *Catholic Church in Louisiana*, 507.

[10]Little Rock *Arkansas Gazette*, 27 March 1906, p. 1. Fitzgerald's telegram of congratulations dated March 26, 1906 in Morris Papers, ADLR. Morris had not heard by early May, see John B. Morris to Bishop Fitzgerald, 3 May 1906, Fitzgerald Papers, ADLR. *Arkansas Gazette*, 14 May 1906, 3.

[11]The Diocese of Little Rock paid for Horan's education and he had been ordained to the priesthood by Bishop Fitzgerald on December 7, 1893 at St. Andrew's Cathedral. Fr. Horan wrote to Bp. Fitzgerald as a seminarian from Rome. Horan to Fitzgerald, 30 December 1888, 12 July 12, 1892. In the latter letter Horan expresses his strong devotion to Our Lady of Good Counsel, as he visited that shrine in Europe in 1892. He named the parish in Little Rock after Our Lady of Good Counsel and served as its first pastor in 1894 even though he had been ordained a priest only for a year. This demonstrates the confidence Bishop Fitzgerald had in this young Irishborn priest. His ordination date is on his certificate of ordination. These letters and documents are found in Fr. Horan Papers, Deceased Priests, ADLR. On Good Counsel see Diocesan Historical Commission, *The History of Catholicity in Arkansas* (Little Rock, AR: Guardian Press, 1925) n.p., (42).

[12]For the sources of Morris' parents see D.H.C., *History of Catholicity in Arkansas*, n.p. (p. 23); Thomas Stritch, *The Catholic Church in Tennessee*, (Nashville, TN: The Catholic Center/Ambrose Printing Co., 1987) 239. The information on Ann Morrissey Morris from a letter of Thomas Stritch to the author, Stritch to Woods, 31 October 1990, letter in possession of the author. Thomas Stritch was the nephew through his mother of Bishop John B. Morris and the nephew through his father of Cardinal Samuel Stritch of Chicago. John Morris' next sibling, his sister, Mary, became a nun and lived in France for years. Thomas Stritch's mother, Ellen, was the fifth child and the third daughter born to John and Ann Morris. Thomas Stritch is a former professor of English and Journalism at the University of Notre Dame.

[13]Morris' career prior to coming to Arkansas in D.H.C., *History of Catholicity in Arkansas*, n.p. (pp. 23-25); Stritch, *Catholic Church in Tennessee*, 121, 223, 225-226, 229. For the career of Cardinal Satolli as the first papal apostolic delegate see Fogarty, *Vatican and the America Hierarchy*, 80-85, 127-142; "Satolli, Francesco." *New Catholic Encyclopedia*, 12:1098.

[14]Little Rock *Arkansas Gazette*, 16 May 1906, p. 3; also see newspaper clipping in Lucey scrapbook, ADLR. In the article Bishop Morris is quoted as saying that he had not received his papers from Rome until Monday, May 14, 1906. Morris wrote Fitzgerald in late May "I am getting things in order for the llth." Morris to Fitzgerald 31 May 1906, Fitzgerald Papers, ADLR.

[15]D.H.C. *History of Catholicity in Arkansas*, n.p. (p. 25). For a better first hand account see Little Rock *Arkansas Gazette*, 12 June 1906, 6. This article contains the text of the Archbishop Moeller sermon. The article can also be found in Lucey scrapbook, ADLR.

[16]Little Rock *Arkansas Gazette,* 24 June 1906, p. 6; Morris quoted in 26 June 1906, p. 6. Also see Little Rock *Arkansas Democrat,* 25 June 1906, p. 3.

[17]Bishop Morris to Bishop Fitzgerald, 21 August 1906, Fitzgerald Papers, ADLR.

[18]Little Rock *Arkansas Gazette,* 3 September 1902, p. 2, also newspaper clipping in Lucey scrapbook, ADLR; Bishop Morris to Bishop Fitzgerald, 25 September 1906, 11 November 1906, 3 December 1906, Fitzgerald Papers, ADLR.

[19]That Kraemer was still vicar general see Kraemer to Morris, 12 October 1906, Morris Papers, ADLR.

[20]Bishop Morris to Bishop Fitzgerald, 18 January 1907, Fitzgerald Papers, ADLR.

[21]On the announcement of Horan replacing Brady at Fort Smith and Horan departing Little Rock see Little Rock *Arkansas Gazette,* 24 October 1906, 3; 12 December 1906, p. 4, also see newspaper clipping in Lucey scrapbook, ADLR. That Horan would stay there until early January, 1936. For a look at Horan's career at Fort Smith see Horan Papers, Deceased Priest File, ADLR.

[22]For a look at Brady's part in the "schism" of 1900 see the previous chapter. For his birth date and date of ordination, see Fr. Kevin Condon, C.M., *The Missionary College of All Hallows, 1842-1891* (Dublin, Ireland: All Hallows College Press, 1986) 361. Fr. Lawrence Smyth's death reported in Fort Smith *New-Record,* 20 November 1900, p. 4. As to his tip that he would succeed Fitzgerald and the quote from prominent clergymen who do not believe, see Little Rock *Arkansas Gazette,* 6 March 1906, p. 6; Little Rock *Arkansas Democrat,* 7 March 1906, 2; newspaper clippings, Lucey scrapbook, ADLR.

[23]Bishop Morris to Fr. James Brady, 28 July 1906, Brady Papers, Deceased Priest File, ADLR.

[24]Bishop Morris to Brady, 25 January 1907, Brady Papers, Deceased Priest File, ADLR.

[25]Morris' warning letters, see Bishop Morris to Fr. James Brady, 8 February 1907, 15 February 1907. This latter letter resulted in his suspension, Morris Papers, ADLR. He was reconciled to the Church in late May 1937, and died in Bellevue, Illinois, on June 3, 1937. Fr. Joseph Mueller to Bishop Morris, 25 May 1937, 3 June 1937, Morris Papers, ADLR. For information on the marriage of Fr. Brady, see Fort Smith *Graphic,* 12 September 1908, newspaper clipping in Lucey scrapbook, ADLR. Other material found in Brady Papers, Deceased Priests File, ADLR.

[26]Little Rock *Arkansas Gazette,* 6 February 1907, 2; also see newspaper clipping, Lucey scrapbook, ADLR. Also see the various notes of congratulations still in the Fitzgerald Papers, ADLR.

[27]This description comes from various newspaper articles in the local press, see Little Rock *Arkansas Gazette,* 21 February, 1907, 1; 22 February 1907, 1; 23 February 1907, 2; 25 February 1907, 2; 26 February 1907, 11; the funeral covered see the above-cited paper, 28 February 1907, 16. For another secondary source for these events, see D.H.C., *History of Catholicity in Arkansas,* n.p. (p. 17).

[28]Little Rock *Arkansas Gazette,* 23 February 1908, 16, also newspaper clipping in Lucey scrapbook, ADLR.

[29]Ibid.

[30]U.S. Department of Commerce and Labor, Bureau of the Census, *Special Report: Religious Bodies, 1906* 2 vols. (Washington, D.C.: Government Printing Office, 1910) 1:160-162.

[31]*Official Catholic Directory, 1907* (Milwaukee, WI: M.H. Wiltzius, 1907) 435.

[32]The report listed Presbyterians as 19,394 with 331 houses of worship throughout the state. U.S. Dept. of Commerce and Labor, *Religious Bodies, 1906,* 1:160-162. In 1850, the Methodists had 25,745 and 168 churches, the Baptists had 18,600 and 114 churches. The Presbyterians had 10, 731 with 52 churches while the Catholics had only 1,600 members with 7 churches. U.S. Department of Interior, *The Seventh Census of the United States, 1850* (Washington, D.C.: Robert Armstrong, 1853) 535, 560-561.

[33]Some other Christian churches below church attendance would be the Christian (Disciples of Christ) 4.9 percent; Presbyterian, 4.8 percent, Episcopalians, 1.0 percent, and the

Lutherans, 0.4 percent. Percentages computed by the author from those numbers provided from U.S. Dept of Commerce and Labor, *Religious Bodies, 1906,* 1:160-162.

[34]U.S. Department of Commerce and Labor, *Religious Bodies, 1906,* 1:66.

[35]The southern states above the national and regional average in percent of church-goers: Louisiana, 50.6%, South Carolina, 45.8; Georgia 42.1; Alabama, 40.8, North Carolina, 40.0. The below average states and their percentage: Mississippi, 38.5; Florida, 35.2; Texas 34.7, Tennessee, 32.1, Arkansas, 30.0. U.S. Department of Commerce and Labor, *Religious Bodies, 1906,* 1:58.

[36]Last Will and Testament of Edward Fitzgerald, with accompanying legal testimony, Fitzgerald papers, ADLR.

[37]Mr. D.O. Loughlin to Bishop Morris, 1 July 1907, Morris papers, ADLR.

[38]Ibid.

[39]Ibid.

[40]Morris to Mr. D.O. Loughlin, 10 July 1907, 26 July 1907, Mr. D.O. Loughlin to Morris, 18 July 1907, Morris papers, ADLR.

[41]William E., Hemingway to Bishop John Morris, 17 September 1907, Morris Papers, ADLR. There is no record of the exact cost of settlement.

[42]Bishop Morris to the Catholic Clergy and People of Arkansas, 4 June 1908, Morris to the Priest of Arkansas, 24 May 1909. These letters and other documents relating to the orphanage can be found in the box labeled St. Joseph's Orphanage, ADLR.

[43]Morris had written in the spring of 1909 that he wanted to see it open by August, later letter confirms that it did not open until late in October. Morris to Mrs. Ella Senyard, 4 March 1909; Morris to B.H. Sansford, 3 August 1909, Morris to T.J. Gaughan, 13 September 1909, 14 October 1909, St. Joseph's Orphanage, ADLR.

[44]D.H.C. *History of Catholicity in Arkansas,* 55; Morris to Fr. Paul Krueger, 29 October 1910, St. Joseph's Orphanage, ADLR.

[45]Minutes of the Little Rock Board of Trade, 20 June 1912. The members of the committee were listed as Frank Ginnocchio, Ed Younger, James Gray, Martin Lally, F.A. Snodgrass, and Edward O'Brien, St. Joseph's Orphanage, ADLR.

[46]*The Southern Guardian,* 25 March 1911, p.4; the title was changed 26 June 1915, l.

[47]D.H.C., *History of Catholicity in Arkansas,* n.p., (p. 59). The last name of the five other lay teachers also given on the same page, O'Rourke, Caveny, Hardington, Means, Falisi. There is a great deal of material on this institution in a box labeled Little Rock College, ADLR.

[48]All of this information and the citation from the Little Rock College Bulletin in the year 1909-1910 is from D.H.C., *History of Catholicity in Arkansas,* n.p. (p. 61-62).

[49]D.H.C., *History of Catholicity in Arkansas,* n.p. (p. 56); as for Diocesan priest studying at Subiaco Abbey consult Fr. Hugh Assenmacher, O.S.B., *A Place Called Subiaco: A History of the Benedictine Monks in Arkansas* (Little Rock, AR: Rose Publishing Company, 1978) 124. There is large box of documentary material on the early Seminary in boxes in ADLR.

[50]D.H.C. *History of Catholicity in Arkansas,* n.p. (pp. 55, 56).

[51]Ibid., n.p. (pp. 55, 56, 63).

[52]Ibid., n.p. (pp. 56, 58). The other seven faculty members by 1923-1924 were Frs. S.J. Peoples, T.J. Martin, E.P. Garrity, J.P. Moran, H.H. Wernke, Edward Soler, J.P. Gaffney, and Cyril Corbato.

[53]Ibid., n.p. (p. 62).

[54]Ibid., n.p. (pp. 62-63). On the Little Rock College School of Pharmacy, 1924-1927 see C. Fred Williams, *A History of Pharmacy in Arkansas* (North Little Rock, AR: Heritage Press, 1982) 52-53. As Professor Williams documents in this short book, the Little Rock College School of Pharmacy was one of many attempts, dating back to the 1890s, to have a state pharmacy school. Not until after World War Two would a stable school be established.

[55]This information was taken from a classic historical work on American nativism between,1860-1925 see John Higham, *Strangers in the Land: Patterns of American Nativism, 1860-1925* (New Brunswick, NJ: Rutgers University Press, 2nd edition, 1988, 1st edition, 1955) 60-62, 84-85, quotation on p. 81.

[56]For a full account of such politics of these political cultures see Paul Kleppner, *The Third Electoral System, 1853-1892: Parties, Voters, and Political Cultures* (Chapel Hill, NC: University of North Carolina, 1979); Robert Kelley, *The Cultural Pattern of American Politics: The First Century* (New York: Random House, 1979).

[57]C. Vann Woodward, *Tom Watson: Agrarian Rebel* (New York: MacMillan Press, 1938, Oxford University Reprint-Paperback Edition, 1978) 416-425. For Watson's hatred of the Jews and his role in the shameful lynching of Leo M. Frank, a Jew falsely accused of murder see pp. 435-450.

[58]For the masthead of *The Menace* quoted in an article on this paper in Arkansas' Catholic paper *The Southern Guardian*, 27 February 1915, 7. For the number of subscribers by 1914, see Higham, *Strangers in the Land*, 180.

[59]Little Rock *Southern Guardian*, 27 February 1915, 1, 7; there is a copy of *The Menace* in the ADLR; Higham, *Strangers in the Land*, 181.

[60]Magnolia (AR) *Liberator*, 2 October 1913, 1-4; 16 October 1913, 1-4; The magazine attacked the Catholic Church and tended to defend Watson from Catholic "attacks". The meeting in Little Rock was announced in the issue, 16 October 1913, 2. No mention of this paper in Frederick Allsopp standard work on Arkansas newspapers so it is unclear how long the paper lasted. *History of the Arkansas Press For a Hundred Years and More* (Little Rock, AR: Parke-Harper, 1922.) For a look at Scarboro's life and career, see a small biographical tribute to the man published after his death in 1932 in the Arkansas History Commission, Little Rock, Arkansas. I could find no evidence that this meeting ever happened on either October 30-31 or November 1-3 at what is now the Old State House. The quote is from a public announcement of the meeting published as an open letter of Rev. J.A. Scarboro to Major Charles B. Taylor of Little Rock, n.d., the copy of the announcement is in the Morris Papers, ADLR.

[61]On Robert Randolph Posey's background see Dallas T. Herndon, *A Centennial History of Arkansas* 3 vols. (Chicago, IL: Clarke Publishing Company, 1922) 3:771-772. For the quote from the bill and whole text of the bill see *Acts of Arkansas, 1915* (Little Rock, AR: Democrat Printing Lithograph Co. 1915) 505-508; quote on p. 507. The *Arkansas Gazette* comment 17 February 1915, 3.

[62]On the actions Posey bill in 1913 it passed the state House of Representatives on March 1 but I could find no record of action in the state Senate. *Journal of the House of Representatives in the State of Arkansas, 1913* (Little Rock, AR: Democrat Printing and Lithograph Co., 1913) 721-722.

[63]For a firsthand treatment of this bill and the debate on it see Little Rock *Arkansas Gazette*, 26 January 1915, 3; 17 February 1915, 3; 3 March 1915, 3; the contents of the bill *Acts of Arkansas, 1915*, 505-508.

[64]*The Southern Guardian*, 16 January 1915, 4; 23 January 1915, 4; 30 January 1915, 4; 13 February 1915, 4; 20 February 1915, 4; 27 February 1915, 2; 6 March 1915, 2; the roll call vote in the state House of Representatives, 26 January 1918, 8; in the state Senate, 6 March 1915, 1. The vote tallies showed what counties they were from.

[65]Mrs. Olivia B. Clarendon to Governor George Washington Hays, March (n.d.) 1915, copy of this letter is in Morris Papers, ADLR.

[66]Ibid.

[67]For a look at Hays' life and career see Richard L. Niswonger, "George Washington Hays" in *The Governors of Arkansas: Essays in Political Biography*, edited by Timothy P. Donovan and Willard B. Gatewood, Jr. (Fayetteville, AR: University of Arkansas Press, 1981) 138-144; last quote found on p. 140.

[68]Abbot Ignatius Conrad's letter to Sheriff J.B. Cook, November 1915, quoted in Assenmacher, *A Place Called Subiaco*, 233.

[69]For Josephs' and Jones' remarks see the Little Rock *Arkansas Gazette*, 2 March 1915, 3; 3 March 1915, 3.

[70]Bishop Morris to Charles N. Hix, president, Hot Spring Branch, Arkansas National Bank, 6 November 1915, Morris Papers, ADLR.

[71]*Acts of Arkansas, 1937* (Little Rock, AR: Democrat Printing and Lithograph Co., 1937) 851.

[72]Stephen J. Ochs, *Desegregating the Altar: The Josephites and the Struggle for Black Priests, 1871-1960* (Baton Rouge, LA: Louisiana State University Press, 1990) 184. I could find no general study of these Southern convent inspection acts, and Ochs gives no more detail on these pieces of legislation. C. Vann Woodward, Watson's biographer, does not mention these efforts. There is a real need for a more detailed look at these acts.

[73]This pamphlet titled "Patriots of Pulaski County, Be On Guard," published by "Patriots of Pulaski County." This pamphlet lists no publisher or date, but says "read before you vote, January 16, 1916." Copy of this material in Morris Papers, ADLR.

[74]This incident related by Msgr. Thomas L. Keany, who was at Little Rock College, to Fr. Joseph Lauro, a seminarian at St. John's and later a priest for the Diocese of Little Rock and a missionary in Peru. This story in Rev. Joseph Lauro and Arthur Orrmont, *Action Priest: The Story of Fr. Joe Lauro* (New York: Morrow Publishing Co., 1970) 264. I could find no account of this incident in newspapers, but Mrs. Rose Capel, born in 1898 and a longtime Catholic resident in Little Rock, attended Little Rock College football games as a young girl and remembers the incident being talked about at the time, but she was not at the game. Author's taped interview with Mrs. Rose Capel, 24 July 1991, tape in ADLR.

[75]For Spurgeon's background see Russellville *Courier-Democrat,* 15 January 1914, 1; 21 January 1914, 1; Assenmacher, *A Place Called Subiaco,* 249.

[76]Assenmacher, *A Place Called Subiaco,* 117, 244249.

[77]For a full account of this see Assenmacher, *A Place Called Subiaco,* 249-251; for some first hand accounts see Little Rock *Arkansas Gazette,* 14 January 1914, 2; 25 January 1914, 6; Russellville *Courier-Democrat,* 14 January 1914, 1; 17 January 1914, 1; 20 January 1914, 1; 21 January 1914, 1; 22 January 1914, 2, 23 January 1914, 1, 24 January 1914, 1.

[78]Bishop Morris' letter to Abbot Ignatius Conrad quoted in Assenmacher, *A Place Called Subiaco,* 251. On the same page Fr. Assenmacher reveals what happened to the "Gospel Wagon."

[79]Morris to Charles Beroad, Ottawa, Canada, 30 March 1914, Morris Papers, ADLR.

[80]For Morris' views about combatting anti-Catholicism in Arkansas, I refer to a taped interview of Msgr. James O'Connell with the author, August 14, 1989, tape in the ADLR. Msgr. James E. O'Connell was a past rector of the seminary and associated with the seminary and Bishop Morris since his arrival in Little Rock in 1932.

[81]Fr. Winand Aretz to J.A. Fraser, Rogers, Arkansas, 26 January 1914, Aretz Papers, Deceased Priests File, ADLR.

[82]There are various letters from these gentlemen to Bishop Morris in his papers, Morris Papers, ADLR.

[83]Bishop Morris Speech to the Board of Trade, 13 September 1909, Morris Papers, ADLR. Also in the Morris papers are letters from the prominent people mentioned in the text.

[84]Morris asked to speak and his acceptance, George Brown to Bishop Morris, 20 March 1914; Morris to Brown 21 March 1914, Morris Papers, ADLR.

[85]Author's interview with Thomas Stritch, July 28, 1989, in South Bend, Indiana. Not until the administration of Governor Sidney S. McMath (19491953) was there any real concerted effort to bring good roads to the state. Jim Lester, *A Man for Arkansas: Sid McMath and the Southern Reform Tradition* (Little Rock, AR: Rose Publishing Company, 1976) 45-49, 129-137. Lester quotes Governor Ben Laney (1945-1949) as saying that in Arkansas "in the late 30s we only drove cars between June and October and then put them away because the roads were too muddy." p. 45.

[86]Charles Brough to Bishop Morris, 20 January 1913; Morris to William Kirby, 8 September 1913, Morris papers, ADLR. Charles Brough did run for governor in a special election after J.T. Robinson resigned in 1913. G.W. Hays won that election, Brough withdrew from the race in April. Niswonger, "G.W. Hays," in Donovan & Gatewood, *Governors of Arkansas,* 139.

[87]The term *ad limina* is a shortened title from the latin phrase *visitation ad limina apostolorum,* meaning literally "a visit to the Pope's doorstep." *Catholic Encyclopedia,* 1:109.

That the U.S. was taken off missionary status in 1908, Fogarty, *Vatican and the American Hierarchy*, 204. That Morris was in Rome when the World War I broke out see Morris to J.K. Conway, 12 September 1914, Morris Papers, ADLR.

[88]*The Guardian*, 15 September 1939, 2.

[89]Fogarty, *Vatican and the American Hierarchy*, 210, 214; D.H.C., *History of Catholicity in Arkansas*, n.p. (55).

[90]D.J. Mier, St. Louis to Bishop Morris, 1 October 1917; quotation from Morris to D.J. Mier, 3 October 1917. Morris Papers, ADLR.

[91]H.L. Remmel to Bishop Morris, 30 July 1918, Morris to H.L. Remmel, 31 July 1918; W.B. Smith to Morris, 26 September 1918; Morris to W. B. Smith, 27 September 1918, Morris Papers, ADLR.

[92]Assenmacher, *A Place Called Subiaco*, 235.

[93]This editorial quoted in Ibid.

[94]Ibid., 238.

[95]On the Immigration Restrictions Acts of 1921, 1924, and the Klan support, see Higham, *Strangers in the Land*, 308-324. This bill was named for Republican Representative Albert Johnson of Washington and Republican Senator David A. Reed of Pennsylvania.

[96]For the revival of the Klan, George B. Tindall, *The Emergence of the New South, 1913-1945* (Baton Rouge, La.: Louisiana State University Press, 1968) 187; for an overall account of the first century of the Klan see David Chalmers, *Hooded Americanism: The First Century of the Ku Klux Klan, 1865-1965* (New York: Oxford University Press, 1965). For the growth of the Klan in the 1920's see Higham, *Strangers in the Land*, 296; William E. Leuchtenburg, *The Perils of Prosperity, 1914-1932* (Chicago, IL: University of Chicago Press, 1958, Paperback edition, 1965), 210. The case is called Pierce (after Governor Walter Pierce) against Society of Sisters in Portland, Oregon.

[97]Terral was defeated for reelection in 1926 over the issue of mismanagement and roads, not owing to his support by the Klan. W. David Baird, "Thomas Jefferson Terral," in Donovan and Gatewood, *The Governors of Arkansas*, 161-167.

[98]Author's conversation with John Healey, August 16, 1991.

[99]Ibid., 143.

[100]Cal Ledbetter, "Joe T. Robinson and the Presidential Campaign of 1928," *Arkansas Historical Quarterly* 45 (Summer, 1986): 95-108.

[101]Bishop Morris to Senator Joseph T. Robinson, quoted in Ledbetter, "Joe T. Robinson and the Presidential Campaign of 1928," 103.

[102]Ibid., p. 113; Donovan and Gatewood, *The Governors of Arkansas*, 172.

[103]Ledbetter, "Joe T. Robinson and the Presidential Campaign of 1928," 113-115.

[104]*The Guardian*, 23 June 1928, 2; 30 June 1928, 2; 7 July 1928, 2.

[105]The two states Smith won outside the South were Massachusetts and Rhode Island. Ledbetter, "Joe T. Robinson and the Presidential Election of 1928," 121.

[106]For a look at the origins of the National Catholic War Council and the National Catholic Welfare Council see Fogarty, S.J., *The Vatican and the American Hierarchy*, 214-220. For a good description of the purpose of the National Catholic Welfare Conference, Rev. Douglas J. Slawson, C.M., "The National Catholic Conference and the Church-State Conflict in Mexico, 1925-1929." *The Americas: A Quarterly Review of Inter-American Cultural History* 47 (July 1990) 55.

[107]Bishop Morris to Archbishop Henry Moeller, 14 September 1922, Morris Papers, ADLR.

[108]Fogarty, *The Vatican and the American Hierarchy*, 220-228.

[109]Bishop Morris to Bishop James Hartley of Columbus, Ohio, 9 May 1922, Morris Papers, ADLR.

[110]Slawson, "N.C.W.C. and the Church-State Conflict in Mexico," 55-93; for the treatment of the church-state conflict and the Cristero Rebellion in Mexico see David C. Bailey, *Viva Cristo Rey: The Cristero Rebellion and the Church-State Conflict in Mexico* (Austin, Texas: University of Texas Press, 1974).

[111]Bishop Morris to Robert Lansing, Secretary of State, 24 January 1917, Morris Papers,

ADLR.

[112]Roger Baudier, *The Catholic Church in Louisiana* (New Orleans, Louisiana: Private Printing, 1939) 523, 534.

[113]For the death of Fr. Matthew Saettele in 1930 see Assenmacher, *A Place Called Subiaco*, 242, and Little Rock *Guardian*, 28 July 1930, 1. Fr. Weibel had left Arkansas and the United States in 1920 and had returned for a few visits until his death in Europe in 1934, see *Forty Years Missionary in Arkansas* translated by Sister Mary Agnes, O.S.B. (Jonesboro, AR: Holy Angels Convent, 1968) 227-237.

[114]Assenmacher, *A Place Called Subiaco*, 262-267, 335-336.

[115]Information on Msgr. Aretz from Artetz Papers, Deceased Priests File, ADLR; that he was second only to the bishop in the Diocese, *The Guardian*, 5 October 1929, 1. That Msgr. Aretz was born in Holland from Albert L. Fletcher, "Reminiscences," unpublished typewritten work, 65, Fletcher Papers, ADLR.

[116]*Official Catholic Directory, 1907* (Milwaukee, WI: M.H. Wiltzius 1907) 435; *Official Catholic Directory, 1909* (Milwaukee, WI: M.H. Wiltzius, 1909) 441; *Official Catholic Directory, 1919* (New York: P.J. Kenedy & Sons, 1919) 501; *Official Catholic Directory, 1929* (New York: P.J. Kenedy & Sons, 1929) 443.

[117]Sr. Henrietta Hockle, O.S.B., "Catholic Schools in Arkansas: A Historical Perspective, 1838-1977." (Ed.D degree, Arkansas State University, 1977) 64.

[118]On making Little Rock College coeducational, see *The Guardian*, 25 August 1928, 3; on the Cathedral renovation and the new organ, see Bishop Morris to Fr. Herman Wernke and Fr. James Moran, Rector of the Cathedral, 21 January 1929, Morris Papers, ADLR; *The Guardian*, 23 March 1962, 1, 3.

[119]*Official Catholic Directory, 1907* (Milwaukee, WI: M.H. Wiltzius, 1907) 435; *Catholic Directory, 1929*, 443.

CHAPTER VIII

[1]Bishop James A. Griffin of Springfield, Illinois to Bishop Morris, 15 February 1929, Morris Papers, ADLR.

[2]That Morris was asked by Mother Katharine Drexel, this request came through Sr. Mary of Grace, President of Xavier University of Louisiana. Sr. Mary of Grace to Morris, 22 July 1932; Morris accepted the invitation to Sr. Mary of Grace, 5 August 1932, both letters in Morris Papers, ADLR. For the ceremony and those in attendance see Roger Baudier, *The Catholic Church in Louisiana* (New Orleans, LA: Private Printing, 1939) 519; for Mother Katharine Drexel's founding of her order of nuns and her Philadelphia's roots see James Hennesey, S.J., *American Catholics: A History of the Roman Catholic Community in the United States* (New York: Oxford University Press, 1982) 104.

[3]A copy of Morris address, dated October 12, 1932 in Morris Papers, ADLR.

[4]Stephen J. Ochs, *Desegregating the Altar: The Josephites and the Struggle for Black Priests, 1871-1960* (Baton Rouge, LA: Louisiana University Press, 1990) 15. Ochs has an excellent survey of Catholic Church and its relationship with blacks from the Colonial era through the papacy of Pope Pius IX, which ended in 1878, 9-48. For other accounts of the "failed mission" of the American churches toward black Americans, 1607-1865 there have been some valuable recent works. These include: Randall M. Miller and Jon L. Wakely, *Catholic in the Old South: Essays on Church and Culture* (Macon, GA: Mercer University Press, 1983); Fr. Cyprian Davis, O.S.B., *A History of Black Catholics in the United States* (New York: Crossroad, 1991) 1-115.

[5]Ochs, *Desegregating the Altar*, 40-41; best account in Davis, *The History of Black Catholics*, 116-122. At the Second Plenary Council opposition led by archbishops outside the Old Southern Confederacy, Archbishop Peter Kenrick of St. Louis and Archbishop John McCloskey of New York. Ironically Bishop Augustin Verot of Savannah, a bishop who had been quite pro-slavery and a staunch defender of the Confederate cause, supported Spalding's call for black evangelization. For Verot's career and that of Archbishop Martin Spalding see Michael V.

Gannon, *Rebel Bishop: The Life and Era of Augustin Verot* (Milwaukee,WI: Bruce Publishing Co., 1964); Thomas W. Spalding, *Martin J. Spalding: American Churchman* (Washington, D.C.: Catholic University of America Press, 1973). On Bishop Patrick Lynch and his efforts, Hennesey, *American Catholics*, 162.

[6]E. Merton Coulter, *The South During Reconstruction, 18651877* (Baton Rouge, LA: Louisiana State University Press, 1947) 338.

[7]Ochs, *Desegregating the Altar*, 16-17.

[8]On the Third Plenary Council and this collection see Hennesey, *American Catholics*, 182; Ochs, *Desegregating the Altar*, 62; Davis, *The History of Black Catholics*, 133135. There are various letters in the papers of Bishops Morris and Fletcher regarding this collection in the ADLR.

[9]Davis, *A History of Black Catholics*, 130; Davis provides a full account of his whole tour of the South and the U.S. between January through late May, 1875. Bishops James Gibbons of Richmond, Patrick Lynch of Charleston, William Gross of Savannah, and William Elder of Natchez, together with Fitzgerald were quite receptive, yet only the Arkansas prelate offered him a huge part of the diocese to evangelize, 126-131. On the founding of the Mill Hill Fathers, or English Josephites and their early work in America see Ochs, *Desegregating the Altar*, 9, 43-85; the date of the Josephites coming to Arkansas, Bishop Fitzgerald to Commission, for Catholic Missions to the Colored People and Indians, 1899, Commission File RG 10, Box 14, Commission Records, Sulpician Archives, Baltimore, Maryland.. All documents quoted come from the Bishop Fitzgerald era, 1887-1907 and were written by Bp. Fitzgerald or his administrator Fr. Fintan Kraemer, O.S.B., and are in the same box. Hereafter this material will be cited as Commission for Catholic Missions, Commission Records, SAB.

[10]Rev. Henry J. Koren, C.S.Sp., *The Serpent and the Dove: A History of the Congregation of the Holy Ghost in the United States, 1784-1984* (Pittsburgh, PA: Spiritus Press, 1985) 117.

[11]Ibid., 119-120.

[12]Ibid., 121, 122.

[13]Ibid., 123.

[14]Ibid., 124.

[15]Bishop Edward M. Fitzgerald to Commission for Catholic Missions, 7 May 1887, 6 September 1887, Commission Records, SAB.

[16]Bishop Fitzgerald to Commission for Catholic Missions, 21 May 1888, Commission Records, SAB.

[17]Bishop Fitzgerald to Commission for Catholic Missions, 21 April 1891, Commission Records, SAB.

[18]Bishop Fitzgerald to Commission for Catholic Missions, 1896, 1898, Fr. Fintan Kraemer to Commission for Catholic Missions, 1900, 1 July 1906; for the numbers estimated see the reports from 50 in 1893 to 250 in 1895, most years to 1899 the numbers were listed at 100, over 200 after 1899. From 1889-1900 the reports are not specifically dated except for the year, yet on the documents it is written that the Bishop must submit them on or before August 1st or 15th. After 1901, the reports are dated 7 May 1901, 7 May 1902, 25 July 1903, 10 July 1904, 30 June 1905. Those written between 1900 to 1906 were penned by Fr. Fintan Kraemer, O.S.B. administrator of the Diocese. All documents found in Commission Records, SAB.

[19]Bishop Fitzgerald to Commission for Catholic Missions, 1897, Commission Records, SAB.

[20]Bishop Fitzgerald to Commission for Catholic Missions, 1895; quote from Fr. Fintan Kraemer to Commission for Catholic Missions, 10 July 1904, Commission Records, SAB.

[21]For the details on Fr. John Michael Lucey, see Diocesan Historical Commission, *A History of Catholicity in Arkansas* (Little Rock, AR: Guardian Press, 1925) n.p. (p. 27-28.) Lucey also kept a large scrapbook of clippings from the newspapers about himself and affairs of Catholic interest. His sketch of the Diocese came at the time of the bishop's jubilee in 1892, and there are other materials on Lucey in the Lucey Papers, Deceased Priests File, ADLR. For Lucey's historical publications see *Publications of the Arkansas Historical Association*, 4 vols. (Little Rock, AR: Democrat Printing and Lithograph Company, 1906, 1917) 2:424-461; 3:201-219.

The dates given as to Lucey's enlistment in the Confederacy and his date of ordination in the published diocesan history is incorrect according to the personal data sheet Lucey filled out for himself just before his death in 1914. That document provides Lucey's birth date and location, Lucey Papers, Deceased Priests File, ADLR.

[22]Lucey's opposition to racial segregation and disenfranchisement, Little Rock *Arkansas Democrat,* 24 January 1890, 3; 11 March 1890, p. 5; Hope *Gazette,* 3 May 1890, p. 4; Little Rock *Arkansas Gazette,* 2 February 1890, 9; Lucey's opposition to lynching, calling it murder and an editorial attacking Lucey for so strong a language in *Arkansas Gazette,* 4 September 1901, 8; 5 September 1901, 4. For an earlier attack by Lucey on lynching see *Arkansas Gazette,* 27 August 1899, 8; 12 October 1899, 4. For an excellent look at Arkansas' segregation laws in the light urban race relations throughout the South see John William Graves, "Jim Crow in Arkansas: A Reconstruction of Urban Race Relations in the Post-Reconstruction South." *Journal of Southern History* 55 (August 1989): 421-448.

[23]Bishop Fitzgerald to Commission for Catholic Missions, 1895, 1899; Fr. Fintan Kraemer to Commission for Catholic Missions, 1900, Commission Records, SAB. On the date of the founding of the Colored Institute which Lucey served as Secretary to the Board of Trustees, using the Sisters of Charity, see Graves, "Jim Crow in Arkansas," 448, n. 87. Also see numerous notices and notes in the Lucey scrapbook from the various commencement exercises and events from institute. That it was located on the east side of Main Street across from Wiley Jones Park see Pine Bluff *Weekly Echo* October 24, 1891; by 1898 Lucey was on the Board of Trustees and overseeing much of the day-to-day operation together with the Sisters of Charity, Pine Bluff *Graphic,* 5 June 1898, 6 June 1898; Pine Bluff *Press Eagle,* 21 June 1898, all the above newspaper citations from papers outside of Little Rock come from clippings in Lucey's scrapbook, ADLR. See also Little Rock *Arkansas Gazette,* 1 November 1898, 4., for another description of the institute by prominent citizens from Little Rock like John G. Fletcher and Morris M. Cohn, then president of the Little Rock Board of Trade. This is also an untitled, author unknown, and undated history of St. Peter's Mission in Parish Records, St. Peter's, Pine Bluff, ADLR.

[24]Fr. Plunkett was born in Ireland in 1861 and came to the U.S. in 1885. Trained to be a Josephite, he was ordained into the Society on April 12, 1898 and sent to Pine Bluff on May 1st. This position he held until October 1, 1898. This and other material on the Josephites who served in Arkansas was sent to the author on 15 July 1991 by Fr. Peter E. Hogan, S.S.J., Archivist for the Society of St. Joseph, Baltimore, Md. I am in his debt. For Fr. Plunkett's work in Tennessee see Thomas Stritch, *The Catholic Church in Tennessee: The Sesquicentennial Story* (Nashville, TN: Catholic Center, 1987) 248, 272-273; 275-276.

[25]Pine Bluff *Graphic,* 19 February 1899, n.p. newspaper clipping from Lucey scrapbook, ADLR.

[26]D.H.C., *History of Catholicity in Arkansas,* n.p. (p.99); for a history of the Sisters of the Holy Family, Davis, *History of Black Catholics in the United States,* 105-109. Fr. James J. Nally, S.S.J., born in Ireland in 1865, came to the U.S. in 1879; ordained a Josephite priest June 19, 1900, sent to Pine Bluff in October, 1900 to replace Fr. Plunkett, S.S.J.; Fr. John J. Ferdinand, S.S.J., born in Rochester, New York in 1863, ordained a Josephite priest on November 1, 1901; came to Pine Bluff a year later. Information on these priests, and the date of the dedication of the brick church of St. Peter's from Fr. Peter E. Hogan, S.S.J., Archivist, Society of St. Joseph, sent to author, 15 July 1991.

[27]In the nineteenth century, the Healy brothers were ordained. Born of an Irish immigrant father and an slave mother in Georgia, James Augustine Healy and Alexander Sherwood Healy were ordained as Diocesan priests for the Archdiocese of Boston; Patrick Francis Healy entered the Society of Jesus. James A. Healy became the first person of black heritage to become a bishop in the United States, Bishop of the Diocese of Portland, Maine from 1875-1900, see his biography Albert S. Foley, S.J. *Bishop Healy: Beloved Outcast* (New York: Farrer, Straust Young, 1954). Patrick F. Healy, S.J., became the first person of black heritage to head an American University, president of Georgetown University 1872-1884. The first full-blooded African-American

to be ordained was Fr. Augustine Tolton, ordained a Diocesan priest in Rome in 1886, where he served in Illinois. For his biography consult, Sr. Caroline Hemesaith, O.F.M., *From Slave to Priest: A Biography of Rev. Augustine Tolton, 1854-1897, First Afro-American Priest in the United States* (Chicago, IL: Franciscan Herald Press, 1973). The first African-American priest in the Society of St. Joseph was Fr. Charles Randolph Uncles, ordained in 1891. Being ordained in 1902, Fr. Dorsey was the first African-American to be ordained to the Catholic priesthood in the United States in this century. This information is found in Ochs, *Desegregating the Altar*, 26-29, 64, 81, 123; Davis, *History of Black Catholics*, 146-162.

[28]The differences between the Josephite minor and major seminary can be found in Ochs, *Desegregating the Altar*, 3; the descriptive quote in the text, p. 145. For the information as to the personal and spiritual background of Fr. John Henry Dorsey sent to author from Fr. Peter E. Hogan, Archivist, Society of St. Joseph, 15 July 1991.

[29]Ochs, *Desegregating the Altar*, 145. 145-147, quote of Fr. Pierre LeBeau, 145.

[30]Ibid., 145-147; Davis, *History of Black Catholics*, 155-162.

[31]On Dorsey's problems with black Protestant ministers and Lucey's opinion of the Josephites see Ochs, *Desegregating the Altar*, 147-149.

[32]Ibid., 149-150.

[33]For Lucey's position about Dorsey's appointment, as well as Lucey's own account of the whole affair see Monsignor John M. Lucey, "The Matter of Rev. J.H. Dorsey of St. Peter's (Colored) Church, Pine Bluff, Arkansas: A Report to the Rt. Reverend John B. Morris, Bishop of Little Rock, November 18, 1907," 1. Unpublished typed manuscript, Dorsey Papers, Deceased Priests File, ADLR.

[34]The "criminal intimacy" quote from Lucey, "The Matter of Rev. J.H. Dorsey," 3; the rest of the material from Ochs, *Desegregating the Altar*, 151, surviving parishioner quoted on p. 153.

[35]Bishop Morris quoted in Ochs, *Desegregating the Altar*, 152.

[36]Ibid., 152-153, quote on p. 153.

[37]Fr. Dorsey quoted in Ibid., 152.

[38]Ibid., 152-155.

[39]Ibid., 155-156; Lucey, "The Matter of J.H. Dorsey," 3-4.

[40]Dorsey's letter quoted in Ochs, *Desegregating the Altar*, 156-157, quote on prejudice, p. 157.

[41]Fr. Murphy quoted in Ibid., 158. Donovan had initially replaced Fr. Dorsey with a Belgian-born Josephite priest named Fr. Joseph Anciaux, S.S.J. (1860-1931); a man who personally sparked a papal investigation of the treatment of black Catholics in the United States in his long confidential report to the Holy Father, Pope Leo XIII, dated June 21, 1903. The Vatican put so much pressure on the American bishops about this that they set up the American Board for Mission Work among the Colored People on April 21, 1906, under the direction of a Monsignor John Burke who worked out of New York City. Morris would have very little to do with this Catholic board, preferring to get money from the older Commission for Catholic Missions to the Colored People and Indians. The Arkansas bishop also refused to allow Anciaux to come to Arkansas, writing Fr. Donovan on October 12, 1907 that he refused "for reasons known only to myself." For Fr. Anciaux's career as a Josephite and his report to the Holy Father and the impact it had on the creation of this special board see Ochs, pp. 126-127, 138-143; Morris' note to Donovan quoted on p. 158. Fr. William A. Murphy, S.S.J., was born in Salem, Massachusetts, and ordained a Josephite priest on June 21, 1905. He stayed at St. Peter's from October, 1907 to May 27, 1909 when he was sent to St. Peter Claver's parish in San Antonio. The dates of Fr. Anciaux's life and the career of Fr. William A. Murphy is found in material sent to the author from Fr. Peter E. Hogan, S.S.J. Archivist of the Society of St. Joseph, 15 July 1991.

[42]Ochs, *Desegregating the Altar*, 156; D.H.C., *History of Catholicity in Arkansas*, n.p. (p.98); Lucey death date in Lucey Papers, Deceased Priests File, ADLR. Kraemer's claim of two hundred and fifty students in 1904, Kraemer to Commission for Catholic Missions, 10 July 1904, Commission Files, SAB; *Official Catholic Directory, 1916* (New York:P.J. Kenedy & Sons, 1916) 511.

[43]Fr. Albert's request for Dorsey to speak in 1913 and his description of Dorsey as a good friend and the bishop's refusal see Fr. John J. Albert, S.S.J. to Bp. Morris, 15 November 1913; Bishop Morris to Fr. John J. Albert, S.S.J., 22 November 1913; on the rainy evening talk in January, 1915, see Fr. Albert S.S.J., to Bishop Morris, 24 January 1915; Bishop demands an apology for inviting him and Albert apologizes, Morris to Albert, 27 January 1915; Fr. Albert to Morris, 28 January 1915. The letters of 1913 are in Parish Records, St. Peter's Pine Bluff, the letters of 1915 in Dorsey Papers, Deceased Priests File, all correspondence in ADLR. For Dorsey's speaking tour and another perspective on Dorsey's visit in 1915, plus his career after the tour and his manner of death see Ochs, *Desegregating the Altar*, 182, 185, 225, 276-277. For Fr. John J. Albert, S.S.J., background and age is from material sent to the author from Fr. Peter E. Hogan, S.S.J., archivist of the Society of St. Joseph, 15 July 1991.

[44]Bishop Morris to Commission for Catholic Missions, 1 July 1907, Commission Records, SAB. For the story of Fr. Krueger's appointment at St. Bartholomew, D.H.C., *History of Catholicity in Arkansas*, 46; on his appointment at Little Rock College; *Official Catholic Directory, 1911* (New York: P.J. Kenedy & Sons, 1911) 476; On his birth date and his background, plus his career after 1912 in Rome and the German army and his failure to return to the U.S., Krueger Papers, Deceased Priests File, ADLR.

[45]D.H.C., *History of Catholicity in Arkansas*, n.p. (4647); *Golden Anniversary: St. Bartholomew Parish, Little Rock, Arkansas, 1909-1960* (Little Rock, AR: Guardian Press, 1960) 57. A copy of this pamphlet in Parish Records, St. Bartholomew's, Little Rock, ADLR.

[46]For a brief history of Society of the Divine Word and their coming to America and the founding of their first mission in the South see *New Catholic Encyclopedia* 15 volumes and index (New York: McGraw-Hill, 1967) 4:923-924; on the work of Fr. Matthew Christman and his Seminaries in Mississippi, and the lack of enthusiasm for black priests in Josephite order under the administration of Fr. Louis Pastorelli, Superior from 1918-1942, see Ochs, *Desegregating the Altar*, 215-270; "German tenacity" quote on p. 250.

[47]Fr. Eugene J. Weibel to Leopoldine Society, Austria, Vienna, 30 November 1898, Austria's Leopoldine Society microfilm, Supplemental Reel 2, frame 231. This quote, and all other quotes from the Leopoldine Society microfilm collection, is from an annotated translation of the letters. Both the film and the annotated translation found in AUND.

[48]Fr. Matthew Saettele, O.S.B., to Leopoldine Society, 28 November 1901, 10 October 1896, Leopoldine Microfilm collection, Supplemental Reel 2, frames 257, 207, AUND.

[49]Fr. Matthew Saettele, O.S.B., to Leopoldine Society, 18 November 1905, Leopoldine Microfilm collection, Supplemental Reel 2, frame 271, AUND.

[50]Fr. Matthew Saettele, O.S.B., to Leopoldine Society, 20 November 1910, Leopolding Microfilm collection, Supplemental Reel 2; frame 275, AUND.

[51]*Official Catholic Directory, 1910* (New York: P.J. Kenedy and Sons, 1910) 451.

[52]On the Elaine Race Riots see Oscar A. Rogers, Jr. "The Elaine Race Riots of 1919," *Arkansas Historical Quarterly* 19 (Summer, 1960): 142-150; Richard C. Cortner, *A Mob Intent on Death: The N.A.A.C.P. and the Arkansas Riot Cases* (Middleton, CT: Wesleyan University Press, 1988).

[53]Davis, *History of Black Catholics*, 164.

[54]Ibid., 165, quote, 166.

[55]Ibid., 163-164, 171-174; Rudd participated later that year in the first Catholic laymen's Congress held in November, 1889 in Baltimore to commemorate the centennial of the creation of the American Catholic hierarchy, p. 175.

[56]Ibid., 175-176.

[57]Ibid., 213.

[58]Ibid., 213-214; Dan Rudd to Bishop Morris, 17 May 1919; the request for money letter dated 23 May 1919; the letter in which Morris gave him the money and expressed his confidence in him, 18 June 1919, various leaflets form the N.A.A.C.P., dated 1919; all documents in Morris Papers, ADLR.

[59]Rudd to Morris, undated; Morris to Rudd, 28 September 1920, both letters in Morris

Papers, ADLR.

[60]Rudd to Morris, 12 July 1926, Morris Papers, ADLR. The letter dated incorrectly as 1896; an obvious mistake, see Davis, *History of Black Catholics,* 312.

[61]Davis, *History of Black Catholics,* 214.

[62]For a look at Morris' negotiations for the Spiritans in 19071908, and the new provincial and his placing the Holy Spirit Fathers in black parishes in the South see Koren, *The Serpent and the Dove,* 188, 260-278.

[63]Ibid., 278-279.

[64]Ibid., 279.

[65]Much of the early story of St. Cyprian's black Catholic church in Helena told in Koren, *Serpent and the Dove,* 280-281; on the one convert on Christmas day, and ten converts by August see Bishop Morris to American Board of Catholic Missions, 1 August 1929, Morris Papers, ADLR. The American Board of Catholic Missions set up by the bishops in 1919 to coordinate solicitation and support of Catholic missions in the United States. This is the first record in the archives of Bishop Morris making a report to this particular board, yet in this report he tells of the exploits of Fr. Murphy in Helena. For the origin of the American Board of Catholic Missions see *New Catholic Encyclopedia,* 1:398.

[66]For the dates of these churches see Parish Records, St. Patrick's, and St. Mary's, both in North Little Rock, ADLR.

[67]For the history of St. Augustine see *Golden Jubilee: St. Augustine's Catholic Church, North Little Rock, Arkansas.* (North Little Rock, AR: Private Printing, 1979), 5. This documents in Parish Records, St. Augustine's, North Little Rock, ADLR. Fr. Joseph H. Haarmann, S.V.D., to Bishop Morris, 27 May 1929, Morris Papers, ADLR.

[68]Bishop Morris to Fr. Bruno Hagspiel, S.V.D., 16 January 1931; for other complaints about Fr. Haarmann see Bishop Morris to Fr. Bruno Hagspiel, S.V.D., 17 December 1930, both letters in Morris Papers, ADLR.

[69]*Golden Jubilee, St. Augustine's Catholic Church,* 5.

[70]Davis, *History of Black Catholics,* 189, 211; Ochs, *Desegregating the Altar,* 225.

[71]Davis, *History of Black Catholics,* 190.

[72]Fr. John F. Thompson's background from material sent to the author Fr. Peter E. Hogan, Archivist, Society of St. Joseph, 15 July 1991. Seymour Jones to Monsignor Winand Aretz, 16 April 1928. In his letter, Mr. Jones mentions that Fr. Thompson had been at St. Peter's for a year and a half. Both of these documents in Parish Records, St. Peter's, Pine Bluff, ADLR. More material on the ten Josephites who served in Arkansas can also be obtained at the Josephite Archives, Baltimore, Maryland.

[73]Fr. John Thompson, S.S.J., to Monsignor Winand Aretz, 1 May 1928, Parish Records, St. Peter's, Pine Bluff, ADLR.

[74]Seymour Jones to Monsignor Aretz, 15 June 1928; 6 August 1928, Parish Records, St. Peter's, Pine Bluff, ADLR.

[75]Fr. Thompson's withdrawal from Pine Bluff is from material sent to the author from Fr. Peter E. Hogan, S.S.J., Archivist, Society of St. Joseph, 15 July 1991. Official Record of Appointment, Fr. Bruno Drescher, S.V.D., 12 October 1928, signed by the Chancellor Fr. Albert L. Fletcher, Parish Records, St. Peter's, Pine Bluff, ADLR.

[76]The number of baptisms and converts while at St. Peter's are taken from Fr. Peter E. Hogan, S.S.J., archivist for the Society of St. Joseph, to author, 15 July 1991.

[77]Bishop Morris to Commission for Catholic Missions to the Colored People and Indians, dated just January, 1927, Morris Papers, ADLR. The two colleges Morris was referring to was that of the Methodist Church, Philander Smith College, and Arkansas Baptist College. There was also the Arkansas Agricultural, Mechanical, and Normal College in Pine Bluff and Shorter College in North Little Rock. This information was taken from T. Harri Baker and Jane Browning, *An Arkansas History For Young People* (Fayetteville, AR: University of Arkansas Press, 1991) 277. Despite the fact the book is geared to young students, it is, in my opinion, the best one volume survey of Arkansas in print.

[78]Bishop Morris to the Commission for Catholic Missions to the Colored People and Indians, January 1927, Morris Papers, ADLR.

[79]Ibid., Indiffentism is "a doctrinal system that exalts the attitude (internal) that all philosophical opinions, all religions, and all ethical doctrines regarding life are equally true and valuable. Accordingly, no one religion contains certain truth. It differs from religious tolerance (in which a religion–considered false–is permitted to exist), from irreligion (in which all religions are judged to be false), from civil religious freedom of conscience (in which the state makes no judgement about the value of various forms of worships), and religious neutralism (in which the state does not become involved in religious controversy). It also differs from practical religious indifference, which is the neglect of religious practice arising from contempt of religion or from psychological, sociological, and environmental factors." *New Catholic Encyclopedia,* 7:469.

[80]Bishop Morris to Commission for Catholic Missions to the Colored People and the Indians, January, 1927, Morris Papers, ADLR.

[81]Ibid.

CHAPTER IX

[1]Records of Bishop Morris' various *ad limina* visits, Morris Papers, ADLR.

[2]There is no published account of Arkansas in the Depression; this material was taken from T. Harri Baker and Jane Browning, *An Arkansas History for Young People* (Fayetteville, AR: University of Arkansas Press, 1919) 287-288.

[3]*The Guardian,* 12 July 1930, 1.

[4]On the closing of the school, see C. Fred Williams, *A History of Pharmacy in Arkansas* (North Little Rock, AR: Heritage Press, 1982) 53, not another until 1946, 55-59.

[5]Morris' circular about financial assistance was sent out on January 1931. In the letters of correspondence, he does tell parish priests to let him know of emergency cases requiring some financial assistance; these circulars in Morris Papers, ADLR.

[6]On the announcement of this affair and the description of the event see *The Guardian,* 21 March 1931, p. 1; 14 May 1931, 1, 4, 5, 7. That Governor Harvey Parnell came to the rally, Governor Harvey Parnell to Fr. John H. Healy, 9 April 1931, Morris Papers, ADLR. A 16mm silent home movie of the event filmed by then Fr. Francis A. Allen is in ADLR.

[7]Born in Nashville, Tennessee, on August 17, 1887, Stritch has once been an altar boy at the cathedral under then Fr. John B. Morris, who inspired the young man to enter the priesthood. Ordained for the Diocese of Nashville on May 21, 1910, Stritch served as pastor in Nashville and Memphis before being named chancellor of the diocese in 1918. In 1921, Pope Benedict XVI made him the second Bishop of Toledo and the youngest bishop in the United States at the time. Nine years later, a year before coming to Arkansas, he became the Archbishop of Milwaukee. Thomas Stritch, *The Catholic Church in Tennessee: The Sesquicentennial Story* (Nashville, TN: The Catholic Center, 1987) 223, 225, 232-236. The author of the sesquicentennial history of the Catholic Church in Tennessee is the son of Thomas Stritch and Ellen Morris Stritch; he graduated from the University of Notre Dame and later served there as a journalism professor and a professor of American studies. As Thomas Stritch points out about his uncle Samuel Stritch, "A good biography of him has yet to be written." p. 234.

[8]*The Guardian,* 14 May 1931, 1, 4; Little Rock *Arkansas Gazette,* 6 May 1931, 1; 7 May 1931, 1, 13; 8 May 1931, 1.

[9]Speech of Bishop Morris on the 25th anniversary of the ordination of Cardinal Stritch, Milwaukee, Wisconsin, 21 May 1935, Morris Papers, ADLR.

[10]Morris invitation to Dougherty's installation, Dougherty to Morris, 17 May 1918; Morris accepts, Morris to Dougherty, 21 May 1918, letters in Morris Papers, ADLR.

[11]Morris to Dougherty, 3 July 1936, Morris Papers, ADLR.

[12]Interview with Msgr. James E. O'Connell, 14 August 1989, audio-tape copy in ADLR. There are still a fair number of priests working in the diocese who came from Philadelphia, Fr. Francis I Malone and his uncle, Fr. Bernard Malone, Fr. George Tribou, Msgr. John O'Donnell, Msgr. William Burke, Msgr. Joseph Burns, Fr. Gus McKee, Fr. Joseph Milan, Fr. John Barnes, and

others, both living and dead, who came to the diocese from the Archdiocese of Philadelphia.

[13]Mundelein's celebration of his silver jubilee in Rome and the career of his Auxiliary Bishop William O'Brien, see *New Catholic Encyclopedia,* 15 vols. (New York: McGraw-Hill, 1967) 10:71; 3:266; Morris' copy of his speech in Morris Papers, ADLR.

[14]Roger Baudier, *The Catholic Church in Louisiana* (New Orleans, LA: Private Printing, 1939) 555; Morris speech given that day, dated May 15, 1935, is in the Morris Papers, ADLR.

[15]Stritch, *Catholic Church in Tennessee,* 321, 323; a copy of Morris' speech, dated October 3, 1937, in Morris Papers, ADLR.

[16]Morris' address at the Eucharistic Congress in New Orleans, n.d; speech on the Golden Jubilee of St. Vincent's Infirmary, May 24, 1938; speech of the Golden Jubilee at Jonesboro, October 4, 1938. Copies of all three speeches found in the Morris Papers, ADLR.

[17]For Morris' problems with his knee by the late 1930s, I have relied on two priests who knew Bishop Morris well in the late 1930s and the last years of his life, Msgr. James E. O'Connell, interview 14 August 1989, Msgr. John Murphy, interview, 17 August 1989. Bishop Morris informed Archbishop Stritch about his knee surgery in 1937. Morris to Stritch, 23 September 1937, Morris Papers, ADLR.

[18]B.A. Brooks to Bishop John B. Morris, 18 November 1938, Morris Papers, ADLR. On the night of the Broken Glass persecution of the Jews see William L. Shirer, *The Rise and Fall of the Third Reich: A History of Nazi Germany* (New York: Simon and Schuster, 1959, Touchstone Paperback Edition, 1960) 430-434. For a firsthand account of the rally see Little Rock *Arkansas Gazette,* 24 November 1938, 1, 9. Other ministers there included Rev. H. W. Smith of the Second Presbyterian Church of Little Rock and Rev. L.M. Sipes of Pulaski Heights Baptist Church of Little Rock.

[19]American Legion Speech, 23 November 1938, copy in Morris Papers, ADLR. Portions of this speech also covered in *The Guardian,* 9 December 1938, 1.

[20]American Legion Speech, 23 November 1938, Morris Papers, ADLR.

[21]Ibid.

[22]Ibid. For Pius XI condemnation of Nazism, see his Encyclical Letter, 14 March 1937, On the condition of the Church in Germany (Washington, D.C.: National Catholic Welfare Conference Publication, 1937).

[23]Fr. Gerald P. Fogarty, S.J., *The Vatican and the American Hierarchy From 1870 to 1965* (Wilmington, DE: Michael Glazier, 1985) 249.

[24]Most of the Catholic bishops, and indeed most American Catholics, were not as outspoken as Morris on Nazi anti-semitism. In the late 1930s, most American Catholic public opinion was more concerned with American neutrality and/or helping Franco or keeping the U.S. from helping the leftist loyalist government in the Spanish Civil War. George Q. Flynn, *Roosevelt and Romanism: Catholic and American Diplomacy, 1937-1945* (Westport, CT: Greenwood Press, 1976) 2-23, 29-55.

[25]Morris used funds from a strapped diocese, Catholic Extension Society and the Board for Catholic Missions to the Colored People and Indians, see Morris to Fr. Bruno Drescher, S.V.D., 17 March 1931; 20 March 1931; 10 December 1931. That the farm might support 300 people and the exact amount of acres is contained in an undated newsletter published at St. Raphael's, called "Smiles from the Sunny South." That Drescher had been in the Society for about 35 years, see Chancellor Albert Fletcher to Edward Rinck, Cincinnati, Ohio, 31 December 1933. Morris wrote Bishop William O'Brien of Chicago that he used a lot of their money for his colored orphanage, Bishop Morris to William O'Brien, 30 December 1932. Most documents in Parish Records, St. Raphael's, Pine Bluff, ADLR. Last letter cited in Morris Papers, ADLR.

[26]Bishop Morris to E.A. Burrow, Editor of the *Ozark* (AR) *Spectator*, 18 July 1934, Parish Records, St. Raphael's, Pine Bluff, ADLR.

[27]The opening program and blessing of St. Raphael's is in the archives. That it revitalized, see letter of Fr. Gregory H. Keller pastor at St. Joseph's Catholic Church in Pine Bluff to Bishop Morris, 22 June 1933, Parish Records, St. Raphael's, Pine Bluff, ADLR.

[28]Fr. Bruno Hagspiel, S.V.D., to Bishop Morris, 10 June 1933; Fr. Gregory H. Keller to

Bishop Morris, 22 June 1933, Parish Records, St. Raphael's, Pine Bluff, ADLR.

[29]Bishop Morris to Fr. Bruno Hagspiel, S.V.D., 26 June 1933; Fr. Drescher to Bishop Morris, 14 September 1933, both in Parish Records, St. Raphael's, Pine Bluff, ADLR.

[30]Exchange used in the text, Mr. Edward Rinck of Cincinnati, Ohio, to Chancellor Albert L. Fletcher, 20 December 1933; Fletcher to Rinck, 31 December 1933; other letters about this matter, Rinck to Bishop Morris, 24 November 1933, Fletcher to Rinck, 3 December 1933; Rinck to Fletcher 14 January 1934, all letters in Parish Records, St. Raphael, Pine Bluff, ADLR.

[31]The careers of the deacon and the priests assigned to St. Raphael's and problems with managing the farms contained in Parish Records, St. Raphael's, Pine Bluff, ADLR. Bishop Morris was aware of the many problems, see his letter of appointment to Fr. Thomas Reynolds, 15 June 1935, but even Reynolds' hard work could not make St. Raphael's a success. This last letter in the collection cited in this endnote.

[32]That the institution started with eight children, see their picture taken about 1932 in Fr. Drescher's undated newsletter and pamphlet, "Smiles from the Sunny South"; as for the amount of 22 by 1937, see Fr. Reynolds to Bishop Morris, 9 April 1937, both documents in Parish Records, St. Raphael's, Pine Bluff, ADLR. Morris wrote in 1933 that the institution could hold 150 orphan children; Bishop Morris to American Board for Catholic Missions, 1933 report, Morris Papers, ADLR.

[33]Chancellor Albert L. Fletcher to Fr. Thomas Reynolds, 18 December 1938, Parish Records, St. Raphael's, Pine Bluff, ADLR.

[34]Bishop Morris to Bishop O'Brien, 4 April 1938, Morris Papers, ADLR.

[35]Ibid. Brother Anthony of the Franciscan Brothers assumed control in January 1938, and was operating the school for the rest of the episcopate of Bishop Morris. For a look at this, the second technical school for blacks in Arkansas, see Parish Records, St. Raphael's, Pine Bluff, ADLR.

[36]Bishop Morris to American Board for Catholic Mission, 1938 report, Morris Papers, ADLR. In the same report, Morris also wrote that "anti-Catholic sentiment hostility has reached even the Negro and he is very wary and suspicious of all the works of the Church."

[37]The foundation of St. Gabriel's Catholic Church and school in Hot Springs are in Fr. Henry J. Koren, *The Serpent and the Dove: A History of the Congregation of the Holy Ghost Fathers in the United States, 1784-1984* (Pittsburgh, PA: Spiritus Press, 1985) 365; "Parish History of St. Gabriel's, Hot Springs," n.a., dated 1954, Parish Histories, St. Gabriel's, Hot Springs, ADLR.

[38]For a brief description of the life and martyrdom of these black African martyrs, *New Catholic Encyclopedia*, 8:1106.

[39]On the history of Holy Martyrs of Uganda Catholic Church in El Dorado see Renee Moon, "Arkansas Black Catholic Homecoming: A Family Strengthening its New Ties and Renewing Its Old Relations," pamphlet/program for a celebration held at St. John's Catholic Center, 27 November 1982, p. 2. Fr. Raymond J. Marmon, born in Jonesboro in 1889, was ordained for the Diocese of Little Rock in 1926, stayed at Holy Martyrs until the Franciscan Fathers took over on January 24, 1952. Marmon's life and career see Marmon Papers, Deceased Priests File, all items in ADLR.

[40]Bishop Morris to William O'Brien, 21 September 1944, Morris Papers, ADLR; documents in Parish Records, St. Raphael's, Pine Bluff, ADLR.

[41]*Official Catholic Directory, 1945* (New York: P.J. Kenedy and Sons, 1945) 526. Also see, Bishop Morris to American Board for Catholic Missions, 28 September 1945, Morris Papers, ADLR.

[42]Bishop Morris to American Board for Catholic Missions, 28 September 1945, Morris Papers, ADLR.

[43]Information on Catholic population, churches, and clergy from *Official Catholic Directory, 1920* (New York: P.J. Kenedy and Sons, 1920) 435; the white population in 1920 stood at 1,279,757, these numbers and the state total conveniently presented in Baker and Browning, *An Arkansas History for Young People*, 308.

[44]Information on Catholic population, churches and clergy from *Official Catholic Directory, 1930* (New York: P.J. Kenedy and Sons, 1930) 452. The white population in 1930 stood at 1,375,315, and the other census numbers for 1930 can be readily found in Baker and Browning, *An Arkansas History for Young People*, 308.

[45]The number of whites in Arkansas that year was 1,466,084; this and the other census numbers for 1940 were taken from Baker and Browning, *Arkansas History for Young People*, 308; information on Catholic numbers from *Official Catholic Directory, 1940* (New York: P.J. Kenedy and Sons, 1940), 445. There was a study of religious bodies in the United States done by the Census Bureau in 1906, 1916, 1926, 1936. By its own admission later, however, only the 1926 reading is accurate. U.S. Department of Commerce, Bureau of the Census, *Historical Statistics of the United States: Colonial Times to 1970* 2 vols. (Washington, D.C.: Government Printing Office, 1975) 1:389. The Census after 1936 no longer took numbers; and information on religious preferences for different states really comes basically from each denomination.

[46]*Extension Magazine* 31 (March 1935) 1, 2, 21. Information about the seminary, as well as a look at the seminarians, chapel, and activities in the seminary in the fall of 1938 on a 16 mm film made by Father (later Msgr.) Francis A. Allen. Copy of this film, as well large boxes of seminary records are in ADLR.

[47]*The Guardian*, 19 June 1942, 13.

[48]Horan's background, titles and positions are revealed in Deceased Priests, ADLR: Diocesan Historical Commission, *The History of Catholicity in Arkansas* (Little Rock, AR: Guardian Press, 1925) n.p. (42, 115, 116).

[49]D.H.C., *History of Catholicity in Arkansas*, n.p. (116). On how Dr. Horon is remembered, see *Arkansas Diamond Jubilee, 1899-1974*, a pamphlet (Fort Smith, AR: Private Printing, 1974), n.p. (15-16). This pamphlet celebrates the founding of the Catholic parish in Fort Smith. Its pre-Civil War name was St. Patrick's, the name changed just prior to the Civil War. The beautiful structure of Immaculate Conception Church built when Fr. Lawrence Smyth was pastor was dedicated by Bishop Edward M. Fitzgerald on June 1. 1899. This had long been a landmark structure at the head of Garrison Street in Fort Smith, n.p. (314).

[50]Story on Horan and the car from a taped interview by Mr. Thomas J. Sexton with Joe B. Miller, a longtime resident of Fort Smith and parishioner at Immaculate Conception. As a young man, he was deeply impressed with Msgr. Horan. Thomas J. Sexton interview with Joe B. Miller, 28 December 1988, Fort Smith, Arkansas. Mr. Miller died in March, 1989. I am grateful to Mr. Thomas J. Sexton for allowing me to use this material.

[51]Morris to Horan, 9 May 1927; Horan to Morris, 21 May 1927, Horan Papers, Deceased Priests File, ADLR.

[52]Horan to Morris, 13 November 1927, Horan Papers, Deceased Priests File, ADLR.

[53]There are numerous letters in Horan's file between him and the bishop concerning complaints in the text between 1930-1935. The letter cited is Fr. Thomas Keaney to Bishop Morris, 21 December 1932, Horan Papers, Deceased Priests File, ADLR. Mr. Miller confirms that much of the parish was hostile or indifferent to Morris owing a lot to the influence of Msgr. Horan, Sexton interview with Miller, 28 December 1988.

[54]Quote on "passive opposition" from Morris to Cardinal Pieto Fumasoni-Biondi, 21 December 1932, Morris to Horan, 20 February 1933; Horan to Morris, 22 February 1933, all letters in Horan Papers, Deceased Priests File, ADLR.

[55]Horan to Morris, 21 June 1935; Fletcher, Chancellor to Fr. Thomas Martin, Consulter of the Diocese, 22 October 1935; that Morris had called for Horan's resignation after talking to the Board of Consultors, see Morris to Cardinal Cicognani, 24 November 1935; last quote from Cicognani to Morris 10 December 1935, petition sent to Cicognani also sent to Morris, all documents in Horan Papers, Deceased Priests File, ADLR.

[56]Horan to Cardinal Cicognani, 7 December 1935; Morris to Cardinal Cicognani, 17 December 1935, both in Horan Papers, Deceased Priests File, ADLR.

[57]Cardinal Cicognani to Horan, 30 December 1935; Horan to Cardinal Cicognani, 3 January 1936; Horan to Morris, 25 February 1936; Fletcher to Horan, 27 February 1936; his death, from

Mercy Hospital in New Orleans, see Auxiliary Bishop Albert Fletcher to Garth Healy, Irish Consulate, Chicago, IL, 9 October 1944. All documents in Horan Papers, Deceased Priests File, ADLR.

[58]For the story of the date this organization started and where it held its first meeting see *The Guardian,* 27 June 1936, 1. The same article listed Ms. Nora Miles as its first president. That the organization is still active, there is a 1991 directory which lists all its past presidents. The directory in the possession of Mrs. Martha McNeil, a long time member of the Catholic Business and Professional Women's Organization.

[59]For the bishop directing all Catholic women's organization into Diocesan Council of Catholic Women see Bishop Morris to the Women of the Diocese, 12 October 1937; the statewide organization met and made up their by laws and constitution on 31 January 1938, both of these documents are in Morris Papers, ADLR.

[60]That the National Council of Catholic Women associated with the National Catholic Welfare Conference, the national Bishop's organization since the 1920s see James J. Hennesey, S.J., *American Catholics: A History of the Roman Catholic Community in the United States* (New York: Oxford University Press, 1981) 245.

[61]Bishop Morris to Archbishop Samuel Stritch, 30 September 1937, Morris Papers, ADLR.

[62]Author's interview with Msgr. John Murphy, Little Rock, Arkansas, 17 August 1989, audio-tape in ADLR.

[63]Author's interview with Msgr. William Galvin, Fort Smith, Arkansas, 24 August 1989, audio-tape in ADLR.

[64]Author's interview with Msgr. James O'Connell, Little Rock, Arkansas, 14 August 1989, audio-tape in ADLR.

[65]Auxiliary Bishop William O'Brien of Chicago to Bishop Morris, 27 February 1941, Morris Papers, ADLR.

[66]Author's interview with Thomas Stritch, South Bend, Indiana, 27 July 1989.

[67]Morris to Patrick Morrissey, 6 February 1934, Morris Papers, ADLR.

[68]Morris to Sr. Madeleine Morris, 24 August 1936; 29 October 1936, Morris Papers, ADLR.

[69]Morris being caught in France, see *The Guardian,* 1 September 1939, 1; 8 September 1939, 1; 15 September 1939, 1.

[70]Morris to Bishop O'Brien, 20 September 1939, Morris Papers, ADLR.

[71]*The Guardian,* 15 December 1939, 1; Little Rock *Arkansas Gazette,* 12 December 1939, 14.

[72]John Gould Fletcher has been the subject of a recent biography, Lucas Carpenter, *John Gould Fletcher and Southern Modernism* (Fayetteville, AR: University of Arkansas Press, 1990).

[73]*The Guardian* 15 December 1939, 1, 8; Little Rock *Arkansas Gazette,* 12 December 1939, 14. For a look at Fletcher's own account of his early life in his own papers, written in the middle 1970s, Bishop Albert Fletcher, "Reminiscences", 1-50, Fletcher Papers, ADLR.

[74]Ibid., That the position was vacant from late 1929 to 1933, see *Official Catholic Directory, 1931* (New York: P.J. Kenedy and Sons, 1931) 458; *Official Catholic Directory, 1932* (New York: P.J. Kenedy and Sons, 1932) 465; *Official Catholic Directory, 1933* (New York: P.J. Kenedy and Sons, 1933) 477. That Fletcher visited Little Italy when he was a young priest see author's interview with Louis Belotti, 25 July 1990, in ADLR. For a look at Fletcher's career, 1920-1940, as he saw it and a long account of his visit to Rome with Bishop Morris, see Fletcher, "Reminiscences," 49-117, Fletcher Papers, ADLR.

[75]*The Guardian* 15 December 1939, 8; Little Rock *Arkansas Gazette,* 12 December 1939, 14.

[76]The affair is described in Little Rock *Arkansas Gazette,* 24 April 1940, 1; 25 April 1940, 1; 26 April 1940, 14; the Diocesan newspaper ran a special edition of *The Guardian,* 3 May 1940, 1-2.

[77]Rev. Hugh Assenmacher, O.S.B., *A Place Called Subiaco: A History of the Benedictine Monks in Arkansas* (Little Rock, AR: Rose Publishing Company, 1977), 266-270, 291-338. These pages cover the career of Abbot Edward Burgert, O.S.B.

[78]For Abbot Paul Nahlen, O.S.B.'s background, see Ibid., 340-346.

[79]Ibid., 339-347; quote on 347.

[80]Ibid., 349-350.

[81]Ibid., 350-351.

[82]Mr. Jewitt became Knight of St. Gregory at St. Andrew's Cathedral on 20 April 1930. On 29 May 1932, he was granted the title of Grand Cross Knight of the Holy Sepulchre. That he would serve as chairman of the St. John's Seminary, Jewitt to Morris, 28 May 1935, presented money for a school for Immaculate Conception in Fort Smith, Jewitt to Morris, 22 October 1935; church in West Memphis, 23 December 1936. These documents and letter are just a sample of documents found in a small box labeled Charles Jewitt, ADLR.

[83]Assenmacher, *A Place Called Subiaco*, 352-354.

[84]Ibid., 371-373.

[85]Flynn, *Roosevelt and Romanism*, 184-224.

[86]Major Thomas Lewis, Office of Selective Service, 24 January 1942; Fletcher to Major Thomas Lewis, 27 January 1942, both letters in Box AA, ADLR.

[87]Auxiliary Bishop Albert Fletcher to Fr. Edward McCormack, 14 April 1944, McCormack Papers, Deceased Priests File, ADLR.

[88]C. Calvin Smith, *War and Wartime Changes: The Transformation of Arkansas, 1940-1945* (Fayetteville, AR: University of Arkansas Press, 1986) 63-75.

[89]Auxiliary Bishop Fletcher to Fr. Hugh Lavery, M.M., in Los Angeles, California, 9 November 1942; Fr. Hugh Lavery, M.M., to Auxiliary Bishop Fletcher, 16 November 1942, Box AA, ADLR.

[90]Auxiliary Bishop Albert L. Fletcher to Fr. Hugh Lavery, M.M., Los Angeles, California, 13 February 1943, ADLR. *Catholic Directory, 1944* (New York: P.J. Kenedy and Sons, 1944) 520; *Catholic Directory, 1945* (New York: P.J. Kenedy and Sons, 1945) 527.

[91]Smith, *War and Wartime Changes*, 74-75; that Fr. Murphy served the German and Italian prisoners at these camps, see author's interview with Msgr. John Murphy, 17 August 1989, audio tape in ADLR.

[92]Assenmacher, *A Place Called Subiaco*, 365.

[93]For the short monastic career of Fred Demara, alias Robert K. French, see Ibid., 358-359. As the book and the movie would indicate, Demara would later have several different careers after leaving Subiaco.

[94]Little Rock *Arkansas Gazette*, 11 June 1942, 1; 12 June 1942, 1; special section and enlarged issue celebrating this event, see *The Guardian*, 26 June 1942.

[95]For a contemporary report of the centennial celebration see Little Rock *Arkansas Gazette* 28 November 1943, *Gazette Magazine*, 3-4; 1 December 1943, 14. The diocesan newspaper ran a special and much enlarged edition celebrating the diocesan centennial with some special articles about Catholic history in Arkansas. There is also a calendar of events in the Diocese, *The Guardian*, 5 December 1943. The quote, "Well, I made it," and the last quotation from about being fatigued is from Morris to Bishop O'Brien, 6 December 1943, Morris Papers, ADLR.

[96]Author's interview with Msgr. James O'Connell, 14 August 1989, audio tape in ADLR. This appointment confirmed in letter to O'Brien, Bishop Morris to William O'Brien, 25 September 1944, Morris Papers, ADLR.

[97]Auxiliary Bishop Fletcher to Auxiliary Bishop William O'Brien, 6 April 1945, Fletcher Papers, ADLR.

[98]*The Guardian*, 8 June 1945, 1.

[99]Hugh Fullerton, American Consulate, Paris, to Bishop Morris, 4 October 1945, Morris Papers, ADLR. This telegram reported the death of Sister Madeleine Morris on July 23, 1945.

[100]Morris to Bishop O'Brien, 6 December 1945, Morris Papers, ADLR.

[101]Bishop O'Brien to Morris, 26 January 1946, Morris Papers, ADLR.

[102]On the date in which Samuel Stritch became Chicago's first Cardinal, see *New Catholic Encyclopedia*, 13:741; Bishop Morris to O'Brien, 27 April 1946, Morris Papers, ADLR.

[103]Auxiliary Bishop William O'Brien to Bishop Morris, 12 September 1946, Morris Papers, ADLR.

[104]Bishop Morris to Auxiliary Bishop O'Brien, 17 September 1946, Morris Papers, ADLR.

[105]*The Guardian*, 25 October 1946, 1, 2; Little Rock *Arkansas Gazette*, 23 October 1943, 1,2.

[106]*Official Catholic Directory, 1906* (Milwaukee, WI: M.H. Wiltzuis, 1906) 410.

[107]*Official Catholic Directory, 1946* (New York: P.J. Kenedy and Sons, 1946) 551.

[108]For Fletcher's own account of his knowledge of appointment see *The Guardian*, 13 December 1946, 2-3; Little Rock *Arkansas Gazette*, 12 December 1946, 1.

[109]Little Rock *Arkansas Gazette*, 11 February 1947, 1; Fletcher's remarks about wearing the various items of predecessors and the number of priests there see, 12 February 1927, 1, 20; for more of his remarks and his comment about placing the diocese into the hands of Sacred Heart of Jesus and Immaculate Heart of Mary and a published account of Bishop Jeanmard, see *The Guardian*, 14 February 1947, 1, 8. Fletcher's sister, Mrs. Marie Fletcher Frame died in 1946 in Texarkana. This fact was brought up in a latter article on the death of the bishop's mother at the age of 90 on June 20, 1958, *The Guardian*, 27 June 1958, 1, 3.

[110]*The Guardian*, 14 February 1947, 2, 3.

CHAPTER X

[1]I have spoken to a number of people who worked with Bishop Fletcher, Mrs. Martha McNeil, James T. Davis, those who still work in the chancery, interview with William W. O'Donnell, former editor of *The Guardian* and Msgr. John O'Donnell, who had many disagreements with Bishop Fletcher, remembered him as being a gracious and gentlemanly person. Author's interview with William W. O'Donnell, 10 September 1991; Author's interview with Msgr. John O'Donnell. Both tapes in ADLR. Also this can be confirmed by Mrs. Elizabeth Parker, who had known Bishop Fletcher since she was a little girl and worked in the chancery under both Bishops Fletcher and McDonald.

[2]On Fulton J. Sheen's life and career, *see Jay P. Dolan, The American Catholic Experience: A History From Colonial Times to the Present* (New York: Doubleday, 1985; Image Paperback edition, 1987) 393.

[3]Msgr. Fulton J. Sheen to Auxiliary Bishop Albert L. Fletcher, 10 March 1946, Fletcher Papers, ADLR.

[4]Auxiliary Bishop Albert L. Fletcher to Msgr. Fulton J. Sheen, 12 March 1946, Fletcher Papers, ADLR.

[5]Bishop Fletcher died in Little Rock on December 6, 1979, *The Guardian*, 14 December 1979, 1; Archbishop Fulton J. Sheen died in New York City on December 9, 1979, *New York Times*, 10 December 1979, lA.

[6]Bishop Fletcher to Auxiliary Bishop William O'Brien of the Archdiocese of Chicago, 28 May 1948, Fletcher Papers, ADLR.

[7]This testimony from people like Mr. James T. Davis who knew Bishop Fletcher well, and two other clerics who worked closely with him, Msgr. James O'Connell and Msgr. John Murphy, and Mrs. Bobby Kruelen, a secretary to Bishop Fletcher. Author's taped interview with O'Connell, 14 August 1989, Murphy, 17 August 1989, Mrs. Kruelen, 25 July 1990. All these tapes in ADLR.

[8]Fletcher to O'Brien, 24 November 1948, Fletcher Papers, ADLR.

[9]Bishop Fletcher "Reminiscences," unpublished typescript copy, 134-136, Fletcher Papers, ADLR. This will hereafter be cited as "Reminiscences."

[10]Helen Wehr Fletcher was the only member of the bishop's family to see him installed as Arkansas' fourth bishop in 1947. She was born January 17, 1868, in Little Rock and she died at St. Vincent's Infirmary on June 20, 1958. The information in the text on the residence of Bishop Fletcher was taken from author's phone interview with Sr. Richard Walter, O.S.B., St. Scholastica's Convent, Fort Smith, Arkansas, 17 October 1991. Sr. Walter had been Bishop Fletcher's housekeeper during the time he went to Crestwood until 1977. That the bishop lived there until two months before his death, see *The Guardian*, 14 December 1979, l.

[11]That Bishop Fletcher set up a Diocesan Resettlement Commission with Fr. Anthony Lachowsky, C.S.Sp., as its head, see his letter to Fr. Thomas Prendergast, editor of *The Guardian*, 17 July 1948; Fletcher to Lachowsky, 26 October 1948. These letters in a Displaced Persons File,

Fletcher Papers, ADLR.

[12]Bishop Fletcher to Msgr. William Castel, New Orleans Archdiocesan Resettlement Bureau, 5 November 1948, Displaced Persons File, Fletcher Papers, ADLR.

[13]Msgr. William Castel to Bishop Fletcher, 9 March 1949, Fletcher to Msgr. Castel, 16 March 1949; Fr. Louis Janesko to Bishop Fletcher, 11 April 1949, Displaced Persons File, Fletcher Papers, ADLR.

[14]Fr. John M. Bann to Bishop Fletcher, 13 April 1949, Displaced Persons File, Fletcher Papers, ADLR.

[15]Bishop Fletcher to Fr. George Carns, 2 February 1950, Fletcher to Lachowsky, 14 February 1951. There are other letters in the Displaced Persons File dealing with efforts by the U.S. Catholic Church and the Diocese of Little Rock to help these displaced European refugees. Fr. Aloysius Wycislo to Mr. Charles Taylor of Little Rock, Fr. Wycislo of N.C.W.C. asks for help for Lithuanians refugees in the U.S. 29 December 1949; Fr. Emile Komora, Catholic Conference for Refugees, to Fr. Joseph Murray, 21 December 1950; Bishop Fletcher to Fr. Henry J. Thessing, C.S.Sp. 1 December 1950. All of the above in Displaced Persons File, Fletcher Papers, ADLR.

[16]Fletcher, "Reminiscences," p. 137-138, 140-142; *The Guardian*, 23 June 1950, 5, 7; Fr. Joseph M. Lauro and Arthur Orrmont, *Action Priest: The Story of Fr. Joe Lauro* (New York: Morrow, 1971) 258.

[17]For the purchase of Marylake by the diocese, as well as a thumbnail history of the building, see *The Guardian*, 22 February 1952, 1. This article mentions that the group was lead by Fr. Edward Soler, O.C.D. Material given to the author by Marylake later indicated that Fr. Felix Da Prato, O.C.D. was the first prior, said the first Mass there and welcomed the novices in 1952. That information and the source of the other information on Marylake from a letter of Fr. Henry Bordeaux, O.C.D. to James M. Woods, 12 February 1992, copy of this letter with the author.

[18]Fletcher, "Reminiscences," 79-112.

[19]The bishop announced through his diocesan paper in 1949 that he would wait until 1950 to go to see the Holy Father. *The Guardian*, 22 April 1949, 1; for coverage of his trip to Rome and his presence at the canonization of this modern Italian Saint, see *Guardian*, 13 June 1950, 1; 25 June 1950, 3. Maria Goretti was a twelve year old Italian girl killed as she refused to submit to rape. Her assailant, Alessandro Serenelli, was still alive, repentant, and present at her canonization. For an account of the life of St. Maria Goretti and her unique canonization ceremony, see *New Catholic Encyclopedia*, 15 volumes (New York: McGraw-Hill, 1967) 6:632; that her attacker was at her canonization, see John J. Delaney, *Dictionary of Saints* (Garden City, NY: Doubleday and Co., 1980) 262.

[20]For an explanation and documentation of this declaration and the dates of its declaration, see *Catholic Encyclopedia*, 1:971-975.

[21]*The Guardian*, 20 August 1950, 1.

[22]On the Marian devotion in post-War, Cold War America, 19451960, see Dolan, *American Catholic Experience*, 385386.

[23]Bishop Fletcher to the Clergy, Religious, and Laity of the Diocese of Little Rock, 6 March 1951. Fletcher Papers, ADLR. This address printed in *The Guardian*, 16 March 1951, 1.

[24]The rally in Little Rock on Sunday, January 20, 1952 at 8 P.M at Robinson Auditorium, the rally in Fort Smith on Wednesday, January 23rd, and in Jonesboro on Friday, January 25, 1952. For coverage of these rallies see *The Guardian*, 5 October 1951, 1; 18 January 1952, 1, 8; 25 January 1952, 1, 8; 1 February 1952, 1, 8; 8 February 1952, 1, 8. There was local coverage of the Little Rock rally in the secular press, Little Rock *Arkansas Democrat*, 21 January 1952, 3. Fr. Peyton, C.S.C., recently passed away, see a note on his death and career in *Arkansas Catholic* 21 June 1992, 16.

[25]For the opening and closing of the Marian year in the Diocese of Little Rock, *The Guardian*, 4 December 1953, 1; 3 December 1954, 1. For the other events given in the text see the above cited newspaper, 3 September 1954, 17 September 1954, 1,5; 15 October 1954, 1; 29

October 1954, 1. For the position of Auxiliary Bishop Shexnayder, *Catholic Encyclopedia,* 8: 317-318.

[26]*The Guardian,* 2 October 1959, 1.

[27]R.A. Bakewell to Bishop Byrne, 12 March 1862, Byrne Papers, ADLR.

[28]On the opening of the Guardian Church Goods Store, see *The Guardian,* 7 July 1950, 1, 8.

[29]On the history of the Guardian Church Goods store after 1950, I have relied on information from a telephone conversation with Michael Lipsmeyer, 18 October 1991. There is also a large amount of material on the Guardian Book Store in ADLR.

[30]For the growth of U.S. Catholics between 1940-1960 see James J. Hennesey, S.J., *American Catholics: A History of the Roman Catholic Community in the United States* (New York: Oxford University Press, 1982) 283, 286; For the U.S. Population in 1960, see U.S. Department of Commerce, Bureau of the Census, *Historical Statistics of the United States: Colonial Times to 1870* 2 vols. (Washington, D.C.: Government Printing Office, 1972) 1:15.

[31]These statistics from Hennesey, *American Catholics,* 287.

[32]*Official Catholic Directory, 1947* (New York: P.J. Kenedy and Sons, 1947) 551; *Official Catholic Directory, 1950* (New York: P.J. Kenedy and Sons, 1950) 416; the total population of Arkansas and the white population numbers of 1,481,507 is taken from T. Harri Baker and Jane Browning, *An Arkansas History For Young People* (Fayetteville, AR: University of Arkansas Press, 1991) 344.

[33]*Official Catholic Directory, 1945* (New York: P.J. Kenedy and Sons, 1945) 529; *Official Catholic Directory, 1950,* 416.

[34]The dedication of the new building, the coming of Cardinal Stritch to the diocese again after 20 years, *The Guardian,* 7 July 1951, 1; 12 October 1951, 1; 19 October 1951, 1-2; 26 October 1951, 1-6; Little Rock *Arkansas Gazette,* 16 October 1951, 1, 2.

[35]For a look at some of the older Catholic parishes in Little Rock-North Little Rock and Fort Smith until 1925, see Diocesan Historical Commission, *The History of Catholicity in Arkansas* (Little Rock, AR: Guardian Press, 1925) n.p. (pp. 3651, 116-121); for the creation of Christ the King, Fort Smith, 1928, see the material in the previous chapter on Dr. Horan and Bishop Morris. As for the dates for the other more recently created parishes in Little Rock and North Little Rock, this is taken from individual parish histories in Parish Records, ADLR.

[36]The year territorial boundaries established, Parish Records, Chancery Files, Diocese of Little Rock. That they were never totally enforced comes from author's interview with William W. O'Donnell, 10 September 1991, ADLR. As will be mentioned in the text later, Mr. O'Donnell worked quite closely with Bp. Fletcher as the editor of *The Guardian.*

[37]For the erection of this parish for the University of Arkansas, see *The Guardian,* 26 July 1957, 1.

[38]For the Catholic population in Arkansas in 1960, see *Official Catholic Directory, 1960* (New York: P.J. Kenedy & Sons, 1960) 517; for the population of the Arkansas and the white population of 1,396,000 for 1960 taken from U.S. Department of Commerce, Bureau of the Census, *Historical Statistics of the United States,* 1:24. The percentage of population decrease in Arkansas, 6.5 percent can be found in Baker and Browning and can be derived from the census data, but they do not provide the numbers, just the percentage. Baker and Browning, *Arkansas History for Young People,* 347.

[39]*Official Catholic Directory, 1920* (New York: P.J.Kenedy & Sons, 1920) 435; *Official Catholic Directory, 1960,* 517.

[40]For the Arkansas Catholic population for 1940, see *Official Catholic Directory, 1940* (New York: P.J. Kenedy and Sons, 1940) 445; the population for Arkansas in 1940 can easily be obtained in Baker and Browning, *Arkansas History for Young People,* 344. The number for 1960 already given in the text.

[41]For Fr. Lauro background, see Lauro and Orrmont, *Action Priest,* 1-181. Fr. Lauro had entered St. John's Seminary during the academic year 1939-1940, but opposition from his pastor prevented him from being accepted as the Chicago archdiocese would not allow him to study for the priesthood in the Arkansas diocese without his pastor's formal permission. pp. 34-41.

[42]Fr. Chinery's background and ordination given in Lauro and Orrmont, *Action Priest*, 185, 186; Fr. Lauro called him Fr. Harry Chinery, 207. Fr. Chinery died in 1973. This information from Msgr. James E. O'Connell given to the author by telephone, 28 October 1991.

[43]Ibid., 187-193; 197-202, 205, 216-221, 226-230.

[44]These two stories in Ibid., 203-204; 223-226.

[45]Ibid., 193-196, the dialogue in the text from p. 195.

[46]In the creation of St. Anthony's, see Fletcher to American Board of Catholic Missions, 30 September 1948, Fletcher Papers, ADLR. In this letter Fletcher provides the name of the first pastor. By 1950, there was a new pastor and the Franciscans still run St. John the Baptist, Fr. Angelus Schaefer, O.F.M., *Official Catholic Directory, 1950,* 414. Franciscans took over El Dorado parish, see Renee Moon, "Arkansas Black Catholic Homecoming: A Family Strengthening Its Ties and Renewing Its Old Relations" Pamphlet/program for a celebration held at St. John's Catholic Center, 27 November 1982, p. 2.

[47]For the creation of Good Shepherd in 1952 and its first pastor, see Rev. Henry J. Koren, C.S.Sp., *The Serpent and the Dove: A History of the Congregation of the Holy Ghost in the United States, 1745-1984* (Pittsburgh, PA: Spiritus Press, 1985) 366.

[48]*Official Catholic Directory, 1955,* (New York: P.J. Kenedy and Sons, 1955) 468.

[49]Bishop Fletcher to American Board of Catholic Missions, 30 June 1952, Fletcher Papers, ADLR.

[50]Bishop Fletcher to American Board of Catholic Missions, 25 August 1955, Fletcher Papers, ADLR; *The Guardian,* 14 October 1955, 1.

[51]The reconstruction of buildings at St. Raphael reported in *The Guardian,* 21 October 1956, 1; 24 October 1958; 31 October 1958, 6; 17 April 1959, 6 *Official Catholic Directory, 1961* (New York: P.J. Kenedy and Sons, 1961) 521. The previous year's directory had listed them being there. *Official Catholic Directory, 1960,* 517.

[52]*Official Catholic Directory, 1960,* 514-517. The directory lists St. Bartholomew's High school as having 101 students and St. Peter's High school as having 50 students. The total number of students in high schools was 754, in elementary schools, 7,839. Of the eleven black parishes all had schools except St. Raphael's, and the three Franciscan parishes in Lake Village, McGehee, and El Dorado.

[53]Bishop Fletcher to American Board of Catholic Missions, 28 June 1954, Fletcher Papers, ADLR.

[54]To the People of the Diocese of Little Rock, Bishop Albert L. Fletcher, 3 August 1954, Fletcher Papers, ADLR.

[55]Lauro and Orrmont, *Action Priest,* 219.

[56]Msgr. John O'Donnell, then a young priest from Philadelphia, was one of the younger priests who felt that Bishop Fletcher moved too slowly on integration. Yet he readily admits that Fletcher was personally no bigot and did help black Catholics behind the scenes. For example, he helped John Gillam, a local black, to secure a loan from a bank that had refused to lend him money. Msgr. O'Donnell is serving as the pastor of Immaculate Conception Catholic Church, North Little Rock. Interview with Msgr. O'Donnell, 31 August 1989, audio-tape in ADLR. This fact confirmed by John Gillam in a telephone conversation with the author, November 5, 1991.

[57]For the background and description of the events during the Little Rock crisis there is a great deal of written material. This taken from various sources: Tony A. Freyer, *The Little Rock Crisis: A Constitutional Interpretation* (Westport, CT: Greenwood Press, 1984) 1-88; another more accessible account see Baker and Browning, *Arkansas History for Young People,* 352-356; for other secondary material on this see Numan V. Bartley, "Looking Back at Little Rock," *Arkansas Historical Quarterly* 25 (Summer 1966): 101-116; Tony A. Freyer, "Politics and Law in the Little Rock Crisis, 1954-1957," *Arkansas Historical Quarterly* 40 (Autumn 1981): 195-219. One could also see the published works of Former Governor Orval Faubus, Daisy Bates, Congressman Brooks Hays, Elizabeth Huckaby, all major participants in the drama. Based on a court action of black members of the Arkansas legislature, Federal District Judge Henry Woods declared unconstitutional the Arkansas state constitutional amendment 44 in 1989. Little Rock

Arkansas Gazette, 1 April 1989, lA, 9A. For a look at the actual court case see *Dietz v. State of Arkansas,* 709F. Supp. 902.

[58]For a narrative of the crisis and its resolution see Freyer, *Little Rock Crisis,* 88-170; for Mrs. Adolphine Fletcher Terry's role in the affair, and her picture taken in 1968, and the fact that most of Little Rock's public schools were not totally integrated until early 1970s, see Baker and Browning, *Arkansas History for Young People,* 362.

[59]*The Guardian,* 20 September 1957, 1.

[60]Ibid.

[61]Ibid., 11 October 1957, 1.

[62]Ibid., 1 November 1957, 1. The show broadcast from 12:30 to 1 pm and was a live show where the Bishop took questions from a group of panelists.

[63]"A Pastoral Letter on the Race Problems", 21 November 1958, Fletcher Papers, ADLR. The bishop's letter was printed in the local Catholic paper, which also reported that the American Catholic Bishops declared that racism was a sin. *The Guardian,* 21 November 1958, 1, 7.

[64]Ibid.

[65]For William W. O'Donnell's background and becoming the first lay editor of Arkansas' weekly Catholic newspaper see author's interview with William W. O'Donnell, K.S.G. 10 September 1991, tape in ADLR. The initials after his name signify that he is a Knight of St. Gregory, a prestigious award granted by the pope to a Catholic layman.

[66]William W. O'Donnell, *America's Race Problem: A Catholic Editor's Analysis* (Little Rock, AR: Guardian Press, 1959); Bishop Albert L. Fletcher, *An Elementary Catechism on the Morality of Segregation and Racial Discrimination* (Little Rock, AR: Guardian Press, 1960), segregation is immoral and so is racial discrimination see pp. 3, 7-8. Copies of both of these works in Integration Box, Fletcher Papers, ADLR.

[67]Fred J. Duff to Bishop Albert L. Fletcher, 12 March 1960, Integration Box, Fletcher Papers, ADLR.

[68]Bishop Fletcher to Carl M. Sherwood, New York, New York, 13 April 1959, Integration Box, Fletcher Papers, ADLR.

[69]Most of this material has no author listed; they are just letters and other material sent to the diocese, see Integration Box, Fletcher Papers, ADLR.

[70]Lauro and Orrmont, *Action Priest,* 252-253.

[71]The story of the relocation of the Carmelite Sisters to western Little Rock is told in Lauro and Orrmont, *Action Priest,* 260-262. For the Bishop's account see Fletcher, "Reminiscences," 140-142.

[72]Bishop Fletcher Quinquennial Report to the Holy Father, 2 November 1959, Fletcher Papers, ADLR.

[73]Assenmacher, *A Place Called Subiaco: A History of the Benedictine Monks of Arkansas* (Little Rock, AR: Rose Publishing Company, 1977) 370-383.

[74]Ibid., 399-440.

[75]Ibid., 338, 384-388,

[76]Ibid., 389-390.

[77]For a look at the Subiaco African experiment see Ibid. 438445.

[78]Ibid., 446-452.

[79]Ibid., 408-418.

[80]Ibid., 413.

[81]Ibid., 400.

[82]For the local coverage of the death of Pope Pius XII and the election of Pope John XIII see *The Guardian,* 7 September 1958, 1; 31 October 1958, 1; 7 November 1958, 1; for the date when Pope John XXIII called for Vatican II see Fr. Gerald P. Fogarty, S.J., *The Vatican and the American Hierarchy From 1870-1965* (Wilmington, DE: Michael Glazier Company, 1985) 384.

[83]Lauro and Orrmont, *Action Priest,* 264-266.

[84]The speaker was Glenn Archer from P.O.A.U., see *The Guardian,* 7 October 1960, 1. On the Rev. Vaught's opposition, I base that on the recollections of Bishop Lawrence F. Graves, then

Msgr. Graves, vice-chancellor of the diocese. Author's interview with Bishop Graves, 16 May 1988, audio tape in ADLR. Also, I refer to a conversation with Stephen Hanley, a member of Immanuel Baptist Church, who remembers that Rev. Vaught spoke out against the Kennedy candidacy. Author's conversation with Mr. Hanley, August 19, 1991.

[85]*The Guardian*, 11 November 1960, 1. The Editor of *The Guardian* said they did this because the paper tried to stay out of politics, unless some moral issue was involved. Interview with Mr. O'Donnell, K.S.G., 10 September 1991, audio tape in ADLR.

[86]For the announcement of the new Catholic High school see *The Guardian*, 22 August 1958, 1. For a more behind the scenes look at the decision to move to this area and its movement there by 1960 consult author's interview with Msgr. William Galvin of Fort Smith, 24 August 1989, audio tape in ADLR. Msgr. Galvin was then the rector at Catholic High School.

[87]For the integration of Catholic High School, see Bishop Fletcher's report to American Board of Catholic Missions, 10 September 1963, also author's interview with Msgr. William Galvin, 24 August 1989, audio tape in ADLR. Ms. Carol Blow still works in the Social Services Department of the Diocese of Little Rock. A graduate of St. Augustine's black Catholic school in North Little Rock, she still remains active in this predominantly black Catholic parish in North Little Rock. For another confirmation that Catholic High integrated by 1962 and the information as to St. Bartholomew's High school department staying open until 1971, the author relies upon his telephone conversation with Mr. John Gillam on 5 November 1991. Mr. Gillam, a native of Little Rock, was raised as a Catholic in St. Bartholomew's parish and is still a member of that parish.

[88]Bishop Fletcher to American Board of Catholic Missions, 10 September 1963; 10 August 1964; 11 August 1965, Fletcher papers, ADLR.

[89]Bishop Fletcher to American Board of Catholic Missions, 26 August 1966, Fletcher Papers, ADLR. Fr. Warren Harvey's attendance see *Arkansas Catholic*, 27 June 1989, 1,9.

[90]Bishop Fletcher to American Board of Catholic Missions, 14 August 1967, Fletcher Papers, ADLR.

[91]Bishop Fletcher to American Board of Catholic Missions, 11 September 1969, Fletcher Papers, ADLR.

[92]Bishop Fletcher to American Board of Catholic Missions, October 1972, Fletcher Papers, ADLR.

[93]On the Glenmary Missioners, see the agreement between Bishop Fletcher and Fr. Clement Borchers, Superior General of Glenmary, concerning their work in the Diocese. The agreement is dated 28 May 1963, and the document is in the Active Missions File, Archives of the Glenmary Home Missioners, Cincinnati, Ohio. For this and other information on the Glenmary Fathers in Arkansas, I am indebted to Mr. Don Buske, Archivist, Glenmary Fathers. For the material on Subiaco and the quote see Assenmacher, *A Place Called Subiaco*, 401.

[94]*Official Catholic Directory, 1950*, 416; *Official Catholic Directory, 1960*, 517.

[95]*The Guardian*, 31 August 1962, 1,2.

[96]Ibid., 2 November 1962, 1,2; 9 November 1962, 1,3.

[97]According to press reports in the spring of 1964 the building was to be open by January 1965, it would not happen for more than a year later. Ibid., 20 March 1964, 1; opened for occupancy and the bishop's blessing on April 29, 1965, Ibid., 23 April 1965, 3.

[98]Bishop Fletcher, "Reminiscences," p. 147; Author's taped interview with Msgr. James E. O'Connell, 14 August 1989, tape in ADLR; Bishop Fletcher to Bishop William O'Brien, Auxiliary Bishop of Chicago, Director of the Catholic Church Extension Society, 26 March 1958, Fletcher Papers, ADLR.

[99]Boileau background, his education, and his return to St. John's see *The Guardian*, 12 January 1962, 1; Boileau being the first Catholic priest to open a session of the Arkansas General Assembly since 1864 see Ibid., 15 February 1963, 1. He was born in 1930 in Kalamazoo, Michigan, Priests File, Chancery, Diocese of Little Rock.

[100]*The Guardian*, 21 May 1965, 1.

[101]Dolan, *American Catholic Experience*, 369; Stephen J. Ochs, *Desegregating the Altar:*

The Josephites and the Struggle for Black Priests, 1871-1960 (Baton Rouge, LA: Louisiana State University Press, 1990) 347-348.

[102]The creation of the local chapter had the blessing of Bishop Fletcher, John J. O'Connor to Bishop Fletcher, 27 May 1960, Fletcher Papers, ADLR. This information also confirmed by a telephone conversation with Ken Oberste of Little Rock, 5 November 1991. Oberste was president of the Little Rock chapter of C.I.C. during the early 1960s.

[103]This information taken from conversations with two past presidents of the Little Rock branch of the C.I.C., Ken Oberste and Ms. Kathleen Woods. As to the bishop's end of the affairs, consult the author's taped interview with Bishop Lawrence Graves, 16 May 1966, copy of tape in ADLR. Bishop Graves was a close friend of Bishop Fletcher and served for a time, 1969-1973, as the Auxiliary Bishop of Little Rock. Bishop Fletcher on joining the C.I.C. see *The Guardian*, 2 October 1964, 10. People active in the organization never remember Bishop Fletcher joining the organization, or attending any meetings, but a few people close to the bishop like the editor of *The Guardian*, William W. O'Donnell, did attend on occasion. Author's conversation with Kathleen Woods, 9 November 1991. There is no record in the bishop's papers that he joined the C.I.C.

[104]Little Rock *Arkansas Gazette*, 26 March 1965, lA; 4 April 1965, lA.

[105]For an account of his visit see Little Rock *Arkansas Gazette*, 29 January 1967, 8A; *The Guardian*, 20 January 1967, 1,2; 3 February 1967, 1. Bishop Perry, who died in 1991, is the first full African-American as a Catholic bishop. For Bishop Perry's stay at St. Peter's in 1949-1950 see *The Guardian*, 21 October 1949, 7; Parish Records, St. Peter's, Pine Bluff, ADLR.

[106]*The Guardian*, 14 June 1957, 1.

[107]Ibid., 23 March 1962, 1, 3.

[108]Ibid., 25 August 1961, 1.

[109]For Fletcher arrival date back in Little Rock see *The Guardian*, 4 December 1962, 1. On the dates of John XXIII's death and the decision by Paul VI to continue the council see Hennesey, *American Catholics*, 310. For a good short description of what was discussed at each of the four sessions of Vatican II and what was approved when, which is outside the topic of this book, see August Franzen and John P. Dolan, *A Concise History of the Church* (New York: Herder & Herder, 1969) 432-438.

[110]On the invitation of Protestants and Orthodox Christians to Vatican II, see Hennesey, *American Catholics*, 310; the quote from a W.P. Campbell to Bishop Fletcher, 13 December 1962, Fletcher Papers, ADLR.

[111]Franzen and Dolan, *Concise History of the Church*, 432, 439. That the council was not all that revolutionary but flowed out of the different movements in the church in the 1940s and 1950s see Dolan, *American Catholic Experience*, 425.

[112]On the American contribution at the Second Vatican Council and the theological influence of John C. Murray, S.J., on church-state relations and religious freedom see Fogarty, *Vatican and the American Hierarchy*, 368-398; Dolan, *American Catholic Experience*, 425; Hennesey, *American Catholics*, 310; Fr. Michael Perko, S.J., *Catholic and American: A Popular History* (Huntingdon, IN: Our Sunday Visitor Press, 1989) 290292.

[113]Fletcher, "Reminiscences," pp. 144-146, 148; on Graves as being his aide see *The Guardian*, 27 September 1962, 1. Author's interview with Bishop Lawrence P. Graves, 16 May 1988, audio tape in ADLR. In a document dated 13 May 1970, Fletcher outlined nine things he thought were important about the Second Vatican Council. Religious liberty is number #8 and he supported that strongly.

[114]This can be seen from the fall editions of *The Guardian*, 1962-1965; Author's interview with William W. O'Donnell, K.S.G., audio-tape in ADLR. That affairs were handled by Msgr. Joseph A. Murray the chancellor, consult author's tape with Msgr. James O'Connell, then rector of the Seminary, 14 August 1989; interview with Msgr. John Murphy, 17 August 1989, both audio tapes in ADLR.

[115]That Fletcher was there every day, consult author's interview with Bishop Lawrence P. Graves, 16 May 1988, audio-tape in ADLR. Bishop Fletcher to William O'Donnell, 25 September

1963; the last quote from the bishop appeared in *The Guardian*, 1 October 1963, lA.

[116]Fletcher, "Reminiscences," 148, quote on p. 147.

[117]Ibid., 148.

[118]*The Guardian*, 9 November 1962, 1.

[119]Bishop Fletcher to Msgr. Murray, 5 November 1963, reprinted in *The Guardian*, 15 November 1963, lA.

[120]*The Guardian*, 25 October 1964, 3A.

[121]On Fletcher's attempt to address the Second Vatican Council at the last session, a session quite busy, from author's interview with Bishop Lawrence Graves, 16 May 1988, audio tape in ADLR. The bishop's written interventions on marriage, war and peace, and the sacraments. The nine are in Fletcher Papers, ADLR. That he attempted 13 interventions from conversation author's conversation with William W. O'Donnell 31 August 1992, and Msgr. James E. O'Connell, 1 September 1992.

[122]Franzen & Dolan, *Concise History of the Church*, 437-438.

[123]Bishop Fletcher apparently wrote his own personal recollections of the council in a document dated 13 May 1970, Fletcher Papers, ADLR. On the council's action in renaming the N.C.W.C. to N.C.C.B. see Fogarty, *Vatican and the American Hierarchy*, 400.

[124]*The Guardian*, 15 December 1965, 1.

[125]Bishop Fletcher's return, see Ibid., 17 December 1965, 1; date of the opening of the First Vatican Council and the closing date of the Second being on December 8 in the years, 1869, 1965, Franzen and Dolan, *Concise History of the Church*, 388, 438.

[126]For a look at the coverage of this event see Little Rock *Arkansas Gazette*, 28 April 1965, 8A; 29 April 1965, 1, 18A; 2 may 1965, 10A; 3 May 1965, 2A; a full Jubilee edition of *The Guardian*, 30 April 1965, 1-44; 7 May 1965, 1.

[127]On Bishop Fletcher's award and address are reported in *The Guardian*, 6 May 1966, 1, 2; 27 May 1966, 1. The actual speech is in the Fletcher Papers, ADLR.

[128]Both of these statements in letters given to the diocese and printed in *The Guardian*, 8 September 1959, 1; 15 September 1959, 1.

[129]On the anticommunism in the American Catholicism from 19451965 see Hennesey, *American Catholics*, 288-294. It should be pointed out that the Senator Joseph McCarthy of Wisconsin, who led an anti-communist demagogic campaign in the early 1950s, was an Irish Catholic who "drew disproportionately from Catholics of recent immigrant background." p. 293.

[130]Ibid., 320-321; Dolan, *American Catholic Experience*, 451.

[131]For Catholic participation in the John Birch Society in late 1950s and early 1960s see Ibid., 316-317; Franzen and Dolan, *Concise History of the Church*, 382; Perko, *Catholic and American*, 307, 308.

[132]The advertisements for Fr. Fenton's speech were given in various issues of *The Guardian* prior to his address in late January 1967. Fr. Fenton conducted an interview with local reporters and he was quoted in the Little Rock *Arkansas Gazette*, lB; Little Rock *Arkansas Democrat*, 24 January 1967, 3.

[133]For some comments and criticisms of Fr. Fenton's visit see letters to the editor in the Little Rock *Arkansas Gazette*, 4 February 1967, 4A, 1 March 1967, 6A, 14 March 1967, 6A.

[134]Report of the meeting, *The Guardian*, 27 January 1967, 1.

[135]Ibid., 6 January 1967, 1. The author's family was one of the original members of this parish and information about where they met and the church building from my own recollections as a parishioner during my high school years.

[136]The cost to the diocese by 1967 to keep the seminary open was taken from author's interview with Bishop Graves, 16 May 1988, audio tape in ADLR; *The Guardian*, 19 August 1966, 1.

[137]Author's interview with Msgr. James E. O'Connell, 14 August 1989, audio-tape in ADLR.

[138]On Fr. James F. Drane's background see his Priests file, Chancery, Diocese of Little Rock. Also see article on him in *Life*, 8 September 1967, 33-34, 36, 38. His book on eastern Europe called *Pilgrimage to Utopia* (Milwaukee, WI: Bruce Publishing Company, 1965). On the

Death of God lectures and Drane's removal from the post in Little Rock *Arkansas Gazette,* 12 October 1966, 7A; 13 October 1966, 7A; 26 October 1966, 3A; 12 November 1966, 15A; 13 November 1966, 15A.

[139]On the papal commission and the speculation about the lifting of the ban on artificial contraception see Hennesey, *American Catholics,* 328; Dolan, *American Catholic Experience,* 435.

[140]The two quotes are from Little Rock *Arkansas Gazette,* 20 June 1967, 7A; 25 June 1967, 3E; for the rest of the articles, see the issues 21 June 1967, 7A; 22 June 1967, 7A; 23 June 1967, 7A, quote from; 25 June 1967, 3E.

[141]Ibid., 25 June 1967, 3E.

[142]*The Guardian,* 7 July 1967, 7.

[143]Fletcher, "Reminiscences," 155.

[144]On the announcement of the closing of St. John's Seminary, *The Guardian,* 14 July 1967, 1; Fletcher, "Reminiscences," 151; Author's interview with Bishop Lawrence P. Graves, 16 May 1988, audio tape in ADLR.

[145]Fletcher to Msgr. Kenneth G. Stack, Chicago, IL, 18 July 1967, Fletcher Papers, ADLR.

[146]Fletcher, "Reminiscences," 157, 154-155; both quotes on p. 157.

[147]Author's interview with Msgr. James O'Connell, 14 August 1989, audio-tape in ADLR. For the records of Frs. Clancy and Boileau see Priests file, Chancery, Diocese of Little Rock.

[148]*Life,* 8 September 1967, 33-34, 36, 38.

[149]Drane's side of the story, and a good account of his life up to 1969 told in James F. Drane, "A Continuing Vocation," in *Why Priests Leave: The Intimate Story of Twelve Who Did* (New York: Hawthorne Books, 1969) 58-72. Also see James F. Drane, *Authority and Institution: A Church in Crisis* (Milwaukee, WI: Bruce Publishing Company, 1969).

[150]For the date of *Humanae Vitae* see Hennesey, *American Catholics,* 328; Perko, *Catholic and American,* 297; Bishop's letter in *The Guardian,* 6 September 1968, 1, 2.

[151]References to plans for the new chancery building and it construction in 1967-1968, and the movement of the diocesan newspaper offices taken from a phone conversation with Mr. William W. O'Donnell, K.S.G., the former editor of the paper. Also this author was a member of Christ the King parish at that time and the parish used the seminary's main chapel for its church from January, 1967 through October, 1969. I remember the construction of that new chancery building on the seminary grounds at the time.

[152]Author's interview with Msgr. James O'Connell, 14 August 1989, audio-tape in ADLR.

[153]Fletcher, "Reminiscences," 158-159; Bishop Fletcher received word on March 5, 1969 and it was announced in Catholic paper two days later. *The Guardian,* 7 March 1969, 1.

[154]For an explanation of Canon Law in the Catholic Church see *New Catholic Encyclopedia,* 3:29-53.

[155]For the life of Bishop Lawrence P. Graves see his career outlined in *The Guardian,* 7 March 1969, 1-2; also author's interview with Bishop Lawrence Graves, 16 May 1988, audio-tape in ADLR. That he was auditor during the 1960s see *Official Catholic Directory, 1965* (New York: P.J. Kenedy and Sons, 1965) 558.

[156]Little Rock *Arkansas Gazette,* 25 April 1969, lA; 26 April 1969, lA; 2B; *The Guardian,* 25 April 1969, 1; 2 May 1969, 1-2.

[157]These impressions coming from people who knew Bishop Fletcher, Mrs. Martha McNeil and Mrs. Elizabeth Parker, also the impression which Bishop Graves had, author's interview with Bishop Graves, 16 May 1988, audio tape in ADLR. Mrs. Parker and Mrs. McNeil work in the chancery office, 1992.

[158]Assenmacher, *A Place Called Subiaco,* 421, 422. The author remembers that the parish councils operated by the late 1960s. I served as a youth representative on the parish council of Christ the King in 1969-1970; and the general impression was that they were in operation in almost every parish. On the new liturgy replacing the old by the end of the decade, around 1969 see Dolan, *American Catholic Experience.* 429; Perko, *Catholic and American,* 292-293.

[159]Jerry Heil and Barry Findley to Bishop Fletcher, 21 November 1971, Fletcher Papers, ADLR. In this letter, Heil and Findley promised to have the Serra Club help and advise the

bishop in setting up such a program.

[160]The event is described and Bishop Reed quoted in Little Rock *Arkansas Gazette*, 5 June 1970, 15A.

[161]Ibid.

[162]*The Guardian*, 16 October 1970, 4. At first a group home for children, yet evolved some two decades later into a day care center. *Diocese of Little Rock, Catholic Directory, 1991* (Little Rock, AR.: Arkansas Catholic Press, 1991) 55.

[163]Fletcher, "Reminiscences," 158. Msgr. Murray was serving as vicar general at the time of his death, *Official Catholic Directory, 1970* (New York: P.J. Kenedy and Sons, 1970) 416.

[164]Lauro's work in South America see Lauro and Orrmont, *Action Priest*, 275-357, conversation between Fletcher and Lauro in 1968, p. 357.

[165]Newspaper clipping, Little Rock *Arkansas Gazette*, 21 April 1971, n.p. Clipping in the possession of Msgr. James E. O'Connell.

[166]Bishop Fletcher to Wilbur Mills, 1 September 1966, Fletcher Papers, ADLR; on conscientious objectors, *The Guardian*, 17 July 1970, 1.

[167]U.S. Catholic Bishops, "Resolution on Southeast Asia," quoted in Hennesey, *American Catholics*, 321.

[168]Ibid.

[169]Fletcher's defense of his action at the bishops' meeting in *The Guardian*, 3 December 1971, 1.

[170]Ibid.

[171]Ibid., 25 February 1972, 1.

[172]For the exact numbers between 1965-1980 see Hennesey, *American Catholics*, 329.

[173]Fletcher, "Reminiscences," 149.

[174]Fletcher, "Reminiscences," 159-161; author's interview with William W. O'Donnell, K.S.G., 10 September 1991, audio-tape in ADLR.

[175]Little Rock *Arkansas Gazette*, 5 July 1972, 1; *The Guardian*, 5 July 1972, 1, 2.

[176]*The Guardian*, 5 July 1972, 2.

CHAPTER XI

[1]On the overall activities of the Sisters of Loretto in Arkansas see Sr. Matilda Bennett, S.L. "Sisters of Loretto: One Hundred and Fifty Years." (Unpublished manuscript, Loretto Motherhouse, Nerinckx, Kentucky). Sr. Bennett's work is undated yet the title indicates that it was probably written around early 1960 as the order was founded on April 25, 1812. For a look at this order and its foundation see Fr. Clyde F. Crews, *An American Holy Land: A History of the Archdiocese of Louisville, 1775-1985* (Wilmington, DE: Michael Glazier Publishing, 1987) 15, 61, 89-91.

[2]Sr. Mary Teresa Carroll, R.S.M., *Leaves from the Annals of the Sisters of Mercy* (New York: Catholic Publishing House, 1889) 328-333; The Sisters of Mercy of Arkansas with Jane Ramos, *Arkansas Frontiers of Mercy: A History of the Sisters of Mercy in the Diocese of Little Rock* (Fort Smith, AR: St. Edward's Press, 1989) 44-52. The formal title of the order is the Religious Sisters of Mercy, usually identified by the initials R.S.M. In referring to the recent publication on the Mercy sisters in Arkansas, I will cite the authors as Ramos, et. al. for simplification.

[3]Ramos, et. al., *Arkansas Frontiers of Mercy*, 52-54.

[4]Ibid., 51.

[5]Ibid., 54-56, 203.

[6]On the number of postulants who left Ireland see Ibid., 55. For a contemporary account of this ceremony see Little Rock *Arkansas Gazette*, 27 June 1851, 3. For Spalding's career as Bishop of Louisville, 1850-1864, and Archbishop of Baltimore, 18641882 see Crews, *An American Holy Land*, 133-154; Thomas W. Spalding, *The Premier See: A History of the Archdiocese of Baltimore, 1789-1989* (Baltimore, MD: Johns Hopkins University Press, 1989) 178-206.

[7]The background to these first five women who made their professions as sisters in Arkansas in 1851 is found in Ramos, et. al., *Arkansas Frontiers of Mercy,* 55-56; quote on p. 56. The religious names of these sisters listed on pp. 203-204.

[8]Ibid., 48.

[9]Ibid., 83-86. This recent history also provides a good description of their journey to Arkansas and what it must have been like to come from Ireland to a frontier river town such as Little Rock. pp. 59-81.

[10]For the announcement of the opening of the St. Mary's Female Institute, as it was first called, see newspaper clipping, from an unnamed and undated paper, found in AANO. Mother Teresa's Farrell's name appears at the bottom of the clipping. Ramos, et. al., *Arkansas Frontiers of Mercy,* 86-87, 89.

[11]Ramos, et. al, *Arkansas Frontiers of Mercy,* 89-90.

[12]Ibid., 94-96; Bishop Byrne to Archbishop Anthony Blanc 22 May 1853, Blanc Papers, AANO.

[13]Ramos, et. al., *Arkansas Frontiers of Mercy,* 100.

[14]In the Catholic almanac for 1855, St.Anne's convent is listed as the Motherhouse for the Mercy Sisters in Arkansas. *Metropolitan Catholic Almanac, 1855* (Baltimore, MD: John Murphy, 1855) 206; that Bishop Byrne separated them and the last quote taken from Ramos, et.al, *Arkansas Frontiers of Mercy,* 101.

[15]For the names of the women who came to Arkansas and professed see Ramos, et. al., *Arkansas Frontiers of Mercy,* 101-102. Bishop Byrne supposedly brought back nine postulants, yet his letter to Archbishop Blanc dated November 1859 states that he only had three with him. Bishop Byrne to Archbishop Blanc, 21 November 1859, Blanc Papers, AANO.

[16]Ramos, et. al., *Arkansas Frontiers of Mercy,* 103-105. That eastern Arkansas, and particularly the area around Helena, was the richest area of the state see James M. Woods, *Rebellion and Realignment: Arkansas Road to Secession* (Fayetteville, AR: University of Arkansas Press, 1987) 5-31.

[17]Ramos, et. al., *Arkansas Frontiers of Mercy,* 113.

[18]Ibid., 112-113; for the state's attack on Fort Smith see Woods, *Rebellion and Realignment,* 157.

[19]Ramos, et. al., *Arkansas Frontiers of Mercy,* 118-119, quote on p. 119. All of the episodes discussed in earlier chapter.

[20]Ibid., 123-124.

[21]Ibid., 126-127, 128.

[22]Little Rock *Arkansas Gazette,* 11 December 1875, 4: Ramos, et. al., *Arkansas Frontiers of Mercy,* 129.

[23]Ramos, et. al., *Arkansas Frontiers of Mercy,* 133-134.

[24]Ibid., 135-137.

[25]Ibid., 138. The number of Mercy sisters from Ireland, 98, and from Newfoundland, 53, amounted to 151 to just 69 from Arkansas and other areas. This meant that the Irish and Newfoundland area accounted for 68.6% the Arkansas Mercy sisters from 1851-1929. The Irish alone accounted for 44.5% pp. 165, 166.

[26]Ibid., 135-137; 138, 139.

[27]Sr. Louise Sharum, O.S.B., *Write the Vision Down: A History of St. Scholastica Convent, Fort Smith, Arkansas, 1879-1979* (Fort Smith, AR: American Printing and Lithograph Co., 1979) 1-8.

[28]Christina Schuler on March 15th, Katherina Hawerott on April 10th, Apollonia Ehalt on June 9th. Ibid., 13-14.

[29]Ibid., 16, 20-21.

[30]Ibid., 22-23, 26.

[31]Ibid., 36-37.

[32]Ibid., 27, 28, 39-48, 174.

[33]Ibid., 50-51.

[34]Ibid., 51-53.

[35]Sr. Agnes Voth, O.S.B., *Green Olive Branch* (Chicago, IL: Franciscan Herald Press, 1973) 48, quote on p. 48. Although the title does not indicate it, this books is the history of the Olivetan community in Arkansas. Sr. Mary Agnes Voth also did the translation from the Father Eugene J. Weibel's account called *Forty Year Missionary In Arkansas* (St. Meinrad, IN: St. Meinred's Abbey Press, 1968). On the same page Sr. Mary Agnes quotes this Fr. Enright saying that in Arkansas "even the dogs are so emaciated that they leaned against fence rails to bark." This comment corresponds to the state's poor reputation which was spread by the then quite popular joke book, *On A Slow Train Through Arkansas* (Lexington, KY: University of Kentucky Press Reprint Edition, 1985).

[36]Voth, *Green Olive Branch,* 51.

[37]On Sr. Renggli birth and her travels to America see Ibid., 3135; 51, 52. Sr. Voth gives her birth date as of January 1, 1848, reports her crossing the Atlantic in 1874 and mistakenly claims she was twenty-seven at the time of her trip to America, while claiming correctly that she was just short of turning forty when she first came to Arkansas.

[38]Ibid., 51-52.

[39]Ibid., 48, 55.

[40]Ibid., 56, 60-62.

[41]Ibid., 64, 65, 66.

[42]Ibid., 83.

[43]Ibid., 79-83; 210.

[44]Ibid., 83-84.

[45]Ibid., 84-86, 87, 94. Sr. Voth also provides a brief history of the European order, see pp. 87-94, 98-104.

[46]Ibid., 105, 119, 120, 147.

[47]Ibid., 113-119, 124, 127, 132.

[48]Crews, *An American Holy Land,* 87-88.

[49]For the location of this the first St. Vincent's run by the Sisters of Charity of Nazareth see Hannah F. Peck, "St. Vincent's Infirmary, 1888-1987: The History of a Roman Catholic Hospital in Little Rock, Arkansas." (Master's thesis in Public History, University of Arkansas at Little Rock, 1987) 16. For the construction of the original building, either by convict or slave labor, see Dan Durning, "Those Enterprising Georges: Early German Settlers in Little Rock." *Pulaski County Historical Review* 23 (June 1975): 21-37, especially pp. 29-31. As of the writing of Durning's article, the house was still standing.

[50]Peck, "St. Vincent's Infirmary," 25-30. Peck reports that in 1898, Bishop Fitzgerald had initially opposed the move to the Tenth and High location as he believed it would too far out from downtown Little Rock. Sr. Hortense finally convinced him to go along with the move. p. 29.

[51]This information on the Sacred Heart Academy and Annunciation Academy from the a letter from Sr. Mary Collette Crone, S.C.N., Archivist, Motherhouse of the Sisters of Charity, Nazareth, Kentucky to James M. Woods, 5 March 1992. I grateful to her for this information. Their Colored Industrial School was covered in earlier chapter, but there is a primary source description of the facility when the Sisters of Charity were there see Little Rock *Arkansas Gazette* 1 November 1898, 4.

[52]*Official Catholic Directory, 1960* (New York: P.J. Kenedy and Sons, 1960) 517.

[53]*Catholic Directory, 1900* (Milwaukee, WI: M.H. Wiltzius, 1900), 361; for the School Sisters of Notre Dame and their activities see Sr. M. Henrietta Hockle, O.S.B., "Catholic Schools in Arkansas: A Historical Perspective, 1838-1977." (Ed.S thesis, Arkansas State University, 1977) 19, 20. On their withdrawal from Conway and Morrilton and their efforts in the 1980s in Pine Bluff and North Little Rock, this material from Sr. Mary Richard Eckerle, S.S.N.D., to James M. Woods, 9 March 1992. This letter in the hands of the author and I am in Sr. Mary Richard Eckerle's debt.

[54]Ramos, et. al., *Arkansas Frontiers of Mercy,* 144.

[55]Little Rock *Arkansas Gazette,* 17 August 1878, 4. A picture of this building can be found

in Diocesan Historical Commission, *A History of Catholicity in Arkansas* (Little Rock, AR: Guardian Press, 1925) n.p. (p. 99); Ramos, et. al., *Arkansas Frontiers of Mercy,* 112.

[56]On the sisters wanting to remove from downtown as early 1883 see Ramos, et. al., *Arkansas Frontiers of Mercy,* 147. For Bp. Fitzgerald's letter see Bishop Fitzgerald to Sr. Mary Joseph Scary, R.S.M., 31 July 1904, Fitzgerald papers, ADLR. This letter quoted more fully in Ramos, pp. 149-150.

[57]Bishop Morris assisted the move to Pulaski Heights by buying their property in at Seventh and Louisiana and these funds, together with donations from local benefactors, enabled the Mercy sisters to purchase the land and erect their new building. Ramos, et. al., *Arkansas Frontiers of Mercy,* 150; beautiful picture of this building as it appeared some seventeen years later, D.H.C., *History of Catholicity in Arkansas,* n.p. (p. 170).

[58]Ramos, et. al., *Arkansas Frontiers of Mercy,* 151-154.

[59]Ibid., 146.

[60]Ibid., 174-177.

[61]D.H.C., *History of Catholicity in Arkansas,* n.p., (p. 71). the completion of the gymnasium and auditorium in January and the pool completed by May, 1930. *The Guardian,* 18 January 1930, 1; 10 May 1930, 6.

[62]Ramos, et. al., *Arkansas Frontiers of Mercy,* 162-163.

[63]Voth, *Green Olive Branch,* 139; Sr. Henrietta Hockle, "Catholic Schools in Arkansas," 62, 82-83. Sr. Hockle reports that first school in 1927 had only thirteen students and two teachers. A small two room structure was built at the corner of Tyler and I streets by 1932. In 1944, three more classrooms were added, as well as an auditorium, kitchen, and library. In 1945 Holy Souls began to offer all eight grades and in 1946 they graduated their first seven students. (p. 83).

[64]Voth, *Green Olive Branch,* 141, 142, 144.

[65]Voth, *Green Olive Branch,* 172, 173, 175; Hockle, "Catholic Schools in Arkansas," 88.

[66]Voth, *Green Olive Branch,* 143-144; 298-300. This is still in operation as of 1991. *Diocese of Little Rock, Catholic Directory, 1991* (Little Rock, AR: Arkansas Catholic Publication, 1991) 55.

[67]For some documentation on the Brothers of St. Paul see Kraemer Papers, Deceased Priests File, ADLR.

[68]On the Armstrong Springs school and the erection of Morris School for Boys see Hockle, "Catholic Schools in Arkansas," 63-65; *Diocese of Little Rock, Catholic Directory, 1991,* 53.

[69]Hockle, "Catholic Schools in Arkansas," 60. There is also a promotional pamphlet on this order, *Sisters of Our Lady of Charity: Hot Springs National Park, Arkansas* (Hot Springs, AR: Connelly Press, 1951) 1-16. This pamphlet lists not author and a copy of it is in ADLR. For the more recent information about St. Michael's school taken from letter of the Superior, Sr. Theresa Marie Lalancette, O.L.C.R, to James M. Woods, 12 February 1992, letter in possession of the author. I am grateful for her assistance.

[70]*Official Catholic Directory, 1909* (Milwaukee, WI: Wiltzius, 1909) 436.

[71]Msgr. Healy's background, Healy Papers, Deceased Priests File, ADLR.

[72]Hockle, "Catholic Schools in Arkansas," 86.

[73]*Official Catholic Directory, 1940* (New York: P.J. Kenedy and Sons, 1940) 445.

[74]The eleven listed for the year 1945 include, Sisters of Our Lady of Charity of Refuge, Missionary Sisters-Servants of the Holy Ghost, Sister Servants of the Holy Heart of Mary, Dominican Sisters of the Third Order, Sisters of Divine Providence, School Sisters of Notre Dame, and Sisters of Charity of the Incarnate Word. These seven were in addition to the four older orders, Sisters of Mercy, Fort Smith Benedictines, Olivetan Benedictines and the Sisters of Charity of Nazareth. *Official Catholic Directory, 1945* (New York: P.J. Kenedy & Sons, 1945) 528, 529.

[75]*Official Catholic Directory, 1965* (New York: P.J. Kenedy and Sons, 1965) 561-562.

[76]*Official Catholic Directory, 1945,* 528, 529.

[77]Peck, "St. Vincent's Infirmary," 51.

[78]That he was made a Monsignor in 1942, the documents in his personal papers. On being

named vicar general soon after Bishop Fletcher was named the Ordinary of Little Rock, Bishop Fletcher to Msgr. Healy, 8 July 1947. All of this in Healy Papers, Deceased Priests File, ADLR.

[79]*The Guardian,* 8 June 1951, 1, 8.

[80]Ibid., 12 December 1952, 1, 9.

[81]Hockle, "Catholic Schools in Arkansas," 92.

[82]Ramos, et al., *Arkansas Frontiers of Mercy,* 189.

[83]This information on the Dominican Sisters from Illinois and their coming to Arkansas to manage this hospital in northwest Arkansas is from information given to the author by Srs. Catherine Dominic Stack, O.P., and Mary Veronica Doolin, O.P., to James M. Woods, 19 March 1992. I am grateful to the sisters for this information.

[84]For the information on this new organization, Hospitals, ADLR. On the list of member hospitals, there is a facility called just Clarksville Hospital, but the Catholic directory calls it St. Hildegarde's. Also the Roger's Memorial Hospital appears in the 1955 directory. *Official Catholic Directory, 1955* (New York: P.J. Kenedy and Sons, 1955) 469.

[85]The hospital in Van Buren is listed in the 1955 directory, yet for some reason it is not listed as a member of the Arkansas Catholic Hospital Association. *Official Catholic Directory, 1955,* 469. The hospital in Eureka Springs is not listed in the 1960 directory, but it is by 1965. *Official Catholic Directory, 1965* (New York: P.J. Kenedy and Sons, 1965) 561. For Fr. Lauro, the opening of the facility in Eureka Springs, and the Olivetan Benedictines staffing it see Voth, *Green Olive Branch,* 256.

[86]Sr. Mary Magdalen Kelly, O.C.D., Prioress, "Carmel of St. Teresa of Jesus, Little Rock, Arkansas," article in *Carmel in the United States, 1790-1990* (Eugene, OR: Queen's Press, 1990) 173. This particular book has not an author but is a collection of articles about these particular Carmelite convents. This material sent to the author by Sr. Mary Magdalen Kelly, O.C.D., Prioress of Little Rock's Carmel of St. Teresa of Jesus. The word "carmel" usually refers to Carmelite house, convent, or monastery.

[87]At their small cemetery is buried the foundress of this monastery. This information and material from the text found in Ibid., 174. Fr. Joseph M. Lauro and Arthur Orrmont, *Action Priest: The Story of Father Joe Lauro* (New York: Morrow Publishing Company, 1971) 260-261. On the altar breads for Arkansas's Catholic, Episcopal, and Methodist churches see Sr. Mary Magdalen Kelly, O.C.D. to James M. Woods, 13 February 1992, letter in possession of the author.

[88]Ramos, et. al., *Arkansas Frontiers of Mercy,* 182, 183.

[89]Ibid., 181, 182.

[90]Ibid., 168-169, 188, quote from Sr. Werner Keith, R.S.M. on p. 185.

[91]Ibid., 189.

[92]Voth, *Green Olive Branch,* 216-217.

[93]Bishop Fletcher quoted in Ibid., 235.

[94]Mother Philippa Wavrick born in Burke, Idaho on July 10, 1910. Her baptized name was Cecilia and her father, a farmer, had moved to Hardy, Arkansas when she was small. Ibid., 238-239, 268-271.

[95]Ramos, et. al., *Arkansas Frontiers of Mercy,* 194

[96]Sharum, *Write the Vision Down,* 53.

[97]Ibid., 55-60.

[98]Ibid., 60-64.

[99]Bishop Fletcher to Sr. Innocence Wallmeier, O.S.B., 16 May 1950, letter quoted in Ibid., 89. For Sr. Wallmeir's work in liturgical chant see pp. 88-89.

[100]Ibid., 89-90.

[101]Ibid., 102-125. For the additional information on the order since the mid-1970s, I have relied on information from Sr. Louise Sharum, O.S.B., to James M. Woods, 2 March 1992. 1-6. Copy of this material in possession of the author. I am grateful to Sr. Sharum for all her help on the history of her community.

[102]Information on the closing of Catholic academies in Helena and Pine Bluff from Sr. Mary Collette Crone, S.C.N., Archivist, to James M. Woods, 5 March 1992, letter in possession of

the author. The author is grateful to Sr. Crone for her assistance.

[103]*The Guardian,* 11 December 1954, 1,2; Peck, "St. Vincent's Infirmary," 51-64, 82-83; Fr. Walter J. Clancy, Director of Catholic Hospitals and Social Services, to Bishop Albert L. Fletcher, 16 July 1968, Hospitals, ADLR.

[104]Peck, "St. Vincent's Infirmary," 74-80.

[105]For Mr. Weintraub's administration see Ibid., 81-83.

[106]Peck, St. Vincent's Infirmary," 91-105; author's telephone conversation with Mr. Larry Whitt, Senior Vice President for Engineering, St. Vincent's Infirmary Medical Center, 10 January 1992.

[107]Ramos, et. al., *Arkansas Frontiers of Mercy,* 195; *Arkansas Catholic,* 20 December 1991, 2.

[108]Ramos, et. al., *Arkansas Frontiers of Mercy,* 196-197.

[109]Ibid., 197-198.

[110]*Official Catholic Directory, 1965* (New York: P.J. Kenedy & Sons, 1965) 561; *Official Catholic Directory, 1980* (New York: P.J. Kenedy & Sons, 1980) 473.

[111]*Official Catholic Directory, 1990* (New York: P.J. Kenedy & Sons, 1990) 502.

[112]The number of Catholic religious sisters in the United States in 1965 was 181,421, by 1990, that number fell to 126,517. The number of 1965 from Fr. James J. Hennesey, S.J., *American Catholics: A History of the Roman Catholic Community in the United States* (New York: Oxford University Press, 1982) 329; the 1990 numbers from Official *Catholic Directory, 1990* (New York: P.J. Kenedy & Sons, 1990) general summary, 1.

[113]Ramos, et. al., *Arkansas Frontiers of Mercy,* 191.

[114]Ibid., 194-195.

[115]Ibid., 193; *The Guardian,* 22 May 1970, 3; 23 May 1975, 3.

[116]*The Guardian,* 30 September 1977, 1.

[117]Ramos, et. al., *Arkansas Frontiers of Mercy,* 193-194; that the old main building was torn down in 1983 see Sr. Jan Hayes, R.S.M., "History of Mount St. Mary Academy, 1851-1987." (Unpublished typed manuscript, copy in St. Mary's Convent, Little Rock, Arkansas, 1987) 33. There is also a copy in the ADLR.

[118]Sr. Troillett's appointment and background in *Arkansas Catholic,* 10 March 1991, 1. As of the September, 1992, Sr. Troillett is still principal at Mount St. Mary's.

[119]On the closing of St. Scholastica's Academy see Sharum, *Write the Vision Down,* 83; on the closing of St. Joseph's Orphanage see The *Guardian,* 16 October 1970, 4; yet St. Joseph's continues as a Day Care center as of 1991, *Diocese of Little Rock, Catholic Directory, 1991,* 55; on the hospital in Van Buren see Fr. James R. Savary, Diocesan Director of Catholic Hospitals and Charities, to Bishop Albert L. Fletcher, 6 April 1972, Hospitals, ADLR.

[120]Voth, *Green Olive Branch,* 271; Sr. M. Rita Sprurder, O.S.B., to Fr. James R. Savary, Director of Catholic Hospitals and Charities, 6 April 1976, Hospitals, ADLR.

[121]Voth, *Green Olive Branch,* 267, 280-281, 313. For the dedication of the new convent and quotes from Bishop McDonald's remarks during this occasion see Sr. Henrietta Hockle, O.S.B., *Promises Kept: Reflections of a Century: The Olivetan Benedictine Sisters, Jonesboro, Arkansas* (Little Rock, AR: Porbeck Printing Company, 1986) 10.

[122]This information of the creation of Michael Meagher later St. Michael's Hospital in Texarkana from material sent to me by Sr. Mary Monica LeFleur, CCVI, Congregational Archives, Houston, Texas to James M. Woods, 12 March 1992. I am most grateful for this packet of information which was sent to me and remains in the possession of the author.

[123]This information contained in a latter from Srs. Catherine Dominic Stack, O.P., and Mary Veronica Doolin, O.P., to James M. Woods, 19 March 1992. Letter in possession of the author. I am grateful to Srs. Stack and Doolin for their assistance.

[124]The sixteen other than the four mentioned in the text are: Daughters of Mary of the Cross, Franciscan Sisters of Our Lady of Perpetual Help, Franciscan Sisters of Perpetual Adoration, Missionary Franciscans of the Immaculate Conception, Sisters of St. Jane of Penance and Charity of Tifflin, Ohio, Daughters of Charity, Daughters of Our Lady of Fatima, Dominican

Sisters, Missionaries of Charity, Our Lady of Charity of Refuge, Order of Discalced Carmelites, School Sisters of Notre Dame, Sisters of Charity of the Incarnate Word, Medical Mission Sisters, Ursulines of Louisville, Kentucky, Franciscan Lay Sisters at Little Portion, see *Diocese of Little Rock: Catholic Directory, 1991*, 47-51.

[125]*Official Catholic Directory, 1965*, 561; *Official Catholic Directory, 1980*, 473. Nationally there has also been a marked decline. In 1965, the American Catholic Church operated 10,879 grade schools and 2,413 high schools. Fifteen years later these numbers were 8,149 grade schools and 1,527 high schools. Hennesey, *American Catholics*, 323.

[126]Hockle, "Catholic Schools in Arkansas," 93.

[127]Personal biographical material given to the author by Sr. Henrietta Hockle, O.S.B., 19 December 1991. Sr. Henrietta Hockle, O.S.B., "Catholic Schools in Arkansas: A Historical Perspective, 1838-1977." (Ed.S. degree, Arkansas State University, 1977).

[128]Author's interview with Sr. Henrietta Hockle, 19 December 1991 in her office. St. John's Catholic Center, Little Rock. Bishop McDonald gave this address to the Diocesan Board of Education on January 24, 1978.

[129]On the Trinity school in Fort Smith, Ramos, et. al., *Arkansas Frontiers of Mercy*, 192. That Trinity is located in St. Scholastica's convent, this information provided me by Sr. Louise Sharum, O.S.B., to James M. Woods, 2 March 1992. I am grateful for help on matters dealing with the Fort Smith Benedictines. For the other information in the text, I have relied on Author's interview with Sr. Henrietta Hockle, 19 December 1991, and telephone conversation with Sr. Hockle, 9 January 1992.

[130]*Arkansas Catholic*, 24 November 1989, 5; author's conversation with Sr. Hockle, 19 December 1991. Brother William Rhody, F.S.C., Executive Director of the National Federation of Nonpublic School State Accrediting Associations to Sr. Henrietta Hockle, O.S.B, Executive Director of the Arkansas Nonpublic School Accrediting Association, 13 November 1989. Copy of this letter provided to the author by Sr. Henrietta Hockle and is in the author's possession. In this letter, the Arkansas chapter is welcomed as part of the national federation.

[131]The number of students enrolled in Catholic schools and for religious instruction outside of regular school hours in the Diocese of Little Rock is from the *Official Catholic Directory, 1991* (New York: P.J. Kenedy and Sons, 1991) 520.

[132]This brief synopsis of the Confraternity of Christian Doctrine program from *New Catholic Encyclopedia*, 15 vols. (New York: McGraw-Hill, 1967) 4:155.

[133]*New Catholic Encyclopedia*, 4:155.

[134]This description of this office and its ministry taken from a letter, Sr. Maria Kleinschmidt, D.C., to James M. Woods, 7 February 1992, letter in possession of the author. I am grateful to Sr. Kleinschmidt for her help in this matter.

[135]For the work of the Daughters of Charity of St. Vincent De Paul, their central American province based out of St. Louis, I have relied upon information supplied by Sr. Maria Liebeck, D.C., dated fall, 1992 to the author. This material is also found Daughter of Charity file, ADLR.

[136]Much of this information on the history of the Social Services department for the Diocese of Little Rock comes from a two-page "History of Catholic Social Services," which is both unsigned and undated. It seems to have been written in the early 1970s, as that is when the narrative ends. Much of this information is confirmed by the *Official Catholic Directories*. This history found, Social Services, ADLR.

[137]Ibid., also see Voth, *Green Olive Branch*, 309; on the information regarding her retirement and the appointment of Sr. Joan Pytlik D.C., in December 1991 from Sr. Catherine Markey, O.S.B., diocesan archivist to James M. Woods, 29 January 1992. Letter in author's possession.

[138]"History of Catholic Social Services," 1; "List of Expenditures of the Westside Medical Clinic, February 16, 1971 to September 23, 1971." This document provides the date the opening of this clinic from the files of Ms. Karen DiPippa, Coordinator of the Westside Medical Clinic. I am grateful to Ms. DiPippa for this information.

[139]"History of Catholic Social Services," 1-2.

[140]Fr. James R. Savary is listed as Director of Catholic Social Services in *Official Catholic Directory, 1975* (New York: P.J. Kenedy and Sons, 1975) 437; *Official Catholic Directory, 1980,* 470.

[141]Author's interview with Mr. Dennis C. Lee, Director of Catholic Social Services. 19 December 1991. His appointment by 1985 see *Official Catholic Directory, 1985* (New York: P.J. Kenedy and Sons, 1985) 485.

[142]Author's conversation with Ms. Antje Harris. L.S.W., Director of Diocesan Adoption Services, 20 December 1991.

[143]Mr. Dennis C. Lee, "Summary of Programs, Catholic Social Services." This document supplied to the author by Mr. Dennis C. Lee. I am grateful for his assistance. Also see *Diocese of Little Rock, Catholic Directory, l991,* 5, 6, 7.

[144]Ibid., *Diocese of Little Rock, Catholic Directory, 1991,* 57, 58.

[145]Fr. John P. Fisher to Mr. J. J. Fuller, American Bauxite Mining Company, 8 January 1921, Mexican Missions, ADLR.

[146]For the concerns about Hispanic migrant workers in the Diocese during Bishop Fletcher's era see Monsignor John Bann to Bishop Albert L. Fletcher, 5 January 1952; Charles M. McCoy to Monsignor John Bann, 18 April 1954; Monsignor Joseph A. Murray to Fr. John Manchino, 26 October 1965; Fr. Manchino to Bishop Fletcher, 13 January 1966, Mexican Missions, ADLR

[147]*The Guardian,* 5 March 1976, 1, 3.

[148]*Official Catholic Directory, 1991,* 516; *Diocese of Little Rock, Catholic Directory, 1991,* 5. This author attended such a Spanish mass at Our Lady of Holy Souls parish on August 18, 1991, celebrated by Fr. David LeSieur.

CHAPTER XII

[1]Author's interview with Bishop Andrew J. McDonald, 9 September 1991, audio-tape in ADLR. Bishop McDonald would not be the first native Georgian, that honor belonging to Bishop James Augustine Healy, a mulatto son of an Irish immigrant father and a black African mother, who eventually became the second Bishop of Portland, Maine, 1875-1900. See his biography, Fr. Albert S. Foley, S.J., *Bishop Healy: Beloved Outcaste* (New York: Farrar, Straus, and Young, 1954). Savannah has a sizable Irish minority as part of its population and every year it celebrates its Hibernian heritage with a parade that the local press claims is second only to that of New York city's famous St. Patrick Day's parade. *Savannah Morning News,* 15 March 1991, Diversions Sections, 1. There is a recent dissertation on the making of Irish community in antebellum Savannah, see Edward M. Shoemaker, "Strangers and Citizens: The Irish Immigrant Community in Savannah, 1837-1861" (Ph.D. dissertation, Emory University, 1990).

[2]For the Catholic population in 1970 *Official Catholic Directory, 1970* (New York: P.J. Kenedy and Sons, 1970) 420; for the population of Arkansas in 1970 see U.S. Department of Commerce, Bureau of the Census, *Historical Statistics of the United States: Colonial Times to 1970,* 2 vols. (Washington, D.C.: Government Printing Office, 1975) 1:24.

[3]Information of Bishop Andrew J. McDonald taken from author's interview with Andrew J. McDonald, fifth Bishop of Little Rock, 9 September 1991, at the chancery, audio-tape in ADLR. For another source for the Bishop's early life see *Arkansas Catholic,* 6 May 1988, 5, 6, 7.

[4]Author's interview with Bishop McDonald, 9 September 1991, audio-tape in ADLR.

[5]For over a century, there has been no published history of the Diocese of Savannah, although there is a biography of its third bishop, see Fr. Michael V. Gannon, *Rebel Bishop: The Life and Era of Augustin Verot, Confederate Bishop and the "Enfant Terrible" of the First Vatican Council* (Milwaukee, WI: Bruce Publishing Co., 1964). For a general history of Savannah diocese, which up to 1950 included the entire state of Georgia, see *New Catholic Encyclopedia,* 15 vols. (New York: McGraw-Hill, 1967) 12:1102-1103.

[6]Author's interview with Bishop McDonald, 9 September 1991, audio-tape in ADLR.

[7]Ibid.

[8]Ibid., On the tape, Bishop McDonald mentioned Bishop Walsh's family had been from Savannah, yet he was born across the river in South Carolina.

[9]Ibid.

[10]Ibid.

[11]Ibid.

[12]*New Catholic Encyclopedia*, 12: 1102-1103; 1:1010; *Official Catholic Directory, 1991* (New York: P.J. Kenedy and Sons, 1991) 963. For another source for the background of Thomas Joseph McDonough, see Fr. Clyde F. Crews, *An American Holy Land: A History of the Archdiocese of Louisville, 1775-1985* (Wilmington, DE: Michael Glazier, Inc., 1987) 318.

[13]Author's interview with Bishop Andrew J. McDonald, 9 September 1991, audio-tape in ADLR. Thomas J. McDonough became Archbishop of Louisville, 1967-1982, see Crews, *An American Holy Land*, 318-321. For a look at when Bishop Frey came to Savannah sede *Official Catholic Directory, 1991* (New York: P.J. Kenedy & Sons, 1991) 963.

[14]Author's interview with Bishop Andrew J. McDonald, 9 September 1991, audio-tape in ADLR.

[15]Ibid., For a written account of the events in the Bishop's life from June-September, 1972 written a year after these events see Bishop Andrew J. McDonald, "From Georgia Cracker to Arkansas Razorback" (unpublished typed manuscript, July 2-3, 1973) 1. This work is in McDonald Papers, ADLR. Only the author and title will be cited hereafter.

[16]Ibid.; McDonald, "From Georgia Cracker to Arkansas Razorback," 1-2.

[17]On Bishop McDonald's earlier visits to Arkansas, author interview with Bishop McDonald, 9 September 1991, audio-tape in ADLR. On the creation of Memphis, see Thomas Stritch, *The Catholic Church in Tennessee: The Sesquicentennial Story* (Nashville, TN: The Catholic Center, 1987) 353.

[18]Savannah *Morning News*, 6 September 1972; lD, 8D; Little Rock *Arkansas Gazette*, 6 September 1972, 9A. For the members of his family and the death of his older sister Josephine, Bishop McDonald to James M. Woods, 9 December 1991, letter in possession of the author. Other sources of this event, author's interview with Bishop McDonald, 9 September 1991, audio-tape in ADLR. McDonald, "From Georgia Cracker to Arkansas Razorback," 5.

[19]Little Rock *Arkansas Gazette*, 7 September 1972, lB; author's interview with Bishop McDonald, 9 September 1972, audio-tape in ADLR; McDonald, "From Georgia Cracker to Arkansas Razorback," 5.

[20]For a description of the ceremony, the quote taken from Little Rock *Arkansas Gazette*, 8 September 1972, 20A; for more detailed coverage see *The Guardian*, 8 September 1972, 1; 15 September 1972, 1-12; McDonald, "From Georgia Cracker to Arkansas Razorback," 5.

[21]Little Rock *Arkansas Gazette*, 8 September 1972, 20A.

[22]This quote and the announcement of the new ecclesiastical province and the name of the new Bishop of Tulsa, *The Guardian*, 22 December 1972, 1. The news was not revealed until December 19, but the document from Rome was dated December 13.

[23]The terms Prefect Apostolic and Vicar Apostolic are more fully explained in the *New Catholic Encyclopedia*, 11:727; 14:638-639. A vicar apostolic can be compared to an abbot who holds the rank of a bishop, but he does not rule a diocese, only a particular monastic community.

[24]For a survey of Catholicism in Oklahoma until 1973 see Fr. James D. White, "The Roman Catholic Church in Oklahoma: The Second 100 Hundred Years," in Oklahoma City *Journal*, 31 January 1973, 12-27. Another study of an earlier period, see Thomas E. Brown, *Bible Belt Catholicism: A History of the Roman Catholic Church in Oklahoma, 1905-1945* (New York: U.S. Catholic Historical Society, 1977).

[25]Oklahoma's Catholic population was 114,000 compared with Arkansas' 55,293. This compares with Oklahoma's overall state population according to the U.S. Census in 1970 of 2,559,000 compared with Arkansas' 1,923,000. Numbers of Catholics from *Official Catholic Directory, 1970*, 420, 587; census numbers from U.S. Dept of Commerce, Census Bureau, *Historical Statistics of the United States*, 24, 33.

[26]*The Guardian*, 9 February 1973, 1.

[27]Archbishop John R. Quinn to Bishop McDonald, 16 February 1973, McDonald Papers, ADLR. Interestingly, neither Quinn nor Gunter would stay in Oklahoma very long; four years later both would move to new dioceses. Archbishop John R. Quinn became archbishop of San Francisco and Bishop Gunter became the bishop of Beaumont, Texas.

[28]Even before coming to Arkansas, Bishop-elect McDonald had asked that Graves be continued as his auxiliary and that he would be his vicar general and auxiliary bishop, with the approval of Rome, *The Guardian*, 15 September 1972, 1; 27 October 1972, those positions listed in the 1973 Catholic Directory, see *Official Catholic Directory, 1973* (New York: P.J. Kenedy and Sons, 1973) 424.

[29]On Bishop Graves' appointment, see *The Guardian*, 29 December 1972, 1; and author's interview with Bishop Lawrence Graves, 16 May 1988, audio-tape in ADLR.

[30]Author's interview with Bishop Lawrence Graves, 16 May 1988, audio tape in ADLR; *The Guardian*, 25 May 1973, 1.

[31]On the announcement and the delay, and the report of the ceremony, see *The Guardian*, 22 June 1973, 3; 6 July 1973, 1; 20 July 1973, 1; 14 September 1973, 1.

[32]*The Guardian*, 25 May 1973, 1.

[33]The years of Bishop Lawrence Graves as Bishop of Alexandria is taken from *Official Catholic Directory, 1987* (New York: P.J. Kenedy and Sons, 1987) 10.

[34]*The Guardian*, 2 October 1972, 1, 3; his column, 9 March 1973, 1. One can see scattered issues throughout the 1970s of the bishop's column in the diocesan paper.

[35]*Diocese of Little Rock, Catholic Directory, 1991* (Little Rock, AR: Arkansas Catholic Publication, 1991) 3.

[36]Minutes of the Social Service Committee Meeting, "Christopher Homes," 26 February 1970, Social Services, ADLR. The people who initiated this project were Bishop Fletcher, Auxiliary Bishop Graves, Fr. Charles F. Kordsmier, and Fr. James R. Savary, then the diocesan Social Service Director.

[37]*Catholic Directory, Diocese of Little Rock, 1991*, 50-51.

[38]Author's interview with Sr. Annella Willett, O.S.B., 23 March 1990, audio-tape in ADLR. Also information provided to me by Mr. Dennis P. Lee, director of Catholic Social Services, Diocese of Little Rock, April 16, 1992. This information in the possession of the author.

[39]The Arkansas Interfaith Hunger Task Force was initiated by the Episcopal Diocese of Arkansas under the leadership of the Rev. Emery Washington and Mrs. Madge W. Brown in 1975. In 1976, they decided to broaden their activities by gaining support from other denominations. This information from Mrs. Madge W. Brown, "The Arkansas Inter-Faith Hunger Task Force," an unpublished, undated history of the organization. A copy of this document given to the author by Mrs. Diane Hanley, a Catholic laywoman currently active in the Task Force. I am grateful to her for this assistance.

[40]On the beginnings of this project, see *The Guardian*, 23 April 1976, 1; 14 April 1978, 1; when it opened is from information supplied to the author by Mr. Dennis P. Lee, 16 April 1992.

[41]On Fr. Schneider's appointment, see Bishop Andrew J. McDonald to Fr. Albert J. Schneider, 10 November 1982; for the newly constituted Arkansas Interfaith Conference see Report of the 1st Annual Assembly of the Arkansas Interfaith Conference of Church and Synagogues, November 8, 1983. The first meeting in which Catholic and Jewish representatives were admitted as members was held at Temple B'Nai Israel in Little Rock. Both of the above cited documents in Ecumenical Affairs, ADLR.

[42]This event announced in the local paper, and the Arkansas's Catholic newspaper gave a description of the event. Little Rock *Arkansas Gazette*, 27 April 1985, 16A; *The Guardian*, 3 May 1985, 1.

[43]For Catholic efforts with the Billy Graham Crusade in 1989 see *Arkansas Catholic*, 15 September 1989, 8.

[44]Telephone conversation with Msgr. John F. O'Donnell, 6 December 1991; Parish Records, St. Peter Church, Pine Bluff, ADLR. The directory for 1975 listed the school, but the school omitted the following year, *Official Catholic Directory, 1975* (New York: P.J. Kenedy & Sons,

1975) 425; *Official Catholic Directory, 1976* (New York: P.J. Kenedy & Sons, 1976) 445.

[45]On St. Augustine's closing see *Golden Jubilee: A History of St. Augustine's Catholic Church, North Little Rock, Arkansas, 1929-1979* (North Little Rock, AR: Privately Printed, 1979) 5, pamphlet found in Parish Records, St. Augustine's Church, North Little Rock, ADLR. For St. Bartholomew's closing see Sr. Mary Agnes Crabb, S.Sp.S., principal of St. Bartholomew's School, to Bishop Andrew J. McDonald, 31 January 1976, McDonald papers, ADLR. The directory for 1976 lists both schools being open, but not the following year, *Official Catholic Directory, 1976,* 444; *Official Catholic Directory, 1977* (New York: P.J. Kenedy and Sons, 1977) 447.

[46]*Official Catholic Directory, 1985* (New York: P.J. Kenedy & Sons, 1985) 451; *A Century of Ministry: A History of St. Peter's Catholic Church, Pine Bluff, Arkansas* (Pine Bluff, AR: Private Printing, 1989) 3. This pamphlet found in Parish Records, St. Peter's Church, Pine Bluff, ADLR.

[47]For the number of priests in the U.S. in 1966 and the number in 1991 see Hennesey, *American Catholics,* 287; *Official Catholic Directory, 1991* (New York: P. J. Kenedy and Sons, 1991) general summary, 1.

[48]These statistics taken from *Official Catholic Directory, 1965* (New York: P.J. Kenedy & Sons, 1965) 561; *Official Catholic Directory, 1980* (New York: P.J. Kenedy & Sons, 1980) 473; *Official Catholic Directory, 1990* (New York: P.J. Kenedy & Sons, 1990) 502.

[49]Jay P. Dolan, *The American Catholic Experience: A History From the Colonial Times to the Present* (Garden City, NY: Doubleday and Company-Image Paperback Edition, 1985) 437.

[50]*Official Catholic Directory, 1965,* 561; *Official Catholic Directory, 1980,* 473; *Official Catholic Directory, 1990,* 502.

[51]Author's interview with Bishop McDonald, 9 September 1991, audio-tape in ADLR.

[52]Bishop McDonald's Quinquennial Report to the Holy Father, Pope Paul VI, 15 August 1974; p. 8, a copy of this report found in McDonald Papers, ADLR. *Official Catholic Directory, 1974* (New York: P.J. Kenedy and Sons, 1974) 426; Msgr. Allen's career and death in October 11, 1988, *Arkansas Catholic,* 14 October 1988, 1, 8. This article gives his birthday as December 5, 1907. For the appointment of Fr. Royce Thomas as vicar general, see Ibid., 16 January 1987, l.

[53]This change can be seen in comparing the directories in 1970 and 1975. *Official Catholic Directory, 1970,* 416; *Official Catholic Directory, 1975,* 437. McDonald's Quinquennial Report, 15 August 1974, 18, McDonald Papers, ADLR.

[54]For Fr. George W. Tribou's background, and that of now Msgr. Galvin please consult author's interview with Msgr. Galvin, 24 August 1989; author's interview with Fr. George W. Tribou, 8 September 1989, copies of both audio tapes in ADLR. For Fr. Tribou being named assistant principal at Catholic High in 1959 see *The Guardian,* 17 April 1959, 1. For a general survey of Catholic High's history for the first 50 years, see Little Rock *Arkansas Gazette,* 16 April 1980, lB-2B. Bill Lewis, a local newspaper reporter, titled a long article this way in 1970: "In a Permissive Age, Catholic High Keeps Discipline." Little Rock *Arkansas Gazette,* 15 February 1970, 4E.

[55]Little Rock *Arkansas Gazette,* 16 April 1980, 2B; author's interview with Fr. George W. Tribou, 8 September 1989, audio-tape in ADLR.

[56]Author's interview with Bishop Andrew J. McDonald, 9 September 1991, audio-tape in ADLR.

[57]Ibid., Little Rock *Arkansas Gazette,* 4 March 1974, 4A; 16 March 1974, lA, 2A; Little Rock *Arkansas Democrat,* 5 March 1974, 5A. This controversy attracted some national attention as a national conservative Catholic weekly attacked Bishop McDonald. *The Wanderer* (St. Paul, Minnesota) 4 April 1974, 1, 4. There is an undated form letter in Bishop McDonald Papers written by a Mr. Richard J. Byrne to "Dear Friend of Catholic High" calling upon parents to stop the supposed merger of Catholic High and Mount St. Mary's.

[58]*The Guardian,* 5 December 1975, 1; 16 September 1976, 1; 30 September 1977, 3.

[59]Author's interview with Bishop McDonald, 9 September 1991, audio-tape in ADLR.

[60]The change announced in May and was ready by December 1975, *The Guardian,* 16 May 1975, 1; 10 October 1975, 1; 5 December 1975, 1.

[61]*The Guardian,* 17 August 1979, 1; for the story of St. Andrew's and his execution on a X-shaped cross, see *New Catholic Encyclopedia,* 1:474.

[62]The beginning of the Permanent Deacon program, *The Guardian,* 27 January 1978, 1; author's interview with Bishop McDonald, 9 September 1991, audio-tape in ADLR. A permanent deacon is an ordained Catholic clergymen who makes promises of obedience to the bishop and celibacy if he is not married. If married, he cannot remarry after his wife dies. He can perform all the sacraments, except confirmation, consecration of the Eucharist, hearing confession or the Sacrament of Reconciliation, and the Anointing of the Sick. The permanent deacons assist the priest at the altar, read the Gospel, preach at Mass, and help in the serving the poor and visiting the sick. For a greater presentation of the theological and historical role of Deacons in the Catholic church, see *New Catholic Encyclopedia,* 4:667-668.

[63]Telephone conversation with Deacon Lawrence Jegley, head of the permanent Diaconate program, 12 December 1991. The number of deacons as of 1991, *Official Catholic Directory, 1991,* 520. The number of 11,000 supplied to the author from Deacon Lawrence Jegley, head of the Diaconate program in the diocese.

[64]For the appointment of Mr. James T. Davis as comptroller see *The Guardian,* 4 May 1978, 1;. On his positions of Mr. Davis see *Diocese of Little Rock, Catholic Directory, 1991* (Little Rock, AR: Arkansas Catholic Press, 1991) 4, 55. Also information sent to me from Mr. Davis, 5 April 1992. I am grateful for his help.

[65]For Deacon William Hartmann's career, I have relied on information given to the author by during our phone conversation, 11 December 1991. I grateful for all his assistance.

[66]For Gregory C. Wolfe's background and career, and his appointment as the first layperson to become vice chancellor in diocesan history see *The Arkansas Catholic,* 4 February 1989, 4; Bishop McDonald's Quinquennial Report, 30 March 1988, McDonald Papers, ADLR; *Diocese of Little Rock, Catholic Directory, 1991,* 4; letter of Mr. Gregory C. Wolfe to James M. Woods, 10 April 1992, letter in possession of the author.

[67]Bishop McDonald to Fred and Tammy Woell, 13 July 1977, McDonald Papers, ADLR. Telephone conversation with Deacon Johnson S. Mattingly, 11 December 1991; Deacon Johnson S. Mattingly to the author, 7 April 1992, letter in possession of the author.

[68]Much of this information on the Little Rock Scripture Study program after 1977 comes from Bishop McDonald's Quinquennial Report, 30 March 1988, McDonald Papers, ADLR; letter of Deacon Johnson S. Mattingly to the author, 7 April 1992. I am grateful for his assistance in this topic.

[69]*Arkansas Catholic,* 17 June 1990, 5.

[70]Author's telephone conversation with Fr. Stephen Binz, 10 September 1992.

[71]On the origin and nature of the *Cursillo* movement and when it came to the U.S., see Hennesey, *American Catholics,* 317. According to the 1992 Catholic Extension Society calendar for 1992, the first *Cursillo* in the United States convened in Waco, Texas on May 27, 1957. See the calendar insert of that date.

[72]Much of this information on the *Cursillo* movement in Arkansas from a telephone conversation with Mr. John Sweeney, the present executive lay director of *Cursillo.* That Msgr. Francis McDevitt was the leader, see *Official Catholic Directory, 1980,* 476; McDevitt's death, see *The Guardian,* 17 July 1981, 1; Fr. Aureli as the new director and Fr. Malone in 1985, see *Official Catholic Directory, 1985* (New York: P.J. Kenedy and Sons, 1985) 451; *Official Catholic Directory, 1991,* 516.

[73]For the Spanish origins of Marriage Encounter and when it entered the United States, see Hennesey, *American Catholics,* 317. For the activities in Arkansas, telephone conversations with Fr. Walter Bracken, S.V.D., 12 December 1991.

[74]On the Pre-Cana program, Fr. John Marconi, Family Life Ministry to James M. Woods, 13 April 1992, letter in possession by the author.

[75]This information on Retrouvaille from Fr. Walt Bracken. S.V.D., to James M. Woods, 13 April 1992, letter in possession of the author. Also phone conversation with Mrs. Rose Kennedy, Secretary to the Family Life Ministry, 5 February 1992. I am grateful to Fr. Bracken, Fr. Marconi,

and Mrs. Kennedy for their assistance.

[76]For a description of the charismatic movement in the Catholic Church see Hennesey, *American Catholics,* 317-318; One Notre Dame historian has estimated that between 1967-1984 8 to 10 million Catholics have been touched by the charismatic movement. Dolan, *American Catholic Experience,*431-432, comment on p. 432. For other information the author has relied on telephone conversation with Fr James E. Mancini, 11 December 1991. Fr. Mancini is pastor at Our Lady of Fatima church in Benton, Arkansas as of 1992.

[77]For Fr. DiOrio's visit to Fort Smith and Little Rock, see *The Guardian,* 21 February 1986, 1; 7 March 1986, 1. On the visit to Good Counsel, *Arkansas Catholic,* 17 September 1986, 1.

[78]On the origins of RENEW and its membership from 1978-1983 see Dolan, *American Catholic Experience,* 431; telephone conversation with Fr. James E. Mancini, 11 December 1991, *Official Catholic Directory, 1985,* 450; special mass date see Bishop McDonald to Pope John Paul II, Quinquennial Report, 30 March 1988, 67. For the closing mass see *The Arkansas Catholic,* 18 September 1987, 1; 25 September 1987, 1; 2 October 1987, 2 October 1987, 1, 2, 4, 6; Fr. James E. Mancini to James M. Woods, 7 April 1992, letter in possession of the author.

[79]For Diocese of Little Rock, the new rite of penance in 1976, and communion in the hand a year later, *The Guardian,* 23 April 1976, 1-3; 2 November 1977, 1.

[80]On amnesty, see *The Guardian,* 30 August 1974, 1. That the bishop received some local criticism for his support for the farm workers and his comment found in Little Rock *Arkansas Democrat,* 29 January 1975, lA, 14A, quote on p. lA. One critic is quoted on p. 14A as saying "Bishop McDonald is certainly a pious man with a desire to do good... But he should stay in the realm of things spiritual."

[81]McDonald to Senator Dale Bumpers, 13 March 1975, McDonald Papers, ADLR.

[82]Senator Dale Bumpers to Bishop Andrew J. McDonald, 26 March 1975, McDonald Papers, ADLR.

[83]Interview with Col. Dutch Dorsch, 14 August 1991; telephone interview with Somphone Vongsaravane, 12 December 1991.

[84]For the passage of Arkansas Right to Work state constitutional amendment see C. Calvin Smith, *War and Wartime Changes in Arkansas, 1940-1945* (Fayetteville, AR: University of Arkansas Press, 1986) 118; for the bishop's campaign to repeal the law see *The Guardian,* 16 July 1976, 1.

[85]Mr. Bob Bailey to Bishop Andrew J. McDonald, 14 October 1976, McDonald Papers, ADLR.

[86]Little Rock *Arkansas Gazette,* 3 November 1976, lA.

[87]For treatment of the Call to Action meeting in Detroit, Michigan in October, 1976 see Dolan, *American Catholic,* 440; for a critical treatment of this event see James Hitchcock, *Catholicism and Modernity: Capitulation or Confrontation* (New York: Seabury Press, 1979) 116-119; author's interview with Bishop Andrew J. McDonald, 9 September 1991, audio-tape in ADLR.

[88]Rev. Hugh Assenmacher, O.S.B., *A Place Called Subiaco: A History of the Benedictine Monks in Arkansas* (Little Rock, AR: Rose Publishing Company, 1977) 453-454.

[89]Ibid., 455-456; quote on p. 455.

[90]Ibid. For a picture of Bishop McDonald blessing the new Abbot, see *The Abbey Message,* 35 (January-February, 1975) 1.

[91]Assenmacher, *A Place Called Subiaco,* 455-456; his career in Africa presented, 440-444. One interesting feature of his family is that the names came from the book of Tobit, one of the seven books of the Catholic Old Testament that are not part of the Protestant or Hebrew Old Testament. His brother was called Tobias and his sister had the name Angela. They are pictured on p. 458. For a fuller treatment of Abbot Raphael DeSalvo career up to his election and the numbers who belong to the Abbey and attend Subiaco see *The Abbey Message* 35 (November-December, 1974) 1-2.

[92]For a description of these activities see *The Abbey Message,* 36 (July-August, 1975), 9; 37 (November-December, 1976), 10; 37 (January-February, 1977), 2; 37 (March-April, 1977), 3; 38

(May-June, 1978), 12; 38 (November-December, 1978), 2; 38 (March-April 1979), 4.

[93]*The Abbey Message*, 39 (September-October, 1978), 3; 41 (November-December, 1980), 2; 42 (November-December, 1981), 2; 44 (July-August, 1983), 4; 44 (September-October, 1983), 2.

[94]*The Abbey Message*, 48 (May-June, 1987), 2; 48 (JanuaryFebruary, 1988), 2; 49 (January-February, 1989, 1; 50 (NovemberDecember, 1989), 1.

[95]*Arkansas Catholic*, 10 November 1989; 1; *The Abbey Message* 50 (January-February, 1990) 1.

[96]*Arkansas Catholic*, 10 November 1989, 1, 4.

[97]For Fr. Jerome's work as a scripture scholar see *The Abbey Message*. 38 (November-December, 1978) 10:50 (January-February, 1990), 6.

[98]*The Abbey Message*, 50 (January-February, 1990), 6. New Subiaco became officially an abbey in 1891, Assenmacher, *A Place Called Subiaco*, 128-129.

[99]This account of Bishop Fletcher's last day given in *The Guardian*, 14 December 1979, 1, 3.

[100]Ibid., 1, 2, 3.

[101]*Official Catholic Directory, 1980*, 473; as for the smallest increase, Ms. Annette King of Conway, had a list of "Catholic Population in Arkansas by Ten Year Increments, 1900-1990." A copy of this in ADLR. I am grateful to Ms. King for this chart and to Sr. Catherine Markey, diocesan archivist for supplying me with this information. For the state population, U.S. Department of Commerce, Bureau of the Census, *The Census of 1980: General Population Characteristic, the United States Summary* (Washington, D.C.: Government Printing Office, 1983) 125.

[102]The Directory number for Catholics in Arkansas in 1900 and 1910 appear as more approximations than real counting. The directory in 1900 stood at 10,000 was at .7 percent with the total Arkansas population at 1,311,564; in 1910 Catholics listed as about 22,000 with a total population of 1,574,449 or 1.3 percent, the same percentage given in 1920. Since that date the number presented in the text. These directory numbers from a chart prepared by Mrs. Annette King, and overall population numbers for Arkansas in 1900 and 1910 in T. Harri Baker and Jane Browning, *An Arkansas History for Young People* (Fayetteville, AR: University of Arkansas Press, 1991) 193, 254.

[103]For the number of Catholics to the white population was 3.0%, the same as it had been ten years earlier. *Official Catholic Directory, 1980*, 473; U.S. Dept of Commerce, *Census of 1980, General Population*, 125. The number of Catholics from *Official Catholic Directory, 1990*, 502; state population totals, white and black see U.S. Department of Commerce, Bureau of the Census, *Statistical Abstract of the United States, 1990* (Washington, D.C.; Government Printing Office, 1990) 26.

[104]For Fr. Joseph M. Biltz's career, see *Arkansas Catholic*, 4 December 1987, 1; also see Biltz Papers, Deceased Priests File, ADLR. The quote from Fr. Biltz found in *The Guardian*, 27 January 1978, 1.

[105]Bishop McDonald to Pope John Paul II, Quinquennial Report, 30 March 1988, p. 61, McDonald Papers, ADLR.

[106]On the draft, see *The Guardian*, 29 February 1980, 8; nuclear freeze, *Guardian*, 4 June 1982, 3; challenge for peace document by the American Catholic Bishops, May, 1983, *Guardian*, 6 May 1983, 1, 4; 8 July 1983, 1; U.S. invasion of Grenada, *Guardian*, 4 November 1983, 1. The Catholic pacifist organization *Pax Christi* founded by Catholic social activist and pacifist Dorothy Day in 1962 and it was initially called just *Pax*. Ten years later it took its present name. Fr. Michael Perko, S.J., *Catholic and American: A Popular History* (Huntingdon, IN: Our Sunday Visitor Press, 1989) 329. Fr. Biltz and a few others organized a Little Rock chapter in February, 1983. *The Guardian*, 25 February 1983, 1.

[107]*The Guardian*, 13 November 1981, 2.

[108]Bishop McDonald to Marcelline E. Giroir, 6 April 1976, McDonald Papers, ADLR.

[109]*Arkansas Catholic*, 4 December 1987, 1.

[110]Sr. Markey's arrival date in Little Rock as archivist and her appointment as both archivist and head of the Office of Justice and Peace is outlined in *Arkansas Catholic*, 8 July

1988, 1, 7. For another source as to when Sr. Markey was hired, see Bishop McDonald to Pope John Paul II, Quinquennial Report, September 1983, 67, McDonald Papers, ADLR.

[111]*Arkansas Catholic*, 9 January 1987, 1.

[112]*Arkansas Catholic*, 8 July 1990, 3; 15 July 1990, 1, 3. According to these reports, the last execution in Arkansas had taken place in 1964.

[113]On Sr. Catherine Markey's appointment as Ecumenical and Inter-Religious affairs, she was recommended for the post by Fr. Albert Schneider, Fr. Schneider to Bishop McDonald, 18 December 1987, Ecumenical Affairs, ADLR. She was appointed to this position, together with being archivist, and head of the Office of Justice and Peace, *Arkansas Catholic*, 8 July 1988, 1, 7; the appointment of Mrs. Jo Ann Bemrich, see *Arkansas Catholic*, 9 January 1991, 5. For the new ecumenical officer see *Diocese of Little Rock Catholic Directory, 1991*, 4.

[114]*The Guardian*, 26 January 1973, 1.

[115]*The Guardian*, 2 April 1976, 1. Along with Bishop McDonald's essay, the very same issue included two pro-life statements by Cardinal Terence Cooke of New York and then Archbishop Joseph Bernardin of Cincinnati, pp. 1, 3.

[116]*Arkansas Catholic*, 3 May 1986, 3.

[117]*The Guardian*, 7 January 1977, 1.

[118]Ibid., 11 June 1982, 3.

[119]Ibid., 1,3.

[120]Ibid., 3.

[121]Ibid., 4.

[122]Author's telephone conversation with Jacki Ragan of National Right to Life, 2 January 1991.

[123]On Jacki Ragan's career working on pro-life activities comes from my conversation with Ms. Anne Dierks who presently directs Respect Life activities for the diocese and is the current president of Arkansas Right to Life. For the Diocese of Little Rock's official endorsement of the 1988 state constitutional amendment see the editorial in *The Arkansas Catholic*, 30 September 1988, 2; That the amendment passed see Little Rock *Arkansas Gazette*, 7 November 1988, lA.

[124]*Arkansas Catholic*, 8 December 1989, 6.

[125]*Arkansas Catholic*, 13 January 1991, 1.

[126]Ibid.

[127]Washington, D.C., *National Right to Life News*, 20 November 1991, 17, 19.

[128]*Official Catholic Directory, 1991*, 516; Mr. Dennis P. Lee, diocesan Social Services Director, to James M. Woods, 13 April 1992, copy of letter in possession of the author.

[129]For the story of John Michael Talbot's career and his Christian and Catholic conversion and his coming to Arkansas see Dan O'Neill, *Troubadour for the Lord: The Story of John Michael Talbot* (New York: Crossways Publishing, 1985); Little Rock *Arkansas Gazette*, 21 October 1984, lC, 8C; *Arkansas Catholic*, 12 February 1988, 7-12; 4 November 1988, 6-8. That the bishop married John Michael and Viola Talbot and approved the new type of society John Michael had sought to establish, see *Arkansas Catholic*, 3 February 1989, 1, 8; 20 May 1990, 8. On the numbers at Little Portion and their document approving their status I have relied on my conversation with a telephone receptionist at Little Portion and my conversation with Ms. Deborah Halter, editor of the *Arkansas Catholic*.

[130]Bishop McDonald to Pope John Paul II, Quinquennial Report, 30 March 1988, 84-87, McDonald Papers, ADLR.

[131]For the project of C.A.S.A. I have relied for this information on my telephone interview with Bishop Andrew J. McDonald, 15 May 1992.

[132]This program was announced in the summer of 1987, *Arkansas Catholic*, 14 August 1987, 1. The author was present at the dedication ceremony Sunday, August 18, 1991.

[133]*Arkansas Catholic*, 24 June 1988, 1.

[134]*The Guardian*, 14 March 1986, 1; *Arkansas Catholic*, 21 March 1986, 2. Bishop McDonald to Pope John Paul II, Quinquennial report, 30 March 1988, 66, McDonald Papers, ADLR.

[135]Bishop McDonald to Pope John Paul II, Quinquennial Report, 30 March 1988, 68, McDonald Papers, ADLR; Ms. Halter's appointment, *Arkansas Catholic,* 24 March 1989, 5.

[136]*Arkansas Catholic,* 9 May 1986, 15.

[137]For the background of Fr. Harvey and the background of the other men ordained on May 28, 1988, see *Arkansas Catholic,* 20 May 1988, 1, 2. Fr. Harvey's nursing degrees were in Practical nursing, Psychiatric nursing, Emergency Technical nursing. I also want to thank Fr. Warren Harvey for some additional information supplied to me. Fr. Warren Harvey to James M. Woods, 31 December 1991, copy of letter in possession of the author. I am grateful for his assistance.

[138]On Fr. Harvey's career and position, Fr. L. Warren Harvey to James M. Woods, 31 December 1991, letter in possession of the author; *Official Catholic Directory, 1991,* 516.

[139]*Arkansas Catholic,* 6 May 1988, 5-7.

[140]Ibid., 23 September 1988, 1; 2 June 1989, 1; *Official Catholic Directory, 1991,* 516.

[141]*Arkansas Catholic,* 13 September 1992, 1; A special commemorative issue of the *Arkansas Catholic* was issued a week earlier to celebrate the twentieth anniversary of his episcopal ordination, Ibid., 6 September 1992, 11-23.

Biographical Note

James M. Woods

James M. Woods is a native of Little Rock, Arkansas, and the son of U.S. District Judge Henry and Kathleen Woods. He received his early education from Holy Souls School and Catholic High. After attending Hendrix College, he transferred to the University of Dallas where he obtained a B.A. degree in History in 1976. Three years later, Rice University awarded him a M.A. degree in History; he then earned his Ph.D. in American History from Tulane University in 1983. He has published articles in U.S. and Latin American History, and this is his second book on Arkansas history. He is currently Associate Professor of History at Georgia Southern University in Statesboro, Georgia, where he is a active member of St. Matthew's Catholic Church. James and his wife, Becky, are the parents of two children, Matthew and Teresa.

Index

Since this whole manuscript is about Arkansas, I have avoided giving it a particular index entry. All cities, towns, and geographical entities are in Arkansas unless otherwise designated. All members of the hierarchy are listed according to their highest ecclesiastical position.